379.157 Ros
Rosado, Luis A.
TExES bilingual generalist EC-6
(192) /

34028082535841
CY $28.95 ocn694396572
01/29/13

LEARN, TEACH...

SUCCEED...

With **REA's TExES™ Bilingual Generalist EC-6 (192)** test prep, you'll be in a class all your own.

WITHDRAWN

WE'D LIKE TO HEAR FROM YOU!

Visit **www.rea.com** to send us your comments

REA: THE LEADER IN TEACHER CERTIFICATION PREP

TExES™ BILINGUAL GENERALIST EC-6 (192)

TEXAS EXAMINATIONS OF EDUCATOR STANDARDS™

Luis A. Rosado, Ed.D.
Professor
Director, Center for Bilingual and ESL Education
The University of Texas, Arlington

Margarita Lara, Ed.D.
Associate Professor
Texas Southern University

And the Editors of
Research & Education Association

Free!
Diagnostic Exam
www.rea.com/texes

Research & Education Association

Planet Friendly Publishing
✔ Made in the United States
✔ Printed on Recycled Paper
Text: 10% Cover: 10%
Learn more: www.greenedition.org

At REA we're committed to producing books in an Earth-friendly manner and to helping our customers make greener choices.

Manufacturing books in the United States ensures compliance with strict environmental laws and eliminates the need for international freight shipping, a major contributor to global air pollution.

And printing on recycled paper helps minimize our consumption of trees, water and fossil fuels. This book was printed on paper made with **10% post-consumer waste**. According to the Environmental Paper Network's Paper Calculator, by using this innovative paper instead of conventional papers, we achieved the following environmental benefits:

Trees Saved: 5 • Air Emissions Eliminated: 878 pounds
Water Saved: 823 gallons • Solid Waste Eliminated: 259 pounds

Courier Corporation, the manufacturer of this book, owns the Green Edition Trademark.
For more information on our environmental practices, please visit us online at **www.rea.com/green**

Research & Education Association
61 Ethel Road West
Piscataway, New Jersey 08854
E-mail: info@rea.com

TExES™ Bilingual Generalist EC-6 (192)

Published 2013

Copyright © 2012 by Research & Education Association, Inc. Prior edition copyright © 2007 by Research & Education Association, Inc. All rights reserved. No part of this book may be reproduced in any form without permission of the publisher.

Printed in the United States of America

Library of Congress Control Number 2011929892

ISBN-13: 978-0-7386-0961-4
ISBN-10: 0-7386-0961-7

The competencies presented in this book were created and implemented by the Texas Education Agency (TEA) and Educational Testing Service (ETS®). Texas Examinations of Educator Standards and TExES are trademarks of the Texas Education Agency. For all references in this book, TEA is a trademark of the Texas Education Agency. In addition, ETS® is a registered trademark of Educational Testing Service. All other trademarks cited in this publication are the property of their respective owners.

LIMIT OF LIABILITY/DISCLAIMER OF WARRANTY: Publication of this work is for the purpose of test preparation and related use and subjects as set forth herein. While every effort has been made to achieve a work of high quality, neither Research & Education Association, Inc., nor the authors and other contributors of this work guarantee the accuracy or completeness of or assume any liability in connection with the information and opinions contained herein and in REA's software and/or online materials. REA and the authors and other contributors shall in no event be liable for any personal injury, property or other damages of any nature whatsoever, whether special, indirect, consequential or compensatory, directly or indirectly resulting from the publication, use or reliance upon this work.

Cover image: JGI/Blend Images/Getty Images

REA® is a registered trademark of
Research & Education Association, Inc.

About the Authors

Dr. Luis A. Rosado is the Director of the Center for Bilingual and ESL Education at the University of Texas at Arlington. He holds degrees from the University of Puerto Rico, Boston State College, and Texas A & M University–Kingsville. He has published in the areas of parental involvement, cross-cultural communication, and Spanish linguistics. Dr. Rosado has more than 19 years of teaching experience at the elementary, high school, and college levels. He has taught in Puerto Rico, Massachusetts, and Texas.

Dr. Margarita Lara is an Associate Professor in the Department of Curriculum & Instruction at Texas Southern University. She earned her Ed.D. in Curriculum & Instruction (Bilingual Education), at the University of Houston, Houston, Texas. Dr. Lara's publications appear in journals such as Teacher Education and Practice, The Journal of Educational Issues of Language Minority Students, Academic Exchange. In addition to classroom teaching, her academic work includes the development of Curriculum guides in collaboration with Project U.S.A. (Urban Scientists in Action), the Houston Zoological Association and Texas Southern University. Dr. Lara is the Director of the Post Baccalaureate Alternative Route to Certification, and a university supervisor for candidates in clinical practice.

About Research & Education Association

Founded in 1959, Research & Education Association (REA) is dedicated to publishing the finest and most effective educational materials — including study guides and test preps — for students in middle school, high school, college, graduate school, and beyond.

Today, REA's wide-ranging catalog is a leading resource for teachers, students, and professionals. Visit *www.rea.com* to see a complete listing of all our titles.

REA Acknowledgments

We would like to thank REA's Larry B. Kling, Vice President, Editorial, for supervising development; Pam Weston, Publisher, for setting the quality standards for production integrity and managing the publication to completion; Kathleen Casey, Senior Editor, for project management; Alice Leonard, Senior Editor, and Diane Goldschmidt, Senior Editor, for preflight editorial review; Barbara McGowran and Marjorie Roueche for copyediting the manuscript; and Christine Saul, Senior Graphic Artist, for cover design.

We also gratefully acknowledge Caragraphics for typesetting the manuscript.

About the Authors

Dr. Luis A. Rosado is the Director of the Center for Bilingual and ESL Education at the University of Texas at Arlington. He holds degrees from the University of Puerto Rico, Boston State College, and Texas A & M University–Kingsville. He has published in the areas of parental involvement, cross-cultural communication, and Spanish linguistics. Dr. Rosado has more than 19 years of teaching experience at the elementary, high school, and college levels. He has taught in Puerto Rico, Massachusetts, and Texas.

Dr. Margarita Lara is an Associate Professor in the Department of Curriculum & Instruction at Texas Southern University. She earned her Ed.D. in Curriculum & Instruction (Bilingual Education), at the University of Houston, Houston, Texas. Dr. Lara's publications appear in journals such as Teacher Education and Practice, The Journal of Educational Issues of Language Minority Students, Academic Exchange. In addition to classroom teaching, her academic work includes the development of Curriculum guides in collaboration with Project U.S.A. (Urban Scientists in Action), the Houston Zoological Association and Texas Southern University. Dr. Lara is the Director of the Post Baccalaureate Alternative Route to Certification, and a university supervisor for candidates in clinical practice.

Note to Readers

The terms "Before Common Era (BCE)" and "Common Era (CE)" are being used in place of the traditional "Before Christ (BC)" and "anno Domini (AD)" to identify historical periods. The new terms are more inclusive and are widely used on standardized tests.

CONTENTS

INTRODUCTION 1

About This Book 1
About the Test 1
How to Use This Book 2
TExES Bilingual Generalist EC-6 (192) Study Schedule 3
Scoring REA's Practice Test 4
Test-Taking Tips 5
The Day of the Test 5

DOMAIN I: BILINGUAL EDUCATION 7

Competency 001 7
Competency 002 26
Competency 003 36
Competency 004 47

DOMAIN II: ENGLISH LANGUAGE ARTS AND READING 57

Competency 005 (Oral Language) 57
Competency 006 (Phonological and Phonemic Awareness) 65
Competency 007 (Alphabetic Principle) 67
Competency 008 (Literacy Development) 70
Competency 009 (Word Analysis and Identification Skills) 76
Competency 010 (Reading Fluency) 79
Competency 011 (Reading Comprehension and Application) 81
Competency 012 (Reading, Inquiry and Research) 86
Competency 013 (Writing Conventions) 90
Competency 014 (Written Communication) 95
Competency 015 (Viewing and Representing) 100
Competency 016 (Assessment of Developing Literacy) 102

DOMAIN III: MATHEMATICS 111

Competency 017 (Mathematics Instruction) 111
Competency 018 (Number Concepts and Operations) 127
Competency 019 (Patterns and Algebra) 134
Competency 020 (Geometry and Measurement) 141
Competency 021 (Probability and Statistics) 152
Competency 022 (Mathematical Processes) 154

DOMAIN IV: SOCIAL SCIENCE 161

Competency 023 (Social Science Instruction) 161
Competency 024 (History) 172
Competency 025 (Geography and Culture) 194
Competency 026 (Economics) 205
Competency 027 (Government and Citizenship) 206

DOMAIN V: SCIENCE 213

Competency 028 (Safe and Proper Laboratory Processes) 213
Competency 029 (Scientific Inquiry) 215
Competency 030 (Impact on Daily Life) 221
Competency 031 (Unifying Concepts and Processes in Science) 222
Competency 032 (Theory and Practice of Teaching Science) 223
Competency 033 (Assessments in Science Learning) 225
Competency 034 (Physical Science: Forces and Motion) 226
Competency 035 (Physical Science: Changes in Matter) 227
Competency 036 (Physical Science: Energy) 229
Competency 037 (Physical Science: Energy and Matter) 232
Competency 038 (Life Science: Structure and Function of Living Things) 234
Competency 039 (Life Science: Reproduction and Heredity) 240
Competency 040 (Life Science: Adaptation and Evolution) 242
Competency 041 (Life Science: Organisms and the Environment) 243
Competency 042 (Earth and Space Science: Earth Systems) 244
Competency 043 (Earth and Space Science: Cycles in Earth Systems) 247
Competency 044 (Earth and Space Science: Weather and Climate) 249
Competency 045 (Earth and Space Science: Solar System and the Universe) 250

DOMAIN VI: FINE ARTS, HEALTH, AND PHYSICAL EDUCATION **255**

Competency 046 (Visual Arts) 255
Competency 047 (Music) 264
Competency 048 (Health) 272
Competency 049 (Physical Education) 282
Competency 050 (Theater) 290

PRACTICE TEST **294**

Answer Key and Domain Competencies 321
Answer Explanations 325

INDEX **357**

Introduction

About This Book

REA's *TExES Bilingual Generalist EC–6 (192)* test is a comprehensive guide designed to assist you in preparing to take the TExES (Texas Examinations of Educator Standards) test which is required for teaching in Texas. To enhance your chances of success in this important step toward your career as a teacher in Texas schools, this test guide:

- presents an accurate and complete overview of the TExES Bilingual Generalist, EC–6 (192)
- identifies all of the important information and its representation on the exam
- provides a comprehensive review of every domain
- presents sample questions in the actual test format
- provides diagnostic tools to identify areas of strength and weakness
- provides a full-length practice test based on the most recently administered TExES test
- replicates the format of the official exam, including level of difficulty
- supplies the correct answer and detailed explanations for each question on the practice test, which enables you to identify correct answers and understand why they are correct and, just as important, why the other answers are incorrect.

This guide is the result of studying many resources. The editors considered the most recent test administrations and professional standards. They also researched information from the Texas Education Agency (TEA), professional journals, textbooks, and educators. This guide includes the best test preparation materials based on the latest information available.

About The Test

Below are the domains used as the basis for the TExES Bilingual Generalist EC–6 (192), examination, as well as the approximate percentage of the total test that each competency occupies. These competencies represent the knowledge that teams of teachers, subject area specialists, and district-level educators have determined to be important for beginning teachers. This book contains a thorough review of these competencies, as well as the specific skills that demonstrate each area.

Domains		Percentage
I.	Bilingual Education	32%
II.	English Language Arts and Reading	22%
III.	Mathematics	13%
IV.	Social Studies	13%
V.	Science	12%
VI.	Fine Arts, Health, and Physical Education	8%

Who Administers the Test?

The TExES is developed and administered by Educational Testing Service (ETS) in cooperation with the Texas State Board for Educator Certification (SBEC) and the Texas Education Agency. A test development process was designed and is implemented to ensure that the content and difficulty level of the test are appropriate and based on a state aim of aligning the school curriculum from grade to grade, from kindergarten through college.

When Should the TExES Be Taken?

The test should be taken just before or after graduation for those seeking certification right out of school. The TExES is a requirement to teach in Texas, so if you are planning on being an educator, you must take and pass this test.

The TExES is usually administered five times a year at several locations throughout Texas. The usual testing day is Saturday, but the test may be taken on an alternate day if a conflict, such as a religious obligation, exists.

The TExES Registration Bulletin offers information about test dates and locations, as well as registration information and how to make testing accommodations for those with special needs.

To receive a registration bulletin, contact:

ETS—TExES Educator Certification
P.O. Box 6001 Program
Princeton, NJ 08541-6001
Phone: (800) 205-2626
Email: texes-excet_inquiries@ets.org

Registration bulletins are also available at education departments of Texas colleges and universities.

The Texas State Board for Educator Certification (SBEC) can be reached at (888) 863-5880 or (512) 469-3008 or via e-mail at sbec@sbec.state.tx.us. You can also find information about the test and registration on the SBEC website at *www.sbec.state.tx.us/.*

Is There a Registration Fee?

To take the TExES, you must pay a registration fee. If you are using the registration form, all fees must be paid in full by personal check, cashier's check, or money order payable to ETS. All payments must be made in U.S. dollars. Cash will not be accepted. Online and phone payments can be made by credit/debit card (American Express®, Discover®, JCB®, MasterCard® and VISA®). Any credit/debit card branded with one of the above five accepted credit card logos can be processed. Online payments can also be made with an electronic check (e-check). Funds must be from a U.S. bank.

How to Use This Book

How Do I Begin Studying?

Review the organization of this test preparation guide.

1. To best utilize your study time, follow our TExES Independent Study Schedule. The schedule is based on a seven-week program, but can be condensed to four weeks if necessary.
2. Take the **diagnostic test online at *www.rea.com/texes.***
3. Review the format of the TExES.
4. Review the test-taking advice and suggestions presented later in this chapter.
5. Pay attention to the information about domains, content, and topics on the test.

6. Spend time reviewing topics that stand out as needing more study.
7. Take the practice test, review the explanations to your answers carefully, study the competencies that your scores indicate need further review.
8. Follow the suggestions at the end of this chapter for the day before and the day of the test.

When Should I Start Studying?

It is never too early to start studying for the TExES. The earlier you begin, the more time you will have to sharpen your skills. Do not procrastinate! Cramming is not an effective way to study, since it does not allow you the time needed to learn the test material.

Studying for the TExES Bilingual Generalist Test

It is very important for you to choose the time and place for studying that works best for you. Some individuals may set aside a certain number of hours every morning to study, while others may choose to study at night before going to sleep. Other people may study during the day, while waiting in line, or even while eating lunch. Only you can determine when and where your study time will be most effective. Be consistent and use your time wisely. Work out a study routine and stick to it.

When you take the practice tests, simulate the conditions of the actual test as closely as possible. Turn your television and radio off, and sit down at a quiet table free from distraction. As you complete each practice test, score your test and thoroughly review the explanations to the questions you answered incorrectly; however, do not review too much at any one time. Concentrate on one problem area at a time by reviewing the question and explanation, and by studying our review until you are confident that you have mastered the material.

Keep track of your scores. By doing so, you will be able to gauge your progress and discover general weaknesses in particular sections. Give extra attention to the reviews that cover your areas of difficulty, as this will build your skills in those areas.

Your TExES Bilingual Generalist Study Schedule

This study schedule allows for thorough preparation for the TExES. The course of study here is seven weeks, but you can condense or expand the timeline to suit your personal schedule. It is vital that you adhere to a structured plan and set aside ample time each day to study. The more time you devote to studying, the more prepared and confident you will be on the day of the test.

Week	Activity
1	**Take the diagnostic exam** which is located online at *www.rea.com/texes*. The score will indicate your strengths and weaknesses. Make sure you simulate real exam conditions when you take the test. Afterwards, score it and review the explanations, especially for questions you answered incorrectly.
2	**Review the explanations for the questions you missed, and review the appropriate chapter sections.** Useful study techniques include highlighting key terms and information; taking notes as you review the book's sections; putting new terms and information on note cards to help retain the information.
3 & 4	**Reread all your note cards, re-fresh your understanding of the exam's competencies and skills, review your college textbooks, and read over class notes you've previously taken.** This is also the time to consider any other supplementary materials that your counselor or the Texas State Department of Education suggests. Review the Department's website at *www.sbec.state.tx.us/*.
5	**Begin to condense your notes and findings.** A structured list of important facts and concepts, based on your note cards and the book's competencies, will help you thoroughly review for the test. Review the answers and explanations for all missed questions.

6	**Have someone quiz you using the index cards you created.** Take the practice test, adhering to the time limits and simulated test-day conditions.
7	**Review your areas of weakness using all study materials.** This is a good time to re-take the practice test.

Format of the Test

The TExES Bilingual Generalist EC–6 (192) includes 185 scorable multiple-choice items and approximately 15 non-scorable items. Your final scaled score will be based only on scorable items.

All multiple-choice questions are designed to assess your knowledge of the domains and related skills mentioned above and reviewed in this book. In general, the multiple-choice questions are intended to make you think. You are expected in most cases to demonstrate more than an ability to recall factual information; you may be asked to think critically about the information, analyze it, consider it carefully, and compare it with knowledge you have, or make a judgment about it.

Answering the multiple-choice questions is straightforward. You will have four choices labeled A, B, C, and D. You must mark your choice on a separate answer sheet. You should have plenty of time in which to complete the test, but be aware of the amount of time you are spending on each question so that you allow yourself time to complete the whole test. Although speed is not very important, a steady pace should be maintained when answering questions. Using the practice tests will help you prepare for this task.

About the Review Sections

The reviews in this book are designed to help you sharpen the basic skills needed to approach the TExES, as well as provide strategies for attacking the questions.

Each teaching competency is examined in a separate chapter. The skills required for all six-competency areas are extensively discussed to optimize your understanding of what the 192 Bilingual Generalist EC–6 test covers.

Your schooling has taught you most of what you need to answer the questions on the test. The education classes you took should have provided you with the know-how to make important decisions about situations you will face as a teacher. Our review is designed to help you fit the information you have acquired into specific competency components. Reviewing your class notes and textbooks together with our competency reviews will give you an excellent springboard for passing the exam.

Scoring REA's Practice Test

How Do I Score My Practice Test?

There are 185 multiple-choice questions on the TExES Bilingual Generalist practice test. You must get 66% or more of the 122 questions correct to pass.

If you do not achieve a passing score on the practice test, review the detailed explanations for the questions you answered incorrectly. Note which types of questions you answered wrong, and re-examine the corresponding review. After further review, you may want to re-take the practice tests.

When Will I Receive My Score Report and What Will It Look Like?

Approximately four weeks after the exam you will be mailed a score report. The report will indicate whether you have passed the test. It will also include:

- a total test scaled score that is reported on a scale of 100–300. The minimum passing score is a scaled score of 240. This score represents the minimum level of competency required to be an entry-level educator in this field in Texas public schools.
- your performance in the major content domains of the test and in the specific competencies of the test. This information may be

useful in identifying strengths and weaknesses and can be used in preparing for the test should you need to retake it.

- information to help you interpret your results.

You will not receive a score report if you are absent or choose to cancel your score.

Test-Taking Tips

Although you may not be familiar with tests like the TExES, this book will help acquaint you with this type of exam and help alleviate your test-taking anxieties. Listed below are ways to help you become accustomed to the TExES, some of which may be applied to other tests as well.

- **Tip 1.** Become comfortable with the format of the TExES. When you are practicing, stay calm and pace yourself. After simulating the test only once, you will boost your chances of doing well, and you will be able to sit down for the actual TExES with much more confidence.
- **Tip 2.** Read all of the possible answers. Just because you think you have found the correct response, do not automatically assume that it is the best answer. Read through each choice to be sure that you are not making a mistake by jumping to conclusions.
- **Tip 3.** Use the process of elimination. Go through each answer to a question and eliminate as many of the answer choices as possible. By eliminating two answer choices, you have given yourself a better chance of getting the item correct since there will only be two choices left from which to make your guess. Do not leave an answer blank; it is better to guess than to not answer a question on the TExES test.
- **Tip 4.** Place a question mark in your answer booklet next to answers you guessed, then recheck them later if you have time.
- **Tip 5.** Work quickly and steadily to avoid focusing on any one problem too long. Taking the practice test in this book will help you learn to budget your precious time.
- **Tip 6.** Learn the directions and format of the test. Familiarizing yourself with the directions and format of the test will not only save time, but will also help you avoid anxiety (and the mistakes caused by getting anxious).
- **Tip 7.** Be sure that the answer circle you are marking corresponds to the number of the question in the test booklet. Since the test is multiple-choice, it is graded by machine, and marking one wrong answer can throw off your answer key and your score. Be extremely careful.

The Day of the Test

Before the Test

On the day of the test, make sure to dress comfortably, so that you are not distracted by being too hot or too cold while taking the test. Plan to arrive at the test center early. This will allow you to collect your thoughts and relax before the test, and will also spare you the anguish that comes with being late.

You should check your TExES registration information to find out what time to arrive at the testing center.

Before you leave for the test center, make sure that you have your admission ticket and two forms of identification, one of which must contain a recent photograph, your name, and signature (i.e., driver's license). You will not be admitted to the test center if you do not have proper identification.

You must bring several sharpened No. 2 pencils with erasers, as none will be provided at the test center.

If you would like, you may wear a watch to the test center. However, you may not wear one that makes noise, because it may disturb the other test takers. Dictionaries, textbooks, notebooks, calculators, briefcases, or packages will not be permitted. Drinking, smoking, and eating are prohibited. NOTE: For this test, scientific calculators are permitted during the test, but they are provided at the test center. You do not need to bring a calculator of your own.

During the Test

The TExES is given in one sitting without breaks. Procedures will be followed to maintain test security. Once you enter the test center, follow all of the rules and instructions given by the test supervisor. If you do not, you risk being dismissed from the test and having your scores cancelled.

When all of the materials have been distributed, the test instructor will give you directions for filling out your answer sheet. Fill out this sheet carefully since this information will be printed on your score report.

Once the test begins, mark only one answer per question, completely erase unwanted answers and marks, and fill in answers darkly and neatly.

Can I Retake the Test?

If you don't do well on the TExES, don't panic! You can take it again, and in fact many candidates do. A score on the TExES that does not match your expectations should not change your plans about teaching. You can register to retake it at any subsequent test administration. To retake a test, submit a new registration along with the correct payment. It is recommended that you wait for your scores before reregistering. If you choose to register again for the same test before receiving your scores from a previous administration, you assume responsibility for test fees and any applicable late or emergency registration fees for both test dates.

After the Test

When you finish your test, hand in your materials and you will be dismissed. Then, go home and relax—you deserve it!

CHAPTER

Domain I: Bilingual Education

1

Competency 001

The bilingual education teacher understands the foundations of bilingual education and the concepts of bilingualism and biculturalism and applies this knowledge to create an effective learning environment for students in the bilingual education program.

This chapter addresses the historical development, major court cases and significant events that affected the development of bilingual education in the United States. In addition, the chapter describes the federal, state and local policies and the various program models that address the needs of English language learners.

Historical Development of Bilingual Education

Colonial Period

Bilingualism and multilingualism have been prevalent features in the history of the United States. People from many language backgrounds founded the initial thirteen colonies. Among the languages used during the colonial period were English, German, French, Dutch, Swedish, and Welsh (Crawford 2004). Linguistic tolerance and multilingualism were typical features of colonial America. As part of this tradition, during the Revolutionary War, official documents were printed in English, German, and French to accommodate speakers from those powerful groups (Crawford 2004). This linguistic diversity played an important role in the decision to leave the identification of the official language of the nation out of the Constitution. By taking this action and based on the Tenth Amendment, language and educational issues were relegated to the state legislatures. Thus, whenever schools were established, the state and local governments made a decision on the language used for instruction.

17th–19th Centuries

During the 17th–19th centuries, multiple languages other than English were used as the language of instruction in U.S. schools. German schools were in operation in Philadelphia as early as 1694 (Crawford 2004). In 1890, about 600,000 children were receiving instruction in German in various states in the nation: Pennsylvania, Maryland, Ohio, Indiana, Illinois, Missouri, Nebraska, Colorado, and Oregon. At the same time, Swedish, Norwegian, and Danish were also used as the language of instruction in Wisconsin, Illinois, Minnesota, Iowa, the Dakotas, Nebraska, and Washington. Polish and Italian were used in schools in Wisconsin, Dutch in Michigan, French in Louisiana, Czech in Texas, and Spanish in the Southwest.

In the second half of the nineteenth century, many parochial and public schools in large cities like Baltimore, Cleveland, Indianapolis, and St. Louis were offering dual language education. The bilingual education movement was so strong in the United States that state legislatures in Ohio (1836), Louisiana (1847), and New Mexico (1848) passed laws authorizing instruction in two languages (Crawford 2004). However, during the same period, military conflicts in Europe restricted the immigration of speakers of the colonial languages. Without the linguistic support of new immigrants, the influence of French, Dutch, and German decreased, and English emerged as the national language. With fewer new immigrants, second-generation immigrants stopped using their heritage languages, and bilingual education as official policy disappeared from public view.

Twentieth Century

During the first part of the twentieth century, new immigrants from southeastern Europe arrived in America. They brought with them the many languages of the region. However, these new immigrants did not enjoy the linguistic flexibility of earlier immigrants. New immigrants were expected to Americanize or assimilate, learn English, and abandon their native cultures and languages. By 1919, as part of the Americanization programs for immigrants, 15 state laws called for English-only instruction. English language learners (ELLs) were subjected to severe punishment for using their native languages on the playground or in the classroom. With the new English-only legislation, dual language instruction virtually disappeared in the United States.

1920s through 1960s

From the 1920s through the 1960s, ELLs were submersed in English without any kind of consistent support through their first language (L1). This "sink or swim" approach resulted in academic failure for many ELLs. The term *submersion* was coined to describe this lack of L1 support for language minority students. In the 1940s, as part of the Americanization program in the United States, English as a foreign language was developed as a field of study at the University of Michigan. By the 1960s, the field had evolved into what is known today as English as a second language (ESL). In 1966, the Teachers of English to Speakers of Other Languages (TESOL) was founded to study and improve methods and strategies to teach English.

In 1953, a document published by the United Nations (UN) titled *The Use of the Vernacular Language in Education* provided the foundation for the rebirth of dual language instruction in the United States. In this document, the UN established one of the cardinal points in bilingual education: "It is axiomatic that the best medium to teach a child is his mother tongue" (United Nations Education, Scientific and Cultural Organization, 1953). This document indirectly launched the development of the bilingual education programs of the 1960s.

The actual event that paved the way for modern bilingual education programs was the triumph of the Cuban Revolution in 1959 and the resulting mass exodus of Cubans to the United States. Using funds for the relocation of Cuban refugees fleeing communism, the U.S. government sponsored the creation of the first dual language program of the 1960s in Dade County, Florida. The success of this program at **Coral Way Elementary** in Florida guided other states like Texas to experiment with bilingual programs.

In 1964, Texas implemented a bilingual education program in the United Consolidated ISD (Laredo area) and in the San Antonio ISD (Anderson & Boyer, 1970). In 1965, two new programs were implemented: one in Pecos, New Mexico and second one in Edinburg, Texas. In 1966, similar programs were implemented in California, New Mexico, Arizona and New Jersey. Some of the districts that began bilingual education in 1966 in Texas include: Harlandale (1966), Del Rio (1966), Zapata 1966), Corpus Christi (1967), and Del Valle (1967) (Anderson & Boyer, 1970).

The Civil Rights Act of 1964

Passage of the Civil Rights Act of 1964 and the leadership of African American and Latino advocates provided the momentum needed to secure federal support for the fight against poverty and, eventually, for bilingual education. One component of the legislation, Title VI, specifically prohibits institutions that receive federal funding from discriminating on the grounds of race, color, or national origin. This legislation was eventually used as a foundation for the many court cases that emerged in the 1970s seeking support for the education of language minority students.

Intervention of the Federal Government

Although education is not mentioned in the U.S. Constitution, the federal government has been indirectly involved in education through various legislative initiatives. In 1965, Congress enacted the Elementary and Secondary Education Act (ESEA) to provide financial support for public education. One of the key components of the legislation, Title I, specifically helped children from low socioeconomic backgrounds. In 1968, the legislation added Title VII—The Bilingual Education Act—which provided funding for programs to address the needs of ELLs. Both Title I and Title VII remained major components of the ESEA until 2001, when it was replaced with the No Child Left Behind Act (NCLB). For 31 years, the ESEA legislation regulated the types of services and programs to address the needs of language-minority students in the nation. Following are some of the key changes of that legislation and the effects on bilingual education programs:

- **1968**—The law did not mandate bilingual education but provided funding to support educational programs, prepare bilingual teachers, disseminate materials, and promote parental involvement (Ovando, Combs, and Collier 2006). The legislation was compensatory in nature and did not specify a program model.
- **1973–1974**—Bilingual education was officially mentioned as the model to address the needs of ELLs. However, the type of bilingual program was not addressed.
- **1978**—The legislation specified the **transitional nature** of the approach, which led to the creation of the **early-exit transitional bilingual education programs.** Furthermore, the legislation prohibited the use of federal funding to create language developmental/maintenance programs.
- **1984**—The law allocated funding for alternative programs that did not require minority languages for instruction (Crawford 2004). However, a portion of the legislation also eliminated the 1978 restrictions to the use of funding for maintenance programs and provided special grants to promote "developmental/maintenance bilingual education programs" (Crawford 2004; Ovando, Combs, and Collier 2006). The legislation also allocated more funding for teacher preparation, and **broke away from a compensatory model to an enrichment approach.**
- **1994**—The ESEA legislation was renamed the Improving America's School Act and School Reform. The legislation continued providing remedial and compensatory education to poor students. It allowed the participation of English proficiency students in the bilingual education programs, which opened the door to the implementation of two-way dual language programs. Finally, the legislation **continued sanctioning the use of funding to support developmental/maintenance bilingual education programs** and provided special funding for higher education to prepare bilingual teachers.

No Child Left Behind (NCLB) Act

The NCLB legislation contains two components—Title I and Title III (formerly known as Title VII)—that directly affect the education of language minority students. Title I requires school districts to hire highly qualified teachers. Beginning in 2006, school districts are required to provide evidence that teachers serving low-income language-minority students are fully certified and proficient in the languages used for instruction.

Under the NCLB, the Bilingual Education Act was renamed the **English Language Acquisition, Language Enhancement, and Academic Achievement Act (Title III)**. The aim of the legislation is to promote English language development, but it allows for local flexibility in the implementation of programs. These are some of the key provisions of the legislation:

1. Consolidate services and funding for language minority students with the Emergency Immigrant Education Program.
2. Make local education agencies (LEAs) responsible for the English language growth of ELLs.
3. Provide funds to the states based on a formula using the number of ELLs and immigrant students identified in the state and reported to the federal government.
4. Recognize the important role of parents in the education of their children. LEAs must inform parents of the rationale for placing students in special language programs. Parents can either agree or disagree or question the placement of their child in bilingual education by completing a parental denial form.
5. Require school districts to use 95 percent of the funding for direct instruction for ELLs.
6. Establish mandatory testing in English for reading and language arts for ELLs who have attended school in the United States for at least three consecutive years.
7. Mandate a federal accountability system to ensure that school districts provide effective instruction to ELLs. Based on the accountability system, districts must develop Annual Measurable Achievement Objectives (AMAOs) to monitor student progress in attaining English proficiency and notify parents if the program fails to meet its AMAOs for two consecutive years. After four years of failing to meet the objectives, the state will require the LEA to modify its curriculum, program, and methods of instruction. If the situation is not solved, the entity can lose federal funding.
8. Require all public school campuses, school districts, and the state to be evaluated for Adequate Yearly Progress (AYP).
9. Set **accountability measures** in Reading/Language Arts, Mathematics, and Graduation Rate (for high schools and districts) or Attendance Rate (for elementary and middle/junior high schools).
10. Require every campus, district, or state that is receiving Title I, Part A funds to meet AYP for two consecutive years.
11. Require the Texas Education Agency to establish AMAOs under Title III for the English language acquisition and academic achievement of limited English proficient (LEP) students.
12. Compare the Texas English Language Proficiency Assessment System (TELPAS) against the state's achievement standards (AMAOs).

The AMAOs measure:

- progress in learning the English language, attainment of English language proficiency and
- LEP AYP based on the state's student academic achievement standards.

TELPAS uses multiple-measures:

- Reading: uses multiple choice tests for grades 2–12 (test online)
- Writing: uses holistic scoring (along with writing samples).
- Classroom Observation: measures how well students understand and use language—using a checklist

TELPAS results can be used for:

- assessing and evaluating language and instruction
- reporting purposes

English Language Proficiency Standards (ELPS)

The adoption of the revised ELPS as part of 19 Texas Administrative Code (TAC) Chapter 74, *Curriculum Requirements*, ensures alignment with all academic content areas.

Section 19 TAC §74.4, *English Language Proficiency Standards* (ELPS) outline the instruction school districts must provide ELLs in order for them to have the full opportunity to learn English and to succeed academically. The rule clarifies that the ELPS are to be implemented as an integral part of the

Table 1.1. Reported Measures of TELPAS

Language Area (Área del lenguaje)	Proficiency Ratings (Nivel de dominio)	Comprehension and Composite Scores (Clasificación global y de comprensión)
Listening	Intermediate	Comprehension (How well the child understands English—2.0)
Speaking	Intermediate	TELPAS Composite Score (Overall level of performance in English— 2.0)
Reading	Intermediate	TELPAS Composite Rating
Writing	Intermediate	Spring 2008 Beginning Spring 2009 Intermediate

instructional program in each foundation and enrichment subject of the TEKS.

Section19 TAC §74.4 (b) lists school district responsibilities to fulfill. In fulfilling the requirements of this section, school districts shall:

(1) identify the student's English language proficiency levels in the domains of listening, speaking, reading, and writing in accordance with the proficiency level descriptors for the beginning, intermediate, advanced, and advanced high levels delineated in subsection.

And, in (d) of this section. English Language Proficiency Standards are aligned and linked with Texas English Language Proficiency Assessment System

For details about each of the components of the NCLB, go to the web site for the U.S. Department of Education at *www.ed.gov/nclb/landing.jhtml*.

Legal Documents and Court Cases

Federal Court Cases

Current bilingual education programs came as a result of political activism and court mandates. Some of the most important court cases that laid the foundation for the actual litigation that eventually shaped bilingual education are presented in the next section.

Court Cases That Preceded Litigation for Bilingual Education

The struggle for a meaningful education for linguistic minorities cannot be separated from the struggle for human rights. Based on this premise, two cases that traditionally are not linked to bilingual education litigation will be discussed. These are included here because they represent the beginning of the struggle for human rights and meaningful education for English learners in the United States.

Mendez v. Westminster (1946), Desegregation case for Mexican Americans in CA.

- U.S. District Court (LA) ruling in favor of the plaintiffs based on the Equal Protection Clause (14th Amendment of the U.S. Constitution)
- U.S 9th Federal District Court of Appeals (SF)—upheld the ruling on different grounds (1947):
  - — The California segregation law did not include Mexican Americans. It included other groups like Chinese or Japanese.
  - — Several organizations like the NAACP led by Thurgood Marshall joined the appellate process as amicus curiae (friends of the court).

  - The Court of Appeals did not challenge the "Separate but Equal Doctrine" established in *Plessy v. Ferguson* (1896).
  - Governor Earl Warren repealed the CA segregation laws. He later became Chief Justice of the U.S. Supreme Court and presided over *Brown v. Topeka* (1954).
- ***Brown v. Topeka*** (1954), Desegregation case for African Americans.
  - U.S. Supreme Court ruled that separate educational facilities were inherently unequal and a violation of the **Equal Protection Clause** of the **Fourteenth Amendment** of the **United States Constitution**.

In *Hernández v. Texas* (1954), a jury composed of "all white" members found Pete Hernández guilty of murder in Jackson County, Texas. During the jury selection and as part of the trial, his legal team unsuccessfully challenged the composition of the jury, alleging that people of Mexican descent were not represented on the jury. They suggested that having a "white only" jury clearly discriminated against the defendant. They alleged that people of Mexican ancestry represent a special classification different from whites. The legal team appealed the case to the Texas Supreme Court on the grounds that an "all white" jury could have not been impartial in the Hernandez case.

The Texas Court of Criminal appeals denied the motion on the grounds that individuals of Mexican descent were not a special classification under the meaning of the 14th Amendment of the Constitution. The defendant appealed the case to the U.S. Supreme court, where the Supreme Court ruled unanimously in favor of Hernández, ordering the case to be retried with a jury of peers selected without regard to ethnicity. The Court also held that the 14th Amendment protects and addresses not only the white and black racial classifications, but also other groups like Mexican Americans (The Oyez Project, 2010). This landmark case extended the equal protection clause of the 14th Amendment to Mexican Americans and other minority groups in the nation (Collier & Thomas, 2009).

The identification of Mexican Americans as a group different from whites was further challenged in a segregation case in ***Cisneros v. Corpus Christi ISD*** (1971). In this court case, the plaintiffs argued that the district's Mexican American students were grouped with African Americans to comply with the desegregation ruling mandated under ***Brown v. Topeka*** (1954). The Court found in favor of the plaintiffs and ordered integration of the three groups—white, black and Mexican American (1971).

In ***Diana v. Board of Education*** (1970), Diana, a Spanish-speaking student from Monterey County, California, was placed in a mildly retarded classroom due to her low IQ scores derived from an English test. The court ruled that Spanish-speaking students should be retested in their native language to avoid errors in placement.

Serna v. Portales (1972 and 1974) was the first successful court case seeking support for bilingual education. In 1972, a federal court mandated that the school district in Portales, New Mexico, implement a bilingual-bicultural curriculum, revise assessment procedures to monitor Hispanic students' academic achievement, and recruit bilingual personnel. The Portales Municipal Schools appealed, but the 10th U.S. District Court of Appeals upheld the decision in 1974, based on the ***Lau v. Nichols*** ruling handed down the same year.

In ***Lau v. Nichols*** (1974), Kinney Lau, representing 1,790 Chinese students, initiated a class action suit against the San Francisco Unified School District seeking support for Chinese students who were failing school because they could not understand English. In 1974, the U.S. Supreme Court, based on the Civil Rights Act of 1964 and the Office for Civil Rights (OCR) Memorandum of 1970, found in favor of the plaintiffs. However, the court did not specify a remedy and left it up to the district to decide how to comply with the mandate of providing "meaningful education" to students of limited English proficiency. In the consent decree that followed, the San Francisco Unified School District agreed to provide bilingual-bicultural education. Although the court did not dictate a specific remedy in the Lau ruling, this landmark case provided the momentum and foundation for other litigations in progress, and it became the de facto tool for the implementation of bilingual education in the United States.

In **A.S.P.I.R.A.** ***v. New York*** (1974), Aspira, a community-based organization, sued the City of New York seeking relief for the large number of ELLs in the city. While the case was being heard, the Lau ruling was handed down, and the litigation ended in a consent decree—that is, the district agreed with the demands of the plaintiffs. The court mandated a citywide assessment and identification of students in need of special language services and the implementation of a districtwide bilingual education program that addressed the identified needs of ELLs.

In ***Rios v. Reed*** (1977), the issue of program quality to meet the needs of ELLs was put to the test. In this litigation, a federal court ruled that the Patchogue-Medford School District in New York had violated the rights of ELLs by providing a "half-hearted" (Crawford 2004, p.11) bilingual program that relied mostly on ESL and did not include a bicultural component. The court upheld the importance of teaching English to students but also recognized the need to provide meaningful education while accomplishing the language goal. This ruling clearly called for the use of L1 instruction for the content areas while developing English proficiency. The *Rios v. Read* decision provided the foundations for the development of the many bilingual education programs founded later in the 1980s and beyond.

In ***Castañeda v. Pickard (1981)***, the quality of the bilingual program was addressed again when the school district of Raymondville, Texas, was charged with violating the Equal Educational Opportunities Act (EEOA) of 1974. As a result of the *Castañeda* decision, the Fifth Court of Appeals mandated a three-step process to develop quality bilingual education programs. The court ruled that program implementation must be based on sound research, with adequate resources and opportunities for students to have access to the full curriculum. These guidelines were used as the model implementation process to enforce the Lau Remedies (discussed later in the chapter).

In ***U.S. v. the State of Texas*** (1981 and 1982), U.S. District Judge William Wayne Justice ordered the state of Texas to offer a bilingual education program for Mexican American students in kindergarten through grade 12. The judge indicated that the state had segregated children to inferior schools and had "vilified" the language and culture of the Mexican American children. Although the ruling was reversed a year later, the case led the governor of Texas to appoint a bilingual education task force to draft a state plan for bilingual education. The work of the task force was instrumental in the drafting of Senate Bill 477, the current Bilingual Education Law in Texas.

In ***Plyler v. Doe*** (1982), the court ruling guarantees the rights of undocumented immigrants to free public education. Public schools are prohibited from denying children of undocumented workers admission to school, requiring parents of students to disclose their immigration status, or requiring Social Security numbers. In 1994, California voters passed Proposition 187 in an attempt to slow down immigration. It required school personnel to report to law enforcement agencies and the federal Immigration and Naturalization Service children or personnel unable to prove their legal immigration status. Based on *Plyler v. Doe*, the reporting requirements of Proposition 187 were declared unconstitutional. The judge ruled that immigration is a federal responsibility and the states do not have the option of establishing their own systems.

Roles of the Federal Government and the Office for Civil Rights

Three documents provide the foundation for litigation seeking support for language-minority students:

- **Title VI of the Civil Rights Act of 1964**—Title VI prohibits discrimination on the basis of race, color, or national origin in any program receiving federal funding.
- **Office for Civil Rights Memorandum of 1970**—The OCR, part of the U.S. Department of Health, Education, and Welfare, issued this memorandum to school officials nationwide, requiring districts to offer appropriate instruction to address the educational needs of language minority students. The document also prohibited the use of data relying strictly on language as the key reason for assigning students to special education programs. Based on the historical value of the memorandum, the OCR incorporated its content into the compliance procedure

for Title VI of the Civil Rights Act of 1964 (Castro Feinberg 1990).

- **Equal Educational Opportunities Act of 1974**—The EEOA prohibits states that receive federal funds from denying equal educational opportunity to people based on race, color, sex, or national origin. This civil rights statute provided additional support for the *Lau* ruling and put more pressure on districts to offer meaningful education to ELLs. Unlike Title VI of the Civil Rights Act of 1964, the EEOA applied to all schools, not just those receiving federal funding.

Using the OCR memorandum, the Equal Educational Opportunities Act, and the *Lau* ruling, the OCR instituted the **Lau Remedies** in 1975. The 1974 ruling in *Lau v. Nichols* received little attention until a year later, when the U.S. secretary of education introduced a document to guide districts in the implementation of the *Lau* ruling. Called the Lau Remedies, this document described the process for identification and evaluation of students in bilingual education programs. It further established that school districts must not assign students to classes for the mentally retarded on the basis of criteria that measures language development in English.

The document also mandated bilingual education for elementary schools and ESL instruction for older students. Further, it described the guidelines for exiting students from the program and the professional standards required for teacher participation in the program. The Lau Remedies evolved into the de facto compliance standards of the OCR. However, in 1980, the Reagan administration described the Lau Remedies as unreasonable and eliminated them.

In 1981, Senator S. I. Hayakawa of California initiated a campaign to declare English the official language of the United States and to eliminate bilingual education. The **English-only movement** gained momentum through the 1980s and remains viable. Currently, 24 states have passed legislation banning dual language instruction.

In 1985, the **English-plus movement** was founded by the League of United Latin American Citizens (LULAC) and the Spanish American League against Discrimination (SALAD) as a reaction against the English-only movement. The influence of this group led to increased funding for bilingual education in 1994 and increased interest in the growth of developmental or late exit programs in the nation.

Official Endorsement of Dual Language Instruction

In 2000, the outgoing secretary of education, Bill Riley, officially endorsed dual language education:

> "Proficiency in English and one other language is something that we need to encourage among all young people. That is why I am delighted to see and highlight the growth and promise of so many dual-language bilingual programs across the country. . . . That is why I am challenging our nation to increase the number of dual-language schools to at least 1,000 over the next five years, and with strong federal, state and local support we can have many more."

State Bilingual Education Legislation

Historical Background

In 1969, New Mexico and Texas became the first two states in this country to pass legislation repealing English-only laws, opening the path to bilingual education legislation. Massachusetts, in 1971, became the first state in the United States to mandate bilingual education.

Texas Governor Dolph Briscoe signed into law the Bilingual Education and Training Act (Senate Bill 121) in 1973. This legislation mandated bilingual education from grades 1 through 6. In 1981, the Texas legislature passed the state's current bilingual education law, (Senate Bill 477). It mandated bilingual education through the elementary grades, bilingual or ESL for middle schools, and ESL for high schools. The history of bilingual education in Texas has been characterized by multiple legal challenges and court cases. Here is a time line of key events that shaped bilingual education in Texas:

- **1918**—Following the lead of many other states in the nation, Texas instituted the English-only rule in education. During this time, ELLs were submerged in English-only instruction. Although some children survived and learned English, others could not cope and dropped out of school.
- **1920**—Schools in southern Texas began offering home-based reading and writing instruction in Spanish—the *"Escuelitas"* program. This program was active until the 1960s (Rodríguez 1996).
- **1964**—Under the leadership of Superintendent Harold Brantley, the Laredo School District became the first in Texas to offer bilingual education. District [illegible] San Antonio, McAllen, El Paso, and other[illegible]rs followed Laredo's lead and started bilingual education programs for Mexican-Ar[illegible] children.

Pasadena Public Library

Library name: PC
User name: Gonzalez, Liliana

Date charged: 7/28/2022, 11:01
Title: TExES, Texas Examinations of Educator Standards,
Item ID: 34028082535841
Date due: 8/18/2022,23:59

You saved this much by using your library today!: $28.95

To renew, visit www.pasadenalibrary.org.
Have library card number and
PIN to renew.

[illegible] Representa- [illegible] Bernal, the [illegible]he English- [illegible]03. The bill [illegible]ingual edu- [illegible]-but not re- [illegible]ugh grade 6 [illegible]s and Texas [illegible]ted English [illegible]

[illegible] in Texas re- [illegible]ding to im- [illegible]grams (Ro- [illegible]

[illegible]xas Educa- [illegible]ment of the [illegible]ining Act. It [illegible]m grades 1 [illegible]

[illegible]gual educa- [illegible]ms for chil- [illegible]ade 12. Bi- [illegible]ed through [illegible] or ESL for [illegible]high school [illegible]

Chapter 89 Commissioner's Rules

The commissioner of education, with the State Board of Education, has issued rules guiding the implementation of the state's education laws. Titled the *Commissioner's Rules Concerning State Plan for Educating Limited English Proficient Students* (19 Texas Administrative Code, Chapter 89, Subchapter BB, 1996), the rules provide a detailed interpretation of bilingual education and special language programs, as authorized by the Texas Education Code (TEC §§29.051–29.064, subchapter B). School districts follow this document for implementing and administering bilingual and special language programs.

Goals of Bilingual and ESL

- To enable limited English proficient students to become competent in comprehension, speaking, reading, and composition of the English language through the development of literacy and academic skills in the primary language and English.
- To enable limited English proficient students to master English language skills, as well as mathematics, science and social studies, as integral parts of the academic goals for all students.
- To enable ESL students to become competent in the comprehension, speaking, reading, and composition of the English language through the integrated use of second language methods.
- To enable ESL students to master English language skills, as well as mathematics, science and social studies, as integral parts of the academic goals for all students.

Components of the Bilingual Program

- Affective Component: Introduces basic concepts of the school environment in both the native language (L1) and English (L2) and instills confidence, self-assurance, and develops a positive identity with the student's cultural heritage as well as the culture of the U.S.

- Linguistic Component: Instruction in L1 and L2 is used to develop and master ELLs skills in comprehension, speaking, reading, and composition.
- Cognitive Component: Instruction in L1 and L2 is used to develop and master ELLs Essential Knowledge & Skills (TEKS) and higher order thinking skills in mathematics, science, health, and social studies as well as other content areas.

Programs Under the Legislation

1. Bilingual education from Kindergarten through the elementary grades (EC-6)
2. Districts shall provide a bilingual education program by offering a dual language program in prekindergarten through the elementary grades.
3. Districts are authorized to establish a bilingual education program at grade levels in which the bilingual education program is not required under subsection (a) of this section. This statement allows the implementation of dual language programs in K–12 schools.
4. Bilingual education, instruction in ESL, or other transitional language program approved by the state in post-elementary grades through grade 8.
5. Instruction in ESL in grades 9–12
6. Voluntary Pre-K bilingual program

Home Language Survey

New students to the district are required to complete a home language survey containing two basic questions: What language is spoken in your home most of the time? What language does your child speak most of the time? If the answer to any of these questions is a language other than English, the child must be tested for language dominance or proficiency.

Screening for Admission to the Program

Students in kindergarten through grade 2 are tested using an oral language proficiency test approved by the state. Two of the best-known instruments are the Woodcock Muñoz Language Survey and the Language Assessment Scales (LAS). Students in grades 3 through 12 take an oral proficiency test; can take the Texas Assessment of Knowledge and Skills (TAKS) or the State of Texas Assessments of Academic Readiness (STAAR), and a norm-referenced test, if available. Using the results of these tests and the input of teachers, administrators, and a parent representative, the Language Proficiency Assessment Committee (LPAC) makes placement decisions within four weeks of initial enrollment.

Identification of LEP Students

Districts shall administer the following to students who have a language other than English as identified by the Home Language Survey:

1. in PK through Grade 1, an oral language proficiency test, within 4 weeks of their enrollment), and
2. in Grades 2–12, a TEA-approved oral language proficiency test and the English reading and English language arts sections from a TEA-approved norm-referenced measure (40th Percentile),or another test approved by TEA.

Students with Special Needs

- The Admission Review and Dismissal Committee (ARD) in conjunction with the Language Proficiency Assessment Committee (LPAC) shall determine an appropriate assessment instrument and appropriate level of peformance in determining the proficiency level of LEP students according to the individualized education program (IEP).
- The decision for entry into a bilingual education or ESL program shall be determined by the ARD committee in conjunction with LPAC.

Exit and Reclassification of LEP students

1. TEA-approved tests that measure the extent to which the student has developed oral and

written language proficiency and specific language skills in English;

2. Satisfactory performance on the reading assessment instrument, or a TEA-approved English Language Arts assessment instrument administered in English, or a score at or above the 40th percentile on both the English reading and the English language arts sections of a TEA-approved norm-referenced assessment instrument for a student who is enrolled in Grade 1 or 2; and
3. results of a subjective teacher evaluation
4. passing grades on all subjects and
5. reclassification decision of LPAC and ARD (if applicable).

In making the final decision, the LPAC must take into account the overall academic performance of the child, teachers' evaluation, and parental input. Once in the program, students cannot be exited in grades K to one (1); thus, the earliest grade for reclassification is second grade.

Two-Year Monitoring Services

On reclassification as a fluent English speaker, a student is monitored for two years to ensure success in the English-only classroom. The LPAC evaluates the student's academic performance in class and the results of the TAKS and additional instruments used in school to measure progress. If the student experiences academic problems, the LPAC has the option of returning the child to the bilingual or ESL program or making the necessary changes to be sure he or she is successful.

Language Proficiency Assessment Committee

The LPAC is a committee composed of at least one administrator, teachers, and a parent representative. This committee regulates admission, treatment, dismissal, and follow-up services to students in the bilingual or special language program. Once students are exited from the program, the LPAC follows their progress for two years and makes decisions based on data.

Functions of the LPAC

1. Designate the language proficiency level of each LEP student.
2. Designate the level of academic achievement of each child;
3. Designate, subject to parental approval, the initial instructional placement of each student in the required program;
4. Facilitate the participation of students in other special programs for which they are eligible provided by the district with either state or federal funds; and
5. Reclassify students as English proficient in accordance with the criteria established.

Documentation Required for Bilingual/ ESL Students

The student's permanent record shall contain documentation of all actions impacting students.

1. the identification of the student as LEP;
2. the designation of the student's level of language proficiency;
3. the recommendation of program placement;
4. parental approval of entry or placement into the program;
5. the dates of entry into, and placement within, the program;
6. the dates of exemptions from the criterion-referenced test, criteria used for this determination, and additional instructional interventions provided to students to ensure adequate yearly progress;
7. the date of exit from the program and parent notification; and
8. the results of (two-year) monitoring for academic success, including students formerly classified as LEP

Bilingual Education in the World

There are more bilingual or multilingual countries in the world than monolingual (Tucker, 1999). However, fewer than 25% of the world's 200 countries officially recognize more than one language (Tucker, 1999). A list of countries with official dual or multilingual language policy follows:

Countries that are officially bilingual or multilingual (Anderson & Boyer, 1977; Grosjean, 1982):

- **Canada**—French and English
- **Belgium**—Flemish, French, and German
- **Finland**—Finnish and Swedish
- **Ireland**—English and Gaelic
- **Israel**—English and Hebrew
- **Singapore**—Chinese, Malay, Tamil, and English
- **South Africa**—Afrikaans and English
- **Switzerland**—German, French, Romansh, and Italian

Multilingual Countries

Some policymakers in the United States see language diversity as a threat to national security and cohesion. However, several countries in the world have multiple linguistic groups who still manage to keep their integrity as nations. For example, India uses Hindi and English as lingua francas (common languages) to communicate with speakers of 200 additional languages, 33 of which have more than 1 million speakers (Grosjean 1982). In India, the average citizen speaks two or three languages. In China, Mandarin is the unifying language of the government, but Cantonese and many other languages are used within the country. In Hong Kong, English is used as the language for business. The South African government recognizes nine official languages in addition to English and Afrikaans. In Paraguay, Spanish is the official language, but Guarani is the national language of the indigenous population. Ninety percent of the people in Paraguay speak Guarani as their first language, and half of the population is bilingual.

In Sweden, non-native children receive instruction in L1 while developing proficiency in Swedish. By the fifth grade, instruction in all subject areas is done in two languages. Similarly, in China, children receive instruction in L1 with gradual introduction to Chinese in the second grade. Canada is probably one of the best examples of a bilingual nation. Its experiments with immersion programs have been used as a model in the United States.

The American Council on the Teaching of Foreign Languages estimates that about 3 percent of high school students can be considered bilingual, and only 5 percent become bilingual after college (Ovando, Combs, and Collier 2006). Bilingualism and multilingualism seem to be the rule in the world, but in the United States, it is still considered the exception.

Bilingual and ESL Program Models

Several bilingual education programs are available to meet the language needs of ELLs in Texas. A summary of these programs follows.

Early-Exit Transitional Bilingual Education Programs

The early-exit transitional bilingual education (TBE) program is the program of choice for most school districts in the United States. In Texas, Senate Bill 2, Chapter 29B, calls for transitional bilingual education. The main goal of the program is to mainstream students as quickly as possible. This program promotes literacy in L1 and offers native language instruction in kindergarten through grade 2 with at least 45 minutes of ESL instruction. Traditionally, the transition to English begins officially in third grade, and by grade 4, students are mainstreamed or placed in a class using the sheltered English approach (discussed later in the chapter). In a self-contained elementary model, a bilingual teacher provides instruction in L1 and L2. In the upper-elementary grades, one instructor might teach in L1 while an ESL specialist promotes language development. Unfortunately, this program is perceived as remedial, too complex for teachers to be able to follow all the guidelines and not long enough for ELLs to develop English proficiency.

A TBE program can be implemented as early exit or late exit, depending on the time in the program (NCELA 2006). However, based on the significant differences between the two programs, they are treated separately in this chapter.

Late-Exit Dual Language Programs

Under the late-exit model, programs offer four or more years of treatment. Although originally designed for students in kindergarten through grade 12, most programs are implemented through fifth or sixth grade. Two types of late-exit programs are described in this section: developmental bilingual education (DBE) and dual language immersion programs.

Developmental Bilingual Education

The developmental bilingual education program emerged in the 1970s as an alternative to the transitional bilingual education model (Crawford 2004). The program is also known as maintenance bilingual education or **bilingual-bicultural education**, and more recently has been labeled **one-way bilingual education**. In this program, language minority children with a common language are placed in a program where they are encouraged to maintain their native language and add English to be able to function academically and socially in both languages. Opponents of bilingual-bicultural education have attacked the program for its failure to place sufficient emphasis on English development. As a result of this opposition, the program was declared ineligible to receive federal funding in 1978 (Crawford 2004). However, the program was reauthorized in the Bilingual Education Act of 1984 under the name *developmental bilingual education* (DBE).

The DBE program appears to be similar to the early-exit TBE program but does have fundamental differences. A comparison of the two programs is presented in Table 1-2.

Two-Way Dual Language Immersion

The two-way bilingual education program is a form of developmental bilingual education because it promotes the maintenance of both languages. The program serves language majority (native English speakers) and language minority students (ELLs) in an instructional setting where both groups learn from each other in a peer-teaching situation. In addition to the language benefits of peer instruction, the program contributes to a better cultural understanding among children in the group (Christian 1994). This program views students as gifted, as opposed to the compensatory and deficient perspective of the early-exit model. The positive nature of the program and its inclusion of language majority students make funding and supporting it more palatable to the general public.

Table 1-2. Comparison of the DBE and TBE Programs

Transitional Bilingual Education	Developmental Bilingual Education
Length of the Program – Approximately 2–3 years	Length of the Program – Approximately 4–5 years
Remedial and subtractive in orientation. The native language is seen as a problem that needs to be eradicated. Students begin with two languages and end with only one.	**Enrichment and additive in orientation**– The native language is seen as an asset that should be preserved. Students begin with different levels of proficiency in L1 and L2 and finish with similar levels of proficiency in both languages.
Literacy in L1 – The early-exit nature of TBE does not allow sufficient time for the child to become proficient in L1, thus, they do not benefit from possible language skills transferred from L1 to L2.	**Literacy in L1** – The late exit nature of the program allows more time to develop the proficiency in L1. With a stronger literacy background, they can transfer literacy skills from L1 to L2.

Program Implementation

The program is implemented in a variety of ways throughout the United States. These versions are structured based on content or percentages of instruction by language.

By Content

In one model, some of the content areas are delivered in L1 and others in L2. For example, social studies and mathematics can be delivered in L1, and art and music can be presented in L2. Switching the language of instruction is done to expose students to the content areas in both languages. Teachers are generally organized in one of two ways:

- **Two Teachers (Mixed) or Team Teaching.** This approach uses two classrooms with one teacher delivering instruction in the minority language and the second teaching in the majority language. At a specific point in the day or week, students switch teachers. One of the benefits of this system is that students identify the teacher with a given language, which discourages **code switching**.
- **Single Teacher.** In this approach, one teacher alternates the use of the languages across disciplines. The teacher must be fully bilingual and must guide students to separate the uses of the two languages. Because students know that the teacher is bilingual, they often switch from one language to the other; thus, the teacher has to make an extra effort to guide students to communicate in the language of instruction.

By Time Percentages

In some two-way programs, a specific percentage of the instructional time is assigned to each of the two languages. Three types of models are possible:

- **Balanced Program, or the 50/50 Model.** In this model, students receive equal instructional time in L1 and L2. This percentage is maintained throughout the program. This is the second-most popular model in the United States, implemented by 33 percent of the programs.
- **Minority/Majority Language Program, or the 90/10 or 80/20 Model.** In this model, the largest percentage of instruction is done in the minority language, which means that language majority students are placed in an immersion format. This is the type of program used in Canada, with English speakers learning French as a second language. The amount of instruction in the majority language increases to a point where balanced instruction is achieved (50/50) by third or fourth grade. This is the most popular model in the United States, implemented by 42 percent of the programs.

  The 90/10 model of the two-way bilingual program uses the minority language for initial instruction (90 percent) and 10 percent for native language development. Thus, language majority students are exposed to an immersion program. However, because language minority students receive instruction in their native language, they are not part of the immersion model. Instead, they are exposed to maintenance or developmental bilingual education.
- **Combination Program.** This type of program combines native language instruction with dual language. Students in this approach are homogenously grouped by their native language for a portion of the day to received native literacy instruction. For example, native English speakers receive instruction in English and native Spanish speakers receive it in Spanish. For the remaining part of the day, they are grouped heterogeneously to receive dual language instruction. Only 2 percent of the programs in the United States have implemented this approach (Howard and Sugarman 2001).

Program Organization

The two most common formats for the dual language program are the **half-day** and the **one-day** alternating organizations.

- **Half-Day Alternating Bilingual Program**—In this type of organization, morning lessons are delivered in one language and the second language in the afternoon. To cover all content areas in both languages, the program alternates the languages used in the two portions of the day.

- **One-Day Alternating Bilingual Program**—Under this type of organization, one full day is delivered in English, and the following day the content is delivered in Spanish.

Alternating approaches to bilingual content area avoid the repetition of lessons in each language within the class period. However, for students with very limited proficiency in one of the languages of instruction, the alternating model may not be appropriate because the student may miss too much content during the time that teaching is in the second language.

Canadian Immersion Programs

A total immersion program was initiated in Montreal, Canada, in the early 1960s for native English-speaking students who wanted to learn the minority language, French. In this program, language majority students (English speakers) are immersed in the second language (French). English language support is provided in the community and in the home environment. From kindergarten to first grade, students receive content and literacy instruction in the second language. Literacy instruction is developed initially in French and later in English. English language arts instruction begins in second grade and increases proportionally from that point. In third grade, instruction is equally distributed between the two languages—50 percent each. After third grade, English instruction increases proportionally until reaching a ratio of 60 percent English to 40 percent French by sixth grade. In grades 7 through 12, students are offered courses in French to maintain their proficiency.

Historical Development of the ESL Field

English as a second language is a system of instruction designed to teach language to children whose native language is other than English. The term *ESL* evolved from the field of foreign language instruction as part of the Americanization efforts of the late nineteenth and early twentieth century (Crawford 2004). In 1941, English as a foreign language became a field of study under the leadership of researchers at the University of Michigan (Ovando, Combs, and Collier 2006). As part of their research efforts, the University of Michigan began preparing teachers to teach English abroad. In the 1960s, the field shifted its emphasis and began preparing teachers to teach English to American immigrants. With this new emphasis, the field of ESL was created. Following the creation of the field of study, the association called TESOL—Teachers of English to Speakers of Other Languages—was founded in 1966. Currently, the term *ESL* or *ESOL* (English for speakers of other languages) is used to describe a system of instruction used in public schools to meet the needs of English language learners.

ESL is part of the curriculum in most school districts in the United States. The field is perceived as compensatory and transitional in nature. Currently, ESL is used mainly in two educational settings:

- ESL is a component of Bilingual Education-where students receive native language instruction and language development through ESL. In early-exit transitional bilingual education models, ESL is the bridge used to move students from native language instruction to instruction in English. In late-exit programs, like one-way and two-way dual language programs, ESL is used to develop the English proficiency needed to receive instruction in a dual language format.
- ESL is also used as a "program" in situations where bilingual education is not feasible because of the large number of foreign languages spoken in the district. In this case, the program is designed to support instruction while students develop the English proficiency to function in the all-English classroom.

English as a Second Language and Special Language Programs

ESL or ESOL is a component of bilingual education programs in the elementary classroom. Students in a self-contained (one instructor teaches all subjects) bilingual education program receive content instruction in L1 and receive at least 45 minutes of ESL instruction to promote English language development. In a variation of the self-contained model, one instructor teaches the content area in L1 and a second teacher pulls out the child to provide ESL instruction. A description of this and other models using English-only instruction follows.

ESL Pullout

One of the first approaches used in public school to teach English to ELLs was the pullout system. In this system, students spend most of the day in mainstream classes and are "pulled out" of their classes for one or two periods per day to receive English instruction. This approach is perhaps the most expensive and least effective of the ESL methods currently used (Crawford 2004; Thomas and Collier 1997). Although schools with a large number of ESL students may have a full-time ESL teacher, some districts employ an ESL teacher who travels to several schools to work with small groups of students scattered throughout the district. This program has been criticized for its cost and its shortcoming (Crawford 2004; Ovando, Combs, and Collier 2006).

Structured English Immersion

Structured English immersion (SEI) was conceptualized in the 1980s under the auspices of the U.S. Department of Education, the leadership of conservative members of Congress, and the English-only movement (Crawford 2004). The origin of SEI can be traced to the Baker and de Kanter Report (1981), a Department of Education commissioned study to investigate the effectiveness of transitional bilingual education programs in the United States. In this study the researchers concluded that the literature did not provide consistent evidence of the effectiveness of TBE programs.

Despite the multiple flaws of the study (Crawford 2004; Ovando, Combs, and Collier 2006), it convinced legislators to search for a different way to address the language needs of ELLs. After analyzing the success of the French bilingual immersion programs in Canada, the researchers proposed a similar program to replace TBE. The model is today known as the structured English immersion program. Contrary to the additive nature of the Canadian bilingual immersion programs, the SEI is a subtractive program designed to teach English only. In the self-contained ESL classroom, the teacher delivers instruction in English to ELLs. To ensure comprehension, teachers use techniques to simplify and contextualize instruction. Through the use of "sheltered instruction," children learn content and language concurrently.

Sheltered English or ESL Content

This model, developed in the 1980s, represents a shift from programs that emphasize only English language development to more content-based ESL instruction (Crawford 2004). The sheltered English approach attempts to make academic instruction in English understandable to ELLs while promoting English language development. In this approach, teachers use hands-on activities, concrete objects, simplified speech, and physical activities to teach concept development in the content areas. Before this model, ESL teachers taught language development at the expense of content area instruction; thus, students were falling behind academically.

Sheltered English or ESL content is used mostly at the secondary level and is most effective for students with intermediate-to-advanced proficiency in English. It focuses on the delivery of content in contextualized situations with the addition of language objectives. Two of the better-known commercial programs that emphasize content and language development are the CALLA model developed by Chamot and O'Malley (1994) and the SIOP model developed by Echevarria, Vogt, and Short (2000). The former was developed for secondary students and the latter addressed both the elementary and secondary levels.

Newcomer Centers

Newcomer centers address the needs of recent immigrants or students who are new to the English language. In a newcomer center, ESL is used to support ELLs in their linguistic and cultural adjustment to life and schooling in the United States. The program provides linguistic and psychological support to unschooled and other nontraditional English language learners. This program was designed mostly for students in middle and high school; however, today it is also used at the elementary level.

The instructional language approach and methods used in newcomer centers vary by district and state. Some centers provide intensive English language development, and others adopt a sheltered English approach in which students can keep up academically while developing proficiency in English. Traditionally, students remain in the center a year or less before they are sent to mainstream classrooms.

Research on Program Effectiveness

AIR Study

The 1978 American Institutes for Research (AIR) study was the first and one of the largest national studies on the effectiveness of federally sponsored Title VII programs (Dannoff et al. 1978). The study encompassed 8,200 students in 38 schools from 10 states. It compared the performance of ELLs (Spanish speakers) in bilingual education programs with the performance of Latino students in the all-English program. The study found few differences in the performance of students in the two models. Bilingual education proponents challenged the study's methodology and identified the following flaws (Crawford, 2004):

- did not control for quality of bilingual program
- did not look at the various type of districts to establish program needs
- did not control for background variables (e.g. initial language proficiency assessment of language proficiency)
- many students in the study had been exited from the bilingual program.
- the study lacked clarity

Ramírez Study

The 1992 Ramírez study was a U.S. government-sponsored study comparing the effectiveness of three program models: early-exit (TBE), late-exit (developmental TBE), and structured English immersion. This longitudinal study began in 1984 and involved more than 2,000 children attending schools in California, Florida, New Jersey, New York, and Texas. A preliminary report issued in 1986 showed that students in the late-exit bilingual education programs were outperforming students in the immersion programs. Keith Baker, program director for the study and a proponent of structured English immersion, quickly dismissed the report and insisted that conclusions should not be drawn from incomplete data. After the initial report, data from the study were kept secret until the final report was released in 1992.

According to Ramírez (1992), the complexity of the study design did not permit a direct comparison of the three models. Instead, the direct comparison was done only between the structured English immersion and early-exit models. This comparison revealed no significant differences in student performance in mathematics, reading, and English language acquisition as measured by the Comprehensive Test of Basic Skills (CTBS).

Ramirez (1992) found the growth curves for ELLs in late-exit instructional programs continued to grow in English Language Arts and Reading and mathematics, catching up to the mainstream group. Early exit and mainstream programs had gains in the lower grades, however, growth declined as they progressed to a higher grade.

Thomas and Collier Study

Thomas and Collier (1997, 2002) conducted a longitudinal study on the school effectiveness for language minority students involving more than 700,000 students from five large urban and suburban school districts. The study examined the performance of ELLs in the various programs available: early-exit, late-exit, and ESL models. The researchers identified some key predictors of academic success, for example:

- The delivery of cognitively complex on-grade-level academic instruction through students' first language (at least through grades 5 or 6) and cognitively complex on-grade-level academic instruction through L2 for part of the school year have a definite impact in the achievement of ELLs.

- Students in two-way bilingual classes outperform their counterparts being schooled in monolingual classrooms, and they sustained the gains all the way through high school.

Programs for Language Minority Students

When English language learners in the United States begin their schooling, they are academically behind their native English-speaking counterparts. To improve their chances of catching up academically with monolingual English speaking peers, a special type of program is required. Two of the programs currently available are accelerated learning and critical pedagogy.

Accelerated Learning

Accelerated learning is a concept that emerged from the work of Levin (1987). The main purpose of the program is to enhance and enrich learning among students in at-risk situations to allow them to catch up academically with their peers. This approach relies heavily on enrichment strategies taken from the gifted-and-talented programs and effectively employs the strengths that children bring from home.

According to the North Central Regional Educational Laboratory (NCREL), the accelerated learning concept is based on the following cardinal principles:

- setting high expectations for all students;
- identifying and eliminating achievement gaps by the end of elementary school;
- implementing an interdisciplinary curriculum that emphasizes hands-on activities, critical thinking and the use of problem-solving using real life situations;
- creating meaningful involvement of parents, and empowerment of teachers; and
- using the language and culture of minority students and incorporate them in daily school activities and used as teaching tools.

Critical Pedagogy

Critical pedagogy is a concept that emerged from the work of the Brazilian educator Paulo Freire (1970). Freire believes that children are not exposed to a curriculum that reflects their reality and are not guided to analyze or question that reality. Critical pedagogy guides students to identify real-life problems, reflect on them, gather information, share it with peers, and collectively find solutions. In this approach, students become active learners and participants in their own reality. Students develop a deep and relevant knowledge of life, develop problem-solving skills, and become protagonists in their quest for knowledge and discovery.

According to Martin Ryder (2005) from the University of Colorado, most current educational principles—such as the concept of student-centered learning, negotiated curriculum, differentiated curriculum, and many more elements of "cutting edge education"—have their origins in critical pedagogy. The approach has the potential to empower linguistic minorities in the United States.

Strategies Used in Bilingual Education

Reciprocal Teaching

In this instructional activity, teachers and students engage in a dialogue about class content (Palincsar 1986). This dialogue is based on the use of four strategies:

- **Summarizing**—Students present the main content in their own words.
- **Question Generating**—Students identify the most significant content and design questions to test their own knowledge in their quest for knowledge.
- **Clarifying**—Students are guided to identify specific parts of the text that might create comprehension problems related to the technical vocabulary, idiomatic expressions, and concepts.
- **Predicting**—Students are guided to predict the content based on prior knowledge and information gathered from the readings.

Preview-Review Approach

In this traditional approach, the teacher introduces the content in one language and presents the body of the lesson in the second language. The teacher provides an overview of the content and introduces the technical vocabulary needed to understand the lesson in the second language. After the body of the lesson is completed, the lesson might be reviewed by grouping students by language dominance, with reinforcement activities conducted in L1, or by using the concurrent approach. In view of the required separation of languages typical in dual language instruction, this strategy is rarely used in bilingual education.

Concurrent Approach

In this traditional approach, both languages are used to deliver instruction. It requires a special ability to provide equivalent content rather than literal translations. In addition, teachers must have a strong knowledge of content area terminology in both languages. This strategy is rarely used as the main medium to deliver content in modern dual language programs.

For a comprehensive list of terminology related to linguistically diverse students and bilingual education, see the glossary on the website for the National Clearinghouse for English Language Acquisition at *www.ncela.gwu.edu*.

Key Principles of Competency 001

- The total language immersion programs in Canada are designed for both English speakers and English language learners (i.e., French students). The structured English immersion programs in the United States are designed mostly to teach English language learners.
- The benefits of the additive nature of developmental bilingual education are cultural reinforcement and continued cognitive growth in L1 that enhances student learning and reinforces cognitive development in L2.
- Strategies to promote biliteracy and biculturalism should incorporate materials from the students' native cultures and readings in L1. Materials should include English language versions of stories, folktales, and other narratives from the students' home cultures to validate and affirm those culture.
- Maintenance bilingual education provides the most extensive instruction in L1.
- Since the 1960s, bilingual education has gradually shifted from the early-exit model to the late-exit and models.
- Students who develop cognitive-academic skills in L1 have a better chance of succeeding academically in L2.
- If a student has mastered Spanish STAAR but is not ready to study content areas in English, the LPAC should allow the student to stay in the bilingual program.
- A bilingual education program should emphasize a student's personal and cultural self-esteem and present the learning of English as an additive component rather than a replacement for the student's native language.
- To improve their chances of achieving academic parity with native English speakers, ELLs should receive content area and language arts instruction in L1 and L2 for at least six years (Ovando, Combs, and Collier 2006).

Competency 002

The beginning bilingual education teacher understands processes of first- and second-language acquisition and development and applies this knowledge to promote students' language proficiency in their first language (L1) and second language (L2).

Stages of Language Development

Language learning appears to be the result of some combination of innate ability and environmental influences. Children have to be exposed to language in natural settings to acquire it. Imitation appears to be a learning strategy for young children who frequently use it through age 2, but the strategy decreases in effectiveness as language learning becomes more complex (Stewig and Jett-Simpson 1995). Children at the one-word stage use imitation as a strategy for language development. They appear to pay attention to the ends of sentences and words. For example, when a mother asks "Do you want me to pick you up?," the child might point to the mother and say, "Up, up." This linguistic behavior is probably the result of the limited short-term memory typical of children at this stage of development. However, imitation cannot explain idiosyncratic statements like "I goed home yesterday," which shows some degree of language creativity and manipulation. That is, the child conceptualizes the function of the regular past tense but over generalizes and applies the rule to an irregular verb form—*to go*. Children are rule makers and often invent strategies to assist them in figuring out how the language operates.

Language is initially acquired in meaningful social settings. The type of the social interaction will determine the type and quality of language that the child will develop. In mainstream American culture, parents often allow their children opportunities to become full-fledged participants in conversation with adults. Children who have been given these opportunities often come to school with stronger language skills than do children who are excluded from adult conversation (Rosado 2005).

English language learners come to school with a developed variation of language or **dialect** that reflects their social structure. Their pronunciation, vocabulary, grammar and rules of discourse vary from the formal language they are exposed to in a school setting. ELLs use language in various contexts in a social setting, thus acquiring different **register**s or language that is used for specific purposes. ELLs bring a wealth of language to the school setting, yet the assessments used by schools are not linguistically appropriate for ELLs thus, there's a mismatch between the language features, dialect, pronunciation and registers of the students and the assessments (Sousa, 2010).

Children acquire language in highly contextualized situations. They expect language to make sense, and they try to discover and negotiate meaning. Table 1–3 presents an overview of the process of L1 acquisition and compares it with equivalent stages in L2 acquisition.

Components of Language

Language is a system composed of several subsystems: phonology, morphology, syntax, lexicon, discourse, and pragmatics. Effective ESL teachers need to clearly understand how these components are acquired in L1 and L2 and how they affect language and cognitive development.

Phonology is the study of the sound system of the language. The basic unit of sound is the phoneme. English has 44 phonemes (sounds) represented by 26 graphemes (letters). An English phoneme can be represented by more than one grapheme, and often the grapheme-phoneme correspondence is inconsistent. English also has many consonant digraphs—two or more letters representing one sound. Here are some examples of digraphs:

gh-	ghost	**gn-**	gnat
kn-	know	**-ght**	thought
pn-	pneumonia	**ps-**	psychology
rh-	rhythm	**wr-**	write
sc-	scene	**sch-**	school

The lack of grapheme-phoneme correspondence in the English language creates problems for ELLs.

Table 1-3. Stages in the Acquisition of L1 and L2

First Language	Second Language
1. Babbling Stage, 0–10 Months • Sends and receives messages • Uses reflexive crying to communicate • Produces vowel- and consonant-like sounds • Identifies the voice of the parents and family members • Understands intonations patterns (e.g., anger, statements, questions, etc.)	**1. Preproduction or Silent Stage** • Communicates with gestures and actions • Lacks receptive vocabulary and shows problems comprehending messages • Some prefer to remain silent (silent phase) • Might experience frustration and anxiety • Relies heavily on nonverbal communication, which can lead to miscommunication
2. Holophrastic Stage 11–18 Months (One-Word Stage) • Understands word concepts • Conceptualizes complete ideas through one-word sentences • Uses adults as tools	**2. Early Speech Production** • Increases comprehension • Communicates using *yes* or *no* and one-word statements • Expands receptive vocabulary • Understands language in contextualized situations
3. Telegraphic Stage, 18 Months and Up • Conceptualizes whole sentences • Uses the minimum number of words to get the point across • Uses content words with high semantic values (e.g., nouns, verbs, adjectives, etc.) • Conceptualizes and imitates the reading and writing processes	**3. Speech Emergence** • Communicates in phrases using words with high semantic context: nouns verbs, and adjective • Continues gaining receptive vocabulary • Communicates more effectively in contextualized situations, face-to-face interactions • Understands more than what he/she is able to communicate
4. School Age • Improves language skills through explicit instruction (deductively) • Formal teaching is introduced • Learns the social functions of the language • Develops a personal communication style or idiolect • Gets exposed to different registers (dialects)	**4. Intermediate Fluency** • Communicates using simple sentences • Overgeneralizes because of intralingual and interlingual interference • Becomes more acculturated and feels more comfortable in school
	5. Advanced Stage Develops the academic language and might be ready to be mainstreamed

For example, the word *through* has seven graphemes representing only three phonemes.

Spanish has a very consistent grapheme-phoneme correspondence. The language has 26 graphemes to represent 25 to 27 sounds. With the notable exception of the *h*, every letter is pronounced in Spanish. This consistency can lead to negative transfer when Spanish-speaking ELLs attempt to pronounce every single letter in English words like ***island*** or ***thought***.

Morphology is the study of the structure of words or word formation. Words are made up of units of meaning called **morphemes**. The word *cars* is made of two morphemes: the basic or root word *car* and the letter indicating plural, *s*. Morphemes are classified into two large categories: derivational and inflectional. **Derivational morphemes** refer to the type of morpheme that can (but may not) change the syntactic classification. These are loans from foreign languages—mostly from Greek and Latin—and can be used as prefixes and suffixes. For example, the word *subconsciously* contains the root word *consci* and three derivational morphemes: The first (*sub-*) is the prefix morpheme, the second (*-ous*) is an adjectival suffix morpheme, and the third (*-ly*) is a suffix that creates an adverb. Transforming the word *subconscious* to *subconsciously* changes the syntactic classification from an adjective to an adverb.

Inflectional morphemes do not change the syntactic classification and typically follow derivational morphemes. There are eight types of inflectional morphemes: present participle (*-ing*), third-person singular (*-s*), possessive (*-'s*), plural (*-s, -es*), regular past tense (*-ed*), past participle (*-en*), the comparative (*-er*), and the superlative (*-est*). All inflectional morphemes are native of English, and they are always placed at the end of the word. For example, the word *greater* is composed of the adjective *great* and the comparative *er*. Adding the inflectional ending to change the word *great* to *greater* did not affect the syntactic classification of the word; both words are adjectives.

Syntax describes the organization of words in a sentence. English has specific syntactic rules to account for the grammaticality of the sentence, the order of words and morphemes, structural ambiguity, and the grammatical and logical relations within sentences (Fromkin and Rodman 1988). Seven of the most common sentence structures in English are listed below:

A **lexicon** is the vocabulary of a language. It is also the most changeable component of language. Words can change meaning based on context. For example the word *hot* can refer to temperature, fashion, or luck, and its meaning depends on the context of usage.

Semantics is the meaning system of a language and is based on the culture and context of the conversation. It uses literal and implied meanings to achieve this goal.

- **Denotation** refers to the literal meaning of words and ideas. A sign that reads "Dog Bites" seems obvious, because all dogs have that capability (literal meaning). However, pragmatics of communication will guide people to go beyond literal meaning and understand the intended meaning of the statement—the dog is aggressive and might attack.
- **Connotation** refers to the implied meaning of words and ideas. Idiomatic expressions frequently use implied meaning as a communication tool; thus, speakers need to know the implied cultural framework to understand them. English language learners might have problems getting the meaning intended in idiomatic statements like "passing the buck." They might know the two meanings of the word *buck*—male deer or a dollar—and still be unable to understand the implied meaning—passing the responsibility to someone else.

Discourse is the ability of speakers to combine sounds into words, words into sentences and larger units in a cohesive manner to achieve oral or written communication. The cohesive devices used in L1 might be different from the ones required in L2.

Pragmatics is the role of context in the interpretation of communication. Pragmatics describes the hidden rules of communication shared by native speakers of the language. Often these rules are not evident for English language learners.

Cognates and False Cognates

Cognates are words pronounced and spelled similarly in two languages. Cognates were developed as a result of the association of modern languages with classical languages like Arabic, Greek, and Latin. Because of the influence of these three cultural groups—Arab, Greek, and Roman—in mathematics, natural sciences, and social studies, many cognates are used in these subjects. Teachers need to make children aware of the similarity of this vocabulary and guide students to transfer cognates from L1 to L2. For a list of cognates from various languages, see Kress (1993). Examples of Spanish cognates are: *abandon* (abandonar), *accent* (acento), *accept* (aceptar), *band* (banda) and *bank* (banco), *family* (familia), *animal* (animal). There is an enormous count of cognates used by Spanish speakers.

A false cognate is a word that resembles a word in a second language but has a different meaning. For example, the English words *embarrass* and *support* resemble the Spanish words *embarazar* (to get pregnant) and *soportar* (to tolerate), and this similarity can create communication problems. Teachers can guide students to identify cognates and false cognates and use this knowledge to expand their academic vocabulary.

Theories of L1 Acquisition

There are three main theories of L1 acquisition: the behaviorist, the innatist, and the interactionist (Peregoy and Boyle 2005). The **behaviorists** believe children are born with a clean slate—*tabula rasa*—and language is added through imitation of parents and caregivers. Specifically, children add information to the *tabula rasa* through the process of stimulus, response, and reinforcement. That is, children hear a word, link the word to a concept, imitate the pronunciation of the word, and get rewarded for their efforts. This theory explains the initial stages of L1 acquisition but fails to explain the linguistic creativity typical of children beyond the initial stage. When a parent tells a 3-year-old boy, "**You** stink" and the child replies by saying "**I** stink," the response shows that the child is not merely repeating or mimicking the speech of the adult but is processing and hypothesizing language rules.

Innatist or nativist theory takes the opposing view that children are born with innate capabilities for language learning. They believe that children are born with what Noam Chomsky called a language acquisition device (LAD). The LAD is equipped with a grammar template or universal grammar enables children to construct the grammar of their native language through the process of hypothesis testing. According to Chomsky, children develop the rules of their language with minimal support from their parents. The role of adults in this theory is restricted to building the lexicon of the language and teaching rules to develop sociolinguistic competence.

Interactionists, on the other hand, reemphasize the importance of both nature and nurture as vital components for language mastery. They conceptualize the existence of the LAD but believe that the role of parents and caregivers in the innatist theory is too narrow in scope. Interactionists believe that caregivers play a vital role in adjusting language to facilitate language acquisition. Parents and caregivers become sympathetic listeners and provide needed language support through conversational scaffolding. Parents scaffold conversation by repeating and modeling the words that the child produces, checking for understanding by prompting questions at the end of the child's statements, and by making the child feel confident in his or her ability to communicate. The interactionist theory is currently the prevailing theory used to explain the process of L1 acquisition.

Theories of L2 Acquisition

Healthy young children acquire a first language in natural settings with minimum conscious effort. Following this universal achievement, researchers in L2 acquisition studied L1 acquisition to identify ways in which this process can be replicated to teach a second language. Their views are presented based on the three dominant theories of L1 acquisition—behaviorist, innatist, and interactionist.

Behaviorists' Views of L2 Acquisition

Behaviorists see L2 learning as a process of habit formation through the use of stimulus, response, and reinforcement. Following these principles, the behaviorist developed the Audio Lingual Method. The method uses imitation, repetition, and reinforcement to teach a second language. They promote the use of memorization of dialogues and pattern drills as a foundation to teach the grammar of the language. Errors are corrected immediately to avoid the formation of bad linguistic habits, and reinforcement is used to maintain the correct structures. This method influenced the teaching of second and foreign languages during the 1950s and 1960s, but its influence virtually ended in the late 1970s.

Innatists' Views of L2 Acquisition

Following Chomsky's view of language, innatists developed the creative construction theory. Proponents of this theory suggest that L2 learners follow similar strategies and make the same kinds of errors as native speakers in the process of language mastery. Following these principles, Krashen (1983) developed one of the most comprehensive theories of L2 acquisition. This theory comprises the following five hypotheses.

1. **Acquisition versus Learning**—Acquisition and learning represent two different processes. Acquisition takes place through meaningful and natural language interaction with speakers of the language with no conscious efforts to comply with grammar conventions. It is meaning driven and characterized by language discovery in a low-anxiety environment. In opposition, learning describes the formal and highly restrictive activities typically found in a teacher-centered classroom instruction. It directly teaches students the rules of grammar v. using language to communicate.

   Educational Implications—Strategies that resemble the process of L1 acquisition can promote L2 acquisition. Teachers need to use inductive teaching and promote language development through fun and interactive activities that lead to self-discovery.

2. **Comprehensible Input**—Children must understand the content of the communication in the target language to acquire the language. However, for real acquisition to take place, the input must be slightly above the current linguistic level of the learner. In other words, language is acquired by understanding input that contains linguistic structures that are beyond the current level of linguistic competence.

   Educational Implications—Teachers need to implement meaningful activities in contextualized situations to ensure that ELLs understand the content of the communication. ESL methods used in the classroom should attempt to recreate the way that children acquire a first language—that is, the Total Physical Response (TPR) and Natural Method (NM). Both the TPR and NM use of commands, concrete objects and highly contextualized situations to make language comprehensible.

3. **The Monitor Hypothesis**—Learners exposed to formal language instruction develop an internal mechanism enabling them to assess language and make corrections. However, to use this language editor, children must have explicit knowledge of the rules and time to apply them.

   Educational Implications—The monitor hypothesis has limited implications for the development of the speaking ability in L2. However, teachers can guide students to internalize the rules to a point where the rules become automatic and can easily be applied in a subconscious fashion. Conscious knowledge of the rules can be beneficial to polish the language and to monitor writing samples.

4. **Affective Filter Hypothesis**—Students perform better when they feel motivated and relaxed. When they are relaxed, the affective filter is lowered, allowing linguistic input in the LAD.

Educational Implications—Teachers should create a low-anxiety environment in which students feel secure. Students should not be forced to communicate before they are ready. Teachers should allow students to remain silent but provide them with comprehensible input to develop the language needed to begin oral communication.

5. **Natural Order Hypothesis**—ESL students acquire English structures in a predictable sequence with small variations depending on the influence of L1. This sequence is guided by the communicative value of the structures and the frequency of required usage. For example, forms of the verb *to be* are used more frequently and convey more information than the third-person singular; thus, they are acquired earlier.

   Educational Implications—Teachers should avoid following a grammatical sequence when teaching English. Instead, developing rich linguistic activities encourage students to use various structures. The communicative acts and the needs of the learners will determine the acquisition sequence of the language structures.

Interactionists' Views in L2 Acquisition

Krashen's concept of comprehensible input is an important part of the interactionist view of L2 acquisition. Interactionists emphasize the way that native speakers deliver comprehensible input and the way they negotiate meaning with ELLs.

Educational Implications—Teachers should be encouraged to use nonverbal communication, drawing, and modified speech (foreign talk) to deliver comprehensible input. They should also develop strategies for ELLs to interact with native speakers and negotiate meaning in real-life situations.

Interdependence of L1 and L2

A strong cognitive and academic development in the first language has a positive effect in the acquisition of the second language. Academic skills and content knowledge, literacy development, and metacognitive strategies transfer to L2 (Ovando, Combs, and Collier 2006). Cummins (1991) calls this interdependence the common underlying proficiency (CUP). The concept of the CUP has been used as an argument in favor of bilingual education.

Age and L2 Acquisition

Critical-Period Hypothesis

Researchers have conceptualized the possibility of a critical period for the acquisition of languages. They place this critical period from two years of age to puberty. During this period, the lateralization of the brain occurs and language functions are assigned to specific parts of the brain. The lateralization of the brain affects mostly the development of native-like pronunciation. That is, a child exposed to a new language during the critical period can develop a near-native accent, while a child coming in contact with a second language after puberty might develop a foreign accent.

The critical-period hypothesis suggests that children might have an advantage over adults in the development of pronunciation. Children are also more willing to take risks than adults; thus, they might develop the language faster. Adults, on the other hand, have developed a "language ego," which might affect their willingness to seek contacts with native speakers to practice the language.

The Threshold Hypothesis

Cummins (1991) believes that language learners should arrive at a given academic and literacy level in L1 before attempting to transfer elements of it to a second language. This age-appropriate threshold is generally reached after 4 or 5 years of effective instruction in L1. This theory explains why ELLs taught in only in L2 may experience academic difficulties in school, while ELLs who receive services through a late-exit program may have cognitive advantages over monolingual students (Baker and Jones 1998).

Levels of L2 Proficiency

The American Council for the Teaching of Foreign Languages (ACTFL) identified five levels of oral language proficiency. These levels resemble the four levels identified by Krashen for L2 learners listed in Table 1-2. Teachers need to have a clear understanding of the stages of L2 proficiency and use these as a foundation for planning instruction and assessing academic and language progress.

Novice (Preproduction and Early Production Stages)

- Communicates minimally with memorized materials as in colors, days of the week, numbers, foods, days of the week, names of family members
- Experiences difficulties in producing sentence-type utterances, and encounters difficulties in being understood by native speakers
- Produces discrete words and phrases but might not be able to put them together coherently

Educational Implications—Teachers should use strategies from the total physical response and natural methods to deliver comprehensible input. To contextualize instruction, teachers should provide opportunities for active listening and use visual and concrete objects. Hands-on and group activities give students the opportunity to support each other. Teachers should avoid direct corrections. Students need help developing the functional vocabulary they need to be successful in daily life. Idioms should be introduced in contextualized situations to ensure student comprehension.

Intermediate

- Creates language by combining or recombining learned elements
- Asks and answers questions as well as initiates and minimally sustains conversations about familiar topics: home, school, friends, personal history, and family members
- Produces discrete sentences and strings of sentences

Educational Implications—Teachers should continue providing contextualized instruction and avoid direct correction in communication activities. If students communicate unintelligibly, teachers should ask for clarification or repetition. Corrective feedback should be given indirectly by modeling, using foreign talk (exaggeration). Instruction should begin with questions that require one-word answers (yes/no and either/or questions) until students are ready to respond to questions that require more language input.

Advanced

- Progresses from sentence-level utterances to paragraph-length connected discourse and narrates and describes present, past, and future activities
- Talks about various concrete topics: personal background, family, travel, interests, and events personally experienced or read about
- Expresses facts, reports accidents, and makes comparisons, but may have difficulties supporting an opinion with examples or arguing against an opposing view

Educational Implications—Teachers should guide students in developing oral and written narratives, analyzing their work, and self-correcting and model pronunciation. Technical vocabulary from the content areas should be discussed before students begin reading for content.

Superior (Advanced fluency)

- Participates effectively in most formal and informal conversations on topics connected to practical, social, professional, and abstract concerns
- Supports opinions and hypothesizes about abstract topics, offering detailed narration and description with native-like discourse strategies
- Produces extended discourse

Educational Implications—Teachers should continue expanding academic vocabulary development and polishing pronunciation. Because fluency can be deceptive at this level, teachers should check for comprehension continuously.

can be deceptive at this level, teachers should check for comprehension continuously.

ESL Strategies for all Levels of English Proficiency

Comprehensible Input—ELLs understand messages above their current level of proficiency if the message is made comprehensible—or understandable—explain a concept clearly

Make lessons visual—use visual representations of new vocabulary and use graphs, maps, photographs, drawings and charts to introduce new vocabulary and use graphic organizers to simply stories and text

Link new information prior knowledge—know students' schema—how much information they already know—and how can you make it connect to the new knowledge presented

Determine key concepts for the lesson—simply key concepts and make them comprehensible—set language objectives

Modify vocabulary—help student pronounce new words, give simple definitions and if possible, provide a visual

Use cooperative learning—give the ELLs practice in using the academic language with other students—give many opportunities for alternative types of assessment as in oral assessment, drawings and acting out the concept or skill

Modify Testing and Homework for ELLs

Teachers should allow alternative types of assessment: oral, drawings, physical response (e.g., act-it-out), and manipulatives as well as modification to the test. Homework and assessment should be directly linked to classroom instruction and students should be provided with study guides so that they know what to study.

Source: Haynes (2010). Seven teaching strategies for classroom teachers of ELLs. EverythingESL.net. Retrieved March 10, 2011, from *www.everythingesl.net/inservices/*

Personality Factors and L2 Acquisition

Extroversion

Extroversion describes people who are outspoken and have well-developed social skills. Extroverted people seek contacts and negotiate meaning with native speakers of the language. Extroversion can be linked to the interpersonal intelligence described by Gardner (1983;1999). This type of personality definitely contributes to second-language acquisition.

Tolerance for Ambiguity

Tolerance for ambiguity is the ability to avoid frustration in instructional situations characterized by lack of organization and guidance. To cope with these situations, most people create their own structures to complete tasks. Students who can cope with ambiguity are generally good language learners and do better academically.

Positive Self-Esteem

Self-esteem is defined as the value that people assign to themselves. Research asserts that having a positive self-esteem correlates to language learning and academic success in school. Students with positive self-esteem are risk takers, which also correlates with language learning.

Impulsiveness versus Reflection

The impulsive student attempts to address an issue or answer a question without having a clear view of what the issue or question entails. The reflective student, on the other hand, analyzes the issue or question before making an attempt to address or answer it. Impulsive students might develop a second language faster than reflective students, but students who take the time to analyze will develop a more polished form of the language.

High Anxiety

Environments characterized by high stress can impair learning and L2 acquisition. However, some levels of anxiety (e.g., facilitating anxiety) can guide students to take responsibility for the learning process and become effective language learners.

Other Factors Influencing Second Language Acquisition

Instrumental Motivation versus Integrative Motivation

Highly motivated students perform well in school. Students with **integrative motivation** want to learn the language because it will enable them to socialize and interact effectively with native speakers. L2 learners with **instrumental motivation** want to acquire the language to accomplish a specific task—for example, to travel to a country or to pass a language test. Both motivations seem to contribute to L2 acquisition, as long as the motivation to learn continues.

Previous Schooling or the Absence of Schooling

Students with strong academic backgrounds are able to transfer academic and language skills to the new language. However, students who have experienced interrupted schooling or have never attended schools represent a unique challenge to educators. Most of these students need to receive assistance to fill their linguistic and academic gaps before they can be placed in regular classrooms. Traditionally, they are served in newcomer centers or through ESL pull-out programs.

Socioeconomic Background

Traditionally, students from low socioeconomic backgrounds do not receive the verbal, literacy, and social stimulus they need to do well in school. Most of these students are served through specialized programs sponsored with funds from Title I of the No Child Left Behind legislation.

Age of Initial Exposure

The age of exposure seems to play a role in the acquisition of a second language. Children who are exposed to the language before puberty seem to have advantages over older students in the acquisition of a native-like pronunciation. However, older students might have advantages over younger ones in the acquisition of grammar and the abstract components of the language.

Home and Community Environment

Children living in ethnic enclaves where L1 is used extensively might not get adequate support in the second language. Because these children have very little need for the second language to function in their environment, they are not highly motivated to learn the language.

Expected Time of Residence in the Country

Students who plan to remain in the country for an extensive period will make an effort to learn the language. However, transitory or migrant students might not have the motivation to learn the language because they know that eventually they will return home.

Language Variation and Modification

Pidginization

Pidginization occurs when speakers of two different languages come in contact and, because they do not understand each other, they develop a simple combined form of both languages. This transitional language is called pidgin. By definition, a pidgin language cannot have native speakers. If the pidgin becomes the native language of a group, then it is called a creole. **Creolization** refers to the process in which a pidgin becomes the native language for a given group. For example, in Haiti, French speakers and speakers of African languages came into contact and developed a pidgin. Eventually, the pidgin became the native language of a large segment of the population in the nation and officially became a French creole—a new language.

Lingua Franca

Lingua franca refers to a common language used for communication in multilingual communities. For example, English and Hindi are often used in India as lingua franca to facilitate communication among speakers of the multiple languages spoken in the nation.

Interlanguage

An interlanguage describes a transitional construction students develop in the process of mastering a second language. It is usually caused by language interference or by the complexity of the structure of the second language. Interlanguages are developmental in nature and generally disappear once students achieve complete mastery of L2. When the nonstandard structures of the inter language persist, they are said to be **fossilized**. For example, ELLs of Spanish background might use features of Spanish as a foundation for pronouncing English, creating nonstandard constructions like *espeak* and *estring*.

Language Interference

The interference of L1 over the structures of L2 can cause students to make errors. For example, because Spanish does not have the voiced alveolar sound *z*, Latino students might substitute the sound with its equivalent in Spanish, *s*. This substitution can result in nonstandard homonyms when speakers replace the *z* for *s*, creating confusion with words like *zoo*, which can be pronounced as *Sue*.

Language Transfer

Positive transfer occurs when the structures of L1 help in the acquisition of the structures of L2. For example, most concepts related to Spanish writing transfer to English. Children do not have to learn to read again; instead, they need to learn the vocabulary and the syntactic and semantic features of the language to obtain meaning.

Code Switching

Code switching describes the process of alternating the use of two languages within a sentence (intrasentential) or across sentences (intersentential). For example, the first sentence in the following list uses two languages, making it intrasentential. The sentences in the second example use English in the first sentence and Spanish in the second, making it intersential.

1. Me encanta ir a los movies on Christmas Day.
2. On Christmas Eve, my parents take me to church and then to dinner. Después de la cena es que empieza la verdadera fiesta.

Code switching is a natural process in bilingual communities; however, teachers need to be sure that students separate L1 and L2 and use each appropriately and consistently.

Dialects

A dialect is defined as a mutually intelligible variation of a standard language or official variety. Dialects can be identified as regional and social. Physical and social isolation promotes the development of dialects. For example, during the American colonial period, the nation had three identified dialects—northern, midland, and southern. Social dialects describe systematic language variations typical of people from a specific social class. For example, Standard American English is spoken mostly by middle-class, educated Americans, while **Ebonics** is spoken by mostly low-income black youths.

Ebonics

Ebonics combines features of Standard American English and African languages. It might have started as a pidgin and for a time functioned as a creole. However, through contacts with speakers of Standard American English and through a process called **decreolization**, it eventually became a dialect of Standard American English. Most features of Ebonics can be found among the speech of southern white speakers but it is more frequent among black speakers. Following are some features of Ebonics (Fromkin and Rodman 1988; Peñalosa 1980):

Double Negatives—two forms of negation are used

Example: **I don't** want to know **nothing** about you.

Copula Deletion—This omission occurs in Standard American English phrases that use contractions (phonological issue). Contractions can be confusing for English language learners. Speakers of Ebonics solve this problem by deleting the contracted verb form, resulting in a nonstandard form.

Example: **He crazy** for *He's crazy*; **They happy** for *They're happy*.

Use of the Habitual Tense—"The habitual indicates continuation of an action or a state over time, rather than a temporary condition or action which takes place only once" (Peñalosa 1980, 152). The tense exists in some African languages, but it does not exist in Standard American English. It is not a simplification of the verb *to be* but the creation of a new tense.

Example: "He be home early from school." This example implies that the child gets home early every day—the habitual.

Deletion of Postvocalic *Rs*—As in some British dialects and the Bostonian dialect, the *r* following a vowel is dropped.

Examples: **park** and **for** become **pak** and **fo**.

Simplification of Final Consonant Clusters

Examples: **Firs** for *first*; **car** for *card*.

Activities to Teach Standard English

- Create or gather from students' examples of dialectical variations and rewrite them using Standard English and vice-versa.
- Develop role-plays where students need to use the vernacular and the standard forms.
- Ask students to write compositions, highlight vernacular expression and ask them to find a different way (standard) of saying the same thing.

Competency 003

The beginning bilingual education teacher has comprehensive knowledge of the development and assessment of literacy in L1 and the development and assessment of biliteracy.

Patterns and Stages of Literacy in L1 and L2

Oral language development is acquired universally with minimum explicit instruction. Literacy instruction on the other hand, is not universally acquired and requires substantial explicit instruction

Key Principles of Competency 002

- Language Development occurs more readily in situations where language is nurtured and modelled in various contexts—making it meaningful.
- Components of language (phonology, morphology, syntax, lexicon, semantics, pragmatics)
- Theories of L1 and L2 Acquisition—Behaviorist, Innatist, and Interactionist
- Interdependence of language—Cognitive and academic language proficiency in L1 has a positive effect in the academic acquisition of L2
- Age and Acquisition (Critical Period Hypothesis—there's a critical period when students develop language proficiency—2 years to puberty)
- Personality factors in L2 (e.g., self-esteem, high anxiety, tolerance for ambiguity)
- Language variation (e.g., dialects, registers, code switching, language transfer)

and practice (Peregoy and Boyle 2005). The process of literacy development is similar in both L1 and L2 (Urzúa 1987; Hudelson 1984). However, there are two principles that teachers must take into account when promoting biliteracy among English language learners:

- Given the appropriate instructions, ELLs can benefit from literacy instruction in L2 before they have developed proficiency in L1 (Urzúa 1987; Hudelson 1984). Moreover, formal literacy instruction in L2 can also support the development of literacy in L1.
- Research suggests that proficiency in L1 makes the development of proficiency in L2 easier because the skills are transferable (Cummins 1981; Tragar and Wong 1984).

Reading Readiness versus Emergent Literacy

The reading readiness perspective was the dominant reading theory in the latter part of the twentieth century. In this perspective, reading was delayed until children developed their speaking ability and they were able to perform specific reading subskills linked to auditory and visual discrimination as well as visual motor skills. Students developed these skills by age 6, which in theory delayed formal reading instruction until first grade. However, researchers noticed that some children were able to read before first grade with minimal or no formal reading instruction. To accommodate this kind of learner, a new view or perspective was conceptualized: the emergent literacy perspective.

In the **emergent literacy** perspective, literacy can emerge naturally among children without formal reading instruction. Literacy development is perceived as a process that is parallel to oral development and emerges when children see adults engaging in meaningful literacy activities, like reading newspapers, writing notes, and looking at environmental print—street signs, billboards, and other printed material children see all around them. Children observe these literacy activities and begin engaging and imitating the literacy process. Because this development occurs mostly at home, family literacy practices become an important component of the process of becoming literate.

Stages of Reading

Lapp et al. (2001) suggest that children go through three stages of literacy development: emerging readers, early readers, and newly fluent readers.

Emerging Readers

Children at the emerging stage of reading demonstrate curiosity for print and understand that print contains meaningful messages. They mimic the reading behaviors of adults and subconsciously acquire print conventions, like directionality and print awareness. Children at this stage also begin developing phonemic awareness—that is, recognizing the connection between letters (graphemes) and sounds (phonemes). Children use illustrations and other graphic representations to obtain meaning and to make predictions about the story. They are also able to retell a story that has been read to them. This type of metalinguistic awareness is a key factor in the development of reading and writing.

Early Readers

Early readers begin to connect words with their written representations (e.g., using phonics to decode) and recognize a number of sight words. Additionally, they begin to develop an awareness of features of printed text, like punctuation, bond print, and text format. Early readers can retell stories with specific details about the plot and characters. They effectively use illustrations, sentence structure and punctuation, and their own experiences to make sense of print. They begin to recognize the meanings of words in various contexts and understand the difference between narrative and nonnarrative texts. Children at this stage enjoy listening to narratives and begin choosing their favorite stories.

Newly Fluent Readers

Newly fluent readers begin to internalize the cuing or decoding system of the language and exhibit some degree of fluency. They use inferences, deduction, and their experiences to infer meaning from text and to develop generalizations. They can discuss the point of view of the author and identify similarities and differences between two stories. As newly fluent readers become more fluent, reading independence emerges, and many of the cuing systems of the language become automatic.

Instructional Implications of the Reading Stages

Children at the early stages of reading can be immersed in various functional reading and writing experiences that display the purpose of literacy while demonstrating and modeling the process of reading and writing. At school, teachers can use routine activities to provide a rich print environment. For example, teachers can post classroom rules, read them to the children, and rehearse the meaning of each rule. They can also post signs identifying parts of the classroom, equipment, and guidelines for activities in the learning centers. Teachers can enrich dramatic play centers with functional print, including lists, phone books, and props, to encourage children to experiment with reading and writing during play activities. Finally, it is important for teachers to guide children to be successful in their attempts to develop literacy; thus, teachers should accept and celebrate the progress of ELLs in their gradual progress toward biliteracy.

Role of Environmental Print in Early Reading

Environmental print describes forms of written communication available to children in their community. Some of the most common print materials are road and store signs, magazines available in public areas, shopping guides, and announcements in billboards. Parents can use these high-profile written samples to motivate children to read and to guide them to discover the meaning and information available in their environment.

Home Environment and Early Literacy

At home, parents can model literacy through functional daily activities like reading newspapers and magazines, writing a grocery list, clipping coupons, putting notes on the refrigerator, labeling things around the house, and posting rules. Parents can also read to their children and guide them to notice parts of books. They can also read stories with simple and predictable story lines, ask children to predict the content of a story based on pictorial clues, and ask children to identify the parts of a story that they like the most or the part they do not like. Parents can also use computer programs and interactive books to promote literacy in fun and relaxed ways. The captions on television can also be used to guide children to link spoken vocabulary with its written representation.

Classroom Activities to Promote Early Literacy Skills

In the school environment, children get exposed to explicit instruction in reading, including reading conventions, the alphabetic principle, sound–symbol correspondence (graphophonemic awareness), and common sight words (Peregoy and Boyle 2005). All these components are presented through whole texts, like poems, songs, and short stories. Once students begin to make sense of simple texts, instruction is supplemented with explicit phonics and sight word instruction.

Daily classroom routines can enhance literacy development. Here are a few examples of enriching activities:

- Write the daily schedule and guide students to follow the activities during the day.
- Post classroom rules and procedures and rehearse them
- Develop a dictionary wall containing vocabulary words that students can already read and continue adding new words.
- Develop an attendance pocket chart with the date and two sections labeled "present" and "Class Roster." Print cards with the names of students and organize them alphabetically. In the morning, guide students to move their names from the section labeled "Class Roster" to the section labeled "present." At the

end of the day, guide students to move their name back and place them in alphabetic order. Teachers can also guide students to read and change the date.

— Post students' writing samples inside and outside the classroom.

— Use language experience charts or the language experience approach

Language Experience Approach

The language experience (LEA) approach to literacy is based on the assumption that students' experiences need to be used as a bridge to new ideas and concepts. This approach was developed as an alternative to using basal readers to teach initial reading instruction to language-minority students. Proponents of the LEA felt that the vocabulary, topics, and ideas of the stories in basal readers did not match the schemata (background knowledge) and the vocabulary of language-minority students and that this discrepancy created comprehension problems. To provide reading opportunities that better matched students' schemata, the LEA has students share an activity or experience, like a science experiment or an activity on the playground. After the initial activity, students are guided to talk about it and to dictate a story to the teacher. Once the story is written, the teacher reads the story while pointing to the words as they are read. Following this initial reading, students join the teacher in a choral reading. After the second reading, students copy the story and take it home. The next day, the story is read again and is used for a variety of follow-up activities. For example, teachers can use a cloze activity, deleting key words from the story—to check for comprehension. The story can also be used to teach grammar conventions and to promote vocabulary development.

Key Components of the Early Reading Process

Big books contain short repetitive stories that can easily be used to teach sight words and the sound–symbol correspondence. The size of the letter permits children to follow the story while the teacher reads and points to the words. This activity is ideal to promote interest in reading for students at the emergent stage of reading.

Sight words are high-frequency words introduced to children visually for easy recognition. Traditionally, teachers use flash cards and games to teach sight words found in stories. Practice of word recognition and meaning can be done with students organized by whole group, small groups, or peer groups. A strong foundation of sight words can support students in the emergent and early stages of reading.

Phonics instruction is used to guide students to recognize words based on the way they are pronounced. Students apply rules to "sound out" words, and based on the way the words sound, students are able to recognize and assign meaning to them. Phonics instruction should always be introduced within a meaningful context. First, the teacher reads the story and allows the children to enjoy it; then the teacher can introduce the skills for word recognition.

Phonics instruction is a bottom-up reading model because it proceeds from the parts to the whole. Typically, it is introduced in a specific sequence (Peregoy and Boyle 2005):

1. Consistent single consonants—*m, p, t*
2. Short and long vowels—*ca t* (short) and *bo y* (long)
3. Word families, or onset and rime— *-ake*, as in *lake*, *bake*, *take*
4. Digraphs (two consonants combined to produce one sound)—*ch-*, *th-*
5. Blends (two or more consonants combined to produce a blended sound)—*pl-*, *cl-*, *scr-*
6. Rules for syllabication

Bottom-Up and Top-Down Models of Reading

The **bottom-up** approach to reading is driven by a process for constructing meaning from letters, words, sentences, paragraphs, and whole texts. It is an inductive and skill-based process based on the principles of behaviorist psychology. This behaviorist approach is best represented by the phonics reading program. Teachers who practice a bottom-up approach emphasize the teaching of discrete skills in a sequential and systematic manner. A product of this approach is the concept of reading readiness, which gained momentum in the 1960s and became a prerequisite for formal reading instruction as in basal readers.

A **top-down** approach to reading relies on the schemata (prior knowledge) that readers bring to the text in their attempt to derive meaning from print. It is a deductive approach that proceeds from the whole to the parts. It begins with whole text, sentences, and words. In this approach, recognizing each word is not a prerequisite for comprehending the passage. Teachers generally do not interfere with students' oral reading and encourage students to use the context or meaning of the passage to identify unrecognized words. The best representation of the top-down model is the **whole language approach**. From its beginnings in the 1960s, the whole language approach was the program of choice in public schools during the 1980s and 1990s. Phonics instruction came back at the start of new millennium, and today teachers are using a **balanced reading** approach that combines features of both phonics and whole language.

Narrative and Expository Writing

Narrative writing describes events or tells a story using context and often repetition to communicate ideas. It uses a predictable format containing three major components—beginning, middle, and end. In the beginning, the characters, the setting, and the problem are introduced. In the middle, the topic is further developed, creating a climax. In the end, the problem is usually solved. Children are generally able to identify this format and use it to make predictions and obtain information. ELLs who are exposed to this format in L1 can easily transfer this information to L2.

Expository writing, on the other hand, provides an explanation of processes or concepts. It uses more technical vocabulary and is less redundant and contextualized than narratives. This kind of technical writing is more succinct, linear, and hierarchical in its development. The information in expository writing is structured topically, chronologically, or numerically. In the topic format, the information is organized into chapters, each covering a topic and divided into subtopics. For example, a chapter on the Amerindians of Texas might be organized by types of Indian groups and by the location, economic activities, and cultural features of each group or chronologically from past to present. The information can also be supplemented with charts, graphs, tables, and other graphic representations arranged numerically, particularly for ELLs.

Development of Writing

Children at the emerging and early stages of writing use several strategies to convey meaning in writing. Before learning conventional spelling, students in the emergent stage of literacy use drawing as a way to convey meaning, followed by scribbling and inventing letters (pseudoletters) that they might be able to read. Eventually, they use phonetic spelling to produce nonstandard words they can read.

Phonetic spelling represents an advanced degree of the emergent literacy stage and the beginning of the development of the **alphabetic principle**—the idea that sounds are represented by letters and letter sequences (Peregoy and Boyle 2005). As part of the alphabetic principle, children notice the **graphophonemic units**—sound-symbol correspondences—of the language. Graphophonemic awareness leads the child to notice the individual sounds that comprise spoken words, which leads to **phonemic awareness**. The development of phonemic awareness prepares children for formal phonics instruction and is the foundation to becoming fluent readers and writers. The development of writing follows a path similar to the reading stages (Lapp et al. 2001).

Characteristics of Emerging Writers

Children at the emerging stage of writing understand that writing symbolizes speech. They use a combination of drawings, scribbles, and conventional letters to convey written communication. First, children use the initial letter of a conventional word to represent the entire word. This invented spelling represents a degree of phonemic awareness because children are actually connecting the sound of the word with its equivalent graphic representation.

Early Writers

Children at the early stages of writing are developing phonemic awareness and use that knowledge to progress through the stages of spelling development. Children's phonetic spelling becomes more conventional as they begin to use rules for capitalization and punctuation. Despite the use of phonetic spelling, their writing is generally comprehensible.

Newly Fluent Writers

Newly fluent writers consistently use conventional grammar, spelling, and punctuation. They are beginning to use prewriting strategies to achieve a writing function (e.g., writing for a specific purpose or responding to a prompt). They are able to produce unique writing samples that contain a beginning, middle, and end. With guidance, they can revise and edit their written work.

Activities for Children at Each Stage of Writing

Children at the various stages of writing can benefit from real-life and functional writing activities. Some examples of activities to accomplish this kind of writing are labeling objects, note taking, writing about a drawing, and writing a list. These activities, together with the concepts and strategies that follow, can promote writing skills among ELLs.

Word families are words that have common spelling patterns in English. The main purpose of teaching English word families is to help students recognize frequently occurring letter patterns in the language, like *-ack* in words like *pack*, *back* and *lack*. Word families are introduced through the use of onsets and rimes. **Onset** refers to the initial consonant or consonant clusters of a syllable. **Rime**, or **phonogram**, refers to the combination of vowels and consonants that follow the onset. The *p* in *pump* is called the onset and the *ump* is the rime. Traditionally, onset and rimes are introduced with monosyllabic words. Examples of common word families are listed here:

Journal Writing

Teachers can use three kinds of journal writing to guide students toward writing for meaningful purposes:

- **Personal Journals**—Students analyze their experiences and write for self-expression. Teachers can be involved only when invited to do so.
- **Dialogue Journals**—Students communicate with teachers, adults, or other students about topics of interest. Teachers respond to the content of the writing by modeling standard language usage without overemphasizing corrections.
- **Reflective Journals**—Students reflect on particular situations or content. This type of journal can be used for self-assessment.

A **learning log** is another type of functional journal in which students provide a summary of the elements they have learned and analyze difficulties experienced during the learning process. Teachers can use the information presented in learning logs to provide additional support or to reteach concepts.

Language Logic

The language logic in Standard American English progresses in a linear fashion without allowing for digression. Speakers of English are expected to progress from point A to point B with minimal deviations from the topic. Russian, Spanish, and most Romance languages have a linear structure, but the grammar allows for a great deal of digression in formal and informal interactions. Native American and Semitic languages allow for even more flexibility and digression from the linear approach. When ELLs or speakers of English dialects impose the logic of their native language on the logic of Standard American English, communication problems can occur. ESL teachers need to guide ELLs in using the linear logic of English. Through prewriting activities, teachers can help students organize their thoughts following the linear progression. Process writing can guide children to organize ideas and write using the linear progression required in English.

Process writing is designed to guide students to write following specific steps:

1. **Prewriting** activities are used to generate and organize ideas. Once children identify the task, they are guided to develop an outline or a web to ensure that the ideas are interconnected and follow a logical pattern. In this stage, teacher can help ELLs organize their ideas following a linear progression.
2. **Drafting** is putting the ideas in writing, keeping in mind audience and purpose.
3. **Conferencing** with the teacher or peers provides feedback to the writer.
4. **Revising** is done based on the input from conferencing and emphasizes the overall content of the piece and the clarity of ideas.
5. **Editing** is done to correct for spelling, grammar, punctuation, and mechanics.
6. **Publishing** represents that final step of the process in which the document is presented in final form and can be shared with an audience.

Formal and Informal Literacy Assessment

Assessment describes the process of gathering data to make instructional or programmatic decisions. It can be done formally or informally. **Formal assessment** is conducted using formal standardized or norm-referenced tests and criterion-referenced tests.

Standardized or **norm-referenced testing** is used to measure a student's performance in various skills and types of content. These tests are administered at set intervals using a professionally developed instrument. Norm-referenced tests compare the scores of students in other geographic locations using a ranking order based on the students' performance. Results are reported based on **percentiles** on a normal curve. For example, a student who scored 1300 on a test with a possible maximum of 1600 can receive a percentile of 70, which means that 30% of the students who took the test on that day scored higher than the student. The same student can retake the test and score lower but receive a higher percentile because the overall group did not do as well as the initial group. Norm-referenced tests compare the performance of students, not necessarily the mastery of specific standards or objectives. The Texas bilingual education law requires that students score in at least the fortieth percentile to become candidates for reclassification as fluent English speakers.

Criterion-referenced tests are used to indicate the level of mastery attained on specific standards or instructional objectives. Results are presented based on the percentage of questions answered correctly. Traditionally, a score of 70 percent is required to indicate mastery of the objectives. Teacher-made tests and state-approved tests like the Texas Assessment of Knowledge and Skills (TAKS) are criterion-referenced tests because they are designed to test the mastery of the state curriculum—the Texas Essential Knowledge and Skills (TEKS). The bilingual education law in Texas requires that students pass the reading and language arts portions of the TAKS test to become candidates for reclassification as fluent English speakers.

Informal assessment is often linked to the concepts of **authentic, on-going** and **performance assessment**. This type of assessment is part of instruction and is generally done to assess students' progress. Results of informal assessment can be easily incorporated into teaching. Following are the most common types of informal assessment used in the language classroom:

- **Observation** is used to assess a student's use of language in various instructional settings. In this type of assessment, teachers observe and record specific language features, such as the use of irregular and regular past tense verbs or the use of the vernacular when the standard version is required.
- **Skill checklists** are used to track the student's development by noting which skills have become part of the linguistic child's repertoire. Traditionally, the characteristics of the stu-

dent at each stage of language development are used to develop the checklist.

- **Portfolio assessment** is used to document in a variety of ways the progress of a child as a language user. Traditionally, teachers collect samples of student work at each stage of the process. To assess language proficiency, teachers can collect taped oral performances in a various settings and samples of writing in L1 and L2, including published works.
- **Conferencing** gives teachers and students opportunities to discuss language development. Teachers meet with children to assess their performance and to identify activities and instruction needed for student progress.
- **Peer review** involves students in the evaluation process and builds their evaluative and interactive skills. For this approach to be effective, teachers need to discuss with students the guidelines for evaluation. Traditionally, teachers use student evaluations when assigning official grades.
- **Self-assessment** empowers students by making them responsible and reflective of their performance in school. Teachers can guide students to self-assessment using checklists, inventories, conferences, and portfolios. Self-assessment is one of the main components of student-centered practices and one of the foundations of the constructivist learning theory.

Formative and Summative Evaluation

Evaluation can be divided into two main components—formative and summative. **Formative evaluation** is informal assessment done during instruction or right after instruction. The main purpose of formative evaluation is to monitor and improve instruction and consequently student learning. It provides ongoing feedback that can be incorporated in the teaching-learning cycle. It is generally conducted informally and consists of observation, questioning, worksheets, and teacher feedback to students. It is important to note that ELLs may need to be assessed using various assessment measures due to their level of English proficiency. Be sure to provide many opportunities for ELLs to produce what they know using alternative ways of assessing their knowledge and skills.

Summative evaluation is formal assessment done after instruction or after a grading period and is used to document mastery and for reporting purposes. Summative evaluation is conducted at specific times in the year with the use of formal instruments like chapter tests, final exams, term papers, and projects. The main purpose of summative evaluation is to document performance after instruction is completed.

Assessment before Instruction: Learning About Students

Teachers can obtain valuable information about their students before the first day of class. Although this information should not be used to prejudge students, it can give teachers an idea of their students' needs and strengths. Some of the documents available for teachers are described here (McMillan 2004).

School records contain valuable information teachers can use to develop an overview of their students. By examining and appropriately using grades from previous years, results of standardized tests, health records, and other documents in the permanent school records, teachers can prepare to take care of the identified instructional, emotional, and medical needs of the children entering their classrooms. However, as with any kind of information, teachers must be cautious when analyzing data about ethnic and linguistic minorities to avoid inaccurate interpretations and stereotyping.

Standardized test scores can offer teachers clues about the potential of students in their classrooms. However, teachers should not use standardized test results alone when making instructional decisions. There are two types of standardized scores:

- **Norm-Referenced Achievement Test Batteries**—Although these tests are commonly used to show achievement and to predict performance of children in the classroom, teachers must use results from these kinds of test with caution because the tests often fail to measure the potential of language minority students and ELLs. Teachers should also investigate how closely the test objectives reflect the state curriculum and use the information as a foundation to plan for initial instruction. Standardized tests can produce three types of scores to indicate the relative strength and weaknesses of students:

- **Percentile rank** indicates the percentage of the norm group that is at, over, or under the student's raw score. It does not indicate the percentage of correct items.
- **National Curve Equivalent (NCE) score** is similar to the percentile rank but uses raw scores to produce the results. This measure is generally used in educational research because it represents a better view of the achievement of students.
- **Grade equivalent score** measures how a child performed in terms of grade-level expectations. However, teachers must interpret this kind of score cautiously. For example, if a child in third grade scores 4.1 on a test, it does not necessarily mean that the child is ready to enter fourth grade. It only means that the child is performing well above his or her third-grade peers. The **Texas Learning Index (TLI)** is a test that produces grade equivalent scores.

Criterion-referenced and standard-based achievement tests are designed to determine if students have mastered the objectives of their grade level and have the knowledge and skills to be promoted to the next grade level. Results of criterion-referenced tests are reported based on percentages or based on mastery/no mastery. The TAKS and the STAAR are criterion-referenced tests that measure the objectives of the TEKS—the state curriculum for grades 3 through 12. The TAKS is being phased out, to be replaced by the STAAR for all grades by 2016.

State Testing Program

As part of the accountability system for educators in Texas, the state has a very comprehensive assessment system, overseen by the Student Testing Division of the TEA. Some of the tests required for each grade level in Texas are described here.

Kindergarten through Grade 2

- **Tejas LEE (El Inventario de Lectura en Español de Tejas)** shows proficiency in Spanish reading. The test is given twice a year to children in the bilingual (Spanish) education program. The test is designed to identify early reading difficulties in Spanish. It covers basic skills like phonics, word segmentation, blending, phonemic and phonological awareness, and reading comprehension.
- **Texas Proficiency Reading Inventory (TPRI)** is equivalent to the Tejas LEE, covering similar language components, but is administered in English.
- **Texas Observation Protocol (TOP)** is a checklist designed to record the English progress of ELLs in listening, speaking, reading, and writing. This test is one of two tests developed by the TEA to comply with the accountability requirement of the NCLB.

Grades 3 through 12

The **Texas Assessment of Academic Skills (TAKS)** and the State of Texas Assessments of Academic Readiness (STAAR) measure the statewide curriculum (TEKS). Table 1-4 presents the assessment schedule by discipline (TEA 2004):

Table 1-4.
Schedule of TAKS/STAAR Examinations

Subject	Administered
Mathematics	3–8
Reading	3–8
Writing	4 and 7
Science	5 and 8
Social Studies	8

Table 1-4. *(continued)*	
End-of-Course High School Assessments (9th Grade and Up)	
English I, English II, English II	**Upon Completion of Course**
Algebra I, Geometry, Algebra II	
Biology, Chemistry, Physics	
World Geography, World History, U.S. History	

The Spanish versions of the tests are available in grades 3 through 6 (TEA 2004). Satisfactory performance on the tests are required for grade promotion and to obtain a high school diploma.

End-of-course (EOC) examinations measure the statewide curriculum of certain high school courses (Algebra I, Biology, English II, and U.S. History) to ensure that high academic standards are being met. Demonstrating satisfactory performance on EOC tests became an additional means for students to be eligible to graduate beginning in the 1998–1999 school year.

The **State-Developed Alternative Assessment (SDAA)** assesses special education students in grades 3 through 8 who are receiving instruction in the TEKS but for whom the statewide assessments are an inappropriate measure of academic progress. This test assesses students in the areas of reading, writing, and mathematics at the appropriate instructional level, as determined by their Admission, Review, and Dismissal (ARD) committee, rather than at the assigned grade level. The SDAA is administered on the same schedule as the TAKS and the STAAR and is designed to measure annual growth based on the Individualized Education Plan (IEP) designed by the ARD committee. The SDAA assessment is part of the state accountability system.

Language proficiency testing is used to determine and document language dominance or proficiency in L1 and L2 (English). When the test is not available in a student's native language, only the English version is administered. Results of the tests are used as one criterion for making entry and exit decisions in the bilingual or ESL program.

The **Reading Proficiency Test in English (RPTE)** measures ELLs' annual growth in English reading proficiency and is used, along with the English and/or Spanish tests, to provide a comprehensive assessment system for English language learners. ELLs in grades 3 through 12 are required to take the RPTE until they achieve a rating of advanced high. This test, together with the TOP, constitutes the Texas English Language Proficiency Assessment System required in the NCLB legislation.

The **Texas English Language Proficiency Assessment System (TELPAS)** was designed to comply with the accountability system required in the federal NCLB legislation. The legislation requires that ELLs be assessed yearly in all language skills: listening, speaking, reading and writing. Students begin taking the TELPAS test in kindergarten and stop participating when they are exited from the bilingual or ESL program. The test for the early grades is different from that for the later grades.

- **Kindergarten through grade 2**—TELPAS consists of the TOP only. This test uses classroom observations to assess listening, speaking, prereading, and prewriting skills in English.
- **Grades 3 through 12**—TELPAS consists of the listening, speaking, and writing components of the TOP and the RPTE. The RPTE assesses reading development and reports results based on reading proficiency. Both the TOP and the RPTE report results based on the following levels: beginning, intermediate, advanced, and advanced high. ELLs stop taking the RPTE when they reach the advanced high level.

Under the accountability provisions in the NCLB, all public school campuses, school districts, and the state are evaluated for **adequate yearly progress (AYP)**. The state plan for meeting federal AYP requirements and related information is available online at *www.tea.state.tx.us/ayp*.

Linguistically accommodated testing (LAT) for ELLs must meet the following requirements (TEA 2006):

- It must not include explanations or definitions of mathematical terminology, concepts, or skills.

- Test administrators may be allowed to translate words, phrases, or sentences as requested by students.
- Students may request that words, phrases, and sentences be read aloud.
- Spanish-speaking students in grades 3 through 6 may refer to both the English and Spanish test items to enhance linguistic accessibility.
- Bilingual, monolingual, and ESL dictionaries may be used to find the meanings of appropriate words.
- Test administrators may prepare written bilingual glossaries of appropriate words.
- Test administrators may prepare written and pictorial ESL glossaries of appropriate words.
- Test administrators may simplify the language used in certain test questions (in writing or orally).
- Pictures and gestures may be used by the test administrator to illustrate the meanings of appropriate words.

The **Academic Excellent Indicators System (AEIS)** reports pull together a wide range of information on the performance of students in each school and district in Texas every year. These reports are posted online in the fall. In addition, Texas annually rates its public schools and districts on the academic performance of their students.

Key Principles of Competency 003

- Identify patterns and stages of Literacy in L1 and L2 (i.e., developing phonemic awareness)
- Make the classroom environment print rich—plays an important role in developing literacy skills in L1 and L2
- Reading Components can be developed early through various activities (e.g., phonemic awareness, phonics, vocabulary, reading fluency, and reading comprehension)
- Use language experience charts (i.e., connection between speech and print)
- Develop writers (e.g., emerging writers, early writers and newly fluent writers)
- Develop activities for each stage of writing (e.g., word families, onset and rime, journal writing)
- Use formal and informal literacy assessments (e.g., norm-referenced and criterion-referenced and other alternative assessments)
- Know state assessments used in Texas (see section in this chapter to review)
- Make instructional modifications to deliver the statewide curriculum (TEKS) to students at various stages of literacy development in L1 and L2
- Support students affected by personal factors such as interrupted schooling, literacy status in L1, and literacy experience.
- Explicitly teach language features that can create confusion among ELLs: antonyms (opposites); homonyms (similar spelling and pronunciation but different meaning, like *to*, *two*, *too*); homophones (same pronunciation but different meaning, like *night*, *knight*); homographs (spelled the same way); and acronyms (words formed from the initial letters of other words, e.g., *radar*, *sonar*, and *laser*).

Competency 004

The beginning bilingual education teacher has comprehensive knowledge of content-area instruction in L1 and L2 and uses this knowledge to promote bilingual students' academic achievement across the curriculum.

Differentiating Instruction: Second Language Proficiency

The American Council for the Teaching of Foreign Languages (ACTFL) identified five levels of oral language proficiency: novice, intermediate, advanced, and superior. These levels resemble the four levels identified by Krashen for L2 learners: preproduction, early production, intermediate, advanced proficiency, and superior (advanced fluency). Teachers need to have a clear understanding of these stages and use them as a foundation for planning instruction and assessing language development and academic progress. The following sections list the abilities of the ELL at each stage of development and describe how teachers should work within each stage.

Novice (Preproduction and Early Production Stages)

- Communicates minimally with memorized materials
- Responds briefly to questions with words and phrases such as familiar vocabulary: colors, numbers, foods, days of the week, names of family members
- Experiences difficulties in producing sentence-type utterances and encounters difficulties in being understood by native speakers
- Produces discrete words and phrases but might not be able to put them together coherently

Educational Implications—Teachers should use strategies from the total physical response and natural methods to deliver comprehensible input. To contextualize instruction, teachers should provide opportunities for active listening and use visual and concrete objects (i.e., functional vocabulary). Hands-on and group activities give students the opportunity to support each other.

Intermediate

- Creates language by combining or recombining learned elements
- Asks and answers questions as well as initiate and minimally sustain conversations about familiar topics like home, school, friends, personal history and family members.
- Can be understood by sympathetic learners and listeners, although limited in grammatical accuracy
- Produces discrete sentences and strings of sentences

Educational Implications—Teachers should continue providing contextualized instruction and avoid direct correction in communication activities. If students communicate unintelligibly, teachers should ask for clarification or to repeat. Corrective feedback should be given indirectly by modeling, using foreign talk (exaggeration). Instruction should begin with questions that require one-word answers (yes/no and either/or questions) until students are ready to produce responses that require more language input. By highlighting errors, teachers can provide opportunities for self-correction.

Advanced Proficiency

- Progresses from sentence-level utterances to paragraph-length connected discourse
- Narrates and describes present, past, and future activities
- Talks about various concrete topics: personal background, family, travel, interests, and events they have experienced or read about
- Expresses facts, report accidents, and make comparisons, but may have difficulty supporting an opinion with examples or arguing against an opposing viewpoint
- Produces paragraph discourse

Educational Implications—Teachers should guide students in developing oral and written narratives, analyzing their work, and self-correcting. Technical vocabulary from the content areas should be discussed before students begin reading for content. Teachers need to identify sounds that can cause language interference and begin polishing pronunciation.

Superior (Advanced Fluency)

- Participates effectively in most formal and informal conversations on topics connected to practical, social, professional, and abstract concerns
- Supports opinions and hypothesizes about abstract topics, offering detailed narration and description with native-like discourse strategies
- Functions effectively with most native speakers
- Produces extended discourse

Educational Implications—Teachers should continue expanding academic vocabulary development and polishing pronunciation. Because fluency can be deceptive at this level, teachers should check for comprehension continuously.

Assessing Language Development

Dichotomy of BICS and CALP

Cummins (1979) conceptualized language proficiency based on two components—basic interpersonal communication skills (BICS) and cognitive academic language proficiency (CALP). BICS make up the social language that children acquire after two to four years of exposure to a language. The social language is characterized by face-to-face communication in highly contextualized situations. Conversely, the CALP makes up the academic language that children need to be successful in the mainstream English-only classroom. It takes from four to seven years to develop this kind of proficiency. Academic language development leads to the use of higher-order thinking skills.

Students in bilingual and ESL programs have to demonstrate English language proficiency to be reclassified as fluent English speakers. BICS are commonly assessed informally and with one of the various language proficiency tests approved by the state—for example, the Woodcock-Muñoz Language Survey and the Language Assessment Scales (LAS). The CALP component is assessed through a criterion-referenced test—the TAKS and the STAAR—and through norm-referenced achievement tests. The state bilingual education law mandates that an ELL pass the reading and language arts components of the statewide assessment to be a candidate for reclassification. Additionally, an ELL has to pass the tests in grades 3 through 12 to be promoted and to graduate from high school. Students unable to pass the test are given extra academic support and the opportunity to retake the test. If a student is unable to pass the test after this support, the school must decide whether to retain the child. Texas state law also indicates that students in the bilingual and ESL programs must score at least at the fortieth percentile in a norm-referenced achievement test to be considered for reclassification.

Interdependence of the First and Second Languages

Studies suggest that a strong cognitive and academic development in L1 have a positive effect in the acquisition of L2. Academic skills and content knowledge, literacy development, and metacognitive strategies transfer to L2 (Ovando, Collier, and Combs 2006). Following this principle, the Language Proficiency Assessment Committee (LPAC) allows students in the Spanish-English bilingual program to take the test in Spanish in grades 3 through 6. The knowledge of the content demonstrated in Spanish can transfer to the English test once students develop the academic language needed to take the English version.

Threshold Hypothesis

Cummins (1979) believes that language learners should arrive at a given academic and literacy level in L1 before attempting to transfer elements from L1 to L2. This threshold is generally obtained after four or five years of effective L1 instruction, which clearly points to the fact that once students develop CALP in the first language, they can transfer that proficiency to the second language.

Vocabulary Transfer

Students who are literate in Spanish (L1) at a level commensurate with their grade placement bring strong word recognition skills to English (L2). This transferability is supported by the historical and linguistic connection between the two languages, which have affected the development of vocabulary. There are many affixes from Greek and Latin common to Spanish and English. Most of these affixes are used in academic areas like science, law, and mathematics. This connection has resulted in the development of numerous cognates—words similar in two languages. The CALP that students need to be successful in the regular classroom can be delivered through this comparison. A few examples of the connection between English and Spanish are listed here:

Greek Prefixes	English	Spanish
anti-	antifreeze	anticongelante
anfi-	amphibious	anfíbio
auto-	autobiography	autobiografía
bio-	biography	biografía
demo-	democracy	democracia
Latin Prefixes	**English**	**Spanish**
ante-	antecedent	antecedente
bi-	bicycle	bicicleta
extra-	extraordinary	extraordinario
infra-	infrared	infrarojo
inter-	international	internacional
Suffixes	**English**	**Spanish**
-ist	artist	artista
-or	actor	actor
-logy	biology	biología
-al	canal	canal
-tion/-ción	nation	nación

Alternative Methods of Assessing ELLs

When assessing ELLs, teachers have to take into account the stage of language development of the child to be sure that language issues do not interfere in the assessment of the intended concepts. Assessment techniques that can be used to minimize the impact of language include the following:

- Structured observation using a checklist
- Dramatizations like role-playing or readers' theater
- Drawings to represent ideas and to support demonstrations or explanations
- Fill-in-the-blanks with word banks

Consider the following when assessing ELLs:

- Be aware that students from culturally diverse backgrounds might express knowledge and understanding differently.
- Be aware that ELLs might have an understanding of concepts but might not have the vocabulary to express the knowledge.
- Organize activities to monitor student growth
- Organize one-to-one interviews with ELLs to explore how much they know.

Techniques to Promote CALP and Content Mastery

Teachers need to implement various activities to teach the state curriculum (the TEKS) at the grade and level of complexity required of English native speakers. Some of the techniques to facilitate content mastery are described here.

Scaffolding was originally used to describe the way in which adults support children in their efforts to communicate in L1. The same concept is used to facilitate language and content development for ELLs. The term alludes to the provisional structure used to provide support during the construction of a building and eliminated when the structure is complete. Following this analogy, ELLs receive support to make content cognitively accessible to them until they achieve L2 mastery, and once this is accomplished, the language support is eliminated.

Graphic organizers are used to show relationships using visuals. These are some of the most common organizers:

A semantic web or tree diagram shows relationships between main ideas and subordinated components.

- A time line presents a visual summary of chronological events.

- A flowchart shows cause-and-effect relationships.
- A Venn diagram uses circles to compare and contrast elements of two or more distinct components and can be used in all content areas.

The **SQ4R** is a study strategy in which the learner is engaged during the whole reading process. The acronym stands for **survey**, **question**, **read**, **reflect**, **recite**, and **review** (Tomas and Robinson 1972). Readers engage in the following:

(S) Survey—survey material and make predictions by generating questions

(Q) Questions—generated questions from the predictions

(4R) Readers read actively to answer questions **(1R)**; read and summarize **(2R)**, read and recite key terms and concepts **(3R)** and evaluate their comprehensive by reviewing what they read **(4R)**.

Reciprocal teaching (Palincsar and Brown 1984) is an instructional activity designed for struggling readers. The teacher engages students in a dialogue about specific portion of a text. The dialogue is structured to elicit four strategies:

1. Summarizing the content of a passage
2. Asking a question about the main idea
3. Clarifying difficult parts of the content
4. Predicting what will come next

Strategies to Integrate Language Arts with Content in L1 and L2

Integrated Language Arts

The integrated language arts curriculum integrates reading, writing, speaking, and listening. It incorporates students' experiences with the aims of the curriculum.

Whole Language Approach

The main principle of the whole language approach (WLA) is that language should not be separated into discrete components or skills but experienced as whole system of communication. Authentic text is preferred—especially, literature and the use of language for personal communication. The concepts and strategies associated with the WLA include the following:

- Reading aloud to children
- Journal writing
- Sustained silent reading
- Higher-order thinking skills
- Student choice in reading materials
- Frequent conferences between teachers and students

Language Across the Curriculum

In this approach, teachers in all content areas carry out language development activities associated with their individual content area.

Language Experience Approach

This approach is based on the assumption that students' prior experiences need to be used as a bridge to new ideas and concepts. The steps in the process are as follows:

1. Students share an activity or experience.
2. The teacher leads students to talk about it.
3. Students dictate the story to the teacher.
4. The teacher copies the story and reads it to the students.
5. The teacher reads the story a second time, and students join in choral reading.
6. Students copy the story.
7. Follow-up activities include cloze activity (gap filling) and assembling the composition or the paragraph, among others.

Content-Based Language Programs

CALLA Model

The cognitive academic language learning approach (CALLA) is an ESL model developed by Chamot and O'Malley (1994) designed to promote English language development through the content areas. It is based on cognitive psychology, with students becoming active participants in the learning process by constructing knowledge. The CALLA model comprises three learning strategies: metacognitive, cognitive, and social.

Metacognitive strategy is a way to conceptualize how learning takes place or being aware of one's own learning. It has two main components: organization and planning for learning, and self-monitoring and self-evaluating (Reiss 2005).

Here are some strategies for **organizing** and **planning for instructions:**

- Keeping track of short and long-term assignments with a due date
- Segmenting long tasks into smaller manageable parts
- Identifying specific strategies to facilitate learning of various kinds of content
- Organizing information to study for a test

Strategies for **self-monitoring** and **self-evaluating** include the following:

- Assessing weaknesses and strengths in the content
- Identifying the preferred and easiest strategy for learning the content
- Conducting continuous self-assessment and progressing toward mastery of the content

Cognitive strategies are techniques to improve understanding and increase retention of information and the ability to apply new information. These are some of the specific strategies:

- Linking and making connections between current and new content
- Analyzing the interrelatedness of and the elements that could transfer from L1 and L2
- Identifying and isolating key concepts while reading or listening for comprehension
- Note taking, emphasizing important concepts in a lesson
- Developing strategies for self-assessment of test content
- Visualizing information as a way to remember information
- Creating charts and graphs to synthesize and present content
- Classifying and organizing information as a way of remembering

Social strategies describe techniques in which students learn from each other or learn by interacting in groups. These are some of those strategies:

- Working in pairs or in groups to complete projects and solve problems
- Asking questions for clarification or making requests
- Seeking support from peers to complete an assignment or to study for a test
- Observing and interacting with people from diverse backgrounds to learn about them

Most students can benefit from explicit instruction in learning strategies. ELLs need help to cope with the demands of learning both a new language and academic content. The CALLA is designed to assist ESL students to succeed in school by providing transitional instruction from ESL programs to grade-level English content instruction.

Sheltered English

Sheltered English is an instructional approach designed for ELLs at the intermediate and advanced levels of language proficiency. The main purpose of the approach is to make content comprehensible for ELLs (Echevarria, Vogt, and Short 2000). As the name implies, children are "sheltered" from the pressure of competing with native English learners. To deliver the comprehensible input, content instruction is linguistically simplified through contextualized instruction, visual aids, hands-on activities, and body language. These are most important strategies used in the sheltered English approach to modify language and make it comprehensible:

- Control the length and complexity of the sentences, keep them short and simple.

- Introduce technical vocabulary before beginning the lesson.
- Use repetition, restatement, and paraphrasing to clarify concepts.
- Control the speed of delivery, and use various intonations to emphasize important concepts.
- Supplement oral presentations with diagrams, graphic organizers, and manipulatives to make content easier to understand.
- Guide students in using role-play to represent important concepts.
- Use linguistic modifications, such as repetition and pauses during speech (Parker 1985).
- Make the presentation of content more interactive with comprehension checks.
- Use cooperative learning strategies.
- Organize of content around thematic units.
- Use graphic organizers to simplify content.
- Emphasize the gist of the concepts instead of details.

Like the CALLA, sheltered English is more effective for classrooms with students from multiple language groups who are at least at the intermediate level of English language development (Schifini 1985).

Cooperative Learning

Cooperative learning is teaching strategy designed to create a low-anxiety learning environment where students work together in small groups to achieve instructional goals.

Key Principles of Competency 004

- Stages of development for ELLs—novice (preproduction and early production), intermediate, advanced proficiency and superior (advanced fluency)
- Interdependence of L1 and L2—cognitive and academic language proficiency in L1 has a positive effect in the acquisition of cognitive and academic proficiency in L2
- Cummins Research on CUP (common underlying proficiency) and CALP (cognitive academic language proficiency).
- Strategies to develop language proficiency in Language Arts and content area instruction (Whole Language, CALLA, Sheltered English)

References

Anderson, T. & Boyer, M. (1977). Bilingual Schooling in the United States. Southwest Educational Development Laboratory, Austin, Texas. Available: www.eric.ed.gov/ERICDocs/

Baker, C., and S. Jones. 1998. *Encyclopedia of bilingualism and bilingual education*. Philadelphia, PA: Multilingual Matters.

Baker, K., and A. de Kanter. 1981. *Effectiveness of bilingual education: A review of the literature*. Washington, DC: Office of Planning, Budget and Evaluation. U.S. Department of Education.

Chamot, A., and J. O'Malley. 1994. *The CALLA handbook: Implementing the cognitive academic language learning approach*. Reading: MA: Addison-Wesley.

Cisneros v. Corpus Christi Independent School District-467 F2nd 142 (1971). United States Court of Appeals, Fifth Circuit. Retrieved April 29, 2010, from Open Juris http://openjurist.org/.

Collier and Thomas (2009). Educating English Learners for a Transformed World. Dual Language Education of New Mexico: Albuquerque, NM.

Christian, D. 1994. *Two-way bilingual education: Students learning through two languages*. Education Practice Report 12. Washington, DC: Center for Applied Linguistics.

Crawford, J. 2004. *Educating English learners: Language diversity in the classroom*. 5th ed. Los Angeles: Bilingual Education Services, Inc.

Cummins, J. 1979. Linguistic interdependence and the educational development of bilingual children. *Bilingual education paper series*, vol. 3, no. 2. ERIC Document Reproduction Service No. ED 257 312.

———. 1981. The role of primary language development in promoting educational success of minority students. In *Schooling and language minority students: A theoretical framework*, ed. California State Department of Education, 3–49. Los Angeles: Evaluation, Dissemination and Assessment Center, California State University.

———. 1991. Interdependence of first- and second-language proficiency in bilingual children. In *Language processing in bilingual children*, ed. E. Bialystok, 70–89. Cambridge: Cambridge Press.

Dannoff, M., G. Coles, D. McLaughlin, and D. Reynolds. (1978). *Evaluation of the impact of ESEA Title VII Spanish/English bilingual education program*. Vol. 3. Palo Alto, CA: American Institutes for Research.

Echevarria, J., M. Vogt, and D. Short. (2000). *Making content comprehensible for English language learners: The SIOP model*. Needham Heights, MA: Allyn and Bacon.

Freire, P. 1970. *Pedagogy of the oppressed*. New York: Continuum.

Fromkin, V., and R. Rodman. 1988. *An introduction to language*. 4th ed. New York: Holt, Rinehart, and Winston.

Gardner, H. (1983). *Frames of mind: The theory of multiple intelligences. New York: Basic Books.*

Gardner, H. (1999). *Intelligence reframed. Multiple intelligences for the 21st century. New York: Basic Books.*

Genzuk, M. (1988, reprinted (2010). Bilingual schooling: A Historical Perspective. www-rcf.usc.edu/

Sousa, David A. (2010). *How the brain learns*. Corwin Press: Sage Publications.

Grosjean, F. 1982. *Life with two languages: An introduction to bilingualism*. Cambridge, MA: Harvard University Press.

Howard, E., and J. Sugarman. 2001. *Two-way immersion programs: Features and statistics*. Washington, DC: Center for Applied Linguistics. www.cal.org/.

Hudelson, S. 1984. Kan yo ret an rayt en ingles: Children becoming literate in English as a second language. *TESOL Quarterly* 18: 221–238.

Kagan, S. 1985. *Cooperative learning resources for teachers*. Riverside, CA: Spencer Kagan.

Krashen, S. D. and Terrell, T. D. (1983). *The natural approach: Language acquisition in the classroom. Hayward, CA: Alemany Press.*

Kress, J. 1993. *The ESL teacher's book of lists*. West Nyack, NY: The Center for Applied Research in Education.

Lapp, D., D. Fisher, J. Flood, and A. Cabello. 2001. An integrated approach to the teaching and assessment of language arts. In *Literacy assessment of second language learners*, eds. S. Rollins Hurley and J. Villamil Tinajero, 1–24. Boston, MA: Allyn and Bacon.

Levin, H. 1987. Accelerated schools for disadvantaged students. *Educational Leadership* 44(6): 19–21.

McMillan, J. 2004. *Classroom assessment: Principles and practice for effective instruction*. 3rd ed. Boston: Pearson.

North Central Regional Educational Laboratory (NCREL). n.d. *Accelerated learning*. www.ncrel.org.

National Clearinghouse for English Language Acquisition and Language Instruction Educational Programs (NCELA). 2006. *Glossary of terms related to the education of linguistically and culturally diverse students*. www.ncela.gwu.edu.

Ovando, C., M. Combs, C. C. and Collier, V. P. 2006. *Bilingual and ESL classrooms: Teaching in multicultural contexts*. 4th ed. Boston: McGraw-Hill.

Palincsar, A. S. and Brown, A. (1984). *Reciprocal Teaching of Comprehension-Fostering and Comprehension Monitoring Activities. Cognition and Instruction, 1(2), 117–175.*

Parker, W. C. 2001. *Social studies in elementary education*. 11th ed. Columbus, OH: Merrill Prentice-Hall.

Peñalosa, F. 1980. *Chicano sociolinguistics*. Rowley, MA: Newbury House Publishers, Inc.

Peregoy, S., and O. Boyle. 2005. *Reading, writing, and learning in ESL: A resource book for K–12 teachers*. 4th ed. New York: Pearson.

Ramírez, D. 1992. Longitudinal study of structured English immersion strategy, early-exit and late-exit transitional bilingual education programs for language-minority children [executive summary]. *Bilingual Research Journal* 16 (Winter/Spring): 1–2.

Reiss, J. 2005. *Teaching content to English language learners: Strategies for secondary school success*. White Plains, NY: Pearson.

Riley, R. 2000. *Excelencia para todos—Excellence for all: The progress of Hispanic education and the challenges of a new century*. Speech delivered at Bell Multicultural High School, Washington, DC, March 15.

Rodríguez, R. 1996. Bilingual education. In *The handbook of Texas online. www.tshaonline.org/.*

Rosado, L. 2005. Cross-cultural communication: A Latino perspective. *Academic Exchange Extra*. January.

Ryder, M. 2005. *Critical pedagogy*. Denver: University of Colorado School of Education.

Schifini, A. 1985. *Sheltered English: Content area instruction for limited English proficiency students*. Los Angeles County Office of Education.

Stewig, J. W. , and Jett-Simpson, M. 1995. *Language arts in the early childhood classroom*, Belmont, CA: Wadsworth.

Texas Education Agency (TEA), Student Assessment Division. 2010. STAAR information booklets.

TEA. 1998. *Academic achievement of elementary students with limited English proficiency*. Policy research report 10.

———. 2005. *LPAC decision-making process for the Texas assessment program (grades 3–12): Procedural manual and forms for the 2005–2006 school year*.

The Oyez Project, Hernandez v. Texas, 347 U.S. 475 (1954).

Thomas, W. P. and V. P. Collier (2002). *A national study of school effectiveness for language minority students' long term academic achievement*. Washington, D.C.: Center for Applied Linguistics.

Thomas, W.P. and V. P. Collier. (1997). *School effectiveness for language minority students*. NCBE Resource Collection Series No. 9. Washington, DC: National Clearinghouse for Bilingual Education.

———. 2002. *A national study of school effectiveness for language minority students' long-term academic achievement*. Santa Cruz, CA: Center for Research on Education, Diversity, and Excellence.

Tomas, E., and H. Robinson. 1972. *Improving reading in every class: A source book for teachers*. Boston: Allyn and Bacon.

Tragar, B., and B. Wong. 1984. The relationship between native and second language reading and second language oral ability. In *Placement procedures in bilingual education: Education and policy issues*, ed. C. Rivera, 152–164. Clevedon, England: Multicultural Matters.

Tucker, R. 1999. A global perspective on bilingualism and bilingual education. *CAL Digests*.

United Nations Scientific and Cultural Organization (1953). The use of the vernacular language in education. Monographs on fundamental education VII. Paris. Author Unknown

Urzúa, C. 1987. "You stopped too soon": Second language children composing and revising. *TESOL Quarterly* 21: 279–305.

CHAPTER

Domain II: English Language Arts and Reading

2

Competency 005 (Oral Language)

The teacher understands the importance of oral language, knows the developmental processes of oral language, and provides the students with varied opportunities to develop listening and speaking skills.

This chapter addresses basic linguistic concepts, stages of oral language development, phonological and phonemic awareness, the alphabetic principle, development in reading and writing and viewing and representing.

According to research in oral language development, language does not develop in isolation. Children internalize language that makes sense to them or is comprehensible (Echevarría, Vogt and Short, 2008). Peregoy and Boyle (2005) have identified comprehensible input and social interaction as the two most important elements of oral language development. Noam Chomsky explains the development of language in terms of children having an innate ability to acquire language. So how exactly do children develop language?

Language acquisition results from the combination of innate ability, imitation of what is said and heard, and multiple environmental influences. Children are said to be born with innate abilities and mechanisms to develop language. Noam Chomsky called this mechanism a Language Acquisition Device (LAD). According to Chomsky, humans possess an "internal grammar" or set of linguistic principles that are activated for all languages. Interestingly, the LAD is considered universal, as the LAD adapts depending on the language being learned. However, it should be noted that linguists have argued that language only emerges if this internal mechanism is triggered by stimuli from people in the child's environment.

Imitation is a learning strategy that young children frequently use to replicate someone's behaviors, actions, phrases by observing and repeating their caregiver's phrases and words. Imitation decreases in effectiveness as language learning becomes more complex. Due to memory limitations, infants appear to pay more attention to the ends of sentences or words. For example, a question such as, "Do you want to go out?" might receive a reply of "out." This reply probably means, "Yes, I want to go out."

After age two, imitation alone cannot meet the communication needs of children. It is at this point when they become creative rule makers. Toddlers begin testing language rules on their own as a way of trying to figure out how language operates. For example, imitation alone cannot explain idiosyncratic statements such as "I goed out yesterday." These nonstandard utterances show that the child is field-testing language rules. In this case, the child is testing the rule for the formation of the regular past tense and has applied it to an irregular verb. This type of overgeneralization characterizes the process of first language acquisition during most of the early childhood years. Thus, modeling becomes very important in presenting the target language to ELLs. Also, teachers must consistently model developmentally appropriate language structures to ELLs.

All teacher candidates need a clear understanding of the basic components of language, which are phonology, morphology, syntax, lexicon, semantics, and pragmatics.

Phonology—the study of the sound system—phonemes (basic units of sound) and graphemes (letters)—**through**—has 7 letters (graphemes) and 3 sounds (phonemes /th,r,u/

Morphology—the study of the structure of words—morphemes (smallest unit of meaning (e.g. cars has 2 morphemes—1) the root word car and 2) the "s" for plural

Types of Kernel Sentences

1.	**Noun**	**Intransitive Verb**	**Predicate Nominative**
Example:	Katrina	was	a hurricane.
2.	**Noun**	**Intransitive Verb**	**Predicate Adjective**
Example:	Katrina	was	destructive.
3.	**Noun**	**Transitive Verb**	**Direct Object**
Example:	*Bear Mountain*	won	an Oscar.
4.	**Noun**	**Transitive Verb**	**Indirect Object Direct Object**
Example:	President Bush	provided India	with nuclear technology.

Syntax—word sequence in a sentence—there are 4 kernel structures)

Lexicon—is the vocabulary of a language—words change based on context and culture

Semantics—conveys meaning based on context and cultural—connotation (implied meaning as in many idiomatic expressions) and denotation (literal meaning).

Both connotation and denotation present a challenge to (ELLs) because they generally lack the familiarity with American culture that native speakers have. Teachers need to teach idioms in a contextualized situation and also need to describe their intended meanings.

Pragmatics describes how context can affect the interpretation of communication. Pragmatics describes the hidden rules of communications understood by native speakers of the same language. Native speakers often call these rules "common sense rules." However, these rules might be only common to native English speakers and not ELLs. Thus, teachers need to familiarize ELLs with the variations in language. In English, a person greets another person with a routine statement such as "how are you?" The rules of pragmatics require the receiver to answer with a generic statement such as "not bad," "I am OK," or "fine." ELLs and people who are new to the culture might misinterpret the routine question as a literal inquiry and try to answer it directly, which often creates confusion.

Language Is Learned in Social Settings

Engagement in conversational dialogue provides children with the vocabulary and the format of conversations (Stewig and Jett-Simpson 1995). Parents do not always engage in direct language teaching but they help language acquisition by communicating with the child and using the adult version of the language. As a result of this linguistic support, most children come to school with a strong vocabulary and language background. Conversely, some ethnic and linguistic groups might not follow the same pattern of linguistic interaction with children. The expression "Children are to be seen, not heard" represents an example of how some groups view the appropriate interaction of children with adults. Children who are brought up in a society where participation in adults' conversations is restricted might not have the same language development and will begin school behind their classmates.

Children are Concerned with Meaning

Children quickly understand that the main purpose of language is communication. They are not concerned with grammar, and they just want to communicate to get their needs met. Because of this, direct error correction has little impact in the language development of preschool children. They expect language to make sense and rely on sympathetic listeners to understand them. Therefore, modeling is always the best way to support language development in preschool children.

Stages of Language Development

The process of first language acquisition is characterized by certain stages, which are regulated by the maturation process and by the level and quality of exposure to the native language. It is difficult to assign a definite age for each of these stages, but we will provide an average age in order to develop a working framework for readers. A description of these stages follows.

Babbling or Pre-Language Stage (0–6 months)

Children at this state send and receive messages and use reflexive crying to communicate with caregivers. They play vocally by producing multiple linguistic and non-linguistic sounds, (e.g., *mmm*, *gugu*, *dada*). Infants can identify the voices of parents and family members, and they are able to follow certain commands. They also begin understanding the intonation patterns used to convey anger or excitement and the patterns used to ask questions.

Holophrastic One-Word Stage (11–19 months)

Children at the one-word stage begin imitating inflections and facial expressions of adults. They recognize their name, and follow simple instructions presented in contextualized situations. Children begin using adults as tools by pointing to objects and requesting assistance. They understand **word concepts** and use these to conceptualize complete ideas.

Two-Word Stage (13–24 months)

At the two-word stage, children begin producing rudimentary types of sentences. These constructions are characterized by a combination of two types of words—Pivot and Open words. **Pivot** refers to words that can be used to accomplish multiple functions, i.e., *no, up, all, see, more,* and *gone*. The **open** class contains words that are generally used to refer to one concept. Words like *home, milk, doggy, juice, pants,* and *shoe* are words that are used mostly to refer to one particular situation. Based on the vocabulary limitations of this stage, children use combinations of these two classes to create the subject and the predicate of the sentence. Some possible examples of utterances produced at this stage are: "See baby," "see mommy," "no more," and "all gone."

Telegraphic Stage (18–27 months)

The telegraphic stage represents a higher degree of linguistic development in which the child goes beyond the two-word stage. Most of the words used at this stage are **content words** with high semantic value that can be used in multiple situations. Some examples of function words are nouns, adjectives and verbs. The use of **function words**, such as prepositions and articles, is very limited at this stage because they do not convey as much information as content words. The typical sentence at this stage consists of subject, verb, object or adjective format. Some possible examples of utterances produced at this stage are: "no more TV," "milk all gone," and "that's not nice."

Two to Three Years

At age two children have about 200 to 300 words in their speaking repertoire, and generally can produce short rudimentary sentences. They also begin using prepositions and pronouns with some level of inconsistency. The vocabulary of three-year-olds grows to about 900 to 1000 words. Three-year-olds begin creating three- to four-word sentences. They are able to follow two-step commands and engage in short dialogues about familiar topics. In schools with programs for three-year-olds, children get exposed to informal and formal registers—variants of a language used for a particular purpose depending on the social setting. Children begin to request instead of demand, use courteous vocabulary, and begin following conversation formats.

Age Four

Four-year-olds generally have about 1,500 words in their speaking repertoire. They use more complex sentence structures, but their speech still contains pronunciation problems and overgeneralizations. Four year-olds are able to understand more than what they are able to verbalize. They can answer factual questions in contextualized situations, but have difficulties explaining the rationale for their answers.

Age Five

Five-year-olds have a vocabulary of about 2,100 words and a working knowledge of the grammar of the language. They may have problems dealing with compound sentences and sentences with embedded meaning. They are beginning to understand time concepts and use verbs accordingly. Most children at this stage have mastered the use of the progressive (-ing), regular past tense (-ed), and plurals (-s). Irregular verbs still constitute a challenge for five-year-olds. They are able to identify and produce specific sounds and blends (combinations of phonemes like in the word *block*). The vocabulary continues to increase as children have more contact with peers and teachers in school.

Age Six and Seven

Six- to seven-year-olds have a speaking vocabulary of about 2,100 words and a comprehension vocabulary of more than 20,000 words. They use well-constructed sentences using all parts of speech. They still might have problems with certain words and structures, but their speech is fluent and clear. However, speakers at this age might still have problems with words containing sounds like /v/, /th/, /ch/ and /sh/. Some children will use the sound of the /w/ in place of the required /r/ and /l/ sounds. They are able to separate words into syllables and begin decoding written language. They are beginning to understand and address questions that call for reasons for an action. For example, they can explain their actions and answer questions such as "Why did you pick number five as the answer?" After age six, the child continues to polish their language skills, and add new and more sophisticated vocabulary.

Age Eight to Ten

The speaking repertoire of eight-year-olds continues growing and improving. They begin using relative pronouns clauses (i.e., The boy *that* you met yesterday is my friend.) They also begin to use subordinated clauses that begin with *when, if, and because* (i.e., *If* you bother me, I am going to tell the teacher). The gerund is also becoming common for speakers of this age (i.e., *Cheating* is bad). Children begin using more complex sentences, vocabulary, and verb construction. Their speech is more coherent though the use of connectors like *first, during, after,* and *finally*.

Assessing the Speaking Ability

Intelligibility

A child's speaking ability is generally assessed informally in class as part of daily activities. First, teachers have to determine if the speech of the child is **intelligible** and can be understood by native speakers with minimum effort. Communication or intelligibility problems in native speakers can be caused by developmental issues, the use of dialectical variations, or speech disorders. To assess the speech of the child, teachers need an understanding of the developmental patterns in the process of language mastery, and use these patterns as a foundation for assessing a child's performance. Teachers should also develop an understanding of features from dialects spoken in the community to avoid confusion with features that contrast with Standard English. For example, speakers of **Ebonics**, a language variant used by some African American children, and speakers of the **Boston dialect** drop the /r/ after a vowel. One example of this is in the statement "...pa**r**k the ca**r** in Ha**r**va**r**d yard" [Pa**h**k the ka**h** in Ha**h**vud ya**h**d]. In this case, the omission of post-vocalic *Rs* cannot be identified as a pronunciation problem. Because of this, teachers need a working knowledge of the dialects used in the community in order to make accurate assessments of the children's speech.

Language Interference

Teachers have to take into account how the first language of an ELL interferes in the pronunciation of English. Phonologically, language interference can happen at the word or sentence level. The most noticeable form of language interference happens when students use the phonology of their first language to pronounce words in English. For example, most Spanish dialects do not use the /v/ sound; instead, they replaced it with the /b/ sound. This feature creates semantic problems when native Spanish speakers pronounce the English word, *vowel* as ***b**owel*, which can create an embarrassing situation for the speaker.

Korean and Japanese speakers might also experience language interference when using the English /r/ sound because this sound is not present in their language. Chinese has both the /r/ and /l/ sounds; however, native Chinese speakers may experience problems with these two sounds when learning English. This is because they have the tendency to substitute the /r/ with the /l/ sound. This feature can create semantic problems when native Chinese, Korean, and Japanese speakers pronounce the English word ***rice as lice***. A second type of interference can be caused by the application of incorrect **word stress** in English. For example, in Standard English most speakers will place the primary stress of the word *com.po.**si.**tion* on the second to last syllable, but never on the last syllable. However, Spanish speakers and speakers of Caribbean English might place the primary stress on the last syllable, resulting in nonstandard English pronunciation. Language interference can create communication problems and potentially embarrassing situations for ELLs. Thus, teachers have to become aware of conflicting language sounds and provide appropriate language support to ELLs.

Communication Style and Culture

Culture plays an important role in the way that people communicate orally and in written form. In oral communication, English uses a linear rhetorical pattern that allows little flexibility to deviate from the topic. Other languages like Spanish, Russian, and Arabic allow for a more flexible progression to convey information. This flexibility is identified as a **curvilinear** approach, because it allows speakers the option of deviating from the main topic without being penalized. This cultural and linguistic difference can create problems in assessing the speaking capabilities of children who are native speakers of languages other than English. Teachers have to be vigilant to determine how the first language (L1) and culture affect the performance of children in the second language (L2).

Speaking Checklist

The speaking ability can also be assessed in the classroom with a structured checklist identifying specific features that teachers want to observe. Lapp et al. (2001) developed an instrument to assess the speaking ability called The Speaking Checklist. A summary of key elements is presented below.

Speaking Checklist

1. Sticks to the topic
2. Builds support for the subject
3. Speaks clearly
4. Takes turns and waits to talk
5. Talks so others in the group can hear
6. Speaks smoothly
7. Uses courteous language
8. Presents in an organized and interesting way
9. Supports the topical thesis
10. Answers questions effectively
11. Is comfortable speaking publicly
12. Maintains listeners interest
13. Volunteers to answer in class

The Texas Education Agency (TEA) also developed a new instrument to comply with the No Child Left Behind (NCLB) state accountability system: this is called the Texas Observation Protocol (TOP). This instrument was designed to assess the language proficiency of ELLs in Texas. This instrument contains a speaking component that assesses the speaking ability based on four language proficiencies: Beginning, Intermediate, Advanced, and Advanced High (TEA,

2006). This instrument is also an observation tool that uses holistic scoring, administered by teachers in the bilingual or ESL classroom. A performance that is scored at the Advanced High proficiency is generally required to be reclassified as a fluent English speaker. A description of the Advanced High proficiency follows:

1. ELLs are able to participate in extended discussion in a variety of social and grade-appropriate academic topics.
2. ELLs are able to communicate effectively using abstract and concrete content-based vocabulary during classroom instruction.
3. ELLs are able to use complex English grammar structures and complex sentences at a level comparative to native speakers.
4. ELLs rarely make linguistic errors that interfere with overall communication.
5. ELLs rarely use pronunciation that interferes with overall communication.

Listening and Speaking

Language uses a complex system for creating meaning through socially shared conventions. During the first months of life, babies are active listeners. Long before they can respond orally, they communicate non-verbally by waving their arms, smiling, or wiggling. They are also capable of communicating their needs and wants through non-verbal communication, including body language and crying. Through listening, they develop the receptive language needed to begin communicating orally. Although listening is used extensively in communication, it does not receive much attention at school.

While there is no well-defined model of teaching listening skills, some theorists link listening skills to reading skills. They feel that reading and listening both make use of similar language comprehension processes. Listening and reading both require the use of skills in phonology, syntax, semantics, and knowledge of the structure of text, and both language skills seem to be controlled by the same set of cognitive processes. A number of studies suggest that the teaching of listening can be done by engaging in the kinds of activities that have been successful in developing reading, writing, and speaking proficiencies. For example, teachers can guide students' listening activities by setting a purpose for listening, providing questions before and after the listening activity, and encouraging children to forge links between the new information that was just heard and the knowledge already in place. In addition, children need to be coached in the use of appropriate volume and speed when they speak, and in the rules to participate in discussions.

Communication Disorders

A communication disorder occurs when a person's speech interferes with the ability to convey messages during interactions with community members. The four classifications of language disorders are disorders in voice, fluency, articulation, and language processing (Piper, 2003).

Voice Disorders

Voice disorders describe any type of distortion of the pitch, timber, or volume of spoken communication. There are two types of voice disorders: phonation and resonance. **Phonation** disorder describes any kind of abnormality in the vibration of the vocal fold. For example, *hoarseness* or extreme breathiness can interfere with comprehension. **Resonance** disorder describes abnormalities created when sound passes through the vocal tract. The most typical example of resonance disorder occurs when the sound passing through the nasal cavity changes oral sounds to nasal, which is called *hyper-nasal sounds*. This type of disorder should not be confused with the nasal quality of Southern dialects like the Texas twang.

Fluency Disorders

Fluency disorders refer to any kind of conditions that affect the child's ability to produce coherent and fluent communication. The most common types of fluency disorder are caused by *stuttering* and *cluttering*. Stuttering is characterized by multiple false starts or the inability to produce the intended sounds. Cluttering occurs when children try to communicate in an excessively fast mode that makes comprehension difficult.

Teachers have to be cautious when assessing ELLs who might experience temporary fluency dysfunction, such as hesitations, false starts, and repetition that are created by anxiety or confusion with the two languages. Often ELLs stutter because they cannot find or might not know the appropriate word in English. Allowing students to code-switch from English to their first language can be used as a temporary remedy to stuttering. Additionally, children new to the language often use the intonation pattern and the speed of delivery of their native language.

Articulation Problems

Children may have problems with specific sounds that can cause unintelligibility and the production of esthetically displeasing sounds. The most common articulation disorder is *lisping*. **Lisping** is a term used when children (or adults) produce the sound /s/, /sh/, /z/, and /ch/ with their tongue between the upper and lower teeth. Some other sounds that can present challenges to children are the /w/, /l/, and /r/ sounds. Some of these problems might be developmental and will eventually be eliminated, while others might require speech therapy. Elmer Fudd and Sylvester the Cat, two popular cartoon characters, are well known for exhibiting these speech features (i.e., Sylvester lisping, and Elmer having difficulties with the /r/ sound as in "wabbit.")

Language Processing

Language processing disorders are generally caused by a brain-based disturbance called aphasia. Three types of aphasia are known: receptive, expressive, and global.

Receptive aphasia, or "sensory aphasia" results from a lesion to a region in the upper back part of the temporal lobe of the brain. Receptive aphasia creates problems with listening comprehension and retrieval of words from memory. People affected with this condition have the tendency of repeating formulaic phrases and producing unintelligible sequences of words or sounds.

Expressive aphasia results from damage to the lower back part of the frontal lobe. This damage affects the speaking ability and causes specific problems with articulation and fluency. The speech produced is often very slow including multiple hesitations and problems with the supra-segmental features of language including intonation, rhythm, and stress. The sentences produced are generally very short and contain only the necessary features to convey the message. Their speech resembles the speech of children at the telegraphic stage of first language development.

Global aphasia is also a brain-based disorder that affects both the receptive and expressive features of language. Children with this kind of severe impairment of articulation and fluency produce minimal speech and their comprehension is very limited. This type of language disorder is also known as "irreversible aphasia," which suggests that little can be done to help children suffering from this condition.

Activities to Promote Oral Communication

The best way to promote oral communication is to guide students into using language in meaningful situations. In classroom situations, teachers can organize activities to resemble real-life situations in order to promote communication among students. Some of these activities are described below.

Dramatic Play

Dramatic play using prompts is an ideal activity to develop communication that resembles real-life situations. Students are given a situation and a specific role to play, and they improvise probable communications. For example, one child can play the role of a parent, another role of a student in trouble, and a third student can play the role of a teacher.

Language Play

Language play involves the use of language in rhyme, alliteration, songs, and repeating patterns to amuse children. Tongue twisters are commonly used to practice pronunciation and language patterns. Through these activities, children acquire language knowledge in a relaxed and fun environment. Teachers can also use nursery rhymes, poems, and stories that contain rhyme to introduce these language features.

Show and Tell

In show and tell, children bring artifacts and personal items to class. They show the object and describe its features to the class. In addition to the obvious benefit of oral communication, this kind of activity can be used to promote home and cultural pride.

Hand-Puppet Show

Hand puppets, finger-puppets, and string-puppets can be used to promote communication confidence among children. Students speak using the puppet as a cover for any errors made in communication. The use of puppets is an enjoyable and motivating activity for young learners.

Pair Interview

Another interesting strategy to promote oral communication is pair interview. In this strategy, children are paired to learn information from each other and then report their findings to the larger group. This strategy is ideal for the first day of class when students want to get to know each other.

Presentations to Address Different Audiences

Preparing children to communicate what they think and know is common practice in classrooms. Depending on the children's age, the expectations surrounding the ways in which they share this information orally will vary. For instance, kindergarten teachers should not expect their students to deliver a 20-minute presentation. Instead, giving their students an opportunity to deliver presentations in a nonthreatening environment and activity (e.g., show-and-tell) can lead them to begin appreciating the art of public speaking from a very young age. As children enter elementary school, the expectations change considerably. For instance, elementary students are expected not only to use correct language when speaking, but to have accurate information when creating a presentation. To this end, students are expected to also find reliable information and sources when investigating a topic of interest or one assigned. Elementary students also learn that a topic of a presentation can be delivered to multiple and different audiences as to inform students of recycling, for example, or present the same topic to business people in the community.

Key Principles of Competency 005

- Promote the development of listening skills by implementing listening activities as a routine in the daily schedule.
- Have students role play specific events in history.
- Present listening skills for various purposes.
- Provide instruction and opportunities for children to evaluate the content of their own spoken messages.
- Select and use appropriate technologies to develop children's oral communication skills.

Competency 006 (Phonological and Phonemic Awareness)

The teacher understands phonological and phonemic awareness and employs a variety of approaches to help children develop phonological and phonemic awareness.

Importance of Phonological and Phonemic Awareness for Reading

Phonological and phonemic awareness constitute the foundation for the development of the metalinguistic awareness that children need to become successful language learners and effective readers.

Phonemic awareness refers to the ability of a child to understand that words have smaller components called sounds, and these sounds together create syllables and words. Phonemic awareness is the basic linguistic principle required to develop an understanding of oral and written communication.

Phonemic Stress

Phonemic stress can be taught through the use of nursery rhymes, short poems, or stories like the traditional Humpty Dumpty character of Mother Goose nursery rhymes. The sound of these rhythmic patterns in an enjoyable and relaxed environment introduces children to the sounds and music of language.

Alliteration is a literacy technique used to emphasize phonemes by using successive words that begin with the same consonant sound or letter. Tongue twisters are the best known form of alliteration. Children can repeat tongue twisters for fun and at the same time, develop an awareness of the sound-symbol correspondence. In the following example, the /p/ sound is emphasized:

Peter **P**iper **p**icked a **p**eck of **p**ickled **p**eppers.

Phonological awareness

Phonological awareness is the ability to recognize and manipulate components of the sound system of a language. It includes the ability to segment words into smaller units like syllables and phonemes (sounds). Phonological awareness also encompasses the ability to identify and separate words within a sentence, identify stress in individual words, and identify the intonation pattern used in sentences.

Syllabication

Syllabication is an important component of phonological awareness. It refers to the ability to conceptualize and separate words into their basic pronunciation components, which are syllables. Syllables can be as a simple as one vowel, or can be a combination of vowels and consonants. For example, the word *elegant* contains three syllables (el/**e**/gant), one of which is a vowel alone. Phonemes are the basic unit of a syllable, and syllables constitute the basic units for the pronunciation of the English language. Consequently, syllables influence the rhythm of the language, poetic meter, and word stress. Syllabication can be taught using the appropriate voice intonation in order to indicate the beginning and ending of a syllable. Teachers often use clapping to indicate syllable boundaries.

Word Stress

English has at least four levels of word stress but, for practical purposes, we only need to be concerned with the first two: main stress and secondary stress. Word stress can affect the ability to understand words, and can also alter meaning. For example, the word *pervert* can have two meanings depending on how it is pronounced. With the stress on the next to last syllable (*pérvert*) it becomes a noun, but if the stress is placed on the last syllable (*pervért*) it becomes a verb.

Intonation Patterns

The intonation pattern describes the pitch contour of a phrase or a sentence that is used to change the meaning of the sentence. In English, there are utterances that might appear to be identical but convey a different meaning. In the question below, the rising point at the verb *are* makes the utterance a question, while a slight change of intonation to the pronoun, *you*, changes the utterance to a reply to the question.

Question	How **are** you?
Reply	How are **you**?

Special Considerations when Teaching Phonemic and Phonological Awareness

1. It is easier to break sentences into words, and break words into syllables than to break syllables into phonemes, whole to part and then reverse the process.
2. Begin teaching phonemic awareness using short monosyllabic words like consonant-vowel-consonant i.e., *bat* and *cat*, before introducing more difficult ones (onset and rime).
3. Teachers should introduce sounds in initial position, then sounds in final position, and finally (the most difficult ones) the phonemes in medial position.
4. Teachers should introduce phoneme awareness first with simpler concepts like rhyming and initial phoneme identification, and then introduce blending and segmenting words into syllables.
5. When teaching sound–symbol correspondence, introduce sounds that present the least chance for distortion. Sounds like the **nasal** /m/ and **sibilant** /s/ represent easier sounds for the child than the brief sounds created with **stop** sounds like /p/, /t/, and /k/.

Teaching Phonemic and Phonological Awareness

Teachers can promote the phonemic and phonological knowledge through a variety of strategies. A list of these strategies follows:

Introduce blending by guiding children to identify the word created when the following sounds are blended: /b/, /a/, and /t/.

- Guide children to identify a word like *tape* and then remove the onset and ask the child: "What word is left when we remove the first sound?" (answer: *ape*.) Then ask students, "Is this a word?"
- Teach word segmentation by saying a word, and then guiding children to identify the sounds that they hear. Teachers can begin with simple monosyllabic words like *car* and then expand to more sophisticated words.
- Use onsets and rhymes to teach the sound-symbol relationship. Guide children to create new words by substituting the first letter of monosyllabic words. For example, using the word *ring*, the child can replace the initial sounds to create additional words *sing*, *king*, and *spring*. This activity has two purposes: it emphasizes phonemic awareness and, at the same time, teaches how word families can support vocabulary development.
- Teachers should lead children to segment or separate the sounds in words. Begin with words with consistent sound-symbol correspondence, like *bag* and *lag*, and later expand to words that contain clusters/blends like in the word ***splash*** and diagraphs like in the word ***ch**urch*.
- Introduce minimal pairs, which are sets of words that differ in only one phoneme like *pail* and *bail*, to guide students to notice the difference. Teachers should pronounce both words and ask students if the words are the same or different. Initially, contrast words with initial consonant sounds like in *pat* and *bat*, and later expand to include more sophisticated contrasting pairs like in **bit** and **beet**.
- Say words and guide children to identify the number of sounds that they hear. Initially, avoid stop sounds because children might have difficulties perceiving the brief sound represented by these sounds.
- Guide children to recite nursery rhymes or children's songs and then guide them to repeat the rhyme or song, changing the initial word. For example, a simple Mother Goose rhyme like *Go to bed, Tom!* can be used to replace the parts of the rhyme. For example, students can repeat "*Go to bed, Tom!, Tired or not, Tom, Go to bed, Tom*." Students can then replace Tom with other names. Students can also replace the initial sound of each line to create standard and non-standard words. For example, guide children to substitute the initial sound of each major word to see how it

sounds and to determine if the change created a word that they can recognize, i.e, *So* to *Sed*, *Som*, *So* to *Sed*, *Som*. In addition to teaching the phoneme system, children are guided to understand how phonemes can alter meaning.

Balanced Reading Program

The development of phonemic and phonological awareness is important to preparing students for formal reading instruction. However, a strong reading program must go beyond these components to incorporate a balanced reading program. The concept of a balanced reading program emerged as a result of the work of Catherine Snow, Susan Burns, and Peg Griffin (1998). The balanced reading program encompasses best teaching practices from two traditionally opposing reading instruction programs: the **skills-based** approach, which emphasizes phonics instruction, and the **meaning-based** approach, which promotes reading comprehension and enrichment. The researchers concluded that a balanced reading program, one that incorporates the best principles of phonics (skills-based) and whole language (meaning-based) instruction, can best address the reading needs of all children.

Competency 007 (Alphabetic Principle)

The teacher understands the importance of the alphabetic principle for reading English and provides instruction that helps students understand the relationship between spoken language and printed words.

The alphabetic principle has been described as the ability to connect letters with sounds, and to create words based on these associations. Children learning to read must develop an understanding that letters and letter patterns represent the sounds of spoken English (TEA, 2002).

How is the Alphabetic Principle Learned?

Traditionally, children go through specific stages in the process of learning new words and mastering the alphabetic principle (Ehri, 1998). Preschoolers are exposed to components of the alphabetic principle through their environment. They can identify the logo of stores like Wal-Mart or Burger King by their design instead of by the specific letters contained in the logo. But because they are not connecting the letters and the sounds of the logo, this stage is generally considered a **pre-alphabetic phase** (U.S. Dept. of Education 2006). At home, children might also get exposed to the alphabet song, which most of them learn in a subconscious manner. Eventually, children engage in a **partial alphabetic** phase as they get exposed to alphabet block playing and concrete letter objects that are typical in early childhood programs. They begin connecting the shape of the letters with the sound that they represent. Children are also often exposed to children's literature and books in which the sound-symbol correspondence is carefully controlled. Children also begin connecting initial letter with the sound of the names of peers, like the N of Nancy and A of Alex.

A third phase of learning new words is identified as the **full alphabetic stage**. At this stage, children begin making connections between the letters, the sounds that they represent, and the actual meaning of the word. Children get very excited during this stage because they are beginning to "crack" the written code of the language. In the fourth and last stage of development, called the **consolidated alphabetic stage**, children begin conceptualizing that they can use components of words that they know to decode new words. They begin discovering how they can create new words with the use of onsets, rhymes, and other letter sequences. One of the main purposes of phonics instruction at this stage is to guide children into understanding the connection between the grapheme and phoneme and the sequence that they create to form words and sentences. This knowledge allows students the opportunity to expand the number of words that they recognize instantly (sight words), which prepares them for literacy.

Teaching the Grapheme-Phoneme Correspondence

- The introduction of the grapheme-phoneme correspondence can be presented through games, songs, and other engaging activities;

but eventually, the correspondence should be presented explicitly. Teachers have to bring the skills to the surface level and make students aware of the concepts and skills that they need to learn in order to become effective readers. Teachers should take into account the complexity of the language and the maturity level of the children when introducing children to the alphabetic principle. A list of considerations and strategies for teaching the grapheme-phoneme connection follows.

- The introduction of the letter-sound correspondence should be guided by the potential support of the children's efforts to become readers. That is, introduce the spelling of the letters that the child is most likely to encounter in text. For example the letters *m, a, t, s, p,* and *h* are used more frequently in writing than letters like *x, q*, or consonant diagraphs like *ght* or.
- It is also important to begin instruction in the grapho-phonemic relationship using sounds that present the least possible distortion or confusion with other sounds. Some of the sounds that are easier to perceive are the nasals /m/, /n/, the fricatives /f/, the sibilant /s/, and the English retroflex /r/.
- Teachers should postpone the introduction of less clear phonemes like the nasal /ng/, the distinction between the sibilants /s/ and /z/, the troublesome sounds in English like the voiced th in the word them, and the voiceless counterpart in words like think.
- Introduce words with one or two consonants and one short vowel sound such as in the words on and car. Later, long vowel sounds can be introduced.
- Next, add consonant blends like try, followed by digraphs like th, sh, and ch in words like thanks, show, and chop. Digraphs can lead students to recognize common words such as this, she, and chair. Introduce single consonants and consonant blends or clusters in separate lessons to avoid confusion.
- Avoid voiceless-stop sounds (/t/, /p/, /k/) at the beginning or middle of words because the short duration of these phonemes makes them difficult to perceive. Teachers should postpone the introduction of conflicting letter-sound correspondence of phonemes like the /b/ and /v/ or /i/ and /e/, or visually
- confusing graphemes like the b and d or p and g.

Types of Writing Systems

Modern writing systems can be categorized into several classifications. Three of the most commonly used classifications are pictographic, syllabic, and alphabetic. ***Pictographic*** writing systems are designed to represent words or ideas with a visual image representing the concept. Pictographic writing was the first type of written language developed in the history of civilizations. Pictograms are used today in road signs and public buildings. For example, the figure of a spoon and a fork are pictographs that represent a restaurant, and a figure of a woman or man represents restroom facilities by gender.

Syllabic writing represents syllables with signs, and syllabic writing is more efficient than a pictographic writing system. Japanese is a syllabic language composed of about 100 syllables. The Japanese syllabic system is ideal because the entire language can be phonologically represented by a relatively small number of syllables and the language does not have consonant clusters.

Alphabetic writing system uses the sounds of the language as a basic unit for writing. English uses an alphabetic writing system that is based upon phonetic signs. Theoretically in this system, each symbol represents one unit of sound. However, this principle works better with languages with more consistent sound-symbol relationship. Many alphabetic languages like Spanish are more phonetically consistent than English. An analysis of the grapheme-phoneme correspondence of English follows.

The Grapheme-Phoneme Correspondence of English

The connection between graphemes and phonemes in English is not always consistent. English has

26 graphemes to represent 44 phonemes. The consonant system is more consistent than the vowel system. English has five letters to represent 12 vowel sounds, which makes decoding and pronunciation more challenging. This inconsistency is partially caused by the evolution of the English language and the influence of multiple languages in the development of Modern English. Teachers need to be proactive by identifying these troublesome areas and organizing instruction to address these issues. Some of the potential areas of concern are:

1. Graphemes can represent multiple phonemes. For example the grapheme ***s*** can represent multiple phonemes: car**s-/z/**, call**s-/z/**, **sugar-/sh/**, mi**ssion-/sh/**, and walk**s-/s/**. This grapheme-phoneme inconsistency represents a challenge when attempting to use a phonic approach to teach reading.
2. English has graphemes that represent a sound in some words and remains silent in other words. For example, the graphemes *s* and *l* become silent in the following examples without giving readers a reliable clue for this change: *island*, *calm*, and *palm* (Some speakers will make an attempt to pronounce the /s/ and /l/ in these words).
3. English has multiple consonant diagraphs, which are two or more letters representing one sound.
   - Gh – Ghost
   - Gn – Gnat
   - Kn – Know
   - Ght – thought
   - Pn– Pneumonia
   - Ps– Psychology
   - Rh– Rhythm
   - Wr– Write
   - Sc– Scene

   This inconsistency presents a challenge to native English speakers as well as ELLs.
4. English uses multiple contractions in daily communication. These can create listening comprehension problems for students and especially for ELLs. Teachers should introduce contractions together with the long version of the words to avoid confusion. Table 2-1 presents a few examples of the type of confusion that contractions can cause.

Table 2-1. Contractions in English

Contractions	Regular form	Possible Confusion
They're	They are	there and their
He's	He is/He has	his
He'll	He will	Hill, hell or heel or heal
You're	You are	your

5. English has multiple initial consonant clusters, which require students to be able to blend the sounds and at the same time recognize the sounds of individual phonemes. These sounds also represent a challenge for native Spanish speakers because Spanish does not have words that begin with particular letter sequences that exist in English. These types of clusters occur in medial positions and they are always preceded by the vowel **e**, such as in the words **esp**ero, **esc**apar, and **est**ar. Based on this feature, Latino children will place an **e** in front of English words containing the following clusters: sp (as in speak), sc (school), st (street), spr (spring), scr (scream), str (stream), sm (small), sn (snow), and sl (slate).
6. A lot of English words end in consonants and consonant clusters (e.g., ra**t**, co**rd**, fi**rst**, and ca**rd**.) Young native English-speaking children and ELLs may have difficulties blending clusters at the end of the words. For native Spanish speakers, these clusters represent a unique challenge because Spanish does not have words that end in consonant clusters. Based on this feature, Spanish-speaking children, and possibly most children in early childhood, may tend to simplify final consonant cluster in English. For example, the word *board* might become *boar*.

Key Principles of Competencies 006 and 007

- Recognize that there will always be variation in students' alphabetic skills development, so plan accordingly.
- Take into consideration that not all languages are alphabetic and that some of your students may struggle when being asked to write in a way that is different from their language.
- The use of both formal and informal assessment tools and instruments can provide a more complete picture of a child's development than the use of only one type of tool.

Competency 008 (Literacy Development)

The teacher understands that literacy develops over time, progressing from emergent to proficient stages, and uses a variety of approaches to support the development of students' literacy.

Literacy Development

Literacy development generally begins at home when parents begin reading stories to their children. Through such activities, they are helping their child to hear the similarities and differences in the sounds of words. As a result of linguistic stimulation, children begin to manipulate and understand sounds in spoken language, and eventually they will practice this understanding by making up rhymes and new words on their own. When children are able to follow the written text together with the oral production, they begin to learn the names of the letters and the different sounds that each letter represents. Finally, children link the letters of the alphabet with the sounds of the words they speak. At this point children begin developing the phonemic and phonological awareness needed to become emergent readers.

Stages of Reading Development

Children go through three main stages of reading development: emergent readers, early readers, and fluent readers (information on the stages of reading can be found in Competency 003).

Emergent Readers

Emergent readers understand that print contains meaningful information. They imitate the reading process and display basic reading readiness skills like directionality movement, i.e., eye movement from top to bottom and from left to right. Emergent readers can participate in shared reading activities and are able to follow and match words with their pronunciation when teachers point to the words as they are read.

Early Readers

Early readers have mastered reading readiness skills and are beginning to read simple text with some degree of success. They are also developing an internal list of high frequency words in print. Their reliance on picture clues has decreased now that they can get more information from print.

Newly Fluent Readers

Newly fluent readers can read with relative fluency and comprehension. They are able to use several cuing systems to obtain meaning from print, i.e., semantic, structural, visual, and grapho-phonemic cuing systems. They self-monitor their reading, and can identify and correct simple errors with minimum external support. They ask clarification questions to develop an understanding of the content. Children at this stage are not totally independent readers but with practice and support from teachers, they soon become fluent and independent readers.

Literacy Development in School

As the child enters school, formal reading instruction begins. How children should be taught to read is a subject that stirs up intense debate. Basically, it comes down to a discussion about starting points, and how to proceed with instruction. The two most common approaches used to teach reading in public schools are the skills-based approach, and the meaning-based approach. The skills-based approach is also called the bottom-up approach and the meaning-based is also known as the top-down approach (information on these approaches can also be found in Competency 003, Chapter 1).

Bottom-Up Approach (Skills-Based)

The **bottom-up approach** proceeds from the specific to the general, or from the parts to the whole. This approach begins with phonemes and graphemes, and continues by expanding to the syllable, words, sentences, paragraphs, and then whole reading selections. The best representation of this approach is phonics instruction.

Phonics is a method of teaching beginners to read and pronounce words by teaching them the phonetic value of letters, letter groups, and syllables. Because English has an alphabetical writing system, an understanding of the letter-sound relationship may prove helpful to the beginning reader. However, this view of reading instruction is that these relationships should be taught in isolation, in a highly sequenced manner, followed by reading words that represent the regularities of English in print. The children are asked to read decodable texts by sounding out words in stories with controlled vocabulary.

Writing instruction follows in the same way. Children are asked to write decodable words, and fill in the blanks with decodable words in sentences in workbooks. This is based on the assumption that once the children progress past this initial reading instruction time frame meaning will follow.

Modern approaches to phonics instruction have made the stories more enjoyable and interesting. For example, the *Progressive Phonics Book* series, which is available through the Genki English website, uses computer sound technology, visuals, and more involving stories to engage the reader. The following is an example of this approach.

Don't Scowl at My Vowel

I don't mind it if my dog
Tries to **pat** me with his **paw**
But I don't like it if my **cat**
Tries to scratch me with her **claw**.

The assumption is that textual meaning will become apparent in time. Furthermore, it must be stressed that teaching phonics is not the same as teaching reading. In summary, the skills-based approach begins reading instruction with a study of single letters, letter sounds, blends and digraphs, blends and digraph sounds, and vowels and vowel sounds in isolation, and in a highly sequenced manner. The children read and write decodable words, with a great emphasis on reading each word accurately, as opposed to reading to comprehend the text as a whole.

The Genki English website provides examples of strategies to use for phonics instruction. This site also provides free use of games, songs and stories. The Genki English websites can be accessed at *www.genkienglish.net/phonics.htm*.

Top-Down Approach (Meaning-Based)

Another approach to promoting literacy is the **top-down approach**. This approach begins with the whole and then proceeds to its individual parts. That is, the top- down approach begins with whole stories, paragraphs, sentences, words and then proceeds to the smallest units of syllables, graphemes, and phonemes. The approach that best represents this view is the **Whole Language Approach**. The Whole Language Approach grew out of the work of Dr. Kenneth Goodman, who was a leader in the development of the psycholinguistic perspective. This approach suggests that to derive meaning from text, readers rely more on the structure and meaning of language than on the graphic information from the text. One of Dr. Goodman's contributions to the field was a process called **miscue analysis**, which is a process that begins with a child reading a selection orally, and an examiner noting variations of the oral reading from the printed text. Each variation from the text is called a miscue and is analyzed for type of variation. Previously, teacher candidates were urged to read and reread texts with young children until the child could read every word in the text perfectly. Goodman suggested, however, that only miscues that altered meaning needed to be corrected, while other, unimportant miscues could be ignored.

Whole-language advocates stress the importance of reading high-quality children's literature and extending the meaning of the literature through conversation, projects, and writing. Instead of fill-in-the-blank workbooks, children are encouraged to write journals, letters, and lists, and to participate in writing workshops. Word recognition skills, including phonics, are taught in the context of reading and writing, and are taught as those things relate to the text in hand. Children are taught to ask themselves, "Does it look right? Does it sound right? Does it make sense?" The children are taught that the reason people read books is to make meaning. Thus, the focus of this approach is on both comprehension and making connections. The main flaw of the Whole Language Approach is that it makes heavy instructional demands on the teacher.

Balanced Reading Program

Today, many classrooms are places where young children enjoy learning to read and write in a balanced reading instructional program. Research into best practice strongly suggests that the teaching of reading requires solid skill instruction, including several techniques for decoding unknown words. These techniques include but are not limited to, phonics instruction embedded in interesting and engaging reading and writing experiences with whole and **authentic literature-based** texts to facilitate the construction of meaning. In other words, this approach to instruction combines the best skill instruction and the whole language approach in order to teach both skills and meaning as well as to meet the reading needs of individual children.

Some of the reading strategies used in a balanced literacy program are:

- Teacher-directed/reading to students (read aloud)
- Shared reading, guided reading and reading workshops
- Student-directed reading and independent reading
- Teacher-directed writing, writing to/for students as part of classroom routines, and process writing
- Shared writing as in language experience/interactive writing, writing workshops
- Student-directed writing and independent writing activities

Children's Literature

Genre is a particular type of literature that can be classified in multiple categories. Some of the most common genres used in elementary schools are science fiction, biography, and traditional literature, including folk tales, fables, myths, epics, and legends. Classifications of genre are largely arbitrary and are based on conventions that apply a basic category to an author's writing. Classifications give the reader a general expectation of what sort of book is being chosen. Teachers today are expected to share a wide range of texts with children. The most common type of books for children is picture books. **Picture books** are books in which the illustrations and the text work together to communicate the story. It is a very good idea to share picture books with children in several different formats. Sometimes, able teachers simply read the book to the child without showing any of the pictures. The story is then discussed, and the children are asked if they would like the book to be reread, this time with the pictures being shared. Typically, this technique sparks a lively conversation about why the book with its illustrations is better than hearing the words alone.

Traditional Literature

Traditional literature comprises the stories that have their roots in the oral tradition of storytelling and have been handed down from generation to generation. This genre also includes the modern versions of these old stories. Teachers can read and share multiple versions of old stories, and then compare and contrast each version. It is also interesting to read a number of folktales and keep track of the elements that these old stories have in common, and also to guide children towards noticing where these old stories show up in their day-to-day lives. Children enjoy sharing what they notice. Some examples of folk literature are:

- Animal tales where the characters are animals exhibiting human characteristics, e.g., *Anansi the Spider*.
- Fables where the main characters are also animals and these present a moral, e.g., *The Tortoise and the Hare*.
- The *Pourquois Tales* comprise stories from around the world that explain how things were created. Every culture may have a different version of the way things were created, e.g., *How the Sea was Created*, and *The Legend of the Bluebonnet*.
- Wonder tales describe stories of enchantment in far away lands. Traditionally, it presents the themes of Good vs. Evil, e.g., *Snow White*.
- Noodle head tales are stories of lovable fools. These stories include individuals that are not very bright, but manage to survive and often succeed.
- Cumulative tales represent stories where the information is presented in a sequence and all the events in the sequence are repeated, e.g., *The Gingerbread Man* and *The Three Little Pigs*.
- Tall tales describe the story of legendary people or fictitious characters that manage to accomplish great things in life, e.g., *Paul Bunyan*, *John Henry*, and *Pecos Bill*.
- Ghost stories have traditionally been used to regulate the behavior of children. For example, the Boogie Man has been used in multiple cultures to scare children and encourage them to behave properly. In the Mexican culture, the Boogie Man is called "El Cucuy," and in the Puerto Rican culture he is called "El Cuco."

Multicultural Literature

Multicultural literature is a term used to describe literature other than traditional European stories. Traditionally, these are stories from countries throughout the world that are written by people from those countries. Original works of people from other countries are regularly used in American public schools. The term **authentic multicultural** has been used to describe literature written by members of particular cultural groups that represent their own reality. Some examples of literature that reflect the Latino experience are *The Gold Coin* by Alma Florada, *Chato's Kitchen* by Gary Soto, *Hairs-Pelitos* by Sandra Cisneros, *Friends from the Other Side* by Gloria Anzaldua, *When I was Puerto Rican* by Esmeralda Santiago, and *Tomas and the Library Lady* by Pat Mora.

Modern Fantasy

Modern fantasy is a genre that presents make-believe stories that are the product of the author's imagination. Often, they are so beyond the realm of everyday life that the stories can't possibly be true. Extraordinary events take place within the covers of these books. Fantasy allows a child to move beyond the normal life in the classroom, and speculate about a life that never was, and may never be. Fantasy is a genre that typically sparks intense discussions, and provides ample opportunities to illuminate the author's craft for the child. The popular *Harry Potter* series by J. K. Rowling is a perfect example of both the genre and the debate generated by this type of fiction.

Historical Fiction

Historical fiction is fiction that is set in the past. This type of fiction allows children to live vicariously in times and places they cannot experience in any other way. This type of fiction often has real people and real events depicted, with fiction laced around them. Historical fiction informs the study of social studies. Examples include *Don't You Know There's a War on?* by James Stevenson (WWII), *Klara's New World* by Jeanette Winter (Swedish immigrant family), *A Horse Called Starfire* by Betty Boegehold (Native Americans' first encounter with the horse), and *Wagon Wheels* by Barbara Brenner (an African American boy and family in 1870 Kansas).

Nonfiction

Nonfiction books have the real world as their point of origin. These books help to expand the knowledge of children when they are studying a topic; however, these books need to be evaluated for accuracy, authenticity, and inclusion of the salient facts. Nonfiction books can be used to support the teaching of content and to promote higher-level comprehension skills.

Biography

Biography is a genre that deals with the lives of real people. Autobiography is a genre that deals with the life of the author. These books invigorate the study of social studies because, through careful research, they often include information that transforms a name in a textbook into a person that one may like to get to know better.

Poetry

Poetry is a genre that is difficult to define for children, except as "not-prose." Poetry is the use of words to capture something: a sight, a feeling, or perhaps a sound. Poetry needs to be chosen carefully for a child, as poetry ought to elicit a response from the child—one that connects with the experience of the poem. All children need poetry in their lives. Poetry should be celebrated and enjoyed as part of the classroom experience, and a literacy-rich classroom will always include a collection of poetry to read, reread, savor, and enjoy. *The Owl and the Pussycat* by Edward Lear, Mother Goose Rhymes, Limericks, and Haiku are all poems or type of poems that appeal to young children.

In summary, today there is an overwhelming variety of children's literature from which to choose. When selecting books for use in a classroom, a teacher has a number of issues to consider. Is the book accurate, aesthetically pleasing and engaging? Bear in mind that all children deserve to see positive images of children like themselves in the books they read, as illustrations can have a powerful influence on their perceptions of the world. Children also need to see positive images of children who are not like themselves. Teachers need to provide children with literature that depicts an affirming, and multicultural view. There should be sex equity (i.e., males and females) in the literature. Teachers have to keep in mind that students may not understand the genre of "fiction" or other genres. A very wise teacher and author explained fiction as "make believe."

Some of the concepts and terminology to describe literature follow:

1. Information about the story including the author and illustrators, the publishing company, and even the International Standard Book Number (ISBN)
2. Terminology to describe the characters of the story (the protagonist, the antagonist or villain, animals, humans)
3. For older students introduce the point of view of the author. A story's point of view can be first person (the author is one of the characters of the story, and the narrator), the omniscient point of view (the narrator is an outsider who knows what the characters are thinking or feeling), or the limited point of view, or subjective consciousness (the narrator is not a character in the story). In the limited point of view, the narrator guides readers to see the story from a point of view of one of the characters. The narrator also conveys information that might seem unnatural coming from a character in the story.
4. The setting refers to the geographical location and the general environment and historical circumstances of the story.
5. The theme of the story. The plot tell us what happens and the theme tells us why it happens. Some examples of themes are: problems of growing up, maturing, linguistic and cultural adjustment, love and friendship, family issues, and achieving one's identity.
6. Literary Style, which includes description of the following:
   - Exposition: It is usually used to introduce the background information and to understand or introduce characters
   - Dialogue: Communication among the characters
   - Vocabulary: Word choice, use of concrete vs. abstract terminology, i.e., Is the language vocabulary appropriate for the intended audience?

- Imagery: The use of words to create sensory impressions. It conveys sights, sounds, textures, smells, and tastes.
- Tone: The author's mood and manner of expression. It might be humorous, serious, satirical, passionate, sensitive, childlike, zealous, indifferent, poignant, or warm.
- Analysis of the story. It might be multicultural or traditional, or include possible stereotypes, sexism, religious issues, controversial elements, or words or ideas that might create controversy.

Fostering the Home-School Connection in the Development of Reading

Teacher candidates need to understand the impact that fostering the home-school connection can have on student achievement (Health, 1983). Working with families and other professionals to promote student learning is therefore key in the development of students' literacy skills.

Ethnographic research conducted by Shirley Brice Heath demonstrated that home literacy and the expectations surrounding literacy opportunities and events can vary and differ from those provided at school (Heath, 1983). Teacher candidates must therefore work closely with parents to identify commonalities and differences in literacy practices, and build on both of these to establish a stronger home-school connection. When the experiences of parents and families are taken into account in the teaching and learning process, students and their families feel valued and welcome. Likewise, whenever parents can see that the child's literacy learning experiences at home are considered in school (e.g., when a child writes a poem about their family and this is shared in a poetry reading in class), their work as "primary teachers" is reinforced. Many strategies exist to develop the home-school connection. Some of these include:

- Make parents and families feel welcome in your classroom and school
- Display materials (e.g., stories of families) in the classroom
- Create a home-school journal that can be used as formative assessment
- Display signs in an assigned area in your classroom in their language
- Give parents and families an opportunity to share their personal, cultural, and linguistic experiences in the classroom.
- Provide parents with flexible meeting times to accommodate their schedules
- Provide parents with strategies they can use to reinforce literacy skills at home.

Key Principles of Competency 008

- Discuss folk tales from around the world and guide students to discuss common features and unique features (oral activities).
- When assessing the literal comprehension of students in the emergent stage of reading development, provide students with visual aids and ask them to explain what happened in the story.
- The invented spelling of emergent readers can be used to determine their ability to apply phonic skills.
- To teach the connection between spoken and written words to emergent readers, the teacher should use a big book and point to each word as she/he reads the story aloud.
- Use a "story tree" or "story map" containing parts of the story to teach critical analysis of literature. A story map contains the following parts: setting (where did the story take place?), characters, plot (what is the main problem?), resolution (how did the story end?).

Competency 009 (Word Analysis and Identification Skills)

The teacher understands the importance of word identification skills (including decoding, blending, structural analysis, sight word vocabulary and contextual analysis) and provides many opportunities for students to practice and improve word identification skills.

Word Analysis Skills and Identification Skills

Word analysis refers to the way that children approach a written word in order to decode and obtain meaning from it.

Vocabulary Sight Words

Vocabulary building is a skill that needs to be practiced daily in the classroom. Research suggests that fluent word identification needs to be accomplished before a child can readily comprehend text. If a child needs to painstakingly analyze many words in a text, the memory and attention needed for comprehension are absorbed by word analysis, and the pleasure in a good story is lost. Typically, children who are just beginning to read, decode each word as they read it. Through repeated exposure to the same words, instant-recognition vocabulary grows. These words are called sight words.

Dolch Words

In 1948, Edward W. Dolch identified 220 of the most frequently used words in the English language. He believed that if children were exposed to these words and learned to recognize them as sight words, they would become fluent readers. Some examples of Dolch words are: *a*, *an*, *am*, *at*, *can*, *had*, *has*, *ran*, *the*, *after*, *but*, *got* and *away*. The introduction of these sight words can expedite the decoding process and develop fluency among early readers.

Decoding Clues

In addition to working on placing sight words into readily available memory, there is sound research suggesting that students can use **context clues** to help identify unknown words. This body of research further suggests that instruction can help improve students' use of context clues. There are three main kinds of context clues: **semantic, syntactic, and structural**.

Semantic Clues

Semantic clues require a child to think about the meanings of words, and what is already known about the topic being read. For example, when reading a story about hawks, teachers can help children to activate prior knowledge about the bird, and to develop an expectation that the selection may contain words associated with hawks, such as *predator*, *carnivorous*, *food chain*, and *wingspan*. This discussion might help a child gain a sense of what might be reasonable in a sentence. For ELLs who might not be familiar with the hawk, teachers need to identify equivalent species from their geographical area.

Syntactic Clues

The word order in a sentence might also provide clues to readers. For example, in the sentence, "Hawks are _____," the order of the words in the sentence indicates that the missing word must be an adjective. This open-ended sentence can lead students to words such as *carnivorous*, *predators*, or other descriptors for the bird. Furthermore, the illustrations in the book can often help with the identification of a word. A picture of a hawk eating prey can lead students to the words *predator* or *carnivorous*. When context clues are combined with other clues such as phonics and structural clues, accurate word identification is usually possible.

Structural Clues

Another strategy to provide clues to readers is to pay attention to letter groups because there are many groups of letters that frequently occur within words, which are called morphemes. These specific clusters of letters can be taught. Common **derivational morphemes** in the form of prefixes, suffixes, and **in-**

flectional endings should be pointed out to students. An analysis of derivational and inflectional endings follows.

Derivational Morphemes Most of the derivational morphemes come from foreign languages like Greek and Latin, and they represent relatively consistent meanings. For example, the meaning of the prefixes *pre*, *anti*, and *sub* is very consistent in English and in other languages; namely pre=before, anti=against, and sub=under.

A large number of English prefixes are common to multiple western languages such as Spanish, French, and German. See Table 2-2 below for examples for English and Spanish.

Table 2-2. Examples of Common Prefixes in English and Spanish

Roots	Meaning	Words in English	Words in Spanish
bio	life	symbiosis	simbiosis
phobia (fobia)	fear of	xenophobia	xenofobia
phono (fono)	sound	phonetics	fonética
photo (foto)	light	photography	fotografía
geo	land, earth	geology	geología

Derivational morphemes can change the syntactic classification of the word. That is, by adding a morpheme to a word it can be changed from a verb to a noun or from an adjective to an adverb. Table 2-3 presents some examples of syntactic changes.

Children who are guided to recognize derivational morphemes will have a definite advantage when decoding words.

Inflectional Morphemes Inflectional morphemes do not change the syntactic classification, and typically follow derivational morphemes in a word. These are native of English and always function as suffixes. English has eight inflectional endings.

Table 2-3. Derivational Morphemes and Syntactic Changes

Type of Modification	Word 1	Word 2
Verb to a noun	To Drive	Driver
Adjective to an adverb	Cautious	Cautiously
Adjective to a noun	Aware	Awareness

1. Short Plural **s**, e.g., Two *car***s**, three *pen***s**
2. Long plural **es**. Use long plurals after ch, sh, s, z, and x, e.g., *churches*, *washes*, *cases*, and *boxes*
3. Third person singular s, e.g., Mary *walks* quickly
4. Possessive **'s**, e.g., Martha**'s** boy
5. Progressive **ing**, e.g., She is *walk***ing**. The gerund is not included in this group, i.e.,**Walking** is good for your health.
6. Regular past tense **ed**, e.g., He work**ed** very hard
7. Past participle **en** or **ed, e.g.,** She has beat**en** the system, or It has been ruin**ed**
8. Comparative and superlative **er** (**better**), and **est** (**best**), e.g.,—Alex Rodríguez is **better** than Derek Jeter, or He is the rich**est** player in the major leagues. Understanding the meaning of these morphemes can definitely enhance students' decoding and comprehension skills. The best practice for helping students gain skill in word-recognition is to provide students with authentic reading and writing activities in the classroom.

Words That Can Create Comprehension Problems for Children

There are words that children can decode but they might have problems identifying the intended meaning. Some of these difficult words include homonyms and homophones. **Homonyms** are words that have the same sound and the same spelling but differ in meaning. Homonyms are common in the content areas and can create comprehension problems. The context will determine the meaning of the words. Examples of homonyms are presented in Table 2-4.

Table 2-4. English Homonyms

Word	Meaning 1	Meaning 2
Club	A place to socialize	A wooden stick
Fine	A penalty	To imply good or okay
Bank	Margins of a river	A place that holds money
Rock	Type of music	A stone

Homophones are words that sound the same but they are spelled differently and have different meaning. Examples of homophones are: blew and blue, cents and sense, heir and air, wait and weight, hear and here, eight and ate, to, two, and too, there and their, deer and dear, hair and hare. **Homographs** are words that are spelled the same way but have more than one pronunciation and different meanings. For example, the word *bow* has two pronunciations, the first referring to the front part of a ship or the way that people bend to salute; the second referring to the decorative knot used in clothing. Consider the use of the word in the following sentence: The Japanese ambassador wore a red *bow*, stood on the *bow* of the ship and graciously *bowed* to the audience.

Compound Words

Compound words are created when two independent words are joined to create a new word. Often, knowing the meaning of the two words will guide students to understand the meaning of the compound word. For example, the compound word *birdhouse* is composed of the words *bird* and *house*. With this information, children can understand that the new word refers to a refuge or a house for birds. However, there are some examples of compound words where the two words can create confusion among children. Examples of these deceptive compound words are *butterfly*, *nightmare*, and *brainstorm*.

Key Principles of Competency 009

- Children develop word analysis and decoding skills in a predictable sequence
- Word identification skills are very important in developing fluent readers
- Use formal and informal procedures for assessing word identification skills
- Teach word recognition in a simple-to-complex progression
- Teach students to recognize high-frequency irregular words
- Teach children ways to identify vowel-sound combinations
- Provide instruction in how to use structural cues to recognize word meaning
- Uses formal and informal assessments to plan and adjust instruction

Competency 010 (Reading Fluency)

The teacher understands the importance of fluency for reading comprehension and provides many opportunities for children to improve their reading fluency.

Reading Fluency

Reading fluency is the ability to decode words quickly and accurately in order to read text with the appropriate word stress, pitch and intonation (or prosody). Reading fluency requires automaticity of word recognition and reading with prosody to facilitate comprehension. **Automaticity** is the quick and accurate recognition of letters, words, and language conventions. Automaticity is achieved through continuous practice using texts written at the reading level of the child.

Fluency and Comprehension

Fluency is a prerequisite for language comprehension. Children struggling with fluency devote their time to mastering their language skills, which is an effort that takes away from the effort that they should be placing on reading comprehension. When students read aloud in class, the main purpose of the activity is to develop fluency. If after reading aloud, teachers ask the child comprehension questions, the child will most likely have to read the same passage silently to be able to respond to the questions. Thus, teachers should separate these two activities—read silently for comprehension, and read aloud to promote fluency.

What Is the Expectation?

Chapter 110.3 TEKS for English language arts and reading suggests that the typical child in first grade should be able to read about 60 words per minute (wpm) and the rate should increase by 10 words in each grade, i.e., second grade (70 wpm), third grade (80 wpm), and fourth grade (90 wpm). To determine the number of words per minute read, a simple formula is used; namely, words read in a minute, minus errors, equals word per minute (UT system/TEA, 2002). The expectation is that children in the first to fourth grade will be able to read independently with minimum difficulty, i.e., finding no more than 1 in 20 words difficult.

How Do We Teach Fluency?

Teachers can use several strategies to promote reading fluency. Descriptions of these strategies follow.

Guided Oral Repeated Reading

Teachers can promote opportunities for **guided oral repeated reading** using text at the reading level of the child. Teachers, parents and peers can provide support and feedback for these students. Allow the child to read the same story repeatedly to develop fluency.

Choral Reading

Reading in group is another activity used to promote reading fluency. This activity is ideal for ELLs and struggling readers because pronunciation and fluency problems will not be publicly noticed and they can use the model provided by fluent readers.

Pairing Students

Pairing proficient readers with ELLs or struggling readers can benefit both groups—the proficient child receives additional practice reading, and the ELLs and struggling readers are able to listen to fluent readers. ELLs and struggling readers can also read to their partners and receive input.

Interactive Computer Programs

Using interactive reading programs can provide individualized reading support for children. These computer programs often contain colorful pictures and interesting stories. The child should have the option of clicking on the words or pictures in order to have the selected word read aloud or to get animation of the word's meaning. The program can also read a story at normal speed while the child follows the highlighted words in a printed text.

Silent Sustained Reading

Guiding the child to read continuously for about 20 minutes a day can definitely improve reading fluency. This activity is also used to teach the child to read silently without moving their lips.

Readers' Theatre

This activity has been used successfully to emphasize reading fluency. In this activity, a story is modified so that various characters have to read portions of the text. Students rehearse their reading part, and then create a theater format to present the reading. Children enjoy this new approach and it improves reading fluency.

Developing Reading Fluency

Pointing to words while reading helps students see the letter-sound correspondence; however, this practice can also affect the development of reading fluency. Second graders should be guided to discontinue this practice. Continuous monitoring of reading fluency is required to insure children develop and maintain reading fluency when they are exposed to more challenging text. To be sure that students maintain reading fluency, teachers can conduct individual assessment using teacher-developed check-lists or more standardized processes like running records.

Assessing Reading Fluency

A running record is an assessment strategy designed by Mary Clay (2002) to assess students' word identification skills and fluency in oral reading. As the teacher listens to a student read a page, the teacher uses a copy of the page to mark each word the child mispronounces. The teacher writes the incorrect word over the printed word, draws a line through each word the child skips, and draws an arrow under repeated words. In this activity teachers can identify the type of error made and can then provide additional support to individual learners.

Key Principles of Competency 010

- Reading fluency includes rate, accuracy, and intonation
- Children's reading rate and fluency affect their comprehension
- Teacher applies norms to identify and monitor children's fluency levels
- Provide students with many opportunities to develop fluency
- Foster collaboration with families to promote reading fluency

Competency 011 (Reading Comprehension and Application)

The teacher understands the importance of reading for understanding, knows the components and processes of reading comprehension and teaches students strategies for improving their comprehension, including using a variety of texts and contexts.

Reading Comprehension

Helping students read for understanding is the central goal of reading instruction. Comprehension is a complex process involving the text, the reader, the situation, and the purpose for reading. There are a number of factors that come into play as a child attempts to comprehend a passage. First, students cannot understand texts if they cannot read the words. Thus, a teacher who is interested in improving students' comprehension skills needs to teach them to decode well. In addition, children need time during the school day to read texts that are easy for them to read, and also have time to discuss what has been read. Children need to read and reread easy texts often enough that decoding becomes rapid, easy, and accurate. It has been noted frequently in the literature that children who comprehend well have bigger vocabularies than children who struggle with reading.

Research suggests that English language learners need systematic, high quality literacy instruction from the beginning. According to the Report of the National Literacy Panel on Language-Minority Children and Youth (August & Shanahan, 2006), "instruction that provides substantial coverage in the key components of reading (identified by the National Reading Panel, 2000)—such as phonemic awareness, phonics, fluency, vocabulary, and text comprehension—have clear benefits for English language learners, but not sufficient. Oral proficiency in English is critical, as well, but overlooked in instruction" (August & Shanahan, 2006, p.4).

Background Knowledge

Reading comprehension can be affected by **prior knowledge**, and readers who possess rich prior knowledge about the topic of a reading often understand the reading better than classmates with less prior knowledge. A discrepancy between the schema intended by the author and the schema that the reader brings to the reading process can create confusion and comprehension problems. This is especially important for students from linguistically and culturally diverse backgrounds, who might not possess the cultural information to understand stories written for middle class American students.

Pre-Reading Activities

Prior knowledge also affects interest. Generally, students like to read about somewhat familiar topics. This is an area in which the skill and interest of the teacher can play a significant role. Teachers should identify interests in children and find appropriate stories to match their interests. An able teacher can also make a previously unfamiliar topic seem familiar through **pre-reading activities** during which prior knowledge is activated, new prior knowledge is formed, and interest is stirred up. Teachers of ELLs often have to spend more time in pre-reading activities than the actual time devoted to reading the stories.

Setting the Purpose for Reading

A good teacher will set a clear purpose for reading, and ask the students to gain an overview of the text before reading, to make predictions about the upcoming text, and then to read selectively based on their predictions. Best practice suggests that children should be encouraged to generate questions about ideas in text while reading. Successful teachers encourage children to construct mental images representing ideas in text, or to construct actual images from texts that lend themselves to this kind an activity.

Linking Prior Knowledge to New Knowledge

A successful teacher will help readers to process text containing new factual information through reading strategies, and helping children to relate that new information to their prior knowledge. Questioning techniques is a simple but powerful mechanism to guide children to link current knowledge to new knowledge. Through questioning, teachers guide children to question the facts, intent of the author, and also to check the answers through text verification. It is through conversation that children are able to compare their predictions and expectations about the content. It is also through these conversations that children see the need to revise their prior knowledge when compelling new ideas are encountered that conflict with prior knowledge. As part of these ongoing conversations, teachers will become alert to students who are applying the incorrect schema as they read, and will be able to encourage use of more appropriate knowledge. These conversations help children figure out the meanings of unfamiliar vocabulary words based on context clues, the opinions of others, and sometimes through the use of appropriate source materials such as glossaries, dictionaries, or an appropriate selection in another text.

Story Grammar

Children should be encouraged to analyze stories using the story-grammar components of setting, characters, problem or problems encountered by characters, attempts at solution(s) to the problem, successful solution, and ending. Teachers can use graphic organizers to present a visual clue of these components. Story frames can be modified to introduce various components of literature, as well as an assessment tool to check for comprehension.

As children's comprehension grows more sophisticated, they become critical readers. This means that they grow in an understanding that comprehension can go beyond the denotative components of the facts portrayed in text. With skillful instruction, children come to read not only what a text says, but also how the text portrays the subject matter. Students recognize the various ways in which every text is the unique creation of a unique author, and they also learn to compare and contrast the treatment of the same subject matter in a number of texts. For example, teachers can introduce the multiple versions of stories like *Cinderella* in order to discuss how stories can represent similar themes using unique settings and situations. Examples of variations on Cinderella are *Mufaro's Beautiful Daughters: An African Tale*, by John Steptoe; *Yeh-Shen, a Cinderella Tale from China*, by Ai-Ling Louie; and *The Egyptian Cinderella*, by Shirley Climo.

Teachers can help students grow in comprehension through the following stages: comprehend what a text says in some authentic way; comprehend author's purpose; recognize the elements of the text, and how the text was assembled; and finally, engage in text interpretation (i.e., detect and articulate tone and persuasive elements; discuss point of view, and recognize bias). Over time, and with good instruction, children learn to infer unstated meanings based on social conventions, shared knowledge, shared experience, or shared values. They make sense of text by recognizing implications and drawing conclusions, and they move past the point of believing the content of a selection simply because it was in print.

Reflecting Reading—Bias in Traditional Stories

Traditional children's stories are filled with episodes of violence, sexism, and stereotypes. Fairy tales like *Cinderella* and *Snow White* portray women as weak creatures in need of support and rescuing. They also present old people as ugly and often as evil, e.g., the evil witch. Killing is also rampant in stories such as *Hansel and Gretel* where the main characters are left to die in the woods, and then are imprisoned by an "ugly and old witch," whom they eventually kill. Thievery and killing are also promoted in the story of *Jack and the Beanstalk*. In the original story, the main character, Jack, steals from the "ugly" giant and kills him. Teachers should not ignore violence and bias in literature, and they should use these stories as a foundation to guide children to discuss and challenge bias and stereotypes.

Teachers can use traditional stories to examine controversial events in the stories. Teachers can lead children to discuss the actions of characters like Jack in *Jack and the Bean Stalk* who steals the golden goose from the giant. Teachers can also introduce new stories and modern versions of traditional stories where stereotypes and violence are challenged. For example, in the Disney's version of the Chinese story of *Mulan*, the main character challenges the stereotypical role of women when she joins the Army disguised as a man in order to save the honor of the family and become a national heroine. In the *Paper Bag Princess*, the protagonist presents the idea that women do not always need to be saved by men or to marry a man who will protect them. In this story, the princess saves the prince from the dragon and eventually she decides not to marry him. Guiding children to examine themes and bias in literature can make them better readers and, more importantly, they can become reflective learners.

Monitoring Comprehension

Children need to be taught to monitor their own comprehension, and to decide when they need to exert more effort, or to apply a strategy to make sense of a text. The goal of comprehension instruction is for the child to reach a level at which the application of strategies becomes automatic. In summary, comprehension is maximized when readers are fluent in all the processes of skilled reading—from the decoding of words to the articulation and easy application of the comprehension strategies used by good readers. Therefore, teachers need to teach predicting, questioning, seeking clarification, relating to background knowledge, constructing mental images, and summarizing.

Monitoring Reading Comprehension in Pre-Literate Children

Story Retelling is a strategy used with young children to assess listening and reading comprehension. This strategy can also assess sentence structure knowledge, vocabulary, speaking ability, and knowledge about the structure of stories.

An informal or more structured checklist can be used to assess a student's comprehension, sentence structure knowledge, and vocabulary development as they retell a story. Any checklist for listening comprehension should assess the ability of the child to (Lapp & et al., 2001):

1. retell the story with details.
2. show evidence of comprehension of the story line and plot, including the characters, setting, author's intention, and literal and implied meaning
3. show evidence that the child understood major ideas and the ideas that support it
4. apply background information to the selection
5. analyze and make judgments based on facts
6. retell the selection in sentences that make grammatical sense
7. retell the story using sentences that include standard usage of verbs, adjectives, conjunctions, and compound sentences
8. use a rich and meaningful vocabulary with minimal use of slang and colloquial expressions
9. adapt spoken language for various audiences, purposes, and occasions
10. listen for various purposes including critical listening to evaluate a speaker's message, and listening to enjoy and appreciate spoken language

Reading Strategies

Looking at strategies used by proficient readers can help teachers make skillful choices of activities that will maximize student learning. Anne Goudvis and Stephanie Harvey (2000) offer the following suggestions for useful activities.

Activating Prior Knowledge

Readers pay more attention when they relate to the text. Readers naturally bring their prior knowledge and experience to reading, but they comprehend better when they think about the connections they make between the text, their lives, and the larger world. This strategy is especially important when teaching children from diverse cultural and linguistic backgrounds. One of the strategies used to explore a child's background and schema is the KWL chart. A KWL chart is a chart that asks students to describe what they **K**now, **W**ant to know, **L**earned and still want to learn; children can benefit from what others already know, what others want to learn, and what areas others had difficulty understanding.

Predicting or Asking Questions

Questioning is the strategy that keeps readers engaged. When readers ask questions, even before they read, they clarify understanding and forge ahead to make meaning. Asking questions is also at the heart of thoughtful reading. A variation of this strategy is to give students a true or false question about the content to be read. Once the students complete the questions, they then read to corroborate the answers.

Visualizing

Active readers create visual images based on the words they read in the text. These created pictures in turn enhance their understanding.

Drawing Inferences

Inferring is when the readers take what they know, garner clues from the text, and think ahead to make a judgment, discern a theme, or speculate about what is to come.

Determining Important Ideas

Thoughtful readers grasp essential ideas and important information when reading. Readers must differentiate between less important ideas and the key ideas that are central to the meaning of the text.

Synthesizing Information

Synthesizing information involves combining new information with existing knowledge to form an original idea or interpretation. Reviewing, sorting, and sifting important information can lead to new insights that change the way readers think.

Repairing Understanding

If confusion disrupts meaning, readers need to stop and clarify their understanding. Readers may use a variety of strategies to "fix up" comprehension when meaning goes awry.

Confirming Predictions

As students read and after they have finished reading, they should confirm the predictions they originally made. There is no wrong answer. One can confirm negatively or positively. Determining if a prediction is correct is a goal.

Using Parts of Book

Students should use book parts—such as charts, diagrams, indexes, and the table of contents, to improve their understanding of the reading content.

Reflecting

An important strategy is for students to think about, or reflect on, what they have just read. Reflection can be just thinking, or it can be more formal, such as a discussion or writing in a journal.

While providing instruction in a subject area, the teacher needs to determine if the reading material is at the students' level of reading mastery. If not, the teacher needs to make accommodations either in the material itself or in the manner of presentation.

Assessing Comprehension

A frequent device for assessing comprehension is the use of oral or written questions. A question may be **convergent**, which indicates that only one answer is correct, or **divergent**, which indicates that more than one answer is acceptable. Most tests, however, include a combination of question types.

Another device for checking on comprehension is a **cloze test**, or a passage with omitted words the test taker must supply. The test maker must decide whether to require the test taker to supply the exact word or to accept synonyms. Passing scores reflect which type of answer is acceptable. If assessing an understanding of meaning is the intent of the exercise, the teacher might accept synonyms and not demand the surface-level constructs, or the exact word.

The speed at which a student reads helps to determine comprehension, up to a point. The faster a student reads, the better that student comprehends, with some limitations. In general, the slow reader who must analyze each word does not comprehend as well as the fast reader. It is possible, however, to read too fast. Most students have had the experience of having to reread materials. For example, reading a chapter in preparation for a test may be read more slowly or reread as compared to reading a short story for pleasure or reading to get the main idea of a story.

Semantic mapping can also be used as a strategy to make direct connections between the vocabulary or words they are learning in the classroom and those that they may have seen, heard or learned previously. The strategy generally works as follows:

- place a word or phrase representing the story in the middle of the board/paper/transparency; may have 3–5 preselected categories.
- have students brainstorm related words in each category
- have students scan the text to locate more words that may fit
- have students include personal connections with the book.
- include more categories and key words to add to the map

Semantic mapping is an excellent strategy for students to see the connections among all the concepts presented as well as facilitating their recall and comprehension of important information from a text or story.

Key Principles of Competency 011

- Vocabulary can be taught both directly and indirectly.
- A variety of techniques should be used in the classroom.
- Students should be taught that some words have multiple meanings.
- Semantic mapping can help students make explicit relationships between words (Nagy, 1988).
- Building and activating schema or prior knowledge is necessary in students' literacy development.
- Meaningful discussion of key concepts and words can show students the relationship and connections between words.
- The four writing skills—speaking, listening, reading, and writing—are interrelated.

Competency 012 (Reading, Inquiry and Research)

The teacher understands the importance of research and inquiry skills to students' academic success, and provides students with instruction that promotes their acquisition and effective use of those study skills in the content areas.

Transition from "Learning to Read" to "Reading to Learn"

Children from pre-K to second grade spend most of the language arts portion of their day trying to decode and make sense of written language. The main purpose of this stage is to read for pleasure. Traditionally, short stories with pictures that have a specific structure and predictable story line are used to guide the child in the process of "learning to read." However, in the upper elementary grades, the needs of the children go beyond decoding and reading for pleasure, and "reading to learn" becomes the main task. The "reading to learn" stages require students to decode written language, understand the content, and obtain vital information from the content. One important component of the process of "reading to learn" is to understand how text is organized in the content areas. Children need to identify key components of the organizational format and identify the type of information offered. Teachers have to guide children to notice and study the structure of text, including the table of contents, titles, subtitles, and headings.

Structure of Text

Students need to look closely at the structure of text in order to comprehend it. To accomplish this task, skillful teachers guide the students through a picture, table, and graphic walk-through of the text while asking questions and pointing out useful text features to the students. Most texts have titles, subtitles, headings, glossaries, and bolded words. What techniques were used to make them stand out? Figuring out the structure of a text helps readers to read more efficiently. Children can anticipate what information will be revealed in a selection when they understand textual structure. Understanding the pattern of the text helps students organize ideas. Authors have a fairly short list of organizational patterns to choose from. The following are the most common patterns:

- Chronological order relates events in a temporal sequence—beginning to end
- Cause-and-effect relationships between described events
- Problem description, followed by solutions
- Comparisons and/or contrasts to describe ideas to readers
- Sequential materials, presented as a series of directions—prescribed order

Once children understand how information in the content areas is organized, they can become more efficient readers.

Becoming More Efficient Readers

Students with strong comprehension skills and decoding ability are now ready to become more efficient readers by practicing the techniques of scanning and skimming to get content information. In **scanning**, children are guided to look for specific information in text. Children are taught to use headings, indices, bolding and italics to guide them to specific words or content. In **skimming**, students read major headings, table of contents, bold letters, graphic materials, and summary paragraphs to get the main idea of the content.

Study Skills

Students need to know how to study the information that has been presented to them in texts and other media. Graphic organizers help students to review material, and help them to see the relationships between one bit of information and another. For example, a Venn diagram helps students identify how things are alike and different. A Venn diagram can also be used to help students recognize how a single topic is treated in two readings, or how two books, animals, or ecosystems are alike and different. The student labels the two overlapping circles, and lists items that are unique to each one in each respective circle. In the area in the center where there is overlap, the student records the elements that the two items have in common.

Another skill students need to master is **note taking**. Unless a teacher wants to read passages directly out of an encyclopedia or other source material, he or she should take the time to actively teach note-taking techniques. Teachers should also think up an authentic task that requires students to accomplish higher-level manipulation of the given information. First, help the children to formulate a researchable question. Second, have them highlight the words that might be used as keywords in searching for information. Third, have students brainstorm in groups of other words to be used as keywords. Next, ask then to list appropriate sources. Finally, as they skim articles, they can fill in the chart with little chunks of information.

Graphic Organizers

Graphic organizers help students improve organizational skills, and provide a visual representation of facts and concepts and their relationships within an organized framework. The ability to organize information and ideas is fundamental to effective thinking.

To increase reading comprehension among ELLs, allow students to share information about the story or passage. Through this activity, students can help each other using peer scaffolding and oral language interaction. Semantic mapping can be used before and after readings to organize materials in new ways highlighting connections among ideas. See graphic organizers for K–12 teachers by clicking on the following link: *http://www.teachervision.fen.com/graphic-organizers/printable/6293.html*

Think-Aloud

This strategy allows the teacher and students to problem solve together. The teacher poses a question to students and then, the teacher, group of students, or entire class responds at the same time. This strategy can be easily used to increase reading comprehension in the content areas.

Summarizing and Organization of Content

When children are guided to summarize and organize content, they are using basic reading comprehension and taking this content to higher level of thinking including evaluation, analysis, and synthesis. By guiding children to go beyond the literal meaning and guiding them to reorganize content requires students to develop a deeper understanding of content. Guide students to reorganize content (study skills) by creating their own tables, charts, and graphs.

Study Plans

To increase content comprehension, teachers might acquaint students with several study plans to help them read content materials. Many of these plans are well known and easily accessed, and the teacher and the students can simply select the plan(s) that works best for them within various subjects. Students may use **mnemonic devices**, or memory-related devices, to help them remember the steps in reading a chapter effectively. Several other strategies follow.

SQ4R

Students often use plans like the **SQ4R** plan when reading text in content areas. The acronym stands for **survey, question, read, reflect, recite, and review** (Tomas & Robinson, 1972). An explanation of the different components of the SQ4R follows:

Survey During the **survey (S)** part, readers examine the headings, illustrations, bold letters, and major components of the text in order to develop predictions and generating **questions (Q)** about the topic.

Question The student may wish to devise some questions that the chapter will probably answer. Through these questions, students establish the purpose for reading and the questions serve as a reading guide. If the chapter has questions at the end, the student can also study these before reading the chapter.

Read (1R) During the next stage, students read while looking for answers to the questions previously generated and/or those questions written by the publishers, which are usually located at the end of the section.

Write (2R) Students monitor their comprehension as they write a summary of the story or text. Creating a summary allows students opportunities to internalize and make their own interpretation of the content.

Recite (3R) The student attempts to answer orally, or in writing, the student-developed questions or the questions at the end of the chapter.

Review (4R) Finally, students **review** the text to evaluate the accuracy of their answers and to show how much they learned about the content.

Reciprocal Teaching

Reciprocal teaching is an instructional activity designed for struggling readers in which the teacher engages students in a dialogue about specific portions of a text (Palincsar, 1986). The main purpose of this activity is to guide children to construct meaning and to monitor reading comprehension. The dialogue is structured to elicit four components: summarizing, asking a question, clarifying and predicting what will come next.

DRTA

The acronym **DRTA** stands for Directed Reading/Thinking Activity. This teacher-directed strategy helps students to establish a purpose for reading a story or reading expository writing from a content book (Reuzel & Cooter, 1992). The teacher models the process of creating and correcting predictions as the story progresses to strengthen comprehension. DRTA has three main steps: develop background by reading titles, pictures, etc.; making predictions; and confirming predictions.

Reading Comprehension in the Content Areas

To assist children and especially ELLs in reading material that may be beyond their reading level, teachers can incorporate the following strategies.

- Tape-record selected passages that students can listen to while reading along in the text.
- Pair children in a tutor/tutee arrangement or in a small group reading format
- Introduce the technical vocabulary of the content areas prior to reading. Introduce elements such as connotation (implied meaning) and denotation (literal meaning), and idioms in the way they are used in text.
- Teach content vocabulary through direct, concrete experiences as opposed to definitions. Definitions can lead to misinterpretations since additional words are required to define the term. Teaching vocabulary in a contextualized situation is particularly important for ELLs because they often rely on translations that do not always represent the intended concept. For example, in English, the word *bayou* is used extensively in Texas and Louisiana. However, *bayou* is very difficult to define for someone who has never seen one. What is the difference between a bayou, a creek, a swamp, or a marshland? How big is a bayou? If an adult has difficulty answering these questions, imagine how young children may struggle!
- Introduce instructional strategies for self-monitoring reading comprehension. In this kind of strategy, students read aloud a passage and then pause to question themselves about the meaning of the passage.

Representations of Information for a Variety of Purposes

Charts, tables, graphs, pictures, and print and non-print media are examples of materials used to present information. Readers should realize that these representations are important. Their purpose is to present information and to encourage interpretation. A graphic can expand a concept, serve as an illustration, support points, summarize data, organize facts, add a dimension to the content (such as a cartoon adding humor), compare information, demonstrate change over time, or furnish additional information. Through graphics, the reader can interpret, predict, and even apply information with some careful observation. The questions that teachers use can make a difference in the ability of students to focus on and clarify the information derived from graphics. See charts by clicking the following link: *www.42explore.com/graphs.htm*

Many students initially skip over graphics, or may just notice their presence without reading them. These students may not have been taught how to use multiple representations of information. Even students who have some training in the use of graphic information may not be able to transfer that knowledge to other content areas, or may have trouble going from print to graphic and then back to print.

Adults can help students use multiple representations of information by using open-book and guided reading. A teacher can demonstrate how to use a chart or graph by using an overhead projector. Even a graphic that appears uncomplicated may challenge a reader's interpretive skills. Many inferences may be necessary for even the simplest visual aid or graphic. Modeled reading may also be an effective technique to use.

Pictures and other graphics can arouse interest and stimulate thinking. Additionally, graphics can add clarity; prevent misunderstandings; show step-by-step developments; exhibit the status of things, events, and processes; and demonstrate comparisons and contrasts (Vacca and Vacca 1989).

Strategies for Developing Critical-Thinking Skills

Critical-thinking skills include analysis, synthesis, and evaluation. Benjamin Bloom (1956) created a taxonomy for categorizing levels of thinking processes typical in school children. The taxonomy presents a structure to categorize the levels of thinking required in order to ask and answer questions. These questions have traditionally been used to guide children from the basic recalling of information (**knowledge**) and understanding information (**comprehension**) to use higher-order thinking skills such as analysis, synthesis, and evaluation. Recalling and understanding are important parts in reading comprehension; however, teachers need to move children beyond the literal and toward explicitly stating ideas. Teachers have to guide children to analyze (**analysis**) the ideas presented in text and then to make inferences (**analysis**), to assess their inferences (**evaluation**), draw conclusion about the ideas (**synthesis**) and perhaps to apply the ideas to new situation (**application**). Children who are able to go beyond the literal and explicit information in text develop a deeper understand of the content areas and are able to manipulate the content at higher levels of thinking. Bloom's Taxonomy has been revised—see page 224 of this review to see the new version or click on the following link to view the old and the new Bloom's Taxonomy versions: *www.odu.edu/educ/roverbau/Bloom/blooms_taxonomy.htm*.

Linguistic Accommodation Testing for ELLs and Special Education Students

The State of Texas provides for linguistic accommodation for ELLs and special education children taking the content portion of the examination in grades 3–8 in order to ensure that reading comprehension does not interfere in assessing content mastery. Based on specific recommendation from the Admission, Review, and Dismissal (ARD) and/or the Language Proficiency Assessment Committee (LPAC), districts can allow linguistic accommodations for special education and ELLs students when taking the basic skills test. A list of allowed linguistic accommodations follows (TEA, 1005).

1. Presenting the information in two languages side by side
2. Allowing the test administrator to read the questions or translate words, phrases, and sentences
3. Using dictionaries to find translations
4. Allowing the use of bilingual or English-language glossaries
5. Allowing the test administrator to present the information using simple language
6. Using visual and non-verbal communication to make content clear

Strategies like the linguistic accommodation testing (LAT) can be used to enhance reading comprehension of special populations in the content areas.

Competency 013 (Writing Conventions)

The teacher understands the conventions of writing in English and provides instruction that helps students develop proficiency in applying writing conventions.

Connection between Spelling and Phonological and Alphabetic Awareness

The transition from oral language development to written communication requires students to develop an awareness of the following concepts (Peregoy and Boyle, 2005):

1. Print carries meaning and it conveys a message
2. Spoken words can be written and preserved
3. English reading/writing follows a specific direction; that is, from left to right, and top to bottom
4. Spoken language is composed of phonemes and these sounds can be represented by specific letters of the alphabet (alphabetic principle)
5. As an alphabetic language, English has a sound-symbol correspondence but often it is inconsistent
6. Spoken language can be used as a foundation for spelling (phonics)

Spoken and Written English

The productive skills of language—speaking and writing—are interconnected. A strong oral development can facilitate the development of written communication. However, because spoken language is generally more informal that written language, teachers need to be sure that students use formal language when writing.

English favors the use of active voice as opposed to passive voice in both oral and written communication. For example the sentence *Katrina devastated the city of New Orleans*, is stronger and more effective than a sentence using the passive voice such as *The city of New Orleans was devastated by Katrina*. To provide support in this area, guide students to work with a partner in converting passive sentences to active sentences; then guide them to discuss how these changes affect the tone and meaning of the sentences. If a student is having problems connecting sounds to written text, teachers can provide phonics instruction. Guiding students to "sound out" words as a foundation for spelling can improve written performance.

Developing Readiness for Writing

A visit to an early childhood classroom shows that children spend the bulk of the time singing, playing with blocks and puzzles, cutting figures with scissors, playing with clay, drawing, and painting. By looking at this picture, lay people might question the value of instruction in early childhood. However, the reality is that children are doing intensive work on developing the fine motor skills needed to master pre-reading skills such as pencil grip, appropriate paper position, and the first strokes of representing the shapes of letters and words.

Stages of Spelling

As children begin to name letters and read print, they also begin to write letters and words. Writing development seems to occur at about the same time as reading development—not afterward, as traditional reading readiness assumed. Whole language seeks to integrate the language arts rather than sequencing them. Just as change has marked educators' beliefs about reading instruction and the way that reading develops, change has also marked the methods and philosophies behind the teaching of writing in the schools.

Drawing is the beginning of children's attempt to convey a message in written form. Teachers can use this interest to introduce writing skills by guiding them to add words to drawings to supplement the information. Initially, the children can dictate the story to teachers until they feel comfortable enough to write it on their own. The development of written communication generally follows a predictable sequence beginning with scribbling, then developing pseudo letters and invented words until conventional spelling is achieved. An analysis of the stages of spelling follows.

Scribbling

In this phase, children pretend that they are writing. Eventually, they develop letter-like symbols. This stage represents an awareness of the difference between writing and drawing to communicate. Scribbling is different from drawing because in scribbling, the child purposely scribbles from left to right and often also follows the top to bottom progression.

Pseudo Letters

In this phase, the child attempts to create forms that resemble letters but these forms cannot always be identified as such. The child becomes aware that the alphabet contains characters of different shapes and attempts to reproduce these in a random way resulting in some form of invented spelling.

Random Letters

In this phase, a child creates individual letters from the alphabet in an attempt to create words. The letters are randomly selected with no clear connection with the phonemes that they are to represent. That is, children are not producing phonetic spelling at this stage. They write letter strings and often leave a space between strings, which suggest that they are beginning to understand word boundaries.

Invented Spelling

At this stage, the child tries to connect the sounds (phonemes) and the letters (graphemes) to create words resulting in non-standard writing. This phonetic spelling is often represented by a single letter or a series of letters, which represent the phonemes contained in the intended word. A child can write an *M* to represent the word mother and often they can point to the word. They can also use strings of letters, mostly consonants, to represent a word. For example, a kindergartener wrote the word *park* as *Prk*, producing the three consonants and omitting the vowel. Because the phoneme-grapheme correspondence of vowels is not consistent, children generally have problems writing them.

Transitional Spelling

Eventually, children discontinue over-reliance on phonetic spelling and begin noticing visual clues and developing a knowledge of word structure. Sight word training becomes very important at this stage. Students begin producing more standard spelling and attempt self-correction. Writing samples might become difficult to read because students erase continuously in an attempt to self-correct. Some inflectional endings (plurals, comparative, superlative, past tense, and present progressive) may appear in writing samples. Students may continue having problems with words with double vowels, like *book* and *feed*, and words containing consonant diagraphs like ***th**rough* or *eight*.

Conventional Spelling

At this stage, children spell most words using conventional spelling. They still may have problems with consonant diagraphs, homonyms, contractions, compound words, as well as prefixes, suffixes, and more difficult letter combinations.

In addition to the traditional spelling stages, students also go through specific stages of writing. Lapp (2001) divided the process into three stages: emerging, early writer, and newly fluent writers. A summary of these stages follows (Lapp and et al., 2001).

Characteristics of Emerging Writers

Students at the emerging stage of writing development are generally able to:

- Dictate an idea or a complete story
- Use initial sounds in their writing
- Use picture, scribbles, symbols, letters, and/or known words to communicate a message
- Understand that writing symbolizes speech

Educational Implications

Read stories to children and ask them to retell the story while you record it. Then, read the story back to the child to emphasize the connection between speech and print. When children begin writing words or pseudo words, ask them to read it to you, and if necessary, provide conventional spelling as an alternative. Use the *Language Experience Approach* to guide children to connect spoken words with their written representations. That is, guide children to dictate words and sentences while you record them on the board. Read the words while pointing to them. Then, ask students to copy the sentences. The next day, review the sentences written and use them for additional language development. Introduce writing for functional tasks like labeling objects and places in the classroom, writing the plan of the day, taking notes, and listing names or things to remember.

Early Writers

Typically, children at the early stage of writing exhibit the following behavior:

- Understand that a written message remains the same each time it is read
- Utilize their knowledge of sounds and letters
- Incorporate feedback in revising and editing with assistance and modeling
- Begin to use conventional grammar, spelling, capitalization, and punctuation

Educational Implications

Guide children to read and reread the same information to establish a connection between letters and sounds. Identify specific words and divide them into syllables to establish a connection between the sounds within a syllable. Take expressions that are commonly used in children's literature and oral communication and guide them to hear word boundaries. For example, children at this stage might write the statement "Once upon a time" as "Oncesoponditim," which represents the way the expression is produced orally without appropriate word boundaries. Model the writing process using a LCD projection system or the traditional chalkboard. Think aloud while you are writing and ask for guidance from students, e.g., Do we need a comma here or a final period? Do we need a capital A in the word "american"? In the writing samples of children, use peer input for editing and guiding students to conduct self-corrections. Instead of making direct error corrections, ask questions leading children to examine the grammaticality of the sentences and to make their own corrections.

Characteristics of Newly Fluent Writers

Newly fluent writers are generally able to:

- Use prewriting strategies to achieve their purposes
- Address a topic or write to a prompt creatively and independently
- Organize writing to include a beginning, middle, and end
- Consistently use conventional grammar, spelling, capitalization, and punctuation
- Revise and edit written work independently and/or collectively
- Produce many genres of writing

Educational Implications

Use prewriting activities to plan for writing using an outline that indicates the sequence of ideas. This activity is especially important for children whose native language does not require the use of the linear progression that are required in English writing. The outline will guide children to comply with this linear rhetorical pattern. Provide interesting writing prompts to children to guide their writing. You may use the prompt used on post TAKS released tests available on line. Traditionally, the Texas Education Agency releases the tests used in its yearly examinations. For information on previously released tests see the Texas Education Agency, Student Assessment Division at: *www.tea.state.tx.us/index3.aspx?id=44&menu_id=79.*

Continue using peer editing and encourage self-corrections. Guide students to produce different kinds of writing such as response to literature, journal writing, writing to convince someone, or writing to argue a point.

Writing Expectations

Children in kindergarten through fourth grade are expected to progress through stages of writing and develop conventional spelling and coherent compositions. The fourth-grade examinations require students to develop a coherent piece of writing free of major errors. It is also expected that children produce and refine compositions for general and specific audiences. Children are required to edit their work and the work of others based on clarity of ideas, and coherence and the conventions of writing.

Strategies for Using Writing Conventions

The main objective of writing is to put ideas in writing in a logical pattern. Once this is accomplished, students have to check for writing conventions—grammar, punctuation, and capitalization. Some of the strategies to introduce writing conventions are listed below.

1. **Modeling**—introduce writing samples where conventions are used appropriately or present a writing sample to the whole class that contains typical errors in English conventions and ask them to provide corrective feedback.
2. **Sentence Builders**—The teacher provides students with a list of words by syntactic categories (articles, adjectives, nouns, verbs, and conjunctions), and guides the children to produce sentences using each component.
3. **Punctuation**—Use sentences where commas or periods are necessary to deliver the intended ideas and guide students to use punctuation to clarify the intended message. For example, in the sentence *Mary, a student from Italy, requested bread, coffee and olive oil for breakfast*, it is not clear if Mary wants coffee mixed with olive oil or just coffee and also olive oil. In this case a comma is needed for clarification.
4. Assess writing samples to identify common problems across the group, and design lessons to address identified problems. For example, if students are producing words like *bred* and *sale boat* in place of *bread* and *sailboat*, provide training in vowel diagraph and compound words. A vowel diagraph is more than one vowel that produces one sound, e.g., beach. A consonant diagraph is more than one consonant that produces only one sound, e.g., thought.

Connecting Discourse

Connecting discourse is a definite challenge to students in the early grades. Children generally produce choppy sentences without transition words or phrases to connect ideas or paragraphs. Most of these connectors are not used in daily speech unless students have had some speech training or an academic preparation in the area; thus, teachers need to teach connectors directly. When writing a composition, teachers can provide a list of possible connectors to guide students to use them. Examples of connectors are presented in Table 2-5.

Table 2-5. Connectors Used in Writing

Writing Task	Sample Connectors
Sequencing	First, second; after, meanwhile, then, lastly, finally, at the beginning, next, following that, before, in conclusion…
Result	Therefore, consequently, then, as a result, thus, hence, as a consequence…
Conclusion	To conclude, in conclusion, as a final point, lastly, finally, at the end, bring to a close, terminate, finish,
Contrast	On the other hand, instead, on the contrary, as opposed to, as an alternative, in its place, conversely, then again, in contrast…
Opinion	According to, as far as I know, in my opinion, I believe, from my point of view…
Condition	Unless, provided that, as soon as, so that, except, only if, given that, as long as, if…
Adding Information	Besides, also, even, additionally, moreover, furthermore, likewise, further, as well…

Dependent and Independent Clauses

Another way to minimize the use of choppy sentences in compositions is by guiding children to combine sentences in one of the following ways:

1. Use conjunctions such as *and, but, or, nor, or yet*. For example, *My car is beautiful, but it is getting old*. Notice that in the sentence, there are two independent clauses joined by a coordinate conjunction, *but*. A comma is required before the conjunction.
2. Join two complete sentences with a semicolon. For example, the sentence *Maricela is a highly intelligent student; she was the Valedictorian of the 2006 class*. Notice that lower case is used after the semicolon.
3. Use dependent and independent clauses. For example, the sentence *Although Dora is my friend, she did not vote for me*. Notice that in this case, the use of a dependent linking word *although* at the beginning clause made the second clause necessary to complete the whole idea. The last statement makes sense by itself, but it becomes a more complete sentence when used together.

Strategies to Promote Written Communication

Reading to students can provide multiple benefits to children. It develops print awareness and understanding of the intonation pattern of the language. It helps students understand the use of commas and punctuation in a text or story. It also provides a model of fluent reading together with the appropriate intonation and pauses of the language. Children can be exposed to different kinds of writing (genre) like prose fiction, biography, tables, and short stories. Finally, they are exposed to the story framework, which is the setting, characters, plot, climax, and resolution. Oral reading and the discussion of a story framework will help students in connecting the oral presentation to the written presentation of language.

Dictated Materials—The Language Experience Approach

Children's individual or group-dictated stories, which can be written on experience charts, guide children to connect spoken language with its written representation. The teacher can record student's dictation or ask them to talk into a tape recorder. When the teacher is recording the stories, saying each word aloud while writing it down can be helpful to the students. To assist students in developing the knowledge of clauses and phrases, read the story placing a hand under each phrase as it is read. Students can also read the story in choral reading, in pairs, or individually.

Interactive Journals

Writing in journals provides students opportunities to use language authentically in literary contexts. Teachers and students can have a designated time for journal writing to communicate on a daily basis. This gives students the freedom to use their own mechanics and invented spelling. Because the purpose of written journals is to communicate, teachers should not correct children's journal writing, but should write comments on content and provide encouragement and reassurance. Some of the key advantages of interactive journals for children and teachers follow.

Advantages of Journal Writing for Students

- develop writing to communicate
- develop ownership in students writing
- develop writing within meaningful contexts
- develop a personal interaction with the teacher and with peers;
- develop non-threatening environment for

Advantages of Journal Writing for Teachers

- Teachers learn about each child's interest, ideas, and everyday concerns
- Teachers interact and communicate on an individual basis with each child
- Teachers model standard convention or writing in the context of authentic communication

Using Routines as Literacy Events

Several routine activities can be modified to promote reading and writing development. Some of these activities are:

- Taking attendance: Using a chart with students' names on it. In the morning, students get their card and move it to the chart showing that they are present. Students can also be placed in alphabetical order, which uses indirect teaching to deal with that concept.
- The daily weather report: Use pictures and words representing the climatic conditions, i.e., cloudy, clear, raining. Students will move the cards showing the prevailing weather conditions for the day.
- Students select the appropriate card showing the days of the week.
- Students organize a calendar of events for the day or for the month
- Teachers use notes to communicate with students.

Key Principles of Competency 013

- Plan many opportunities to develop students' writing at each stage.
- Use numerous strategies to develop writing in the classroom and know what to expect of the students in each level of proficiency (emerging writers, early writers, and newly fluent writers).

Competency 014 (Written Communication)

The teacher understands that writing to communicate is a developmental process and provides instruction that promotes children's competence in written communication.

Writing is a developmental process that requires students to go through a series of steps to complete a written product (see processes below).

The writing process includes the knowledge and use of prewriting strategies like:

- brainstorming and using semantic mapping, outlining, reading and research;
- developing writing for various audiences and purposes (e.g., expressive, informative, persuasive);
- using text genres and structures (e.g., letter, poem, story, play); and strategies (e.g., peer conferences);
- developing skills for drafting, editing, revising, proofreading, and publishing materials.

Children also need knowledge of English grammar and mechanics to revise their writing. It includes revising given texts in terms of sentence construction like:

- revise run-on sentences and misplaced modifiers;
- revise subject-verb and pronoun-antecedent agreement;
- revise verb forms, pronouns, adverbs, adjectives, and plural and possessive nouns;
- revise capitalization, punctuation, and spelling.

Students need to analyze and revise written work in relation to style, clarity, organization, intended audience, and purpose. This includes revising text prepared for a given audience or purpose, and improving organization and unity. This can be done by adding transition words and phrases, reordering sentences or paragraphs, deleting unnecessary information, and adding a topic sentence. Another strategy is to increase text clarity, precision, and effectiveness through word choices.

Dr. Donald Graves, a professor of education at the University of New Hampshire, developed an approach to writing instruction called *process writing* (1983). His notion is simple. Teach children to write the way real writers write. What do writers do? They tend to write about what they want to write about. Then they may read about the subject, talk about the subject, take notes, or generally fool around with the topic before they compose. Then they may write a draft, knowing up-front that they are not done at this point. Writers may share the draft with others, and end up writing all over it. They may also go over every sentence, thinking about word choice, and looking for vague spots, or spots where the piece falls off the subject. Writers may then revise the draft again, share it again, revise it again, and so on, until they are satisfied with the product. Then they publish it.

Another aspect of process writing is celebration. Children are invited to share their work with the class. After a young author reads their piece, classmates ought to offer affirmations and suggestions. Able teachers should have children save each piece of paper generated in the writing process, and store them in a personal portfolio for review. A summary of process writing together with strategies for each phase is presented in Table 2-6 (Peregoy & Boyle, 2005).

New Trends in Writing

In addition to process writing, there is a new trend emphasizing specific elements of the writing process. The best known system is called the 6+1 Writing Traits. This system, which was developed by the Northwest Regional Education Laboratory (NREL), emphasizes seven elements of the writing process (2006). These elements are described below.

1. **Ideas**—how ideas are presented in the writing sample
2. **Organization**—the internal structure of the writing sample

Table 2-6. Process Writing

Phase	Purpose	Strategies
Prewriting	To generate and gather ideas for writing; to prepare for writing; to identify purpose and audience for writing; to identify the main ideas and supporting details; to write more coherently	Talking and discussing the topics; brainstorming, clustering, questioning, reading, keeping journal in all content areas; to discuss experiences with partner
Drafting	Getting ideas in writing; getting first draft that can be evaluated according to purpose and audience for paper	Fast writing; daily writing; journal of all types: buddy journals, dialogue journal and learning journals
Revising	Reordering arguments or reviewing scenes in a narrative; reordering supporting details; reviewing or changing sentences	Shortening sentences; combining sentences; peer response groups; teacher conferences
Editing	Correcting spelling, grammar, punctuation, mechanics…	Peer editing groups; proofreading; computer programs for spelling; mini-lessons
Publishing	Sharing writing with one another, with students and parents; showing that writing is valued; creating a classroom library; motivating writing	Writing may be shared in many formats; paper placed on bulletin boards, papers published with computers, paper shared in school book fairs…

3. **Voice**—the uniqueness of the author and how ideas are projected
4. **Word Choice**—the vocabulary used to convey meaning
5. **Sentence Fluency**—the flow of ideas and the use of connectors
6. **Conventions**—the use of capitalization, punctuation and spelling
7. **Presentation**—how the final product looks in print.

The Texas Education Agency developed a similar writing program emphasizing similar components. These components are described below.

1. **Focus and Coherence**—how the main idea is introduced and supported in the composition
2. **Organization**—the organization of ideas including connectors
3. **Development of Ideas**—how the ideas are presented and supported in writing
4. **Voice**—the uniqueness of the author and how ideas are projected
5. **Conventions**—the use of capitalization, punctuation and spelling

Both the 6+1 Writing Traits and the Texas writing program guide children to demonstrate knowledge of writing traits. To assess their performance, both programs develop a four-point rubric for each of the writing traits. A description of the lowest and highest points of the rubric used by TEA to assess TAKS writing is presented in Table 2-7 on page 98.

Identifying the Characteristics of Modes of Writing

Writing serves many different functions. The main functions are to narrate, to describe, to explain, and to persuade. Students need to be aware of each of these functions.

The **narrative** is a story or an account. It may recount an incident or a series of incidents. The account may be autobiographical to make a point. The narrative may be fiction or nonfiction.

The purpose of **descriptive** writing is to provide information about a person, place, or thing. Descriptive writing can be fiction or nonfiction. Description is a powerful tool in advertisement.

The purpose of **expository** writing is to explain and clarify ideas. Students are probably most familiar with this type of writing. While the expository essay may have narrative elements, the storytelling or recounting aspect is minor and subservient to the explanation element. Expository writing is typically found in many textbooks.

The purpose of **persuasive** writing is to convince the reader of something. Persuasive writing fills current magazines and newspapers, and permeates the World Wide Web. The writer may be trying to push a political candidate, to convince someone to vote for a zoning ordinance, or even to promote a diet plan. Persuasive writing usually presents a point, provides evidence, which may be factual or anecdotal, and supports the point. The writer's intent is to persuade.

Authors choose their form of writing not necessarily just to tell a story but also to present an idea. Whether writers choose the narrative, descriptive, expository, or persuasive format, they have something on their minds that they want to convey to their readers.

Writing for a Variety of Occasions, Purposes, and Audiences

The writer must consider the audience, the occasion, and the purpose when choosing the writing mode. The writer's responsibility is to write clearly, honestly, and cleanly for the reader's sake and so the **audience** is very important. After all, writing would be pointless without readers. The teacher can designate an audience for students' writing. Knowing who will read their work, students can modify their writing to suit the intended readers. For instance, a fourth-grade teacher might suggest that the class take their compositions about a favorite animal to second graders and allow the younger children to read it. The writers soon will realize that they need to use manuscript and not cursive writing, to employ simple vocabulary, and to omit complex sentences when they write for their young audience.

Table 2-7. Rubric for the TAKS Writing (TEA, 2004)

Focus and Coherence: 1 Point	Focus and Coherence: 4 Points
Individual paragraphs and/or composition as a whole are not focused. It may shift abruptly from idea to idea, making it difficult for the reader to understand how the ideas included in the composition are related.	Individual paragraphs and the composition as a whole are focused. This sustained focus enables the reader to understand and appreciate how the ideas included in the composition are related.
Organization: 1 Point	**Organization: 4 Points**
The writer's progression of thought from sentence to sentence and/or paragraph is not logical. Sometimes weak progression results from an absence of transition or from the use of transitions that do not make sense. At other times, the progression of thought is simply not evident even if appropriate transitions are included.	The writer's progression of thought from sentence to sentence and/or paragraph is smooth and controlled. The writer's use of meaningful transitions and the logical movement from idea to idea strengthen this progression.
Development of Ideas: 1 Point	**Development of Ideas: 4 Points**
The writer presents one or more ideas but provides little or no development of those ideas.	The writer's thoughts and specific development of each idea creates depth of thought in the composition, enabling the readers to truly understand and appreciate the writer's ideas.
Voice: 1 Point	**Voice: 4 Points**
The writer does not engage the reader, therefore failing to establish connection.	The writer engages the reader and sustains this connection throughout the composition.
Conventions: 1 Point	**Conventions: 4 Points**
There is little or no evidence in the composition that the writer can correctly apply the conventions of the English language. Severe and/or frequent errors in spelling, capitalization, punctuation, grammar, usage, and sentence structure may cause the writing to be unclear or difficult to read. These errors weaken the composition by causing an overall lack of fluency.	The overall strength of the conventions contributes to the effectiveness of the composition. The writer demonstrates a consistent command of spelling, capitalization, punctuation, grammar, usage, and sentence structure. When the writer attempts to communicate ideas through sophisticated forms of expression, he/she may make minor errors as a result of these compositional risks. These types of errors do not detract from the overall fluency of the composition.

The **occasion** also helps to determine the elements of writing. The language should fit the occasion. Students should keep in mind that particular words may have certain effects, such as evoking sympathy or raising questions about an opposing point of view.

The **purpose** helps to determine the format (narrative, expository, descriptive, or persuasive) and the language of the writer. The students, for instance, might consider the appropriateness of written material for a specific purpose such as a business letter, a communication with residents of a retirement center, or a thank-you note to parents.

In selecting the mode of writing and the content, the writer might ask the following:

> What would the audience need to know to believe you or to accept your position? Imagine someone you know (visualize her or him) listening to you declare your position or opinion and then saying, "Oh yeah? Prove it!" What evidence do you need to prove your idea to this skeptic? With what might the audience disagree? What common knowledge does the audience share with you? What information do you need to share with the audience? The teacher might wish to have the students practice selecting the mode and the language by adapting forms, organizational strategies, and styles for different audiences and purposes.

Types of Writing

Teachers need to encourage children to write for meaningful purposes. Meaningful writing can be easily incorporated as part of daily classroom activities and can enhance not only writing skills, but also content area mastery. Some of the types of writing are: functional writing (used to achieve a purpose as in writing a grocery list) and journal writing.

- **Personal journals** are used to record personal information and to encourage self-analysis of their experiences. This is a personal document and it is up to the child to make it available to others.
- **Dialogue journals** promote written communication among students and between the teacher and students. The main purpose is to communicate not to teach writing skills. Teachers can model writing when they reply to children.
- **Reflective journals** are used to respond in writing to specific situations or problems. It is often shared with the teacher for input.
- **Learning logs** are commonly used in the content areas to record elements discussed in class. In this logs, students describe what they have learned and elements where they have difficulties. Teachers read the document and act on request for assistance.

Integrating Technology with Language and Content

Teachers should feel encouraged to use state-of-the-art technology to motivate children to write and monitor their writing. **Word processing** programs have features that can help children with editing. Elements like spell check, definitions of terms, thesaurus, and even suggestions for sentence constructions, are commonly available in programs like Microsoft Word. However, teachers have to teach children how to use and take advantage of these features. For example, the real function of a spell checker is not only to identify misspelled words, but to free students from the pressure of spelling. Students are encouraged to put their ideas in writing without stopping to check for spelling. Once they finish the content of the writing, they can take care of superficial elements like spelling. However, children should be guided to pay attention to corrections and to learn from them.

Electronic Dialogue Journals

The Internet can be used to expand the use of dialogue journals. Teachers can contact schools in other states or countries to initiate an electronic "pen pal" system involving more mature or advanced writers.

Projection Systems

Computers with the appropriate projection system can be used to display students work and to model writing.

Key Principles of Competency 014

- Teachers need to know of the processes involved in writing (e.g., process writing).
- Teachers need to know the types of writing (e.g., descriptive, expository and persuasive).
- Teachers need to know the TExES assessments expectations for writing for their grade level.
- Teachers need to be able to plan, develop and assess the writing skills of students based on the state writing assessment rubric expectations.

Competency 015 (Viewing and Representing)

The teacher understands skills for interpreting, analyzing, evaluating, and producing visual images and messages in various media and provides students with opportunities to develop skills in this area.

According to the TEKS (1998), students in EC-6 grades need to develop the necessary skills to create and understand images and messages in a variety of media. The skills required by the students increase in complexity as they move from lower elementary grades to upper elementary. For instance, students in grades 1–3 are required to produce visual representations of the information they are learning in school or the tasks they are involved in (e.g., creating an image summarizing a story read). Students are also required to know how to discuss the visual representations they have created. In grades 4–6, students need to be able to understand, interpret, analyze, critique, and produce these visual representations as well as discuss their meaning or significance through the use of multiple media, including newsletters, charts, and electronic presentations, among others. Students are also required to understand the author's purpose and choice of various elements that were used by him/her to get their message across through the use of multiple media. The characteristics and functions of the various different types of media are explained below.

Types and Characteristics of Media

Media is considered to be any means used to convey information to others. There are at least three main types of media available. These include print, visual, and electronic media. **Print media** is what is used to disseminate information in print form such as that found in newspapers, magazines, and direct mail. Print media is static; that is, once it is published, the information cannot be changed. **Visual media** incorporates the use of visual imagery to either complement or supplement the message being carried. Visual media can also stand by itself. For example, photographs and paintings can convey meaning without the need of including texts. Moreover, visual media is also an integral part of print media to illustrate messages. As such, visual media can take many forms, including photography, film, and even cartoons. Visual media can be either static (e.g., still photograph) or dynamic as seen in movies or videos. In addition to incorporating print and visual imagery, **electronic media** requires the use of an external device such as a television, computer, or personal assistant device to display the information and images being presented. Electronic media is used in many different fields including journalism, fine arts, commerce, education, and communications. A primary type of electronic media that encompasses different electronic tools is the Internet, where one can find blogs, email, Web sites, etc.

Technology changes at a rapidly, and teachers must keep this in mind when working with students. In fact, many of the tools that are used for presenting information are improved and refined every day. For instance, the process for creating photographs has evolved from creating these on plates and then film to now being created digitally.

In this information era, beginning teachers should also understand that there is a vast array of possibilities to create and display information by making use of existing types of media. In fact, as the need for using and sharing massive amounts of information with others becomes necessary, some of these types of media will take precedence over others. Take, for instance, the use of electronic media such as the use of online sources.

Representing Messages and Meanings through Media

Charts, tables, graphs, pictures, and print and nonprint media are examples of materials used to solely present or summarize information and/or to complement the message being conveyed. For instance, a chart can be used to summarize large amounts of information without the need to use extensive written explanations. Students should understand that visual representations are important and that the purpose for using them is to present information and to facilitate the communication of the message. Visual images should also be used to make information more understandable. A graphic can expand a concept, serve as an illustration, support points, summarize data, organize facts, add a dimension to the content (such as a cartoon adding humor), compare information, demonstrate change over time, or furnish additional information. Through graphics, the reader can interpret, predict, and even apply information with some careful observation. Actively questioning students as they create visual images (e.g., asking them what they are trying to convey or how they think someone will interpret their image) as well as providing ongoing feedback may allow students to specifically focus on and clarify the information that is being presented and that can be derived in such graphic formats.

Understanding How Students May Interpret and Evaluate Visual Images

It is important for teachers to realize that even a graphic that appears uncomplicated may challenge a reader's interpretive skills. Many inferences may be necessary for even the simplest visual aid or graphic. Many students may initially skip over graphics, or may just notice their presence without interpreting them. Likewise, students may only focus on the graphic aspects being presented in such visual media but not focus on the complementary or written explanations. Even students who have some training in the use of graphic information may not be able to transfer that knowledge to other content areas, or may have trouble going from print to graphic and then back to print. In either case, students may not have been taught how to use multiple representations of information. Teachers can help students use multiple representations of information by using open-book and guided reading. A teacher can also demonstrate how to use a chart or graph through the use of electronic tools including overhead projectors and interactive whiteboards. Examples of presentations and steps toward creating an effective presentation can be shared with the students. Resources and software that would be useful as "mentor texts" (Dorfman & Cappelli, 2007) can give students representative examples of how to best select images to use in parallel with the text (e.g., consideration of how the image parallels or complements the text).

Visual design can be thought of as containing its own grammar (Kress & van Leeuwen, 2001). Teachers can help students to understand and apply the elements of such visual grammar by teaching its component parts (Wysocki, Johnson-Eilola, Selfe & Sirc, 2004):

- Visual impact: the ways in which the overall visual design appeals to the reader (e.g., through detail, layout, use of color).
- Visual coherence: the ways in which the design of the piece creates a sense of unity and wholeness (e.g., by use of shapes, line, imagery).
- Visual salience: using design features to generate a certain effect (e.g., through varying size, colors, clip art, etc.)

- Organization: the layout of the page to create a unique pattern, especially one that is understandable to the reader (e.g., through consideration of how the different aspects of the layout might be arranged).

Of course, these features of visual literacy overlap and can be used flexibly to guide students towards creating an awareness of the visual literacy that parallel and differ from the features of print literacy.

Modeling how to read, complement, and interpret visual images should be done by teachers whenever students are required to create visual images as part of their work in the classroom. Pictures and other graphics can arouse interest and stimulate thinking. Additionally, graphics can add clarity, prevent misunderstandings, show step-by-step developments, exhibit the status of things, events, and processes, and demonstrate comparisons and contrasts (Vacca and Vacca 1989).

Integrating Technology for Producing Communications

Teachers should provide students with opportunities to use state-of-the-art technology and tools to not only motivate children to read, write, and monitor their writing, but to create various kinds of communications products with a variety of media. For instance, one could assume that the goal for using word processor software is to simply record written information. Interestingly, with the advances in technology, such software has improved their features to even offer writers assistance with the actual editing of their documents. Other uses for this type of software include creating semantic maps, tables, charts, and graphs. Writing-related elements like spell check, definitions of terms, thesaurus, and even suggestions for sentence constructions are commonly available in programs like Microsoft Word. The real function of a spell checker is not only to identify misspelled words, but also to free students from the pressure of getting spelling right, at least at the drafting stage. Students should be encouraged to put their ideas in writing without stopping to check for spelling. Once they finish the content of the writing, they can take care of other important elements like spelling. Students should, however, be aware that there may be cases in which the spell checker may be ineffective. Therefore, children should be guided to pay attention to corrections and to learn from them.

Teachers have to teach children how to use and take advantage of programs available for communicating and creating electronic products in their classrooms. Some of these products include creating a classroom newsletter, a multimedia presentation, and a video response to a group project. Students should be aware that they must keep their audience and purpose for creating such products in mind whenever they are creating their pieces. Students should also make sure that the language being used is appropriate and understandable for their audience.

Competency 016 (Assessment of Developing Literacy)

The teacher understands the basic principles of literacy assessment and uses a variety of assessments to guide literacy instruction.

Knowledge and Use of Literacy Assessment

The two main types of assessment are formal and informal. Both have a place in the classroom, particularly in the literacy classroom. The effective teacher understands the importance of ongoing assessment as an instructional tool and uses both informal and formal assessment measures. Any grouping of students should come about after the consideration of several assessments, and the grouping should be flexible enough to consider individual differences among the students in each group.

Informal Assessments

Teachers can learn valuable information by simply observing their students at work. Many school districts use a type of inventory/report card to inform adults at home about the progress that children are making. Experienced teachers usually develop, through trial and error, their own means of assessing the skills of students in their classes. Teachers can also develop their own informal reading assessment. The purpose of these assessments is to collect meaningful information about what students can and cannot do. A **running record** is a way to assess students' word identification skills and fluency in oral reading. In a running record, the teacher uses a copy of the page to mark each word the child mispronounces as the teacher listens to a student read a page. The teacher writes the incorrect word over the printed word, draws a line through each word the child skips, and draws an arrow under repeated words.

Reading Levels

Reading specialists have identified three reading proficiency levels—independent, instructional, and frustration. If the student reads 95% of the words correctly, the book is at the child's **independent level**. If the student reads 90% to 94% of the words correctly, the book is at the child's **instructional level**, which means the child can perform satisfactorily with help from the teacher. If the student reads 89% or fewer words correctly, the book is probably at the child's **frustration level**. These reading levels are determined based on the ability of children to answer comprehension questions after reading passages. Reading levels are generally assessed through reading informal reading inventories.

Informal Reading Inventories

Informal reading inventories are informal assessment instruments designed to identify the reading levels of children. Most basal reader books contain some type of informal reading inventory. These are graded (by reading levels) passages that include comprehension questions. Teachers begin with a passage at the reading level of the child and continue increasing the complexity until the child is not able to respond to the comprehension questions.

Asking a child to retell a story is another type of informal assessment. The ability to retell a story is an informal type of assessment that is useful to the teacher, parent, and eventually, the child. Informal assessment measures can also include observations, journals, written drafts, and conversations.

The teacher may make **observations** during individual or group work. Usually, the teacher makes a **checklist** of competencies, skills, or requirements, and then uses the list to check off the ones a student or group displays. A teacher wishing to emphasize interviewing skills could devise a checklist that includes personal appearance, mannerisms, confidence, and addressing the questions asked. A teacher who wants to emphasize careful listening might observe a discussion with a checklist that includes paying attention, not interrupting, summarizing the ideas of other members of the group, and asking questions about others.

Checklists give teachers the potential for capturing behaviors that cannot be accurately measured with a paper-and-pencil test, such as following the correct sequence of steps in a science experiment, or including all important elements in a speech in class. One characteristic of a checklist that is both an advantage and a disadvantage is its structure, which provides consistency but inflexibility. However, an open-ended comment section at the end of a checklist can help overcome this disadvantage.

Anecdotal records are helpful in some instances, such as capturing the process a group of students uses to solve a problem. These anecdotal records can be useful when giving feedback to the group. Students can also be taught to write explanations of the procedures they use for their projects or science experiments.

Portfolios

Portfolios are collections of students' best work. They can be used in any subject area where the teacher wants students to take more responsibility for planning, carrying out, and organizing their own learning. Like a portfolio created by an artist, model, or performer, a student portfolio provides a succinct picture of the child's achievements over a certain period. Portfolios may contain essays or articles written on paper, videotapes, multimedia presentations on computer disks, or a combination of these.

Teachers should provide, or assist students in developing, guidelines for what materials should go in their portfolios because it would be unrealistic to include every piece of work in one portfolio. Using portfolios requires that the students devise a means of evaluating their own work. A portfolio should not be a scrapbook for collecting handouts or work done by other individuals, but it can certainly include work by a group in which the student was a participant.

One disadvantage of portfolios is the amount of time required to teach students how to develop meaningful portfolios and the time it takes to assess the portfolio. However, as students become more proficient at self-assessment, the teacher can spend more time in coaching and advising students throughout the development of their portfolios. Another concern is that parents may not understand how the teacher will grade the portfolios. The effective teacher devises a system that the students and parents understand before work on the portfolios begins.

Miscue Analysis

Miscue analysis is an assessment procedure to assess oral reading. Miscues refer to any deviation from text made during oral reading. The procedure for its implementation follows.

1. Select reading material a little bit above the current reading level of the child. The complete story should be about 500 words in length.
2. Provide a copy of the selection to the child.
3. Get a copy of the selection that is triple spaced to allow room to write comments.
4. Audiotape the reading.
5. Provide instructions to the child, and tell the student that you cannot help him/her during the reading
6. Ask questions about the story.
7. Let the reader listen to the tape recording and then analyze it.
8. Look for consistent miscues and pay special attention to initial and final clusters/blends and diagraphs.

Running Records

Running records is a form of ongoing assessment designed to identify early reading difficulties in children. The teacher evaluates the reading performance of individual children based on checklists.

Through informal observations and through the use of inventories (formal and informal), teachers should be able to determine the **learning styles** of their students. Student learning styles play an important role in determining classroom structure.

Formal Assessments

Formal measures may include teacher-made tests, district exams, and standardized tests. Both formative and summative evaluations are part of effective instruction. **Formative evaluation** occurs during the process of learning when the teacher or the students monitor progress while it is still possible to modify instruction. **Summative evaluation** occurs at the end of a specific time or course of study. Usually, a summative evaluation applies a single grade or score to represent a student's performance.

The effective teacher uses a variety of formal assessment techniques. Teacher-made instruments are ideally developed at the same time as the planning of goals and outcomes, rather than at the last minute after the completion of the lessons. Carefully planned objectives and assessment instruments serve as lesson development guides for the teacher. Paper-and-pencil tests are the most common method for evaluating student progress.

Criterion-Referenced Tests

In **criterion-referenced tests (CRTs)**, the teacher attempts to measure each student against uniform objectives or criteria. CRTs allow the possibility that all students can score 100 percent on the test because they understand the concepts being tested. Teacher-made tests should be criterion-referenced because the teacher should develop them to measure the achievement of predetermined outcomes for the course. If teachers have properly prepared lessons based on the outcomes and, if students have mastered the outcomes, then scores on CRTs should be high.

The **Texas Assessment of Knowledge and Skills** (TAKS) and the State of Texas Assessments of Academic Readiness (STAAR) is a basic skills test for children in grades 3 to 12. This criterion-referenced test assesses the implementation and the mastery of the Texas Essential Knowledge and Skills (TEKS)—the Texas state curriculum.

Norm-Referenced Tests

The purpose of a **norm-referenced test (NRT)** is to compare the performance of groups of students. This type of test is competitive because a limited number of students can score well. A plot of NRT scores resembles a **bell-shaped curve**, with most scores clustering around the center, and a few scores at each end. The **midpoint** is the average of test data; and therefore, half of the population will score above average and half below average. The bell-shaped curve is a mathematical description of the results of tossing coins. As such, it represents the chance or normal distribution of skills, knowledge, or events across the general population. A survey of the height of sixth-grade boys will result in an average height, with half the boys being above average height, and half below. There will also be a very small number with heights far above average and a very small number with heights far below average; but, most heights will cluster around the average. A **percentile score** (not to be confused with a percentage) is a way of reporting a student's NRT score. The percentile score indicates the percentage of the population whose scores fall at or below the student's score. For example, a group score at the eightieth percentile means that the group scored as well as or better than 80 percent of the students who took the test. A student with a score at the fiftieth percentile has an average score. Percentile scores rank students from highest to lowest. By themselves, percentile scores do not indicate how well the student has mastered the content objectives. **Raw scores** indicate how many questions the student answered correctly and are, therefore, useful in computing a percentage score.

The Texas Education Agency (TEA) has a comprehensive list of approved norm-reference tests that districts can choose from to assess achievement of students in the state. This list includes the California Achievement Test (CAT), Stanford Achievement Test (SAT), and the Iowa Test of Basic Skills (ITBS), among others.

Performance-Based Assessment

Some states and districts are moving toward performance-based tests, which assess students on how well they perform certain tasks. Students must use higher-level thinking skills to apply, analyze, synthesize, and evaluate ideas and data. For example, a content-based performance-based assessment might require students to read a problem, design and carry out a laboratory experiment, and then write summaries of their findings. The performance-based assessment would evaluate both the processes students used and the output they produced. An English performance-based test might ask students to first read a selection of literature and then write a critical analysis. A mathematics performance-based test might state a general problem, require students to invent one or more methods of solving the problem, use one of the methods to arrive at a solution, and write the solution and an explanation of the processes they used.

Performance-based assessment allows students to be creative in solutions to problems or questions, and it requires them to use higher-level skills that can be applied to various content areas. There are weaknesses in this approach, however. This type of assessment can be time consuming. Performance-based assessment often requires multiple resources, which can be expensive. Teachers must receive training in applying the test. These tests are more authentic measures of student achievement than traditional tests.

Classroom Tests

Teachers must consider fundamental professional and technical factors when constructing effective classroom tests. One of the first factors to recognize is that test construction is as creative, challenging, and important as any aspect of teaching. The planning and background that contribute to effective teaching are incomplete unless evaluation of student performance provides accurate feedback to the teacher and the student about the learning process.

Good tests are the product of careful planning, creative thinking, hard work, and technical knowledge about the various methods of measuring student knowledge and performance. Classroom tests that accomplish their purpose are the result of the development of a pool of items and refinement of those items based on feedback and constant revision. It is through this process that evaluation of students becomes valid and reliable.

Tests serve as a valuable instructional aid because they help determine student progress and also provide feedback to teachers regarding their own effectiveness.

Student misunderstandings and problems that the tests reveal can help the teacher understand areas of special concern in providing instruction. This information also becomes the basis for the remediation of students and the revision of teaching procedures. Consequently, the construction, administration, and proper scoring of classroom tests are among the most important activities in teaching.

Authentic Assessments

Paper-and-pencil tests and essay tests are not the only methods of assessment. Other assessments include projects, observations, checklists, anecdotal records, portfolios, self-assessments, and peer assessments. Although these types of assessments often take more time and effort to plan and administer, they can often provide a more authentic measurement of student progress.

There are advantages and disadvantages to essay tests. Advantages of essay questions include the possibility for students to be creative in their answers, the opportunity for students to explain their responses, and the potential to test for higher-level thinking skills. Disadvantages of essay questions include the time students need to formulate meaningful responses, and the time teachers need to evaluate the essays. In addition, language difficulties can make essay tests extremely difficult for some students, including ELLs. Consistency in evaluating essays can also be a problem for some teachers, but an outline of the acceptable answers—a scoring rubric—can help a teacher avoid inconsistency.

Using Rubrics for Assessment

A **rubric** is a checklist with assigned point values. To construct a rubric, a teacher uses the lesson objectives. Students should receive an explanation of the rubric *before* starting to work on their writing assignment, and they can use the rubric as a guideline while they are preparing their writing assignment. The teacher can use the rubric to evaluate student work after the student has completed the assignment. Teachers should model what is expected by discussing the rubric.

Scoring Compositions

Holistic scoring is used to evaluate the composition and writing performance of students in Texas. The whole writing sample is scored based on a pre-established criteria contained in a rubric. The writing rubric used to score the performance on the exam is based on four levels. Students need to score at level three or four to pass the test.

Educator's Guide to TEKS-Based Assessment (TEA, 2004)

The writing portion of the fourth grade test is assessed based on two objectives:

1. The student will, within a context, produce an effective composition for a specific purpose.
2. The student will produce a piece of writing that demonstrates command of the conventions of spelling, capitalization, punctuation, grammar, usage, and sentence structure.

These objectives are integrated into the five components of effective writing approved by the TEA and used for scoring the writing component of the state assessment, which are focus and coherence, organization, development of ideas, voice, and conventions. (See previous chapter for detailed explanations of these components.) The rubric has a four-point scale based on the five components of the writing process and is used to assess the writing performance of children. Table 2-8 presents a description of the four levels of performance where four is the maximum scored possible.

Table 2-8. Criteria for Evaluation Compositions Based on a Four-Point Scale

Point Scale
4. An excellent paper that is well organized and displays facile use of language, content, and mechanics.
3. A paper that demonstrates adequate organization, content, language use, and handling mechanics. It may lack imagination and creativity.
2. A lower-half paper that is weak in content, organization, style, and/or mechanics.
1. An unacceptable paper that addresses the topic but is weak in organization, content, and language use and is full of errors in mechanics.

Ongoing Assessment

Ongoing assessment provides teachers with updated information about the progress and challenges that children are facing in writing. This information can then be easily incorporated in daily instruction.

The State of Texas Assessments of Academic Readiness (STAAR) will replace the TAKS, which has been in place since 2003—STAAR includes the 12 end-of-course (EOC) assessments mandated by SB 1031 in 2007 and the new grade 3–8 assessments mandated by HB 3 in 2009. The new tests will focus on ***readiness*** for subsequent grades. These new tests will be phased in for the 2011–2012 school year—click on the following link to view *www.tea.state.tx.us/student.assessment/staar/*. A comparison of TAKS and STAAR skills and rigor can be found in this TEA web link.

Assessing English Language Learners

Texas English Language Proficiency Assessment System (TELPAS) was designed to comply with the accountability system required in the No Child Left Behind (NCLB) legislation (TEA, 2006). The legislation requires that ELLs are assessed yearly in all language skills—listening, speaking, reading, and writing. Students begin taking TELPAS in kindergarten and only stop participating when they are exited from the program.

This system is composed of two testing components: the Reading Proficiency Tests in English (RPTE) and the Texas Observation Protocols (TOP). Both assessment instruments were especially developed for ELLs. The RPTE is an assessment that measures reading skills of ELLs, which are word meaning, supporting idea, summarization, analyzing, and evaluating. RPTE is given in a booklet in a multiple-choice format. The TOP is an assessment that measures four language skills through classroom observation and daily interactions. It is graded holistically. Both assessments are broken down into four levels: beginning, intermediate, advanced, and advanced high.

Listening, speaking, reading, and writing are assessed with the TOP in kindergarten to second grade. In grades 3 and up, listening, speaking, and writing are assessed by the TOP, and reading is assessed with the RPTE. To assess the writing component, at least five writing samples a year are collected for ELLs in grades 2 through 12, and assessed holistically to comply with the four language levels mentioned earlier—beginning, intermediate, advanced, or advanced high level. ELLs stop taking the RPTE when they reach the advanced high level of the combined TOP and RPTE scores.

The modified alternative assessment measures for special education populations can be accessed by clicking on the following link *www.tea.state.tx.us/index3.aspx?id=3636&menu_id=793*.

Diversity in the Classroom

The effective teacher appreciates human diversity. An empowered instructor recognizes how diversity in the classroom creates an environment in which everyone accepts and celebrates both the diversity and the uniqueness of individuals. In that environment, the teacher and the students view race, ethnicity, religion, national origin, learning style, and gender of learners as strengths that foster learning with and from each other.

Assessing Diverse Learners

The purpose of both formal and informal assessments in the classroom is to improve the instruction and the learning of all students. It is important for the teacher to (1) analyze and interpret the information gathered through informal and formal means, (2) to use test results professionally to help all students in the classroom to learn to the best of their ability, and (3) to take into account diversity when teaching and assessing children. The use of criterion-referenced, norm-referenced, performance-based, classroom, and authentic assessments is essential to giving the child, the teacher, and the parents a complete picture of the child's progress.

References

Anderson, P. F. 1995–2005. The Mother Goose Pages *www.personal.umich.edu/~pfa/dreamhouse/nursery/rhymes.html*

August, D., & Shanahan T. (EDs.). (2006). Developing literacy in second-language learners: A report of the National Literacy Panel on Language-Minority Children and Youth. Mahwah, NJ: Lawrence Erlbaum Associates.

Bloom, B. S. ed. 1956. Taxonomy of educational objectives: The classification of educational goals: Handbook I, cognitive domain. New York; Toronto: Longmans, Green

Browning Schulman, M. & Payne, C. D. (2000). Guided reading: Making it work. New York: Scholastic, Inc.

Clay, M. M. 2002. An observation survey of early literacy achievement 2nd ed. Portmouth, NH: Heinemann.

Echevarria, J., Vogt, M.E., & Short, D (2008). Making content comprehensible for English learners: The SIOP Model. 2nd Ed. Bloston: Pearson/Allyn and Bacon.

Ehri, L. 1998. Grapheme-phoneme knowledge is essential for learning to read words in English. In Word recognition in beginning literacy, eds J. Metsala and L. Ehri, 3–40. Mahwah, NJ: Erlbaum.

Goudvis, A. and Harvey, S. 2000. Strategies that work. Portland, ME: Stenhouse.

Graves, D. H. 1983. Writing: Teachers and children at work. Portsmouth, NH: Heinemann Educational Books.

Lapp, D., Fisher, D., Flood, J. and Cabello, A. 2001. An integrated approach to the teaching and assessment of language arts. In Literacy assessment of second language learners, eds S. Rollins Hurley and J. Villamil Tinajero, 1–24. Boston, MA: Allyn and Bacon.

Martin, K. and Doris, D. 2006. Cinderella stories. The Children's Literature *www.ucalgary.ca/~dkbrown/cinderella.html*

National Institute of Child Health and Human Development (NICHD). (2000). Report of the National Reading Panel. Teaching children to read: An evidence-based assessment of the scientific research on reading and its implications for reading instruction. (NIH Publication No. 00-4769). Washington, DC: U.S. Department of Health and Human Services.

Northwest Regional Education Laboratory. 2006. 6+1 Writing Trait. www.nwrel.org/assessment/definition

Palincsar, A. S. 1986. Reciprocal teaching. In Teaching reading as thinking. Oak Brook, IL: North Central Regional Educational Laboratory.

Peregoy, S. F. and Boyle, O. F. 2005. Reading, writing, and learning in ESL: A resource book for K–12 teachers. 4th ed. New York: Pearson.

Peregoy, S. F. & Boyle, O. F. 2005. Reading, writing, and learning in ESL: A resource book for K–12 teachers 4th ed. New York: Pearson.

Piper, T. 2003. Language and learning: The home school year. 3rd ed. Columbus, Ohio: Merrill Prentice Hall.

Progressive Phonic Book (2006). The Genki, English, website. www.genkienglish.net/phonics.htm

Reuzel, R. D., & Cooter, R. 1992. Teaching children to read: From basals to books. New York: Macmillan Publishing Co.

Snow, C. E., Burns, M. S., & Griffin, P. Eds. 1998. Preventing reading difficulties in young children.

Washington, DC: National Academy Press. http://books.nap.edu/html/prdyc/

Stewig, J. W. and Jett-Simpson. 1995. Language arts in the early childhood classroom. Belmont, CA: Wadsworth.

TAKS 2005. Chapter 110. 3 English Language arts and reading. Subchapter A. Elementary. Texas Education Code, §28.002.

TEA 2002. Guidelines for examining phonics and word recognition programs, Texas Reading Initiative. http://www.tea.state.tx.us/reading/products/products.html.

TEA 2004. TAKS Scoring Guide for 4th Grade Writing Composition. Released tests. www.tea.state.tx.us/student.assessment/resources/release/taks/2004/g4sg.pdf

TEA 2005. Linguistically Accommodated Testing (LAT) Supplement to the TAKS and SDAA II. Test Administrator Manuals. Student Assessment Division. www.tea.state.tx.us/student.assessment/admin/rpte/LAT_TA_supp.pdf#xml=http://www.tea.state.tx.us/cgi/texis/webinator/search/xml.txt?query=Linguistic+accommodations&db=db&id=f8b138c3acf474d6

TEA 2006. Texas Observation Protocol (TOP). Rater Manual Grades K-12. Texas English Language Proficiency Assessment System (TELPAS). Austin, TX: Texas Education.

TEA 2006. Texas English Language Proficiency Assessment System (TELPAS). Texas Student Assessment Program Coordinator Manual.

Texas Education Agency. 2004. Division of Student Assessment. TAKS Released test. *www.tea.state.tx.us/student.assessment/resources/release/taks/index.html*

TEA. 2011. Texas Education Agency. State Texas Assessment of Academic Readiness (STAAR) Resources. Retrieved from http://www.tea.state.tx.us/student.assessment/staar/

Tomas, E., & Robinson, H. 1972. Improving reading in every class: A source book for teachers. Boston: Allyn and Bacon.

U.S. Department of Education 2006. A closer look at the five essential components of effective reading instruction. http://www.tea.state.tx.us/reading/readingfirst/readingfirst.html

UT System/TEA. 2002. Effective fluency instruction and progress monitoring. http://readingserver.edb.utexas.edu/downloads/primary/guides/Fluency_Presentation.PDF#search='Reading%20fluency'

Vacca, R. T., and Vacca, J. A. 1989. Content area reading. 3rd. Glenview, IL: Scott Foresman.

CHAPTER

Domain III: Mathematics

3

Competency 017 (Mathematics Instruction)

The teacher understands how students learn mathematical skills and uses that knowledge to plan, organize, and implement instruction and assess learning.

This chapter will discuss content that beginning teachers need to know in order to plan, organize, implement and assess instruction for concepts outlined in the Texas Essential Knowledge and Skills (TEKS) for Mathematics.

In 2000, the National Council of Teachers of Mathematics (NCTM) published the Principles and Standards for School Mathematics. The national organization's goals include the development and improvement of mathematics education. In the NCTM publication, the association identified six principles and ten standards that children in K–12 ought to master. The document guides states and district curricula development and specifies the mathematics content knowledge students should develop.

Principles of Mathematics

The NCTM (2000) identified six principles that should guide mathematics instruction. These include: equity, curriculum, teaching, learning, assessment, and technology. These are defined as follows:

- **Equity**—Excellence in mathematics education requires equity: high expectations and strong support for all students.
- **Curriculum**—A curriculum must be coherent, focused on important mathematics, and well-articulated concepts across the grades.
- **Teaching**—Effective mathematics teaching requires understanding of what students know and need to learn and then challenging and supporting students to learn it well.
- **Learning**—Students must learn mathematics with understanding, actively building new knowledge from experience and previous knowledge.
- **Assessment**—Assessment should support the learning of important mathematics concepts, and furnish useful information to both teachers and students.
- **Technology**—Technology is essential in teaching and learning mathematics; it influences the teaching of mathematics and enhances students' learning.

Standards for Mathematics

The Content Standards describe the five strands of content that students should learn; and the Process

Standards highlight ways of acquiring and applying content knowledge.

Content Standards

1. **Number and Operations.** This standard deals with understanding numbers, developing meanings of operations, and computing fluently.
2. **Algebra**. Algebraic symbols and procedures for working with them are a towering mathematical accomplishment in the history of mathematics, and are critical in mathematical work. Algebra is best learned as a set of concepts and techniques tied to the representation of quantitative relations and as a style of mathematical thinking for formalizing patterns, functions, and generalizations.
3. **Geometry**. Geometry has long been regarded as the place in high school where students learn to prove geometric theorems. The Geometry standard takes a broader view of the power of geometry by calling on students to analyze characteristics of geometric shapes and make mathematical arguments about the geometric relationship, as well as to use visualization, spatial reasoning, and geometric modeling to solve problems.
4. **Measurement**. The study of measurement is crucial in the school mathematics curriculum because of its practicality and pervasiveness in so many aspects of life. The Measurement standard includes understanding the attributes, units, systems, and processes of measurement as well as applying the techniques, tools, and formulas to determine measurements.
5. **Data Analysis and Probability**. Students must formulate questions and collect, organize, and display relevant data to answer key questions. Additionally, it emphasizes learning appropriate statistical methods to analyze data, making inferences and predictions based on data, and understanding and using the basic concepts of probability.

Process Standards

1. **Problem Solving**. Students require frequent opportunities to formulate, grapple with, and solve complex problems that involve a significant amount of effort. Students are able to acquire ways of thinking, habits of persistence and curiosity, and confidence in unfamiliar situations that serve them well outside the mathematics classroom.
2. **Reasoning and Proof**. Mathematical reasoning and proof offer powerful ways of developing and expressing insights. Students are able to identify patterns, structure, or regularities in both real-world and mathematical situations. They make and investigate mathematical conjectures; and develop and evaluate mathematical arguments and proofs.
3. **Communication**. Mathematical communication is a way of sharing ideas and clarifying understanding. Through communication, ideas become objects of reflection, refinement, discussion, and amendment.
4. **Connections**. Mathematics is an integrated field of study. When students connect mathematical ideas, their understanding is deeper and more lasting, and they come to view mathematics as a coherent whole.
5. **Representations**. Mathematical ideas can be represented in a variety of ways: pictures, concrete materials, tables, graphs, number and letter symbols, spreadsheet displays, and so on.

Texas Mathematics Standards

Standard 1—Number Concepts:

The mathematics teacher understands and uses numbers, number systems and their structure, operations and algorithms, quantitative reasoning, and technology appropriate to teach the statewide curriculum (Texas Essential Knowledge and Skills [TEKS]) in order to prepare students to use mathematics (TEA, 2009a).

Standard 2—Patterns and Algebra:

The mathematics teacher understands and uses patterns, relations, functions, algebraic reasoning, analysis, and technology appropriate to teach the statewide curriculum (Texas Essential Knowledge and Skills [TEKS]) in order to prepare students to use mathematics.

Standard 3—Geometry and Measurement:

The mathematics teacher understands and uses geometry, spatial reasoning, measurement concepts and principles, and technology appropriate to teach the statewide curriculum (Texas Essential Knowledge and Skills [TEKS]) in order to prepare students to use mathematics.

Standard 4—Probability and Statistics:

The mathematics teacher understands and uses probability and statistics, their applications, and technology appropriate to teach the statewide curriculum (Texas Essential Knowledge and Skills [TEKS]) in order to prepare students to use mathematics.

Standard 5—Mathematical Processes:

The mathematics teacher understands and uses mathematical processes to reason mathematically, to solve mathematical problems, to make mathematical connections within and outside of mathematics, and to communicate mathematically.

Standard 6—Mathematical Perspectives:

The mathematics teacher understands the historical development of mathematical ideas, the interrelationship between society and mathematics, the structure of mathematics, and the evolving nature of mathematics and mathematical knowledge.

Standard 7—Mathematical Learning and Instruction:

The mathematics teacher understands how children learn and develop mathematical skills, procedures, and concepts, knows typical errors students make, and uses this knowledge to plan, organize, and implement instruction; to meet curriculum goals; and to teach all students to understand and use mathematics.

Standard 8—Mathematical Assessment:

The mathematics teacher understands assessment and uses a variety of formal and informal assessment techniques appropriate to the learner on an ongoing basis to monitor and guide instruction and to evaluate and report student progress.

Standard 9—Professional Development:

The mathematics teacher understands mathematics teaching as a profession, knows the value and rewards of being a reflective practitioner, and realizes the importance of making a lifelong commitment to professional growth and development.

Mathematics and English Language Learners

Contrary to popular belief, mathematics is not a universal language. It is a language with special nomenclature and unique concepts. Even the way that people perform mathematical processes is often different. For example, in Mexico and the Dominican Republic the processes used for division differ from the process used in the United States. In Mexico the problem is set up in a similar fashion but most of the steps are done mentally, as opposed to the American way, where students write every single step as part of the process. For example, in the problem, 11 divided by 2, children in Mexico are taught to multiply 5 by 2 and get 10, but they do not write the 10 under the 11; they do it mentally and write the remainder below the 11. In the Dominican Republic, children do not use the traditional division bracket used in the United States and Mexico; instead, they use a bracket similar to an elongated L, and they place the divisor inside the bracket and the dividend outside. Thus children from Mexico and the Dominican Republic might experience confusion when asked to perform division the "American way."

Table 3-1 illustrates the three different processes used to perform division. The use of Arabic numbers does not present problems for English language learners (ELLs). The real challenge is to comprehend the explanation of the process in a language that ELLs have not yet mastered. Providing examples of mathematics process and modeling while describing them can definitely improve comprehension. Students who enjoy inductive teaching—learning through examples—will definitely benefit from this approach. However, children who enjoy the deductive approach—learning step by step—might experience comprehension problems.

Table 3-1.
Processes of Division Use

American	Mexican	Dominican
$\begin{array}{r} 5 \\ 2\overline{)11} \\ -10 \\ \hline 1R \end{array}$	$\begin{array}{r} 5 \\ 2\overline{)11} \\ 1R \end{array}$	$\begin{array}{rr} 11 & 5 \\ -10 & 2 \\ 1R & 10 \end{array}$

The Nomenclature of Mathematics

In addition to the obvious English communication problems, English learners face a number of challenges with the technical vocabulary or the nomenclature of mathematics for at least three reasons. First, the mathematics classroom tends to abound in assumptions concerning students' prior knowledge of specialized terms such as denominator, subtraction, minuend, divisor, subtrahend, and others. Second, the terms that have one meaning in one subject domain can assume an entirely different meaning in the vocabulary of mathematics; these terms include quarter, column, product, rational, even, and table. Finally, the vocabulary tends to encompass a variety of homophones (words pronounced in the same way but have different meanings) and can be troublesome for English learners who are unaccustomed to the new language. The Table 3-2 lists various mathematic terms and structures that may be confusing for all students.

Table 3-2. Terminology of Mathematics

Terminology	Generic Meaning	Mathematical Meaning
Even	Equal amount, same level	Numbers divisible by 2
Faces	Front of human head	Surface of a geometric solid
Plane	Flat surface, aircraft, or without adornment	A two-dimensional surface
Mean	Not nice, or to express a particular message	Arithmetic average of a set of values
Right	Correct, proper, or a direction	Forming a 90° right angle
Sum/Some	A small amount	Answer to addition problem
Volume	Loudness of sounds	Quantity of Liquid
Unfamiliar Structures		
Technical terms (e.g., equation, exponents, inequalities, quotient)		
Varied degrees of focus on problem solving versus computation and notation.		
Use of passive voice for most problem-solving questions and statements.		
Use of various mathematical symbols unfamiliar to ELLs (e.g., π, \$, $<$, $=$, $\pm$, and $\neq$).		
Multiple words or phrases indicating the same operations (e.g., fractional parts, divide, separate, equivalent parts, etc.)		
"If . . . then . . ." problem statements that are unclear.		
Cultural specific examples in word problems drawn from unfamiliar situations.		
Focus on problem solving using culturally bias strategies or context unfamiliar to ELLs.		
Multiple words with similar meanings (e.g., mean mode, median, and range).		
New information that does not fit with prior knowledge of subject matter (e.g., time, temperature, money, measurement, use of manipulative in the classroom).		

More Math Strategies for ELLs

Auditory/Oral Strategies

- Use simple sentence structures.
- Avoid jargon, idiomatic speech, and figurative language.
- Use think-a-louds to engage students in oral mathematical discourse.

Model Language and Vocabulary

- Use appropriate cognates used in math for Spanish speakers.
- Provide alternatives for oral presentations as in using presentation software.

Visual Strategies

- Write key mathematical words as you discuss them, pronouncing clearly and slowly.
- Identify language that might confuse ELLs; for example, determine volume.
- Connect verbal, written, and pictorial or symbolic representations of the same word.
- Explain any structural patterns found in expository text.
- Use charts, graphs, visuals in ELLs first language to help with math concepts.
- Have ELLs focus on headings, subheadings, charts, graphs, visuals.
- Point out contextual clues that help with meaning, for example, table, operation.
- Have ELLs keep a personal word story notebook—key math vocabulary for each lesson.

Instructional Strategies

- Teach key vocabulary explicitly and reinforce it consistently.
- Post mathematical symbols with word definitions and examples.
- Reinforce math concepts and vocabulary by providing visuals and graphic organizers such as T-charts and Venn diagrams.
- Move from concrete manipulatives, to visuals, to abstract concepts.
- Make strategic use of the first language in the introduction of new concepts.
- Use word generation charts to help ELLs with math vocabulary and English language acquisition (e.g., word—math language meaning—everyday language meaning—other forms of the word—cognates in ELLs' first language—and examples of how the word was used in the lesson.

Scaffolding Strategies

- Have ELLs restate their understanding of concepts.
- Demonstrate your thought process and have students do the same.
- Provide sentence prompts for ELLs to use the new academic language such as "another way of saying this is. . . ."
- Use K-W-L charts to help ELLs verbalize what they know, what they need to know to understand the concept, and at the end, what they have learned.
- Use manipulatives, interactive games, and technology as thinking tools.
- Encourage ELLs to use graphic organizers, diagrams, gestures, and sketches to aid in thinking and in communicating with others.
- Provide ELLs with corrective/positive feedback using prompts, gestures, encouragement, and praise. ELLs from various cultures may react quite differently to criticism.
- Provide handouts that help students structure, organize and guide their work, such as skeleton notes, summaries of past concepts, and outlines of future topics to be covered.

Assessment Strategies

In assessing ELLs' competence in mathematics, it is important to distinguish between content errors and/or language errors; thus, a series of formative assessments can be very useful tools in distinguishing between language and content knowledge. See strategies below:

- Gather sufficient data related to ELLs prior knowledge and experiences to help them make connections in their new learning.
- Check for accuracy of their prior knowledge.
- Design assessments to uncover specific gaps that might exist in the ELLs' mathematical knowledge and experience.
- Demonstrate the use of mathematical tools as in calculators, rulers, computers and software.
- Incorporate a variety of assessments to get a clear picture of the students' performance.
- Prepare ELLs for assessment by incorporating the strategies that activate their prior knowledge as in the various organizers already mentioned.
- Use body language and facial expression to check for understanding of your ELLs.
- Observe and assess students as they work in groups and provide encouragement for interaction and contribution.
- Guide students in acquiring self-monitoring skills that help them identify difficulties they have in understanding what they know, need to know and do.
- Provide timely and frequent feedback on their growth in English academic language.
- Conduct frequent briefing sessions with ELLs to assess their understanding of concepts.
- Differentiate assessment by adjusting the assessment tools and strategies to meet their needs.
- Provide bilingual dictionaries (1st language/English), personal word books and notebooks when taking exams.
- Use assessment to guide further instruction to meet the students' needs.

Developmentally Appropriate Instruction

Children develop a basic understanding of numbers as early as two years of age or even at a younger age. Infants and toddlers understand the concepts of "one" or "more," usually within the context of food. Rote counting or the verbal repetition of numbers begins at around the age of 2–3 years. This rote memorization can be used as a foundation for building understanding of number concepts of combining, separating, and naming amounts using concrete objects as soon as language develops. In their effort to develop the idea of amount, children must first know the language of number words (Fuson & Hall, 1983). Sometimes children appear to be counting when, in fact, they are naming the objects. For example, when a child has eight red blocks and begins to count out loud, "One, two, three, four, five, six, seven, eight," pointing to each block as he/she goes, and then says, "Eight," we need to ask questions. "How do you know?" or "show me eight" will tell us whether the child recognizes that the entire set makes up "eight" or that the last block is named "Eight." They need to understand that the idea of amount is inclusive of all the previously counted blocks, not just the name of the last block.

Children should be encouraged to think about numbers and the quantity of objects in meaningful situations. For example, children may be asked to hold up five crayons or hand out five crayons to each student. Kamii (2000) states that to deepen quantification knowledge students should compare sets in real-life situations rather than just count out objects. It is important for children to use movable objects, moving to larger quantities, in order to create their own internal mental relationships while interacting with various types of objects (Pepper & Hunting, 1998).

In making the move from quantification to computation, it is helpful to pose an addition question using concrete objects. Using a context for the objects helps children to make their own sense and helps them to develop their own autonomy about the operation of addition. For example, a simple addition problem can be introduced by putting beads on a string and asking children to add or subtract the various colors to create a necklace or bracelet. Many times children will prefer to "use paper and pencil" instead of objects, so they can externalize their own ideas and use drawings instead. This is probably why children do not choose to use counters to solve word problems (Kamii, 2000).

Several materials or concrete objects can be used to help children demonstrate the mathematics of the problems. It is important to distinguish between discrete models, such as counters, and continuous models, such as number lines that children might choose for solving problems. Personal algorithms can grow directly from meaningful experiences acting out problems, whether through direct modeling or counting until the mathematics concepts make sense to the child.

Cognitive Development and Mathematics

The cognitive development of children in Pre-K through grade 6 represents a special challenge when attempting to learn the symbolic and abstract representation used in mathematics. Children are expected to learn an entire organized discipline, usually represented in symbolic form. They may learn to deal with symbols well enough to perform arithmetic operations. However, having learned arithmetic procedures is not sufficient for real understanding of the concepts that symbolic manipulations represent. It is not guaranteed that children will be able to use those concepts to solve problems.

As a developmental biologist, Jean Piaget (1896–1980) observed and recorded the intellectual abilities of infants, children, and adolescents. His stages of intellectual development were related to brain growth and led him to conclude that the thinking and reasoning of children was dominated by preoperational thought—a pattern of thinking that is egocentric, centered, irreversibly and non-transformational (Piaget & Inhelder, 1969). His theory concerned the growth of intelligence, the emergence and acquisition of schemata-schemes of a child using "developmental stages" to explain how children acquire new information. Piaget divided schemes that children use into four main stages, these include:

- Sensorimotor stage (birth–2 years)
- Preoperational stage (years 2–7)
- Concrete Operational stage (years 7–11)
- Formal Operational stage (years 11–adult)

The importance of these stages of development as conceptualized by Piaget is the recognition of the child's ability to integrate symbolic referents (objects or experiences) and to interpret the mathematical concept. Children about six years old (first graders in the Preoperational stage) tend to fix their attention on a single aspect of a relationship. For example, if two rows of the same number of coins are lined up, one-to-one, equally spaced, and children are asked if the number of coins in the two rows are the same, they are likely to judge the two to be equal. When the appearance of one of the rows is changed, either by spreading the coins out further or stacking them, the child is more likely to judge them as being unequal. Their response is not based on logical reasoning but on their own perception.

According to Piaget, the **Preoperational** stage of development includes the following processes: symbolic functioning, centration, intuitive thought, egocentrism, and inability to conserve. Children in the **Concrete Operational** stage exhibit the developmental processes of: decentering, reversibility, conservation, serialization, classification, and elimination of egocentrism. The **Formal Operational** stage of cognitive development begins around eleven years of age (puberty) and continues into adulthood. The characteristics of this stage focus on the ability to use symbols and think abstractly.

Sperry Smith (2008) reports that children in the Preoperational stage experience problems with at least two perceptual concepts—**centration** and **conservation**.

1. **Centration**—Characterized by a child focusing only on one aspect of a situation or problem. For example, take two 5″ × 8″ cards and roll each into a tube, rolling one the short way and the other the long way. Tape them to make cylindrical containers. Fill each tube with beans to compare how much each holds. A preschool child might judge the quantity of beans in the tall cylinder to be more than the shorter based on their perception of tall and short.
2. **Conservation**—Understanding that quantity, length, or number of items is unrelated to the arrangement or appearance of the object or items. This limitation can affect children's ability to measure volume and to understand

the value of money. For example, children may think a nickel is worth more than a dime because the coin is larger, or that five nickels are more than a quarter.

During the Concrete Operational stage of cognitive development—second to seventh grades—children experience rapid growth in cognitive development. This stage is characterized by the ability to think logically about concrete objects or relationships. Some of the characteristics of children at this stage are as follows:

- **Decentering**—Where the child can take into account multiple aspects of a problem to solve it. Can form conclusion based on reason rather than perception;
- **Reversibility**—Where the child understands that the objects can be changed, then returned to their original state. Can determine that

  $4 + 4 = 8$ and $8 - 4 = 4$,
  is the original quantity.
- **Conservation**—Where the child understands that quantity, length, or number of items is unrelated to the arrangement or appearance of the object. Can discern that if water is transferred to a pitcher it will conserve the quantity and be equal to the other filled cup.
- **Seriation**—Where the child is able to arrange objects in an order according to size, shape, or any other attribute. Can arrange geometric forms by shape, size, color, and thickness of the form.
- **Classification**—Where the child can name and identify sets of objects according to appearance, size, or other characteristic. Can arrange objects based on characteristics.
- **Elimination of Egocentrism**—Where the child is able to view things from another's perspective. Can retell a story from another child's perspective.

Since Piaget completed his work, contemporary researchers (often referred to as neo-Piagetian and post-Piagetian researchers) found that Piaget had underestimated the abilities of children in the preschool and early elementary years. Even before the second or early third grade, some students develop more sophisticated thinking and reasoning skill, especially if they have had adequate instruction and opportunities to interact with adults and competent peers (Vygotsky, 1986). Children's intellectual development appears to proceed continuously, and their cognitive development is influenced by their culture and by instruction (Santrock, 2003). This relates to cognitively guided instruction (CGI) (Carpenter, Fennema, Franke, Levi, & Empson, 1999; Flavell, 1985; Kamii, 2000). The CGI model depends heavily on a well-developed structure of how children learn a given topic and on the ability of the teacher to assess the knowledge of each child and provide appropriate experiences.

Mathematics in Real-Life Situations

Mathematical concepts are an integral part of our daily life. Children should be encouraged to pay attention to daily activities and identify the mathematical principles used to perform the activity or the task. A simple visit to the local supermarket requires some level of mathematical development to communicate effectively. For instance, reading product labels requires an understanding of weights and measurements. It also requires knowledge of the standard and metric systems and the value of money. Without this kind of knowledge, it would be practically impossible to make intelligent decisions.

Consider the following situation:

> A consumer is trying to decide between two products—a kilogram of coffee for $3.99 or 2 pounds of the same coffee for $3.99. What item represents the best value?

In order to make this decision, the consumer must have an understanding of the standard and metric systems of measurement. Most consumers in the United States will probably go with 2 pounds because they are familiar with the standard system of measurement. However, this option is not the best value for the money because 1 kilogram is equivalent to 2.2 pounds. Parents can present this kind of problem to children and ask them to help in the decision-making process. When mathematics is used in real-life situations, it becomes more meaningful and easier to internalize.

Manipulatives in Mathematics

Children can benefit from group instruction and the use of concrete objects and manipulatives. Manipulatives can be use to provide "hands-on-learning" for kindergarten to high school students. Manipulatives enhance student understanding, enable students to have conversations that are grounded in a common model, and help students recognize and correct their own misconceptions in concept attainment. Manipulatives are an excellent way for students to develop self-verbalizing learning strategies. As they use the senses of sight, touch, and hearing, students should be encouraged to talk their way through each problem, either with peers or to themselves. Physical materials can model the situation and illuminate some of the aspects of the processes of various operations, such as multiplication and division. It is important that the concept is first understood by the student and that the manipulative is appropriate for the concept in order for the materials to be used in ways that make sense. Teachers have to ask good questions and listen to students explain their thinking to know whether they have abstracted the idea from the physical models.

Games are highly motivational for children in pre-kindergarten through grade 6. A simple game using dice can be used to teach counting, place value, and probability. Color tiles, unifix cubes, two-color counters, and pattern blocks can be used to teach sequencing, patterns, odd and even numbers, probability, and statistics. Children learn best when they can manipulate materials to check their understanding and link what they are learning to real-life situations. For example, they learn about fractions initially outside the school. Often they hear adults use fractions in various conversations:

- You can have half of my cookie.
- The dishwasher is less than half full.
- I need to buy two and a half yards of ribbon.
- My gas tank is half full.
- Do you have any quarter-inch plywood?
- The recipe calls for two-thirds of a cup of Rice Krispies.
- May I have half a pound of sliced turkey?

Numbers and fractions represent a challenge to elementary students. From their experiences, a number of ideas about fractions take shape informally in children's minds. They may have heard of one-half, one-fourth, and one-third of a unit—but not two-thirds or three-fourths. Therefore, their understanding may be incomplete and confused. Children think of "half" as any part of a whole, rather than one of two equal parts, and refer to one-half being larger than another. For example, they may say, "My half is bigger than yours." Additionally, they may not understand relationships, such as three-fourths of an inch is one-fourth less than one inch. Classroom instruction should build on children's previous experiences and focus within the context of real life before moving to the symbolic representations. Fractions may be taught using fraction kits, where students cut and label the pieces to relate the fractional notation to the concrete pieces and compare the sizes of fractional parts. They are able to see that $\frac{1}{4}$, for example, is larger than one-sixteenth, and they can measure to prove that two of the $\frac{1}{8}$ pieces are equivalent to $\frac{1}{4}$. Table 3–3 presents an analysis of fractions.

Use of Technology

As rapidly as technology is changing and improving, educators are having difficulty keeping up with those advances and how to use technology to improve instruction. Clearly changes need to be made in how schools acquire access to these new advances. These changes must be equitably implemented so that students who live in poverty have the same access to technology and challenging mathematics as their affluent peers. The newest advancements in hand-held computers present educators with both opportunities and responsibilities.

Digital videos provide opportunities for students to evaluate their own explanations of problem solutions. Students may present their videos and discuss similarities and differences in approaches to solving problems. These may be uploaded onto a website to allow for online discussions using discussion board tools, blogs, and various communication tools with

Table 3–3. Equivalent Fractions

<table>
<tr><td colspan="16">One Whole = $\frac{1}{1}$</td></tr>
<tr><td colspan="8">One-half = $\frac{1}{2}$</td><td colspan="8">One-half = $\frac{1}{2}$</td></tr>
<tr><td colspan="4">One-fourth = $\frac{1}{4}$</td><td colspan="4">One-fourth = $\frac{1}{4}$</td><td colspan="4">One-fourth = $\frac{1}{4}$</td><td colspan="4">One-fourth = $\frac{1}{4}$</td></tr>
<tr><td colspan="2">One-eighth = $\frac{1}{8}$</td><td colspan="2">$\frac{1}{8}$</td><td colspan="2">$\frac{1}{8}$</td><td colspan="2">$\frac{1}{8}$</td><td colspan="2">$\frac{1}{8}$</td><td colspan="2">$\frac{1}{8}$</td><td colspan="2">$\frac{1}{8}$</td><td colspan="2">$\frac{1}{8}$</td></tr>
<tr><td>$\frac{1}{16}$</td><td>$\frac{1}{16}$</td><td>$\frac{1}{16}$</td><td>$\frac{1}{16}$</td><td>$\frac{1}{16}$</td><td>$\frac{1}{16}$</td><td>$\frac{1}{16}$</td><td>$\frac{1}{16}$</td><td>$\frac{1}{16}$</td><td>$\frac{1}{16}$</td><td>$\frac{1}{16}$</td><td>$\frac{1}{16}$</td><td>$\frac{1}{16}$</td><td>$\frac{1}{16}$</td><td>$\frac{1}{16}$</td><td>$\frac{1}{16}$</td></tr>
</table>

other students. Students can develop effective presentations, online resources, wikis, and other projects for sharing with learners around the world. Additional digital presentation tools may help students to develop effective presentations that communicate mathematic ideas. Programs such as PowerPoint and HyperStudio allow students to integrate graphics, digital images and video, and text into their presentations.

Learning Environment

The Professional Standards for Teaching Mathematics (NCTM, 2007) presents six standards for the teaching of mathematics, organized under four categories: tasks, discourse, environment, and analysis. These are crucial in shaping what goes on in mathematics classrooms. These four strands are integrated and interdependent, and they include the following:

- TASKS are the projects, questions, problems, constructions, applications, and exercises in which students engage.
- DISCOURSE refers to the way of representing, thinking, talking, and agreeing and disagreeing that teachers and students use to engage in these tasks.
- ENVIRONMENT represents the setting for learning.
- ANALYSIS is the systematic reflection in which teachers engage.

The teacher of mathematics should create a learning environment that fosters the development of each student's mathematical ability, by doing the following:

- provide and structure the time necessary to explore sound mathematics and grapple with significant ideas and problems;
- use the physical space and materials in ways that facilitate the learning of mathematics;
- provide a context that encourages the development of mathematical skill and proficiency;
- Respect and value students' ideas, ways of thinking, and mathematical dispositions.

Included in the Professional Standards for Teaching Mathematics are five major shifts in the environment of mathematics classrooms from current practice to teaching for the empowerment of students. These major shift areas include:

1. Classrooms as mathematical communities—away from classrooms as simply a collection of individuals;
2. Logic and mathematical evidence as verification—away from the teacher as the sole authority for right answers;

3. Mathematical reasoning—away from merely memorizing procedures;
4. Problem solving—away from an emphasis on mechanistic answer-finding;
5. Connecting mathematics, its ideas, and its applications—away from mathematics as a body of isolated concepts and procedures.

Strengthening Mathematical Concepts

Using Manipulatives and a Variety of Tools

In addition to the manipulative used in mathematics, the typical classroom contains a variety of instructional materials (See Table 3–4) to support children in the learning process. Teachers should be

Table 3–4. Materials used in the Mathematics Classroom

Types of Manipulatives and Instructional Materials					
Grades K–1	Grade 2	Grade 3	Grade 4	Grade 5	Grades 6
Beads, string, sewing cards	Blocks	Base Ten Blocks	Geometric solids	Cuisenaire rods	Cuisenaire rods
Snap cubes, straws	Cubes	Tangrams	Geoboards	Virtual manipulative	Virtual manipulative
Color tiles	Chips	Pattern blocks	Calculators	Calculators	Calculators
Two-color counters	Measuring cups	Playing cards	Protractors	Graduated cylinders	Attribute logic block
Macaroni, beans, cereal, candy, raisins, crackers	Attribute Shapes	Scales: customary & metric	Tangrams	Timers	Algebra tiles
Buttons, sticks, stones, shells	Money models	Magnetic numbers, chalk boards	Pentominoes	Metric beaker set for volume	Video games
Paper Clips	Number lines	Spinners, dice	Graphing paper	Metric trundle wheel	Math software games
Toothpicks	Dominoes	Calendar	Fraction kit	Fraction tower cubes	iPods
Legos	Unifix cubes	Fractional shapes	Platform scale	Connecting cubes	Balance Metric weight set
Egg cartons	Clock faces	Games	Customary weight set	Board games	Computer/ internet
Teddy Bear counters	Ruler, yard stick, metric stick	Measuring tape	Metric weight set	Fraction tiles	Smart boards
Board games	Balance scales	0–99 Charts	Graphing boards	Geoboards	Digital cameras, camcorders
Pictographs	Linear graphs	Bar Graphs	Scatter plot graphs	Pie charts & graphs	Computer templates

encouraged to use these to make mathematics more engaging and meaningful to children.

The Texas Essential Knowledge and Skills (TEKS) Curriculum

The Texas Essential Knowledge and Skills (TEKS) is the state's required curriculum. The implementation of TEKS for Mathematics requires a well-balanced curriculum beginning in Kindergarten and continuing through grade 12 (See: TAC, Chapter 111—The provisions of §111.11 adopted to be effective September 1, 1998, 22 TexReg 7623.).

Pre-kindergarten content has been aligned with the TEKS and may be found at the Texas Education Agency, Pre-kindergarten Curriculum Guidelines (1999a) online at: *www.tea.state.tx.us/curriculum/early/prekguide.html*.

Both the TEKS and the Pre-kindergarten Curriculum Guidelines incorporate the principles and standards of the NCTM, which provide early experiences and exploration of number concepts using concrete objects to learn about one-to-one correspondence. In the first and second grade, students continue exploring number concepts and begin learning basic computation skills. In third through the fifth grades, they continue developing number concepts to include multiplication, division, fraction and decimal representations, geometric principles, and algebraic reasoning. Table 3-5 presents the focal points from Pre-kindergarten through grade 6.

Analysis of Teaching and Learning

The teacher of mathematics should engage in ongoing analysis of teaching and learning by doing the following:

- observing, listening to, and gathering other information about students to assess what they are learning;
- examining effects of the task, discourse, and learning environment on students' mathematical knowledge, skills, and dispositions.
- challenging and extending students' ideas;
- adapting or changing activities while teaching;
- making plans, both short- and long-range;
- describing and commenting on each student's learning to parents and administrators, as well as to the students themselves.

Making Connections with the Real World

The U.S. Department of Labor (2008–09) developed a list of the top professions that require a strong knowledge in mathematics. Some of the most prominent jobs are accountants and auditors, computer programmers, computer scientists, computer engineers and system analysts, economists and marketing research analysts, managers, mathematicians, operations research analysts, statisticians, and financial planners. The best way to link mathematics to real jobs or activities is to guide students to develop a list of jobs available in their community. For example, a unit about community helpers will yield a large list of occupations, such as nurses, physicians, sanitary workers, home builders, landscapers, plumbers, carpet and tile installers, among others. Teachers can assign readings about these professions and invite community sources to describe and demonstrate how they use mathematics in their profession. The interactive and concrete approach can easily present the need for mathematics in our daily lives.

One of the key challenges in promoting interest in mathematics is to convince children that mathematics plays an important role in their lives. Based on this assumption, teachers need to introduce mathematics concepts in a problem-solving format using real-life situations.

Using Thematic Units

Thematic instruction is the organization of curriculum content based on themes or topics. Thematic instruction integrates basic disciplines like reading, math, music, art, and science with the exploration of broad subjects like American Indians, Six Flags over Texas, state symbols, river systems in Texas, the rain forest, recycling resources, and so on. The selection

Table 3-5. Mathematics Curriculum: Number Concepts Strand for Pre-K–Grade 6

Grade Level	Numbers and Operations
Pre-K	1. Exploration of concrete models and materials, begins to arrange sets of concrete objects in one-to-one correspondence, count by ones to 10 or higher, by fives or higher, and combine, separate, and name "how many" concrete objects. 2. Begin to recognize and describe the concept of zero (meaning there are none), to identify first and last in a series, to compare the numbers of concrete objects using language (e.g., "same" or "equal," "one more," "more than," or "less than").
Kindergarten	1. Uses whole number concepts to describe how many objects are in a set (through 20) using verbal and symbolic descriptions, uses sets of concrete objects to represent quantities given in verbal or written form (through 20), uses one-to-one correspondence and language such as more than, same number as, or two less than to describe relative sizes of sets of concrete objects, and names the ordinal positions in a sequence such as first, second, third, etc. 2. Begins to demonstrate part of and whole with real objects. 3. Sorts to explore numbers, uses patterns, and able to model and create addition and subtraction problems in real situations with concrete objects.
First	1. Ability to create sets of tens and ones using concrete objects to describe, compare, and order whole numbers, reads and writes numbers to 99 to describe sets of concrete objects using sets of concrete objects and pictorial models. 2. Separates a whole into two, three, or four equal parts and use appropriate language to describe the parts. 3. Models and creates addition and subtraction problem situations with concrete objects and writes corresponding number sentences. 4. Identifies individual coins by name and value and describes relationships among them.
Second	1. Uses concrete models of hundreds, tens, and ones to represent a given whole number (up to 999) in various ways. Begins to use place value to read, write, and describe the value of whole numbers to 999, uses models to compare and order whole numbers to 999, and records the comparisons using numbers and symbols (<, =, >). 2. Uses concrete models to represent and name fractional parts of a whole object (with denominators of 12 or less). 3. Models addition and subtraction of two-digit numbers with objects, pictures, words, and numbers, solve problems with and without regrouping, and is able to recall and apply basic addition and subtraction facts (to 18). 4. Determines the value of a collection of coins up to one dollar and describes how the cent symbol, dollar symbol, and the decimal point are used to name the value of a collection of coins.

(continued)

Table 3-5. *(Continued)*

Grade Level	Numbers and Operations
Third	1. Uses place value to read, write (in symbols and words), and describes the value of whole numbers and compares and orders whole numbers through 9,999. 2. Uses fraction names and symbols to describe fractional parts of whole objects or sets of objects and compares fractional parts of whole objects or sets of objects in a problem situation using concrete models. 3. Selects addition or subtraction and uses the operation to solve problems involving whole numbers through 999. 4. Applies multiplication facts through 12 by using concrete models and objects (up to two digits times one digit), uses models to solve division problems, and number sentences.
Fourth	1. Uses place value to read, write, compare, and order: whole numbers through 999,999,999 and decimals involving tenths and hundredths, including money, using concrete objects and pictorial models. 2. Uses concrete objects and pictorial models to generate equivalent fractions. 3. Uses multiplication to solve problems (no more than two digits, times two digits) and uses division to solve problems (no more than one-digit divisors and three-digit dividends). 4. Uses strategies, including rounding and compatible numbers to estimate solutions to addition, subtraction, multiplication, and division problems.
Fifth	1. Uses place value to read, write, compare, and order whole numbers through 999,999,999,999 and decimals through the thousandths place. 2. Identifies common factors of a set of whole numbers, uses multiplication to solve problems involving whole numbers (no more than three digits times two digits) and uses division to solve problems involving whole numbers (no more than two-digit divisors and three-digit dividends), including solutions with a remainder.
Sixth	1. Compares and orders non-negative rational numbers, generates equivalent forms of rational numbers including whole numbers, fractions, and decimals, uses integers to represent real-life situations. 2. Able to write prime factorizations using exponents, identifies factors of a positive integer, common factors, and the greatest common factor of a set of positive integers.

of the theme can be done schoolwide, by grade, or by individual teacher.

Thematic planning provides opportunities for the students to hear similar information in various instructional segments and from a variety of sources. Additionally, it allows students opportunities to apply cognitive processes and creativity through content-area instruction based on real-life situations.

Planning and Organization of Thematic Units

There are several important elements that teachers must consider when planning thematic units. The basic steps are as follows (Fredericks, Blake-Kline, and Kristo, 1997).

Selecting the Theme of Interest to Students: "The Solar System"

Designing the Integrated Curriculum: using (TEKS) as the guiding force—identify the key objectives to involve each content area and the materials needed to implement instruction.

Gathering Materials for the Unit

- The materials should focus on objectives for each of the content areas.
- Materials should include narratives, expositions, drama, poems, and a variety of materials and resources books, magazines, newspapers, movies, Internet materials, videotapes, and audiotapes.
- Materials should also represent a range of thinking abilities and literacy development, including materials written in a language other than English.
- Materials should represent the home as well as the school culture and language of the students.

Designing Instruction: ensure that instruction is developmentally appropriate and that knowledge and skills are integrated throughout the content areas used in the thematic unit.

Arranging Thematic Materials and Activities

Traditionally, thematic units are organized into three main segments—introduction to the unit, presentation of the content, and a closing activity. The opening activity is designed to motivate children and to get them interested in the theme. Children are exposed to the goals and the steps in the presentation of the theme. The presentation of the content is done through various coordinated lessons and activities. The closing activity is designed to review and pull together the concepts learned and to celebrate the mastery of the content.

Types of Questioning Strategies

It should be clear for all teachers to use questions that do not have simple yes/no answers. Questions should focus students' thinking, require them to think critically, and help them to "clarify or justify their ideas orally and in writing." Good questions "elicit language and challenge each student's thinking" (NCTM, 2000, p. 35). Teachers need to model these questioning strategies. See the following chart with the NCTM proposed five types of questions strategies teacher should use.

Using Formal and Informal Assessment

The Texas Assessment of Knowledge and Skills (TAKS) and, now, the State of Texas Assessments of Academic Readiness (STAAR) is the state assessment for reading, math, writing, science, and social studies. The TAKS test evaluates student learning based on the state-required curriculum, the Texas Essential Knowledge and Skills. It is a "high-stakes" testing system that provides accountability for districts, schools, administrators, teachers, and students. By law, Texas students must pass the TAKS test to be promoted at certain grade levels and graduate from high school.

Table 3-6. Questioning Strategies for Mathematics Discourse

The NCTM Professional Standards propose five types of questions that teachers should ask to elicit justification and reasoning, in the following:

Category 1—Questions that help students learn how to make learning math meaningful.

"Do you agree? Disagree with the correct answer?"

"Does anyone use a different strategy to get the correct answer, explain it?"

Category 2—Questions that help students to become self-reliant and determine whether something is mathematically correct.

"Does that make sense?"

"Tell me what makes this a reasonable solution to the task?"

Category 3—Questions that help students learn to reason mathematically.

"What have you tried that has worked or not worked?"

"How could you explain this in your own words?"

Category 4—Questions that help students learn to solve problems.

"What would happen if...?"

"What would happen if not...?"

"What pattern do you see, and how would you explain your answer?"

Category 5—Questions that relate to helping students connect mathematics, its ideas, and its applications.

"Have we solved a problem that is similar to this one?"

"Can you write another problem like this one?"

Source: Charles Al. Dana Center, Mathematics TEKS Toolkit. UT-Austin. Available online at: *http://www.utdanacenter.org/mathtoolkit/support/questioning.php*.

Competency 018 (Number Concepts and Operations)

The teacher understands concepts related to numbers, operations and algorithms, and the properties of numbers.

Number Concepts and Algorithms

One of the key challenges in mathematics education is the teaching of technical vocabulary and concepts. Teachers as well as students need to have an understanding of the key terms used in mathematics to communicate effectively in the classroom. An algorithm is an established and well-defined step-by-step problem solving method used to achieve a desired mathematical result. A summary of key mathematical terms and concepts follows.

Integers

An integer is a whole number that includes all positive and negative numbers, including zero. This may be represented on a number line that extends in both directions from 0. You might have –45, –450,000, 0, 234, or 78,306. Integers do not include decimals or fractions. The set of integers: {..., –6, –5, –4, –3, –2, –1, 0, 1, 2, 3, 4, 5, 6...}

You can represent many real-life situations with integers.

Natural Numbers

A natural number is a positive integer or a non-negative integer. There is a small difference because non-negative integers also include "0." A list of positive integers would only include whole numbers, but not zero. Natural numbers include 1, 2, 3, 4, 5 ... ∞ (Note: ∞ is the symbol for infinity). They are all whole numbers. Natural numbers do not include negative numbers, fractions, or decimals.

Rational Numbers

A number that can be expressed as a ratio or quotient of two non-zero integers is known as a rational number. Rational numbers can be expressed as common fractions or decimals, such as $\frac{3}{5}$ or 0.6. Finite decimals, repeating decimals, mixed numbers, and whole numbers are all rational numbers. Non-repeating decimals cannot be expressed in this way, and are said to be irrational.

Irrational Numbers

An irrational number is a number that cannot be represented as an exact ratio of two integers. The decimal form of the number never terminates and never repeats. Examples: The square root of 2 ($\sqrt{2}$) or Pi (π).

Real Numbers

A real number describes any number that is positive, negative, or zero and is used to measure continuous quantities. A real number also includes numbers, which have decimal representations, even those with infinite decimal sequences (e.g., Pi (π)).

Exponential Notation

Exponential notation is a symbolic way of showing how many times a number or variable is used as a factor. In the notation 5^3, the exponent 3 shows that 5 is a factor used three times; that is calculated in the following way: $5^3 = 5 \times 5 \times 5 = 125$.

Scientific Notation

Scientific notation is a form of writing a number as the product of a power of 10 and a decimal number greater than or equal to 1 and less than 10.

Example: $2{,}400{,}000 = 2.4 \times 10^6$,
$240.2 = 2.402 \times 10^2$,
$0.0024 = 2.4 \times 10^{-3}$

Absolute Value

The absolute value is the number's distance from zero on the number line. This action ignores the + or – sign of a number. $|x|$ is the graphic used to describe the action of absolute value. Example: $|-5| = 5$ or $|5| = 5$.

Expanded Form

The expanded form of an algebraic expression is the equivalent expression without parentheses, for example the expanded form of $(a + b)^2$ is $a^2 + 2ab$

$+ b^2$. A way to write numbers that shows the place value of each digit, for example: 263 = 200 + 60 + 3 or 263 which is equal to 2 hundreds, 6 tens, and 3 ones.

Expanded Notation

Expanded notation is showing place value by multiplying each digit in a number by the appropriate power of 10.

Example: $523 = 5 \times 100 + 2 \times 10 + 3 \times 1$ or
$5 \times 10^2 + 2 \times 10^1 + 3 \times 10^0$

Estimating

Estimating is generally done by rounding the numbers to the nearest decimal place required for accuracy. For example, a sum 23 + 35 can be solved easily by rounding 23 to 20 and 35 to 40 to obtain the estimation 20 + 40 = 60.

Place Values

Place Values are the basic foundation for understanding mathematic computation. A simple number like 1984 can be explained based on the positions of the numbers in the value scale. See the example in Table 3-7.

Table 3–7.
Place Value

Thousand	Hundred	Ten	One
1000	900	80	4
1	9	8	4

Fractions, Decimals, and Percentages

A fraction is a number that represents part of a whole, part of a set, or a quotient in the form $\frac{a}{b}$ which can be read as a divided by b.

Finding Equivalent Fractions or Simplification of Fractions

To identify an equivalent fraction, follow these steps using the example $\frac{2}{4}$:

- Find a number that can be divided evenly into the numerator and the denominator. For example, in the fraction $\frac{2}{4}$, the number 2 can be divided evenly into (2) and (4).
- Divide the numerator and denominator by 2 and get the result: $\frac{2}{4} = \frac{1}{2}$

Adding and Subtracting Homogeneous Fractions

When adding or subtracting fractions with the same denominator (homogeneous fractions), add or subtract the numerators—the denominator remains the same, for example: $\frac{2}{5} + \frac{1}{5} = \frac{3}{5}$; $\frac{7}{9} - \frac{5}{9} = \frac{2}{9}$.

Changing Improper Fractions to Mixed Numbers

To change an improper fraction, like $\frac{5}{2}$, to a mixed number, divide the numerator by the denominator and represent the remainder as a fraction, for example: $2\frac{1}{2}$.

$$\frac{5}{2} = 2\overline{)5} \quad 2\frac{1}{2}$$
$$\underline{-4}$$
$$1$$

Adding and Subtracting Mixed Numbers

To add and subtract mixed numbers, see the examples and follow the rule provided.

$$\begin{array}{r} 2\frac{5}{10} \\ +1\frac{4}{10} \\ \hline 3\frac{9}{10} \end{array} \qquad \begin{array}{r} 7\frac{9}{12} \\ -5\frac{4}{12} \\ \hline 2\frac{5}{12} \end{array}$$

Add or subtract the fractions, then add or subtract the whole numbers. "Borrow" from the whole numbers if necessary to complete the operation as needed.

Changing Mixed Numbers to Fractions

To change a mixed number, multiply the denominator by the whole number; then add the result to the numerator to obtain the new numerator.

$$2\frac{3}{4}=\frac{2\times4+3}{4}=\frac{8+3}{4}=\frac{11}{4}$$

Adding Fractions with Different Denominators

To work with these kinds of fractions, it is necessary to rename fractions using a common denominator. For example, to rename the fractions $\frac{1}{2}$ and $\frac{2}{3}$, it is necessary to find a common denominator between them. In this case the lowest common denominator is 6, because both of the original denominators are factors of 6. That is, $\frac{1}{2}$ can be written as $\frac{3}{6}$, and $\frac{2}{3}$ can be written as $\frac{4}{6}$. $\frac{3}{6}$ and $\frac{4}{6}$ now can be added: $\frac{7}{6}$

Multiplying Fractions

Multiplying fractions involves multiplying the numerator together and the denominators together (horizontally), then simplifying the product.

$$\frac{2}{3}\times\frac{3}{4}=\frac{6}{12}=\frac{6\times1}{6\times2}=\frac{1}{2}$$

If the numbers to be multiplied are mixed fractions, first rewrite them as "improper" fractions like $\frac{6}{2}$ and then proceed to multiply as described earlier.

Dividing Fractions

To perform this operation, invert the second fraction (the one doing the dividing) and multiply the numbers as described earlier. In the case of $\frac{1}{5}$ divided by $\frac{3}{8}$, follow these steps: Invert the second fraction $\frac{3}{8}$ to $\frac{8}{3}$. Proceed to multiply.

$$\frac{1}{5}\div\frac{3}{8}=\frac{1}{5}\times\frac{8}{3}=\frac{8}{15}$$

Decimal Numbers

Decimal numbers are fractional numbers that are written using base ten. A mixed decimal number has a whole number part as well, for example: 0.28 is a decimal number and 3.9 is a mixed decimal number.

Adding and Subtracting Decimals

Decimal numbers are fractions whose denominators are powers of 10 (i.e., 10, 100, 1000, and so forth). For example: 0.098 is equivalent to $\frac{98}{1000}$. To add or subtract decimal numbers, arrange them vertically, aligning decimal points then add or subtract as for whole numbers. See the following example.

$$\begin{array}{r} 23.5 \\ \underline{+20.4} \\ 43.9 \end{array}$$

The decimal point remains in the same location.

Multiplying Decimals

Multiplication of decimals does not require aligning decimal points; the numbers can be arranged vertically, with right justification. The numbers can then be multiplied as if they were whole numbers. The numbers of digits to the right of the decimal point in the product should be equal to the sum of the number of digits to the right of the decimal point in the two factors.

$$\begin{array}{r} 1.25 \\ \underline{\times\ 0.6} \\ 0.750 \end{array}$$

Count the number to the right of the decimal and place it accordingly.

Dividing Decimals

Division of decimals is done like traditional whole number division. The number of digits to the right of the decimal point in the divisor is how far the decimal point in the answer (quotient) should be moved to the right.

$$0.3\overline{)1.44} = 3\overline{)14.4}\ \ 4.8$$

Percent

Percent is another way of expressing a fractional number. Percent always expresses a fractional number in terms of $\frac{1}{100}$ or 0.01's. Percents use the "%" symbol (e.g., 40 parts out of 100 is 40%).

$$100\% = \frac{100}{100} = 1.0$$

$$25\% = \frac{25}{100} = 0.25$$

As shown in these examples, a percent is easily converted to a common fraction or a decimal fraction. To convert a decimal to a common fraction, place the percent in the numerator and use 100 as the denominator (simplify as necessary). To convert a percent to a decimal fraction, divide the percent by 100, or move the decimal point two places to the left.

$$25\% = \frac{25}{100} = \frac{1}{4} \text{ and } 25\% = 0.25$$

To convert a common fraction to a percent, follow this procedure: 1) Carry out the division of the numerator by the denominator of the fraction, and 2) round the result to the hundredths decimal place. To convert the decimal to a percentage, move the decimal point two places to the right (adding 0's as placeholders, if needed) and round as necessary.

$$\frac{1}{4} = 1 \div 4 = \frac{25}{100} = 0.25 = 25\%$$

$$\frac{2}{7} = 2 \div 7 = 0.286 \approx 29\%$$

If you wish to find the percentage of a known quantity, change the percent to a common fraction or a decimal fraction, and multiply the fraction times the quantity. The percentage is expressed in the same units as the known quantity. For example, to find 25% of 360 books, change 25% to 0.25 and multiply times 360, as follows: $0.25 \times 360 = 90$. The result is 90 books. (Note: The known quantity is the base, the percent is the rate, and the result is the percentage.)

Number Theory

Teacher candidates have to have a solid command of basic number theory. Some of the elements required for elements covered in the EC-6 curricula are discussed next:

Prime Factorization

You can use exponents to write the prime factorization of a number. Every composite number can be written as a product of prime numbers. This is called the prime factorization of the number. When a factor is repeated in a prime factorization, express the repeated factor using an exponent. A factor tree can also help you find the prime factorization of a composite number. It does not matter which factor pair you start with, as long as you continue factoring until you have only prime numbers. See example from 6th grade TAKS Exam study guide (TEA, 2009b) available online at: *http://ritter.tea.state.tx.us/student.assessment/resources/guides/study/G6MathE-SG.pdf.*

What is the prime factorization of 48 using exponents?

- $48 = 3 \times 16$
- $48 = 3 \times 2 \times 8$
- $48 = 3 \times 2 \times 2 \times 4$
- $48 = 3 \times 2 \times 2 \times 2 \times 2$

The prime factorization of 48 is 3×2^4.

The exponent 4 shows how many times the base number 2 is used as a factor. The factor 3 is used only once. It has an exponent of 1. Exponents of 1 do not need to be written because they are implied. Prime factorizations are usually written in order from least to greatest base number. The prime factorization of 48 can also be written $2^4 \times 3$.

Greatest Common Divisor (GCD)

The greatest common divisor (GCD) of two or more non-zero integers is the largest positive integer that divides into the numbers without producing a remainder. This is useful for simplifying fractions into their lowest terms, for example: GCD (42, 56) = 14.

$$\frac{42}{56}=\frac{3\times14}{4\times14}=\frac{3}{4}.$$

Although 42 and 56 are divisible by larger numbers (21 and 28, respectively), the largest number, which is a factor of both 42 and 56, is 14.

Common Multiple

A common multiple is a whole number that is a multiple of two or more given numbers, for example: The common multiples of 2, 3, and 4 are 12, 24, 36, 48 . . .

Composite Number

A number greater than zero which is divisible by at least one other number besides one (1) and itself resulting in an integer (i.e., it has at least 3 factors). For example: 9 is a composite number because it has three factors: 1, 3, and 9.

Basic Operations

Some of the basic operations covered in the EC-6 Curricula are discussed below.

Addition

Addition is the mathematical operation of combining two or more numbers into a sum. Addition in mathematics refers to the process of combining two or more digits into one number. In addition of whole numbers, the key element is to align the numbers based on place value—ones, tens, hundreds, thousands, and so forth. Following the alignment, proceed to add beginning with the ones—in a right to left progression.

$$\begin{array}{r} 25 \\ +32 \\ \hline 57 \end{array}$$

Step 1: Add the numbers in the ones place (5 + 2 = 7).

Step 2: Add the numbers in the tens place (2 + 3 = 5).

Subtraction

Subtraction is the process/operation of removing objects from a larger group, or finding parts of a whole. It is the opposite of addition and/or finding parts of a whole. Subtraction is indicated by the minus sign (–). When a number is subtracted from another number, the resulting number is smaller than the minuend. The minuend is the quantity from which the subtrahend is deducted in subtraction. The difference is the result of the subtraction, as in the following:

> From a group of 25 cars, 20 were sold. How many are left?

The child might know the operation but may not understand that the word "left" in the problem calls for subtraction. Teachers need to develop a list of key words linked to each of the four basic operations.

See the following operation.

$$\begin{array}{rl} 25 & \text{(minuend)} \\ -\ 20 & \text{(subtrahend)} \\ \hline 05 & \text{(remainder or difference)} \end{array}$$

Step 1: Beginning with the ones, subtract the bottom numbers from the top numbers.

Step 2: Subtract the tens using the same process to get the results.

Like addition, subtraction is a process in which children must see their learning task as one of making sense of whatever they are studying. It is not appropriate to teach children how to do a procedure without teaching them how to reason. Students should not be expected to do things by rote or be made to say things they do not honestly understand. Additionally, the complexity of the language can create problems for all children, especially for ELLs. For example, some common phrases used in forming subtraction word problems include: (1) How many are left or left over? (2) How many more are needed? (3) How many less or fewer? (4) How many more than? (5) How many would you have if a half were subtracted? Words and phrases used for explaining subtraction include: Minus, take away, decrease, reduce, deduct, remove, less than, and how many do you need to take away to get a certain number.

Children need to make sense of the procedure. The most obvious message to a child is that addition and subtraction require that you follow the "rules." Teaching "what to do" in mathematics is a widespread practice in the classroom. However, it is important to understand that teaching procedures and teaching procedures in relation to their meaning are two very different approaches to teaching mathematics. Have children describe their thinking processes and explain why their answers make sense. When children understand why, their understanding and skills can be applied more easily to new tasks.

Multiplication

Multiplication is a mathematical operation of combining groups of equal amounts; and may be described as repeated addition and/or the inverse of division. Traditionally, multiplication requires students to memorize the multiplication facts and develop computation facility. After memorizing all the "times tables," children learn to multiply with paper and pencil, first practicing with one-digit multipliers (24 × 5 = ___) and progressing to two-digit and three-digit multipliers, etc. Word problems provide a way for children to being applying the concepts of multiplication in various situations. Example of the steps in the process, include the following example:

$$\begin{array}{rl} 95 & \text{(factor)} \\ \underline{\times\ 7} & \text{(factor)} \\ 665 & \text{(product)} \end{array}$$

Step 1: Multiply 7 × 5 = 35.

Step 2: Since the number has more than one digit (i.e., 3 tens and 5 ones), place the 3 at the top of the tens column and the 5 in the ones column.

Step 3: Multiply the digit in the tens place (9) 7 × 9 = 63.

Step 4: Add the 63 to the 3 placed in the tens place; this equals 66.

Step 5: Place the 66 on the left of the ones to obtain the final result is 665.

Teachers should link multiplication to real-world contexts. Having children explore with groups of objects helps children link the idea of multiplication as repeated addition. Children need to interact with the concept of multiplication pictorially by drawing sets of objects, symbolically by writing the multiplication sentences (4 × 6 = 24), and verbally by reading the sentences (4 sets of 6 equals 24; 4 groups of 6 equals 24; and/or 4 times 6 equals 24). Children need opportunities to see mathematics in their daily lives, not as existing only in the classrooms or on the pages of their textbooks.

Division

Division is a mathematical operation involving two numbers that tells how many groups there are or how many are in each group. The symbol for division is ÷ or /.

$$\begin{array}{r} 7\ \text{R2} \\ 8\overline{)58} \end{array}$$

Step 1: Place the divisor outside the bracket on the left-hand side and the dividend inside the bracket.

Step 2: Examine the first digit of the dividend. If this is smaller than the divisor, then take both numbers of the dividend.

Step 3: Identify how many times the divisor (8) can fit into the dividend (58).

Step 4: Place the result on top of the bracket (i.e., 7).

Step 5: Multiply the quotient (7) with the divisor (8)–56.

Step 6: Subtract 56 from 58 to identify a possible remainder.

Step 7: Place the remainder on the quotient (i.e., R2).

Counting Techniques for Solving Problems

Students use counting techniques to solve mathematic problems. Some of the techniques are presented next.

- Use networks, traceable paths, tree diagrams, Venn diagrams, and other pictorial representations to find the number of outcomes in a problem situation. Example: In a motel there are 4 different elevators that go from Joan's room to the pool and 3 different doors to the pool area. Use a tree diagram to show how many different ways Joan can get from her room to the pool.

- Use the fundamental counting principle to find the number of outcomes in a problem situation. Example: You are getting dressed one morning when you realize that you have far too many choices. You have 6 shirts to choose from, 4 pairs of jeans, and 3 pairs of shoes. Ignoring color coordination, construct a tree diagram or other pictorial representation to show how many different outfits you could assemble.
- Use combinatorial reasoning to solve problems. Example: You know that your locker combination contains the numbers 2, 4, 6, and 8, but you have forgotten the order in which they occur. What is the maximum number of combinations you need to try before your locker opens?
- Use counting techniques to solve probability problems. Example: In the last example, what is the probability that your locker opens with the first combination you try?
- Use simulations to solve counting and probability problems. Example: A panel of 12 jurors was selected from a large pool that was 70% male and 30% female. The jury turned out to be 11 men and 1 woman. Suspecting gender bias, the defense attorneys asked how likely is it that this situation, or worse, would occur purely by chance. Simulate this situation using a random number generator to select 12 numbers, letting 0, 1, and 2 represent women and 3, 4, 5, 6, 7, 8, and 9 represent men. Note the number of times that 11 or 12 men are chosen.

Order of Operations

Students may first learn the distributive property when they are learning order of operations. The distributive property is expressed in math terms as the following equation: $a\ (b + c) = ab + ac$. You can read this as the product of a and $(b + c)$ is equal to the sum of a times b and a times c. When you're looking at an equation like this, you can see that the multiplication part distributes evenly to all the numbers within the parentheses. It would be incorrect to multiply ab and just add c, or to multiply ac and add b. The distributive property reminds us that everything within the parentheses needs to be multiplied by the outside number.

In mathematics, we encounter many problems in which the solution involves a series of calculations. An arithmetic expression is evaluated by following these ordered steps: (1) simplify within grouping symbols such as parentheses or brackets, starting with the innermost; (2) apply exponents—powers and roots; (3) perform all multiplications and divisions in order from left to right; (4) perform all additions and subtractions in order from left to right.

For example: What is the correct answer to $3 + 2 \times 6 = n$?

Should we go "left to right" and just do the + first and get 30, or do we do the multiplication first and get 15? In order to avoid confusion and get the correct answer, mathematicians decided long ago that all calculations should be done in the same order. You may have learned the order of operations as being: *Please Excuse My Dear Aunt Sally*! The words in this sentence stand for Parentheses, Exponentiation, Multiplication, Division, Addition, and Subtraction (PEMDAS). So what is the correct answer for our problem? The order of operations would say that in the absence of parentheses, you would multiply 2 by 6 first, and then add 3. So, the answer would be 15. If you were to add $3 + 2 = 5$, then multiply 5×6 that would be 30, a very different answer!

Front-End Estimation

Estimation is used to make an approximation that is still close enough to be useful. When using front-end estimation, use the leading or the left-most digit to make an estimate, for example: Estimate the sum of 594, 32, and 221.

An initial estimate would be $600 + 0 + 200 = 800$.

Rounding Numbers

Rounding may be used to estimate a sum, difference, or product and to make mental approximations.

This is done by rounding all the numbers first to nearest ten or hundred and then performing the operation. The rules for rounding are:

- If the digit is 0, 1, 2, 3, or 4, round down.
- If the digit is 5, 6, 7, 8, or 9, round up.

For example, in addition, add in this way by rounding up or down: 532 + 385 + 57 = 500 + 400 + 60 = 960. The result is less precise, but easier to perform mentally in most cases. This example is sometimes referred to front-end estimation using the leading, or left-most digit to make an estimate quickly and easily.

Rounding may also be used to reduce the number of digits in a number. The term "digit" in mathematics is a number symbol (e.g., 1, 2, or 3) used in numerals to represent numbers (these are real numbers or integers) in positional numeral systems. In this case, the purpose for rounding is to have fewer digits in the answer when dividing numbers with remainders. For example, if we are dividing a 20 cm long wire into 3 equal pieces, we would divide 20 by 3 to get the length of each piece. This example would be calculated in the following manner:

$$\frac{20}{3} = 6.6666666666666666\ldots$$

The 6 repeats an infinite number of times. This is known as a repeating decimal. Typically, we would round the answer based on the required number of decimal places. By "decimal places" we refer to the number of digits to the right of the decimal point. Usually rounding to the tenths or hundredths place is sufficient. We could round the answer (6.666…) to the nearest hundredths place. In our example, 6.666…, the next digit in the thousandths place is 6, so we would round up, giving 6.67 as the desired answer.

Repeating Decimal

A decimal in which one or more digits repeat infinitely, for example: 0.3333... or $0.\overline{3}$ (with line over the 3) and 5.27272… or $5.\overline{27}$.

Competency 019 (Patterns and Algebra)

The teacher understands concepts related to patterns, relations, functions, and algebraic reasoning.

Numbers and Their Properties

Numbers have basic properties that can help simplify mathematics problem solving and reasoning skills. Some of these are:

Commutative Property

The order of the addends or factors does not change the result.

$a + b = b + a$ and $a \times b = b \times a$

Addition: $6 + 8 = 14$ is the same as $8 + 6 = 14$

Multiplication: $5 \times 8 = 40$ is the same as $8 \times 5 = 40$

Associative Property of Multiplication and Addition

The order of the addends or product will not change the sum or the product.

$(a + b) + c = a + (b + c)$ and
$(a \times b) \times c = a \times (b \times c)$

Addition: $(2 + 3) + 5 = 10, 2 + (3 + 5) = 10$

Multiplication: $(2 \times 3) \times 5 = 30, 2 \times (3 \times 5) = 30$

Property of Zero

The sum of a number and zero is the number itself, and the product of a number and zero is zero.

Addition: $8 + 0 = 8$

Multiplication: $8 \times 0 = 0$

Distributive Property

You can add and then multiply or multiply then add.

$a(b + c) = (a \times b) + (a \times c)$

$8(5 + 2) = (8 \times 5) + (8 \times 2) = 56$

Linear and Nonlinear Functional Relationships

Many functions can be represented by pairs of numbers. When the graph of those pairs results in points lying on a straight line, a function it is said to be linear. When not on a line, the function is nonlinear.

A real-valued function for a real variable is a rule that assigns to each real number x in a specified set of numbers, called the domain of f, a single real number $f(x)$. The variable x is called the independent variable. If $y = f(x)$ we call y the dependent variable. A function can be specified in the following ways: 1) numerically by the means of a table, 2) algebraically by means of a formula, or 3) graphically by means of a graph. A numerical specified function is listed in Table 3–8:

Table 3–8.
Numerical Specified Function

x	0	1	2	3
$f(x)$	3.01	–1.03	2.22	0.01

Then, $f(0)$ is the value of the function when $x = 0$. From the table, we may have the following values: $f(0) = 3.01$ and $f(1) = -1.03$

An algebraically specified function: Suppose you had function f specified by $f(x) = 3x^2 - 4x + 1$. Then:

$f(x) = 3x^2 - 4x + 1$ (Substitute 2 for x)
$f(2) = 3(2)^2 - 4(2) + 1$

The answer: $f(2) = 12 - 8 + 1$, this would $= 5$

$f(-1) = 3(-1)^2 - 4(-1) + 1$ (Substitute –1 for x)
$= 3 + 4 + 1$, this would $= 8$

A linear function is one whose graph is a straight line (that is why it is called "linear"). A linear function is one of the most fundamental and important relationship concepts as a foundation for advanced mathematics. A linear function is one which always satisfies the following: $f(x + y) = f(x) + f(y)$ and $f(\alpha x) = \alpha f(x)$. In this definition, x and y are input variables and α is a constant.

For example: Consider the function $f(x) = 2x$. Assuming there are two input values ($x = a + b$), the function now becomes $f(x) = f(a + b) = 2(a + b) = 2a + 2b$. We see that if we substitute ($x = a$ and then $x = b$) we obtain $f(a) = 2a$ and $f(b) = 2b$ where we see that $f(a + b) = f(a) + f(b)$ and satisfies the first rule. Checking the second constraint we have $f(\alpha x) = 2\alpha x$ which is equivalent to $\alpha f(x) = \alpha 2x$ due to the associative/commutative properties of multiplication.

A non-linear function is one that does not satisfy the constraints stated previously. For example, the function $f(x) = x^2$ is non-linear because $f(a + b) = (a + b)^2 = a^2 + 2ab + b^2$ is not equal to $f(a) + f(b) = a^2 + b^2$.

Algebraic Pattern

An algebraic pattern is a set of numbers and/or variables in a specific order that form a pattern. An example would be a chart showing the distance in feet if Max travels on his bicycle a different number of seconds. Given the chart below, what is one way to find the number of feet Max travels on his bicycle in 1 second?

# of seconds	6	8	9
# of feet	90	120	135

First, students need to be able to understand the algebraic pattern presented in the chart and how the numbers are listed. Students should divide the number of feet by the number of seconds to find the correct answer. However, in this problem the answer 15 does not answer the test question. Students need to be able to tell which operation they used to derive the answer to the question.

Algebraic Expression

An algebraic expression is a mathematical phrase that is written using one or more variables and constants, but which does not contain a relation symbol (e.g., $5y + 8$).

A variable or an unknown is a letter that stands for a number in an algebraic expression.

Coefficients are the numbers that precede the variable to give the quantity of the variable in the expression. Algebraic expressions are comprised of terms, or groupings of variables and numbers. An

Function

Functions can be used to understand how one quantity varies in relation to (is a function of) changes in the second quantity. For example, there is a functional relationship between the price per pound of a particular type of meat and the total amount paid for ten pounds of that type of meat. You can see that values of one variable determine the values of another.

Patterns

A pattern can be a design (geometric) or sequence (numeric or algebraic) that is predictable because some aspect of it repeats. Examples: Numeric pattern that adds increments of 3's: 4, 7, 10, 13... Algebraic pattern that adds one to the multiple: x, x2, x3, ... An example is when students are asked to identify patterns using fact families, as in the following:

Example from TAKS Objective 2

(3.6) (C) identify patterns in related multiplication and division sentences (fact families) such as $2 \times 3 = 6$, $3 \times 2 = 6$, $6 \div 2 = 3$, $6 \div 3 = 2$.

This student expectation lists only one fact family: *such as* $2 \times 3 = 6$, $3 \times 2 = 6$, $6 \div 2 = 3$, $6 \div 3 = 2$

However, there are many other fact families students may use to identify patterns in multiplication and division sentences.

Source: Grade 3 TAKS Mathematics Information Booklet, p. 11

algebraic expression with one term is called a monomial; with two terms, a binomial; with three terms, a trinomial; with more than one term, a polynomial.

For example, $2ab - cd$ is a binomial algebraic expression with variables a, b, c, and d, and terms $2ab$ and $(-cd)$. 2 is the coefficient of ab and -1 is the coefficient of cd.

$x^2 + 3y - 1$ is a trinomial algebraic expression using the variables x and y, and terms x^2, $3y$, and (-1); $z(x - 1) + uv - wy - 2$ is a polynomial with variables z, x, u, v, w, and y, and terms $z(x - 1)$, uv, $(-wy)$, and (-2).

Operations with algebraic expressions are governed by various rules and conventions.

- In addition and subtraction, only like algebraic terms (same exponent) can be added or subtracted to produce a simpler expressions. For example, $2x^3$ and $3x^3$ can be added together to get $5x^3$, because the terms are like terms; they both have a base of x^3. You cannot add, say, $7m^3$ and $6m^2$ because they are unlike bases. (Note: To evaluate an algebraic expression means to simplify it using conventional rules.)
- When multiplying exponential terms together, the constant terms are multiplied, but the exponents of terms with the same variable bases are added together, which is somewhat counterintuitive. For example, $4w^2$ multiplied by $8w^3$ gives $32w^5$ (not $32w^6$, as one might guess).
- When like algebraic terms are divided, exponents are subtracted. For example, $\frac{2x^7}{5x^3}$ becomes $\frac{2x^{7-3}}{5} = \frac{2x^4}{5}$.

Multiplication of Binomials

In algebra, it is frequently necessary to multiply two binomials. Binomials are algebraic expressions of two terms. The FOIL method is one way to multiply binomials. FOIL stands for "first, outer, inner, last": Multiply the first terms in the parentheses, then the outermost terms, then the innermost terms, then the last terms, and then add the products together. For example, to multiply $(x + 3)$ and $(2x - 5)$ you multiply x by $2x$ (the first terms), x by -5 (outer terms), 3 by $2x$ (inner terms), and 3 by -5 (last terms). The four products ($2x^2$, $-5x$, $6x$, and -15) add up to $2x^2 + x - 15$. If the polynomials to be multiplied have more than two terms (trinomials, for instance), make sure that each term of the first polynomial is multiplied by each term of the second. The opposite of polynomial multiplication is factoring. Factoring a polynomial means rewriting it as the product of factors (often two binomials). The trinomial $x^2 - 11x + 28$, for instance, can be factored into $(x - 4)(x - 7)$. (You can check this by "FOILing" the binomials.) When attempting to factor polynomials, it is sometimes necessary to factor out any factor that might be common to all terms first. The two terms in $5x^2 - 10$, for example, both contain the factor 5. This means that the expression can be rewritten as $5(x^2 - 2)$.

Algebraic Relationship

To express the relationship between two or more numbers using an algebraic expression. The algebraic relationship which represents 2, 4, 6, 8... is $2n$ (where $n = 1, 2, 3, ...$) and the algebraic relationship which represents 4, 7, 10, 13, ... is $3n + 1$ (where $n = 1, 2, 3, ...$).

Algebraic Solution

An algebraic solution is the process of solving a mathematical problem using the principles of algebra.

Performing Operations with Negative and Positive Numbers

When performing operations on negative and positive numbers, the key component is to pay attention to the sign—the positive or negative value. Rules for multiplication and division are the same—two positives and two negatives make a positive, and mixing negative with positive makes a negative. See the following examples.

- negative × negative = positive ($-6 \times -5 = 30$)
- positive × positive = positive ($6 \times 5 = 30$)
- positive × negative = negative ($6 \times -5 = -30$)

Graphs and Symbolic Representations

A graph is an image or chart representation used to show a numerical relationship. On the TExES, teacher candidates are required to study graphs, charts, and tables and answer questions based on the information presented. A table is a systematic or orderly list of values, usually in rows and columns. They are often organized from a function or relationship. Four kinds of graphs are generally used in grades PK to grade 6—pictorial, bar, pie, and line.

Pictorial graphs are the most concrete representation of information. They represent a transition from the real object graphs to symbolic graphs (Sperry Smith, 2008). These are usually used to introduce children to graphing in PK through grade 1. For example, the teacher can use pictures of pizzas and hot dogs to represent the number of children that prefer one food over the other.

Bar graphs are used to represent two elements of a single subject. For example, the bar graph that follows presents the number of books read by a group of students. This graph presents in a concrete fashion that child E was the top reader with 5 books, while child A is the one with the lowest number of books read.

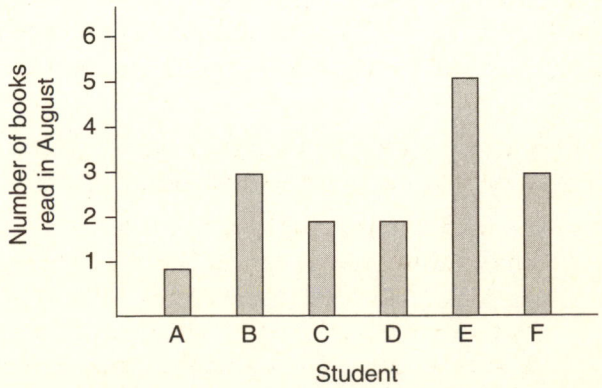

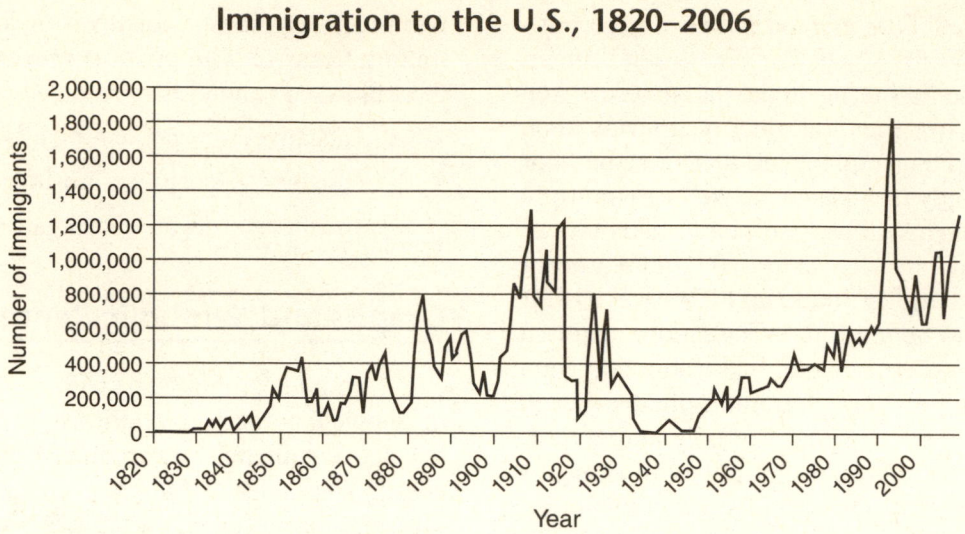

Line graphs present information in a similar fashion as the bar graphs, but it uses points and lines. This type of representation is more abstract for children and is therefore more challenging for them. A line graph tracks one or more subjects. One element is usually a time period over which the other element increases, decreases, or remains static. The following line graph depicts U.S. immigration statistics from 1820 to 2000.

Pie charts are used to help visualize relationships based on percentages of a subject. The figure is divided based on the percentages out of a possible 100%. This graph appears to be easy to read, which is deceptive. It requires an understanding of percentages, which makes it inappropriate for children in the early grades. A pie graph representing food preferences follows.

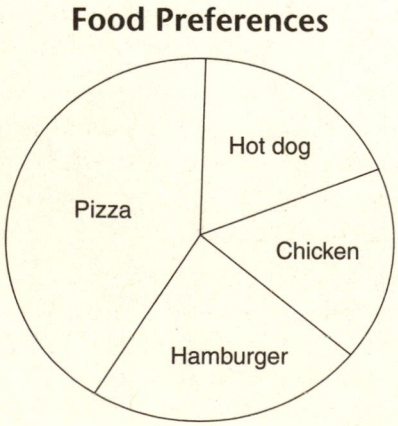

Identifying Patterns using Concrete Models

Kindergarten students begin to use concrete models to construct, describe, extend, and determine what comes next in repeating patterns. In order to identify and construct repeating patterns, students must be able to identify the attributes of the objects in the pattern. Therefore students sort objects by their attributes, before they begin constructing their own patterns. Students construct patterns with two (AB, AAB, ABB) or three (ABC) elements. As students become more familiar with the structure of patterns they are able to begin to think about how two patterns are similar and different.

By Grade 5, students continue their work from Grades 3 and 4 by examining, representing, and describing situations in which the rate of change is constant. Students move from using concrete models, to figures and numbers. Throughout their work, students use tables, graphs, and equations and between those representations and the situation they represent. Their work with symbolic notation is closely related to the context in which they are working. By moving back and forth between the contexts, their own ways of describing general rules in words, and symbolic notation, students learn how this notation can carry mathematical meaning.

Linear and Nonlinear Functions

As stated previously, a linear function is one whose graph is a straight line. An equation whose graph is a straight line is called a linear function. A linear function has an equation that can be written in the form of $y = mx + b$. A linear function has a constant rate of increase or decrease. The constant rate of change is the slope of the line and is represented by m in the equation. It can be written in this form:

Function form: $f(x) = mx + b$

Example: $f(x) = 3x - 1$

$(m = 3, b = -1)$.

Equation form: $y = mx + b$

Example: $y = 3x - 1$

Here is a partial table of values of the linear function $f(x) = 3x - 1$.

x	–4	–3	–2	–1	0	1	2	3
y	–13	–10	–7	–4	–1	2	5	8

The linear equation has $m = 3$ (slope), $b = -1$ (y-intercept). You will notice that $x = 0$ gives $y = -1$, the value of b. Numerically, b is the value of y when $x = 0$. On the graph, the corresponding point (0,–1) is the point where the graph crosses the y-axis, and we say that $b = -1$ is the y-intercept of the graph. The role of m in the equation $y = mx + b$ means that the value of y increases by $m = 3$ for every increase of 1 in x. This is caused by the term $3x$ in the formula.

On the graph, the value of y increases by exactly 3 for every increase of 1 in x, the graph is a straight line rising by 3 for every 1 we go to the right. We say that we have a rise of 3 units for each run of 1 unit. Similarly, we have a rise of 6 for a run of 2, a rise of 9 for a run of 3, and so on. Thus we see that $m = 3$ is a measure of the steepness of the line; we call m the slope of the line. Geometrically, the graph rises by m units for every 1 unit move to the right; m is the slope of the line.

Non-linear functions are not linear and have an exact solution. An example is $x^2 + x - 1 = 0$. This may be written as $f(x) = C$, where $f(x) = x^2 + x$ and $C = 1$. Though nonlinear, this simple example may be solved exactly using a quadratic formula and is very well understood. To determine whether the function is linear or nonlinear, see the following examples:

$y = 4x$	$y = x^2 + x - 2$	$y = 7/x$
Linear, $y = 4x$ can be written as $y = mx + b$	Nonlinear, $y = x^2 + x - 2$ cannot be written as $y = mx + b$	Nonlinear, $y = 7/x$ cannot be written as $y = mx + b$

Problem-Solving Situations into Equations Involving Variables

The role of operations in problem solving involves developing critical thinking and rational powers. The uses of operations in problem solving include: applications, study of patterns and relationships, translation of word problems with a variety of structures and situations into symbolic representations using equations, and the selection of problem solving strategies.

Proportional Reasoning

Proportional reasoning is important in preparing students for algebra. Students in 5th grade begin to use a ratio chart to solve proportion problems. Proportions present a challenge for students because proportions are difficult for students to grasp because two values are related in a certain way that may be solved using multiplication. Students can be influenced by the context, so it is important to expose students to various examples, as in the following types of problems:

1. The office copier uses 5 reams of paper every 2 weeks. At the end of 6 weeks, how many reams of paper will the office copier use within this period of time?
2. Each table in the restaurant has a vase with three long-stem roses. The restaurant has fifteen tables; how many flowers are there altogether?

3. The soccer coach orders new soccer balls for the team. She orders 3 out of 4 soccer balls in the school colors. If she orders 36 soccer balls, how many of these will be painted in the school colors?

Linear Function—Data Sets

A mathematical linear function refers to a first-degree polynomial function of one variable. In analytic geometry, the term linear function is sometimes used to mean a first-degree polynomial function of one variable. These functions are called "linear" because they are precisely the functions whose graph in the Cartesian coordinate plane is a straight line. Such a function can be written as $f(x) = mx + b$ (called slope-intercept form), where m and b are real constants and x is a real variable. The constant m is often called the slope or gradient, while b is the y-intercept, which gives the point of intersection between the graph of the function and the y-axis. Changing m makes the line steeper or shallower, while changing b moves the line up or down.

Examples of functions whose graph is a line include the following:

- $f_1(x) = 2x + 1$
- $f_2(x) = \frac{x}{2} + 1$
- $f_3(x) = \frac{x}{2} - 1$

The graphs of these are shown below:

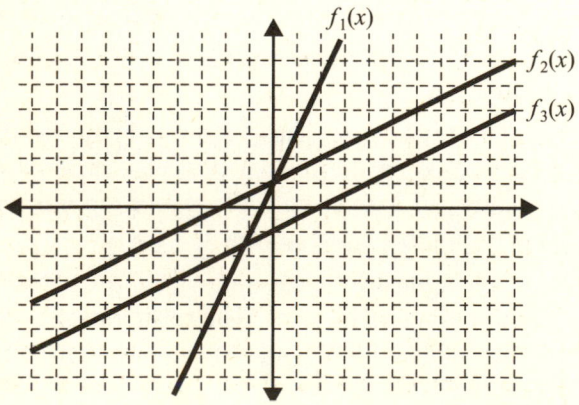

Variables, Equations and Inequalities

Equations

An equation is a mathematical sentence stating that two expressions are equal. Many mathematical expressions include letters called variables. Variables are classified as either free or bound. For a given combination of values for the free variables, an expression may be evaluated, although for some combinations of values of the free variables, the value of the expression may be undefined. Thus an expression represents a function whose inputs are the values assigned the free variables and whose output is the resulting value of the expression.

For example, the expression $\frac{x}{y}$ evaluated for $x = 10$, $y = 5$, will give 2; but is undefined for $y = 0$.

The evaluation of an expression is dependent on the definition of the mathematical operators and on the system of values that is its context. See Formal Semantics and Interpretation (logic) for the study of this question in logic.

Two expressions are said to be equivalent if, for each combination of values for the free variables, they have the same output, i.e., they represent the same function. Example:

The expression $\sum_{n=1}^{3}(2nx)$ has free variable x, bound variable n, constants 1, 2, and 3, two occurrences of an implicit multiplication operator, and a summation operator. The expression is equivalent with the simpler expression $12x$. The value for $x = 3$ is 36.

The '+' and '–' (addition and subtraction) symbols have their usual meanings. Division can be expressed either with the '/' or with a horizontal dash, i.e., $x / 2$ or $\frac{x}{2}$ are perfectly valid. Also, for multiplication one can use the symbols $\times$ or a "·" (dot), or else simply omit it (multiplication is implicit); so: $\times x2$ or $2x$ or $2 \cdot x$ or $x \cdot 2$ are all acceptable (please notice in the first example above how the "times" symbol resembles an "x" and also how the "." symbol resembles a decimal point, so to avoid confusion it's best to use one of the later two forms).

An expression must be well-formed. That is, the operators must have the correct number of inputs, in the correct places. The expression 2 + 3 is well formed; the expression * 2 + is not, at least, not in the usual notation of arithmetic.

Algebraic Inequality

An algebraic inequality is a statement that is written using one or more variables and constants that shows a greater than or less than relationship. Example: $2x + 8 > 24$.

Solving an algebraic inequality means finding all of its solutions. A "solution" of an inequality is a number which when substituted for the variable (for example, x) makes the inequality a true statement. An algebraic inequality is defined as a statement that is written using one or more variables and constants that shows a greater than or less than relationship. As in the case of solving equations, there are certain manipulations of the inequality, which do not change the solution. Consider the algebraic inequality in the following example: $2x + 8 > 24$.

Here is a list of possible manipulations:

1. Adding/subtracting the same number on both sides: $2x + 8 > 24$ has the same solution as the inequality $2x > 16$. (The second inequality was obtained from the first one by subtracting 8 on both sides.)
2. Switching sides and changing the orientation of the inequality sign: $2x + 8 > 24$ has the same solution as $24 < 2x + 8$ (We merely switch sides and turned the ">" into a "<".)

Last, the operation which is at the source of all the trouble with inequalities:

3a. Multiplying/dividing by the same POSITIVE number on both sides.

3b. Multiplying/dividing by the same NEGATIVE number on both sides AND changing the orientation of the inequality sign.

This does not seem too difficult. The inequality $2x \leq 6$ has the same solution as the inequality $x \leq 3$. (We divided by +2 on both sides.) The inequality $-2x > 4$ has the same solutions as the inequality $x < -2$. (We divided by (–2) on both sides and switched ">" to "<".).

The inequality $x^2 > x$ does not have the same solutions as the inequality $x > 1$. (We were planning on dividing both sides by x, but this is not possible, because we do not know whether x will be positive or negative). In fact, it is easy to check that $x = -2$, that solves the first inequality, but does not solve the second inequality.

Consider the inequality: $2x + 8 > 24$

The basic strategy for inequalities and equations is the same: isolate x on one side. Following this strategy, let's move +8 to the right side. We accomplish this by subtracting 8 on both sides (Rule 1) to obtain $(2x + 8) - 8 > 24 - 8$, after simplifying we obtain $2x > 16$. Once we divide by +2 on both sides (Rule 3a), we have succeeded in isolating x on the left: $2x/2 > 16/2$, or simplified, $x > 8$. All real numbers greater than 8 solve the inequality. We say that the "set of solutions'" of the inequality consists of all real numbers greater than 8.

An algebraic inequality is an algebraic statement about the relative size of one or more variables and/or constants. Inequalities are used to determine the relationship between these values. Example: Taking x as a variable and saying, "x is less than 5," may be written as $x < 5$.

Competency 020 (Geometry and Measurement)

The teacher understands concepts and principles of geometry and measurement.

Geometry and measurement are significant strands of mathematics. In the elementary classroom, children's experience in geometry should provide for the development of the concepts of direction, shape, size, symmetry, congruence, and similarity in using two-dimensional and three-dimensional shapes. Experiences for children should begin with exploring, playing, and building with shapes using familiar objects and a wide variety of concrete materials.

Concepts and skills in the measurement strand of mathematics deal with making comparisons between what is being measured and the standard for measurement. Children need first-hand experiences with measuring activities that require them to practice the skill. Additionally, children should be aware that measurement is never exact, but is actually an estimation. However, it is important that children learn to practice making estimates. Measuring gives children practical applications to apply their computation skills. It also provides a way to link geometric concepts to number concepts.

The van Hiele Theory

Although the van Hiele theory (van Hiele, 1986) has been recognized for its role in describing the levels of thinking associated with the learning of geometry, it has also been developed as a general theory of mathematics education. In 1988, Fuys, Gedds, and Tischler interpreted much of that work. The van Hiele theory is a stage theory, set out in levels. The theory does not stop at the description of "levels of thinking," but provides a foundation for understanding the movement between these levels, and the role of the teacher in assisting with this progression. The theory goes beyond the concerns of Piaget, who did not address the question of how students may be encouraged to progress from level to level. The van Hiele theory, in addition to describing levels of thinking, offers an important addition. This is the notion of stages of learning as means by which the learner may be assisted to use higher level thinking skills. Five such stages are specified in Table 3–11 (van Hiele, 1986):

Principles and Properties of Geometry

A fundamental concept of geometry is the notion of a point. A point is a specific location, taking up no space, having no area, and frequently represented by a dot. A point is considered to have no dimensions. In other words, it has neither length nor breadth nor depth.

Through any two points there is exactly one straight line; straight lines are two-dimensional. Planes (think of flat surfaces without edges) are two-dimensional, meaning they have infinite length and breadth but no depth. From these foundational ideas you can move to some other important geometric terms and ideas.

- A segment is any portion of a line between two points on that line. It has a definite start and a definite end. The notation for a segment extending from point A to point B is $\overline{AB}$.
- A ray is like a line segment, except it extends forever in one direction. The notation for a ray originating at point X (an endpoint) through point Y is $\overrightarrow{XY}$.

Formulas for Lengths, Perimeters, Area, and Volume

Finding the Perimeter

The perimeter of a two-dimensional (flat) shape or object is the distance around the object (think of a fence, for example). Perimeter is measured in linear units (e.g., inches, feet, and meters). See the chart for the formulas used to find perimeter:

Perimeter of a Square	$P = 4s$
Perimeter of a Rectangle	$P = 2l + 2w$ or $P = 2(l + w)$

The perimeter of a square is found by multiplying four times the measure of a side of the square. This relationship is commonly given by the formula $P = 4s$, where s is the measure of a side of the square. For example, if a square has $s = 5$ feet, then the perimeter of the square is given by $P = 4(5 \text{ feet}) = 20$ feet.

The perimeter of a rectangle is found by adding twice the length of the rectangle to twice the width of the rectangle. This relationship is commonly given by the formula:

$P = 2l + 2w$, where l is the measure of the length and w is the measure of the width. For example, if a rectangle has $l = 10$ m and $w = 5$ m, then the perimeter of the rectangle is given by $P = 2(10 \text{ m}) + 2(5 \text{ m}) = 30$ m.

Table 3–11. van Hiele's Levels of Geometric Thinking

What the teacher needs to know	What the learner can do
van Hiele's Level 0—Visualization Learners develop a mental picture of each shape; therefore, teachers need to provide a multitude of good physical examples and nonexamples for exploration.	**Learner able to:** • Select a specific shape from a set of shapes; • Sort and match shapes; • Identify shapes in the environment; • Point out a baseball diamond, etc.
van Hiele's Levels 1—Analysis Learners begin to talk and notice the properties of the shapes. Teachers can focus on the various components of the geometric shape.	**Learner able to:** • Predict a shape's final form after just seeing only a part of it; • List several attributes of each shape; • Can subdivide a shape into parts, describe the various pieces, and create a shape from parts.
van Hiele's Levels 2—Informal Deduction Students stop relying on visualization, they now use relationships to make a conclusion. Focus on the first two levels for students in K–8.	**Learner able to:** • Recognize that squares belong in both the rectangle and rhombus category; • Use "if" statements describing the shape; • Divide a rectangle into two congruent triangles; • Identify parallelograms based on the criteria regarding opposite equal angles.
van Hiele's Levels 3—Formal Deduction Focus on higher levels of geometry; using various theorems to teach how two triangles are congruent (e.g., side-angle-side theorem).	**Learner able to:** • Make deductions and to support those deductions; • Do high school level geometry including construction of their own proofs involving quadrilaterals drawn on a sphere.
van Hiele's Levels 4—Rigor Associated with college-level geometry.	**Learner able to:** • Compare different geometries at the proof level.

The perimeter of a triangle is found by adding the measures of the three sides of the triangle. This relationship can be represented by $P = s_1 + s_2 + s_3$, where s_1, s_2, and s_3 are the measures of the sides of the triangle. For example, if a triangle has three sides measuring 3 inches, 4 inches, and 5 inches, then the perimeter of the triangle is given by

$P = 3$ inches + 4 inches + 5 inches = 12 inches.

Finding the Area

The area of a rectangle is found by multiplying the measure of the length of the rectangle by the measure of the width of the rectangle. This relationship is commonly given by $A = l \times w$, where l is the measure of the length and w is the measure of the width. For example, if a rectangle has $l = 10$ m and $w = 5$ m, then the area of the rectangle is given by $A = 10 \text{ m} \times 5 \text{ m} = 50 \text{ m}^2$.

The area of a square is found by squaring the measure of the side of the square. This relationship is commonly given by $A = s^2$, where s is the measure of a side. For example, if a square has $s = 5$ ft, then the area of the square is given by $A = (5 \text{ ft})^2 = 25 \text{ ft}^2$.

Volume

Volume refers to how much space is inside of three-dimensional closed containers. It is useful to think of volume as how many cubic units could fit into a solid. If the container is a rectangular solid, multiplying width, length, and height together computes the volume.

If all six faces (sides) of a rectangular solid are squares, then the object is a cube.

Cube

A cube is a three-dimensional solid figure. This figure has 6 faces, 12 edges, and 8 vertices. The number of faces, edges and vertices can be identified visually, or through the application of the following formula:

Formula for the figure: $F + V = E + 2$

- **Vertex:** A vertex is the union of two segments or point of intersection of two sides of a polygon.
- **Faces:** Each of the plain regions of a geometric body is a face.
- **Edge:** An edge is a line segment where two faces of a three-dimensional figure meet.

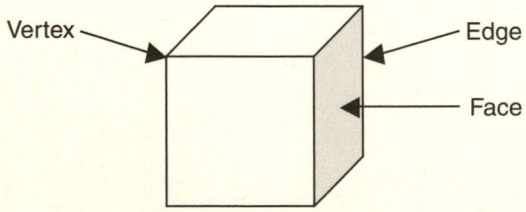

Using Triangles to Explore Geometric Relationships

Sufficient evidence for congruence between two triangles can be shown through the following comparisons:

- **SAS** (Side-Angle-Side): If two pairs of sides of two triangles are equal in length, and the included angles are equal in measurement, then the triangles are congruent.
- **SSS** (Side-Side-Side): If three pairs of sides of two triangles are equal in length, then the triangles are congruent.
- **ASA** (Angle-Side-Angle): If two pairs of angles of two triangles are equal in measurement, and the included sides are equal in length, then the triangles are congruent.
- **AAS** (Angle-Angle-Side): If two pairs of angles of two triangles are equal in measurement and a pair of corresponding sides equal in length, then the triangles are congruent.

Points, Lines, Angles, Lengths, and Distances

Points

Points are most often considered within the framework of Euclidean geometry, where they are one of the fundamental objects. Euclid originally defined the point vaguely, as "that which has no part." In two-dimensional Euclidean space, a point is represented by an ordered pair, (x, y), of numbers, where the first number conventionally represents the horizontal and is often denoted by x, and the second number conventionally represents the vertical and is often denoted by y. This idea is easily generalized to three-dimensional Euclidean space, where a point is represented by an ordered triplet, (x, y, z), with the additional third number representing depth and often denoted by z.

Many constructs within Euclidean geometry consist of an infinite collection of points that conform to certain axioms. This is usually represented by a set of points. As an example, a line is an infinite set of points of the form $L = \{(a_1, a_2, \ldots, a_n)\ [a_1c_1 + a_2c_2 + \ldots a_nc_n = d\}$, where c_1 through c_n and d are constants and n is the dimension of the space. Similar constructions exist that define the plane, line segment, and other related concepts.

In addition to defining points and constructs related to points, Euclid also postulated a key idea about points. He claimed that any two points can be connected by a straight line, this is easily confirmed under modern expansions of Euclidean geometry, and had grave consequences at the time of its introduction, allowing the construction of almost all the geometric concepts of the time. However, Euclid's axiomatization of points was neither complete nor definitive, as he occasionally assumed facts that didn't follow directly from his axioms, such as the ordering of points on the line or the existence of specific points, but in spite of this, modern expansions of the system have since removed these assumptions.

Angles

When two rays (or lines) share an endpoint, an angle is formed. Typically, a degree is the unit of measure of the angle created. If a circle is divided into 360 even slices, each slice has an angle measure of 1 degree.

- If an angle has exactly 90 degrees it is called a right angle.
- Angles of less than 90 degrees are acute angles.
- Angles greater than 90 degrees but less than 180 degrees are obtuse angles.
- If two angles have the same size (regardless of how long their rays might be drawn), they are congruent. Congruence is shown this way: $\angle m \cong \angle n$ (read "angle m is congruent to angle n").

Angle Measure

Angles are often measured in degrees. A circle has a measure of 360°, a half-circle 180°, a quarter-circle 90°, and so forth. If the measures of two angles are the same, then the angles are said to be congruent as stated earlier. Three types of angles are commonly identified—right, acute, and obtuse.

- Right angles measure 90°.
- Acute angles measure less than 90°.
- Obtuse angles measures more than 90° but less than 180°.

In addition to the traditional type of angles, combinations of two angles are classified as complementary and supplementary.

- Supplementary angles add up to 180°.
- Complementary angles add up to 90°.

Vertical (Opposite) Angles

If two lines intersect, they form two pairs of equal angles. The measures of vertical angles are equivalent; that is, vertical angles are congruent.

Parallel and Perpendicular Lines

Parallel Lines

Parallel and perpendicular are important concepts in geometry. Consider the two parallel lines that follow, and the third line (a transversal), which crosses them. Note that among the many individual angles created, there are only two angle measures: (30° noted in the figure) and 150° (180° – 30°).

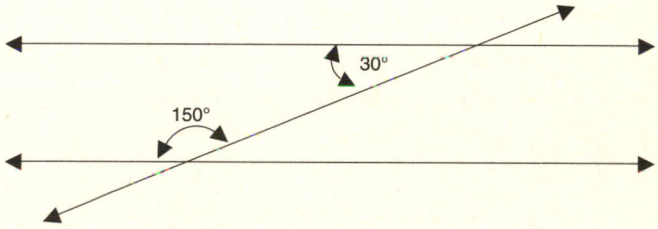

Perpendicular Lines

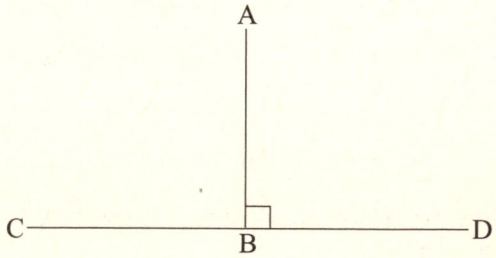

Two- and Three-Dimensional Figures

Circle

Finding the circumference of a circle, you would use the following formula:

$C = 2\pi r$ or $C = \pi d$ (pi is the ratio of a circle's circumference to its diameter).

The value of π is the same for all circles; approximately 3.14159. The approximation 3.14 is adequate for most calculations. In the formula the d represents the diameter and the r stands for the radius of the circle.

Diameter and Radius

The diameter of a circle is a straight line segment that goes from one edge of a circle to the other side, passing through the center. The radius of a circle is half of its diameter (from the center to an edge). A chord is any segment that goes from one spot on a circle to any other spot (all diameters are chords, but not all chords are diameters).

Triangles

Properties of Triangles

The sum of the measures of the angles of a triangle is 180°. Triangles are three-sided polygons. There are three types of triangles—isosceles, equilateral, and scalene.

- An isosceles triangle is a polygon with at least two equal sides and two equal angles.
- If the measures of all sides of the triangle are equal, then the triangle is called an equilateral triangle (this means all angles will be equal).
- A scalene triangle is a polygon with three unequal sides.

Problem: Find the measures of the angles of a right triangle if one of the angles measures 30°.

Solution: Since the triangle is a right triangle, one angle of the triangle measures 90°. We know the sum of the measures of a triangle is 180°, so that $90° + 30° + x° = 180°$. Solving for $x°$, we get $x° = 60°$. The measures of the angles of the triangle are 90°, 60° and 30°.

Formulas for Basic Polygons

Area of a square	$A = s^2$
Area of a rectangle	$A = lw$ or $A = bh$
Area of a triangle	$A = \frac{1}{2} bh$ or $A = bh/2$
Area of a trapezoid	$A = \frac{1}{2}(b_1 + b_2)h$ *or* $A = \frac{(b_1 + b_2)h}{2}$
Area of a circle	$A = \pi r^2$
s = side, l = length, w = width, b = base, h = height, π = pi	

Polygons

A polygon is a many-sided plane figure bounded by a finite number of straight lines or a closed figure on a circle bounded by arcs. These figures are described based on the number of sides. Some of the most common are the following:

- Three-sided polygons are triangles.
- Four-sided polygons are quadrilaterals.
- Five-sided polygons are pentagons.
- Six-sided polygons are hexagons.
- Eight-sided polygons are octagons.

If two polygons (or any figures) have exactly the same size and shape, they are congruent. If they are the same shape, but different sizes, they are similar.

The following are formulas for finding the areas of basic polygons (formally defined as closed, coplanar geometric figures with three or more straight sides). Abbreviations used are as follows: A stands for area, l stands for length, w stands for width, h stands for height, and b stands for length of the base.

Triangle (a three-sided polygon): $A = \frac{b \times h}{2}$

(Note that, as shown in the figure that follows, the height of a triangle is not necessarily the same as the length of any of its sides.)

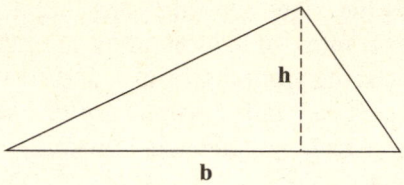

Rectangle (a four-sided polygon with four right angles): $A = l \times w$

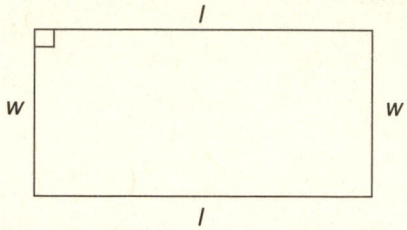

Parallelogram (a four-sided polygon with two pairs of parallel sides): $A = l \times h$ (Note that, as with triangles, and as shown in the figure below, the height of a parallelogram is not necessarily the same as the length of its sides.)

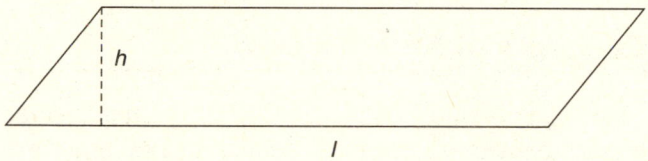

Circle The area of a circle can be found by squaring the length of its radius, then multiplying that product by π. The formula is given as $A = \pi r^2$ (pi is the ratio of a circle's circumference to its diameter).

The value of π is the same for all circles; approximately 3.14159. (The approximation 3.14 is adequate for most calculations.) The approximate area of the circle shown below can be found by squaring 6 (giving 36), then multiplying 36 by 3.14, giving an area of about 113 square units.

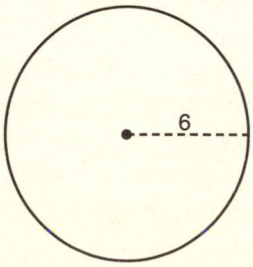

Here are several commonly used volume formulas:

The volume of a rectangular solid is equal to the product of its length, width, and height; $A = l \times w \times h$. (A rectangular solid can be thought of as a box, wherein all intersecting edges form right angles.)

A prism is a polyhedron—a three-dimensional solid consisting of a collection of polygons—with two congruent, parallel faces (called bases) and whose lateral (side) faces are parallelograms. The volume of a prism can be found by multiplying the area of the prism's base by its height. The volume of the triangular prism shown hereafter is 60 cubic units. (The area of the triangular base is 10 square units, and the height is 6 units.)

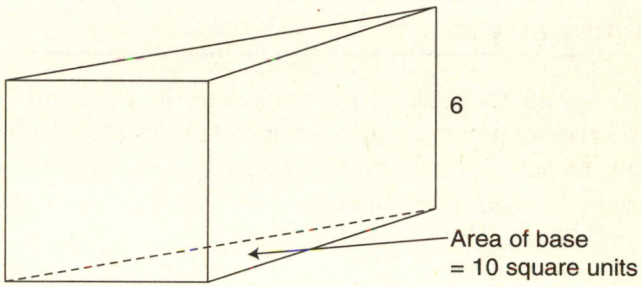

A cylinder is like a prism in that it has parallel faces, but its rounded "side" is smooth. The formula for finding the volume of a cylinder is the same as the formula for finding the volume of a prism: the area of the cylinder's base is multiplied by the height. The volume of the cylinder in the following figure is approximately 628 cubic units ($5 \times 5 \times \pi \times 8$).

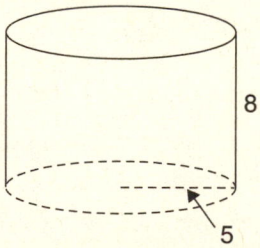

A property of all triangles is that the sum of the measures of the three angles is 180°. If, therefore, the measures of two angles are known, the third can be deduced using addition, then subtraction. Right triangles (those with a right angle) have several special properties. A chief property is described by the Pythagorean theorem, which states that in any right triangle with legs (shorter sides) a and b, and hypotenuse (the longest side) c, the sum of the squares of the sides will be equal to the square of the hypotenuse ($a^2 + b^2 = c^2$).

Note that in the following right triangle, $3^2 + 4^2 = 5^2$.

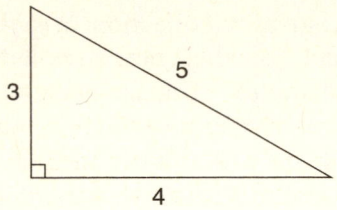

Symmetry

Symmetry—The correspondence in size, form, and arrangement of parts on opposite sides of a plane, line, or point. For example, a figure that has line symmetry has two halves that coincide if folded along its line of symmetry.

Lines of Symmetry

Polygons may have lines of symmetry, which can be thought of as imaginary fold lines that produce two congruent, mirror-image figures. Squares have four lines of symmetry, and non-square rectangles have two, as shown in the following figures. Circles have an infinite number of lines of symmetry.

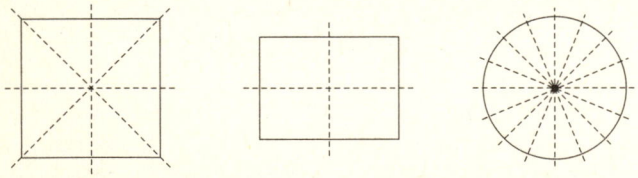

Tessellations

The arrangement of polygons that forms a grid is called a tessellation; however, other shapes may also tessellate. A tessellation is a pattern formed by the repetition of a single unit or shape that, when repeated, fills the plane with no gaps and no overlaps. Familiar examples of tessellations are the patterns formed by paving stones or bricks, and cross-sections of beehives. (See Math Forum at: *http://mathforum.org/geometry/rugs/symmetry/grids.html.*)

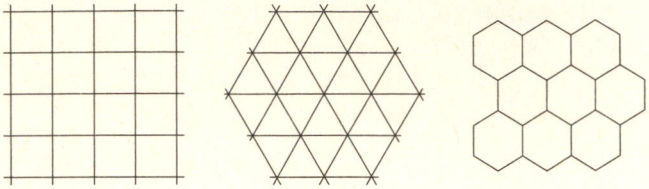

square grid triangular grid hexagonal grid

Grids

Grids are usually based on regular polygons: squares, equilateral triangles, and hexagons. Or they can be based on rectangles, parallelograms, and rhomboids.

Concepts of Measurement

Concepts and skills in the Measurement strand of the math curriculum all deal with making comparisons between what is being measured and some suitable standard of measure. Measurement offers opportunities for interdisciplinary learning in social studies, geography, science, art and music. Key to the development of skills in measurement is allowing for various types of measurement activities. Children need firsthand practice with measuring and making estimates in measurement. The principles of measurement involve understanding of the attributes of length, capacity, weight, area, volume, time, temperature, and angles. Being able to measure connects mathematics to the environment and gives children practical applications for computation skills. The ability to use measurement tools: rulers, thermometers, measuring cups, and scales to estimate is a necessary skill for children to develop. According to Burns (2000), concepts in measurement include four stages in learning when developing classroom activities. Instruction should progress using the four stages of measurement.

Concepts in Measurement Include Four Stages in Learning

1. Comparing objects by matching—ordering items based on size
2. Comparing a variety of objects for measuring—using body parts, blocks, cubes, etc.
3. Comparing objects using standard units—using standard and metric systems
4. Comparing using suitable units for specific measurements—choosing standard units

Time

There are two kinds of clocks: analog and digital. The digital represents the time using Arabic numbers separating the hours from the minutes with a colon (12:45), which makes it relatively easy to read. However, the analog clock uses two hands to represent the hours and minutes based on 60 minutes for an hour and 60 seconds for a minute. Students must have a mathematical understanding of each of the numbers on a face when using analog clocks.

Time
1 year = 365 days
1 year = 12 months
1 year = 52 weeks
1 week = 7 days
1 day = 24 hours
1 hour = 60 minutes
1 minute = 60 seconds

Temperature

Temperature is measured using a thermometer, which is filled with mercury (a liquid metallic element that expands with heat). The Fahrenheit scale is used in the U.S., whereas the Celsius scale is used in countries throughout the world. The Celsius scale is specifically useful in scientific experimentation. Water boils at 212°F or 100°C, and freezes at 32°F or 0°C.

Money

Teaching the concept of money involves the understanding of base ten. Children learn how to relate each denomination to pennies and understand the relationship between the other coins. Use real currency to introduce this concept. Children begin by observing the various coins and their attributes. They learn to associate the value for each of the coins and make equivalences. Suggest that students begin by counting out a bag of coins and then trade out the various coins for larger denominations, for example 5 pennies for one nickel, etc.

Translations, Rotations, and Reflections

Translation (also called a slide)—In geometry a translation simply means moving. Every translation has a direction and distance. This is known as a transformation that moves a geometric figure by sliding. Each of the points of the geometric figure moves the same distance in the same direction. This may be shown on a graph by moving the figure without rotating or reflecting it.

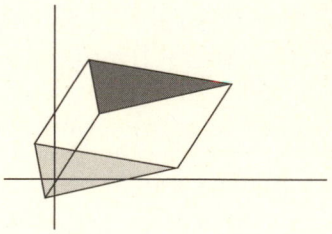

Rotation (also called a turn)—In geometry this is known as a transformation that means a rotation or to turn the shape around. Each rotation has a center and an angle for movement around a given number of degrees.

Reflection (also called a flip)—This is known as a transformation that means to reflect an object or to make the figure/object appear to be backwards or flipped. It produces the mirror image of a geometric figure.

Conversions Within and Between Measurement Systems

Units of Measurement

TEKS require that students in kindergarten through grade 6 become familiar with and apply knowledge of measurement using both U.S. Customary (standard) and metric systems. Table 3–12 provides a comparison of these two units of measurement.

Customary Units

- Linear measurement: Customary units of length include inches, feet, yards, and miles.
- Measurement of mass: Customary units of weight include ounces, pounds, and tons.
- Volume measurement: Customary units of capacity include teaspoons, tablespoons, cups, pints, quarts, and gallons.

Metric Units

- Linear measurement: Metric units of length include millimeters, centimeters, meters, and kilometers. The centimeter is the basic metric unit of length, at least for short distances. There are about 2.5 centimeters to 1 inch. The kilometer is a metric unit of length used for longer distances. It takes more than 1.5 kilometers to make a mile.
- Measurement of mass: Metric units of weight include grams and kilograms. The gram is the basic metric unit of mass (which for many purposes is the same as weight). A large paper clip weighs about 1 gram. It takes about 28 grams to make 1 ounce.
- Volume measurement: Metric units of capacity include milliliters and liters. The liter is the basic metric unit of volume. A liter is slightly larger than a quart, so it takes less than four liters to make a gallon.

Table 3–12. The Customary and Metric Systems

Customary System	Metric System
Linear 12 inches (in.) = 1 foot (ft.) 3 feet (ft.) = 1 yard (yd.) 1,760 yards (yds.) = 1 mile (mi.) 5,280 feet (ft.) = 1 mile (mi.)	**Linear** 10 millimeters (mm) = 1 centimeter (cm) 100 centimeters (cm) = 1 meter (m) 1000 meters (m) = 1 kilometer (km)
Capacity and Volume 1 gallon (gal.) = 4 quarts (qt.) 1 gallon (gal.) = 128 fluid ounces 1 quart (qt.) = 2 pints (pt.) 1 pint (pt.) = 2 cups (C.) 1 pint (pt.) = 16 fluid ounces (oz.) 1 cup (C.) = 8 fluid ounces (oz.)	**Capacity and Volume** 1 liter (L) = 1000 milliliters (ml) 1 liter (L) = 1.0556 quarts (qt.)
Mass and Weight 1 ton = 2000 pounds (lbs.) 1 pound (lb.) = 16 ounces (oz.)	**Mass and Weight** 1 kilogram (kg) = 1000 grams (g) 1 gram (g) = 1000 milligrams (mg)

Logical Reasoning

The development of logical reasoning is closely related to children's language development. Elementary mathematics instruction should help students learn to organize ideas, understand what they are studying, and explain their thinking as they solve problems. Activities should provide students with opportunities to make generalizations and conclusions, to justify them with logical arguments, and to be able to communicate their reasoning to others. Mathematics is a way of thinking, rather than a body of facts. This is an important distinction for children to understand. Critical thinking and logical reasoning aid students in clarifying their thought processes and may apply this skill in all curriculum areas.

In the early grades through grade 3, logical thinking should be introduced using an informal approach. There should be many opportunities for children to explore, manipulate, and experience concrete objects to identify their attributes, to make comparisons, to classify by their characteristics and to make generalization about their properties. The use of words such as all, some, if, then, or not helps children gain knowledge with the language used in logic. In upper elementary grades, students should be provided with learning activities involving deductive and inductive reasoning.

Deductive Reasoning

This requires moving from the assumption to conclusion. Deductive reasoning is reasoning from the general to the specific, and it is supported by deductive logic. Students use this type of reasoning in daily life, for example: "It is raining so I need to take my umbrella to school." Note that conclusions reached via deductive reasoning are only sound if the original assumptions are actually true.

Inductive Reasoning

This involves examining particular instances to come to some general assumptions. This type of reasoning is informal and intuitive. When thinking inductively, students make hypotheses, extend thought patterns, use analogies, and make reasonable conclusions from examining what appears to be a large enough body of evidence. Students use this type of reasoning regularly in life situations, for example: If I do my homework all this week, I think my mother will take me to the concert on Saturday. With inductive reasoning, a general rule is inferred from specific observations (which may be limited). Moving from the statement, "All fish that I have ever seen have fins" (specific but limited observations) to "All fish have fins" (a general proposition) is an example of inductive reasoning. Conclusions arrived using inductive reasoning are not always necessarily true.

Axiomatic Structure

An axiom is a mathematical rule. This basic assumption about a system allows theorems to be developed. For example, the system could be the points and lines in the plane. Then an axiom would be that given any two distinct points in the plane, there is a unique line through them.

Apply Reasoning Skills

Reasoning skills include drawing conclusions using the principles of similarity, congruence, parallelism, and perpendicularity; and using inductive and deductive reasoning. Geometric figures are similar if they have the exact same shapes, even if they do not have the same sizes. In transformational geometry, two figures are said to be similar if and only if a similarity transformation maps one figure onto the other. In the figure that follows, triangles A and B are similar.

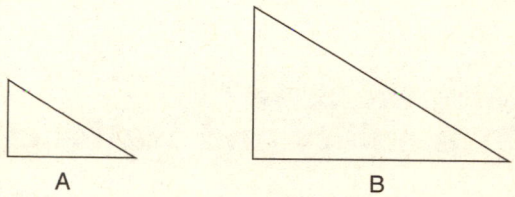

Corresponding angles of similar figures have the same measure, and the lengths of corresponding sides are proportional.

In the following figure, rectangles A and B are congruent.

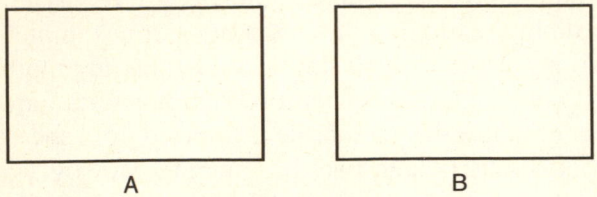

The corresponding sides are congruent, meaning that figures are congruent if they have the same shape and size (Congruent figures are also similar.)

Straight lines within the same plane that have no points in common (that is, they never cross) are parallel lines. Note that the term parallel is used to describe the relationship between two coplanar lines that do not intersect. Lines that are not coplanar—although they never cross—are not considered to be parallel. Coplanar lines crossing at right angles (90°) are perpendicular.

An example of how logical reasoning can be used to solve a geometry problem is given hereafter. (In this case deductive reasoning is used to find the measure of $\angle J$.)

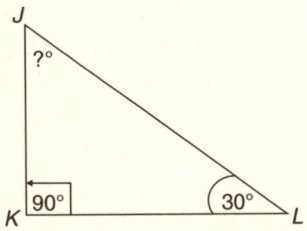

The sum of the measures of the three angles of any triangle is 180° (a general proposition). The sum of the measures of $\angle K$ and $\angle L$ is 120°, therefore the measure of $\angle J$ is 60° (a specific proposition).

Competency 021 (Probability and Statistics)

The teacher understands concepts related to probability and statistics and their applications.

Statistics is the science or study of data. Statistical methods are used to describe, analyze, evaluate, and interpret information. The information is then used for predicting, drawing inferences, and making decisions. Data analysis involves both probability and statistics. Probability gives a way to measure uncertainty and is essential for understanding statistical methods. It explains data sets to give a type of generalized statistic, to make a prediction, or to infer something beyond the specific data collected. Probability is used to create experimental and theoretical models of situations involving probabilities.

There is some general agreement with regard to six underlying facts about the learning and teaching of data analysis. These include the following:

Research on Teaching Data Analysis

1. Problem solving approach to teaching is consistent with how learners develop data analysis knowledge. (Lajoie, Jacobs, & Lavigne, 1995)
2. Concept knowledge must be developed first before developing procedural knowledge. This can then be further developed using problem solving, for example understanding the concept of sample before gathering data to analysis a problem/situation. (Horvath & Lehrer, 1998)
3. Concepts and procedures are interdependent. (Konold & Higgins, 2003)
4. Statistical representations can become more sophisticated using technology and as students have more experiences with data. (Friel, S.N., Curcio, F.R., & Bright, G. W. (2001))
5. Data organization can be improved by using technology tools. (Konold, 2002; Lehrer & Romberg, 1996)
6. Teachers must sequence instruction based on developmental age-appropriate situations and so students may examine certain types of situations before other types. For example, students should study situations in which all outcomes are equally likely before studying situations in which all outcomes are not equally likely. (Horvath & Lehrer, 1998)

Probability

Learning probability and statistics provides real applications of arithmetic. When basic computation skills are used in context, students have the opportunity to see the advantages and limitations of their calculations. Most arithmetic is done with a degree of uncertainty, for example estimating costs, making calculations of needed building materials, approximating estimated time of arrival (ETA) on trips, and estimating time for baking or cooking food.

A set of data can be described by its range, mean, median, and/or mode.

The **range** of a set of data is the difference between the greatest and the least numbers in the data set. Subtract to find the difference.

The **mean** of a set of data is the average of the data values. To find the mean, add all the data values and then divide this sum by the number of values in the set.

The **median** of a set of data is the middle value of all the numbers. To find the middle value, list the numbers in order from the least to greatest or from greatest to least. Cross out one value on each end of the list until you reach the middle. If there are two values in the middle, find the number halfway between the two values by adding them together and dividing their sum by 2.

The **mode** is the value (or values) that appear in a set of data more frequently than any other value. If all the values in a set of data appear once, the set does not have a mode.

Studying probability and statistics should involve real problems and/or simulations. A theoretical or abstract approach is not appropriate for students in elementary mathematics. The approach should be based on experiments that draw on children's experience and interests. Children's intuition needs to be challenged. Once they understand or can say what "should happen" in a situation, then they may be able to conduct experiments to test their predictions. Basic to probability and statistics are the following steps:

1. Data Collections
2. Sampling
3. Organizing and Representing Data
4. Interpreting Data
5. Assigning Probabilities
6. Making Inferences

Probability is a way of describing how likely it is a particular outcome will occur. A random event occurs when a selection is made without looking. A fraction can be used to describe the results of a probability experiment in this way: 1) the numerator of the fraction is the number of favorable outcomes for the experiment. 2) The denominator of the fraction is the number of all the possible outcomes for the experiment.

Example:

Gabrielle is randomly choosing a marble from a bag containing three marbles—1 red marble, 1 blue marble, and 1 green marble. What is the probability that she will choose a green marble on a single pull?

- There is 1 green marble in the bag. There is 1 favorable outcome.
- There are 1 + 1 + 1 = 3 marbles in the bag. There are 3 possible outcomes.

$$\text{Probability of choosing a green marble} = \frac{\text{Number of favorable outcomes}}{\text{Total number of possible outcomes}} = \frac{1}{3}$$

The probability that Gabrielle will choose a green marble on a single pull is $\frac{1}{3}$, or 1 out of 3.

Students need to demonstrate an understanding of probability and statistics and be able to do the following: 1) use experimental and theoretical probability to make predictions; and 2) use statistical representations to analyze data. A sample space is the set of all possible outcomes of an experiment. For example, if you flip a coin, it will land either heads or tails. Students learn to list all the possible outcomes: heads or tails. Sample spaces may also be listed on a chart or tree diagram.

Permutations—All possible arrangements of a given number of items in which the order of the items makes a difference, for example the different ways that a set of four books can be placed on a shelf.

Jones, Langral, Thornton, and Mogill (1999) have developed a four-stage framework that attempts to explain the learning process for probability. Learners begin at the subjective level, at which they are easily swayed by personal experiences when making probabilistic statements. At the second level, transitional learners begin to recognize the importance of organizing information. The third level involves students becoming informal quantitative thinkers. Finally, students work at the purely numerical level in which they understand the nuances of numerical argument and use sophisticated procedures to determine numerical facts.

Students should learn to read graphs, making quick visual summaries as well as further interpretations and comparisons of data through finding means, medians, and modes. Students use tables, line graphs, bar graphs, circle graphs, line plots, and pictographs to organize and display data. This is a helpful strategy used in problem solving. A line plot represents a set of data by showing how often a piece of data appears in that set. It consists of a number line that indicates the values of the data set. An X is placed above the corresponding number each time that value appears in the data set, for example the heights of 10 twelve-year-old girls were measured and recorded. A line plot is used to record the data from a chart. Then, students may make comparisons of the range of height, find the tallest or shortest girl, and interpret the data found.

In real-world problems, students may sample a part of a population. Students need to learn the difference between random and nonrandom samples and the importance this difference makes in statistical studies, for example to determine the percentage of people who are left-handed. Students would not poll famous athletes as a random sampling.

For students to fully understand data analysis, all frameworks and researchers agree that student should generate their own data. They should work with simulations that model real situations. They should use dice, spinners, two-color counters, and coins. As students begin to understand how to gather their own data, they need to be consciously aware of any graphical representations they might choose to use, recognizing the difference between discrete and continuous situations. Finally, technology is a highly useful tool in data analysis and in making sense of the data.

Competency 022 (Mathematical Processes)

The teacher understands mathematical processes and knows how to reason mathematically, solve mathematical problems, and make mathematical connections within and outside of mathematics.

The National Council of Teachers of Mathematics (NCTM) and the Texas Essential Knowledge and Skills (TEKS) have emphasized the importance of teaching mathematical reasoning for children from kindergarten through grade 12. TEKS requires children to explore mathematical reasoning as early as kindergarten. This requirement presents a challenge for teachers since the ability to perform operations involving logical reasoning requires some level of cognitive maturity and the ability to think abstractly. From kindergarten to grade 2, children must understand the principles and patterns of the number system and the symbols used to represent numbers. Principles of measurement and basic geometry are also introduced early in the process. In grades 1 and 2, children begin using quantitative reasoning and basic algorithms for addition and subtraction. Beginning in grade 3 and continuing throughout elementary school, students continue improving their basic knowledge of the number system and the abstraction of mathematical reasoning. Children begin exploring basic algebraic, geometric, and spatial reasoning. They also master multiplication facts and division. Word problems and mathematical reasoning are heavily emphasized in third-grade preparation for TEKS, which is offered in grades 3 to 12.

Logical Reasoning

Teachers must create opportunities to motivate children to engage in exploratory mathematics to develop logical thinking. For the early grades this exploration can be done in learning centers, where children have the opportunity to work with blocks, shapes, and other manipulatives. Learning centers are designed to exposure children to manipulatives, which are used to teach mathematical concepts in an indirect fashion through student-selected activities.

In addition to exposure to mathematics concepts in learning centers, teachers use instructional strategies to apply mathematics concepts in real-life situations. For example, a role-play activity involving ordering food in a restaurant may be simulated in the classroom. A group of children can be given a budget to order food in a restaurant. This type of activity may guide children to understand basic mathematical concepts, including calculating sums of money, giving change, understanding percentages to determine an appropriate gratuity or sales tax, and the use of mathematics in daily life.

Logical reasoning is thinking of something in a way that makes sense. Thinking about mathematics problems involves logical reasoning. You can use logical reasoning to find patterns in a set of data. You can then use those patterns to draw conclusions about the data that can be used to solve problems. Finding patterns involves identifying characteristics that numbers or objects have in common. Look for the pattern in different ways. A sequence of geometric objects may have some property in common. For example, they may all be quadrilaterals or all have right angles.

Problem-Solving Strategies

Solving problems involves more than just numerical computation; logical reasoning and careful planning also play important roles. Strategies may include, but are not limited to: acting it out, drawing a picture or graph, using logical reasoning, looking for a pattern, using a process of elimination, creating an organized chart or list, solving a simpler but related problem, using trial and error (guess and check), working backwards, writing an equation. Here are some of the steps using in solving problems.

Steps to follow when solving problems:
Understand the problem Organize the information you are given and identify the question. You may be given extraneous information that is not needed to solve the problem.
Choose a strategy and/or make a plan After you have organized the information, decide how to use this information to find an answer. Think about the math concepts that apply to the situation. Identify the order in which you will find new information and carry out your strategy.
Carry out the plan After you have chosen a problem-solving strategy, use the strategy to work out the problem. Go step-by-step through your plan, writing down important information at each step.
Check your answer Check your answer to see if it makes sense. Does it answer the question? Is it stated in the correct units? Is it reasonable? You can estimate the solution and then compare the estimate to your answer. They should be approximately equal.

Developmental Considerations

Children in Pre-K through kindergarten might have problems understanding basic number systems and how numbers are presented symbolically. They might have difficulties dealing with measurement activities that require them to master the principle of conservation. They might think that an apple split in half is more than a single apple, or a soda drink in a tall and narrow glass might be more than the same liquid poured in a shorter and wider glass. These cognitive and reasoning limitations tend to disappear as children develop. By first grade, the principle of conservation is generally acquired.

Mathematics instruction in kindergarten through grade 6 involves not only knowing mathematical processes but also being able to determine when a given process is required. Children must develop the ability to reason through word problems and understand the type of answer required. Most third graders can do addition, subtraction, multiplication, and even division. However, they might have difficulties with word problems and problem-solving activities that require them to identify the appropriate mathematical process. They might also have problems understanding questions involving multiple steps and deciding on the appropriate answer. The word problem that follows represents an example:

> Joe can place a maximum of 5 apples in a paper sack. If he needs to put 32 apples in sacks, how many sacks does he need?

In this example, most students will know that the problem calls for division—32 divided by 5—which will yield the expected number of 6.4. Some students will provide 6.4 as the answer, but the real question is: "How many sacks does Joe need?" Children will have to reason that paper sacks cannot be divided; thus the answer cannot be 6.4 but 7 paper sacks.

Mathematical reasoning is crucial for understanding and using mathematics. This type of contextual or situational reasoning is certainly important, and questions such as the preceding one have a solid place in the curriculum and on state tests. Logical reasoning is the foundation for understanding mathematics and its use in life.

Historical Development of Mathematics

Every culture has developed some form of functional mathematics concept. In most cases, accomplishments of these civilizations have been transmitted to and enhanced by other groups. This transmission of knowledge and its cumulative effects have resulted in the creation of the modern-day mathematics used around the world. Some of the key civilizations that impacted the development of mathematics in the Western world are discussed in the following sections.

Egyptians and Babylonians

The first mathematicians that impacted the development of modern-day mathematics were from the ancient civilizations of Babylon and Egypt around the third millennium BCE. The ancient Egyptians wrote numbers using hieroglyphs to represents the numbers 1, 10, 100, 1,000, 10,000, and 1,000,000. They used numbers into the millions for practical purposes like managing resources and for building large-scale public structures like temples and pyramids.

The Babylonians made great advances in science, math, and specifically in astronomy. They also developed tables for multiplication, division, and square and cube roots. One of the greatest accomplishments of Babylonian civilization was the development of a number system with a base of 60. This number system constituted the foundation for the advanced mathematics evolution that followed the Egyptians and Babylonians.

Greeks

The Greeks built on the accomplishments of the Egyptians and Babylonians and further developed the field of mathematics. Most historians believe that the formal study of mathematics as a discipline began with the Athenian Greek school of Thales and Pythagoras. Some authorities identify Thales and Pythagoras as the founders of Greek mathematics. Thales (640–550 BCE) was a merchant who traveled extensively and became acquainted with Egyptian mathematics. Some of his contributions include the following: a circle is bisected by the diameter, angles at the base of an isosceles triangle are equal, and a semicircle creates a right angle. Pythagoras, his former pupil, followed Thales's ideas and eventually became one of the leading figures of Greek mathematics. Pythagoras taught that there is a basic relationship between harmony and mathematics. He developed the Pythagorean Theorem. It was after the early Athenian Greeks that the Alexandrian Greeks emerged as the leaders in the study of science and mathematics. Around 300 BCE, Ptolemy founded the university at Alexandria in Egypt, which became the center of learning for the Western world.

This institution became the leading force in the study of mathematics, contributing multiple discoveries and some of the greatest thinkers of the time. Two of the leading figures that emerged during this period were Archimedes and Euclid.

Archimedes calculated the distances of the planets from the Earth and constructed a spherical planetarium imitating the motions of the sun, moon, and six then known planets. He also made multiple discoveries with scientific and military applications. Euclid was one of the most influential Greek mathematicians in the world. He is believed to have learned geometry from the students of Plato. He is famous for providing a complete record of the mathematics accomplishments of Ancient Greece. He wrote several books on the elements of geometry. His mathematics knowledge has served as the standard mathematics textbook for over two thousand years.

The Greeks also discovered that real numbers could not accurately express all mathematical values. Based on this need, they developed the concept of irrational numbers. An irrational number cannot be expressed as a fraction. In decimal form, numbers do not repeat in a pattern or terminate; they continue to infinity. Some examples of irrational numbers are as follows:

$\pi = 3.141592654...$ and $\sqrt{2} = 1.14121356...$

Hindus

Around the fifth century CE, the Hindus developed a system of mathematics that allowed for astronomical calculations. They developed a technique of computation, which later influenced the development of modern-day algebra.

Arab Contributions

The Arabs were the first civilization to solve sophisticated algebraic equations currently used in science and engineering, for example quadratic equations. They also developed and perfected geometric algebra. Arab mathematicians used the work of the Greeks in geometry and improved the development of the field. They founded non-Euclidian geometry and made advances in trigonometry. The greatest contributions of the Arabs were the development of the numeric system, which resulted in the spread of the cumulative knowledge of mathematics to the world.

The Concept of the Zero

Some historians believe that the concept of zero used today originated in India around 650 CE. Others suggest that it was perfected from the work of Greek astronomers. However, all seem to agree that eventually, the Arabs used the concept of the zero to develop the current system of enumeration used in the world. The concept of zero was also developed separately by the Mayans in 700 CE; however, there is no evidence to suggest that the Mayan concept of zero impacted the development of mathematics beyond the Maya empire in Central America. The zero that we know today came from the Hindu tradition.

The Number System

The number system used in modern days is described as an Hindu-Arabic numeration system. It uses numbers from 1 to 9 and the zero. Historians seem to agree that the Hindus contributed to the development of the base-10 digit system and the Arabs perfected it and spread it through the world.

The cumulative knowledge of the Babylonians, Egyptians, and Greeks was translated from Greek into Arabic. At the same time, the mathematic accomplishments of the Hindus were also translated into Arabic. The collective knowledge of these civilizations and the improvement and innovations developed in the Arab world became the mathematics of Western Europe and, over a period of several hundred years of further development, became the mathematics of the world.

Contributions from Other Civilizations

Other civilizations, like the Mayans and the Aztecs, made significant progress in mathematics. The Mayan civilization around 700 BCE developed an elaborate calendar and the mathematical concept of zero. The Mayans also had highly advanced knowledge of astronomy, engineering, and the arts.

The Aztec civilization flourished around 1325 BCE. The Aztecs were also skilled builders and engineers, accomplished astronomers, and mathematicians. Like the Egyptians, they used mathematic principles for functional purposes like engineering to build pyramids, palaces, plazas, and canals.

There are other places in the world that developed significant accomplishments in mathematics. China, Japan, and several kingdoms from Africa are examples of civilizations that made sizeable progress in mathematics; however, their accomplishments did not have a direct impact on the development of mathematics in the Western world. For a detailed analysis of the historical development of mathematics and the contribution of various civilizations, see the "History of Mathematics" website, maintained by David E. Joyce of Clark University in Worcester, Massachusetts. (*http://aleph0.clarku.edu/~djoyce/mathhist/*)

Developments of Mathematics Education in the U.S.

In the last half-century, the American education system has made important changes in the teaching of mathematics. Some of the key changes are listed below.

1950s to 1960s

- Significant changes in content of elementary mathematics programs
- New content added
- Standard content taught at earlier grade levels

1970s

- Slowing down of content changes
- Attention and focus on "system of delivery" of content

Late 1970s, early 1980s

- Back to basics movement
- Heavy emphasis on drill and practice

Late 1980s

- Increased emphasis on teaching concepts and problem solving

1990s

- Increased use of computers and calculators for computation
- Increased emphasis on estimation, problem solving, and higher-level thinking
- Release of Professional Standards for Teaching Mathematics (1991)

2000s

- Increased emphasis on assessment, equity, technology, learning, teaching and curriculum standards
- Use of literature and cultural connections with mathematics and its implication in teaching
- Increased emphasis on research-based instructional strategies

References

Burns, M. 2000. About teaching mathematics: A K-8 resource. Sausalito, CA: Math Solutions Publications.

Carpenter, T.M., E. Fennema, M. L. Franke, L. Levi, and S. B. Empson. 1999.

Children's mathematics: Cognitively guided instruction. Portsmouth, NH: Heinemann.

Fredericks, A. D., B. Blake-Kline, and J. V. Kristo. 1997. Teaching the integrated language arts: Process and practice. New York: Longman.

Friel, S.N., F. R. Curcio, and G. W. Bright. 2001. Making sense of graphs: Critical factors influencing comprehension and instructional implication. Journal of Research in Mathematics Education, 32(2), 124–158.

Flavell, J.H. 1985. Cognitive development. 2nd ed. Upper Saddle River, NJ: Prentice Hall.

Fuson, K. 1988. Children's counting and concepts of numbers. New York: Springer.

Fuson, K. C., and J. W. Hall. 1983. The acquisition of early number word meanings: A conceptual analysis and review. The development of mathematical thinking, ed. H. P. Ginsburg, pp. 49–107. Orlando, FL: Academic Press.

Fuys, D., D. Gedds, and R. Tischler. 1988. The van Hiele model of thinking in geometry among adolescent. Journal of Research in Mathematics Education Monograph #3. Reston, VA: NCTM.

Horvath, J.K. & R. Lehrer. 1998. A model-based perspective on the development of children's understanding of chance and uncertainty. In Reflections on statistics: Learning teaching, and assessment in grades K–12, ed. S.P. Lajoie, pp. 121–148. Mahwah, NJ: Lawrence Erlbaum Associates.

Jones, G.A., C. W. Langrall, C. A. Thorton, and A. T. Mogill. 1999. Student's probabilistic thinking in instruction. Journal for Research in Mathematics Education, 30(5), 487–519.

Kamii, C. 2000. Young children reinvent arithmetic: Implications of Piaget's theory. New York: Teacher College Press.

Konold, C. 2002. Teaching concepts rather than conventions. New England Journal of Mathematics Education, 34(2), 69–81.

Konold, C. and T. Higgins. 2003. Reasoning about data. A research companion to principles and standards for school mathematics, eds. J. Kilpatrick, W.G. Martin, and D.E. Schifter, Reston, VA: NCTM.

Lejoie, S.P., V. R. Jacobs, and N. C. Lavigne. 1995. Empowering children in the use of statistics. Journal of Mathematics Behavior, 14(4), 401–425.

Lehrer, R. and T. Romberg. 1996. Exploring children's data modeling. Cognition and Instruction, 14(1), 69–108.

National Council of Teachers of Mathematics 2007. Professional standards for teaching mathematics. http://toolkitforchange.org/toolkit/view.php?obj=1039&menu=i (accessed August 20, 2009)

National Council of Teachers of Mathematics 2000. Principles and standards for school mathematics. Reston, VA: NCTM.

Pepper, C. and R. P. Hunting. 1998. Preschooler's counting and sharing. Journal for Research in Mathematics Education, 29(2), 14–183.

Piaget, J. and B. Inhelder. 1969. The psychology of the child. New York: Basic Books.

Santrock, J.W. 2003. Children, 7th ed. Boston, PA: McGraw-Hill.

Sousa, D. (2011). *How the ELL Brain Learns*. Corwin: A Sage Company.

Sperry Smith, S. 2008. Early childhood mathematics, 4th ed. Boston, MA: Allyn and Bacon.

Texas Education Agency. 2009a. Texas Essential Knowledge and Skills. Texas Administrative Code (TAC), Title 19, Part II Chapter. Texas Essential Knowledge and Skills for Mathematics.

Texas Education Agency. 2009b. TAKS Exam study guide available online at http://ritter.tea.state.tx.us/student.assessment/resources/guides/study/G6MathE-SG.pdf

U. S. Department of Labor 2008–09. Bureau of Labor Statistics, U.S. Department of Labor Occupational Outlook Handbook, 2008–09 edition, Bulletin 2700. Superintendent of Documents, U.S. Government Printing Office, Washington, DC: Author. http://www.bls.gov/OCO/ (accessed August 1, 2009)

van Hiele, P.M. 1986. Structure and Insight. Orlando, FL: Academic Press.

Vygotsky, L. S. 1986. Thought and language (new rev. ed.) Cambridge, MA: MIT Press

CHAPTER

Domain IV: Social Science

4

This chapter discusses social studies history, geography and culture, economics, and government and citizenship content that beginning teachers need to know in order to plan, implement, and assess students' performance as delineated in the TEKS standards.

Competency 023 (Social Science Instruction)

The teacher uses social science knowledge and skills to plan, organize, and implement instruction and assess learning.

Social Studies Curricula

Social studies is an umbrella term used to encompass the disciplines of history, geography, civics and government, economics, and psychology. All five components are intertwined with the standards or strands shown in Figure 4-1, which were developed by the National Council for the Teaching of Social Studies in 1997 (NCTSS 2006). The Texas Education Agency (TEA) used these strands and curriculum standards as a foundation to develop the state social studies curriculum for kindergarten through grade 12.

Texas Essential Knowledge and Skills (TEKS) in Social Studies

The Texas Essential Knowledge and Skills (TEKS) is the state curriculum for kindergarten to grade 12. The TEKS organizes the social studies content inductively, from the known to the unknown. In this vertical alignment, children begin learning about the self in kindergarten and expand their knowledge with each successive grade, eventually encompassing the community, the state, the nation, and the world. A summary of the key components of the social studies curriculum covered in kindergarten through grade 6 follows.

Kindergarten—Child, Home, Family, and Classroom

- The child as an individual
- Home and families
- State and national heritage
- Patriotic holidays and the contribution of historical characters

Grade 1—Child's Relationship to the Classroom, School, and Community

- The concept of chronology developed by distinguishing among past, present, and future

Figure 4-1. Social Studies Strands

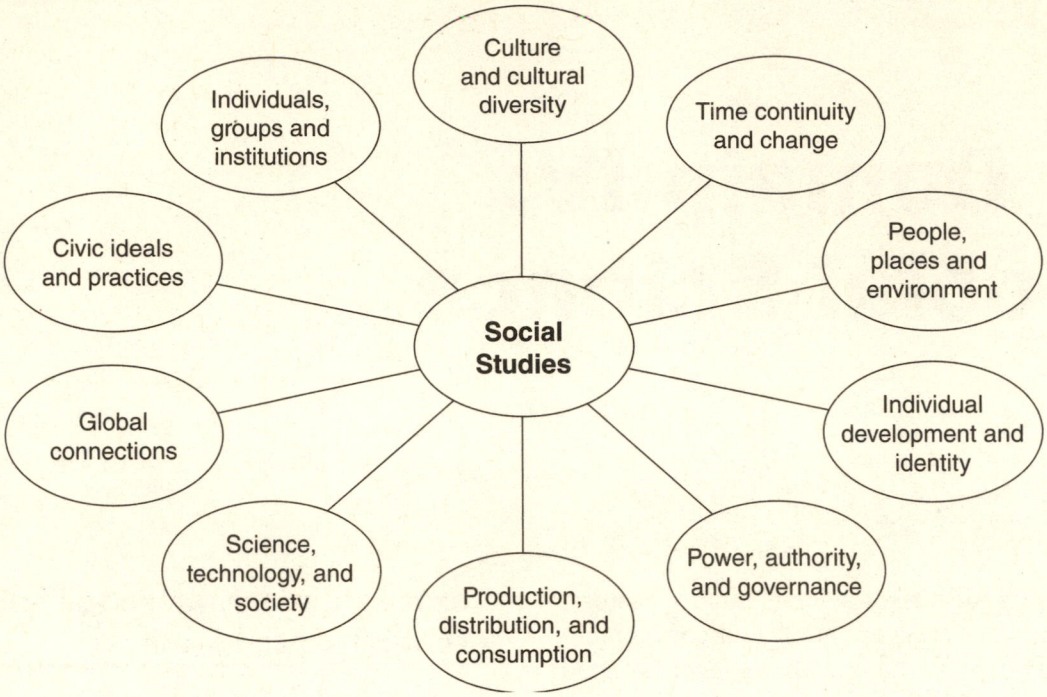

- Anthems and mottoes of Texas and the United States

Grade 2—Local Community

- Impact of significant individuals and events in the history of the community, state, and nation
- Concepts of time and chronology by measuring calendar time by days, weeks, months, and years
- Relationship between the physical environment and human activities
- Functions of government and services that it provides

Grade 3—How Individuals Change Their Communities and the World

- Past and present heroes and their contributions
- People who overcame obstacles
- Economic, cultural, and scientific contributions made by individuals

Grade 4—History of Texas

- History of Texas from its beginning to the present
- Events and individuals of the nineteenth and twentieth centuries
- Human activity and physical features of regions in Texas and the Western Hemisphere
- Native Americans in Texas and the Western Hemisphere
- European exploration and colonization
- Types of Native American governments
- Characteristics of Spanish and Mexican colonial governments

Grade 5—United States History

- History of the United States from its early beginnings to the present

- Major events and significant individuals of the late nineteenth and twentieth centuries including contributions of famous inventors and scientists
- Regions of the United States that result from physical features and human activity
- Characteristics and benefits of the free enterprise system
- Roots of representative government
- Important ideas in the Declaration of Independence
- Meaning of the Pledge of Allegiance
- Fundamental rights guaranteed in the Bill of Rights
- Customs and celebrations of various racial, ethnic, and religious groups in the nation

Grade 6—People and Places of the Contemporary World

- People and places of the contemporary world
- Societies from the following regions in the world: Europe, Russia and the Eurasian republics, North America, Middle America, South America, Southwest Asia-North Africa, Sub-Saharan Africa, South Asia, East Asia, Southeast Asia, Australia, and the Pacific Realm
- Influence of individuals and groups from various cultures on selected historical and contemporary events
- Different ways of organizing economic and governmental systems

Using Maps and Globes

Symbolic representation can pose challenges for children in kindergarten through grade 4, and even students in fifth and sixth grades. Maps and globes are tools for representing space symbolically. In the early grades, the main purpose for using globes is to familiarize children with the basic roundness of the earth and to begin developing a global perspective. It can also be used to study the proportion of land and water. In kindergarten through third grade, teachers should use a simplified 12-inch globe. Generally, this type of globe uses no more than three colors to represent land elevation and no more than two colors to represent water depth. For this age group, the globe should include only the largest rivers, cities, and oceans. In grades 4 through 6, students can use a 16-inch globe containing additional details. Generally, seven colors are used to represent land elevation and three colors to represent water depth.

Activities for Students in Kindergarten through Grade 6

Teaching map concepts in kindergarten through grade 4 should include the following activities:

- Stress that the globe is a very small representation of the earth.
- Show children how land areas and water bodies are represented on the globe.
- Identify major land and water bodies.
- Show the location of the North Pole and explain the concept of the Northern Hemisphere, where most of the world's land is located.
- Show the location of the South Pole and explain the concept of the Southern Hemisphere, where most of the world's water is located.
- Show the relationship and location of the Earth in the solar system.
- Use the globe to find the continent, the country, the state, and the city where the children live.
- Encourage children to explore the globe to find places by themselves.
- Compare the size of the continents represented on a globe with their representation on a Mercator projection—the flat representation.

Teaching map concepts in fifth and sixth grade should include the following activities:

- Create and interpret maps.
- Use maps and globes to pose and answer questions.

- Locate major historical and contemporary societies on maps and globes.
- Use maps to solve real-life problems, i.e., using road maps to plan a route to a specific destination.

Latitude and Longitude—Developmental Considerations

The concepts of latitude and longitude are generally covered in fourth grade and up. However, even fourth graders may have difficulty understanding the mathematics involved in the grid system. Children might get confused with these concepts:

- The sizes of the meridians of longitude and the parallels of latitude on a globe and Mercator projection look different.
- The meridians of longitude have a consistent size, but the parallels of latitude vary in size, becoming smaller as they move away from the equator.

They might have problems conceptualizing and separating the Western Hemisphere and the Eastern Hemisphere, or the Northern and Southern hemispheres. Teachers should use concrete materials like a pumpkin to represent these concepts.

Using Technology Information in Social Studies

Research in social studies involves the use of systematic inquiry. Engaging children in inquiry involves the ability to acquire information from various resources. Inquiry involves the ability to design and conduct investigations, which requires students to develop an understanding of key information in social studies content.

To gather content information, students should become familiar with the various resources used in social sciences research. Those resources include primary and secondary sources, encyclopedias, almanacs, atlases, government documents, artifacts, and oral histories. Students are expected to apply critical-thinking skills to organize and use information acquired from a variety of sources including electronic technology. In addition to sources available electronically, students can use commercially developed programs like "Oregon Trails" and "Where in the World is Carmen San Diego?" These kinds of interactive programs can expose students to problem-solving skills and social studies content in a fun and supportive environment.

Integration of Social Studies

As mentioned earlier, the teaching of social studies by definition implies integration of content from five disciplines: history, geography, civics and government, economics, and psychology. However, teachers can go beyond this integration and add components from other content areas. The use of a literature-based approach is an ideal way to integrate social studies with language arts. Through the use of authentic multicultural literature, teachers can expose children to quality reading and the cultures of the many ethnic and linguistic groups living in the United States.

The use of thematic units can also help teachers integrate the content areas. In this approach, a teacher or teachers select a theme and organize content area instruction around it. Thematic instruction can be done in a self-contained classroom or in a departmental format in which several teachers teach the content. Thematic instruction is ideal for English language learners (ELLs) because the use of a common theme in multiple content areas makes content more cognitively accessible for them. The presentation and repetition of content in different subjects and conditions allow students the opportunity to develop English vocabulary while learning content.

Graphic Representations of Historical Information

Information in social studies can be presented in a visual form through the use of graphs and charts to make content accessible to all children, including ELLs.

Graphs

The most commonly used graphs are the pictorial graph, the bar graph, the pie or circle graph, and the line graph. The pictorial graph is the most concrete type of graph because it uses a picture of the object being represented. Bar graphs are more concrete than pie graphs. Although the pie graph appears to be simple enough for children in the elementary grades, students need to understand the concept of percentages to correctly interpret the meaning of this type of graph, and the concept of percentages is not acquired until late in the elementary grades. At first, teachers can use real-life situations to guide students in the construction of graphs. For example, teachers can create a simple graph showing information about students in the classroom, like the number of boys and girls in the classroom or their color or food preferences. Figure 4-2 shows the results of a poll on the favorite foods of first-grade boys and girls.

Figure 4-2.
Food Preferences for Children

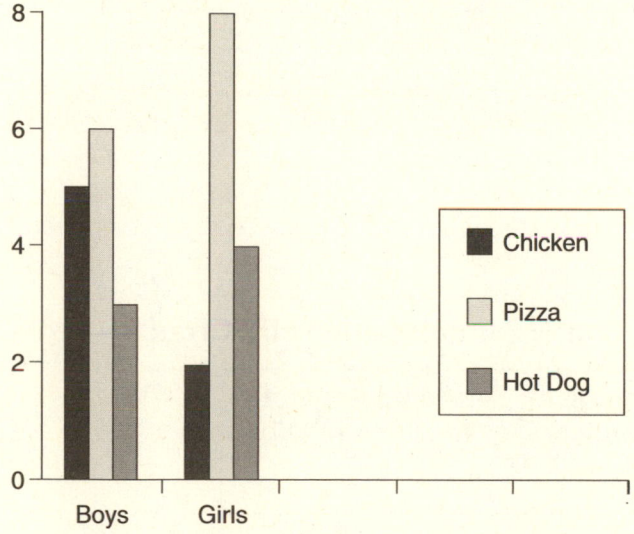

Teachers can use more sophisticated graphs like the pie graph to represent research information. For example, children can take 5 to 10 minutes a day to observe the types of transportation used by people in the neighborhood and prepare a graph similar to the one presented in Figure 4-3. Teachers can use this information to guide children to make inferences about the information contained in the graph. Why are so many people using pickup trucks as a mode of transportation? Why are only a small number of people walking?

Figure 4-3.
Pie Graph—Methods of Transportation

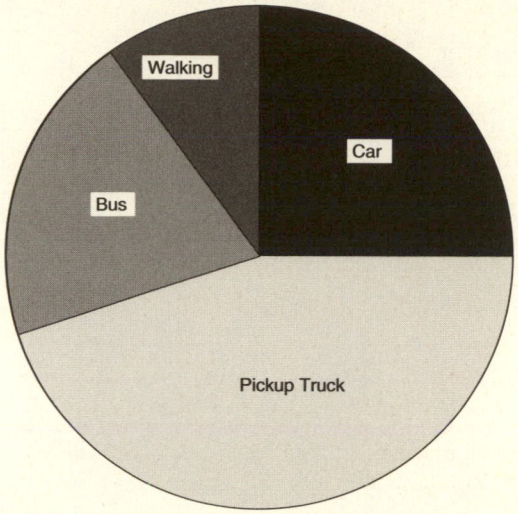

Charts

Charts can be used to record information and present ideas in a concise way. Charts are ideal for promoting concept formation in a concrete fashion. Data retrieval charts are used to gather and keep track of data gathered from research, observation, or experimentation. The chart is constructed to allow the easy comparison of two or more sets of data. For example, students could use the chart shown in Table 4-1 to record information about the foods of the ethnic groups represented in their classroom.

Narrative charts are used to show events in a sequence. For example, students can develop charts showing the steps in making their favorite dishes. A narrative chart can also be used to present a timeline of historical events. An example of a simple timeline is one that shows a child's personal history. Because children in kindergarten through grade 2 might have problems conceptualizing time, initial exposure to timelines should begin with things that they did yesterday, things that they are doing today, and things that will be done tomorrow. Starting in third grade, children can begin introducing more challenging components, like the ones listed in Figure 4-4.

A tabulation or classification chart provides orderly columnar display of information for comparison. For example, Table 4-2 compares data from the 2010 United States census.

Table 4-1.
Data Retrieval Chart—Ethnic Foods

Ethnic Group	Mexican American	Puerto Rican	African American	Italian American
Breakfast	Tortilla/eggs	Bread/eggs	Grits/eggs	Frittata (omelet)
Dinner	Enchiladas/rice	Pinto beans/rice	Collard greens/meat	Spaghetti/meatballs
Special Days	Tamales/menudo	Roasted pork/rice	Glazed smoked ham	Special lasagna

Figure 4-4.
A Timeline—My History

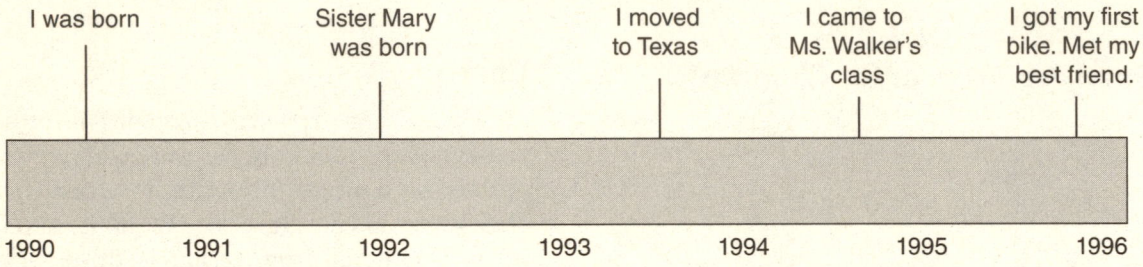

Table 4-2
Tabulation or Classification Chart—U.S. and Texas Populations by Group

Ethnic Group Population	Percentage of U.S. Population	Percentage of Texas Population
Caucasian	72.4%	70.4%
African American	12.6%	11.8%
Asian American	4.8%	3.8%
Hispanic	16.2%	37.6%
Native American	0.2%	0.7%
Total Population	281,421,906	20,851,820

Using developmentally appropriate vocabulary, teachers can guide students to recall or infer data from the chart.

A pedigree chart shows the origin and development of something. Examples are a person's family, the pedigree line of a purebred dog, and the development of a political party. Figure 4-5 presents a pedigree chart.

An organizational chart shows the structure of an organization, like a school or business. Figure 4-6 represents the typical organization of an elementary school.

A flowchart shows a process involving changes at certain points—for example, Figure 4-7 shows a process used to complete an academic degree.

Figure 4-5.
A Pedigree Chart—My Family Tree

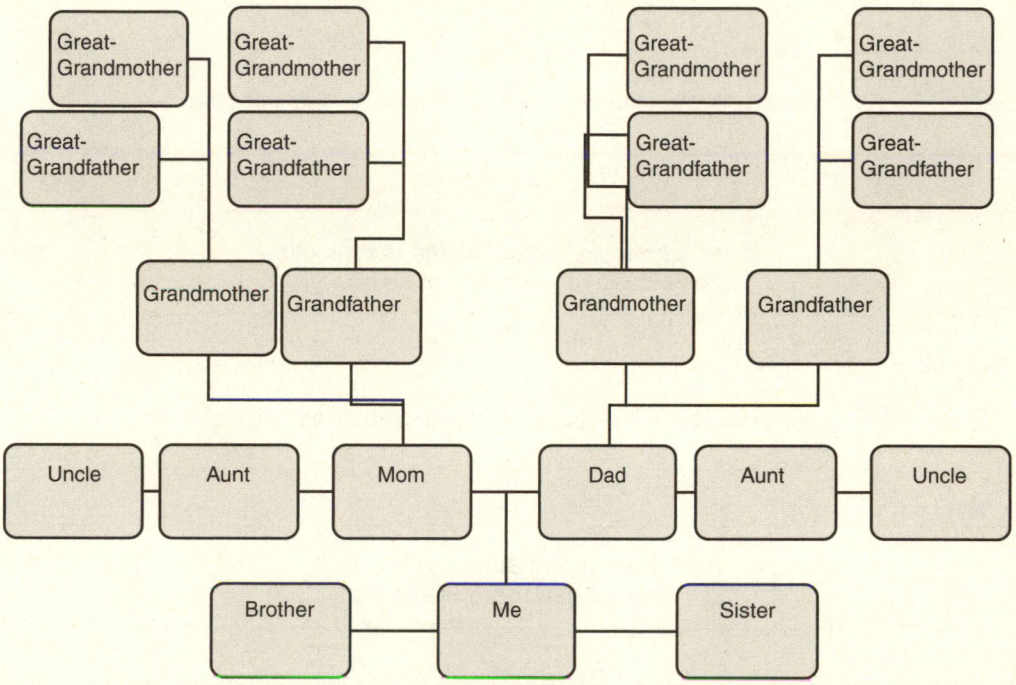

Figure 4-6.
Organizational Chart—Elementary School

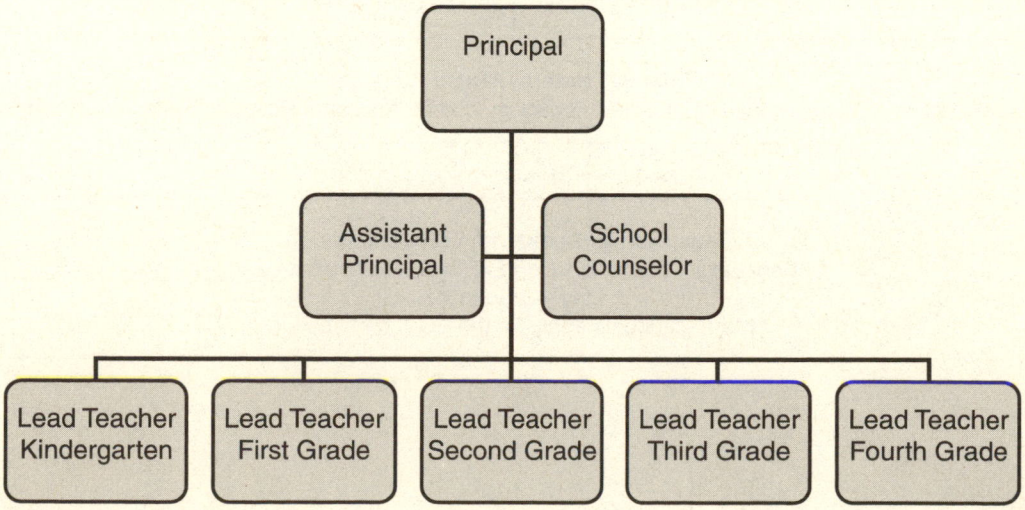

Figure 4-7.
Flowchart for Program Completion

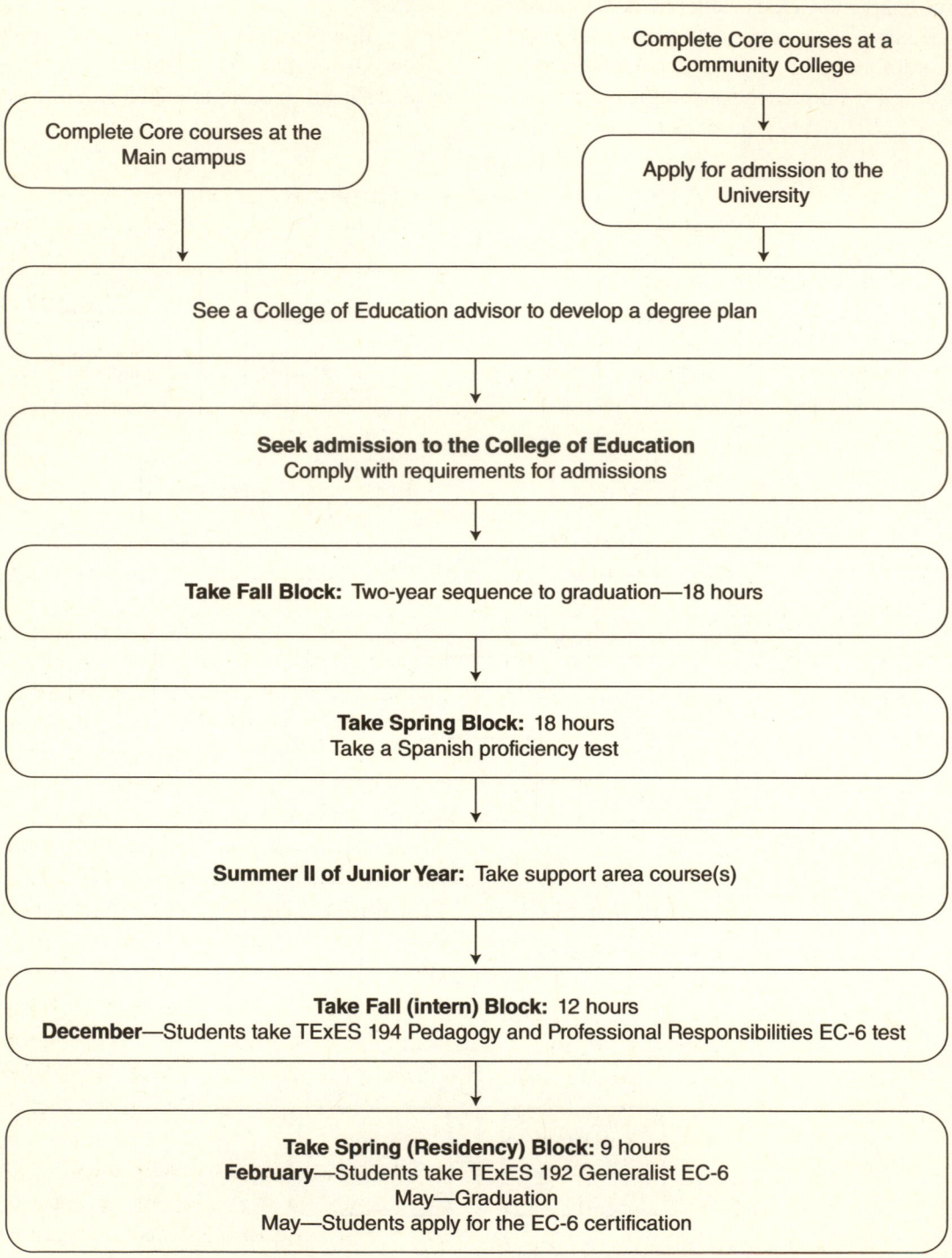

Addressing the Needs of English Language Learners

English language learners can find social studies instruction quite challenging; thus, teachers need to modify instruction to make the content comprehensible for this group. Some textbooks have been written with ELLs in mind. These books use numerous visual and graphic representations to make the content cognitively accessible to children learning English. For example, *Adventure Tales of America*, written by Jody Potts (1994), is an American history book that uses cartoons and illustrations to explain complex concepts like the processes of electing the president and making a bill into law. The illustrations give ELLs the fundamental meanings of important concepts from which teachers can develop lessons.

Other books integrate language instruction with content to deliver both components in a contextualized format. One example is the ESL series titled *Avenues*, published by Hampton Brown (Schifini et al. 2004). This set of books presents ESL lessons in conjunction with content from other disciplines. The integration of content and language is one of the most effective strategies to promote content area mastery and language development.

Cognates and Suffixes

English and most Western languages have been heavily influenced by the Greek and Roman civilizations. The association has resulted in the creation of multiple cognates—words that are similar in two languages. Most of the sophisticated English words in the content areas and especially in social studies are cognates of Spanish and other Western languages. Teachers can use these similarities to expand the vocabulary of students and enhance content area comprehension. Table 4-3 presents examples of the connection between English and Spanish words (Rosado and Salazar 2002–2003).

Table 4-3. Common Greek and Latin Roots and Affixes

Roots/ Affixes	Meaning	English/ Spanish Cognates
Phobia Xeno	Fear of Foreigners or strangers	Xenophobia/ Xenofobia
Phono Logy(ia)	Sound Study of	Phonology/ Fonología
Photo Graphy	Light Graph, form	Photography/ Fotografía
Homo Sapiens	Same, Man Able to Think	Homo sapiens/ homo sapiens
Demo Cracy	People Government	Democracy/ Democracia

Instructional Techniques to Support ELLs

Teachers need to implement a variety of activities to teach the state curriculum to ELLs at the grade level and complexity required of native English speakers. Scaffolding was originally used to describe the way in which adults support children in their efforts to communicate in the native language (L1). The same concept can be used to facilitate language and content development for ELLs. The term scaffolding alludes to the provisional structure used to provide support during the construction of a building. This support is eliminated when the structure is complete. Following this analogy, ELLs receive language support to make content cognitively accessible to them until they achieve mastery in the second language (L2); once that mastery is accomplished, the language support is eliminated.

Sousa (2011) has identified several strategies to help ELLs learn Social Studies content (see below). He suggests that the teacher adjust the strategies based on students' age and level of English proficiency (p. 131).

Preteach reading assignments—discuss, model the features of the textbook (overviews and summaries) in order for students to generate monitoring questions prior to reading the assignment.

Use role plays—for ELLs who do not have the proficiency to engage in dialogue, simply listening to other students' debate will model appropriate language—slowly engage ELLs in simple role plays.

Create analogies—this strategy will help ELLs link the familiar with the unfamiliar—like comparing a President's cabinet to that of the staff at a school.

Be a considerate lecturer—to help struggling ELLs listeners, distribute fill-in-the-blanks lecture guides or graphic organizers before lecturing—use simple familiar language whenever possible.

Use jigsaw groups—collaborative groups provide support in reading and study (e.g. John Kennedy lesson—divide the students into 5 original groups, assign each member in the group a number (experts), then the expert groups can research (1) his childhood, (2) his family life, (3) military service, (4) his Presidency, and (5) the assassination and then come together to teach the original group). Other strategies used with ELLs are listed below.

Graphic organizers are visuals used to show relationships. These are the most common graphic organizers:

- A semantic web or tree diagram shows the relationship between main ideas and subordinated components.
- A timeline presents a visual summary of chronological events and is ideal for showing historical events or events in a sequence.
- A flowchart shows cause-and-effect relationships and can be used to show steps in a process, like the process for admission to a school or program.
- A Venn diagram uses circles to compare common and unique elements of two or three distinct components, such as properties of numbers, elements of stories, or events or civilizations (like the Maya, Inca, and Aztec shown in Figure 4-8).

The SQ4R is a study strategy in which the learner is engaged in the entire reading process. The acronym stands for survey, question, read, reflect, recite, and review. During the survey part, readers examine the headings and major components of the text to develop predictions and generate questions.

Figure 4-8.
Venn Diagram—Three Civilizations

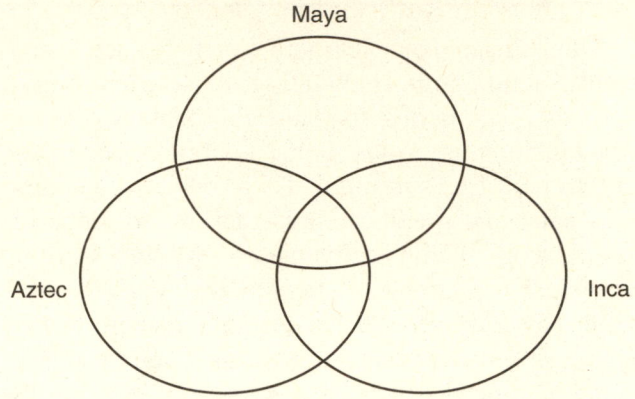

Through these questions, students establish the purpose for reading. As they read, students look for answers to the questions they generated. They monitor their comprehension as they reflect, write a summary, and recite the content they learned. Finally, they review to evaluate how much they learned about the content.

Sheltered English

Sheltered English is an instructional approach designed to make content comprehensible for ELLs (Echevarria, Vogt, and Short 2000). In the program, children are "sheltered" from the pressure of competing with native English learners. To deliver comprehensible input, content instruction is linguistically simplified through contextualized instruction, visual aids, hands-on activities, and body language. Some strategies teachers can use to modify language to make it comprehensible are:

- Control the length and complexity of the sentences. Children respond better to short, simple sentences.
- Introduce technical vocabulary before beginning the lesson.
- Use repetition, restatement, and paraphrasing to clarify concepts.
- Control the speed of delivery, and use a different type of intonation to emphasize important concepts.

- Supplement oral presentations with diagrams, graphic organizers, and manipulatives to make content easier to understand.
- Help students use drawings and graphic organizers to visualize word problems and experiments, and as tools for communication.
- Guide students in using role-play to represent important concepts.
- Use linguistic modifications, such as repetition and pauses during speech (Parker 2001).
- Make the presentation of content more interactive with comprehension checks.
- Use cooperative learning strategies.
- Organize content around thematic units.
- Use graphic organizers to simplify and chunk content.
- Emphasize the gist of concepts instead of details.

Sheltered English is most effective in a classroom with students from many language groups who are at least at the intermediate level of English language development (Schifini 1985).

Academic Vocabulary in Social Studies

Academic vocabulary is the vocabulary needed to understand the concepts of school. In other words, it is the vocabulary of teaching and learning. Marzano and Pickering (2005) emphasize the importance of teaching academic vocabulary to English language learners and recommend a six-step systematic approach that includes direct instruction as well as practice and reinforcement. The steps to teach academic vocabulary are:

- The teacher provides a description, explanation, or example of the new term.
- Students restate the description, example, or explanation in their own words.
- Students create a representation of the word by drawing a picture, symbol, or graphic of the word.
- Students periodically participate in activities that help to add to their knowledge of terms.
- Students discuss terms with one another.
- Students participate in games and activities that reinforce the new term.

Cooperative learning is a teaching strategy designed to create a low-anxiety learning environment in which students work together in small groups to achieve instructional goals. As a result of this instructional arrangement, students with different levels of ability or language development work collaboratively to support each other to ensure that each member masters the objectives of the lesson. This approach can easily be used to deliver content and language instruction. Traditionally, the strategy is delivered in specific steps whereby the teacher will (Arends 1998):

1. **Present Goals**—lesson objectives and motivation.
2. **Present Information**—inform students either verbally or with text.
3. **Organize Students into Learning Teams**—form learning teams along with transitions.
4. **Assist Teamwork and Study**—assist learning teams as work.
5. **Test Students on the Content**—assess students' knowledge of learning materials.
6. **Provide Recognition**—recognize both individual and group efforts and achievements.

To emphasize the cooperative nature of the strategy, specific methods were developed to enrich the lessons. These specialized methods are described in the sections that follow.

Student Teams Achievement Division (STAD)

1. The teacher presents new academic information to students.
2. Students are divided into four- or five-member learning teams.

3. Team members master the content and then help each other learn the material through tutoring, quizzing one another, or carrying on team discussions.
4. Each student receives an improvement score that shows the growth he or she has made.
5. Daily or weekly quizzes are given to assess mastery.
6. Each week, recognized individuals/groups. (Slavin 1986).

Group Investigation

1. Students select a subtopic within a general area.
2. The teacher divides the class into small groups (ethnically and academically heterogeneous).
3. The students and the teacher plan specific learning procedures, tasks, and goals.
4. Students carry out the plan using various sources while the teacher monitors the teams.
5. The students analyze and evaluate information and plan how they can summarize it.
6. The students present their final product.
7. The teacher conducts individual or group evaluation (Thelen 1981).

Think-Pair-Share

This activity was developed as a result of the wait-time research. Wait-time research suggests that pausing for a few seconds to allow children to reflect on the question can improve the quality of the response and the overall performance of children (Rowe 1986).

1. **Think**—the teacher poses a question and asks students to spend a minute thinking alone about the answer. No talking is allowed.
2. **Pair**—Students pair off and discuss what they have been thinking about, sharing possible answers or information.
3. **Share**—Students share their answers with the whole class. The teacher goes around the classroom from pair to pair until a fourth or a half of the class has a chance to report (Lyman 1981).

Numbered Heads Together

This activity was designed to involve more students in the review of materials covered in class.

1. **Number**—the teacher divides the students into teams with three to five members each and assigns a number to each member.
2. **Question**—the teacher asks a question.
3. **Heads Together**—Students put their heads together to figure out the answer and to be sure everyone knows the answer.
4. **Answer**—the teacher calls a number, and students from each group with that number raise their hands and provide the answer (Kagan 1985).

Competency 024 (History)

The teacher understands and applies knowledge of significant historical events and developments, multiple historical interpretations and ideas, and relationships between the past, the present, and the future as defined by the Texas Essential Knowledge and Skills (TEKS).

World History

The World History Encyclopedia divides the history of the world into five periods: the Ancient World, the Middle Ages, the Age of Discovery, Revolution and Industry, and the Modern World (Ganeri, Martell, and Williams 1999). A summary and timeline of key events in each period is presented here:

The Ancient World (4 Million Years Ago to 500 CE)

Study of the ancient world focuses on the development of the first humans, the first farmers, and the first civilizations. It emphasizes the history of the ancient civilizations of Mesopotamia, Sumer, Assyria, Babylon, Egypt, the Indus Valley, megalith Europe, ancient China, Phoenicia, ancient America, ancient Greece, the Celts, the Romans, and empires in Africa and India.

Timeline of the Ancient World

4000 BCE	Homo sapiens appear in various regions in the world
3500 BCE	The Sumerians of Mesopotamia invent writing and the wheel
3100 BCE	Egypt becomes unified
2800 BCE	Building begins in Stonehenge, England
2500 BCE	Indus civilization flourishes in India
1600–1100 BCE	Mycenaean control of Greece
1200–400 BCE	Olmecs civilization flourishes in western Mexico
1000–612 BCE	New Assyrian Empire flourishes
753 BCE	Foundation of Rome
605–562 BCE	King Nebuchadnezzar rebuilds the city Babylon
476–431 BCE	Golden age of Athens
336–323 BCE	Alexander the Great rules the world
27 BCE to 14 CE	Augustus rules as the first Roman emperor
476 CE	Western Roman Empire falls

The Middle Ages (500–1400 CE)

This period includes the Byzantine civilization, the rise of Islam, civilizations of the Americas, the Vikings, the feudal system, the Crusades, Genghis Khan and China, the African kingdoms, and the Hundred Years' War.

Timeline of the Middle Ages (CE)

500	Eastern Roman (Byzantine Empire) at its peak
600	Teotihuacán civilization flourishes in Mexico
600	Rise of Islam
700	Mayan civilization at its height in Central America
700	Feudal system begins in Europe; peasants serve a lord in exchange for protection
711	Moors invade Spain
750	Abbasid dynasty is founded; Arab Empire at its peak
800	Charlemagne crowned emperor of the Holy Roman Empire
900	Rise of Toltec civilization in Mexico
1000	Vikings land in North America
1095	Muslim Turks take Jerusalem and ban Christian pilgrims from the city
1096–1270	Crusades try to rescue Jerusalem from the Muslims
1215	Genghis Khan and the Mongols invade China
1271	Marco Polo travels to China from Italy
1300	Renaissance begins in Europe
1325	Aztecs established Tenochtitlán near modern day Mexico City
1368	Foundation of the Ming dynasty in China
1453	Fall of the eastern Roman Empire (Constantinople)
1454	Gutenberg invents the printing machine
1500	Inca Empire at its peak in Peru

Age of Discovery (1400–1700)

This period includes the Renaissance, the development of the Aztec and Inca civilizations, voyages of discovery from Spain and Portugal, African empires, the Reformation, the Ottoman Empire, and the Ming dynasty.

Timeline of the Age of Discovery

1441	Portuguese begin slave trade from Africa to Europe
1448	Portuguese explorers reach the southern part of Africa
1492	Columbus sails from Spain to America
1492	Spain becomes unified and expels the Moors
1497	Portuguese reach India
1517	Martin Luther begins the religious Reformation in Europe
1520	Suleiman rules the Ottoman Empire
1522	Magellan travels around the world
1535	Spain completes the conquest of the Aztecs in Mexico and the Incas in Peru
1543	Copernicus suggests that the sun is the center of the universe, not the Earth
1571	Europeans defeat the Muslim Ottomans in the battle of Lepanto
1588	England defeats the Spanish Armada and becomes the greatest naval power in the world
1607	England begins the colonization of North America
1609	Galileo uses a new invention, the telescope, to study the universe
1618	Thirty Years' War begins

Revolution and Industry (1700–1900)

This period includes the Russian Empire, the Manchu dynasty in China, the period of Enlightenment in Europe, the growth of Austria and Prussia, the birth of the United States, the French Revolution, the Napoleonic era, the Industrial Revolution, the British Empire, the American Civil War, and the unification of Italy and Germany.

Timeline of the Age of Revolution and Industry

1644	The Manchu overthrow the Ming dynasty of China
1682–1725	Peter the Great rules Russia
1740	Frederick the Great becomes king of Prussia—Domination of Europe
1756–63	Seven Years' War ensues, with France, Austria, and Russia clashing against Prussia and England
1768	James Cook visits regions in the Pacific
1776	America declares independence from England
1789	French Revolution begins with the fall of the Bastille in Paris
1791	As part of the Enlightenment period, Thomas Paine publishes *The Rights of Man*.
1804	Napoleon declares himself emperor of France, beginning the Napoleonic Era
1808	Wars for independence begin in Spanish America
1837–1901	British Empire at its peak under Queen Victoria
1848	Year of revolution in all Europe
1861–65	American Civil War
1869	Union Pacific Railroad links the East and West coasts of the United States

The Modern World (1900–Present)

This period includes the struggle for equal rights for women, World War I, the Russian Revolution, the Great Depression, the rise of fascism, revolution in China, World War II, Israel versus Palestine, the Cold War, the space race, the Korean and Vietnam wars, and globalization.

Timeline of the Modern World

1914	World War I begins when Austria declares war on Serbia and Germany on Russia.
1917	Russian Revolution starts when the Bolsheviks, led by Lenin, seize power from Czar Nicholas II.
1918	World War I ends; Europe is in ruins, and Germany is heavily punished.
1929	Great Depression begins in the United States.
1933	Adolf Hitler achieves power in Germany
1936–39	Spanish Civil War brings Francisco Franco to power.
1939	World War II begins when Germany invaded Poland and Czechoslovakia.
1941	United States enters World War II.
1945	Germany surrenders to the Allied Forces, and Japan surrenders after the United States detonates two atomic bombs in Hiroshima and Nagasaki.
1947	Pakistan and India obtain independence from Great Britain.
1948–49	State of Israel is founded in Palestine, and the Arabs declare war.
1949	Communist Mao Zedong (Tse-tung) gains control of China.
1959	Cuban Revolution
1960	Many countries in Africa gain independence.
1965–72	America participates in the Vietnam War.
1969	Neil Armstrong lands on the moon.
1990	Germany is reunited.
1991	Soviet Union collapses, and the Cold War ends.
1994	Free elections in South Africa and the end of apartheid
2001	9/11 terrorist attack in New York City and Washington, D.C.
2001	War in Afghanistan against the Taliban
2003	War in Iraq
2009	Barack Obama becomes the 44th President of the United States.

For details about these historical periods, go to these websites: Kidipede—History for Kids (*www.historyforkids.org*) and Ancient Mesoamerican Civilizations, created and maintained by Kevin L. Callahan of the University of Minnesota, Department of Anthropology (*www.angelfire.com/ca/humanorigins*).

The Industrial Revolution and Modern Technology

The Industrial Revolution began in England in the mid-eighteenth century. Inventions that made mining of fossil fuel (charcoal) easier provided the energy needed to expand and promote industrial development. Improvements on the steam engine and industrial machines led to the mass production of goods and a better distribution system. The economic growth motivated people to leave the rural areas and move to the cities. The following time line highlights inventions that supported the industrial revolution and modern life:

Timeline of Industrial and Technological Development

1769	Richard Arkwright patents the spinning machine powered by a waterwheel
1810	A German, Frederick Koenig, invents an improved printing press
1831	An American, Cyrus H. McCormick, invents the reaper
1836	Samuel Colt invents the first revolver
1837–1938	Samuel Morse invents the telegraph and Morse code
1846	Ascanio Sobrero, an Italian chemist, invents nitroglycerin
1856	Louis Pasteur invents the process of pasteurization
1858	Jean Lenoir invents an internal combustion engine
1866	Albert Nobel invents dynamite
1876	Alexander Graham Bell patents the telephone
1885	Gottlieb Daimler invents the first gas engine motorcycle
1900	Ferdinand Von Zeppelin invents a hot air balloon called the zeppelin
1903	The Wright brothers invent the first gas-powered airplane
1905	Albert Einstein publishes the theory of relativity: $E = mc^2$
1914	Henry Ford introduces the assembly line and begins building the first American cars
1928	Biologist Alexander Fleming discovers penicillin
1930	Vannevar Bush at the Massachusetts Institute of Technology in Boston invents the analog computer
1940	Peter Goldmark invents modern color television
1946	The atomic bomb is invented
1952	The hydrogen bomb is invented
1955	The antibiotic tetracycline is invented
1959	Jack Kilby and Robert Noyce invent the microchip
1969	The predecessor of the Internet, called the ARPAnet, is invented
1971	Ray Tomlinson invents Internet-based e-mail
1985	Microsoft invents the Windows program
1988	Digital cellular phones are invented
1990	Tim Berners-Lee created the Internet protocol HTTP and the World Wide Web language HTML

Ancient Civilizations of the Americas

Among the most developed ancient civilizations in the Americas were the Mayas, Toltecs, Olmecs, Aztecs, and Incas.

Mayas

One of the earliest civilizations of Mesoamerica was the Mayan who occupied regions of Mexico's Yucatán Peninsula, Guatemala, and Honduras. The Mayas developed a highly integrated society with elaborate religious observances for which they built stone and mortar pyramids. The center of the Maya civilization was the city of Chichén Itzá and its religious centers. The Mayas developed an elaborate calendar, a system of writing, and the mathematical concept of zero. They also had highly advanced knowledge of astronomy, engineering, and art. By the time the Spanish conquerors arrived, most of the Mayan religious centers had been abandoned and the civilization was in decline.

Zapotecs, Olmecs, and Toltecs

Farther north in Mexico, three highly sophisticated civilizations emerged: the Olmecs, Zapotecs, Teotihuacán, and Toltecs. Beginning with the Olmecs, who flourished around 1200 BCE and followed by the Toltecs and Zapotecs, these groups developed highly sophisticated civilizations. They had already begun to use a ceremonial calendar and had built stone pyramids on which they performed religious observances. Teotihuacán is the best-known example of religious ceremonial sites built by these civilizations. They developed a partly alphabetic writing system and left codices describing their history, religion, and daily events.

Aztecs

The Aztec civilization achieved the highest degree of development in Mexico. They had a centralized government headed by a king and supported by a large army. The Aztecs were also skilled builders and engineers, accomplished astronomers and mathematicians. They built the famous city of Tenochtitlan, with many pyramids, palaces, plazas, and canals. At the peak of their civilization, the Aztecs had a population of about five million. For information about the civilizations that emerged in Mexico, go to the Web site Teotihuacán: The City of the Gods, hosted by Arizona State University, at http://archaeology.la.asu.edu/teo/intro/intrteo.htm and the National Indian Education Association website at *www.xmission.com/~amauta/index.htm*.

Incas—Children of the Sun

The Inca civilization covered the modern countries of Ecuador, Peru, and central Chile. Although they were not as advanced in mathematics and the sciences as the Mayans and Aztecs, the Incas had a well-developed political system. They also built a monumental road system to unify the empire. Their civilization was at its peak when the Spanish conquerors arrived in Cuzco, the capital of the empire.

Mound Builders in North America

In North America, two major groups, known as the Woodland and Mississippian peoples, lived in the Great Lakes and Mississippi area. These people built burial mounds dated as early as 500 CE. The Mississippian people built flat-topped mounds as foundations for wooden temples dating from 500 CE. The chiefs and the priests of these groups lived in residences built on the top of the mounds, while the rest of the population lived in houses below. These mound-building civilizations declined gradually and disappeared by the fourteenth century.

Inhabitants of the South and Southwest

In the southwestern United States and northern Mexico, two ancient cultures developed: the Anasazi and the Hohokam. The Anasazi developed adobe architecture consisting of individual apartments, storage areas, and a central plaza. They worked the land extensively, had a highly developed system of irrigation, and made cloth and baskets. The Hohokam built separate stone and timber houses around a central plaza. Neither group developed a written language. Drought and attacks from rival tribes contributed to the decline of these civilizations. Historians believe that the Anasazi built the cliff dwellings at Mesa Verde, Colorado, during the fourteenth and fifteenth centuries to protect themselves from these attacks.

Pueblo Indians

There is evidence to suggest that the Anasazi settled along the Rio Grande and intermarried with the local population, leading to the emergence of the Pueblo people. The Pueblo culture continued to improve the architectural tradition and farming techniques of their predecessors. They were also able to produce drought-resistant corn and squash, which became the foundation of their diet. The Pueblo Indians managed to survive the Spanish conquest and colonization period.

Iroquois

The Iroquois inhabited the area of Ontario, Canada, and Upstate New York for at least 4,500 years before the arrival of Europeans. They hunted and fished, but farming became the main economic activity for the group. The Iroquois had a matrilineal line of descent, with women doing most of the farming to support the community. They developed the Iroquois Confederation to discourage war among the groups and to provide for a common defense.

American History

Colonization

In 1565, the Spaniards established the first successful European settlement in North America near the current city of Jacksonville, Florida. Following the Spaniards, the English attempted to establish a permanent colony on Roanoke, an island off the coast of North Carolina. This colony eventually disappeared. Further north, the Dutch settled colonies in the region of present-day New York and New Jersey. Following the Dutch, numerous private companies received royal charters, or patents, permitting them to begin the colonization process in North America. Three of the first and most successful companies were the Plymouth Company, the Massachusetts Bay Company, and the London Company. The London Company was the first to exercise this patent.

The English Colonies

Thirteen colonies were established on the Atlantic coastline. Three types of colonies developed based on three types of charters: corporate colonies, royal colonies, and proprietary colonies. These were divided in three geographical regions: the New England Colonies, the Middle Colonies, and the Southern Colonies. The New England Colonies consisted of Massachusetts, Connecticut, Rhode Island, and New Hampshire. The economy of the New England colonies was based on farming and very small industries such as fishing, lumber, and crafts. The Middle Colonies consisted of New York, New Jersey, Delaware, Maryland, and Pennsylvania. The economy of the Middle Colonies was based on farming, shipping, fishing, and trading. The Southern Colonies were Virginia, North Carolina, South Carolina, and Georgia. The economy of the Southern Colonies was based on the crops of tobacco, rice, indigo, and cotton plantations. Plantations produced agricultural crops in large scale and exploited workers as well as the environment.

Virginia (1607)

The London Company established the first English colony in Jamestown, Virginia. The leader of the colony was Captain John Smith. Natives of the area captured Smith and sentenced him to death. Pocahontas, daughter of the tribe's chief, intervened and saved his life. Contrary to popular belief, John Smith did not marry Pocahontas; instead, Pocahontas married John Rolfe, a tobacco farmer from the same colony.

Massachusetts (1620)

The Puritans, who fled England to avoid religious persecution, founded Plymouth. The group obtained a patent from the London Virginia Company. Before arriving at their destination, they wrote the Mayflower Compact, a document containing rules to guide life in the community. This compact established the first type of government in North America colonies.

New Hampshire (1623)

Two groups founded the colony of New Hampshire. The first group was led by Captain John Mason, who established a fishing village in 1623. In 1638, a group led by John Wheelwright founded a second settlement called Exeter. That colony began as a proprietorship but eventually became a royal colony.

New Jersey (1623)

The Dutch founded the New Jersey colony in 1623. After taking over the Dutch territory between Virginia and New England in 1664, King George II of England gave these possessions to his brother, the Duke of York. The duke then gave the territory as a proprietary grant to Sir George Carteret and Lord Berkeley. In 1702, New Jersey became an English colony.

New York (1624)

The area of New York was part of New Amsterdam, a possession of the Dutch government. In 1674, the British took control of the territory, and in 1685 New York officially became a royal colony.

Maryland (1633)

In 1632, King Charles I granted a Maryland Charter to Lord Baltimore (George Calvert). In 1633, the colony was established as a refuge for freemen, especially Catholics.

Rhode Island (1636)

Roger Williams founded the Rhode Island colony in 1636, and in 1638 Anne Hutchinson settled an additional part of the colony. Both Williams and Hutchinson had been banned from Massachusetts for their religious and political views and were looking for sanctuary. The colony was initially a corporation and eventually became a royal colony.

Connecticut (1636)

As early as 1633, Dutch traders had established a permanent settlement near Hartford. After the decline of the Dutch influence in the area, Thomas Hooker established the colony of Connecticut. Hooker and his followers were also seeking religious freedom after being expelled from Massachusetts. In 1662, Connecticut obtained a Royal Charter under the leadership of John Winthrop Jr.

Delaware (1638)

The Dutch and Swedish initially settled this colony. With the decline of the Dutch influence in the area, the English took control. In 1682, Delaware was awarded to William Penn.

North Carolina (1653)

By 1653, Virginia colonists began moving south and settling in the North Carolina region. In 1691, the region was officially recognized as a colony, and Charles I granted a royal charter in 1729.

South Carolina (1663)

In 1663, King Charles II created the colony of Carolina by granting the territory, of what is now the region of present-day North Carolina, South Carolina, and Georgia, to loyal supporters. It began as a proprietary colony and became a royal colony in 1719. Sir John Yeamans, a plantation owner from Barbados, founded the city of Charleston in 1670.

Pennsylvania (1682)

As early as 1647, Swedish, Dutch, and English settlers tried to establish permanent settlements in Delaware. In 1681, a large territory, which included Pennsylvania, was granted to William Penn. Penn was a member of a religion persecuted in England, the Quakers. He made Pennsylvania a safe haven for Quakers, and a large number of German Quakers settled in the colony. In 1683, the first group of settlers arrived in Pennsylvania and formed Germantown near Philadelphia.

Georgia (1732)

This colony was founded with two main purposes: to establish a buffer zone from the Spanish settlement south of the colony and to provide a safe haven for poor people.

Table 4-4 summarizes the key historical characters and events of the colonies.

Representative Government in Colonial America

Colonists brought with them their tradition of hard work, individual freedom, and representative government. They believed in the right to elect the people who would represent them in important issues such as taxes. The Virginia House of Burgesses was the first colonial assembly of elected representatives from the Virginia settlement. It was established in Jamestown to represent the colonists in the state of Virginia in the lawmaking process.

The Mayflower Compact was drawn and signed by the Pilgrims aboard the Mayflower. They pledged to consult one another to make decisions and to act by the will of the majority. It is one of the earliest agreements to establish a political body and to give that political body the power to act for the good of the colony.

Indentured Servants

The indentured servant system was used to bring workers to the New World. In practice, the indentured servant would sell him or herself to an agent or ship captain before leaving England. In turn, the contract would be sold to a buyer in the colonies to recover the cost of passage. Criminals and people in debt could also be sold for life or until they paid their debts. This system of provisional servitude was not applied to Africans; instead, permanent slavery was instituted.

Table 4-4.
The Thirteen American Colonies

Colony	Year Established	Colonizer	Historical Features/ Characters
Virginia	1607	London Company	Captain John Smith, John Rolfe, and Pocahontas
Massachusetts	1620	Puritans with a patent from the London Virginia Company	Puritans, Mayflower, Mayflower Compact
New Hampshire	1623	Proprietary colony	Captain John Mason, John Wheelwright
New Jersey	1623	Dutch possession, then a proprietorship	Duke of York
New York	1624	Dutch possession, then a proprietorship	Purchase of the island of Manhattan, Duke of York
Maryland	1633	Proprietorship	George Calvert (Lord Baltimore), the colony served as a refuge for persecuted Catholics
Rhode Island	1636	Corporate colony	Roger Williams and Anne Hutchinson
Connecticut	1636	Corporate colony	Thomas Hooker and John Winthrop
Delaware	1638	Corporate colony	First, under the Dutch, Swedish, and finally under British control William Penn
North Carolina	1653	Proprietorship	King Charles II
South Carolina	1663	Proprietorship, then a charter colony	King Charles II, Sir John Yeamans
Pennsylvania	1682	Proprietorship	William Penn and Quakers
Georgia	1732	Charter colony	James Edward Oglethorpe

The Enlightenment—The Age of Reason

The Enlightenment refers to a period during the seventeenth and eighteenth centuries when people began questioning religious dogmas and emphasizing scientific reasoning and knowledge. The result of this quest for knowledge was the development of modern chemistry and biology. People also began questioning governments and started searching for individual freedom. The search for freedom led countries to seek independence and fight tyranny. For example, the quest for freedom led to the American War of Independence and the French Revolution. The American Revolution motivated the Spanish colonies to seek independence. Some of the leading thinkers of this period were Jean-Jacques Rousseau, John Locke, Charles Montesquieu, Voltaire, and Francis Bacon. The ideas of the Enlightenment quickly reached the British colonies. Many of the leaders responsible for the writing of the Constitution were familiar with the leading thinkers of the movement, and framed the Constitution protecting the natural rights of the individual and limiting the power of the government.

American Revolution

The main reasons for the War of Independence were economic in nature. England, as well as other European nations, had established the mercantilism system to exploit the colonies. This system had three main principles:

1. The wealth of the nation is measured in terms of commodities accrued (gold and silver).
2. Economic activities can increase the power and control of the national government.
3. The colonies existed for the benefit of the mother country.

England used the system of mercantilism quite effectively in the thirteen colonies, but after more than a century of British rule, the colonies were primed for independence, and war with England became inevitable.

Another reason for the rebellion was the cost of the French and Indian War. This war, which was the North American portion of the Seven Years' War, emptied the British coffers, and the British Crown needed a quick way to recover financially. The taxation system that followed the French and Indian War was unbearable for the colonies. The colonies responded with civil disobedience and by boycotting the government of King George. In response to civil disobedience, the British sent troops to Boston, where the groups clashed and several colonists were killed. The event was called the Boston Massacre. One of the best-known boycotts was the Boston Tea Party, in which the colonists dumped tea in the Boston harbor to protest against taxation. All these events and the repression that followed led to the American War of Independence.

Continental Congress

Following the events in Massachusetts, representatives of the colonies met in Philadelphia to discuss the political and economic situation in the colonies. No clear solutions were reached at this congress. Once the hostilities started, the Second Continental Congress met to discuss preparations for war. George Washington was elected commander of the American forces, and war was declared against the British. The congress named a committee, led by Thomas Jefferson, to prepare the Declaration of Independence, which was officially signed on July 4, 1776.

The Declaration of Independence

The Declaration of Independence pronounced the colonies free and independent states. It consists of a preamble, or introduction, followed by three main parts. The first part stresses natural unalienable rights and liberties that belong to all people from birth. The second part consists of a list of specific grievances and injustices committed by Britain. The third part announces the colonies as the United States of America. This document provided the foundation to establish equal rights for all people.

Revolution

The American Revolution began in Massachusetts in the outskirts of the towns of Concord and Lexington. In 1775, while the colonists were preparing for war, hundreds of British soldiers marched against them. Paul Revere warned the colonists of British troop movements, and minutemen took up arms to face the enemy. At Concord, the British were repelled and forced back to Boston. On their way back, American sharpshooters ambushed and killed hundreds of British soldiers. Following this initial victory for the colonists, the battle of Bunker Hill was fought near Boston. In this battle, the British lost large numbers of soldiers but managed to defeat the colonial troops. Later, in Long Island, the British won another decisive victory over the Americans. The French joined the war in support of the Americans, in retaliation for their defeat at the hands of the British in the Seven Years' War. Eventually, with the support of the French, the American troops defeated the British forces in Yorktown, Virginia, in 1781. The Treaty of Paris, officially signed in 1783, ended the war and gave independence to the new nation. For additional details about the American Revolution, go to the web page of HistoryCentral.com at *www.multied.com/Revolt/index.html*.

Articles of Confederation

During the Revolutionary War, the Second Continental Congress ran the government. After independence, the Articles of Confederation defined a new form of government. The new government was composed of representatives, from thirteen independent states, with limited power. The Congress could not declare war or raise an army. They could ask the states for money or for soldiers, but it was up to the states to agree to provide them. Under this type of government, each state printed its own money and imposed taxes on imports from the other states.

On the positive side, the new government provided for a common citizenship—citizens of the United States. It organized a uniform system of weights and measurements and the postal service. It also became responsible for issues related to Native Americans living within the borders of the new nation. The confederation served as the official government of the young republic until 1789, when the states ratified the Constitution.

United States Constitution

After six years under the Articles of Confederation, the leaders of the nation realized that the American government needed revision to bolster its strength. To accomplish this goal, a constitutional convention was held in Philadelphia in 1787. The leaders of this initiative were George Washington, James Madison, Benjamin Franklin, and Alexander Hamilton. From this convention, a new form of government emerged. The Constitution was officially ratified in 1788, and in 1789 George Washington was selected to be the first president of the United States. The republic defined by the Constitution was composed of three branches, the executive, judicial, and legislative, and a system of checks and balances to regulate each branch.

To learn more about historical American documents, go to "A Chronology of U.S. Historical Documents," a website created and maintained by the University of Oklahoma Law Center, at *www.law.ou.edu/hist*.

Policies of the New Nation

Monroe Doctrine

In 1823, President Monroe made clear to European countries that the United States was not going to permit the establishment of colonies in the Western Hemisphere. Monroe also banned European countries from attacking the new American republics that were just becoming established in the early nineteenth century. Nor was the U.S. to become involved in European affairs. This concept of "America for Americans" is known as the Monroe Doctrine.

Manifest Destiny

In 1844, President James K. Polk declared to the world that the United States would eventually become a world power and expand to its natural borders. Some of the borders mentioned were the Pacific to the west and Mexico to the south. Eventually, Polk's expectations became a reality as a result of the war between Mexico and the United States from 1846 to 1848.

Slavery in the United States

The Dutch brought the first African slaves to Virginia in 1619 to work on plantations. From 1640 to 1680, large numbers of slaves were brought to the Americas. With the invention of Eli Whitney's cotton gin, cotton became the economic mainstay of the South, and the demand for labor increased the slave trade. From 1798 to 1808, more than 200,000 African slaves were brought to America, mostly to the southern region.

Beginning in 1774, the North began regulating and eventually prohibiting slavery. By 1804, New York and New Jersey had passed gradual emancipation laws. Meanwhile, the slave trade in the South grew to meet the economic needs of the area. Eventually, the issue of slavery, along with other economic and ideological differences between the regions, resulted in the American Civil War. In 1862, Abraham Lincoln issued the Emancipation Proclamation, granting freedom to slaves in the South. After the war, the Thirteenth Amendment to the Constitution officially abolished slavery. Additionally, in 1866 the Fourteenth Amendment gave African Americans full citizenship, and the Fifteenth Amendment granted voting rights to black men.

Civil War

With the expansion of the United States came additional problems for the young nation. One problem that divided the nation was the issue of slavery. By the 1800s, slavery had been virtually abolished in the North. The northern states' reasons for turning against slavery were primarily economic: the North had become more urban and industrialized than the South, and northern states received large numbers of immigrants who provided the necessary labor. Southern states remained mostly rural and received few immigrants, making slavery the foundation of their economy. With the nation's expansion westward and the addition of new states, the question of slavery became a contentious issue. Any new state would affect the balance between the free and slave states.

The issue of slavery became the main topic of the presidential election of 1860. The candidates were clearly aligned either in favor of or against slavery. The southern Democrats backed a strong proslavery candidate, John C. Breckinridge of Kentucky, while the new Republican Party selected a strong antislavery candidate in the figure of Abraham Lincoln. The election of Abraham Lincoln resulted in the secession of the southern states from the union, the creation of the Confederacy, and the start of the American Civil War. The southern states created the Confederate States of America and selected Jefferson Davis as president.

Battle of Gettysburg

Several battles were fought in this war, but none was as memorable as the Battle of Gettysburg. Fought in 1863, this battle was the most disastrous event of the war and perhaps in the history of the United States. In this battle, more than 50,000 soldiers from the North and the South lost their lives. In a speech delivered on the battlefield in November 1863, President Lincoln eulogized the fallen Union soldiers in a speech known as the Gettysburg Address. After five years of fighting and the loss of thousands of lives and millions of dollars in property, in 1865 the commander of the Confederate army, General Robert E. Lee, surrendered to General Ulysses S. Grant, commander of the Union forces.

Reconstruction Era (1865–1877)

Because the war was fought primarily in the South, that area was practically destroyed. Therefore, the physical reconstruction of the country focused on the South. However, the emotional reconstruction and the reconstruction of American unity had to be done nationwide, and admission of rebel states back into the Union was not automatically granted. The Reconstruction period was characterized by hatred and violence. Because Lincoln was assassinated in 1865, shortly after the end of the war, leadership of the reconstruction effort fell on the shoulders of Andrew Johnson, a southerner who was disliked by the North as well as the South. Eventually, he was impeached and almost removed from power.

A major obstacle to the reunification of the nation resulted from the black codes. These very restrictive laws were passed by southern legislatures to control former slaves. Some black codes restricted free assembly, while others restricted the types of jobs that they could do. In 1867, the U.S. Congress, still composed entirely of northerners, passed legislation to eliminate the black codes. Additionally, Congress required southern states to ratify the Fourteenth Amendment of the Constitution prior to being allowed back into the Union. The Fourteenth Amendment gave citizenship to blacks. Finally, in 1870, the last two states (Texas and Florida) were allowed back in the Union.

Ku Klux Klan

The Ku Klux Klan was one of various secret societies established during Reconstruction to continue the implementation of the black codes and to terrorize African Americans. Members of the group warned blacks not to vote or exercise individual freedoms. The Klan divided the South based on color lines. More subtle legislation was passed in the South to control the progress of African Americans. These new laws were known as Jim Crow laws. Racial separation characterized life in the South and other parts of the nation for most of the twentieth century.

Economic Development

After the reunification of the country, energy was redirected to the economic development and growth of the nation. New inventions, together with the development of the railroad, paved the way to economic recovery. The reconstruction that followed the war also played a vital role in the development of the United States as a solid economic and industrial nation.

Civil Rights Movement

Civil rights are legal and political rights of the people who live in a particular country. In the United States, the Constitution and the Bill of Rights guarantee civil rights to American citizens and residents. The first 10 amendments to the U.S. Constitution are known as the Bill of Rights. Following these initial amendments and as a result of the American Civil War, three additional amendments were added. The Thirteenth, Fourteenth, and Fifteenth Amendments to the Constitution were passed during the Reconstruction era. The 13th Amendment freed all the slaves without compensation to slave owners. The 14th Amendment declared that all persons born in the U.S. were citizens (except Native Americans), that all citizens were entitled to equal rights, and that their rights were protected by due process. The 15th Amendment granted black men the right to vote.

The civil rights movement sought equality for African Americans. Even after the 13th, 14th, and 15th Amendments were added to the Constitution, blacks were denied full civil rights. Discrimination existed throughout the nation. Jim Crow laws enforced strict separation in the South. They were also kept from voting by poll taxes and literacy tests. In the North many qualified African Americans were not able to find good jobs. Segregation rules restricted blacks to separate facilities in public places such as theaters, restaurants, buses, restrooms, and schools. Discrimination also affected other minorities such as Latinos and Native Americans. In 1896, *Plessy v. Ferguson* legalized segregation, allowing "separate but equal facilities" for black and white students.

Several historic events marked the beginning of what is today known as the Civil Rights Movement. In 1947, Jackie Robinson became the first African American to play baseball on a major league team. In 1948, President Truman ordered the integration of the armed forces and introduced civil rights legislation in Congress. The National Association for the Advancement of Colored People (NAACP) challenged the laws of segregation with the Brown v. Board of Education of Topeka case, and in 1954 the Supreme Court ruled that racial segregation in public schools was unconstitutional.

Another important event in the civil rights movement era was the Montgomery Bus Boycott. In December 1955, Rosa Parks, a well-known activist and respected citizen of Montgomery, Alabama, refused to give up her seat on the bus to a white man as Alabama's Jim Crow laws required. She was consequently arrested and sent to jail. Her actions prompted local community leaders of the NAACP to form a new organization called the Montgomery Improvement Association.

The association chose a young Baptist minister, Dr. Martin Luther King Jr., to lead the organization and to direct a boycott of the Montgomery bus company. The boycott began in December 1956 and ended about a year later when the U.S. Supreme Court ruled segregation on buses unconstitutional. This victory gained national attention and Dr. King became one of the most prominent figures of the civil rights movement. He founded the Southern Christian Leadership Conference (SCLC) with other African American leaders. The SCLC favored nonviolent forms of protest such as sit-ins, boycotts, and protest marches. His famous "I Have a Dream" speech took place during the march in Washington in support of the Civil Rights Act of 1964. The eloquent speech and orderly demonstration gained more supporters for the cause. He was assassinated in 1968 in Memphis, Tennessee, but his work resulted in the official Civil Rights Act in 1964.

President John F. Kennedy proposed new civil rights laws as well as programs to help the millions of Americans living in poverty. After Kennedy's assassination in Dallas in 1963, President Lyndon B. Johnson urged Congress to pass the laws in honor of Kennedy persuading the majority of Democrats and some Republicans. The Civil Rights Act passed in 1964 prohibited segregation in all public facilities and discrimination in education and employment.

The Mexican American Civil Rights Movement

During the 1960s Mexican Americans were engaged in the struggle for human rights. As part of the process, the Mexican-American leaders initiated a movement called the Chicano Movement. This movement was cultural as well as political (Rosales Castañeda n.d.). It embraced four main goals: the restoration of land grants, the farm workers' rights, education, and political rights (Mendoza, 2001). The movement also sought to rescue the cultural and linguistic identity of Mexican Americans.

Activist Reies Tijerina initiated the Chicano Movement in New Mexico with the land grant movement, which sought to recover the land taken from the Mexican Americans as a result of the Guadalupe Hidalgo Treaty of 1848 and the eventual annexation of the American Southwest. In Colorado, Rodolfo "Corky" Gonzales founded the Crusade for Justice as a platform for the political movement (Mendoza, 2001). He also defined the movement through his epic poem "Yo Soy Joaquín/I am Joaquin." In this poem he provided a historical development of Mexican-American identity and described their struggles in the United States.

As part of the effort to support the rights of farm workers, human rights leaders Cesar Chávez and Dolores Huertas founded the United Farm Workers (UFW) union. Through the UFW they fought for better working conditions and fair compensation for agricultural workers.

In Texas, the movement focused its attention on the educational and political rights of Mexican Americans. In Crystal City, students took a leadership role organizing Mexican-American voters and joining the political process. As part of this process, Mexican American Student Organization (MAYO), under the leadership of José Ángel Gutiérrez and Mario Compean founded the Raza Unida Party (RUP) in 1970. Through the RUP, they sought to bring greater economic, social, and political autonomy to Mexican Americans (Acosta, n.d.). As a result of this movement, the RUP nominated candidates for mayor, city councils, and school boards in three South Texas cities—Crystal City, Cotulla, and Carrizo. In these communities, the RUP won fifteen seats. This political awakening of the Mexican-American voters in Texas paved the way for better schools and programs for Mexican American and minority children in general.

Women's Rights

While the 19th Amendment to the Constitution guaranteed women the right to vote in 1920, women remained subject of discrimination. The civil rights movement provided the impetus for the women's movement of the 60s. The women's movement attained better employment and professional opportunities for women. The Equal Pay Act of 1963 and the Civil Rights Act of 1964 prohibited discrimination based on gender. In 1966, Betty Friedan, author of *The Feminine Mystique*, and other leaders founded the National Organization for Women (NOW). This organization adopted the activist approach used by the African-American leaders of the civil rights movement. The Equal Rights Amendment of 1972 guarantees women's equal rights.

Temperance Movement—Prohibition

The temperance movement sought to prohibit alcohol consumption in the United States. This movement began in the 1830s, and by 1855 thirteen states had enacted legislation to prohibit the use of alcohol. In 1919 the U.S. Constitution was amended to prohibit alcohol consumption at the national level; this marked the adoption of the 18th Amendment (Cardinale, 2007). However, the prohibition was never fully enforced. Battles between law enforcement agents, like Eliot

Ness, and organized crime characterized the prohibition era. Leaders of organized crime, like Al Capone, made millions selling alcohol. After 14 years of prohibition and unsuccessful attempts to enforce the law, it was finally repealed in 1933 with the 21st Amendment.

Conflicts and Wars

Spanish American War of 1898

The war between Spain and the United States made the United States a world power. As a result of this war, the United States established its power and influence in the Caribbean Sea and Pacific Ocean. Cuba became an independent nation, and the United States gained control of the Philippines, Guam, and Puerto Rico. Eventually, the Philippines became an independent nation, while Puerto Rico and Guam remained U.S. territories. Eventually, the people from Guam and Puerto Rico became American citizens.

World War I

The first global war began in Europe and involved two alliances: the Allies and the Central Powers. The Allies were England, France, Russia, and Italy. The Central Powers were Germany, the Austria-Hungary Empire, Turkey, and Bulgaria. Initially, the Americans remained neutral and benefited extensively from trading with the Allies. America's neutrality was challenged, however, when the Germans developed a new weapon, the submarine, and used it successfully to destroy Allied ships. In 1915, the Germans sank a British liner, the *Lusitania*, killing more than 1,100 passengers, including 128 Americans. Additionally, American cargo ships were sunk, which forced President Wilson to ask Congress to declare war against Germany and the Central Powers. The influx of fresh American forces fostered the Allies' victory in 1918.

With the Treaty of Versailles, the war officially ended. In this treaty, the Central Powers were severely punished and forced to pay for the war. Additionally, the Austria-Hungary Empire was dismembered and new countries were created. The punitive conditions of the Treaty of Versailles created the resentment of the Germans that eventually led to the second global confrontation, World War II.

The Bolshevik Revolution in Russia

In 1917, the Communists, led by Vladimir Lenin, took over the government in Russia. As a result of this revolution, Russia underwent a period of governmental reconstruction to incorporate the communist philosophy in the nation. With a new government in power, Russia withdrew from World War I.

The Great Depression

After World War I, the United States enjoyed a period of prosperity, the golden 1920s. But it all came to an abrupt end on October 29, 1929, when the stock market crashed, initiating a ten-year period that we now call the Great Depression. During the Depression, millions of people lost their capital and jobs. Between 1933 and 1937, President Franklin D. Roosevelt implemented a series of government-sponsored programs, called the New Deal, designed to revitalize the economy and alleviate poverty and despair caused by the Depression.

World War II

The emergence of totalitarian countries like Russia, Germany, and Italy created instability in Europe and eventually led to war. Communist Russia, under the leadership of Stalin, became a threat to European countries. Italy was a fascist, belligerent state where individual liberties were ignored. Germany, under the leadership of Adolf Hitler, was ready to avenge the humiliating treatment it suffered as a result of World War I. In the Pacific, Japan was building an empire that had already conquered parts of China. All these conditions promoted the creation of military alliances that eventually led to World War II. Germany, Italy, and Japan created the Axis powers, and Russia, France, and England became the Allies. The war started with the German invasion of Poland in 1939. Two days later, France and England declared war against Germany. Hitler conquered most of Europe in a relatively short time. France was occupied, and England was brought close to submission. The United States supported the Allies with supplies and weapons but did not send troops. Although it remained neutral for the first few years of the war, the United States joined the Allies when Japan attacked the U.S. naval base in Pearl Harbor, Hawaii, in 1941.

D-Day

With Hitler in full control of Europe, the United States joined England and representatives of the French government to plan and execute the invasion of Europe in 1944. On June 6, General Dwight D. Eisenhower, together with a quarter of a million Allied soldiers, crossed the English Channel into France and launched one of the largest offensives against the German occupying forces. This large attack on Germany was known as D-Day. As a result of the collective effort of the Allies, France was freed from German occupation. With the combined forces of England, Russia, Canada, and the United States, Hitler and the Axis forces were finally defeated.

Yalta Conference

The Allies met in Yalta, Russia, to discuss the terms of the treaty to end the war. In this meeting, the leaders of the Allied forces—Winston Churchill, Joseph Stalin, and Franklin D. Roosevelt—met to discuss peace. Under the terms of peace agreed to at Yalta, Germany was to be divided into four sections, each controlled by an Allied country—Britain, France, Russia, and the United States. The Germans were to pay the Russians for war reparations in money and labor. Poland was divided, and the Russians received control of one section (later they took full control of the nation). Finally, plans were set to organize the United Nations to prevent future conflicts in the world.

Hiroshima and Nagasaki

The United States was fighting the war on two fronts, and the Japanese were dug in for a long military campaign. The best available option seemed to be the atomic bomb—seen at the time as the only way to achieve Japanese surrender. By the order of President Harry Truman, the United States dropped two atomic bombs on the cities of Hiroshima and Nagasaki. The death and destruction caused by these two bombs forced the Japanese government to surrender in 1945, which officially ended WWII.

The Marshall Plan

The Marshall Plan was a U.S.-supported program to rebuild the economic infrastructure in Europe. The United States provided money and machinery for the reconstruction of the continent.

The Holocaust and Creation of Israel

During World War II, Hitler devised a "master plan" to exterminate the Jewish population. Germany placed European Jews in concentration camps and systematically killed millions. This act of genocide is known today as the Holocaust. At the end of the war, under the leadership of Great Britain, the United States, and the United Nations, the state of Israel was created in Palestine. On that same day, the Arab Liberation Army (ALA) was created to fight the Jewish state. This liberation movement has resulted in several wars between Israel and the Arabs. Today, this war has expanded to include Europe and the United States, with many terrorist attacks committed during the new century.

The Truman Doctrine

In response to the threat of the Soviets, Harry Truman issued a proclamation warning communist countries that the United States will help any nation in danger of falling under communist control. This declaration was called the Truman Doctrine. As a result of this doctrine, the United States became involved in two major military conflicts: the Korean War and the Vietnam War.

The Cold War

As a result of the Yalta agreement, Russia became the most powerful country in the region. After taking over Poland and East Berlin, and building the Berlin Wall, a new war emerged between the Soviet Union and the United States—the Cold War. Although war was never formally declared between the two nations, confrontations occurred from 1945 to 1991. In 1963, the two nations were on the verge of nuclear war after Premier Nikita Khrushchev ordered the deployment of nuclear missiles to Cuba. An intense negotiation between Premier Khrushchev and President Kennedy avoided war between the two countries. This most intense confrontation of the Cold War was called the Cuban Missile Crisis.

The Cold War finally ended with the fall of the Soviet Union under the leadership of Mikhail Gorbachev. The fall of the Soviet empire resulted in the reunification of Germany and the creation of multiple smaller countries in Russia that gained independence.

The War on Terrorism

In 2001, terrorists from abroad attacked American soil. The attacks on the twin towers of the World Trade Center in New York and the Pentagon in Arlington, Virginia, on September 11 killed more than 3,000 people. As a result of the attacks, the United States declared war on terrorism and attacked the Taliban regime in Afghanistan. Saudi Arabian militant Osama bin Laden, the mastermind of the 9/11 attacks, eluded capture until May 2, 2011, when he was killed in Pakistan, by American Navy SEALs. The search for weapons of mass destruction led the United States into war with Iraq. Currently, the United States is still fighting to stabilize the region.

History of Texas

Before European Colonization

Several Native American groups inhabited the territory known today as Texas. The three groups living in the coastal plains—the Coahuiltecans, Karankawas, and Caddos—were food gatherers, fishermen, and farmers. When the Spanish arrived in Texas, they made initial contact with these groups. The name Texas came as a result of contact with the Caddos. Attempting to communicate to the Spaniards that they were not hostile, some Caddos identified themselves with the word taysha, which in their language meant "friend" or "ally" (Fry n.d.). When the Spaniards heard the word taysha, they thought the Caddos were identifying the name of the region. From that exchange, the name Texas and the state motto, "Friendship," emerged.

A fourth group, the Jumanos, lived in the mountains and basins of West Texas. The information about this group is limited because they virtually disappeared before the Spaniards arrived in the area. The last two groups are the Comanches and the Apaches. These two groups coexisted with Europeans and resisted the colonization efforts. After they domesticated horses (previously introduced by the Spanish), the Comanches and Apaches became fearless warriors and successful buffalo hunters. The domestication of the horse allowed the development of the culture of the buffalo. When buffalo were later annihilated in the area, these two groups became practically extinct. Table 4-5 presents a summary of Native American groups from Texas.

European Colonization

Cabeza de Vaca

The Spanish exploration of the territory today known as Texas began in 1528, when Cabeza de Vaca and three companions landed in the territory. The four Spaniards made contact with the Caddo in the southeastern part of the state, near modern-day Houston. In his account of the meeting, de Vaca described the Caddo as a very sophisticated Native American group. From there, de Vaca continued exploring the region of modern-day New Mexico and Arizona (Sheppard n.d.). No other significant events happened in the region until 1541, when Francisco Vázquez de Coronado explored Texas.

Francisco Vázquez de Coronado

In response to reports of the mythical Seven Cities of Cibola, Coronado led an expedition of almost a thousand men in search of the golden cities. The expedition left Mexico City and explored the southwestern United States and northern Texas. In 1542, Coronado returned to Mexico empty handed. For the next 140 years, the Texas region remained isolated, and no other attempts were made to colonize it.

Juán de Oñate

In 1595, Oñate received permission from King Philip II of Spain to colonize New Mexico. In 1598, he founded the first European settlement west of the Mississippi in New Mexico.

First Mission in Texas

In 1682, the Spanish established the first permanent settlement in Texas—the mission of Ysleta del

Table 4-5.
Native American Groups from Texas

Regions	Native Group
Coastal plains, flatland	**Coahuiltecan** (Rio Grande Valley) **Economic Activity:** Food gatherers and hunters—roots, beans of the mesquite tree, rabbit, birds, and deer **Features:** Lived in family groups **Karankawa** (Southeastern Texas) **Economic Activity:** Fishing and food gathering **Features:** Lived as nomads and used canoes for fishing **Caddo** (East Texas, Piney Woods) **Economic Activity:** Farming—squash, pumpkins, tobacco, and corn (good food supply) **Features:** Built villages and lived in groups
Central plains, flatland, and hills	**Apache** (Central and western Texas) **Economic Activity:** Farming and hunting **Features:** Lived as nomads, built portable housing called tepees, domesticated horses, and hunted bison
Great Plains, flatland, and hills	**Comanche** **Economic Activity:** Hunters **Features:** Lived as nomads and built portable housing; also domesticated the horse and hunted the buffalo
Mountains and basins	**Jumano** (West Texas) **Economic Activity:** Farming and hunting **Features:** Mostly sedentary and built homes of adobe

Sur near the present-day city of El Paso. After this mission, no serious efforts were made to colonize the area until the French began to threaten the Spanish hegemony in East Texas.

French Influence in Texas

In 1682, Robert de la Salle established a French settlement in Fort Saint Louis in East Texas. A few years later, the Spaniards expelled the French and established a series of missions in East Texas to control the French threat in the region.

San Antonio

In 1718, the Spanish established a mission and a fort—San Antonio de Valero and Fort San Antonio de Bexar—near what is now the city of San Antonio.

These settlements were established to provide protection and support to the settlements in East Texas.

Mexican Independence

During the first part of the nineteenth century, the Spanish empire began crumbling. Mexico obtained its independence in 1821 and took control of the colony of Texas.

Anglo-American Presence in Texas

In 1820, Moses Austin received permission from the Spanish government to bring Anglo-American families to settle in Texas. This agreement was voided when Mexico took control of the territory. Later, Austin's son, Stephen, negotiated with the Mexican government and obtained a similar agreement to allow Anglo-Americans to settle in Texas. By 1835, the settlers were the majority in the region, which antagonized the Mexican government and resulted in war.

Texas War for Independence

Conflicts between Texans and the Mexican government started as early as 1830. The colonists felt that the government was not providing adequate support and protection to Texas. Initially, they wanted to negotiate with the new president, Santa Anna, and sent Stephen Austin to Mexico City to represent the colony. The Mexican government was not willing to negotiate and jailed Austin for a year.

First Battle in Gonzales

The town of Gonzales had a cannon to protect the colonists from the Indians. By order of the government, Mexican soldiers came to take the cannon from the colonists in October 1835. The Texans refused to relinquish their weapon and fired the cannon against the Mexican soldiers. With this incident in Gonzales, the war for Texas independence began.

Sam Houston

A delegation of Texans traveled to Washington, D.C., to secure support from the U.S. government. Sam Houston, a former governor of Tennessee, volunteered to fight for Texas and eventually became the commander-in-chief of the Texas army.

The Alamo and Goliad

The first meaningful battle of the Texas war for independence took place near the present-day city of San Antonio in a small mission and fort known as the Alamo. When the war began, fewer than 200 men, led by Colonel William Travis, protected the Alamo. Eventually, additional historical characters like James Bowie and Davy Crockett joined Travis in defending the fort. In 1836, General Antonio López de Santa Anna and the Mexican army took the fort and killed all its defenders, including Texans of Mexican ancestry. Following this victory, Santa Anna continued marching against the rebels and took the city of Goliad, where more than 300 rebels were killed. These two battles provided the patriotic emotion that resulted in the creation of an army and eventually led to victory against Mexico.

Texas Declaration of Independence

A few days before the Battle of the Alamo, a group of Texans met at Washington-on-the-Brazos to issue a declaration of independence and to form the new government. An interim government for the republic of Texas was established, with David G. Burnet as president and Lorenzo de Zavala as vice president.

Battle of San Jacinto

While the colonists were fighting the Mexican army at the Alamo and in Goliad, General Sam Houston was strengthening the army of the new republic. The Texan army continued retreating ahead of the Mexican forces until they reached the San Jacinto River, near the city of Houston. In a battle that lasted less than twenty minutes, Houston's troops defeated the Mexican army and captured General Santa Anna.

Texas President Burnet and Mexican President Santa Anna signed the Treaty of Velasco, with Santa Anna agreeing to withdraw his troops from Texas in exchange for safe conduct back to Mexico, where he would lobby for recognition of Texas independence. Santa Anna's commitment never materialized, and the Mexican government refused to recognize Texas as an independent republic. Nevertheless, Sam Houston became the president of the new republic, and from 1836 to 1845, Texas functioned as an independent nation. However, the Mexican government still considered it one of its rebellious provinces that it could one day reclaim (Barker & Pohl, 2009).

Republic Period

Despite the economic hardship typical of new nations, Texas managed to remain independent for ten years and was recognized by several nations in the world, including the United States. However, unable to secure its borders and reverse its financial situation, the new nation sought the support of the United States.

Texas Joins the United States

In 1845, Texas became the twenty-eighth state of the American union. Immediately, the U.S. government sent troops to the Rio Grande (which Mexicans considered their territory) to secure the Texas border. The ensuing clashes between Mexican and U.S. forces resulted in Congress declaring war in May 1846.

Mexican-American War

Between 1846 and 1848, Mexico and the United States waged a war that ended with a decisive victory and tremendous land acquisitions for the United States. As a result of the Treaty of Guadalupe Hidalgo, Mexico withdrew its claim over Texas and established the Rio Grande, or Rio Bravo, as it is known in Mexico, as the official border between the two countries. Mexico also ceded California and the territory known today as the American Southwest to the United States. Figure 4-9 presents a timeline of important events in Texas from 1528 to 1861.

Confederacy Period (1861–65)

At the onset of the American Civil War, Texas left the union and joined the Confederacy as a proslavery state. After five years of war, the Confederate army, led by General Robert E. Lee, surrendered to General Ulysses S. Grant, the leader of the Union forces. After the war, the Union forces occupied the South for a

Figure 4-9. Texas Time Line from 1528 to 1861

1528	**1541**	**1682**	**1682**	**1690**	**1718**	**1820**
Cabeza de Vaca lands in Texas	Coronado explores Texas	Mission founded in El Paso	La Salle (French) lands in Texas	First mission in East Texas San Francisco de los Tejas	Mission and fort founded in San Antonio	Austin arrives in San Antonio
1861	**1848**	**1846**	**1845**	**1836**	**1835**	**1833**
Texas secedes from the union	Treaty of Guadalupe Hidalgo	Mexican-American war begins	Texas becomes the 28th state in the union	Battle of San Jacinto, Texas declares independence	Battle of Gonzales marks beginning of Texas revolution	Santa Anna becomes president of Mexico

period of 12 years (1865–1877). This era was called the Reconstruction Period.

Reconstruction Period

During Reconstruction, Texas was briefly under occupation by U.S. troops. Texas was allowed to rejoin the union in 1870. The Ku Klux Klan became very active at this time, terrorizing African Americans in Texas and the southern states.

Economic Development after Reconstruction

After Reconstruction, the Texas economy flourished, largely based on the growth of the cattle industry. Barbed wire was introduced in 1880, and ranchers began using scientific cattle breeding to increase production and improve the quality of meat.

Oil in Texas

In 1901, oil was discovered in the Spindletop Oil Field near Beaumont. The development of the oil industry made Texas the leading producer of oil in the United States. As a result of this boom, cities like Houston and Dallas became large urban and industrial centers.

World Wars and Beyond

As a result of World War I, Texas emerged as a leading military training center. Several military bases were established in the state, bringing economic growth. The rapid development of the aircraft industry and highly technological businesses led to rapid industrialization in the state. By World War II, Texas was a leading state in the defense industry. The modern economy of Texas still relies on agriculture, ranching, and oil production, but new high-technology industries are rapidly becoming the top economic forces in the state.

Six Flags over Texas

The phrase "Six Flags over Texas" describes the different countries that have exerted control in Texas from 1519, when the first European exploration of the region by Cortés took place, to the present:

- Spain (1519–1821)
- France (1685–1690)
- Mexico (1821–1836)
- Republic of Texas (1836–1845)
- United States (1845–1861)
- Texas in the Confederacy (1861–1865)
- Back to the American union (1870–present)

State Facts and Symbols

Texas has adopted the following symbols to represent the state:

- State flower — Bluebonnet
- State bird — Mockingbird
- State tree — Pecan
- State motto — Friendship
- Border states — Oklahoma, Louisiana, Arkansas, and New Mexico
- State song — "Texas, Our Texas," by William J. Marsh and Gladys Yoakum Wright

Key Principles of Competency 023 and 024

- The Enlightenment period of European history (eighteenth century) helped to restore religious unity that had been disrupted by the Protestant Reformation.
- The America Revolution influenced political development in Latin America by demonstrating that it was possible to overthrow European colonial rule.
- The introduction of horses and firearms had a great impact on the colonization of the American plains and the West.
- Early civilizations in Asia and Africa were located near river valleys. Some of these civilizations were Egypt, Mesopotamia, and Persia (Iran). This location provided access to fresh water for crop growing and for human consumption.
- The civil rights movement of the 1960s addressed issues that were major topics during the Reconstruction era following the Civil War—individual and human rights.
- Louis Pasteur's germ theory of diseases was one of the most important breakthroughs of nineteenth-century Europe.
- Every culture has a way to explain the formation of the earth and develops a way to adapt to the physical environment.
- In 1492, Columbus claimed America for Spain. Following that, they established colonies in the Caribbean. In 1519, Spain initiated the colonization of Mexico. Presidios and missions were established to protect the colony and to convert the natives to Christianity.
- In 1598, Juan de Oñate founded the first European settlement west of the Mississippi in New Mexico.
- The first Spanish missions in Texas were established to strengthen the control of Spain in the area and to reduce the threat of the French: San Francisco de los Tejas (1690) in East Texas and Fort San Antonio and the Alamo (1718).

Competency 025 (Geography and Culture)

The teacher understands and applies knowledge of geographic relationships involving people, places, and environments in Texas, the United States, and the world; and also understands and applies knowledge of cultural development, adaptation, diversity, and interactions among science, technology, and society as defined by the Texas Essential Knowledge and Skills (TEKS).

Geography

Geography is the study of the Earth's surface, the organisms that populate it, and their interaction within the ecosystem. Geography can be divided into two main areas: physical geography and cultural geography. Physical geography refers to the physical characteristics of the surface of the Earth and how those features affect life. Cultural geography deals with the interaction of humans with their environment and how that interaction produces changes. Humans can alter the physical environment of the Earth, but the physical environment can also shape humans and their culture. For example, the Incas built the capital of their empire, Cuzco, in the Andes Mountains in what is now Peru. This city has an altitude of 11,152 feet above sea level, where oxygen is scarce and agriculture is a challenge. However, the Incas managed to live and flourish under these conditions. They carved the land for agriculture and built roads and cities. In turn, the environment changed the Incas, who had to evolve to tolerate the low levels of oxygen. Studies conducted on the Indians from Peru suggest that people of the Andes developed genetic adaptations for high-altitude living (Discovery Channel, 2004 March 10) By adapting to the conditions of their environment, inhabitants of the area not only survived but also flourished in less-than-ideal conditions.

Locating Places and Regions on a Map

There are two categories of maps: reference maps and thematic maps. Reference maps show the locations of places, boundaries of countries, states, counties, and towns. Atlases or road maps are examples of reference maps. Thematic maps show a particular topic such as population density or distribution of world religions, and physical, social, economic, political, agricultural, or economic features. A physical map shows the topography of the Earth including land features and elevations. A political map shows how a country is organized. An economic map shows the important resources of a country or region. A historical map is used to show historical events including places of the past. Population maps are used to show where people live in a particular region.

A globe is a scale model of the Earth shaped like a sphere. Because a globe resembles the actual shape of the Earth it shows sizes and shapes more accurately than a Mercator projection map (a flat representation of the Earth). However, the cylindrical shape and portability of Mercator projections makes them more useful than globes.

The Grid System

A grid system is a network of horizontal and vertical lines used to locate points on a map or a chart by means of coordinates. This grid shows the location of places. Latitude and longitude lines form divisions in this grid system that consist of geometrical coordinates used in designating the location of places on the surface of the Earth on a globe or map. The lines measure distances in degrees.

Latitude lines are horizontal lines that run parallel around the Earth measuring the distance north and south of the equator. The equator is identified as the 0 degree line of latitude, and it divides the Earth into the Northern and the Southern hemispheres. The United States is located in the Northern Hemisphere, while Brazil is located in the Southern Hemisphere. Longitude lines are vertical lines that run north and south going east and west. The 0 degree line of longitude is known as the prime meridian. It goes through Greenwich, England, and it divides the Earth into the Eastern and Western hemispheres. The United States is in the Western Hemisphere and Japan in the Eastern Hemisphere.

Geographic Symbols

A compass rose is a design printed on a chart or map for reference. It shows the orientation of a map on Earth and shows the four cardinal directions (north, south, east, and west). A compass rose may also show in-between directions such as northeast or northwest. Symbols are used for a map to contain a large amount of information that can be easily understood. Common symbols used on a map include dots, stars, and small pictures to represent cities or places. Some maps use different colors to represent features such as elevations and divisions. These symbols and colors are defined in the map's key, or legend. A map scale shows the distance between two places in the world. The scale to which a map is drawn represents the ratio of the distance between two points on the Earth and the distance between the two corresponding points on the map.

Time Zones

Time zones are established based on the lines of longitude, or meridians. These lines run from north to south. The prime meridian, or the meridian at 0 degrees, has been set in Greenwich, England. On the other side of the globe is the International Date Line. The prime meridian divides the Earth into the Western and Eastern hemispheres. Following the sunlight as it travels along the rotating Earth, the time decreases moving from east to west. When people travel from China (east) to the United States (west), they save a day; that is, they might spend a day traveling but still arrive on the same calendar day.

The United States has six time zones of one hour difference each—Eastern, Central, Mountain, Pacific, Alaska, and Hawaii. Figure 4-10 represents the six time zones in the United States with a key city for each zone. For more information about time zones, go to the website provided by the National Institute of Standards and Technology (an agency of the U.S. Department of Commerce) and the U.S. Naval Observatory at *www.time.gov/about.html.*

Regions of the World

A world region is an area of the world that shares similar, unifying cultural or physical characteristics that are different from those of surrounding areas. The physical features refer to topographic characteristics like elevation, rivers, and mountains. The cultural features include all the characteristics that distinguish different groups of people, for example: language, religion, government, economics, food, architecture, shared values, and family life.

Geographers have divided the world into ten regions: North America, Central and South America, Europe, Central Eurasia, the Middle East, North Africa, Sub-Saharan Africa, South Asia, East Asia, and Australasia. These divisions are based on physical and cultural similarities. North America consists of Canada, the United States, and Mexico. It is the third largest continent, and it is located between the Arctic Circle and the Tropic of Cancer. Table 4-6 presents an overview of the world regions by physical and cultural features.

Figure 4-10. Times Zones in the United States

West ←					**East**
Hawaii	Alaska	Pacific	Mountain	Central	Eastern
1:00 PM	2:00 PM	3:00 PM	4:00 PM	5:00 PM	6:00 PM
Honolulu	Anchorage	Los Angeles	Phoenix	Dallas	New York City

Table 4-6. World Regions

World Region	Physical Features	Cultural Features
North America	• Consists of Canada, the United States, and Mexico. • The United States is the fourth largest country in the world. • Oil is an important resource in the U.S. • Most of the U.S. has a humid-continental or humid-subtropical climate • Most of Canada has a subarctic or tundra climate. • Over 75% of Canadians live along the Southern border. • The areas of greatest concentration of population in the U.S. are along the East Coast and California. • The climate of Mexico ranges from humid tropical and subtropical to desert and highland. • Mexico has rich mineral resources including oil.	• Europeans colonized this region. • Languages spoken are predominantly English, Spanish, and French. • Most people hold Christian beliefs.
Central and South America	• Includes the countries of Central America, the Caribbean islands, and South America. • The majority of this continuous mass of land is south of the Equator. • South America extends from Point Gallinas in Colombia to Cape Horn. • Part of South America lies closer to the South Pole than any other land mass of this size. • Venezuela is one of the world's leading exporters of oil. • Most of Eastern Central America and equatorial South America have a humid tropical climate.	• Most people speak Spanish, but many other languages are spoken: Portuguese, French, Dutch, English, and several Native American languages and dialects. • Most people hold Christian beliefs, and the Roman Catholic religion is predominant. • Architecture, law, religion, traditions, and language are strongly influenced by Europe's colonial rule of this region. • The many ethnic groups in this region are separated by geographical barriers such as the Andes and the Amazon.

World Region	Physical Features	Cultural Features
Europe	• Western section of the Eurasian continent • Shares a mountain chain, the Alps. • Most of Europe has a temperate climate. • Europe's irregular coastline has many harbors that are important manufacturing and trade centers. • The rivers of Europe are important resources for trade, water, and hydroelectricity. • European population growth rates are the smallest in the world.	• Shares a common history in the Roman Empire and later the Catholic Church and Latin language. • English is the most spoken language in Europe, German and French are also widespread. • Cultural diffusion or shared cultural traits spread throughout Europe. • Ninety percent of all adults ages 15–24 speak a second language and some countries are considered multilingual. • Europeans practice many different religions. • Roman Catholicism is the predominant religion of many European countries. • Most of Northern and Central Europe is Protestant. • Jews live in many parts of Western Europe.
Central Eurasia	• Central Asia and Eastern Europe • United around one continuous mass of land located in the idle of the continent. • Little access to the sea • The borders of Eastern European countries have changed many times. • From WWII to the late 1980s, the Soviet Union controlled Eastern Europe and introduced communism to the region.	• Conquered at different times by the Persians, Mongolians, Tartars, the French, the Germans, and the Russians. • Slavic languages are predominant. • Most people in the Eastern part of the region follow the Eastern Orthodox church, people in the Northern area are mostly Roman Catholic.

(Continued)

World Region	Physical Features	Cultural Features
Middle East	• Consists of the area of southwest Asia and North Africa. • Access to sea water • The majority of the land is desert. • Rich in oil	• While the majority of people follow the religion of Islam there are also groups that follow Christianity and Judaism. • The religion defines the law in many places. • The most ancient of human civilizations. Egyptians, Assyrians, Babylonians, Persians, Greeks, and Romans have left their mark in this region. • This region has been the fighting ground for many religious battles.
North-Africa	• Part of the African continent • Includes Egypt, Libya, Tunisia, Algeria, and Morocco • Extensive coastline • The Sahara desert and the Nile river are two important physical features of this area. • Rich in oil • Egypt is undergoing rapid growth and urbanization, and industrialization.	• The majority of people follow the religion of Islam. • People speak Arabic predominantly. • Religious issues influence the politics of this area.
Sub-Saharan Africa	• Consists of Africa south of the Sahara • Most of the area is a savanna. • Has abundant rain • Extensive coastline • Fertile land • Most people live in the forest zone and the dry savannas. • Agriculture is the predominant activity in West Africa. • Livestock is the predominant economic activity in the northern area.	• Cultural diversity reflects indigenous, Arab, and European influences. • Majority follows tribal beliefs, Christianity, or a combination of both. • Most people speak native African or European languages. • Over 500 ethnic groups live in this region.

World Region	Physical Features	Cultural Features
South Asia	• Consists of a large Indian peninsula that extends into the Indian Ocean. • Abundant rainfall • Strong seasonal winds called monsoons • Rice is an important crop. • One of the most populated regions in the world. • The world's highest mountains are located in the northern area of this region. • Many major manufacturing and trade centers are located along the coast.	• People in South Asia speak many languages. • Predominant beliefs are of Eastern origins such as Buddhism and Hinduism. • Many South Asians are farmers who live in small villages. • Many cultural influences • Through the efforts of Mohandas Gandhi the region gained its independence from Britain in 1947.
East Asia	• Consists of China, Korea, Taiwan, and Japan. • It is the most densely populated region in the world. • Large expanse of coastline.	• Buddhism and Taoism are predominant religions. • Confucian philosophy • People speak Chinese, Japanese, Korean, Mongolian, and many other languages. • Chinese Script or characters influence many of the writing systems of these languages. • Culturally, China has had a major influence in this region.
Australasia	• It is composed of the Australian continent and surrounding islands. • South of the equator	• English is the predominant language of most of the nations in this region. • Population is a large Christian majority.

Regions of the United States

The concept of regions facilitates the examination of geography by providing a convenient and manageable unit for studying the Earth's human and natural environment. The continental United States can be divided into eight broad geographic divisions:

- Laurentian Highlands are part of the Canadian Shield that extends into the northern United States and the Great Lakes area. This area has a hard winter, and agriculture is very limited.
- Atlantic–Gulf Coastal Plains are the coastal regions of the eastern and southern states. It includes New York City in the North, the Mid-Atlantic states to Florida in the South, and all the way west to Texas on the Gulf Coast.
- Appalachian Highlands covers the Appalachian Mountains, the Adirondack Mountains, and New England—the states of Connecticut, Maine, Massachusetts, New Hampshire, Rhode Island, and Vermont.
- Interior Plains and the Great Plains covers the interior part of the United States. Included in this area are the states west of the Appalachians, south of the Great Lakes, and as far west as Montana, Wyoming, Colorado, New Mexico, and northwestern Texas. Most of the nation's wheat, corn, and feed crops are grown in this area.
- Interior Highlands is also part of the interior continental United States. This area includes the Ozark Mountains and the states of Missouri, Arkansas, Kentucky, and part of Oklahoma and Kansas.
- Rocky Mountain System is in the western United States and Canada extending from British Colombia to Montana, Utah, Colorado, and New Mexico. The mountain range is called the Continental Divide, because it separates the eastward-flowing rivers from the westward-flowing rivers. The waters that flow eastward empty into the Atlantic Ocean, and those that flow westward empty into the Pacific Ocean.
- Intermontane Plateaus is a large region that includes the Pacific Northwest, the Colorado Plateau, and the basins of the southwestern United States. This area covers the states of Washington, Oregon, Idaho, part of Utah, New Mexico, and Arizona. It also covers the areas of the Grand Canyon and Death Valley.
- Pacific Mountain System covers the west coast of the United States. This area extends from the Cascade Mountains in the north down the entire west coast through the states of Washington, Oregon, and California.

Texas Regions and Economic Activity

Texas is the second-largest state in the United States. Covering 268,601 square miles, Texas contains five geographic regions. Table 4-7 lists the regions, the key cities, and the main economic activities of each.

Largest Rivers in the World

These are the three largest rivers in the world:

- The Nile (North and East Africa) is the longest river in the world. It originates in Lake Victoria in Uganda and ends in the Mediterranean Sea.
- The Amazon (South America) is the second-largest and the widest river in the world. It originates in Peru, and its mouth is at the Atlantic Ocean off the coast of Brazil.
- The Chang Jiang or Yangtze (China) is the third-largest river in the world. Its source is the Tibetan Plateau, and its mouth is the East China Sea.

For information about the world's largest rivers, go to the Social Studies for Kids website at *www.socialstudiesforkids.com/articles/geography/longestriverstable.htm*.

Largest Rivers in the United States

These are the largest and most important rivers in the United States:

Table 4-7. Regions and Economic Activity in Texas

Region	Key Cities	Main Economic Activities	Key Statistics
Coastal plains, flatland	Dallas, Houston, San Antonio, Austin, Corpus Christi, Laredo	Lumber—East Texas (Piney Woods) Oil—Refineries in Houston Farming—Rice, oranges, cotton, wheat, milo Ranching—Cattle in Kingsville Shipping—Houston	Population—High: 1 of 3 Texans Rainfall—High Distinguishing Mark—Hurricanes
Central plains, flatland and hills	Fort Worth, Arlington, San Angelo, Abilene	Ranching—Cattle, wool (mohair), sheep Farming—Grains	Population—High Rainfall—Medium Distinguishing Marks—Tornadoes, northerlies (cold winds), hailstorms; large ranches
Great Plains Flatland and hill country	Midland, Odessa, Lubbock, Amarillo, Texas Panhandle	Ranching—Cattle, sheep Minerals—Graphite Oil—Odessa and Midland Farming—Wheat	Population—Average Rainfall—Medium Distinguishing Marks—Snowstorms, dust storms, windmills, use of aquifers
Mountains and basins, Rocky Mountains, Davis, Chisos, and Guadalupe, Chihuahuan Desert	El Paso	Ranching—Limited large ranches Mexico-U.S. border economy based on trading of goods produced by the industries established in Mexico—Maquiladoras.	Population—Low Rainfall—Low; hard rain wears out the rocks and land Distinguishing Mark—Big Bend National Park

- The Mississippi is the longest river in the United States and the fourteenth-longest in the world. It begins in Minnesota and ends in the Gulf of Mexico.
- The Ohio River begins near Pittsburgh and runs southwest, ending in the Mississippi River on the Illinois and Missouri borders.
- The Rio Grande begins in the San Juan Mountains of southern Colorado and ends in the Gulf of Mexico. The river is the official border between the United States and Mexico, where it is known as the Rio Bravo.
- The Colorado River begins in the Rocky Mountains and ends in California.
- The Missouri River begins in the Rocky Mountains, flowing north first and then generally southeast across the central United States, ending at the Mississippi River, just to the north of St. Louis, Missouri.
- For information about rivers in the United States, visit WorldAtlas.com. To view the most significant rivers of the continental United States, visit *www.worldatlas.com/webimage/countrys/namerica/usstates/artwork/rivers/uslayout.htm*.

Mountains of the World

With notable exception of the peak known as K2, which is part of the Karakoram Range, the tallest mountains in the world are located in the Himalayas, ranging across the countries of China, Pakistan, Nepal, and Tibet. Table 4-8 lists the top ten tallest mountains. Compared with the world's tallest peaks, the United States' mountains are small. The highest mountain is Mt. McKinley in Alaska. In fact, the state of Alaska has the 16 highest peaks in the United States. A list of the mountains with 16,000 feet or above is presented in Table 4-9. For additional information about the world's mountains, go to the Infoplease.com Web site at *www.infoplease.com/ipa/A0001771.html.*

Table 4-8.
Tallest Mountains in the World

Mountain	Location	Height (in feet)
Everest	Nepal/Tibet	29,035
K2	Pakistan/China	28,250
Kanchenjunga	India/Nepal	28,169
Lhotse I	Nepal/Tibet	27,940
Makalu I	Nepal/Tibet	27,766
Cho Oyu	Nepal/Tibet	26,906
Dhaulagiri	Nepal	26,795
Manaslu I	Nepal	26,781
Nanga Parbat	Pakistan	26,660
Annapurna	Nepal	26,545

Table 4-9.
Tallest Mountains in the United States

Mountain	Location	Height (in feet)
Mt. McKinley	Alaska	20,320
Mt. St. Elias	Alaska	18,008
Mt. Foraker	Alaska	17,400
Mt. Bona	Alaska	16,500
Mt. Blackburn	Alaska	16,390
Mt. Sanford	Alaska	16,237

Deforestation

Deforestation can increase soil erosion and in some instances can lead to tragedies like the mudslides that occurred in 2006 in the Philippines, where thousands of people were buried alive. The rate of soil erosion is most likely to exceed the rate of soil formation in areas like Brazil, where people have cut forests to clear land for farming.

Deposition

Deposition is the process of carrying soil from one place to another, usually by means of water or wind. This process is responsible for the creation of beaches, sand dunes found in desert areas, and landforms created by glaciers.

Map Skills by Grade—Scope and Sequence

In addition to the basic knowledge required in the Texas Essential Knowledge and Skills (TEKS), each student in kindergarten through grade 6 needs to acquire the following specific geography skills and concepts:

Kindergarten

- Understands and uses terms related to location, direction, and distance (up, down, left, right, here, near, far).
- Recognizes a globe as a model of the Earth.
- Recognizes and uses terms that express relative size and shape (big, little, large, small, round, square).
- Identifies school and local community by name.
- Recognizes and uses models and symbols to represent real things.
- Identifies bodies of water—oceans, seas, lakes, rivers, ponds, and bayous (TEKS).
- Identifies landforms—plains, mountains, deserts, hills, and canyons (TEKS).

- Identifies natural resources—water, soil, trees, metals, and fish (TEKS).

Grade 1

- Makes and uses simple classroom maps to locate objects.
- Knows geographical location of home in relation to school and neighborhood.
- Knows the layout of the school campus.
- Identifies state and nation by name.
- Follows and gives verbal directions (here, there, left, right, below, above).
- Distinguishes between land and water symbols on globes and maps.
- Relates locations on maps and globes to locations on the Earth.
- Observes, describes, and builds simple models and maps of the local environment.
- Knows the four cardinal points (TEKS).
- Identifies the physical characteristics of places—precipitation, body of water, landforms, types of vegetation, and climate (TEKS).

Grade 2

- Makes and uses simple maps of the school and neighborhood.
- Interprets map symbols using a legend.
- Knows and uses cardinal directions.
- Locates community, state, and nation on maps and globes.
- Identifies local landforms.
- Differentiates between maps and globes.
- Locates other neighborhoods studied on maps.
- Knows the continents of the world (TEKS).
- Identifies important landmarks—Statue of Liberty and others (TEKS).
- Identifies natural resources (TEKS).
- Identifies aspects of the physical environment, from organisms to communities (TEKS).

Grade 3

- Uses distance, directions, scale, and map symbols.
- Compares own community with other communities.
- Compares urban and rural environments.
- Uses charts to record and present information (TEKS).
- Understands climate and the elements that influence climate like wind velocity, precipitation, and proximity to bodies of water.
- Uses the compass rose as a means of orientation on a map of the Earth (TEKS).
- Uses graphs (TEKS).
- Uses graphic organizers and diagrams to arrange items in meaningful way (TEKS).
- Understands that landforms change through the processes of erosion and deposition (TEKS).
- Understands that regions are areas of the Earth's surface (TEKS).
- Uses scale to represent distances (TEKS).
- Uses timelines to chronologically list events.

Grade 4

- Interprets pictures, graphs, charts, and tables.
- Works with distance, directions, scale, and map symbols.
- Relates similarities and differences between maps and globes.
- Uses maps of different scales and themes.
- Recognizes the common characteristics of the map grid system.
- Compares and contrasts regions on a state, national, or world basis.
- Understands the concepts of adaptation and modification, such as changing the landscape to meet survival needs and building to adjust to a new environment (TEKS).
- Identifies elements that affect the climate (TEKS).
- Uses a compass rose to find true directions.

- Identifies key explorers and their achievements (TEKS).
- Identifies geographic factors that affect the settlement and development of places.
- Understands the connection between climate and vegetation on Earth.
- Identifies global divisions, like the prime meridian, the equator, the Northern and Southern hemispheres, and the Eastern and Western hemispheres (TEKS).

Grade 5

- Uses geographic tools to collect, analyze, and interpret data (TEKS).
- Applies geographic tools such as grid systems, legends, symbols, scales, and compass roses to construct and interpret maps (TEKS).
- Translates geographic data into a variety of formats such as graphs and maps (TEKS).
- Understands the concept of regions and can describe a variety of regions in the U.S. that result from patterns of human activity such as political, population, and economic regions or from physical characteristics such as landform, climate, and vegetation regions (TEKS).
- Locates the 50 states on a map and identifies regions made up by groups of states such as New England and the Great Plains (TEKS).
- Understands and describes location and patterns of settlement as well as their distribution (TEKS).
- Analyzes the location of cities in the United States including capital cities (TEKS).
- Understands how people adapt and modify their environment in order to meet basic human needs (TEKS).
- Analyzes the consequences of human modification of the environment in the United States (TEKS).

Grade 6

- Uses maps, globes, graphs, charts, models, and databases to answer geographic questions.
- Creates maps, graphs, models, and databases (TEKS).
- Poses and answers questions about geographic distributions and patterns from selected world regions and countries (TEKS).
- Compares selected world regions and countries using data from maps, graphs, charts, databases, and models (TEKS).
- Understands the characteristics and relative locations of major historical and contemporary societies (TEKS).
- Locates major historical and contemporary societies on maps and globes (TEKS).
- Identifies and explains geographic factors affecting patterns of population in places and regions (TEKS).
- Understands how geographic factors influence the economic development, political relationships, and policies of societies (TEKS).
- Understands the impact of physical processes on patterns in the environment (TEKS).
- Understands the impact of interactions between people and the physical environment on the development of places and regions (TEKS).

Cultural Diffusion

The term cultural diffusion describes the exchange or transmission of cultural information and lifestyles from people around the world. For example, most people in the world use cotton, a fabric developed in India, and silk, developed in China. Chicken and pigs were originally domesticated in Asia, but by the process of cultural diffusion, these animals are common today in most countries in the world. Many countries are predominantly Christian today, but Christianity was born in the Middle East, a place where most people are Muslim. The Romans facilitated the cultural diffusion of Christianity around the ancient world. Travelers visiting Morocco, a Muslim country in North Africa, may be surprised to hear Puerto Rican salsa and Jamaican reggae music being played in local nightclubs. The popularity of Latin and Caribbean rhythms in a predominantly Muslim country is an example of the powerful effect of cultural diffusion.

Competency 026 (Economics)

The teacher understands the concepts and processes of government and the responsibilities of citizenship; knows how people organize economic systems to produce, distribute, and consume goods and services; and applies social science skills to information, ideas, and issues related to government and economics.

Basic Principles of Economy

Economics is a social science that analyzes the principles that regulate the production, distribution, and consumption of resources in society. It emphasizes how these principles operate within the economic choices of individuals, households, businesses, and governments. Economics can be divided into two main areas: macroeconomics and microeconomics. Macroeconomics is the study of the economy at the world, regional, state, and local levels. Some of the topics include reasons and ways to control inflation, causes of unemployment, and economic growth in general. Microeconomics deals with specific issues related to the decision-making process at the household, firm, or industry levels.

Theory of Supply and Demand

This theory states that prices vary based on balance between the availability of a product or service at a certain price (supply) and the desire of potential purchasers to pay that price (demand). This balance of supply and demand can occur naturally or be created artificially. An example of an artificially created balance is the intentional destruction of a surplus of a given product on the world market to maintain the price level. Another way is to control the production and availability of the product to create a scarcity of a product. For instance, the Organization of Petroleum Exporting Countries (OPEC) often reduces its production of oil to cause an increase in price.

Goods and Services

The use of machines increases the availability of goods and services to the population. This kind of production can decrease the cost of producing the goods and consequently its price. For example, as a result of the division of labor and the use of assembly lines developed by Eli Whitney in 1799, production costs of manufactured goods decreased and productivity increased. Mass production that came as a result of the Industrial Revolution made contemporary families and children more likely to become consumers rather than producers. However, before the Industrial Revolution, especially in colonial America, children were used to produce goods and contribute to the group.

Free Enterprise

Free enterprise is an economic and political doctrine of the capitalist system. The concept is based on the premise that the economy can regulate itself in a freely competitive market through the relationship of supply and demand, and with minimum governmental intervention. One of the main benefits of the system of free enterprise is the competition among businesses that results in a greater choice and better prices for consumers. The system of free enterprise has led to globalization. Globalization can be defined as a continuous increase of cross-border financial, economic, and social activities. It implies some level of economic interdependence among individuals, financial entities, and nations. As a result of globalization, trade barriers have been eliminated and tariffs imposed on imported products have been largely discontinued. In a global market, it is difficult to determine the origins of products. For example, Toyota from Japan and Ford from the United States joined forces to build cars using parts and labor from Mexico.

The concept of economic interdependence describes a positive, close connection between producers and consumers of goods and services within a nation or across nations. This economic interdependence has guided nations to establish large markets of free trade zones like the European Union (EU) trade agreement and the North American Free Trade Agreement (NAFTA) for Canada, Mexico, and the United States. The European Union went a step further; in 2002 they adopted a common currency for the Union—the Euro. As a result of this alliance, the Euro is today one of the strongest currencies in the world.

Money and Banking

Under the presidency of Woodrow Wilson, the Federal Reserve System was established. The main purpose of this institution is to keep the banking industry strong to ensure a supply of currency. The Federal Reserve is run by the Federal Reserve Board of Governors, a seven-member body appointed to a four-year term, with the option of being reappointed to a maximum of fourteen-year terms. Alan Greenspan served as chairman of the Federal Reserve Board from 1987 to 2006. He finished an unexpired term and then served for a full fourteen-year term for a total of eighteen and a half years. The current chair is Ben S. Bernanke. His term will expire in January 2014. The main function of the Federal Reserve Bank is to promote fiscal stability and economic growth in the nation and to regulate inflation and deflation. The Board of Governors controls the flow of money and sets the interest rate that banks use to lend money. They increase the interest rate to control inflation and lower the interest rate when business slows down.

Inflation and Deflation

Inflation reduces the purchasing power of money, which technically affects the value of the currency. Countries generally devalue their currency to keep up with inflation. Deflation is the opposite of inflation: the purchasing power of money increases, thereby lowering the prices of goods and services. In a period of deflation, consumers benefit but industry suffers. The Federal Reserve controls the flow of money and keeps a healthy balance between inflation and deflation.

American Federal Income Tax System

In 1913, the Sixteenth Amendment of the U.S. Constitution allowed the imposition of direct taxation of citizens. This direct taxation is known as the federal income tax.

Interdependence of State, National, and World Economies

The economy of Texas is based primarily on telecommunications, software, financial services, business products and services, semiconductors, biotechnology, and oil and coal. Agriculture and ranching are still viable economic activities, but they are no longer carrying the economy. A large percentage of these products are exported to members of NAFTA—Mexico and Canada—and to the world markets. According to the Texas Economic Update, if Texas were a nation, it would rank as the eighth-largest economy in the world (Strayhorn, 2004).

The Texas economy relies heavily on exports of goods and services. From 2002 through 2005, Texas was ranked as the number one state in terms of export revenues (BIDC 2006). Without its exports, the Texas economy could not sustain its growth. Because of the interdependence of state and global economies, political turmoil and economic problems in the world can have a direct impact on the Texas economy. For example, because part of the economy of Texas is based on petroleum, the decisions of OPEC have a direct impact on the state's economy.

Competency 027 (Government and Citizenship)

The teacher understands and applies knowledge of concepts of government, democracy, and citizenship, including ways that individuals and groups achieve their goals through political systems.

Forms of Government

The U.S. Department of State identifies 26 forms of governments in the world (CIA, n.d).

Some of best-known forms of government listed are communism, socialism, democracy, monarchy, and oligarchy. A description of these types of government follows:

1. Communism is a system in which the state controls economic activity in the nation. The state rejects free enterprise and capitalism; consequently, private ownership is discouraged and often prohibited. Usually the nation is ruled through a one-party system. In theory communism believes that the country should not have social classes, as a way to avoid the oppressor–oppressed dichotomy that exists in the world.
2. Socialism is a system of government in which the central government controls the production and distribution of goods, services, and labor in the nation. The goal is to promote an equitable distribution of resources among the people. In theory, the working class should take over and administer collectively the resources for their benefit and the benefit of the national as a whole.
3. Democracy is a form of government in which the majority rules. In practice it becomes a representative democracy, in which the people elect candidates to represent them in the government.
4. Monarchy is a system in which a king or queen leads the nation. The monarch can have supreme powers and become dictator, or he/she can have limited or ceremonial powers limited by a parliament or a constitution.

There are three main broad classifications for these forms of government based on the number of people in power—government by one person, a group, or by many people:

Rule by One

In this form of government, one person becomes the supreme leader of the nation. Some of the terminology and concepts linked to this type of government are:

- **Autocracy:** Ruler has unlimited power, uses power in an arbitrary manner.
- **Monarchy:** Ruled by a king or queen who holds complete control over the subjects. Ruler sometimes claims birth and divine rights.
- **Dictatorship:** The ruler holds absolute power to make laws and to command the army.

Ruled by a Few

In this system, a group of influential people takes control of the government. Traditionally, they appoint one of their own to function as the supreme leader of the government. Some examples of this type of government are:

- **Theocracy:** Ruled by a group of religious leaders, e.g., the Taliban in Afghanistan.
- **Aristocracy:** A group of nobles controls the economy and the government.
- **Oligarchy:** A small group of powerful and wealthy people rule the nation with the support of the military.
- **Military:** A committee of military officers or a junta becomes the rulers of the nation.

Rule by Many

In this type of government, the citizens of the nation, technically, become the government. In practice, the citizens elect members to represent them and become the government. Some examples of this type of government are:

- **Democracy:** The citizens of the nation directly or through elected members make important decisions, and become part of the government.
- **Constitutional Democracy:** It is a democratic form of government regulated by a constitution.
- **Parliamentarian Monarchy:** The monarch shares the power with the parliament. Often, the powers of the monarch are ceremonial in nature, like in Great Britain.

- **Federal Republic:** A constitutional government in which the powers of the central government are restricted to create semi-autonomous bodies (states or provinces) with certain degrees of self-governing powers, e.g., the United States.

The American Government

The governmental system of the United States has been identified as a federal republic and constitutional representative democracy. It is a federal republic because the U.S. government is limited by law; in this case, the government is limited by the Constitution. It is a constitutional representative democracy because the citizens elect senators and representatives to represent them in Congress.

The Constitution is the supreme law of the nation. It contains a description of the government and the rights and responsibilities of its citizens. The document can be amended with the approval of two-thirds of the House and the Senate and the ratification of individual state legislatures. Amendments to the U.S. Constitution have made it more democratic than the original document. The first ten amendments to the Constitution are known as the Bill of Rights.

Executive Branch

The executive branch of the U.S. government is composed of a president and a vice president elected every four years by electoral votes. The president is the commander-in-chief of the armed forces. He or she appoints cabinet members, nominates judges to the federal court system, grants pardons, recommends legislation, and has the power to veto legislation.

Judicial Branch

The judicial branch is composed of a federal court system that includes the Supreme Court and a system of lower courts—district courts, appeals courts, bankruptcy courts, and special federal courts. Federal judges are nominated by the president of the United States and confirmed by the Senate. All federal judges are appointed for life. The Supreme Court is composed of nine judges, and their ruling is considered final. Some of the major responsibilities of this body are to interpret the Constitution, resolve conflicts among states, and interpret laws and treaties.

Legislative Branch

The legislative branch is composed of the Congress, which is divided in two parts—the Senate and the House of Representatives. The Senate comprises two senators from each state, while the composition of the House is based on the population of each state. The Congress makes the laws of the nation, collects taxes, coins money and regulates its value, can declare war, controls appropriations, can impeach public officials, regulates the jurisdictions of federal courts, and can override presidential vetoes.

System of Checks and Balances

The U.S. Constitution provides for a system of checks and balances among the three branches of the government. In this type of system, individual branches check the others to be sure that no one assumes full control of the central government. The legislative branch can check the executive branch by passing laws over presidential veto (by a two-thirds majority in both houses). This branch exerts control over the judicial branch by refusing to confirm the president's judges. The executive can check the legislative branch by the use of the veto and the judicial branch by appointing federal judges. The judicial branch can check the other two branches through the process of judicial review, which can declare legislation unconstitutional or illegal.

Judicial Review Process—*Marbury v. Madison*

A dispute that occurred as the Thomas Jefferson administration came into power fundamentally altered the system of checks and balances of the American government. In this case, the judicial branch confirmed its power to review and assess the constitutionality of the legislation passed by Congress and signed by the president. This process is now called the judicial review.

Bill of Rights

After the U.S. Constitution was enacted in 1783, the founders felt that additional measures were necessary to preserve basic human rights. The first ten amendments to the U.S. Constitution came to be the

Bill of Rights. A summary of the first ten amendments follows:

First Amendment—separation of church and state; freedom of religion, speech and press; and the right to peaceful assembly

Second Amendment—rights to keep and bear arms

Third Amendment—made it illegal to force people to offer quarters to soldiers in time of peace

Fourth Amendment—rights to privacy and unreasonable searches or seizures

Fifth Amendment—rights of due process, protection against self-incrimination, and protection from being indicted for the same crime twice (double jeopardy)

Sixth Amendment—rights to speedy public trial by an impartial jury and to counsel for one's defense

Seventh Amendment—right to sue people

Eighth Amendment—protection against cruel and unusual punishment

Ninth Amendment—enumeration of specific rights in the Constitution cannot be taken as a way to deny other rights retained by the people

Tenth Amendment—rights not delegated to the federal government by the Constitution are reserved to the states or to the people

Power Sharing Between State and Federal Governments

One of the most significant principles of the U.S Constitution is the concept of power sharing between the federal and state governments. Some of the powers reserved to the federal and state governments follow.

Powers Reserved for the Federal Government

- Regulate interstate and foreign commerce
- Print money and regulate its value
- Establish the laws for regulation of immigration and naturalization
- Regulate admission of new states
- Declare war and ratify peace treaties
- Establish a system of weights and measures
- Raise and maintain armed forces
- Conduct relations with foreign nations

Powers Reserved for State Governments

- Conduct and monitor local, state, and federal elections
- Provide for local government
- Ratify proposed amendments to the Constitution
- Regulate intrastate commerce
- Provide education for its citizens
- Establish direct taxes like sales and state taxes
- Regulate and maintain police power over public health and safety
- Maintain control of state borders

In addition to the powers reserved to the states, the Tenth Amendment of the U.S. Constitution provides additional powers to the state. In this amendment, the powers not specifically delegated to the federal government are reserved for the states.

Local and State Governments

Most states in the United States follow the type of government established in the U.S. Constitution. State governments generally have three branches—executive, legislative, and judicial. The main difference is that the executive branch is led by a governor and the judicial branch is composed of a state court system subordinate to the federal court system. The city government is generally headed by a mayor or city manager with the support of a city council.

Citizenship

The development of civic ideas and practices is a lifelong process that begins in school by observing patriotic holidays, learning about the contribution of historical characters, and pledging allegiance to the American and Texas flags each day. In first grade, encouraging good citizenship continues with the introduction of the American anthem and the mottoes of Texas and the United States. Civic education and the principles of democracy are infused through active participation in community activities. To promote civic responsibility, students can get involved in discussions about issues that affect the community. Teachers encourage students to suggest possible solutions to community problems, while students listen and analyze contributions. Through this exchange, students are guided to practice principles of democracy and to value individual contributions to solve community problems.

In grades K–6, students will become familiar with the meaning and importance of national holidays observed during the year. Holidays with historic significance observed during the year are Memorial Day, Labor Day, Columbus Day, Independence Day, Veteran's Day, and Martin Luther King Jr. Day. Memorial Day honors members of the military who died in war. Labor Day recognizes the importance of workers and labor unions. Columbus Day commemorates the arrival of Christopher Columbus to the Americas. Independence Day commemorates the adoption of the Declaration of Independence. Martin Luther King Jr. Day honors the leader of the civil rights movement. Veteran's Day celebrates all those who have served in our country's armed forces.

Children as early as prekindergarten can be guided to develop civic responsibility. Teachers can promote this sense of responsibility by involving students in real-life situations in which they take civic responsibility. For example, teachers can make children aware of how producing trash can affect the environment. As part of this process, students can be guided to examine the amount of trash that they produce daily and explore ways to reduce it. Promoting a sense of responsibility to the well-being of everyone constitutes the main principle for developing responsible citizenship.

American Symbols

American Patriotic Symbols

Patriotic symbols are visible signs of national pride. The U.S. National Flag, the Pledge of Allegiance, the Statue of Liberty, the Liberty Bell, and the White House are important examples of patriotic symbols.

- The United States of America National Flag has 50 stars representing the 50 states of the Union. The flag's colors are red, white, and blue. The color red represents hardiness and valor, white symbolizes purity and innocence, and blue symbolizes vigilance, perseverance, and justice. Congress approved a new flag with 13 red and white alternating horizontal stripes and 13 stars representing the original colonies in 1777. A star and a stripe were added to the flag each time a state entered the union. Congress set the number of stripes at thirteen in 1818 and approved to continue to add a star for each new state.
- The Pledge of Allegiance is a declaration of patriotism. It was first published in 1892 in *The Youth's Companion* and is believed to be written by the magazine's editor, Francis Bellamy. The original purpose of the Pledge was to be used by school children to celebrate the 400th anniversary of the discovery of America. The Pledge was widely used in morning school routines for many years and received official recognition by Congress on 1942. The phrase "under God" was added in 1954 along with a law indicating the proper behavior to adopt when reciting the Pledge, which includes standing straight, removing hats or any other headgear, and placing the right hand over the heart.
- "The Star-Spangled Banner" is the national anthem of the United States. It was originally a poem written by Francis Scott Key during the Battle of Baltimore in the War of 1812. In 1931, it was made the official national anthem of the United States.
- The Statue of Liberty was a gift of friendship from the people of France to the people of the United States commemorating the United States' 100th anniversary. It is a universal symbol of freedom, democracy, and international friendship.
- The Liberty Bell is a symbol of freedom and liberty. The Pennsylvania Assembly ordered

the Liberty Bell to commemorate the 50th anniversary of Pennsylvania's original constitution, the William Penn's Charter of Privileges. It is traditionally believed that it was rung to summon the people of Philadelphia to hear the Declaration of Independence. It became an icon when the abolitionists adopted it as a symbol of freedom. The abolitionists changed its name from The State House Bell to the Liberty Bell.

- The White House was originally planned by President George Washington in 1791 and was completed in 1800 when its first resident, President John Adams, moved in with his wife, Abigail. It was originally called the President's House. President Theodore Roosevelt christened it with the name *The White House* in 1901, and for over 200 years it has been the home of the U.S. Presidents and their families. It is recognized as a symbol of the Presidency of the United States throughout the world.
- The Great Seal of the United States consists of a bald eagle holding an olive branch and a bundle of arrows. The olive branch represents peace and the arrows represent military strength. The eagle holds a scroll in its beak with the nation's motto: "E Pluribus Unum" which means "Out of many, one."

For additional information about symbols of the United States go to *http://govdocs.evergreen.edu/symbols.html*, a website created and maintained by Evergreen State College in Olympia, Washington, or *http://www.ushistory.org*, a website created and hosted by the Independence Hall Association in Philadelphia.

References

Acosta, T. P. 2009. "Raza Unida Party." *The Handbook of Texas Online.* Texas State Historical Association. http://www.tshaonline.org/handbook/online/articles/RR/war1.html (accessed August 28, 2009).

Arends, R. 1998. *Learning to Teach.* 4th ed. Boston: McGraw-Hill.

Barker, E. C. and J. W. Pohl. 2009. "Texas Revolution." *The Handbook of Texas Online.* Texas State Historical Association. http://www.tshaonline.org/handbook/online/articles/TT/qdt1.html (accessed August 24, 2009).

Business and Industry Data Center (BIDC). 2006. *Overview of the Texas Economy.* Office of the Governor, Economic Development and Tourism. http://governor.state.tx.us/ecodev/business_research/texas_economy/ (accessed October 1, 2009).

CIA World Fact Book. "Central Asia: Russia." https://www.cia.gov/library/publications/the-world-factbook/geos/rs.html (accessed October 1, 2009).

CIA World Fact Book. "Nations: Forms of Government." HistoryGuy.com. http://www.historyguy.com/nations/government_types.html (accessed August 27, 2009).

Echevarria, J., M. Vogt, and D. Short. 2000. "Making content comprehensible for English language learners: The SIOP model." Needham Heights, MA: Allyn and Bacon.

Fry, P. L. "Origin of Name." *The Handbook of Texas Online.* Texas State Historical Association. www.tshaonline.org/handbook/online/articles/TT/pft4.html (accessed August 24, 2009).

Ganeri, A., H. M. Martell, and B. Williams. 1999. *The World History Encyclopedia.* Bath, UK: Parragon.

Kagan, S. 1985. "Cooperative learning resources for teachers." Riverside, CA: Spencer Kagan.

Kerr, A. 2006. "Temperance and prohibition." History Department, Ohio State University. http://prohibition.osu.edu/ (accessed October 1, 2009).

Lyman, F. T. 1981. "The responsive classroom discussion: The inclusion of all students." *In Mainstreaming Digest,* ed. A. S. Anderson, 109–113. College Park: University of Maryland Press.

Marzano, R., and D. Pickering. 2005. "Building academic vocabulary: Teacher's manual." Alexandria, VA: ASCD.

Mayell, H. 2004. "Three high-altitude peoples, three adaptations to thin air." *National Geographic.* http://news.nationalgeographic.com/news/2004/02/0224_040225_evolution.html (accessed October 1, 2009).

Mendoza, V. 2001. Video review of "Chicano! History of the Mexican American Civil Rights Movement." *The Journal for MultiMedia History,* Volume 3. www.albany.edu/jmmh/vol3/chicano/chicano.html (accessed August 28, 2009).

National Council for the Teaching of Social Studies (NCTSS) 2006. "Expectations of Excellence: Curriculum Standards for Social Studies—Executive Summary." www.socialstudies.org/standards/execsummary (accessed October 1, 2009).

Parker, W. C. 2001. *Social Studies in Elementary Education.* 11th ed. Columbus, OH: Merrill Prentice-Hall.

Potts, J. 1994. *Adventure Tales of America.* Dallas, TX: Signal Media.

Rosado, L., and D. Salazar. 2002–2003. "La Conexión: The English/Spanish connection." *National Forum of Applied Educational Research Journal* 15(4): 51–66.

Rosales Castañeda, O. 2006. "The Chicano Movement in Washington State History" Link.org (accessed October 21, 2009) 1967-2006.

Rowe, M. B. 1986. "Wait Times: Slowing Down May Be a Way of Speeding Up." *Journal of Teacher Education,* 37, 43–50.

Schifini, A. 1985. "Sheltered English: Content area instruction for limited English proficiency students." Los Angeles County Office of Education.

Schifini, A., H. García, D. J. Short, E. E. García, J. Villamil Tinajero, E. Hamayan, and L. Kratky. 2004. *Avenues: Success in language, literacy and content.* Carmel, CA: Hampton-Brown.

Seattle Civil Rights and Labor History Project. 2006. http://depts.washington.edu/civilr/Chicanomovement_part1.htm (accessed August 28, 2009).

Sheppard, D. E. "Cabeza de Vaca in North America." Floridahistory.com. 23 www.floridahistory.com/cabeza.html (accessed August 23, 2009).

Slavin, R. 1986. "Student Learning: An Overview and Practical Guide." Washington, DC: Professional Library National Education Association.

Sousa, David. 2011. *How the ELLs Brain Learns.* Corwin Press. A Sage Company.

Strayhorn, C. K. 2004, Fall. "The Rebound is Here." *Texas Economic Update.* Window on State Government. www.window.state.tx.us/ecodata/teufall04/ (accessed August 24, 2009).

CHAPTER

Domain V: Science

5

This chapter includes information on the following topics: practices in science that are safe for all students, processes in scientific inquiry, and appropriate assessments in the various areas of science learning (e.g., physical science, life science, and earth and space science).

Competency 028 (Safe and Proper Laboratory Processes)

The teacher understands how to manage learning activities, tools, materials, equipment and technologies to ensure the safety of all students.

Science Curriculum

The National Science Teachers Association (NSTA, 2006) believes all students, including English Language Learners (ELL), can succeed in science given all the support and equitable opportunities in learning science. Being that teachers play a critical role in the process of teaching and learning of science content, they also need the support and resources to effectively teach science to ELLs. NSTA supports educational policies that allow or encourage the use of students' home language as an instructional support to promote science learning, even within an "English-only Policy (Garcia and Lee, 2008). Sousa (2011) examined studies of how ELLs learn science and stated that the findings reinforce how important it is for ELLs to learn specialized vocabulary in the context of doing science. He further states that this approach allows the brain's mental lexicon to link unusual words with visual representation and physical actions (Sousa, 2011).

According to research, educators teaching ELLs should be well versed in teaching science content as well as pedagogy. Teachers must be able to integrate language learning and science learning. Research has shown that teachers who are well prepared to teach science have a positive attitude in integrating science and literacy. Below are some safety processes that must be followed by all students involved in science inquiry.

Classroom and Laboratory Health and Safety Processes

Teachers must create a safe environment for children involved in scientific inquiry. Here are some of the principles and practices that teachers can follow to reduce risks and protect children:

- Use appropriate personal protective gear, like goggles, laboratory coats, and gloves.

- Use appropriate procedures for cleaning and disposing of materials.
- Adhere to appropriate disciplinary procedures to avoid accidents.
- Use less hazardous equivalent materials when possible; avoid chemicals in their pure form.
- Use polyethylene or metal containers in place of glass.
- Advise children to avoid tasting or ingesting substances or materials.
- Label containers appropriately to avoid confusion.
- Control the use of sharp objects that can puncture the skin.
- Supervise the use of living organisms and the cleaning of instruments.
- Avoid experimenting with human cells and bodily fluids.
- Share the responsibility—students should motivate each other to follow safety procedures.
- Make provisions for students with special needs.
- Prepare and send home an age-appropriate safety contract—parent/guardian signature.
- Organize all materials for each student group—pick up and return of materials—in bins.
- Prepare and practice an emergency plan with students should an accident occur.
- Clearly label and demonstrate the use of safety equipment with students.
- Document all accidents, regardless of how minor—have teacher sign as witness if possible.
- Clearly write, and read to students, the safety precautions for the laboratory before beginning.
- Place posters around the room emphasizing the safety rules of the classroom and laboratory.
- Keep all chemicals and glassware in locked cabinets.
- Maintain regular inventory of all laboratory materials and chemicals.
- Store acids and other caustic chemicals in cabinets close to the floor.
- Students must tie long hair back and tape or roll up sleeves to avoid contact with the fire.

The use of dangerous chemical substances in the elementary classroom is limited in scope. Many laboratory chemicals can be substituted with household products. However, care needs to be taken even when handling household chemicals. It is important to demonstrate safe laboratory procedures for the classroom because household products are still chemicals and pose some level of risk to students. Safety management of chemicals in the classroom requires teachers to have knowledge of those chemicals and their properties. For example, teachers need to be aware that a simple tool like a mercury thermometer can break and pose a danger to children. In general, maintaining safety requires teachers to take the following steps:

- Assess the relative danger of each chemical used in the classroom.
- Label and store chemicals appropriately.
- Implement safety procedures for the use and handling of materials and equipment.
- Follow appropriate procedures for cleaning containers and disposing of chemicals.

Proper Laboratory Procedures and Precision

Scientific experimentation cannot rely solely on our senses to record information. We need to extend what can be observed with our senses by using scientific instruments such as balances, microscopes, beakers, and graduated cylinders to make precise observations and measurements. Science requires the use of standard measuring devices to be sure that the information is clear, accurate, and able to be replicated in experimental settings. The United States uses a combination of the English system of measurement (standard) and the metric system. In fact, the United States is the only technologically developed country in the world that uses the English system for business transactions and for day-to-day activities. However, for international business, engineering, and natural sciences, all countries use a more standardized, precise system of weights and measurement, the metric system. The English system uses pounds, gallons, and inches for measurement, while the metric system uses kilos, liters, and meters. The metric system uses a system of fractions and multiples of units that are related to each other by powers of 10, allowing conversion and comparison of measures simply by shifting a decimal point, and avoiding the lengthy arithmetical operations required by the English system. The TEKS requires the teaching of both the metric and the English systems; however, all scientific data are to be reported using the metric system.

Competency 029 (Scientific Inquiry)

The teacher understands the history and nature of science, process, and role of scientific inquiry, and the role of inquiry in science instruction.

Scientific Inquiry

Scientific inquiry is promoted through hands-on activities and experimentation. From their experiences conducting scientific experiments, students acquire information firsthand and develop problem-solving skills. Children in grades EC-6 are inquisitive and want to understand the environment around them. Teachers can use this interest to provide young students with opportunities to use electronic and printed sources to find answers to their questions and to expand their knowledge about the topic. It is important for children to develop inquiry skills. This can only be accomplished by allowing them to experience science for themselves in hands-on investigations. By doing so, students develop important science inquiry and thinking skills (Table 5-1).

Table 5-1.
Science Thinking Skills (FOSS, 2000)

• Observing: Using the senses to get information
• Communicating: Talking, drawing, and acting
• Comparing: Pairing and one-to-one correspondence
• Organizing: Grouping, seriating, and sequencing
• Relating: Determining cause-and-effect and classification
• Inferring: Super-ordinate/subordinate classification, if/then reasoning, and developing scientific laws
• Applying: Developing strategic plans and inventing

The model of inquiry that best supports science learning is a model known as the learning cycle, consisting of three phases: exploration, concept invention, and application (Lawson, Abraham, and Renner 1989; Marek and Cavallo 1997). Over time, the learning cycle was extended with the addition of two new phases becoming what is known as the 5-E model (Bybee 1989). What follows is some history on the development of inquiry-based teaching via the learning cycle and 5-E model.

The original three-phase learning cycle model developed by Robert Karplus in the early 1960s was based upon the following theoretical foundation:

1. Science must be taught in a way that is consistent with the nature of science, that is, by discovery and investigation which is a "doing-active process."
2. Science must be taught in a way that promotes the students use of independent, critical, and higher-level thinking abilities (e.g., logic). Students use logic and reasoning to find "answers" or explanations for themselves; further discussion and teacher guidance can follow the students' direct experiences.
3. Science must be taught in a way that matches how students learn, described as the mental

functioning model by Piaget (1964). How individuals learn is through mentally experiencing the following three-phase mental process. We first (1) assimilate or "take in" information through our senses from our environment, then we accommodate the information after we understand it (i.e. aha! moment) and (3) third, we organize it into our mental structures. That is, we connect the new idea or what we have just figured out/made sense of, to what we already know, what we experience in everyday life, and connect it to related concepts.

The three phases of learning described by Piaget, assimilation-accommodation-organization, match the original learning cycle's three phases: exploration-concept invention-application. The logic in developing the learning cycle in these three phases was that, given what we know about how children (people) learn, we should be teaching in a sequence or way that matches this learning pattern. Teachers can guide the students through all of these phases of teaching science and give ample opportunities for students to apply what they have learned.

Furthermore, by teaching via the learning cycle, we are teaching in a way that is consistent with the nature of science—as an active, hands-on process characterized by investigation and discovery. The learning cycle and its origins and theory base is more fully described in a book by Marek and Cavallo (1997) titled *The Learning Cycle: Elementary School Science and Beyond.*

Over time, science educators added some additional phases to the learning cycle, namely, the "engage phase," with the idea that teachers need to do something that will gain the students' attention before beginning the exploration phase. Engage can be a demonstration (without explanation) or simply posing a question, challenge, or problem. So the original learning cycle model's first phase, Exploration, became two phases, **Engage** and **Explore**. Though identical, the Concept Invention phase's name was changed to **Explain** and Application phase had the name changed to **Elaborate**, to sustain the alliteration. Assessment or the measurement of learning in the original three-phase model was to take place throughout the learning cycle. However, science educators at the time preferred to have assessment articulated as an additional phase, which again to keep the "E" pattern, was termed **Evaluate**. So the three-phase learning cycle model was expanded into a 5-E Model: Engage, Explore, Explain, Elaborate, Evaluate.

Most importantly, in both models, the learning cycle and 5-E, students are not told the science concept or information before beginning the inquiry, but must discover the concept themselves through hands-on investigation, observation, and collection of data. In using the **Engage** phase (from 5-E) the students' learning experience begins with the teacher posing one or more questions, giving an interesting demonstration, or providing a laboratory guide; but in all of these, this phase captures their curiosity and motivates them to learn. Whether or not an Engage phase is used, students next (or first) experience an **Exploration** phase—and it must be a student-centered hands-on activity, investigation, or experiment. In the Exploration phase, students make observations and gather data on a science idea or topic area. In this phase, students can determine the experimental design or it can be pre-determined by the teacher. The main aspect, however, is that students are doing the lab activity themselves, and have not been told the expected outcome beforehand. For example, students may grow plants in the light and in the dark, and make observations, draw and/or take photos, and measure the plants grown under the two differing conditions over a period of time. All other variables are controlled (soil, water, air); only the light received by the plants is different, which is the variable.

After the observations have been made and data has been gathered by students, the teacher begins the next instructional phase called **Concept Invention**, or in the 5-E model, the **Explain phase.** In this phase the students present and share data with their classmates in a teacher-guided discussion of findings. The teacher uses questions to guide students' thinking and encourages the use of logic and reasoning as they interpret their data. For example, students may post the photos or drawings of plants grown in the dark and in the light, make line graphs of plant height over time, or share qualitative information about how the plant appeared after grown under the two conditions (e.g., plants in the light were green, whereas plants in the dark were yellow and pale). At the end of this phase, the students construct an overall statement that summarizes their data and observations, which is the central science concept. The science vocabulary is then linked to the concept students "invented."

Next the teacher helps students through the **Application** (from the learning cycle) or **Elaborate** (from the 5-E model) in which students use the new concept they learned as it is applied in new contexts. For example, students can create new questions to investigate or hypotheses to test based on what they just learned (the concept) and develop a way to answer their questions or test their hypotheses (e.g., what color of light is best for plants to grow?).They can also go to the Internet to learn more about the concept they just invented. In this phase the teacher can engage students in additional hands-on laboratories, readings, discussions, field trips, and/or writing activities that extend and expand upon the concept. These models of inquiry science teaching and learning are endorsed by NSTA (NSTA, 1998, 2003).

The diagram in **Figure 5-1** shows the inquiry-based learning cycle model as it corresponds to the 5-E model of science teaching. The template shown in **Table 5-2** explains each phase of the learning cycle as it relates to the 5-E Model for structuring inquiry-based science teaching for all students.

Figure 5-1.
The Learning Cycle and 5-E Model

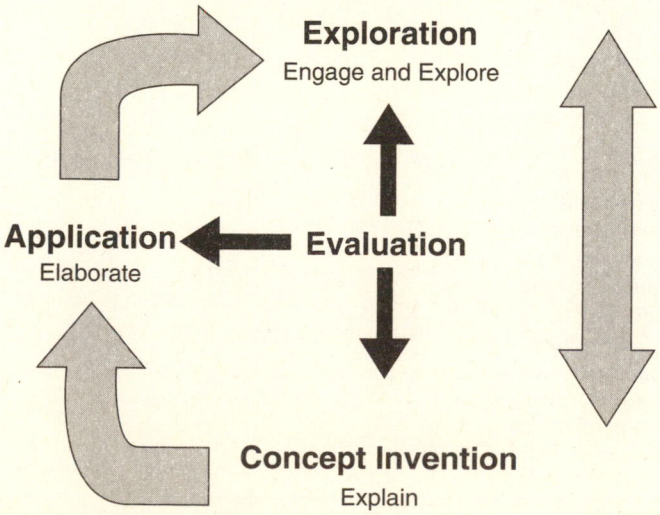

Interpreting Findings in Science Inquiry

In planning and conducting experiments, teachers should guide children to develop an appropriate procedure for testing hypotheses, including the use of instruments that can yield measurable data. Even at the early stages of scientific experimentation, the procedure must be clear and tangible enough to allow replication by other students or scientists. Help students understand the concept of controlling variables and testing only one variable at a time. Students need to learn to be precise in the collection of data and measurements. Ensure the use of the metric system in obtaining all measurement data.

Allowing students to gather their own data and observations for interpretation promotes their critical and logical thinking abilities. It also gives them experience with using appropriate scientific tools, resources, and technology that will lead to accurate organization and analysis of data. The students will be able to experience and practice science skills by verifying their findings, basing findings on evidence, and analyzing sources of error. Having students collect and report their own data also brings the teacher opportunities to discuss scientific ethics with students.

In explaining data collection procedures and display of findings to English language learners, the teacher needs to demonstrate and provide a model of what the end results should look like. In using inquiry, students work in groups, which is particularly helpful for second language learners as they interpret and exchange ideas about data and scientific reasoning.

When students complete their experiments, teachers need to engage them in the process of analyzing their own, and other groups' data for similarities, differences, and variations including error. This occurs in the concept invention or "explain" phase of the learning cycle and 5-E model, and again in any application or "elaborate" activities in which data has been collected. After data has been collected from students' explorations, they display their data in charts and graphs, for example, and communicate their observations and, ultimately, concept statements to the class by posting them on the board and/or through an oral presentation. The data helps them develop conclusions and form new research questions or hypotheses as they evaluate their findings, setting

Table 5-2. Description of the Phases of the Learning Cycle and 5-E Model

Learning Cycle Phases	5-E Model Phases	Explanation of the Phases	
EXPLORATION PHASE	ENGAGE EXPLORE	In beginning of the Learning Cycle's **Exploration** phase and/or in the 5-E Model's **Engage**, the teacher begins with an activity, demo, or probing questions that *does not give away the main concept* s/he wants them to learn—but that motivates students to "want to know." In the **Exploration** or **Explore** phases, the teacher actively involves students in direct, hands-on experiments, activities, and investigations; along with an analysis of their data and findings that lead them toward gaining understanding of main concepts. Guides the students with questions and examples, and allows them to post and discuss data with the class—looking for patterns, and using logic and reasoning.	In both, **Evaluation** of student learning during the learning cycle and the 5-E model's **Evaluate** phase, the teacher uses authentic ways to measure learning in each phase. This authentic evaluation means the teacher checks and measures students' learning using various alternative as well as traditional methods throughout the various phases of the learning cycle/5-E model. Alternative evaluation may involve simple techniques such as asking students questions to respond to verbally or in writing, asking them to draw their understandings, reviewing their journals, checking charts and graphs and mathematical calculations and measurements, reviewing their concept statements, assessing their verbal statements, administering a laboratory practical, and requiring oral and/or visual presentations. The use of more traditional methods includes the administration of short tests or quizzes. In both models, the teacher measures learning *throughout* to gauge students' learning and make adjustments in instruction as needed.
CONCEPT INVENTION PHASE	EXPLAIN	In the **Concept Invention** or **Explain** phase, all data has been collected and now students are to construct and state for themselves the main concept that they have drawn from their exploration and analysis of observations and data. The teacher guides students with questions but does not "tell" students the concept—they invent it from their findings. After the students have stated the concept and/or posted it on the board, the teacher may supply the scientific terminology or labels for the concept and further explain what the students have found.	
APPLICATION PHASE	ELABORATE	The **Application** or **Elaborate** phase takes the concept students have constructed in this learning cycle and uses it in different contexts. In this phase the teacher works to expand and enhance students' understanding of the main concept(s) by applying it to real-world contexts and experiences, using mathematical calculations, additional but related experiments, further discussion on the topic, interactive lectures, computer research and/or simulations, readings, journal writing, and/or *any* teaching methods that will help students gain a more deep and interconnected understanding of the concept, creating a foundation in the learners' minds for future, more complex science and mathematics learning.	

the foundation for new explorations. Students should be able to present pertinent data using graphic representations, and communicate their findings in written and oral forms to others.

In using scientific inquiry as in the learning cycle and 5-E model, scientific vocabulary is introduced after students have had hands-on experiences in the (engage and) exploration phase and have used their observations and data to construct meaning from their experiences in the concept invention or "explain" phase. Once students have had the hands-on direct experience with the concept, and have stated the meaning of their observations, the scientific vocabulary or terms that label the concept can be introduced by the teacher. In the application or elaborate phase, the teacher and students use the new vocabulary in extended experimentation, discussion, readings, writing, and other learning activities.

Introducing terms after students have directly experienced the science inquiry and constructed meaning from their experiences by making a concept statement is especially important for **ELLs** in facilitating the development of understanding of science concepts. For all students, but especially for second language learners, this helps them understand concepts when terms are later re-introduced. By giving students the experience—something they do—and then allowing them to form meaning from their experience in ways that make sense to them, then when the term that labels what they learned is introduced, they are able to link it to prior knowledge and learning experiences in their minds. The terms are now able to build their background knowledge, which is critical for second language learners to understand the language of science. Making a connection between the hands-on activities and scientific vocabulary is beneficial to all students but especially to English language learners (**ELLs**), who can link the actions with the appropriate concept and vocabulary words without engaging in translations.

Promoting Logical Thinking and Scientific Reasoning

Interpreting results is one of the most challenging phases of scientific inquiry for children in EC-6. Students can easily discuss the observable results but might have difficulty interpreting their meaning. The use of appropriate questioning techniques is important in getting students to interpret their findings. Sousa (2011) presents strategies to help ELLs learn and use the scientific method. These are listed below.

- Preparing for a scientific investigation (What do you want to find out and what do your students already know?)
- Collecting Information (What will you examine? Provide many visual aids and graphic organizers because they require minimal language).
- Formulating a hypothesis (What do you think will happen? Show videos and partner ELLs with strong English speakers).
- Testing the hypothesis—procedure or method (What procedure will you follow to find your answer? Model laboratory activities to ELLs and provide visuals).
- Collecting data (What information do you need to answer the question? Provide an outline or a chart for students to record the data.)
- Making and Reporting Observations (What did you find out and what does the information tell you? Show various graphs for reporting data.)
- Reporting the conclusion (Based on the information collected, what is the answer to your question?)

Scientific Tools and Equipment for Gathering and Storing Data

Various tools or instruments are used in scientific experimentation in kindergarten through grade 6. The classroom can be equipped with measuring devices like graduated cylinders, beakers, scales, dishes, thermometers, meter sticks, and micrometers. They might also have anatomical models showing the body systems. Teachers need to learn to use these tools and equipment properly in order to help their students know how to use them and to collect accurate data in their inquiry investigations.

The TEKS requires students to gather information using specific equipment and tools. Examples of the tools required in kindergarten through grade 6 are presented in **Table 5-3** (TEA 2006).

History and Nature of Science, Diversity, and Equity in Science

The history and nature of science provides an important framework for student learning. By learn-

Table 5-3. Tools and Equipment Required in the TEKS

Tools and Equipment	Kindergarten	1st	2nd	3rd	4th	5th	6th
Nonstandard measurements	√	√	√				
Hand lenses	√	√	√	√	√	√	√
Computers	√	√	√	√	√	√	√
Balances	√	√	√	√	√	√	√
Cups and bowls	√	√	√	√	√	√	√
Thermometers		√	√	√	√	√	√
Clocks			√	√	√	√	√
Meter sticks			√	√	√	√	√
Microscopes				√	√	√	√
Safety goggles				√	√	√	√
Magnets				√	√	√	√
Compasses				√	√	√	√
Timing devices					√	√	√
Calculators					√	√	√
Sound recorders					√	√	√
Hot plates						√	√
Burners						√	√
Beakers						√	√
Graduated cylinders						√	√
Flasks (Erlenmeyer and Florence)						√	√
Test tubes and holders						√	√

ing the history of science, students will come to understand that science is changing and dynamic rather than fixed and tentative. They will understand that their own conceptions and understandings of science can change in light of new experimental observations and evidence. Therefore, it is important to use the history and nature of science as a tool to promote students' learning. For example, the students can learn about the earth-centered model of the solar system that prevailed for hundreds of years before Copernicus, and then Galileo supported a new model, which is now the accepted view of a sun-centered model of the solar system. With better tools developed through time and the extension of findings through observations and experiments, our scientific knowledge constantly shifts and changes.

Science for all has long been the theme of science education's guiding documents such as Project 2061, a long-term initiative of the American Association for the Advancement of Science created in 1989, and the National Science Education Standards, published by the National Research Council in 1996. Science for all means that teachers need to help their students abandon stereotypes they may hold of science and scientists. For example, "science is a male-dominated profession." Teachers should help students to more appropriately view science as a field for males and females and for all cultures and ethnicities. To accomplish this goal, teachers need to be aware of their own potential, often not intentional, bias toward science and scientists that may be exclusionary. Posters of scientists displayed in the room should represent male and female scientists of diverse ethnicities and cultures, as well as of many different fields of science, such as environmental science, veterinary medicine, geology, engineering, and architecture, as well as the more traditionally represented physics and chemistry. Likewise, discussions of science and scientific discovery should include contributions from a diverse range of scientists. In giving examples to students, it is important to alternate between the use of "he" and "she," and to use and/or vary examples to be more gender neutral and meaningful to a variety of ethnicities. Ensure that all students rotate roles (e.g. record keeper, materials facilitator) in the laboratory.

Competency 030 (Impact on Daily Life/ Environment)

The teacher understands how science impacts the daily lives of students and interacts with and influences personal and societal decisions.

Science in Daily Life

Students need to be aware of how science is present and plays a role in their daily lives. The functioning of their bodies, the natural environment that is around them, and their everyday use of electrical appliances, bicycles, computers, and cell phones are examples of biological and physical science in their lives. However, students tend to keep the science they learn in school separate from the science they experience in everyday life! It is important that teachers help students connect the science they are learning in school to the world around them to broaden their understandings and promote the usefulness, value, and applicability of science. In the learning cycle and 5-E models, the best time to help students make these connections is in the application/elaboration phase. After students have experienced a hands-on lab activity and constructed an understanding of the concept, the teacher should help them relate that new concept to their everyday lives and see how the concept works in differing contexts. Connecting newly learned concepts to the students' life experiences makes the learning more meaningful for students and helps them retain understanding of the concept for later use. Relating science to what students already know and experience in life helps bridge the disconnections between "school science" and science they observe and experience in everyday life.

Science has brought society many advantages that have served to increase the health and longevity of humans, and to improve the quality of life for all. However, there may be consequences, often unforeseen, to scientific discovery and invention that impacts society and the natural environment, as well as the habitats and survival of the living organisms that share this planet. To better understand these issues, students need to gain scientific knowledge and evidence of what is known. Armed with appropriate background knowledge, students will be in the position to weigh the pros and cons of various scientific discoveries and debate issues that prevail in our global community. Students should be apprised of issues such as global warming, for example, but before taking a position on the topic, they must be prepared with accurate scientific information on the topic. When students are given opportunities to use scientific concepts as support for sound logic and reasoning to debate or evaluate a scientific issue, they are operating at a high cognitive level important to their intellectual development. Equally important is student awareness of the ethical, personal, societal, and economic implications of science, from both positive and negative perspectives. It is important that students fully understand the scientific knowledge that underlies all such complex issues, and can formulate decisions based on this knowledge.

Energy as a source of fuel and electricity is a major issue threatening the economic, environmental, and personal status of living in the U.S. and global society. It is important to know about fossil fuels, their origin, how they are obtained, and how they are used for energy consumption. In addition, it is important to know that fossil fuels are nonrenewable and will one day be expended. Therefore, science must continue to develop and improve upon alternative sources of energy such as wind, hydroelectric, and geothermal. Teachers must be knowledgeable about these other sources of energy and be able to guide students toward understanding how these alternative, renewable energy sources are used and how they impact our society's energy needs.

A significant impact of science on daily life relates to student fitness and health. Childhood obesity is a serious problem in the U.S., and teachers can play an important role in educating children on the negative health issues associated with poor nutrition and a lack of exercise. Students need to learn about factors that impact physical and psychological health and about how to make good choices on such factors, including nutrition, hygiene, physical exercise, smoking, drugs and alcohol. Understanding human biology, therefore, is important for students to realize how obesity and other factors such as substance use/abuse affect their physical and mental health. The topics of heart disease, diabetes, and cancer should be included in the curriculum as ways to help students understand the detrimental effects of unhealthy life choices.

Competency 031 (Unifying Concepts and Processes in Science)

The teacher knows and understands the unifying concepts and processes that are common to all sciences.

Explanatory Framework across Science Disciplines

Science is a way of knowing, a process—it is a systematic way of looking at the world and how it works. This competency focuses on how science uses a regular, consistent method of collecting and reporting data about scientific phenomena. Science is a way of organizing observations and then seeking patterns and regularity in order to make sense of the world. In science we organize evidence, create models, and explain observations in a logical form. We make predictions and hypotheses and test our predictions and hypotheses through controlled experimentation, meaning all variables of the experiment remain constant except for the variable being tested. We repeat experiments multiple times and seek constancy in our findings in form and/or function. We seek patterns and consistency in our observations and data in order to construct explanations and make new predictions.

Science embraces a broad spectrum of subject matter, such as life science, physical science, and earth science, all of which is interrelated. For example, in studying the ecosystem, teachers must understand the biological aspects (e.g., the living organism) and how they interact, as in predator-prey relationships and symbiotic relationships (e.g., parasitism, commensalism), as well as the chemical aspects of the ecosystem (e.g., nitrogen cycle), the geologic or earth science aspects (e.g., the landscape, the water, and the climate) and the physics aspects (e.g., energy transfer, motion). Ecosystems, for example, regardless of location on Earth, share unifying components and characteristics, and teachers must understand this unity. In life science, there is unity of what makes organisms "living"—they all must carry on life functions and are composed of one or more cells. These are the criteria that unify life forms and classify something like a virus, for example, as non-living (it does not carry on the life functions and is not composed of cells).

All scientific observations can be described by their characteristics or "properties." These properties organize the observations according to commonalities, or classification. Observed properties and patterns are centered on space, time, energy, and matter.

Scientific Models

Models are representations of the natural world and universe in order to help better understand how something appears, its form and/or its function. For example, we may make models of the solar system, cells, or an atom to help us better explain its form and function and interactivity with other structures. Such models can be helpful to us in understanding the actual concept the model represents, and scientists often make models for this purpose. However, it is important to understand that, though it represents the actual science phenomena or concept and provides explanatory power, it is not the same as the actual science concept and is limited. Models in science may be physical, as in a physical model of a cell; conceptual, as in a concept map or an analogy; and/or mathematical as in a formula showing relationships, such as d = m/v (formula for density).

Competency 032 (Theory and Practice of Teaching Science)

The teacher has theoretical and practical knowledge about teaching science and about how students learn science.

Developmentally Appropriate Practices

Children's processing of scientific inquiry can begin as early as age three or four. However, teachers must be aware of the stages of cognitive, social, and emotional development of children to appropriately introduce children to science concepts. For example, observing and experimenting with water and colors can easily be done by three or four year-olds, but using microscopes to observe and analyze animal or vegetable cells might be more appropriate for children in third and fourth grades. Students in EC-6 need direct experiences in order to understand concepts. According to Piaget (1964), children are transitioning through stages of development that require direct involvement to make sense of their experience. The model of teaching described earlier, the learning cycle and 5-E model, are based upon promoting the intellectual development of children. Thus, these models of teaching were designed to be consistent with the nature of science—and importantly, to match how children naturally learn (Marek and Cavallo, 1997; Renner and Marek, 1990). It is important that teachers understand the theory and research that underlie such models, as well as know how to use these models in teaching.

Misconceptions or alternative conceptions are a pervasive problem in science teaching and learning. Children tend to view the world from their own perspectives and draw conclusions based on their limited experiences. Once misconceptions are established in learners' minds, they are difficult to change. Therefore, teaching needs to allow children the opportunity for direct experience and collecting evidence. The learning cycle has been established as a teaching model that promotes conceptual change, helps students resolve misconceptions, and leads to more scientifically accurate understandings (Sandoval 1995).

The use of good questions by the teacher is critical to promoting logical thinking and scientific reasoning among students. Good questioning causes students to reflect upon the logic of their data and observations with confidence and also identify possible misinformation or misunderstanding of important concepts. Students learn to effectively use scientific argumentation and respond to challenges to their findings in order to support their conclusions. Teachers use questioning to reveal student learning and assess their progress in forming sound scientific frameworks of understanding.

Teachers can guide students at various levels of development to observe events; and through questioning, teachers can help students develop high-order thinking skills. For example, a teacher can lead children to make predictions while conducting experiments with objects that float or sink in water. By asking students to predict and explain why an object might sink or float, the teacher is leading students to analyze the properties of the object and the water to make an evaluative decision; that is, the children are using analysis and evaluation to complete that simple task. During the 1990's a new group of cognitive psychologist, lead by Lorin Anderson (a former student of Blooms's), updated the taxonomy to make it more relevant to 21st century work. The following guide will help teachers best promote and elevate logical thinking abilities among students. You can view additional information at *www.odu.edu/educ/roverbau/Bloom/blooms_taxonomy.htm*.

1. Use Key Questioning Terms Aimed at the Full Range of the Cognitive Domain.

LEVEL 1: Remember

- Recall or remember factual information.
- List the five Kingdoms.
- Label the parts of the cell in the diagram provided.

LEVEL 2: Understand

- Communicate an idea in a different form.
- Explain heat transfer through conduction.
- Restate what a habitat is in your own words.

LEVEL 3: Apply

- Use what is known to find new solutions or apply in new situation.
- Utilize your understanding of burning to explain why sand works to put out a fire.
- Making use of the clothes you are wearing, "How can you stay afloat for several hours?"

LEVEL 4: Analyze

- Break things and ideas down into component parts and find their unique characteristics.
- Study the diagram of human digestion and reason what the organ marked #7 might be and explain its function.
- Using the given laboratory materials, deduce the identities of the substances labeled "A," "B," and "C."

LEVEL 5: Evaluate

- Use what is known to make judgments and ratings; accept or reject ideas; determine the worthiness of an idea or thing.
- Decide whether or not you agree with the production of more nuclear power plants and provide justification for your decision.
- Make a ruling you would give to car manufacturers on global warming and provide support for your ruling.

LEVEL 6: Create

- Use what is known to think creatively and divergently; make something new or original; pattern ideas or things in a new way.
- Create a burglar alarm system for the classroom.
- Develop a plan for cleaning the pollutants in the Trinity River.

2. Use Questions Beginning with the Words Why, How, What, Where, and When that Probe Students' Thinking.

- How do you know?
- Why do you think that?
- Where did you see a change?
- What is your explanation for this observation?
- When did you notice the change occur?
- What do you think?

Competency 033 (Assessments in Science Learning)

The teacher knows the varied and appropriate assessments and assessment practices for monitoring science learning in laboratory, field, and classroom settings.

Measuring Student Learning

Teaching cannot occur without student learning, and in order to determine that learning is occurring, student progress needs to be assessed on a regular basis. Assessment of learning should occur on some scale, large or small, every class day, and as students move through the learning of concepts, as in the learning cycle and 5-E models. Measuring learning as it is occurring is "authentic assessment" and allows teachers to adjust the instruction according to student learning and potential difficulties in learning. Alternative assessment methods, in addition to the more traditional testing formats (e.g., multiple-choice) should be used to obtain a full picture of what students know and do not know, or can and cannot do. Alternative assessments include techniques such as verbal reports, laboratory practical exams, story writing, developing advertisements or brochures, constructing a concept map, writing essays, creating drawings or models, and developing a play or skit. In each assessment, the concepts to be learned are represented in alternative ways—yet clearly communicate what students have learned and understand.

It is essential that teachers monitor and assess students' understanding of concepts and skills on a regular, consistent basis and use this information to adjust instruction. The results of frequent informal and formal/traditional and alternative assessments should be used as a tool for planning subsequent instruction. Teachers must communicate progress to students so they can learn to self-monitor their own learning and understand what is needed to achieve learning goals.

Assessing the Science Curriculum

As part of the accountability system, Texas has a very comprehensive assessment system to measure the state uniform curriculum—the Texas Essential Knowledge and Skills (TEKS). In this system, students take the assessment tests in grades 3 through 12. However, the science component of TEKS is assessed only in grades 5, 8, and 10. The fifth-grade science test is available in Spanish; thus, Spanish-speaking ELLs can take the test in Spanish. In addition to the required science TAKS examinations, students are assessed through teacher and district developed tests in kindergarten through grade 12.

The study of elementary science includes planning and safely implementing classroom and outdoor investigations using scientific processes, including inquiry methods, analyzing information, making informed decisions, and using tools to collect and record information, while addressing the major concepts and vocabulary, in the context of physical, earth, and life sciences. School Districts are encouraged to facilitate classroom and outdoor investigations for at least 50% of instructional time.

In Grade 5 (TEKS), investigations are used to learn about the natural world. At the end of science instruction, students should understand that certain types of questions can be answered through investigation and methods, models, and conclusions built from these investigations may change as new observations are made. Models of objects and events are tools for understanding the natural world and can show how systems work. They have limitations and, based on new discoveries, are constantly being modified to more closely reflect the natural world. The following environments are studied in 5th grade.

(A) Within the **physical** environment, students learn about the physical properties of matter, including magnetism, physical states of matter, relative density, solubility in water, and the ability to conduct or insulate electrical and heat energy. Students explore the uses of light, thermal, electrical, and sound energies.

(B) Within the **natural** environment, students learn how changes occur on Earth's surface and that predictable patterns occur in the sky. Students learn that the natural world consists of resources, including nonrenewable, renewable, and alternative energy sources.

(C) Within the **living** environment, students learn that structure and function of organisms can improve the survival of members of a species. Students learn to differentiate between inherited traits and learned behaviors. Students learn that life cycles occur in animals and plants and that the carbon dioxide-oxygen cycle occurs naturally to support the living environment. Click on link to view Science TEKS *http://ritter.tea.state.tx.us/rules/tac/chapter112/ch112a.html.*

Competency 034 (Physical Science)

The teacher understands forces and motion and their relationships.

Universal forces include gravity, electricity, and magnetism, which are important to understanding this competency.

Magnetism and Gravity

Magnetism is the force of attraction or repulsion between objects that results from the positive and negative ionic charges of the objects. Usually, the objects are metals, such as iron, nickel, and cobalt. Magnets have two poles that have opposing charges or forces: north (+) and south (–). When the north pole of a magnet is placed close to the north pole of a second magnet, repulsion occurs. When poles of different kinds (north and south) are placed close, they attract one another. The strength of the forces depends on the size and the proximity of the magnets. The charged area around a magnet is called a magnetic field. The Earth is like a large magnet, with opposing forces—the north pole and south pole, and the magnetic field of attraction of Earth that we know as gravity is like that of a magnet. Without gravity, all objects on Earth, including the atmosphere, would not be held onto its surface. Planets and other celestial objects that are more massive than Earth, such as Jupiter, have stronger gravitational forces, and those that are less massive and/or dense, such as our moon, have weaker gravitational forces.

Force and Motion

Force is defined as the action of moving an object by pulling or pushing it. Force can cause an object to move at a constant speed or to accelerate. When force is applied over a distance, work is done. Work is the product of the force acting in the direction of movement and causing displacement. Energy is defined as the ability to do work; when a tow truck uses force to pull a car and move it to a different location, energy is used and work is accomplished. Newton's laws of motion are important to understand in fulfilling this competency. Newton's first law is that an object at rest will remain at rest unless acted upon by an (unbalanced) force, and an object in motion will continue to stay in motion with the same speed and in the same direction unless acted upon by an (unbalanced) outside force. This first law is also called inertia. Newton's second law is that acceleration is produced when a force acts on mass and the greater the mass of the object being accelerated, the greater the amount of force needed to accelerate that object. Newton's third law of motion states that for every action there is an equal and opposite reaction (see *http://teachertech.rice.edu/Participants/louviere/Newton/*).

Force and motion, as well as changes in motion, may be measured through hands-on activities in which variables such as time, speed, distance, and direction can be recorded and graphed, and teachers need to know how to do so. For example, teachers can have students experience and record what happens when an object with higher mass (such as a large marble or ball bearing), collides with an object with less mass (e.g., a small marble or ball bearing). Teachers should also know what happens when the rate of speed is high when the objects collide compared to when the rate of speed is low. The game of pool or billiards is a good example. When forces are unbalanced, it may cause the object to change its motion or position.

Relationships between Force and Motion: Machines, Space, and Geologic Processes

A machine is something that makes work easier. Machines can be as simple as a wedge or a screw or as sophisticated as a computer or gas engine. A simple machine has few or no moving parts and can change the size and direction of a force. A screw, hammer, wedge, and incline plane are examples of simple machines. Simple machines are part of our daily activities. For example, children playing on a seesaw are using a simple machine called a lever. Thus, teachers and their students should know the practical use of these simple machines in everyday life. A complex machine is two or more simple machines working together to facilitate work. Some of the complex machines used in daily activities are a wheelbarrow, a can opener, and a bicycle.

Force and motion is what keeps the sun, Earth, moon, and planets in their orbits and explains the structure and changes of the universe. On Earth, force and motion are found in all geologic processes, explaining phenomena such as tides and tsunamis.

Competency 035 (Physical Science)

The teacher understands the physical and chemical properties of and changes in matter.

Matter

Matter is anything that takes up space and has mass. The mass of a body is the amount of matter in an object or thing, and volume describes the amount of space that matter takes up. Mass is also the property of a body that causes it to have weight. Weight is the amount of gravitational force exerted over an object. It is important not to confuse mass and weight. What students are measuring on their balances in the laboratory is an object's mass. Weight changes as an object goes from one level of gravitational force to another, for example, from Earth to the Moon, because the amount of "pull" on that object is different; but the mass of the object—how much matter or material is in the object—does not change unless we do something to actually take away or add matter to that object.

There are 112 basic kinds of matter, called elements, which are organized into the periodic table. An element is composed of microscopic components called atoms. Atoms are made up of particles called electrons, neutrons, and protons. The mass of the atom is located mostly in the nucleus, which is made up of protons and neutrons. The electron contains little mass and follows an orbit around the nucleus. Molecules are two or more atoms bonded together in a chemical bond. The atoms of a molecule can be more than one of the same kind of atom, as in the naturally occurring oxygen molecule, O_2, or a molecule can be two or more different atoms as in carbon dioxide, CO_2, ammonia, NH_3, and glucose, $C6H1_2O_6$. Compounds have two or more different kinds of atoms in the molecule and a given amount of that substance. In other words, compounds consist of matter composed of atoms that are chemically combined with one another in molecules in definite weight proportions. An example of a compound is water; water is oxygen and hydrogen combined in the ratio of two hydrogen molecules to one molecule of oxygen H_2O. So, you can also call one H_2O a molecule.

Properties of Matter

Matter has physical, thermal, electrical, and chemical properties. These properties are dependent upon the molecular composition of the matter.

Physical Properties

The physical properties of matter are the way matter looks and feels. Physical properties include qualities such as color, density, hardness, and conductivity. Color represents the way matter is reflected or perceived by the human eye. Density is the mass that is contained in a unit of volume of a given substance. Hardness represents the resistance to penetration offered by a given substance. Conductivity is the ability of substances to transmit thermal or electric current.

Thermal Properties

Matter is sensitive to temperature changes. Heat and cold produce changes in the physical properties of matter; however, the chemical properties remain unchanged. For example, when water is exposed to cold temperature (release of heat), it changes from liquid to solid; and when water is exposed to heat, it changes from solid to liquid. With continued heat, the water changes from liquid to gas (water vapor). Water vapor can be cooled again and turned back into liquid. However, through all these states, water retains its chemical properties—two molecules of hydrogen and one molecule of oxygen or H_2O.

Electrical Properties

Matter can be classified as a conductor or nonconductor of electricity. Conductive matter allows the transfer of electric current or heat from one point to another. Metals are usually good conductors, while wood and rocks are examples of nonconductive matter.

Chemical Properties

The chemical properties of one type of matter (element) can react with the chemical properties of other types of matter. In general, elements from the same groups will not react with each other, while elements from different groups may. The more separated the groups, the more likely they will cause a chemical reaction when brought together. A type of matter can be chemically altered to become a different type of matter; for example, a metal trash can will rust if it is left out in the rain.

States of Matter

Matter can exist in four distinct states: solid, liquid, gas, and plasma. Most people are familiar with the basic states of matter, but they might not be familiar with the fourth one, plasma. Plasmas are formed at extremely high temperatures when electrons are stripped from neutral atoms (University of California 2006). Stars are predominantly composed of plasmas. Solids have mass, occupy a define amount of space or volume or have a definite shape, and are more dense than liquids. Liquids have mass, occupy a definite volume, do not have a definite shape, but instead take the shape of their container. Gases have mass, do not have a definite volume, have no definite shape but take the shape of their container, and are the least dense of the three states of matter. Plasma has no definite shape or volume, and is a substance that cannot be classified as a solid, liquid, or gas. When substances change from one state of matter to another, such as ice melting, it is a physical change, and not a chemical change.

Mixtures and Solutions

Mixtures are combinations of two or more substances, where each substance is distinct from the other, that is, made up of two or more types of molecules and not chemically combined. The two substances in the mixture may or may not be evenly distributed, so there are no definite amounts or weight proportions. Mixtures may be heterogeneous, which means an uneven distribution of the substances in the mixture throughout. A mixture may be homogeneous, which means the components are evenly distributed throughout. Examples of mixtures include milk, which is a heterogeneous mixture of water and butterfat particles. The components of a mixture can be separated physically. For example, milk producers and manufacturers remove the butterfat from whole milk to make skim milk.

Solutions are mixtures that are homogeneous, which means that the components are distributed evenly and there is an even concentration throughout. The solute is the substance in the smaller amount that dissolves and that you add into the substance that is in the larger amount—the solvent. Water is a common solvent. Solids, liquids, and gases can be solutes. Examples of solutions are seawater and ammonia. Seawater is made up of water and salt, and ammonia is made up of ammonia gas and water. In these examples, the salt and the ammonia (NH_3) are the solutes; water is the solvent.

Physical and Chemical Changes in Matter

A physical change is a change in a substance that does not change what that substance is made of. Examples of physical changes are melting ice (boiling water), tearing paper, chopping wood, writing with chalk and mixing sugar and water together. In the mixing of sugar with water, or salt with water, even though the sugar or salt may not be visible to the naked eye in the water, it is still there and still has the same composition—that is, the molecules that make up the sugar or salt and water are still the same as when you mixed them. You can evaporate the water and you will recover your sugar or salt crystals.

A chemical change is when the substances that were combined are no longer the same molecules—they have changed to new substances. For example, burning wood, mixing baking soda and vinegar, or a rusting nail, that occurs when the iron of the nail (Fe) combines with oxygen (in the presence of water) to form a new substance—that is, a new molecule is formed, iron oxide Fe_2O_3.

Physical changes can be reversed, whereas chemical changes generally cannot be reversed. Evidence of a chemical change include: the combination of the substances gives off a gas (bubbles are observed), it changes color (not always a chemical change, but may be if the other evidences are also present), it gives off heat and becomes warmer, or absorbs heat and becomes colder (temperature change), and it forms a precipitate (a solid substance). When heat is given off in a chemical change, it is an exothermic reaction; and when heat is absorbed in a chemical change (the combination becomes colder), it is an endothermic reaction. Everyday examples of exothermic reactions are firewood burning or the use of a hand warmer used by many mountain climbers and snow skiers. Examples of endothermic reactions would be a cold pack used in sports injuries or the combination of baking soda and vinegar. (Try it with a thermometer in the vinegar during the reaction and see!)

Chemical Reactions in Everyday Life

Chemical reactions occur in everyday life and are an essential part of our physical and biological world. The burning of gasoline in automobiles is a chemical change—and burning of any kind for that matter. Burning is the combination of oxygen from the atmosphere with substances containing the carbon atom. The proper temperature has to be reached in order to begin this exothermic reaction, but once started, the chemical reaction can continue until the oxygen is used up or is prevented from entering into the reaction. So since gasoline is a fossil fuel (a once living organism), it contains carbon. When we provide the energy it needs to begin the reaction, called activation energy, as long as oxygen is present, the carbon substance will burn. Burning is a chemical reaction because the carbon and oxygen combine to form new substances such as carbon monoxide (CO) and carbon dioxide (CO_2). The same reaction occurs in burning wood, candles, and even in cell respiration—the oxygen we breathe and carry through our bloodstream is combined in our cells with carbon—containing glucose molecules in a type of "controlled" burning. Our bodies give off heat from this reaction, which is why we are able to maintain a fairly high temperature of about 98.6 degrees Fahrenheit. Other examples of chemical reactions in everyday life include chemical batteries, the digestion of food, and cooking/baking. Moreover, the process of photosynthesis, in which plants use sunlight to convert carbon dioxide gas and water into food for the plant, known as glucose (a simple sugar), is also an important chemical reaction responsible for providing food for and sustaining all life on Earth.

Competency 036 (Physical Science)

The teacher understands energy and interactions between matter and energy.

Principles of Energy

Energy is available in many forms, including heat, light, solar radiation, chemical, electrical, magnetic, sound, and mechanical energy. It exists in three states: potential, kinetic, and activation energies. An object possessing energy because of its ability to move has kinetic energy. The energy that an object has as the result of its position or condition is called potential energy. The energy necessary to transfer or convert potential energy into kinetic energy is called activation energy. All three states of energy can be transformed from one to the other. A vehicle parked in a garage has potential energy. When the driver starts the engine using the chemical energy stored in the battery combined with the fuel, potential energy becomes activation energy. Once the vehicle is moving, the energy changes to kinetic energy.

Heat and Temperature

Heat is a form of energy. Temperature is the measure of heat. The most common device used to measure temperature is the thermometer. Thermometers are made of heat-sensitive substances—mercury and alcohol—that expand when heated.

Heat and Light

The most common form of energy comes from the sun. Solar energy provides heat and light for animals and plants. Through **photosynthesis**, plants capture radiant energy from the sun and transform it into **chemical energy** in the form of glucose. This chemical energy is stored in the leaves, stems, and fruits of plants. Humans and animals consume the plants or fruits and get the energy they need for survival. This energy source is transformed again to create kinetic energy and body heat. Kinetic energy is used for movement and to do work, while heat is a required element for all warm-blooded animals, like humans. Cold-blooded animals also require heat, but rather than making it themselves through the transformation of plant sugar, they use solar energy to heat their body. Energy transformation constitutes the foundation and the driving force of an ecosystem. In addition to heat and solar radiation, energy is available in the forms of electricity and magnetism.

Heat Transfer

The transfer of heat is accomplished in three ways: conduction, radiation, and convection. Conduction is the process of transferring heat or electricity through a substance. It occurs when two objects of differing temperatures are placed in contact with each other and heat flows from the hotter object to the cooler object. For example, in the cooling system of a car, heat from the engine is transferred to the liquid coolant. When the coolant passes through the radiator, the heat transfers from the coolant to the radiator, and eventually, out of the car. This heat transfer system preserves the engine and allows it to continue working.

Radiation describes the energy that travels at high speed in space in the form of light or through the decay of radioactive elements. Radiation is part of our modern life. It exists in simple states as the energy emitted by microwaves, cellular phones, and sunshine or as potentially dangerous energy as X-ray machines and nuclear weapons. The radiation used in medicine, nuclear power, and nuclear weapons has enough energy to cause permanent damage and death.

Convection describes the flow of heat through the movement of matter from a hot region to a cool region. In its most basic form, the concept of convection is that warmer air rises and colder air sinks. The colder air contracts and so is denser, thus it sinks; the warmer air is expanded, or more spread out, and so is less dense and rises. Thus, convection occurs when the heating and circulation of a substance changes the density of the substance. A good example is the heating of air over land near coastal areas coupled with the influx of cooler sea breezes offshore. The heated air inland expands and thus decreases in density, causing the cooler, more dense air to rush in to achieve equilibrium. A more common example of convection is the process of heating water on a stove. In this case, heat is transferred from the stove element to the bottom of the pot to the water. Heat is transferred from the hot water at the bottom to the cooler water at the top by convection. At the same time, the cooler, denser water at the top sinks to the bottom, where it is subsequently heated. This circulation creates the movement typical of boiling water. Convection currents created by the combining or colliding of cold and warm air masses is one factor responsible for storms and circular rotation of the air in tornados and hurricanes. Ocean currents are also caused by the collision of cold water and warm water masses in the oceans (Cavallo 2001).

Objects feel warmer or colder to the touch. We refer to that sensation as temperature. The amount of heat energy in an object determines its temperature. Heat energy will transfer from warmer objects to colder objects.

For more information see *http://www.homeofbob.com/science/actPlans/physical/rds/tempByTouchDSCS.html.*

Related Concepts and Facts

- Energy is a property of matter that is related to doing something—heat, chemical change, motion, light, magnetism, nuclear change, electrical.
- Heat can be produced in many ways, such as burning, rubbing, or mixing one substance with another.
- Heat is transferred from a source to a receiver.
- Heat is transferred in predictable ways, flowing from warmer objects to cooler ones, until both reach the same temperature.
- Heat can be transferred during a chemical, electrical, magnetic, light, mechanical, or nuclear reaction.
- Objects that give off light usually give off heat.
- Mechanical energy is usually related to heat through friction.
- Hot and cold objects will transfer heat energy until they reach equilibrium.
- Some materials conduct energy better than others.
- Some materials can transfer heat by contact or at a distance
- Heat is almost always a result of energy transfer.
- Heat can be transferred by touching of particles (collisions of atoms conduction), or through space by rays (radiation) or currents in a fluid (convection).
- Heat energy is the disorderly motion of molecules and in radiation.
- Insulator is a material that has a slower transfer of energy.
- Conductor is a material that easily transfers energy.

Electricity and Magnetism

When you arrange an energy source, such as a battery, a wire, and a light bulb (or motor, or bell, or any electrical device) such that all metal parts are touching (metal is a good "conductor" of energy) in a circle—the bulb will light (the motor will run, the bell will ring, and so on). What has been created by arranging the items in this circle is known as an "electric circuit." The energy from the battery or other energy source is able to "flow" or be transferred through the metal wires and parts of the circuit. A closed circuit is when all metal parts are touching and the electrical charge is able to continue to be transferred through the circuit. A light switch or other "on button" closes the circuit and allows the electricity to flow. An open circuit occurs when there is a break someplace in the flow of electricity through the circuit. A switch or "off button" opens the circuit and stops the electricity flow. When you ring a door bell, you are closing the circuit or allowing all metal parts to touch and send electricity through it to make the bell ring; when you let go of the doorbell button, the circuit is open, and so the flow of electricity stops and so does the ringing of the bell.

Lightning is a form of static electricity which means it is not "flowing" or being transferred through a metal wire, but is caused by friction, much the same as walking across a carpet in socks and getting a shock when a metal doorknob is touched. In both kinds of electricity, the electrons in the atoms of the substance, which are negatively charged, are pulled away from their atom's nucleus, giving the object, or cloud, a negative charge. The negative charge is quickly attracted to a positive charge—in the case of lightning, that positive charge could be something (or someone!) on the ground. The positive charge quickly jumps toward the negative charge and the negative charge quickly jumps toward the positive charge, and a flash of lighting and clap of thunder is heard.

Light Energy

Light energy, and all energy for that matter, travels in waves and in a straight-line path. The electromagnetic spectrum shows the different wavelengths and frequencies of energy, including the small portion that is visible light. The electromagnetic spectrum includes, for example, micro-waves, x-rays, radio waves, infrared radiation, visible light waves, and ultraviolet radiation, all of which have different wavelengths and frequencies that distinguish one type of wave from another (see *http://imagine.gsfc.nasa.gov/docs/science/know_l1/emspectrum.html*).

Visible light is the wavelength of light we can see, which our eyes see as white light. However, this white light is composed of a host of other wavelengths of light that our eyes cannot always distinguish, which we know as the visible light spectrum, or a rainbow. The colors of white light include red, orange, yellow, green, blue, indigo, and violet (although some sources now eliminate indigo as separate from violet), or ROYGBIV. When light, again, traveling in a straight line, hits an object or substance and is bent, it is called refraction. The bending of light waves may result in the colors of light in the spectrum becoming visible, as when we see a rainbow in the sky (the water molecules in the air bend the light) or when light travels through cut glass such as with a prism. **Reflection** is when light waves bounce back, as when looking in a mirror. The principles of reflection and refraction are used in periscopes and telescopes in order to be able to see objects we may otherwise not be able to see. They are often popular in magic shows when objects are said to "disappear." In actuality, the light of the object has been refracted or reflected to a place away from our eyes so that we can no longer see it.

Refraction is also used to our advantage through concave and convex lenses. Concave or convex lenses work such that when light passes through, it changes the focal point. The eye contains a lens, but when light passing through, the eye cannot properly focus on the "screen" known as the retina, the object being viewed may be blurred. Concave or convex lenses are used in eyeglasses to adjust and correct the focal point. These lenses are also used in cameras, microscopes, and telescopes. A spoon is an example of both a concave and a convex lens—if you look into the concave side, you will see yourself upside down. If you look into the convex side of the spoon, you will see yourself right side up. This is due to refraction (and reflection) of light. For more on this topic, see *http://camillasenior.homestead.com/optics4.html*.

Sound Energy

Sound also travels in waves. Sounds are caused by vibrations, such as a guitar string (or a rubber band), or banging on a drum or cymbal. Sound has a certain wavelength, frequency, pitch, and amplitude (loudness). Sound waves must travel through a medium, which may be solid, liquid, or gas. Sound travels best through solids because there are more molecules (particles) to vibrate, and least well through gases.

The types of sound waves are longitudinal and transverse. Longitudinal waves move parallel to the direction the wave moves, and transverse waves move perpendicular to the direction of the wave. For more information and animations on sound waves, see *www.glenbrook.k12.il.us/gbssci/Phys/Class/waves/u10l1c.html*.

Competency 037 (Physical Science)

The teacher understands energy transformations and the conservation of matter and energy.

Electricity

Electricity is the flow of electrons or electric power or charge. The basic unit of charge is based on the positive charge of the proton and the negative charge of the electron. Energy occurs naturally in the atmosphere through light. However, it is not feasible to capture that type of energy. The electricity that we use comes from secondary sources because it is produced from the conversion of primary (natural) sources of energy like fossil fuels that are nonrenewable (natural gas, coal, and oil) and nuclear, and renewable resources such as wind and solar energy. All sources of energy are used to produce a common result—to turn a turbine that generates electricity (see *www.sce.com/kids/science/producing.html*). Electricity that is generated can then be sent through wires for human use, and can be transformed into other forms of energy, including sound, light, heat, and force.

Conservation of Energy

The main principle of energy conservation states that energy can change form but cannot totally disappear. For example, the chemical energy stored in a car battery is used to start the engine, which in turn is used to recharge the battery. Another example of energy conservation is placing merchandise on shelves. Energy was used to do the work (placing merchandise on a shelf) and it was stored as potential energy. Potential energy in turn can be converted to kinetic energy when the merchandise is pushed back to the floor. In this case, work was recovered completely, but often the recovered energy is less than the energy used to do the work. This loss of energy can be caused by friction or any kind of resistance encountered in the process of doing the work. For example, as a vehicle's tires roll across the pavement, doing the work of moving forward, they encounter friction. This friction causes heat energy to be released, as well as kinetic energy.

In essence, energy cannot be created or destroyed, only changed in form. Likewise, matter cannot be created or destroyed, only changed in form. Thus, energy from the sun is changed, for example, to chemical energy when plants use the energy to make glucose in photosynthesis. The energy from the sun is stored in the chemical bonds of the glucose molecule and will be released for use by the organism—the plant itself, or any organism that eats the plant and its glucose—when the molecule's chemical bonds are "broken" by oxygen in cell respiration and/or stored in another chemical form known as ATP. Likewise, electrical energy comes from burning, or breaking the bond of carbon-based molecules as in fossil fuels. This electricity generated is then transformed to another form by first capturing and sending that electrical energy through metal wires originating at the power generating plant, and sending it in a complete, closed circuit to homes, businesses, and industries. There the electrical energy may be transformed to sound, heat, light, and/or mechanical energy. In all cases, the energy is not lost, it is changed in form.

It is important to conserve matter and energy generated from fossil fuels as these are non-renewable sources and will one day be expended. It is also important to continue exploring alternative, renewable forms of energy and electricity generation to meet our society's energy demands and maintain our Earth's clean air and water supplies.

Key Principles of Competency 037

- To help students develop higher-order thinking skills, teachers need to guide students to analyze research data and make extrapolations or inferences based on data analysis.
- Matter is anything that has mass and takes up space.
- Mass is the amount of matter something contains.
- Volume refers to the amount of space taken up by an object.
- The states of matter are solid, gas, liquid, and plasma.
- There are 112 basic kinds of matter called elements.
- Elements are made up of atoms. An atom is the smallest part of matter.
- A compound is a kind of matter made up of two or more elements. A chemical formula describes the kinds of elements present in a compound. The chemical formula of water is H_2O because it has two molecules of hydrogen and one molecule of oxygen.
- Physical properties of matter are the characteristics that can be seen or measured without changing the material.
- Chemical properties of matter are the characteristics that can only be seen when the material changes and new materials are formed; for example, wood burns and turns into ashes.
- Weight is the amount of gravitational force exerted over an object.
- Energy and matter may be changed from one form to another but are not lost.
- Heat is transferred by conduction, convection, and radiation.
- Electric circuits may be open or closed.
- Potential energy is stored energy; kinetic energy is energy in motion or actively being used. Activation energy is the energy it takes to change potential energy into kinetic energy.
- Light travels in waves and in a straight line; light may be refracted or bent and/or reflected.
- Sound is caused by vibrations.

Competency 038 (Life Science)

The teacher understands the structure and function of living things.

Structure and Function

All living things carry on life functions, such as, respiration, nutrition, response, circulation, growth, excretion, regulation, and reproduction, all of which characterize them as living as opposed to nonliving. In addition, all living things are composed of the basic unit of life known as cells. Organisms, as well as individual cells of an organism and single-celled organisms, carry on these life functions using specialized structures. For example, earthworms carry on respiration through their moist skin; plants excrete gases from tiny pores on the underside of leaves called stomata; a single-celled Amoeba ingests food by use of a "false foot" or pseudopodia; and insects respond to chemical attractants called pheromones of the opposite-sex insect for mating.

Animal and Plant Cells

Animal and plant cells are similar in appearance. Animal cells contain mitochondria, small round or rod-shaped bodies found in the cytoplasm of most cells. The main function of mitochondria is to produce the enzymes for the metabolic conversion of food to energy. This process consumes oxygen and is termed aerobic respiration.

Plants cells also contain mitochondria, which allow plants to carry on respiration where they use oxygen and excrete carbon dioxide and water just like animals. However, plants also have specialized organelles called chloroplasts that are used for taking in sunlight and using this energy to convert another gas, carbon dioxide, and water taken in from the roots to make glucose—a simple sugar that is the food for the plant. Chloroplasts contain chlorophyll, which is used in this process of converting light into chemical energy. This process is called photosynthesis. Photosynthesis is the process by which chlorophyll-containing organisms convert light energy to chemical energy.

Cell System

The cell is the basic unit of living organisms and the simplest living unit of life. Living organisms are composed of cells that have the following common characteristics:

- Have a membrane that regulates the flow of nutrients and water that enter and exit the cell
- Contain the genetic material (DNA) that allows for reproduction
- Require a supply of energy
- Contain basic chemicals to make metabolic decision for survival
- Reproduce and are the result of reproduction

Eukaryotic and Prokaryotic Cells

There are two kinds of cells—prokaryotic and eukaryotic. **Prokaryotic** cells are the simplest and most primitive type of cells. They do not contain the structures typical of eukaryotic cells. Some prokaryotic cells have external whiplike flagella for locomotion or a hairlike system for adhesion. Prokaryotic cells come in three shapes: cocci (round), bacilli (rods), and spirilla or spirochetes (helical cells). Bacteria (also called Monera) are prokaryotic cells. For more information and animated illustrations of prokaryotic cells see *www.cellsalive.com/cells/bactcell.htm*.

Eukaryotic cells evolved from prokaryotic cells and in the process became structurally and biochemically more complex. The key distinction between the two cell types is that only eukaryotic cells contain many structures, or organelles, separated from other cytoplasm components by a membrane. The organelles within eukaryotic cells are the nucleus, mitochondria, chloroplasts, and Golgi apparatus. The nucleus contains the deoxyribonucleic acid (DNA) information. The mitochondria have their own membrane and contain some DNA information and proteins. They generate the energy for the cell. The chloroplast is a component that exists in plants only, allowing them to trap sunlight as energy for the process of photosynthesis. The Golgi apparatus secretes substances needed for the cell's survival. For information and animations on eukaryotic cells, see *www.cellsalive.com/cells/3dcell.htm*.

Reproduction

An organism may consist of only one cell, or it may comprise many billions of cells of various dimensions. Cells are composed primarily of water and the elements oxygen, hydrogen, carbon, and nitrogen. Growth in most organisms is caused by nuclear cell division **(mitosis)** and replication **(meiosis)**, in addition to enlargement of the cells themselves. Some cells are complete organisms, such as the unicellular bacteria; others, such as muscle cells, are parts of multicellular organisms. All cells have an internal substance called cytoplasm—a clear gelatinous fluid—enclosed within a membrane. Each cell contains the genetic material containing the information for the formation of organisms.

Classifications of Living Things

Living things are divided into five groups, or **kingdoms**: Monera (bacteria), Protista (protozoans), Fungi, Plantae (plants), and Animalia (animals).

Monera consists of unicellular organisms. It is the only group of living organisms made of prokaryotic cells—the cells with a primitive organization system. Some examples of this organism are bacteria, blue-green algae, and spirochetes.

Protista contains a type of eukaryotic cell with a more complex organization system. This kingdom includes diverse, mostly unicellular organisms that live in aquatic habitats, in both freshwater and saltwater. They are not animals or plants but a unique organism. Some examples of Protista are protozoans and algae of various types.

Fungi are made of multicellular organisms with a sophisticated organization system—that is, containing eukaryotic cells. They exist in a variety of forms and shapes. Because they do not have chlorophyll, they cannot produce food through photosynthesis. Fungi obtain energy, carbon, and water from dead materials. Some examples of these types of organisms are mushrooms, mold, mildews, and yeast.

Plants are multicellular organisms with a sophisticated organization system. In addition to more familiar plants, moss and ferns also fall under this category. Plant cells have chloroplasts, a component that allows them to trap sunlight as energy for the process of photosynthesis. Photosynthesis eliminates carbon dioxide from the environment and produces the oxygen needed for the survival of animals.

Animals are also multicellular with multiple forms and shapes, and with specialized senses and organs. The Animalia kingdom is composed of organisms like sponges, worms, insects, fish, amphibians, reptiles, birds, and mammals. Animals are the most sophisticated type of living organisms and represent the highest levels of evolution. Animals live in all kinds of habitats, and they are as simple as flies or as sophisticated as humans.

For additional information about living things, go to the Web site of the Behavioral Sciences Department of Palomar College, San Marcos, California, at *http://anthro.palomar.edu/animal/default.htm.*

Life Cycles

Life traditionally begins with a seed or a fertilized egg, which goes through metamorphosis until the organism is fully formed. The development and growth of organisms can take days, months, or years, but eventually they all go through similar stages: creation, maturation, reproduction, and death. Some organisms, like insects, go through a short cycle, reproducing once and then dying. Others, like vertebrates, spend more time in the reproductive stage. Some examples of living organisms and the changes that they go through are presented in Table 5-4 on the next page.

Some of the most spectacular metamorphoses (changes from one stage of life to another) are experienced by insects, amphibians, and humans. Insects, like the Darkling Beetle and the butterfly, go through drastic changes in a period of weeks. Frogs go through similar transmutations that allow them to move from an aquatic environment to land. Humans, on the other hand, begin life as microscopic beings and after nine months develop into a six- to nine-pound physically functional individual. The National Science Education Standards (NSES) and the TEKS emphasize that during the elementary school grades, students should be exposed to the concept of life cycles for plants and animals, including humans.

Life Cycle of Plants

The life cycle of plants generally begins with seeds. Mature plants produce the seeds, which are transported through various means: wind, water, hitchhiking on animals, or ingested as food and released as droppings or waste. For the seeds to germinate, they need air, the right amount of heat or proper temperature specific for that seed, and water. They do not need light to germinate or initially sprout, but do need light to grow since they need to carry on photosynthesis for their source of food, and to mature into an adult plant that can reproduce new seeds. Growing plants also need the right kind of soil, sufficient water, and heat/light from the sun. As part of the growth process, plants develop a root system for support and to extract the water and minerals they need from the soil. It is important to understand that fertilizers are not food for the plant—they only provide vitamins and minerals for the plant to help it remain healthy. The only food the plant has is what it makes for itself through photosynthesis.

Through the process of photosynthesis, a plant containing chlorophyll captures energy from the

Table 5-4. Life Cycles of Common Organisms

Organism	Stage 1	Stage 2	Stage 3	Stage 4	Stage 5
Darkling Beetle	Egg (fertilized by male sperm)	Larva—called "mealworm" though not a true worm	Pupa—mealworm curls up into a pupated or sleeplike state	Darkling Beetle	Reproduction—organisms lay eggs Death of the adult
Butterfly	Egg (fertilized by male sperm)	Larva—called caterpillar	Pupa—caterpillar forms a cocoon or chrysalis	Butterfly	Reproduction—organisms lay eggs Death of the adult
Frog	Egg (fertilized by male sperm)	Embryo	Tadpole	Frog	Reproduction—organism lays eggs Death of the adult
Human	Egg (fertilized by male sperm)	Embryo/Fetus	Child through adolescent	Human adult	Reproduction—organisms have live birth of offspring Death of the adult
Trees	Seed with embryo or "baby plant" inside (egg or ovule inside of flower, ovary fertilized by male sperm, nuclei inside of pollen grains)	Sprout	Growing plant	Mature tree	Reproduction—Tree produces flowers with new seeds that are dispersed Death of the adult

sun and converts it into chemical energy. Part of the chemical energy is used for the plant's own survival, and the rest is stored in the stem and leaves. As part of the growth process, some plants produce flowers, which are pollinated by insects or through the wind. That is, the pollen, which contains sperm nuclei, is transferred from the male part of the flower, the stamen, to the female part of the flower, the pistil. Once pollination occurs, the sperm leaves the pollen and travels to the ovules or eggs inside the ovary of the pistil and fertilizes the ovules. The fertilized ovules become the seeds. The ovary swells to become the fruit, and the flower itself dies because it has now served its purpose. The fruits contain, carry, and protect the seeds until they are dispersed to a place where they can sprout, and the cycle of the plant continues.

For information on how this process can be presented to children in the elementary school grades, visit the following site: "The Life Cycle of Plants," at *www.cast.org/teachingeverystudent*. For additional information about photosynthesis, visit the following site: "Exploring Photosynthesis," at *www.botany.uwc.ac.za/ecotree/photosynthesis/photosynthesis1.htm*. An inquiry-based curriculum on the life cycle of plants can also be found in the NSTA publication, *Science and Children* by Cavallo (2005) titled, "Cycling Through Plants."

Life Cycle of Animals

Many animals come from eggs. For some animals, the egg grows inside the female animal and is fertilized by the male, for others such as most fish species, the eggs are fertilized by the male after they have been expelled from the female's body. When fertilized internally, the fertilized egg may be laid externally from the female as in many insects, reptiles, and birds, or it may remain in the body of the female until birth. The egg has an outer lining to protect the animal growing inside. Bird eggs have hard shells, while the eggs of amphibians, like the turtle, have hard but flexible coverings. With the appropriate care and heat, an egg will hatch. After hatching, in some species, the parents protect and feed the newborn until it can survive on its own; in other species, the eggs are left on their own to survive. On reaching adulthood, females begin laying eggs, and the cycle of life continues. Mammals are also conceived through egg fertilization, but the resulting embryo is kept inside the mother until it is mature enough for life outside the womb.

Needs of Living Organisms

Living organisms like plants and animals need to have ideal conditions for their survival. They need nutrients, the appropriate temperature, and a balanced ecosystem to survive and reproduce. A healthy ecosystem must contain an appropriate system for energy exchange or a food chain. The right combination of herbivorous and carnivorous animals is necessary for a healthy ecosystem. The food chain generally begins with the primary source of energy, the sun. The sun provides the energy for plants; plants in turn are consumed by animals; and animals are consumed by other animals. These animals die and serve as food sources for fungi and plants. When this balance is disrupted either by the removal of organisms or the introduction of nonnative species, the ecosystem is affected, forcing animals and plants to adapt or else die. Thus, the common basic needs of all living organisms for survival are: air, water, food, and shelter.

Body Structure and Function

Cells are the basic unit of all living organisms. Within cells there are specialized organelles that carry on all of the life functions at a microscopic/chemical level. For example, the mitochondria carries on cell respiration, and ribosomes assemble proteins for use both inside the cell and out. Teachers should know the parts of the cell, called organelles, and their functions, particularly, the nucleus, mitochondria, chloroplasts (plants only), ribosomes, Golgi, endoplasmic reticulum, vacuoles, and cell membranes. An explanation of organelles may be found at *www.cellsalive.com/cells/3dcell.htm*.

Moving outward from the cell, it is important to know that cells communicate with one another on a chemical level and work together to perform specific functions. The shape of these groups of cells and activity levels differ according to their particular function in the body; for example, muscle cells are long and narrow so they may better respond to stimuli and contract. Groups of cells with similar functions are called tissues. Tissues are organized together to perform a specific life function. A complex system of tissues working together to carry on one of the body's life functions is an organ. A group of different organs working together to support and help carry out a life function and keep the organism alive is called an organ system. Examples of systems include the digestive system, the respiratory system, the immune system, the muscular system, the skeletal system, the nervous system, and the circulatory system. Organ systems are organized into an organism. The order of organization is as follows:

Cells → Tissues → Organs → Systems → Organ Systems → Organism

For more information on the structure and function of organisms, see *www.palmbeach.k12.fl.us/MULTICULTURAL/ESOLCurriculumDocs/Secondary/SciOrganism.pdf*.

Animal and Plant Cells

Animal and plant cells are similar in appearance. Animal cells contain mitochondria, small round or rod-shaped bodies found in the cytoplasm of most cells. The main function of mitochondria is to produce the enzymes for the metabolic conversion of food to energy. This process consumes oxygen and is termed **aerobic respiration**.

Plants cells also contain mitochondria and similar organelles called chloroplasts. Chloroplasts contain chlorophyll, used in converting light into chemical energy. This process is called **photosynthesis**. Photosynthesis is the process by which chlorophyll-containing organisms convert light energy to chemical energy.

Systems of the Human Body

Musculoskeletal System

The human skeleton consists of more than 200 bones held together by connective tissues called ligaments. Movements are effected by contractions of the skeletal muscles, to which the bones are attached by tendons. Muscular contractions are controlled by the nervous system.

Nervous System

The nervous system has two main divisions: the somatic and automatic. The somatic allows the voluntary control of skeletal muscles, and the automatic, or involuntary, controls cardiac and glandular functions. **Voluntary movement** is caused by nerve impulses sent from the brain through the spinal cord to nerves to connecting skeletal muscles. **Involuntary movement** occurs in direct response to outside stimulus. Involuntary responses are called reflexes. For example, when an object presents danger to the eye, the body responds automatically by blinking or retracting away from the object.

Circulatory System

The circulatory system follows a cyclical process in which the heart pumps blood through the right chambers of the heart and through the lungs, where it acquires oxygen. From there it is pumped back into the left chambers of the heart, where it is pumped into the main artery (aorta), which then sends the oxygenated blood to the rest of the body using a system of veins and capillaries. Through the capillaries, the blood distributes the oxygen and nutrients to tissues, absorbing from them carbon dioxide, a metabolic waste product. Finally, the blood completes the circuit by passing through small veins, which join to form increasingly larger vessels. Eventually, the blood reaches the largest veins, which return it to the right side of the heart to complete and restart the process.

Immune System

The main function of the body's immune system is to defend itself against foreign proteins and infectious organisms. The system recognizes organisms that are not normally in the body and develops the antibodies needed to control and destroy the invaders. When the body is attacked by infectious organisms, it develops what we know as a fever. Fever is caused by the body fighting invading molecules. The raised temperature of a fever will kill some bacteria. The major components of the immune system are the thymus, lymph system, bone marrow, white blood cells, antibodies, and hormones.

Respiratory System

Respiration is carried out by the expansion and contraction of the lungs. In the lungs, oxygen enters tiny capillaries, where it combines with **hemoglobin** in the red blood cells and is carried to the tissues through the circulatory system. At the same time, carbon dioxide passes through capillaries into the air contained within the lungs.

Animals inhale oxygen from the environment and exhale carbon dioxide. Carbon dioxide is used by plants in the process of photosynthesis, which produces the oxygen that animals use again for survival.

Digestive and Excretory Systems

The energy required for sustenance of the human body is supplied through the chemical energy stored in food. To obtain the energy from food, it has to be fragmented and digested. Digestion begins at the moment that food is placed in the mouth and makes contact with saliva. Fragmented and partially digested food passes down the esophagus to the stomach, where the process is continued by the gastric and intestinal juices. Thereafter, the mixture of food and secretions makes its way down the small intestine, where the nutrients are extracted and absorbed into the bloodstream. The unused portion of the food goes to the large intestine and eventually is excreted from the body through defecation.

For a detailed analysis of each component of the body system go to the Human Anatomy Online Web site at *http://www.innerbody.com/htm/body.html*.

Competency 039 (Life Science)

The teacher understands reproduction and the mechanisms of heredity.

Reproduction

An organism may consist of only one cell, or it may comprise many billions of cells of various dimensions. For example, cells are complete organisms, such as the unicellular bacteria; others, such as muscle cells, are parts of multicellular organisms. All cells have an internal substance called cytoplasm—a clear gelatinous fluid—enclosed within a membrane. Each cell contains the genetic material containing the information for the formation of organisms. Cells are composed primarily of water and the elements oxygen, hydrogen, carbon, and nitrogen.

Growth in most organisms is caused by nuclear cell division (mitosis.) In mitosis the chromosomes (containing DNA which is the genetic material of the cell or blueprint) first replicate—in humans the 46 chromosomes in the cell double. The cell then divides through a series of steps resulting in 2 new cells that each has the original 46 chromosomes, or the exact copy of the original. Through mitosis, new cells are made, for example, to form a scar after an injury, new bone cells, muscle cells, blood cells, and any cell that is needed by the body throughout life and growth.

However, in single-celled organisms, mitosis is the cell's form of reproduction—making exact copies of the DNA in each of the two "daughter" cells, and is often called binary fission. This type of reproduction is also called asexual reproduction because only one organism (the single cell) is involved and there is no exchange of genetic material or DNA. Thus, the two offspring cells, or daughter cells, are identical to the original or parent cell.

In humans and many other organisms, particularly mammals, another form of cell division occurs only in the reproductive organs (in most called the female ovaries and male testicles) where the DNA is replicated/copied; however, the cell divides twice in a process called meiosis. Meiosis is how sperm and egg cells are formed through a series of steps. The original cell in the female ovary or male testicle first duplicates (replicates) its 46 chromosomes (containing the genetic blueprint material, DNA) and then divides twice, the result is four cells with half the number of chromosomes, or 23 chromosomes each. In forming the egg cell, only one is a viable egg that can be fertilized and the remaining three are polar bodies that eventually dissolve. In the male, all four sperm cells that were formed by meiosis of the original cell are viable and capable of fertilizing the egg. The process is similar in other organisms; however, the number of chromosomes may be different, depending on the particular species—a similar process even occurs in plants, where the flower is the reproductive organ—the ovules are the egg cells, and the pollen contains the sperm. This form of reproduction is known as sexual reproduction, because it requires the combination of DNA between two organisms of the same species (male, female). The fertilization of the egg by sperm cells occurs through copulation in vertebrates, and for fish and some amphibians it occurs through cross-fertilization. Cross-fertilization occurs outside the body; the female lays the eggs (ovum), and the males spray them with sperm to fertilize them.

Plant Reproduction

The reproduction of plants can also be divided into asexual and sexual mechanisms. Asexual reproduction of plants takes place by cutting portions of the plant and replanting them. Sexual reproduction involves seeds produced by female and male plants, which are then cross-pollinated with help from insects or other animals. As mentioned, the flower is the reproductive organ of the plant. The flower consists of several parts that are the male and female reproductive organs. Some flowers may have only the male part, and likewise, some flowers contain only the female part of the same species of plant/tree. So there actually can be a "male" tree and a "female" tree for example. In the flower, the male reproductive organ is the stamen, which is divided into filament and anther. The filament simply holds up the anther, and the anther contains the pollen and in the pollen are the sperm nuclei. Flowers may also contain the female reproductive organ, or pistil, which consists of the ovary, style, and stigma. The ovary contains the egg cells, which in the flower are called ovules. The style is the tube above the ovary, and the stigma is the top of the style which has a sticky substance. The pollen needs to either be manually placed on the stigma, or blown there by the wind, or what usually happens, it needs to stick to the body of a bee or butterfly (who are actually in search of sugary nectar in the flower and not the pollen). When the pollen sticks to the body of the insect, it may then be transferred from the anther (male part) to the stigma (female part). In essence, the sperm nuclei then travel down the style until it reaches the ovules, where fertilization occurs. The fertilized egg then becomes the seed. The ovary of the flower may swell and become the fruit (as in a peach or apple). This process helps protect the seeds and also helps with seed dispersal (animals eat the fruit, the seed has a seed coat that protects it and is indigestible, the animals excretes the seed, unharmed, in its fecal matter). Seed germination—where the seed sprouts into a plant—requires the appropriate quantity of air, water, and heat.

Hereditary Material

Deoxyribonucleic acid or DNA is the hereditary material of living organisms. DNA has as its smallest complete component what is called a nucleotide. A single nucleotide consists of the sugar deoxyribose, a phosphate molecule, and a nitrogen base molecule. There are four nitrogen bases that are paired in the double-helix structure of DNA. These nitrogen bases are adenine, thymine, guanine, and cytosine. In DNA, adenine always pairs with a nucleotide having thymine as its nitrogen base (A-T); and guanine always pairs with a nucleotide having cytosine as its nitrogen base (G-C), and vice versa (T-A; C-G)

In bacteria, also called monera or prokaryotic cells, DNA is in a single strand. In more complex organisms including protista, fungi, animals and plants, all eukaryotic cells, the DNA is arranged in chromosomes, and these chromosomes with its DNA are located in the nucleus (though there is new evidence of DNA in other cell organelles, particularly the mitochondria). The number of chromosomes in the cells of organisms varies from one species to another—but it is the same for all members of that species. Along the strands of DNA that exist inside of chromosomes, there are certain locations that direct specific functions of cells, including hereditary traits, called genes. Certain genes give the cell directions, in the developing embryo for example, for the expression of traits such as eye color, hair color, and leg shape and size. In already developed organisms, as the human adult, other genes (sections of DNA) direct the production of substances and control specific activities and functions. The production of insulin in pancreatic cells, for example, is controlled by certain genes in the chromosomes in the cells of the organ known as the pancreas. In inheritance and cell functions, traits can be controlled or determined by more than one gene, located on the same, or even on different chromosomes. Likewise, there may be several traits influenced by one single gene.

As discussed earlier, the fertilized egg that eventually grows into the organism that then goes through its respective life cycle to adult contains half the number of -chromosomes from the female egg (mother) and half the number of chromosomes from the male sperm (father). In the human, there are 23 chromosomes in the egg and 23 in the sperm, so the fertilized egg and, therefore, the offspring (baby) has 46 chromosomes—which is the normal number for all cells in all organisms of the human species. The 23 chromosomes of the egg have an exact pair or match in the sperm. That matching chromosome contains genes with DNA that direct the same traits. So along the length of chromosome number 20, for example, in the egg cell, you will find it controls the same traits that are along the length of chromosome number 20 in the male sperm. However, the 23 chromosomes in the egg contain the specific qualities or characteristics of the mother; whereas, the 23 chromosomes in the sperm contain the specific qualities or characters of the father. Though more than one chromosome controls eye color—we will use one chromosome as an example. In one of the egg cell's chromosomes, there is a gene that controls eye color, and in the egg this eye color could be "blue." In the same number chromosome in the same location in the sperm cell, there will also be a gene for eye color, but the characteristic of that eye color may instead be "brown." So traits are located on the same number chromosome whether that chromosome originated from the egg or the sperm; however, the quality or characteristic may differ (that is, the pigment color that section of DNA or gene directs the cell to make). The gene for eye color and other traits that are the paired chromosomes in the same location are called alleles. When the egg is fertilized, the directions coded in the DNA alleles are set. In many alleles, one of the traits directed by the gene on one chromosome is dominant, and the other is recessive.

The dominant trait is the one that typically "shows" or is expressed in the offspring. In the case of eye color, brown is usually dominant over blue eye color, so if one of the alleles is for "blue" eyes and the other allele from the other parent is for "brown" eyes, the offspring will show the dominant trait and have brown eyes. It is important to note that environmental factors play an important role in the expression (showing up) of traits in the offspring as they grow and develop. Sometimes environmental stressors, for example, can cause a genetic change in an organism that otherwise may not have been expressed, such as certain food allergies or intolerances.

For more genetics information and activities go to *www.kidsturncentral.com/links/geneticslinks.htm*.

Competency 040 (Life Science)

The teacher understands adaptations of organisms and theory of evolution.

Adaptations and Change over Time

Genetics plays an important role in the ability of organisms to be able to survive and thrive in their environment and, ultimately, produce new offspring where they can pass on similar genetic material, like that which allowed them to survive and thrive, and maybe survive and thrive even better. Some inherited traits, called adaptations, allow the organisms to best survive in their environment and others do not, and may even lead to their demise (and those prevent the prospect of future offspring). Adaptations do not suddenly arise or develop in the lifetime of organisms. They occur gradually in the species over time. For example, if a certain deer-like animal thousands of years ago was particularly fast—that is, it was born with stronger muscle tissue than most, and a better bone and muscle physical structure—perhaps it was better able to run away from predators and survive. Therefore, this deer-like animal was able to survive long enough for it to have offspring with similar genetic material. At the same time, those deer-like animals that were not born with the same muscular and structural soundness as this one were killed as prey before they could reproduce. The animal that was best adapted to its environment (able to run from predators) was the first deer-like animal. In time, those animals that are best suited in this, as well as in other ways, are the organisms who survive, as do their offspring. Those not well adapted perish.

It is also the case that the organism that survives will breed with another that also has better adapted characteristics, and was also able to survive in the natural environment. A change or mutation in the genetic material, that is, the genes that direct the development of a trait, may give rise to a new characteristic that either is or is not better suited for the environment. Over the years, mutations that are better suited to the environment may make the organism appear quite different than it did hundreds, thousands, and millions of years earlier. If the environment itself changes, however, organisms that were able to survive under the previous conditions (climate, water supply, vegetation, landscape) may be unable to survive in the new environmental conditions. Thus, a catastrophic event, such as perhaps a large asteroid striking the Earth, could change the environmental conditions and either lead to the extinction of organisms, or the survival of organisms that would not have survived under the conditions before the strike. Likewise, selective breeding, which is human selection of which organisms breed with another, and thus, control of the genetic material that is passed onto offspring, also effects the change over time of organisms. The combination of genetics, adaptations, changes over time, mutations, selective breeding, and environmental conditions/changes contribute to the concept known as evolution.

Competency 041 (Life Science)

The teacher understands the relationships between organisms and the environment.

Ecology

Ecology studies the relationship of organisms with their physical environment. The physical environment includes light, heat, solar radiation, moisture, wind, oxygen, carbon dioxide, nutrients, water, and the atmosphere. The biological environment describes living and nonliving organisms in the ecosystem. There are three main components of an ecosystem:

- **Producers** are green plants that produce oxygen and store chemical energy for consumers.
- **Consumers** are animals, both herbivores and carnivores. The herbivores take the chemical energy from plants and carnivores take the energy from other animals or directly from plants.
- **Decomposers,** like fungi and bacteria, are in charge of cleaning up the environment by decomposing and freeing dead matter for recycling back into the ecosystem.

Maintaining a Healthy Balance

A successful ecosystem requires a healthy balance among producers, consumers, and decomposers. This balance relies on natural ways to control populations of living organisms and is maintained mostly through competition and predation.

Competition

When a shared resource is scarce, organisms must compete to survive. The competition, which occurs between animals as well as between plants, ensures the survival of the fittest and the preservation of the system.

Predation

Predation is the consumption of one living organism, plant or animal, by another. It is a direct way to control population and promote natural selection by eliminating weak organisms from the population. As a consequence of predation, predators and prey evolve to survive. If an organism cannot evolve to meet challenges from the environment, it perishes.

Adaptation for Survival

Changes in the environment force living organisms to modify their ways and even develop new physical features for survival. For example, the anteater developed a long snout to be able to reach for ants, and frogs developed a long, sticky tongue to catch flies. Adaptation for animals, plants, and even humans is a matter of life or death. Changes in the food chain of animals often force them to change their behaviors and adapt to new conditions.

For example, because their habitats are destroyed when land is developed by humans, raccoons and opossums have learned to coexist with humans and to get new sources of food. Bears have managed to successfully adapt to colder climates by hibernating during the winter while living on the fat they accumulate during the rest of they year. Other animals, like the chameleon or the fox, have developed camouflage to hide from predators. Humans are not exempt from the need to adapt to new situations. For example, humans have had to adapt and use tools to produce, preserve, and trade the food supplies they needed to sustain them. All these examples represent ways in which organisms adapt to deal with challenges in their ecosystem.

Key Principles of Competency 041

- When working with animals, teachers are ethically responsible for their well-being. Teachers need to provide an adequate environment for the survival and development of animals under their care.
- By observing the development of frogs and butterflies, students directly acquire information on the life cycles. Students can also observe how organisms adapt to their environment.
- Fungi obtain energy, carbon, and water from dead material. Fungi do not have chlorophyll, so they cannot produce food through photosynthesis.
- Chromosomes contain the genetic code, or DNA.
- Mitosis describes the process of a cell splitting to create two identical cells.
- Photosynthesis is the process of capturing, storing and converting solar energy. It is also the source of oxygen in the atmosphere.
- Insects have three main parts: head, thorax, and abdomen.
- Humans have several body systems, including the musculoskeletal, nervous, circulatory, immune, respiratory, and digestive/excretory systems.

Competency 042 (Earth and Space Science)

The teacher understands the function and structure of Earth systems.

Structure and Composition of the Earth (Geology)

Landform Characteristics

The formation of deserts, mountains, rivers, oceans, and other landforms can be described in terms of geological processes. Mountains are formed by colliding plates. For example, the Appalachian Mountains in the United States were formed when the tectonic plate carrying the continent of Africa collided with the plate carrying the North American continent 250 million years ago (Badder et. al. 2000). Rivers and natural lakes form at low elevations where rainfall collects and eventually runs down to the sea. The sediment gathered by the rivers in turn accumulates at river mouths to create deltas.

Layers of the Earth

The average circumference of the Earth at the equator is 25,902 miles, and its radius is about 3,959 miles. The Earth is divided into three main parts:

- The **crust** is the outer portion of the Earth where we live. The thickness of the crust varies from about 3 miles to 40 miles, depending on the location. It contains various types of soil, metals, and rocks. The crust is broken down into several floating tectonic plates. Movements of these plates cause Earthquakes and changes in landforms.
- The **mantle** is the thickest layer of the Earth located right below the crust. It is composed mostly of rocks and metals. The heat in the mantle is so intense that rocks and metals melt, creating magma and the resulting lava that reaches the surface.
- The **core** is the inner part of the Earth. It is composed of a solid inner core and an outer core that is mostly liquid. The inner core is made of solid iron and nickel. Despite temperatures in the inner core that resemble the

heat on the surface of the sun, this portion of the Earth remains solid because of the intense pressure there. For more information about the layers of the Earth, go to *http://jersey.uoregon.edu/~mstrick/AskGeoMan/geoQuerry8.html.*

Continental Drift

In 1915, the German scientist Alfred Weneger proposed that all the continents were previously one large continent but then broke apart and drifted through the ocean floor to their present locations. This theory was called the Continental Drift, and it was the origin of today's concept of plate tectonics.

Tectonic Plates

Based on the theory of plate tectonics, the surface of the Earth is fragmented into large plates. These plates are in continuous motion, floating on the liquid mantel and always changing in size and position. The edges of these plates, where they move against each other, are sites of intense geologic activity, which results in Earthquakes, volcanoes, and the creation of mountains. The generator for the movement of the continents/Earth's plates is the mid-Atlantic ridge—a huge volcanic mountain range on the floor of the Atlantic Ocean that is continuously erupting and pushing the plates apart in opposite directions from each other. For more information go to *pubs.usgs.gov/gip/dynamic/understanding.html#anchor5567033.*

Forces That Change the Surface of the Earth

Three main forces and processes change the surface of the Earth: weathering, geological movements, and the creation of glaciers.

Weathering

Weathering is the process of breaking down rock, soils, and minerals through natural, chemical, and biological processes. Two of the most common examples of physical weathering are exfoliation and freeze thaw.

- **Exfoliation** occurs in places like the desert when the soil is exposed first to high temperatures, which cause it to expand, and then to cold temperatures, which make the soil contract. The stress of these changes causes the outer layers of rock to peel off.
- **Freeze-thaw** breaks down rock when water gets into rock joints or cracks and then freezes and expands, breaking the rock. A similar process occurs when water containing salt crystals gets into the rock. Once the water evaporates, the crystals expand and break the rock. This process is called salt-crystal growth.

Weathering can be caused by chemical reactions. Two of the most common examples of chemical weathering are acid formation and hydration. Acid is formed under various conditions. For example, sulfur and rain are combined to create acid rain, which can weather and change the chemical composition of rock. Hydration occurs when the minerals in rock absorb water and expand sometimes changing the chemical composition of the rock. For example, through the process of hydration, a mineral like anhydrite can be changed into a different mineral, namely gypsum.

Erosion

After weathering, a second process called erosion can take place. Erosion is the movement of sediment from one location to the other through the use of water, wind, ice, or gravity. The Grand Canyon was created by the processes of weathering and erosion. The water movement (erosion) is responsible for the canyon being so deep, and the weathering process is responsible for its width (Badder et al. 2000).

Earthquakes and Geologic Faults

The movement of the Earth's plates has forced rock layers to fold, creating mountains, hills, and valleys. This movement causes faults in the Earth's crust, breaking rocks and reshaping the environment. When forces within the Earth cause rocks to break and move around geologic faults, earthquakes occur. A fault is a deep crack that marks the boundary between two plates. The San Andreas fault in central California is a well-known origin of Earthquakes in the area. The epicenter of an earthquake is the point on the surface where the quake is the strongest. The Richter scale is used to measure the amount of energy released by the earthquake. The severity of an earthquake runs from 0 to 9 on the Richter scale. Small tremors occur constantly, but every few months, a major earthquake occurs somewhere in the world. Scientists are researching ways to predict earthquakes, but their predictions are not always accurate.

Volcanoes

Volcanoes are formed by the constant motion of tectonic plates. This movement creates pressure that forces magma from the mantel to escape to the surface, creating an explosion of lava, fire, and ash. The pressure of the magma and gases creates a monticule, or a small cone, that eventually grows to form a mountain-like volcano. Volcanic activity can create Earthquakes, and the fiery lava can cause destruction.

Gravity

Gravity is the force of attraction that exists between objects. Gravity keeps the Earth in its orbit by establishing a balance between the attraction of the sun and the speed at which the Earth travels around it. However, gravity is also responsible for many of the Earth's forces that change the land. For example, when ice melts on the tops of mountains, it is because of gravity that the water will form streams and rivers that flow down the mountain, eventually making its way to the lowest point. Some of the main functions of gravity are listed here:

- Keeping the Earth's atmosphere, oceans, and inhabitants from drifting into space
- Pulling the rain to the rivers and eventually to the sea
- Guiding the development and growth of plants
- Affecting the way that our bones and muscles function

For information about the Earth and space, go to the official website of the National Aeronautics and Space Administration (NASA) at *www.nasa.gov/home/index.html?skipIntro=1*. This site includes special sections for children, students from kindergarten through grade 12, and teachers.

Surface Water and Groundwater

Surface water is the water in streams, lakes and rivers, and all water that is on the surface of the land. Ground water is water that seeps beneath the surface of the land and forms an underground "river" of water. The groundwater seeps into the soil until it reaches an impermeable layer of rock. The water stays on top of this layer and is a source of drinking water. This water may be tapped into via aquifers and wells. For more information, see *http://ga.water.usgs.gov/edu/Earthgw.html*.

The Earth's Atmosphere

The Earth is surrounded by a large mass of gas called the atmosphere. Roughly 348 miles thick, this gas mass supports life on the Earth and separates it from space. Among the many functions of the atmosphere are these:

- Absorbing energy from the sun to sustain life
- Recycling water and other chemicals needed for life
- Maintaining the climate, working with electric and magnetic forces
- Serving as a vacuum that protects life

The atmosphere is composed of 78 percent nitrogen, 21 percent oxygen, and 1 percent argon. In addition to these gases, the atmosphere contains water, greenhouse gases like ozone, and carbon dioxide. The Earth's atmosphere has five layers. The layer closest to the Earth is called the troposphere, and the weather we experience occurs in this layer. For more information on the atmosphere, go to *www.windows.ucar.edu/tour/link=/Earth/Atmosphere/layers.html&fr=t%20t*.

Natural and Human Influences on Earth Systems

It is important to understand that many natural processes on Earth can change its systems. For example, Earthquakes and volcanoes can be destructive and change the structure and composition of the landscape. A tsunami, an enormous wall of water that crashes into shorelines caused by Earthquakes under bodies of water such as oceans, can create a dramatic change in that shoreline. However, human influences may also change Earth systems. The destruction of the rainforests, called deforestation, can change the structure and composition of the land, and on a larger scale, affect the balance of atmospheric gases including carbon dioxide and oxygen levels. Carbon dioxide emissions from factories, automobiles, and airplanes, as examples, may play a role in changing the atmospheric composition as well. Carbon dioxide, called a "greenhouse gas" tends to trap heat energy and result in an overall warming of the atmosphere, which has an impact on climate and plant growth that in turn affects all living organisms on Earth. There are many natural and human influences that contribute to the increase of greenhouse gases in the atmosphere producing what is known as "global warming." Other greenhouse gases include methane (CH_4) and ozone, which is the molecule O_3, that when at the surface of the Earth are components of smog.

It is important to distinguish global warming and the ozone that is in smog from the destruction of the ozone layer (hole in the ozone layer) which is a different phenomenon. Ozone forms a layer at the top of the atmosphere that blocks harmful ultraviolet rays from the sun from reaching the Earth's surface ("good ozone"). The "hole" in the ozone layer means there is a destruction of this ozone layer, and now harmful ultraviolet radiation is reaching Earth's surface where this hole is present. Chlorofluorocarbons, which are found in aerosols, contribute to the destruction of the ozone layer. For more information on greenhouse gases and ozone, go to *http://hvo.wr.usgs.gov/volcanowatch/2005/05_07_28.html*.

Competency 043 (Earth and Space Science)

The teacher understands cycles in Earth Systems.

Rock Types

The hard, solid part of the Earth's surface is called rock. Rocks are made of one or more minerals. Rocks like granite, marble, and limestone are extensively used in the construction industry. They can be used in floors, buildings, dams, highways, or the making of cement. Rocks are classified by the way they are formed. Here are descriptions of the three types of rock:

- **Igneous** rocks are crystalline solids that form directly from the cooling of magma or lava. The composition of the magma determines the composition of the rock. Granite is one of the most common types of igneous rocks and is created from magma (inside the Earth). Once magma reaches the Earth's surface, it is called lava. Lava that has cooled forms a rock with a glassy look, called obsidian.
- **Sedimentary** rocks are called secondary rocks because they are often the result of the accumulation of small pieces broken off from preexisting rocks and then pressed into a new form. There are three types of sedimentary rocks:
  - — **Clastic** sedimentary rocks are made when pieces of rock, mineral, and organic material fuse together. These are classified as conglomerates, sandstone, and shale.
  - — **Chemical** sedimentary rocks are formed when water rich in minerals evaporates, leaving the minerals behind. Some common examples are gypsum, rock salt, and some limestone.
  - — **Organic** sedimentary rocks are made from the remains of plants and animals. For example, coal is formed when dead plants are squeezed together. Another example is a form of limestone rock composed of the remains of organisms that lived in the ocean.
- **Metamorphic** rocks are also secondary rocks formed from igneous, sedimentary, or other types of metamorphic rock. When hot magma or lava comes in contact with rocks or when buried rocks are exposed to pressure and high temperatures, the result is metamorphic rocks. For example, exposing limestone to high temperatures creates marble. The most common metamorphic rocks are slate, gneiss, and marble. For more information, go to *http://jersey.uoregon.edu/~mstrick/AskGeoMan/geoQuerry13.html*.

Rock Cycle

The formation of rock follows a cyclical process. For instance, rocks can be formed when magma or lava cools down, creating igneous rocks. Igneous rocks exposed to weathering can break into sediment, which can be compacted and cemented to form sedimentary rocks. Sedimentary rocks are exposed to heat and pressure to create metamorphic rocks. Finally, metamorphic rocks can melt and become magma and lava again (Badder et al. 2000). An illustration of the rock cycle and forces causing the changes in rock can be found at *www.classzone.com/books/Earth_science/terc/content/investigations/es0602/es0602page02.cfm*.

Minerals

Minerals are the most common form of solid material found in the Earth's crust. Even soil contains bits of minerals that have broken away from rock. To be considered a mineral, a substance must be found in nature and must never have been a part of any living organism. Minerals can be as soft as talc or as hard as emeralds and diamonds. Dug from the Earth, minerals are used to make various products:

- **Jewelry**—Gemstones such as amethysts, opals, diamonds, emeralds, topazes, and garnets are examples of minerals commonly used to create jewelry. Gold and silver are another type of mineral that can be used to create jewelry.
- **Construction**—Gypsum boards (drywall) are made of a mineral of the same name—gypsum. The windows in homes are made from another mineral, quartz.
- **Personal Use**—Talc is the softest mineral and it is commonly applied to the body in powder form.

Water Cycle

The hydrologic cycle describes a series of movements of water above, on, and below the surface of the Earth. This cycle consists of four distinct stages: storage, evaporation, precipitation, and runoff. It is the means by which the sun's energy is used to transport, through the atmosphere, stored water from the rivers and oceans to land masses. The heat of the sun evaporates the water and takes it to the atmosphere from which, through condensation, it falls as precipitation. As precipitation falls, water is filtrated back to underground water deposits called aquifers, or it runs off into storage in lakes, ponds, and oceans.

Tides

The word tides is used to describe the alternating rise and fall in sea level with respect to the land, produced by the gravitational attraction of the moon and the sun. Additional factors such as the configuration of the coastline, depth of the water, the topography of the ocean floor, and other hydrographic and meteorological influences may play an important role in altering the range, interval, and times of the arrival of the tides.

Nutrient Cycles

Nutrient cycles include the carbon and nitrogen cycle. The carbon cycle is the capture of carbon from carbon dioxide in the atmosphere by plants to make glucose. When this glucose is used as food for the plant or other organisms, it is digested, then by respiration, broken apart again into carbon dioxide and returned back to the atmosphere. The process continues in a life sustaining process. More information on the carbon cycle can be found at *www.ucar.edu/learn/1_4_2_15t.htm*.

For the **nitrogen cycle** it is important to recognize that most of the air we breathe is nitrogen, but it is not useful to us in that form, so it is exhaled. Lightning causes nitrogen in the air to combine with oxygen. Certain bacteria that live on the roots of certain plants, called nitrogen-fixing bacteria, are able to take nitrogen in this combined form with oxygen and make it available for use by plants. The plants can incorporate the nitrogen into their plant structure, and when eaten by animals and other organisms, this nitrogen becomes available for use. The nitrogen returns to the soil when the plant or other living organism dies and decays, releasing nitrogen gas back into the atmosphere. Nitrogen is important to all living things because it is a major component of DNA, RNA, and amino acids, which are the building blocks of proteins. A good animation of the nitrogen cycle is found at *www.classzone.com/books/ml_science_share/vis_sim/em05_pg20_nitrogen/em05_pg20_nitrogen.html, and further explanation is located at http://eo.ucar.edu/kids/green/cycles7.htm.*

Competency 044 (Earth and Space Science)

The teacher understands the role of energy in weather and climate.

Weather

The elements of weather include interactions between wind, water (precipitation), wind speed and direction, air pressure, humidity, and temperature. Wind is caused by air masses that have different amounts of heat (temperatures), where there may be a warm air mass that is moving toward a cold air mass for example. Air pressure is related to both the amount of water in the air mass and its temperature (heat content), in that warm air has higher pressure than cold air—warm, high pressure air masses move toward cold, low pressure air masses. One simple rule is that energy always moves from warmer to colder. So, if you open a window on a hot summer day when your air conditioning is on, the cold does not go out—the warm air comes in. The same is true on a larger scale with warm and cold air masses.

Humidity is a measure of the percentage of water that is in the air. Dew point is the temperature at which the air needs to be for the water to condense out of the air in liquid form as precipitation; or it may be observed as "dew." In other words, air has a certain amount of water vapor (water in the gas state) in it (the percent is measured as humidity). That water vapor will turn to liquid water as temperatures drop overnight, in which we observe dew, or when a cold front moves in that lowers the temperature, which can result in a rain or snow storm. For resources and information on weather, go to the National Weather Service education website at *www.nws.noaa.gov/os/edures.shtml.*

Wind is measured by an instrument called an anemometer. Air pressure is measured by a barometer; rain gauges and other instruments measure precipitation. Temperature is measured by a thermometer. Relative humidity is measured by a psychrometer. For more information on these instruments, see *http://schoolscience.rice.edu/duker/winstruments.html.*

Climate

Weather is the conditions of the atmosphere at a given, relatively short period of time. Climate, however, is the weather conditions in an area on a continuous, seasonal basis. The climate is more complex and can be measured by the average variety of weather conditions, such as temperature and precipitation, that occur seasonally in that geographic region of the world over a long period of time. More information, including the contrast between weather and climate, can be found at *www.nasa.gov/mission_pages/noaa-n/climate/climate_weather.html.*

Predicting Weather

Weather can be predicted by tracking weather patterns using maps and charts. These maps have special symbols that indicate, for example, warm and cold air masses, air pressure, and relative humidity in a region. By knowing how air behaves, such as cold air goes down and warm air rises, warmer air always moves toward colder air, and high pressure always moves outward toward lower pressure, we can track the weather and make predictions. Clouds are also an indication of the type of weather occurring in an area. For a summary of predicting weather as well as a description of cloud types, see *www.ussartf.org/predicting_weather.htm.*

Interpreting weather maps is an important skill for weather prediction. The symbols and their meanings can be found at *http://eo.ucar.edu/webweather/forecasttips.html.*

The Earth's Surface and Position as a Factor in Weather and Climate

The Earth's surface is primarily water, and bodies of water affect the weather and climate of an area. Water has a high specific heat, which means that it takes longer to take in heat and longer to release the heat it has absorbed than any other material on Earth. Therefore, coastal areas tend to be warmer than areas inland or away from water, because the water moderates the temperature, even if the locations are at the same latitude. In the U.S., for example, areas in the middle of the country will have greater extreme differences in the cold temperatures in the winter and warm temperatures in the summer compared to a location at the same latitude near the ocean.

Large lakes, such as the Great Lakes, also create a situation called "lake effect" in the winter—the air over the lake is relatively warm, and so can carry water vapor (evaporation). As soon as that air carrying water moves over land, however, it rapidly cools and releases its water (precipitation) in the form of snow over the land. Mountains and other landforms also have an effect on the weather. When air holding water hits a mountain side, it is forced upward which makes the air cool and therefore rain (or snow) on that side of the mountain. This is typically the western side of the mountain in the U.S. as in the mountain ranges of the Rocky Mountains. Once the precipitation is gone from that air mass and the air mass crosses the mountain to the other side, it drops back down and warms, but now it is dry air which may cause an arid region or desert. The Gobi Desert of the U.S. is a result of this phenomenon.

On a much larger scale, the tilt of the Earth itself—as a planet—is responsible for weather and climate. The Earth is on a 23° tilt on its axis in space. This tilt means the Earth's North Pole is pointed away from the sun when it is in one location in its orbit (path around the sun), and toward the sun when it is in the opposite orbital location. This tilt of the Earth results in the seasons, with extreme changes being in locations closer to the North and South poles. See more information on this topic at *www.windows.ucar.edu/tour/link=/Earth/climate/cli_seasons.html*.

Competency 045 (Earth and Space Science)

The teacher understands the characteristics of the solar system and the universe.

Space Science

Galaxies

Galaxies are large collections of stars, hydrogen, dust particles, and other gases. The universe is made of countless galaxies. The solar system that includes Earth is part of a galaxy called the Milky Way.

Stars

Stars like the sun are composed of large masses of hydrogen pulled together by gravity. The hydrogen, with strong gravitational pressure, creates fusion inside the star, turning the hydrogen into helium. The liberation of energy created by this process causes solar radiation, which makes the sun glow with visible light, as well as forms of radiation not visible to the human eye.

The Earth-Sun-Moon System

Movements of Planet Earth

Earth performs two kinds of movement: rotation and revolution. Rotation describes the spinning of Earth on its axis. Earth takes approximately 24 hours to make a complete (360°) rotation, which creates day and night.

While Earth is rotating on its axis, it is also following an orbit around the sun. This movement is called revolution. It takes a year, or 365¼ days, for Earth to complete one revolution. The tilt of Earth as it moves around the sun and its curvature create climate zones and seasons. The zones immediately north and south of the equator are called the tropics—Cancer (north) and Capricorn (south). The Arctic Circle (North Pole) and Antarctic Circle (South Pole) are the area surrounding Earth's axis points. Latitude lines are imaginary horizontal lines around the Earth, and longitude lines are likewise vertical lines around the Earth from the North to the South Poles. These lines form a grid that helps us locate positions on Earth according to the locations specific latitude and longitude.

Phases of the Moon

During each lunar orbit around Earth (about 28 days), the moon appears to go through several stages based on the portion of the moon visible from Earth. The moon does not have its own source of light but reflects the light from the sun. The shape of the moon varies from a full moon, when Earth is between the sun and the moon, to a new moon, when the moon is located between the sun and Earth. A description of the major stages of the moon follows:

- **New Moon**—The moon is not visible to Earth because the side of the moon facing Earth is not being lit by the sun.
- **Crescent Moon**—At this stage between the half moon and the new moon, the shape of the moon is often compared to a banana.
- **Half Moon, or First Quarter**—During this stage, half of the moon is visible.
- **Gibbous Moon**—In this stage, about three quarters of the moon is visible.
- **Full Moon**—The whole moon is visible from Earth.

The term blue moon describes the appearance of two full moons in a single calendar month. The expression "once in a blue moon" represents an event that is not very frequent.

Components of Our Solar System

The sun is the center of our solar system, which is composed of eight planets, many satellites that orbit the planets, and a large number of smaller bodies like comets and asteroids. Short definitions of these terms follows:

- Planets are large bodies orbiting the sun.
- Satellites are moons orbiting the planets.
- Asteroids are small dense objects orbiting the sun.
- Comets are small icy objects traveling through space in an elliptical orbit around the sun.

Planets

The objects in our solar system revolve around our star, which we call the sun. The inner solar system contains the planets Mercury, Venus, Earth, and Mars, in this order. The outer solar system comprises the planets Jupiter, Saturn, Uranus, and Neptune, and a number of dwarf planets, including Pluto, Ceres, Eris and others, with likely more yet to be found (see Table 5-4). More information about our solar system can be found at *http://starchild.gsfc.nasa.gov/docs/StarChild/StarChild.html*.

Table 5.4.
Planets and Dwarf Planets of our Solar System

Inner Planets	Mercury Venus Earth Mars
Outer Planets	Jupiter Saturn Uranus Neptune
Dwarf Planets	Pluto Ceres Eris Haumea Makemake

Key Principles of Competencies 042, 043, 044, and 045

- Our solar system is part of the Milky Way, one of many galaxies in the universe.
- Minerals and rocks are commonly used in our daily life.
- The movement of tectonic plates creates intense geologic activity that results in earthquakes and volcanic activity.
- The Earth's atmosphere protects and preserves life.
- The water cycles are the movement and distribution of water within the Earth's atmosphere.
- The tilt of the Earth causes the seasons.
- Human activities as well as natural processes impact the landscape and processes on Earth.
- Weather is the interaction of many factors, including air temperature, air pressure, and humidity.
- The solar system consists of the sun, inner planets, outer planets, dwarf planets, satellites, asteroids, comets and meteoroids.

References

American Association for the Advancement of Science. 1989. Science for All Americans: A Project 2061 Report on Literacy Goals in Science, Mathematics, and Technology. Washington, DC.

Anderson, L. W., D. R. Krathwohl, et al. Eds. 2001. A Taxonomy for Learning, Teaching, and Assessing: A Revision of Bloom's Taxonomy of Educational Objectives. Boston, MA: Allyn & Bacon (Pearson Education Group)

Badder, W., D. Peck, L. J. Bethel, C. Sumner, V. Fu, and C. Valentino. 2000. Discovery works. (Texas ed.). Boston: Houghton Mifflin.

Bloom, B. S. and D. R. Krathwohl. 1956. Taxonomy of Educational Objectives: The Classification of Educational Goals, by a committee of college and university examiners. Handbook I: Cognitive Domain. NY, NY: Longmans, Green

Bybee, R., Buchwald, C.E., Crissman, S. Heil, D., Kuerbis, P., Matsumoto, C. & McInerney 1989. Science and Technology Education for Elementary Years: Frameworks for Curriculum and Instruction. Washington, DC: The National Center for Improving Science Education.

Cavallo, A.M.L. 2005. Cycling through plants. Science and Children, 4, 22–27.

Cavallo, A.M.L. 2001. Convection connections: Integrated learning cycle investigations that explore convection—the science behind wind and waves. Science and Children, 38, 20–25.

Full Option Science System (FOSS). 2000. Lawrence Hall of Science, University of California, Berkeley, CA.

Garcia, E. and Lee, O. (2008). Creating culturally responsive learning communities. In *Teaching science to English language learners,* eds. A. Rosebery and B. Warren, 147-150. Arlington, VA: NSTA Press.

Lawson, A.E., M.R. Abraham, and J. W. Renner. 1989. A theory of instruction: Using the learning cycle to teach science concepts and thinking skills. NARST Monograph No.?1.

Marek, E. A., & Cavallo, A. M. L. (1997). The Learning Cycle: Elementary School Science and Beyond (Rev. ed.). Portsmouth, NH: Heinemann.

National Science Teachers Association (NSTA). 2009. Science for English language learners. Retrieved March 31, 2011 from http://science.nsta.org/nstaexpress/ELLDraftForMembers.pdf

National Science Teachers Association. 2003. Standards for Science Teacher Preparation: Skills of Teaching (Revised Version). Washington, DC: National Science Teachers Association.

National Science Teachers Association (NSTA). 2002. Elementary school science. Position paper. Retrieved September 22, 2009, from www.nsta.org/positionstatement&psid=8/.

National Science Teachers Association. 1998. Standards for Science Teacher Preparation: Skills of Teaching. Washington, DC: National Science Teachers Association.

National Research Council. 1996 National Science Education Standards. Washington, D.C.: National Academy Press.

Piaget, J. 1964. Cognitive development in children: Piaget, development and learning. Journal of Research in Science Teaching, 2, 176–80.

Renner, J. W., and Marek, E. A. 1990. An educational theory base for science teaching. Journal of Research in Science Teaching. 27(3): 241–46.

Sandoval, J. S. 1995. Teaching in subject matter areas: Science. Annual Review of Psychology, 46, 355–74.

Sousa, David. A. (2011). *How the ELL brain learns*. Corwin Press: Sage, Ltd.

Texas Education Agency (TEA). 2006. Prekinder curriculum guide-lines. Retrieved September 22, 2009, from www.tea.state.tx.us/curriculum/early/prekguide.html#4.

_____. 2006. Texas Essential Knowledge and Skills. www.tea.state.tx.us/teks/.

University of California, Lawrence Livermore National Laboratory. 2006. Plasma: The fourth state of matter. Retrieved September 18, 2009, from http://FusEdWeb.llnl.gov/CPEP/.

CHAPTER

Domain VI: Fine Arts, Health, and Physical Education

6

Competency 046: Visual Arts

The teacher understands concepts, processes, and skills involved in the creation, appreciation, and evaluation of art and uses this knowledge to plan and implement effective engaging visual arts instruction.

This chapter covers art concepts, principles and elements of **art,** style, culture, **music** concepts, and **health and physical education**. The TEKs curriculum is presented for each of these areas for grades K–6.

Fine Arts or Visual Arts?

The term fine arts is an umbrella term used to describe artworks that appeal to people's aesthetic perceptions. The fine arts include music, theater, sculpture, painting, printmaking, and other traditional forms of art. However, the fine arts exclude applied arts or craftwork like basket-weaving, ceramics, and textiles. To include more forms of artistic expression and to encompass these other forms of aesthetic expression, the term visual arts was coined. The term visual arts refers to artistic expression such as sculpture, painting, and printmaking, but it also includes less familiar forms of art like textiles, basket weaving, ceramics, metalworking—blacksmithing and jewelry-making, and more modern art forms like photography and filmmaking. The term visual arts is a more inclusive term and a better descriptor for the arts produced and appreciated in modern society.

Children's Artistic Development

Young children's earliest experiences with the visual arts are much more scientific than artistic in nature. A child making marks by moving a crayon or marker across a surface is concentrating on the sensory experience rather than on self-expression or symbolism. The child is most interested in the texture of the surface, the colors that appear, and the shapes that emerge. It is not until age three or four that the child may notice a similarity between an actual object and a mark that has been made. At this point, the child artist begins to realize that the colors and shapes being applied can symbolize people, objects, and events in reality.

Children of all cultures may experiment in their drawings with variations of the mandala, a circle intersected by lines, and the tadpole person, a circle representing a human head with lines protruding to represent arms and legs. Around age five, children move into drawing individual symbols to represent people and objects. A house, for example, may be consistently represented as a square with a triangle on top, regardless of the appearance of the house in reality. The use of symbolized drawings continues through the early elementary years, when children typically become enamored with repeating a particular theme in their drawings. A scene with a house, a tree, and hills in the background, or one with a spaceship, a planet surrounded by rings and a quarter moon may be repeated many, many times with little variation as the child artist works toward his/her own ideas of perfection. As children move into the middle and later elementary years, they strive increasingly to achieve photographic realism in their artwork. The frustration they may experience at this point will convince some children that they do not have artistic abilities and make them very reluctant to engage in art activities.

Goals in Art Education

The overall goals of art education include developing children's aesthetic perception, providing experiences with many art forms, and facilitating reflections on and discussions of observations and responses to art. Art education provides opportunities for children to develop and extend their own artistic abilities, and exposes children to characteristics and objects of art. Art education empowers children to analyze diverse forms of the visual arts using informed judgments. Because of these important benefits and life skills, art education is an important component of the Texas Essential Knowledge and Skills from grades K–12.

Texas Essential Knowledge and Skills

The state curriculum for fine arts and visual arts is organized around four main strands—perception, creative expression, historical/cultural heritage, and critical evaluation. A summary of the key elements required for children in grades K–6 is presented in Table 6.1 (TEA 2006). Traditionally, these curriculum components are delivered by an art teacher in collaboration with EC-6 teachers. EC-6 teachers should know and understand the visual art curriculum components and be able to integrate them meaningfully throughout their grade-level curriculum.

Art Techniques and Materials

While painting and drawing are familiar activities to most elementary teachers, other techniques and materials used in the visual arts curriculum may be less known. Some of these activities are:

1. **Printmaking:** This is the artistic process of making a print in which color (paint or ink) is applied to an object; the object is then pressed onto a surface. When the object is lifted, a print is left on the surface.
2. **Ceramic:** The use of clay to create ceramics is one of the oldest forms of art. Figurines, tiles, and tableware are made by applying high heat to fresh clay and then cooling the object until it becomes solid.
3. **Textiles:** The textile arts are those that use plant, animal, or synthetic fibers to construct practical or decorative objects, including stitchery, weaving, dying and printing, lace making, knitting, crocheting, and embroidery.
4. **Basket weaving:** This ancient art uses unspun fibers (pine straw, animal hair, hide, grasses, thread, or wood) to create baskets or other forms for artistic or utilitarian purposes.
5. **Metalworking:** The traditional metalworking is the artistic process of working with metals to produce individual pieces, assemblies, or structures, including jewelry.
6. **Photography and filmmaking:** This relatively modern art creates still or moving pictures by recording radiation on a sensitive medium, such as a photographic film or an electronic sensor.
7. **Sculpture:** A sculpture is a three-dimensional artwork made by shaping or combining hard material such as marble, rock, glass, wood, or metal. Some sculptures are created directly by carving in a solid material; others are assembled, built together and fired, welded, molded, or cast.
8. **Computer-generated art:** This relatively new form of art is created through the manipulation of pixels, either through drawing

Table 6.1. Visual Arts Strands for K–6 in Texas

Grade	Perceptions	Creative Expressions	Historical/Cultural	Critical Evaluation
Kindergarten	Identify colors, textures, and forms in the environment	Create artwork using a variety of colors, forms, and line	Share ideas about personal artworks and show respect for different opinions	Express ideas about personal artworks, and the artworks of peers or professional artists
1	Identify art elements such as color, texture, form, and line with emphasis on nature and human-made environments	Invent images that combine color, form, and line, and organize forms to create designs	Demonstrate a basic understanding of art history. Select artwork that show families and groups	Make informed judgment about their personal artworks and the work of peers
2	Continue using color, texture, form, line, space, and art principles, like emphasis, patterns, and rhythm to create artworks	Produce drawings, paintings, prints, constructions, and modeled forms using a variety of art materials	Develop respect for the tradition and contributions in the art of diverse groups	Define reasons for preferences in artworks
3	Continue emphasizing art principles such as emphasis, patterns, rhythm, balance, proportion, and unity in artworks	Express ideas through original artworks using a variety of media. Develop compositions using design skills; and produce drawings, print constructions, and ceramics	Compare artworks from different cultures and link it to different kinds of jobs in everyday life	Apply simple criteria to identify main ideas in original artworks
4	Communicate ideas about self, family, school, and community using sensory knowledge and experiences	Invent ways to produce artworks and to explore photographic imagery using a variety of media and materials	Compare artworks from various groups; identify the role of art in American society	Interpret ideas and moods in original artwork
5	Develop and organize ideas from the environment	Express ideas through original artworks, using a variety of media with appropriate skill	Demonstrate an understanding of art history and culture as records of human achievement	Make informed judgments about personal artworks and artworks of others
6	Develop and organize ideas from the environment	Express ideas through original artworks, using a variety of media with appropriate skill	Demonstrate an understanding of art history and culture as records of human achievement	Make informed judgments about personal artworks and the artworks of others

and painting software or through electronic images stored in the computer. The computer screen serves as the canvas and colored light is the medium.

The Art Classroom

Whether art experiences happen in the art room or the regular classroom, the room should allow for individual seating arrangements as well as small-group and large-group arrangements. There should be areas for the teacher to lecture and display students' work, space for learning centers, areas for drawing, painting, printmaking, creating computer graphics, modeling, and assembling crafts. There should be both natural and artificial lighting in the room. Materials should be stored in cabinets, with access controlled by the teachers. Safety guidelines are critical, and following them is mandatory for students. Ease of cleanup is a requirement; therefore, sinks and surfaces must have durable, cleanable finishes.

Visual Arts Activities for K–6

Throughout the elementary grades, students engage in a variety of art activities such as drawing, painting, designing, constructing, crafts, sculpting, weaving, and finger painting. In grades 3 and 4, students continue perfecting the skills from K through 2 and begin working with new techniques like printmaking, sponge painting, graphics, film animation, and environmental design. In grades 5 and 6, students develop their art from personal experience and direct observation and are expected to demonstrate technical skills.

The elementary curriculum encourages the integration of visual art in the regular classroom, as well as specialized activities in the art room. Appropriate art activities should first of all focus on the self-expression of young artists. While the developing fine motor and perceptual skills of young children may lead to art products that have little resemblance to reality, it is important that children are encouraged to experiment, explore, and express their own ideas through their own efforts. Teacher-made models, pre-cut outlines and templates that standardize art products are not appropriate for elementary age children.

Art materials for the elementary art program include scissors, wet and dry brushes, fabrics, wrapping papers, film, computers, clay, glue, construction paper, crayons, beads, and multiple household items that can be used to create art. Safety is a primary concern during art activities, and toxic substances or potentially dangerous tools should not be allowed in the classroom. While elementary children enjoy variety in the materials they use in their art projects, teachers should recognize that the introduction of new materials leads children to explore the properties of those materials rather than to engage in creative expression. A regular rotation of familiar materials in classroom art projects is most likely to encourage artistic engagement.

Assessment in the visual arts is, of course, based on the individual child's attitudes and dispositions toward engagement in both art production and art appreciation activities. Does the child engage in art production activities willingly and enthusiastically? Is the child willing to try new materials and techniques? Does the child express original ideas in his or her artwork? Does he or she carefully consider the art products of others and discuss the elements and principles of art exhibited? These are questions to be carefully considered by both the EC-6 teacher and the arts specialist during the assessment process.

By relating art production in the elementary curriculum to art products created by artists from other historical eras and cultures, children are introduced to art appreciation and the basic elements and principles of art. An analysis of the elements and principles of arts follow.

Elements and Principles of Art

Art is a way of communicating and expressing ideas, emotions, and experiences. In order to communicate their own ideas and to understand the communications of other artists, children must have knowledge of and be able to use the elements of art. The elements and principles of art are used by artists to create paintings, drawings, and/or designs; they are the basic principles of design.

Elements of Art

The elements of art are the individual components that combine to create artwork—line, shape, space, value, color, and texture (Wallace, 2006). Most works of art have some small aspect of each element. A description of each element follows.

1. Line refers to marks from a pen or brush used to highlight a specific part of a painting or a structure.
2. Shape represents a self-contained, defined area of a two- or three-dimensional area creating a form. There are two basic types of shapes: geometric and organic. The term geometric shapes refers to squares, triangles, circles, and rectangles. Organic shapes describes more natural-looking shapes like leaves, animals, and clouds.
3. Space describes the emptiness around or within objects. Space can be used to create perspective, to create objects or people in different planes, and to create a sense of depth.
4. Value refers to the darkness or lightness of an artwork. Values are commonly used to create the two-dimensional quality of artwork. Values also indicate the source of light in a work and provide a three-dimensional view of figures by suggesting shadows. Values can also represent the mood of the artist and the artwork. Darker values are used to represent sadness, mystery, or formality, while lighter values usually represent contentment and relaxation.
5. Color represents reflected light and the way it bounces off objects. There are three primary colors (red, yellow, blue); three secondary colors (green, orange, violet); and an unlimited amount of tertiary colors, which are colors that fall between the primary and secondary colors, and compound colors. Compound colors are colors containing a mixture of the three primary colors. There also warm colors (such as yellow, orange, and red) and cool colors (such as blue, green, and purple). Artists use all these color combinations to create the environment of the painting.
6. Texture describes the surface quality of a figure or shape. A shape can appear to be rough, smooth, soft, hard, or glossy. Texture can be physical (felt with the hand, e.g., a buildup of paint) or visual (giving the illusion of texture, e.g., the paint gives the impression of texture, but the surface remains smooth and flat).

Principles of Art

The principles of art describe the guidelines that artists follow to create art and to deliver their intended message. Artists use the elements of art to communicate the principles in their creations. The principles of art include emphasis, balance, rhythm, contrast, movement, and harmony (Wallace 2006). A description of these components follows.

1. Emphasis is the technique of making one part of a work standout from the rest of the artwork. It guides viewers to pay attention to specific details or components of the artwork. By making texture different in one area from the rest of the artwork, the artist can also make the target area stand out.
2. Balance refers to the positioning of objects in such a way that none of them overpower the other components of the artwork. Size, space, color, shape, and lighting can be used to create balance. A large shape, for example, that is close to the center can be balanced by a smaller shape that is close to the edge. A large light-toned shape can be balanced by a small dark-toned shape. There are two main kinds of balance: symmetrical and asymmetrical. Symmetrical balance occurs when two halves of a figure coincide creating a mirror image. The line of symmetry is the line that divides the figure in two. The easiest way to identify symmetric figures is to fold the figure in half, and if these two halves are identical, then we can say that the figure is symmetrical. Asymmetrical balance occurs when two sides of an artwork are different. For example, the artwork of the American flag—horizontal lines of different sizes, a smaller rectangle in the upper left corner with stars—makes it asymmetrical.

3. Rhythm describes the type of patterns used in the artwork. For example, placing a repetition of objects evenly spaced presents a regular type of rhythm. Elements increasing or decreasing in size in an artwork presents a progressive rhythm.
4. Contrast is used to create interest through the combination of elements. Contrast is used to break the monotony or repetitious pattern in a work of art. Rembrandt's paintings are well-known for using value (lightness and darkness) to create contrast. He also used lighter values to highlight portions of the paintings.
5. Movement refers to the way that artists produce the appearance of motion. In painting, artists use the element of line to simulate the movement of wind or water. This technique leads viewers to perceive the effects of motion and action through the artwork.
6. Harmony is used to represent a sense of completeness in the artwork. It shows the unity of the artwork. For example, texture and color can be combined to provide a sense of balance and harmony.

While the elements and principles of art provide the foundations of artwork in all media and styles, they also have application in other disciplines and in contemporary occupations. Line, shape, space, and balance are terms with parallel meanings in the field of mathematics, while texture and color are also basic objects in science observations. Similarly, rhythm and harmony are used to describe synonymous concepts in both art and music. Mathematical concepts such as symmetry, angle, distance, and convergence are illustrated in artwork and must be explicitly understood by artists. Similarly, artists regularly explore science concepts related to light, water, and temperature in their work. Engagement in art also requires artists, whether adults or children, to think critically and to problem-solve. Artists must carefully consider how to communicate emotions and ideas in their work, how to convey change and movement, and how to use symbolism. Artists of all ages must also learn to evaluate their own efforts and the work of others.

While art at its most basic is self-expression, the skills and dispositions required of artists have application in other fields and occupations. Architects and interior designers, for example, draw upon the elements and principles of art, as well as other technical skills, to create aesthetically pleasing designs for buildings, landscaping, and interior spaces. Commercial artists may use their abilities in advertising, animation of comics or cartoons, or illustrating print media.

Identifying Characteristics of Style in Works of Art

A style is an artist's manner of expression. When a group of artists during a specific period (which can last a few months, years, or decades) have a common style, it is called an art movement. Art movements are found predominantly in Western cultures and occur in both visual art and architecture.

There are eight main historical periods, with various artistic styles and art movements within each. Although some periods have only one or two unique art styles, the twentieth century has produced 36 unique styles. Descriptions of some of the best-known styles throughout history follow (Witcombe 1995).

The Prehistoric period is characterized by paintings that represent the daily activities of a group of people. The best-known representation of this type of art is the Caves of Altamira, in modern Spain. The Paleolithic peoples of Europe produced small, stylized stone carvings of women as symbols of fertility. These small statues have been found most often in modern France, Italy, and Austria.

The Ancient period produced a large number of masterpieces from varied civilizations, such as the Sumerians, Babylonians, Assyrians, Egyptians, Greeks, and Romans. These civilizations skillfully carved even the hardest rocks, such as granite and basalt, into narratives of battles and historical records. Egyptian statues, like their architectural monuments the pyramids, were often of colossal size in order to exalt the power of the society's leaders and gods. The art of ancient Greece has its roots in the Minoan civilization on the island of Crete, which flourished from about 2500 to 1400 BCE. The palace at Knossos held characteristic wall paintings revealing a civilization enamored with games, leisure, and the beauty of the sea.

The mainland of the Greeks of the Classical period, about 1,000 years later than the ancient period, was fascinated by physical beauty. Fashioned in the human image, with a universal ideal of perfection and guided by a master plan, the Greeks recreated their Olympian gods in their idealized and gracefully proportioned sculptures, architecture, and paintings. In the Hellenistic period (330–30 BCE), the populace, fascinated by physical beauty, appreciated these various objects of art for their beauty alone. The culture of Rome excelled in engineering and building, skills intended to efficiently organize a vast empire and provide an aesthetic environment for private and public use. The Romans built temples, roads, bathing complexes, civic buildings, palaces, and aqueducts. One of the greatest of their artistic and engineering accomplishments was the massive-domed temple of all the gods called the Pantheon, which is today one of the most perfectly preserved of all buildings from the classical period.

The Medieval period (500–1400 CE) also produced large numbers of artistic masterpieces. The Romanesque style of art and architecture was preeminent from about 800 to 1200 CE. By then many local styles, including the decorative arts of the Byzantine Empire, the Near East, and the German and Celtic tribes, were contributing to European culture. Common features of Romanesque churches are round arches, vaulted ceilings, and heavy walls that are ornately decorated—primarily with symbolic figures of Christianity. Realism had become less important than the message. The Gothic architecture flourished during this period with the creation of magnificent ribbed vaulting and pointed roofs. The cathedrals in this style are some of the purest expressions of an age. They combine a continued search for engineering and structural improvement with stylistic features that convey a relentless verticality, a reach toward heaven, and the unbridled adoration of God. Soaring and roomy, the construction of the Gothic cathedrals employed such elements as flying buttresses (structure to reinforce a wall) and pointed arches and vaults; a number of sculptures and stained-glass windows that were, for the worshippers, visual encyclopedias of Christian teachings and stories.

Renaissance (14th to 16th century) artists developed new forms and revived classical styles and values, with the belief in the importance of the human experience on Earth and realism. Great sculptors approached true human characterization and realism as they revived elements of Greek architecture. Like the painters of the period, Renaissance architects took a scientific, ordered approach and emphasized perspective and the calculated composition of figures in space. Art became more emotional and dramatic, and because of this, the use of color and movement increased, compositions were more vigorous, and references to classical iconography and the pleasures of an idyllic golden age increased. Typical examples of this emotional, dramatic art are Michelangelo's magnificent Sistine Chapel frescoes and his powerful sculptures of David and Moses; Leonardo da Vinci's Mona Lisa; Raphael's School of Athens fresco; and the increasingly dramatic and colorful works of the Venetian and northern Italian masters Titian, Correggio, Giorgione, and Bellini.

Baroque style emerged in the 17th century in Europe. The baroque style used exaggerated motion, and elaborate and detailed artwork. The movement produced drama, tension, exuberance, and grandeur in sculpture, painting, literature, and music.

Rococo art characterizes the art of the early eighteenth century. Artists of the Rococo era turned the agitated drama of the baroque style into light, pastel-toned, swirling compositions that seem placed in an idyllic land of a golden age.

Nineteenth-century art was characterized by three elements—romanticism and idealism, realism, and impressionism. In the first half of the nineteenth century, landscape painting in England reached a zenith with the works of John Constable and Joseph Mallord William Turner. Turner's awe-inspiring landscapes form a bridge between the spirit of romanticism and the expressionistic brushwork and realism of the Barbizon School in France, whose chief painters were Charles Daubigny and Jean-Baptiste-Camille Corot. Beginning with Barbizon, the French painters of the nineteenth century concentrated increasingly on the reporter-like depiction of everyday life and the natural environment in a free, painterly (gesture and brushwork) style.

Realism rejected traditional means of composing a picture, academic methods of figure modeling and color relations, and accurate and exact rendering of people and objects in favor of an art that emphasized quickly observed and sketched moments from life, the relation of shapes and forms and colors, the effects of light, and the act of painting itself. The realist pioneers were Gustave Courbet (The Stone Breakers, A Burial at Ormans), Jean-François Millet (The Sower, The Angelus), and Honoré Daumier (The Third-Class Carriage).

Impressionism began with Edouard Manet in France in the 1860s. French artists continually blurred the boundaries of realism and abstraction. They used light and color to capture the impression of images as opposed to the real "real image." The landscapes and everyday-life paintings of impressionist artists like Claude Monet, Camille Pissarro, Auguste Renoir, Alfred Sisley, and Edgar Degas gave way to the more experimental arrangements of form and color of the great postimpressionists: Paul Gauguin, Vincent van Gogh, Georges Seurat, and Henri de Toulouse-Lautrec. Auguste Rodin produced powerful sculptures with the freedom of impressionist style.

Twentieth-century art provided new avenues for artistic expressions:

Surrealism is one of the new trends in painting that emerged in the 20th century. Inspired by the psychoanalytic writings of Sigmund Freud and Carl Jung, artists made the subconscious and the metaphysical important elements in their work. The influence of psychology is especially evident in the work of the surrealist artist Salvador Dali. Dali created non-realistic paintings as revealed in dreams, free of conscious controls of reason and conventions.

Cubism and abstract paintings of Pablo Picasso also emerged during the twentieth century. This new type of art represents the most direct call for the reduction and fragmentation of realistic depiction. Artists challenged common realistic conventions to create new representations of reality or imagination. Cubism is the most important and influential movement of European paintings and sculptures in the early 20th century.

Muralists and social realists between WWI and WWII created art that was physically interesting and whose subjects were accessible to the average person. John Sloan, George Bellows, Edward Hopper, Thomas Hart Benton, Grant Wood, and John Stuart Curry were among those who celebrated the American scene in paintings, frequently in murals for public buildings, and through widely available fine prints. The great Mexican muralists, who usually concentrated on political themes—Diego Rivera, José Clemente Orozco, and David Siqueiros—brought their work to the public both in Mexico and in the United States.

Photorealism also emerged as a new form of art in which paintings resemble photos, lifelike—often portraits, still lifes, and landscapes.

Graffiti is a new and controversial type of art form that emerged in inner cities in America. The controversial nature of this new form of art is caused by the way that the expression is conducted. Traditionally, spray painting and using brushes, the artists create the work on the surface of private and public buildings with or without the approval of the owners. For some people, graffiti is a nuisance while for others, it becomes a liberating response to the pressure of modern-day living.

Art in Other Cultures

The progression of art in China is divided into periods according to the ruling dynasty and the development of technology. The earliest Chinese art products were made from pottery, jade, and, eventually, bronze. Porcelain art forms were introduced in early imperial China and were refined to the extent that in English the word china came to mean high-quality porcelain. Buddhism arrived in China in the first century BCE and strongly influenced artists throughout the country. Calligraphy and painting were popular art forms at this time, with artists working primarily on silk until paper was invented. While classical sculpture was the dominant art form of the Tang dynasty, landscape painting, almost Impressionistic in its portrayal of distance, was dominant during the Song dynasty. Color painting and printing were emphasized during the Ming dynasty and reached their peaks during the Qing dynasty when painters known as Individualists began to use free brushwork to express their ideas more openly. Beginning in the 19th century, Chinese artists were increasingly influenced by Western ideas and techniques. In the early 20th century, social realism was the dominant theme of Chinese artists. During the Cultural Revolution of the mid-20th century, art schools were closed and exhibitions were prohibited. Following the Cultural Revolution, however, art exchanges were established with other countries and artists began to experiment with various themes and methods. Of particular note is artist Wang Yani, a child prodigy whose work since 1975 has exemplified xieyi hua, a freehand style.

Traditional African art was generally intended to both please the viewer and to uphold moral values. Because traditional African art was based in religious and ethical meanings, the human figure was the primary subject. African art was most often created and exhibited or used in ritual contexts that dealt with important moral and spiritual concerns (Ray, 1997).

Native American, or American Indian, art encompasses a broad variety of media and techniques including pottery, woodcarving, weaving, stitchery, painting, beadwork, and jewelry-making. Art forms and symbols vary considerably across Native American tribes. Tribal artisans relied on available natural resources to determine the media in which they worked. Generally, art was used to beautify everyday objects and to create objects of spiritual significance.

For a comprehensive analysis of the history of art visit *http://witcombe.sbc.eduARTHLinks.html*.

Integration of the Arts in the Content Areas

The arts can be easily integrated with other academic content areas. In reading, children draw to represent the main idea of a story. Later in writing, they begin adding words to their drawings. Art appreciation activities also provide an appropriate context for children to notice and discuss details in a painting. Through observation and description, children practice new vocabulary and use descriptive language. Scientific principles like light, color, and texture can be easily introduced through artwork. Likewise, art concepts of space, proportion, and balance can be introduced through mathematics. Artworks in all media provide meaningful contexts for the discussion of culture and history.

Evaluating Works of Art

To judge the quality of a work of visual art, students should be given basic criteria for evaluation. The main principle of the criteria can be derived through questions similar to the ones presented below:

- What is the purpose of the artist? Does the work achieve the purpose?
- Has the artist spoken with a unique voice, regardless of style, or could this artwork just as easily be the work of someone else?
- Is the style appropriate to the expressed purpose of the work?
- Is the work memorable and distinctive?
- Was it created to meet social or cultural needs?
- Has the artist used the elements and principles of art effectively?

After answering such questions, a student might be able to determine the specific timeframe of the painting and the style in which it was painted.

When addressing these questions, students should be able to describe a work of art using terms such as line, color, value, shape, balance, texture, repetition, rhythm, and shape. They should be able to discuss some of the major periods in the history of the visual arts. It is important that students be able to confront a work and judge its aesthetic merits, regardless of their ability to recognize it from memory.

Competency 047: Music

The teacher understands the concepts, processes, and skills involved in the creation, appreciation, and evaluation of music, and uses that knowledge to plan and implement effective and engaging music instruction.

The goal of music education is to develop independent musicians through the use of conceptual teaching of musical skills. It is expected that music teachers be literate in music similar to how an English teacher is literate in language. Teachers of music should be able to teach children how to sing in tune, keep a steady beat, listen to different styles of music appropriately, and perform music expressively. Teachers should also learn and use music terminology and the elements of music. They should also learn the appropriate methodology to integrate music in the content areas, and apply the legal and ethical principles of music education.

Elements of Music

Essential to the understanding of music are the key elements upon which all music is based—rhythm, melody, harmony, form, and expression. Rhythm is the varied lengths of sounds and silences in relation to the underlying beat. Usually children (K–3) confuse beat and rhythm and try to make them the same thing. Beat is the pulse that is felt in the music and rhythm is typically called the melodic rhythm or word rhythm found in the song. Audiate[1] the song *Happy Birthday*; the beat is the underlying pulse and the melodic rhythm is the words to the song. Now audiate *The Star-Spangled Banner*; the beat may or may not be faster or slower (the speed of the underlying pulse of music is called tempo). The beginning of *The Star-Spangled Banner* has the same melodic rhythm as the beginning of *Happy Birthday*. *Happy Birthday* begins with "Happy birthday to you" and has the same melodic rhythm as "Oh say can you see." After this beginning the two songs do not have the same melodic rhythm. Melodic rhythm is identified using musical notation (the writing of music), which includes various types of notes and rests (see Figure 6-1).

Melody is the succession of sounds and silences that may move upward, downward, or stay the same. The "tune" or the singable part of the song is the melody. A musical staff (see Figure 6-2), consisting of five parallel lines and four spaces, is needed to read a musical tune. The pitches are represented by symbols called notes placed on the staff. There are seven letters found in the musical alphabet (A, B, C, D, E, F, G). The clef signs at the beginning of the song determine the pitch level, either higher or lower. Typically,

[1]Audiation is to hear music inside one's head.

Figure 6-1. Notes and Rests

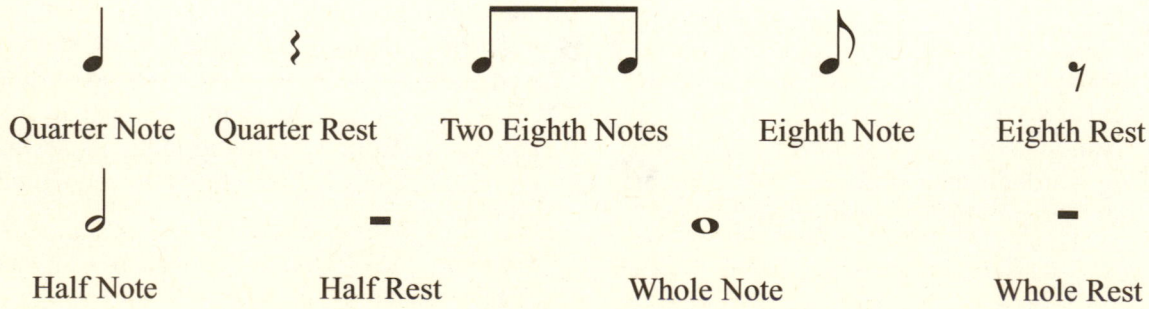

the treble clef is the singing range of women and the right hand on the piano; and the bass clef is the singing range of men and the left hand on the piano (see Figure 6-3).

Figure 6-2. Musical Staff

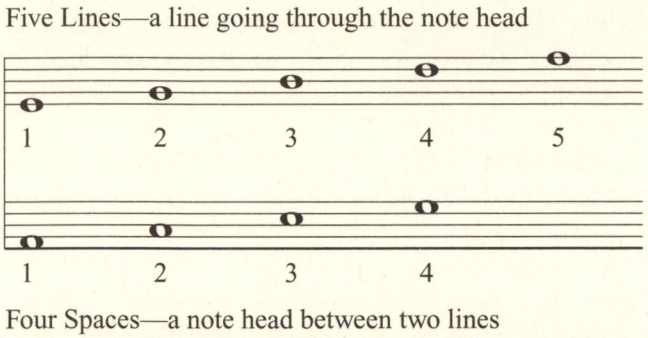

Figure 6-3. Musical Staff with Clefs and Notes

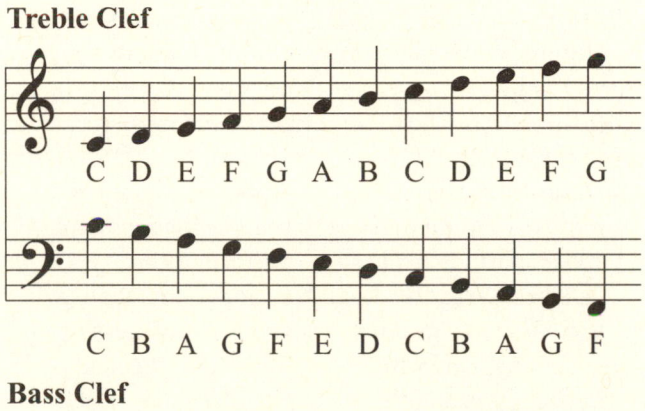

Harmony is usually the accompaniment or supportive sounds to a melody. These accompaniments are typically played by a pitched instrument, such as a piano, guitar, or autoharp. Another way to produce harmony is through the use of singing rounds, such as *Row, Row, Row Your Boat.*

Form is the structure or design of the music. A phrase, which is a musical line that contains groups of pitches, is similar to a sentence in language. Several musical phrases make up a song just like several sentences make up a paragraph. These phrases can define a song. Musical forms are analogous to mathematical patterns. Common forms in elementary music are binary (AB), ternary (ABA), theme and variation (A A1 A2 A3 A4 etc.), and rondo (ABACA).

Expression consists of dynamics and timbre. Dynamics is a term used by musicians to represent the louds and softs in music. Typically, younger children (K–2) confuse dynamics with pitch level or melodic direction. The word "up" in music is usually associated with pitch level (the music moves up or goes higher) whereas, in the home if children are asked to turn up the music or television, the word "up" is associated with a dynamic level (louder). Dynamics are expressed using the Italian language (see Table 6-2).

Table 6-2. Dynamics

Italian Term	Dynamic Level
Piano	Soft
Mezzo piano	Medium soft
Mezzo forte	Medium loud
Forte	Loud

Timbre is defined as tone color in music. This tone color refers to the quality of sound that distinguishes one voice or instrument from another. Kindergarten children distinguish between the four human voices—speaking, whispering, calling, and singing; whereas, first- and second-grade students can identify the timbre of classroom instruments (woods, metals, and skins). Students in grades 2–6 can identify the timbre of singing voices (soprano, alto, tenor, baritone, bass) and orchestral instruments (strings, woodwinds, brass, percussion, and keyboard).

Curriculum Requirements

Texas has developed the Texas Essential Knowledge and Skills (TEKS) for music into four basic strands—perception, creative expression/performance, historical and cultural heritage, and critical evaluation (see Table 6-3). Teachers of music are expected to have their students develop and master each strand within the prescribed state curricula.

Table 6-3. Music Education Strands for K–6 (Texas Education Agency, 2006)

Grade Levels	Perception	Creative Expression/ Performance	Historical/ Cultural Heritage	Critical Evaluation
K–2	Identify the difference between the voices, timbre of voices, and instruments. Use basic music terminology to explain sounds and performances. Identify musical forms (AB, ABA).	Perform a varied repertoire of music from diverse cultures. Read and write music notation. Create rhythmic and melodic patterns.	Sing songs and play musical games from diverse cultures. Identify relationships between music and other subjects. Identify music from various periods of history and culture.	Distinguish between musical concepts (e.g., higher/lower, louder/ softer) in musical performances. Show appropriate audience behavior during live performances.
3–4	Categorize voices, orchestral instruments, and instruments of various cultures. Use standard terminology in explaining music. Identify musical forms (AB, ABA, and rondo).	Perform a varied repertoire of music from diverse cultures. Read and write music notation. Create patterns and simple accompaniments. Identify and interpret music symbols.	Identify excerpts of music representing diverse genres, styles, periods, and cultures. Perform music and movement from diverse cultures and American and Texas heritage.	Define and apply basic criteria in evaluating musical performances. Practice concert etiquette as a participant and exhibit audience etiquette during live performances.
5–6	Distinguish among a variety of musical timbres. Use standard terminology in explaining music. Identify a variety of musical forms.	Perform independently and musically accurate a varied repertoire of music representing styles from diverse cultures. Read, write, create, and arrange music within specified guidelines.	Describe music representing diverse styles, periods, and cultures. Describe various music-related vocations. Perform music representative of diverse cultures, including American and Texas heritage. Relate the other fine arts to music.	Apply and identify criteria for evaluating performances. Evaluate the quality and effectiveness of music and musical performances. Exhibit concert etiquette as an informed, actively involved listener during varied live performances.

Music in the Classroom

Elementary music teachers in Texas typically use two approaches to teach students music, Orff Schulwerk and Kodály.

Orff Schulwerk Method

Orff Schulwerk[2] is a "learning by doing" approach to teaching music. It is based on what is most natural to children: singing, moving, chanting, creating, improvising, and playing instruments. In an Orff classroom every child participates and experiences all aspects of music in a noncompetitive atmosphere. Orff Schulwerk begins with speech because Carl Orff, the creator of Orff Schulwerk, believed that speech is tied to rhythm and rhythm is the strongest musical element. These speech rhythms are transferred to the body in the form of body percussion (snap, clap, patchen[3], and stamping). Special Orff instruments are used to accompany the songs or rhymes. These instruments (unpitched and barred) allow students to be creative, which leads to improvisation and, later, composition.

Unpitched rhythm instruments (e.g., wood block, triangle, claves, drums, finger cymbals, etc.) and melodic instruments or barred instruments (xylophones, metallophones, and glockenspiels) make up the Orff ensemble. Usually, the unpitched instruments play rhythmic figures and add a nice contrast to the Orff ensemble.

The barred instruments are unique to Orff Schulwerk and can be found in classrooms all over the world. "The xylophone and metallophone are similar to traditional xylophones and vibes, but are small and have removable bars" (Lange 2005, p. 9). The easy removal of bars enables children to have greater success during the instrumental experience. "There are three sizes of xylophones and metallophones: bass, alto, and soprano. The bars on the xylophone are made of wood; the bars on the metallophone are made of metal and have a ringing timbre that is important in the ensemble because of the contrast in sound with xylophones" (Lange 2005, p. 9). The glockenspiels are smaller (alto and soprano only) and have removable metal bars, similar to the xylophone and metallophone.

The Orff instruments are typically played in elementary music classes. The classroom music teacher does not teach traditional band and orchestral instruments. Usually, study of these instruments begins in middle school with a specialized band or orchestra teacher. However, the elementary music teacher first introduces these band and orchestral instruments during listening lessons. Learning the names and aural identification of band and orchestral instruments may aid in the selection of playing one of these instruments later in their musical career.

The American Orff Schulwerk Association (AOSA) offers several educational opportunities to teachers around the country. There are six Orff chapters in Texas that offer workshops on several Saturdays throughout the school year and AOSA sponsors a national conference yearly. Also, there are two-week certification courses, offered for graduate credit, at numerous universities around the country. These teacher training courses are divided into three levels, and it is recommended that they be taken over three consecutive summers (American Orff Schulwerk Association 2009).

The Kodály Method

The Kodály Method developed out of Zoltán Kodály's principles as a step-by-step process for Hungarian teachers. This teaching technique is rooted in Hungarian culture, nevertheless can be adapted to other cultures and is used by some Texas music teachers. The main goals of the Kodály Method are to instill the love of music into all children; to have children achieve music literacy; start music education in early childhood; teach music sequentially; use quality folk songs; and cultivate the singing voice. The 3 Ps (preparation, presentation, and practice) is vital to the teaching process in Kodály. These 3 Ps are similar to the whole-part-whole approach in which the teacher prepares a concept, teaches the concept, and then through repetition and review masters that concept. The tools used in Kodály are solfege (do, re, mi, fa, sol, la, ti, do), hand signs (to present a visualization in space of the high-low relationships of

[2] Audiation is to hear music inside one's head.

[3] Patchen is German for patting legs.

the pitches being sung), and rhythm syllables (quarter note = ta, two eighth notes = ti ti, etc.). Other tools include musical flash cards, stick notation (the music notation without the note head) and musical ladders that show the melodic direction of the music.

One primary goal of Kodály is to teach music literacy and singing is the vehicle to achieve this goal. Singing is as important to the current Kodály teacher as it was to Zoltán Kodály himself. Kodály believed that music was "meant to develop one's entire being—personality, intellect, and emotions" (Organization of American Kodály Educators 2009) and used folk songs as his basis of teaching music.

There are professional development opportunities offered in Kodály that are similar to Orff Schulwerk. The Organization of American Kodály Educators (OAKE) has chapters around the country with one large chapter in Texas. Chapters offer Saturday workshops and the OAKE offers national conferences and teacher education programs to further the education of the music teacher (Organization of American Kodály Educators, 2009).

Singing and Repertoire

For young children to learn to sing well they must sing songs that will not strain the undeveloped vocal chords by singing too high or too low. Typically, the classroom teacher sings too low for children and as a result children strain their voices or do not sing along with the teacher. The best singing range for students in K–2 is from D–A (see Figure 6-4). Students in grades 3–6 can sing a little higher, usually from D–D (see Figure 6-5). Children in K–6 have a breathy tone quality and should not be asked to sing louder or project their voice. If a louder sound is necessary, add more children. If an adult asks children to sing louder, children will typically yell instead of sing and therefore damage their voice.

Figure 6-4.
Singing Range of Students in K–2

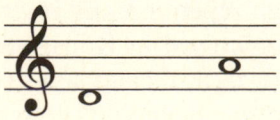

Figure 6-5.
Singing Range of Students in 3–6

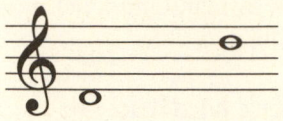

When selecting music for students in K–6, make sure that most of the pitches fall within the desired range listed above. Avoid songs that are too low, which will cause strain and harm to the voice. There are several music collections from around the world that are appropriate for children. When choosing this music try to choose recordings that are as authentic to the culture as possible.

Singing patriotic songs is an important component in the Texas music curriculum. There are national patriotic songs, such as *The Star-Spangled Banner, America*, *America the Beautiful*, and *God Bless America*. Explaining the historical significance behind each song is one of the TEKS standards for music. For example, *The Star-Spangled Banner* was written during the War of 1812 when Francis Scott Key wrote the poem. He was detained on a British ship in the harbor, while the British bombed Fort McHenry in Baltimore, Maryland. Key wrote the poem on an envelope early the next morning when he saw the American flag still flying on the Fort (Star-Spangled Banner n.d.). The poem was later set to a tune written by John Stafford Smith and approved by Congress as the National Anthem on March 3, 1931.

Music has the power to heal wounds and patriotic songs typically help in nationalistic healing. Since September 11, 2001, the singing of *God Bless America*, which can be heard regularly at Major League Baseball games, has played an important part in American culture. For younger students (K–2) *America* (My Country 'Tis of Thee) is an appropriate patriotic song that allows for discussion of American history. Another patriotic song appropriate for middle- to upper-elementary students (grades 3–6) to teach history and culture is *America the Beautiful*. The text of this song was written by an American educator, Katharine Lee Bates, and describes the landscape of the country.

Texas has an amazing history that can be taught in music class through song. *Texas, Our Texas* was adopted in 1929 by the Texas Legislature as the Texas state song. It was modified once in 1959 when Alaska became a state and therefore the wording in the song needed to be changed from "largest" state to "boldest" state in the third line of the song (Texas State Libraries and Archives 2009). Other Texas songs that should be taught in elementary school are *Deep in the Heart of Texas*, *The Yellow Rose of Texas*, and several others that discuss the history and culture of Texas.

Music from diverse cultures is not only one of the TEKS standards for music but is popular in Texas schools. For example, Tejano and Mariachi are prevalent in several districts throughout the state. Tejano music dates back to 1690 when Spain settled the area that is now known as Texas. The music developed over the centuries with new settlers from different parts of the world, thus combining several ethnic backgrounds, Mexican, German, Czech, and Cuban. The featured instrument is the accordion and the Tejano orchestra has been influenced by Mexican, Cuban, German, and Czech brass bands. In addition to the instrumentation, the roots of Tejano include various dance styles, which adds to its diversity and cultural heritage (The Roots of Tejano and Conjunto Music 2009).

Mariachi is a group of musicians that is Mexican in heritage. The instrumentation consists of violins, trumpets, a Spanish guitar, and a guitarrón (a large deep-bodied six-stringed acoustic bass from Mexico). Typically, several of the band members will sing along while playing an instrument. Usually, the group all dress in the same attire with silver studded charro outfits and wide brimmed hats. The size of the group varies from three to fifteen members. Mariachi has become popular in Texas schools, where the band director teaches and leads the group.

Listening

Teaching elementary-aged students how to listen to music and what to listen for in music is important for musical understanding. If students are not taught what to listen for in a piece of music, they will typically begin talking and the music therefore becomes background noise. Preparation of a listening lesson should consist of historical background of the music (e.g., time period and composer biography) followed by information on the music itself (e.g., main theme, instrumentation, musical form, dynamics, etc.). This preparation prior to listening to the music allows for the students to be actively engaged while listening and should ensure greater concert etiquette. Students in grades K–6 are expected to demonstrate appropriate concert etiquette. Whispering, talking, and turning around in a seat are unacceptable in most classical concert settings. MENC: The National Association for Music Education has developed "The Ten Rules of Concert Etiquette" for students and parents. (Editor's note: A former title for the group was the Music Educators National Conference, hence the MENC.) These rules are reproducible for distribution so inappropriate behavior at concerts does not occur. Other inappropriate behaviors, in addition to the three listed above, are the use of dangling jewelry, watch alarms, and chewing gum loudly (National Association for Music Educators 2009). Teaching students the expectations at a concert will benefit everyone involved, performers and audience members alike.

Copyright Law

The Copyright Law of the United States is quite complicated and changes regularly, especially with the technological advances in our society. In order to remain current, it is suggested that before any music is copied, reproduced, performed, or sold that the law be read. If possible, consult an expert. Currently, the copyright protection consists of the following:

- Works created after 1/1/1978—Life of the longest surviving author plus 70 years
- Earliest possible public domain date is 1/1/2048
- Works registered between 1/1/1923 and 1/1/1978—95 years from the date copyright was secured
- Works registered before 1/1/1923—Copyright protection for 75 years has expired and these words are in public domain (Public Domain Information Project 2009).

There was an amendment to the Copyright Protection Law in 1998 called the Sonny Bono Copyright Term Extension Act, which states that works registered before January 1, 1978, are now extended from 75 years to 95 years. That means that no new musical works will enter public domain until January 1, 2019 (Public Domain Information Project 2009).

Music that is public domain, which means that the music does not have an author or the song has exceeded the copyright protection, can be used without securing permission. Songs, such as cowboy songs or folk songs, can be reproduced without obtaining permission; however, the difficultly with public domain is that the original source must be located to make sure the date is correct, it has an unknown author, and that the music has entered public domain. Just because everyone knows a song does not mean that is it in public domain. For example, *Happy Birthday* was written by two women in Kentucky, who were kindergarten teachers, and is highly controversial with regard to the copyright law. It was registered for copyright in the 1930s and then when the Sonny Bono Copyright Term Extension Act was implemented, the copyright for *Happy Birthday* was extended until approximately 2030. With this extension it is illegal to publicly perform *Happy Birthday* without paying the appropriate royalties. That is why restaurant employees no longer sing *Happy Birthday* to their customers.

It is imperative that the copyright law be followed when teaching, distributing, and performing music. The song *Texas, Our Texas* cannot be copied or distributed without permission from Southern Music Company in San Antonio, who owns the copyright (Texas State Libraries and Archives 2009). Remember, copying music is illegal and the fines for copyright infringement are large and enforced.

Evaluation

Evaluation is subjective and evaluating musical performances is no different. The way to add objectivity to evaluating music is to use performance evaluations (rubrics). A well-written rubric gives students positive feedback to improve their performance, and allows the teacher to measure many students performing at the same time. Rubrics identify critical components to be assessed, and communicate acceptable levels of student performance or expected behavior. Any rubrics used should be simple enough to allow the students opportunities for self-assessment. The **RubiStar**, a website from the University of Kansas, provides opportunities for teachers to create their own rubric. This interactive site lets you choose from a list of music assessment components. The system also allows the option to customize the rubric. See an example of a customized version to assess classical concert etiquette for elementary education students. Visit *http://rubistar.4teachers.org/index.php?screen=NewRubric*.

Using these types of rubrics gives elementary grade students the opportunity to develop criteria for evaluating their behavior during musical performance, actual musical performances, and for evaluating music when they become adults and consumers of music.

Table 6.4.
Sample Rubric for Elementary Education Students

Measuring Component	Levels of Performance		
Category	**Best Behavior**	**Needs Improvement**	**Unacceptable**
Entering hall or auditorium	Stands quietly outside the door, then follows usher quietly to assigned seat	Talks in soft voice while waiting and while being seated	Talks in a loud voice while waiting and while being seated
Attention	Listens politely to the music. Has an interested expression almost all the time	Does not appear to be listening or interested, but keeps hands and feet to himself or herself.	Distracts others by talking, moving, rattling things, playing with toys, etc. during the actual performance
Showing appreciation	Claps at an appropriate volume at the end of all musical selections	Does not clap for all selections or claps at the wrong time	Claps too loudly, drawing audience attention, or whistles and screams while clapping

References

American Orff Schulwerk Association (AOSA). www.aosa.org/index.html (accessed May 23, 2011).

Lange, D. M. 2005. Together in harmony: Combining Orff Schulwerk and music learning Theory. Chicago: GIA Publications.

National Association of Music Educators (MENC). www.menc.org/resources/view/rules-for-concert-etiquette (accessed May 23, 2011).

Organization of American Kodály Educators (OAKE). www.oake.org/default.aspx (accessed May 23, 2011).

Public Domain Information Project. www.pdinfo.com/index.php (accessed May 23, 2011).

Shirrmacher, R., and J. E. Fox. 2009. Art and creative development for young children. 6th ed. Upper Saddle River, NJ: Cengage Learning.

Star-Spangled Banner. http://encarta.msn.com/encyclopedia_761575047/Star-Spangled_Banner.html (accessed June 11, 2009).

Texas State Libraries and Archives. http://www.tsl.state.tx.us/ref/abouttx/statesong.html (accessed May 23, 2011).

Texas Education Agency. 2006. Texas Knowledge and Skills. www.tea.state.tx.us/index2.aspx?id=6148/ (accessed May 23, 2011).

The Roots of Tejano and Conjunto Music. http://www.lib.utexas.edu/benson/border/arhoolie2/raices.html (accessed May 23, 2011).

Wallace, L. 2006. Utah Education Network (UEN). www.uen.org/ (accessed May 23, 2011).

Witcombe, C. L. 1995. Art history. Sweet Briar College, VA. http://arthistoryresources.net/ARTHLinks.html (accessed May 23, 2011).

Competency 048: Health

The teacher uses knowledge of the concepts and purposes of health education to plan and implement effective and engaging health instruction.

Enhancing Wellness

In today's world, the leading causes of illness, disease, and death are not infectious by nature, but rather lifestyle related. Heart disease, obesity, and cancer are all influenced by and result from people's chosen behaviors. The key to achieving good health is taking responsibility for your daily actions and creating a proactive lifestyle. Recognizing that you make daily choices that impact your total well-being will enable individuals to experience high-level wellness and avoid disease throughout life.

The benefits of a consistent program of diet and exercise are many and varied. Improvements in cardiac output, maximum oxygen intake, mood stabilization, and enhancing the blood's ability to carry oxygen are just a few of these benefits. Another aspect of health education is the awareness and avoidance of risks that are present in our everyday lives. Some risk factors include being overweight, smoking, using drugs, having unprotected sex, inactivity, and excessive unmanaged stress. Education is the key to minimizing the presence of these risk factors.

Body Systems

The body has a system of interrelated subsystems working together to keep the body functioning properly. Cells are the building blocks of the human body, and tissues are groups of similar cells working together to perform a specific job. An organ consists of many kinds of tissues working together for a larger purpose, and a group of organs working together is called an organ system. There are several organ systems in the human body.

Circulatory System. The heart pumps blood in the circulatory system. The blood passes through the right chambers of the heart and through the lungs, where it acquires oxygen, and back into the left chambers of the heart where it is pumped into the aorta, which branches into increasingly smaller arteries throughout the body. Beyond that, blood passes through tiny, thin-walled structures called capillaries. In the capillaries, the blood gives up oxygen and nutrients to tissues and absorbs metabolic waste products containing carbon dioxide. Finally, blood completes the circuit by passing through small veins, joining to form increasingly larger vessels until it reaches the largest veins, which return it back to the right side of the heart.

Respiratory System. Respiration results from the expansion and contraction of the lungs for gas exchange in the body. In the lungs, oxygen enters tiny capillaries, where it combines with hemoglobin in the red blood cells and is carried to the body's tissues. At the same time, carbon dioxide passes through capillaries into the air contained within the lungs. Inhaling draws air that is higher in oxygen and lower in carbon dioxide into the lungs; exhaling forces air that is high in carbon dioxide and low in oxygen from the lungs.

Digestive System. Food provides the energy required for sustenance of the human body. After the fragmenting of food by chewing and mixing with saliva, digestion begins. Chewed food passes down the esophagus into the stomach, where gastric and intestinal juices continue the digestion process. Thereafter, the mixture of food and secretions makes its way down the alimentary canal using peristalsis (the rhythmic contraction of the smooth muscle of the gastrointestinal tract). The smallest units of food are ultimately absorbed into the blood stream and transported throughout the rest of the body for utilization.

Immune System. The body defends itself against foreign proteins and infectious microorganisms by means of a complex immune system. The immune system is composed of a dual system that depends on recognizing a portion of the surface pattern of the invader and the generation of lymphocytes and antibody molecules to destroy invading molecules.

Skeletal System. The human skeletal system consists of more than 200 bones held together by connective tissues called ligaments. The bones are attached to the skeletal muscles; contractions of these skeletal muscles affect movements.

Nervous System. The nervous system controls muscular contractions. The nervous system has two divisions: the somatic, which allows voluntary control over skeletal muscle, and the autonomic, or involuntary, which controls cardiac and glandular functions. Nerve impulses carried by cranial or spinal cord nerves that connect the brain to skeletal muscles cause voluntary movement. Involuntary movement, or reflex movement, occurs in direct response to outside stimulus. Various nerve terminals, called receptors, constantly send impulses to the central nervous system. Each type of receptor routes nerve impulses to specialized areas of the brain for processing.

Diet and Exercise

Statistics show that Americans get fatter every year. Even though countless books and magazine articles are available on the subject of weight control, often the only place a student gets reliable information about diet is in the classroom. The unfortunate reality is that people who are overweight on average do not live as long as those who are not. Being overweight has been isolated as a risk factor in various types of cancer, heart disease, gall bladder problems, and kidney disease. Chronic diseases such as diabetes and high blood pressure are also aggravated by, or caused by, being overweight. Conversely, being underweight presents a great many dangers to health as well. Our society often places too much emphasis on losing weight and being thin. Women are especially prone to measuring their self-worth by the numbers they read on the bathroom scale. Young girls are especially susceptible to these messages and eating disorders can result.

According to the National Institute of Mental Health (2009) ideal weight and a good body fat ratio should be the goals when trying to lose weight. A correlation may exist between body fat and high cholesterol. Diet and exercise is the key to maintaining a good body fat ratio. Exercise helps keep the ratio low, improves cholesterol levels, and prevents heart disease. In order to lose weight, calories burned must exceed calories consumed.

Metabolism is a set of chemical processes that occur in the body to keep it functioning, growing, responding to the environment, and maintaining life balance. Basal Metabolic Rate (BMR) is the pace at which the body burns the vast majority of calories efficiently at rest. Adjustments in the BMR are slow, occur over time, and are dependent upon the demands put upon the body physically (i.e., exercise) and calorie consumption. If calorie intake is restricted too much, the body goes into starvation mode and operates by burning fewer calories in order to conserve energy. Just a 250 calorie drop a day combined with a 250 calorie burn will result in a loss of one pound a week. Crash diets, which bring about rapid weight loss, are not only unhealthy but also ineffective. Slower weight loss is more lasting. Aerobic exercise is a major component to successful weight loss. Exercise speeds up metabolism and causes the body to burn calories efficiently. Timing of exercise may also enhance the benefits. Exercise before meals speeds up metabolism and helps suppress appetite. Through education, people will be better able to realize that maintaining a healthy weight is crucial to a healthy life and should be a constant consideration.

Along with exercise, a healthy diet is vital to good health, learning, academic achievement, and longevity. The elements of good nutrition, the role of vitamins, elimination of risk factors, and strategies to control weight are all part of a healthy lifestyle. In June of 2011, the USDA changed its symbol for healthy eating from a Food Pyramid to a Healthy Plate. Instead of having Americans consider their daily intake the USDA is encouraging consumers to think about building a healthy diet one plate at at time.

The colorful, four-part plate is divided into four sections (Figure 6-5, on next page). Fruit and vegetables take up an entire half of the plate while one quarter of the plate is reserved for protein and the remaining fourth for grains. A side container represents dairy.

Figure 6-5. Choose My Plate

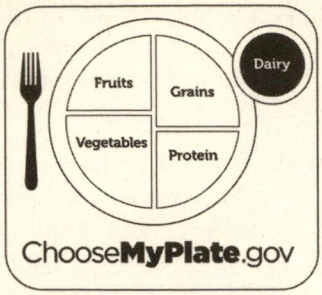

Source: U.S. Department of Agriculture, *MyPlate*, *www.teamnutrition.usda.gov/myplate.htm.*

Recommendations include:

1. One-half of the plate should be whole grains (e.g., bread, cereal, rice, and pasta) and proteins (which should vary between animal protiens and legumes).
2. Vegetables and fruit should comprise the other half of the plate.
3. Milk products should be low-fat (1%) or fat-free.
4. Compare sodium contents in soups and frozen foods and choose lower sodium products.
5. Drink water intead of sugary drinks.

Nutrients are divided into two main groups: macro-nutrients (carbohydrates, proteins, and fats) and micro-nutrients (vitamins and minerals). Most foods contain a combination of the two groups. Complex carbohydrates (e.g., vegetables, fruits, whole grain breads, and cereals) are the preferred energy source for the body and should comprise up to one-half of the diet. These foods provide fiber, which helps digestion, reduces constipation, and reduces the risk of colon cancer. Proteins (e.g., milk, eggs, meat, fish, and beans) are one of our most essential nutrients because the body uses them to build and repair itself in more ways than any other food. Fats (e.g., olive and canola oils) are important to the body for regulating blood pressure, forming cell structures, transporting vitamins, and triggering immune system responses. Vitamins are essential given they perform highly specific metabolic processes in the cells and aid with many other functions such as growth and maintenance of the body. Minerals (e.g., calcium, iron, potassium, and zinc) help build strong bones and teeth, aid in muscle function, and help the nervous system transmit messages. Keeping a balance of nutrients consistently in the body combined with hydration will keep systems functioning appropriately and minimize overall health risk. A world of nutrition information is available to teachers at the Dietary Guidelines for Americans, published by the United States Department of Health and Human Services (2006).

Stress Management

Stress is the product of any change, either negative or positive. Multiple components and situations can cause stress. Some of these are:

- Environmental factors such as noise, air pollution, and crowding
- Physiological factors such as sickness and physical injuries
- Psychological factors such as self-deprecating thoughts and negative self-image

In addition to the normal stressors that everyone experiences, some students may be living in dysfunctional families, some may be dealing with substance abuse and addictions, and some may be experiencing sexual abuse.

People have numerous sources of stress in their lives, and it is important that students and teachers learn acceptable ways to cope with stress. The first step is to recognize the role that stress plays in our daily lives. A teacher might lead a class through a brainstorming activity to help the students become aware of the various sources of stress affecting them. Next, the teacher could identify positive ways of coping with stress, including positive self-talk, physical exercise, proper nutrition, adequate sleep, balanced activities, time management techniques, good study habits, and relaxation exercises.

Students facing stress often experience a wide range of emotions. They may be sad, frustrated, or afraid. Effective teachers realize that students' emotions play a significant role in students' classroom performance and achievement. Thus, they should seek to create a classroom environment supportive of students' emotional needs. They should have appropriate empathy and compassion for the emotional conflicts facing students, as well as a realistic awareness that students need to attain crucial academic and social skills that will give them some control over their environment as they become increasingly independent individuals and, eventually, productive citizens.

The state curriculum for health (Texas Essential Knowledge and Skills) has incorporated objectives and standards to prepare school-age children to face the multiple physical, environmental, and emotional challenges that children face in the United States. Health education teachers and teachers in general are required to teach these health objectives in formal health classes through the integration of health components in the general curricula. Knowledge of the state health curriculum is required for all teachers in the state. An analysis of the health curriculum mandates in Texas follows.

Curriculum Requirements for Health

The Texas Essential Knowledge and Skills (TEKS) contain all the curriculum components in the area of Health. Health education teachers are expected to implement the prescribed state curriculum (Texas Administrative Code 2009a). In conjunction with the national initiative, The Texas Essential Knowledge and Skills provides for the teaching of developmentally appropriate content and strategies for health education to children in grades K–12. Some of the key components of the TEKS require children to develop an understanding of their body, proper nutrition practices, and safety procedures, and to use reliable information to make personal health decisions. Some of the topics introduced in grades K–6 are:

1. Identify and consume healthy food choices
2. Strategies to avoid health and safety risks
3. Strategies for protection against sexual predators
4. Role of media and Internet influencing health decisions
5. Assertive behaviors and strategies to deal with risky situations
6. Gang prevention programs
7. Drugs and alcohol prevention programs
8. Knowledge of the human body
9. Safety procedures in school and the community

Some of the key skills and activities required in the state K–6 curriculum are listed below.

Kindergarten

Children should be able to:

1. Identify types of foods that help the body grow such as healthy breakfast foods and snacks
2. Identify the purpose of protective equipment such as a seat belt and a bicycle helmet
3. Identify how to get help from a parent and/or trusted adult when made to feel uncomfortable or unsafe by another person/adult
4. Demonstrate procedures for responding to emergencies including dialing 911
5. Demonstrate how to seek the help of parents/guardians and other trusted adults in making decisions and solving problems

First Grade

Children should be able to:

1. Name safe play environments
2. Explain the harmful effects of, and how to avoid, alcohol, tobacco, and other drugs
3. Identify and practice safety rules during play
4. Identify common illnesses and diseases and their symptoms
5. Name various members of his/her family who help him/her to promote and practice healthy habits

Second Grade

Children should be able to:

1. Describe and demonstrate personal health habits such as brushing and flossing teeth and exercise
2. Identify the major organs of the body such as the heart, lungs, and brain and describe their primary functions
3. Apply practices to control spread of germs in daily life such as hand washing and skin care
4. Demonstrate refusal skills
5. Identify various media that provide health information

Third Grade

Children should be able to:

1. Describe ways to improve personal fitness
2. Identify types of nutrients
3. Explain the body's defense systems and how they fight disease
4. Relate how protecting the environment promotes individual and community health
5. Describe how the media can influence knowledge and healthy behaviors

Fourth Grade

Children should be able to:

1. Identify information on menus and food labels
2. Explain how to develop a home-safety and emergency response plan such as fire safety
3. Explain how sleep affects academic performance
4. Identify the importance of taking personal responsibility for developing and maintaining a personal health plan such as fitness, nutrition, stress management, and personal safety
5. Identify ways to avoid drugs and list alternatives for the use of drugs and other substances

Fifth Grade

Children should be able to:

1. Apply information from the food guide pyramid to make healthy food choices
2. Calculate the relationship between caloric intake and energy expenditure
3. Explain strategies for avoiding violence, gangs, weapons, and drugs
4. Explain the impact of neglect and abuse
5. Assess the role of assertiveness, refusal skills, and peer pressure on decision making and problem solving

Sixth Grade

Children should be able to:

1. Analyze healthy and unhealthy dietary practices
2. Explain the consequences of sexual activity and the benefits of abstinence
3. Seek the input of parents and other trusted adults in problem solving and goal setting
4. Make healthy choices from among environmental alternatives such as leaving a smoke-filled room or selecting healthy snacks from vending machines
5. Describe chemical dependency and addiction to tobacco, alcohol, and other drugs and substances. (Texas Administrative Code 2009a)

Human Growth and Development

A teacher does not have to be an expert in anatomy and physiology to see the physical changes that accompany students' growth and maturity. The preschool child has trouble grasping pencils and crayons in a manner that facilitates handwriting; however, even most two-year-olds can grasp crayons sufficiently to make marks on papers and thus enjoy the creative excitement of art. Physiological changes play a significant role in the development of children as they increase their control of bodily movements and refine their motor skills. Their ability to engage in simple to complex classroom and playground activities increases as they develop. Teachers must adjust and adapt classroom and playground activities to be developmentally appropriate for students' various skill levels.

Girls, on average, reach maturational milestones before boys. Physical changes may cause embarrassment to both females and males when they draw unwelcome attention. These changes almost always create some discomfort as adolescents find the body they were familiar and comfortable with to be quite different, sometimes seemingly overnight. To facilitate this transition, teachers need to make children aware that these changes are part of their natural development.

Many major factors relate to and are necessary to build both social and emotional health. It is critically important for teachers to develop a basic understanding of the principles of human development and its multiple dimensions (e.g., physical, mental, emotional, and social). Additionally, teachers must appreciate a dynamic and interactive view of human development. This approach to understanding human development is one that recognizes that human beings do not develop in a vacuum.

A constant interaction occurs between people and their environments. Thus, effective teachers must be sensitive to and knowledgeable of both personal characteristics of students (internal factors) and characteristics of their environment. Internal factors, beyond the general characteristics that humans share as they grow and mature, also include students' personality characteristics, their self-concept and sense of self-esteem, their self-discipline and self-control, their ability to cope with stress, and their general outlook on life (attitude).

Empowerment has many components, one of which is self-concept. A good definition of self-concept is what we think and believe to be true about ourselves, not what we think about others and not what they think about us. Related to self-concept is self-efficacy. Simply stated, self-efficacy is the confidence you have in your ability to cope with life's challenges. Self-efficacy refers to your sense of control over life or over your responses to life. Experts say that ideas about self-efficacy get established by the time children reach age four. Therefore, it is all the more important that teachers attempt to help students achieve coping skills and a sense of self-efficacy.

Substance Use and Abuse

Drug and alcohol problems can affect anyone, regardless of age, sex, race, marital status, place of residence, income level, or lifestyle. However, there are certain identifiable risk factors for substance abuse. These factors include individual, familial, social, and cultural characteristics.

Some of the personal characteristics that have been linked to substance abuse are: aggressiveness, emotional problems, inability to cope with stress, and low self-esteem. Feelings of failure and a fragile ego can also contribute to this problem. The presence of physical disabilities, physical or mental health problems, or learning disabilities can add to the student's vulnerability to substance abuse. In many ways, students who are at-risk for academic problems are also susceptible to substance abuse problems.

Associated with substance abuse among youth are several family characteristics. First, and perhaps most important, is the alcohol or other drug dependency of a parent or both parents. This characteristic might relate to another significant factor: parental abuse and neglect of children. Antisocial and/or mentally ill parents are also factors that put children at risk for drug and/or alcohol abuse. Other conditions like family unemployment or underemployment, and parents with little education or who are socially isolated can also become risk factors. Single parents without family or other support, family instability, a high level of marital and family conflict or violence, and parental absenteeism due to separation, divorce, or death can also increase children's vulnerability to substance abuse. Finally, other important factors to consider are the lack of family rituals, inadequate parenting, little child-to-parent interaction, and frequent family moves. These factors describe children without affiliation or a sense of identity with their families or the community. Any of these family factors could lead to a substance abuse problem in a student.

Living in an economically depressed area with high unemployment, inadequate housing, a high crime rate, and a prevalence of illegal drug use are social characteristics that can put an individual at risk for substance abuse. Cultural risk factors include minority status involving racial discrimination, differing generational levels of assimilation, low levels of education, and low achievement expectations from society at large. All the recognized risk factors are only indicators of the potential for substance abuse. They are not necessarily predictive of an individual's proclivity to drug or alcohol abuse. Some children who are exposed to very adverse conditions grow up to be healthy, productive, and well-functioning adults. Yet, knowing the risk factors, teachers are better able to identify children vulnerable to substance abuse and develop prevention education strategies.

Sometimes it can be difficult to tell if someone is using illegal drugs or alcohol. Usually, people who abuse drugs or alcohol (including young people) go to great lengths to keep their behavior a secret. They deny and/or try to hide the problem. However, certain warning signs can indicate that someone is using drugs or drinking too much alcohol: (1) Lying to teachers and family members, (2) Avoiding people who are longtime friends or associates, (3) Having slurred speech, (4) Complaining of headaches, nausea, or dizziness, (5) Having difficulty staying awake in class, and (6) bloodshot, glazed over, and/or squinting eyes. These examples are insufficient to confirm a substance abuse problem, but in combination and when displayed consistently over time, they are strong indicators. Teachers should record their observations and keep written reports of the behavioral changes they witness. Moreover, they should report their suspicions to the appropriate school authorities.

Violence and Abuse

Child abuse is a common problem in the United States. According to the American Academy of Pediatrics, more than 2.5 million cases of child abuse and neglect are reported annually in the nation (Shelov, & Remer, 2009). Half of these cases involves neglect while the other half involves physical and sexual abuse. Despite all the media attention given to child abuse and neglect, many teachers still believe that it cannot happen to one of their students. They may think, "This is a nice neighborhood," or "Most of these students have both a mother and a father living at home." However, abuse and neglect may happen to children, possibly even to one of your students. Abused children typically show signs of over stimulation—being "wired," unruly, and/or belligerent. By contrast, the behaviors of neglected children point to under stimulation—all they want is to be left alone and typically they are unsociable, sedate, and/or withdrawn. The child learns this behavior at home during periods of neglect. The neglect may change the child's behaviors from almost flat (registering no emotion) to anger. Although poor attention, tears, violence, and apathetic behavior may be indicators of either abuse or neglect, neglected children usually have feelings of hopelessness and cannot adequately control their thoughts and emotions. Students either become obsessed by the neglect or refuse to acknowledge that the neglect is really happening.

One of the most obvious visible signs of child abuse is red swelling or bruising caused by being hit. The appearance of marks on a child may be proof of child abuse, and the teacher must report the evidence immediately. Visible signs are also one way teachers can separate real abuse cases from unfounded ones. While marks from the hand, fist, or belt are usually recognizable, other marks in geometric shapes (i.e., eating utensils, paddles, coat hangers, or extension cords) can signify child abuse as well.

In addition to the physical marks, victims of child abuse and neglect can also exhibit nontraditional behaviors. The most common documented characteristics include: (1) frequent illness; (2) hyperactivity disorders; (3) depression; (4) bowel or bladder control problems; (5) impulsivity, aggressiveness, or defiance; and (6) academic difficulties. Neglect is more common than abuse but receives much less attention largely because it does not show easily observable manifestations.

Teachers hope they will never have to manage a disclosure of any kind of maltreatment of a child, although such revelations are the responsibility of these trusted adults and student advocates. Following the disclosure of abuse from a child, it is important for teachers to respond in a calm manner and thank/support the child for bringing this important matter to their attention. Teachers should not question the child about the details; rather gather information and follow-up with administrators, counselors, and/or nurses. The best course of action is to make an immediate referral or report of these suspicions.

Teachers in Texas are required by law to report any suspicion of child abuse or neglect to the Department of Human Services. Thus, they must be vigilant for possible symptoms or indications of child abuse. Failure to file a report of suspicion of child abuse or neglect has consequences, and it can result in legal action against the teacher. After the report, the teacher should realize that the child may feel that the educator has exposed the child's private life. While accepting the child's feeling of betrayal, the teacher can explain that the report was necessary and assure the child of protection against reprisals for telling about the abuse. Sometimes the child benefits from just knowing that others do care about his or her well-being.

Safety and Accident Prevention

Peer counseling, peer mediation, and peer leadership programs have demonstrated little effectiveness for reducing violence, encouraging safety in schools, and preventing accidents. In addition, restricting promotion to succeeding grades for violent students have shown to have negative effects on achievement, attendance, and behavior toward school. Research shows that the most successful programs are those that are multifaceted and linked to a variety of services. Characteristics of such programs include: (1) early start and long-term commitment; (2) strong collaborative leadership that enforces explicit disciplinary policies; (3) ongoing staff development; (4) parental involvement and parental education (e.g., home visits); and (5) role-modeling activities designed to be culturally relevant.

School Violence

School violence is a prevalent feature in most American schools. Some of the elements that contribute to school violence are: (1) overcrowding, (2) poor design and use of school space, (3) lack of disciplinary procedures, (4) student alienation, (5) multicultural insensitivity, (6) rejection of at-risk students by teachers and peers, and (7) anger or resentment at school routines. On the other hand, factors contributing to school safety include (1) a positive school climate and atmosphere, (2) clear and high performance expectations for all students, (3) practices and values that promote inclusion, (4) bonding of the students to the school, (5) high levels of student participation and parental involvement in school activities, and (6) opportunities to acquire academic skills and develop socially. Effective teachers need to be alert to the signs of potentially violent behavior, acknowledging that signs can easily be misinterpreted and misunderstood. Warning signs should be used to get help for children, not to exclude, punish, or isolate them. Some of the imminent warning signs of school violence are: (1) serious physical fighting with peers or family members; (2) serious destruction of property; (3) rage for seemingly minor reasons; (4) detailed threats of lethal violence; (5) possession and/or use of firearms and weapons; and (6) other self-injurious behaviors or threats of suicide. Teachers have to become vigilant to these signs of violence and notify the appropriate authorities of these behaviors. Violence prevention strategies at school range from adding social skills training to the curriculum to installing metal detectors at the entrances to buildings. Schools should teach all students procedures in conflict resolution and anger management, and should explain the school's rules, expectations, and disciplinary policies.

Mental and Emotional Health

Mental and emotional disorders present various emotional and physical signs. Depression can manifest itself in an overall lack of interest in activities, constant crying, or talk of suicide. Anxiety or obsessive thoughts are another indication of a possible mental or emotional disorder. Physical signs include a disruption in eating or sleeping patterns, headaches, nausea and stomach pain, or diarrhea. The teacher needs to consider these signs as a cause for serious concerns and treatment.

Psychotic disorders, such as schizophrenia, are serious emotional disorders. These disorders are rare in young children and difficult to diagnose, although one of the warning signs for psychotic disorders is that the student experiences a complete break from the reality of his or her surroundings. Schizophrenics may have difficulty expressing themselves, resulting in unusual speech patterns or even muteness. Schizophrenics, who are more likely to be boys than girls, may also exhibit facial expressions that are either markedly absent of emotion or overly active.

Infantile Autism

Infantile autism is another serious emotional disorder that appears in early childhood. Characteristics include withdrawn behavior and delayed or absent language and communication skills. Symptoms of autism can appear in children between four and eighteen months of age. Autistic children will usually distance themselves from others and may be unable to experience empathy. In addition, they often cannot distinguish or appreciate humor. Autistic children may have a preoccupation with particular objects or may perform particular activities repeatedly. While autistic children can range in all levels of intelligence, some children may have particular skills in focused areas, such as music or math. Diagnosis might inaccurately determine mental retardation, hearing/auditory impairment, or brain damage. Treatment for autistic children may involve therapy, drugs, or residential living. However, only five percent of autistic children ever become socially well-adjusted adults. Many of these high-functioning autistics are placed in the regular classroom, some with personal aides to facilitate their success.

Eating Disorders

Eating disorders are not due to a failure of will or behavior; rather, they are real, treatable medical illnesses in which certain maladaptive patterns of eating take on a life of their own (National Institute of Mental Health, 2009). The main types of eating disorders are anorexia nervosa (lack of desire or interest in food which results in starvation of the body) and bulimia nervosa (episodes of secretive excessive eating followed by inappropriate methods of weight control such as self-induced vomiting). A third type of problem that exhibits a total lack of control for eating is compulsive overeating or binge-eating disorder. Many professionals have suggested this condition as a formal disorder in today's world although it has not yet been approved as a formal psychiatric diagnosis. Treatments for eating disorders are complex and most often requires professional help (e.g., psychotherapy, support groups, and/or hospitalization).

Healthy Interpersonal Relationships

The social domain of health is manifested in our ability to practice good social skills and maintain comfortable relationships with others. Socially healthy people are effective at communicating respect for others, being tolerant and patient, and accepting differences without compromising relationships. Successful teachers are able to listen intently and recognize the needs and issues of others. Ultimately, effective educators recognize ways they enrich and are enriched by their relationships and use these skills to role-model appropriate behaviors.

To become effective communicators, students need a variety of learning opportunities to practice interpersonal skills in a variety of situations they are likely to encounter (e.g., communicating empathy, resisting peer-pressure, managing conflicts, and asking for help). As a result of practicing such methods, a natural link is established for students to express their healthy intentions when the correct situation/environment arises. Educators should constantly look for ways in which to practice assertive communication including stating a position, offering a reason that makes sense or is healthy, and acknowledging other's feelings.

Health Care Information

The Surgeon General's Report on Health Promotion and Disease Prevention was first released in 1979 creating a public health revolution that emphasized disease prevention and taking personal responsibility for one's health. In 1990, the United States Department of Health and Human Services published Promoting Health/Preventing Disease: Objectives for the Nation, which outlined specific objectives for meeting those goals identified in the earlier Surgeon General's Report. These objectives led to the development of Healthy People 2000, a document that aimed to reduce preventable death and disability and enhance the quality of life for American society. Today, Healthy People 2010 (n.d.) is setting the disease prevention agenda for the United States using science, technology, and education.

Health Care Professionals

School health services typically include a set of policies and programs that assess and protect the health of students. Specifically, the school nurse leads this collaborative effort to direct patient care, screen and diagnose symptoms, promote health counseling services, participate in health promotion and disease prevention, and maintain relationships with allied health professionals and community health service providers. School administrators have the legal responsibility for the safety of all students and for the supervision of the health services program offered in school. Regrettably, many school districts have assigned these tasks to untrained teachers and/or staff, which lead to dangerous practices for the students, teachers, and school district.

Like other states, Texas has a legislative mandate requiring all children to be immunized against certain communicable diseases (e.g., polio, diphtheria, measles, mumps, rubella, chicken pox, and hepatitis) prior to enrolling in public school. All policies governing communicable diseases should be available to teachers and school employees to promote collaboration and risk reduction. Teachers should always be proactive in obtaining information when a child who suffers from a communicable disease can safely return to school. In addition to any formal instruction in health, other teachers should integrate the content areas (e.g., social studies, science, art, and music) to health-related issues. Examples of topics that can be integrated easily into other content areas are:

1. the effects of pollution on health and occupational-related disease (e.g., "black lung" disease)
2. the health care options available to people in different parts of the world and in different economic circumstances
3. differentiation between communicable and noncommunicable diseases
4. the importance of washing hands frequently

Older children should be able to explain the transmission and prevention of communicable diseases, and all children should learn which diseases cannot be transmitted through casual contact.

Students as young as kindergartners and first graders can learn how to recognize advertisements that might lead them to unhealthy behavior (e.g., for candy or sugar-laden cereal). By third or fourth grade, children should be able to demonstrate that they are able to make health-related decisions regarding advertisements in various media. Teachers can encourage students to: (1) avoid alcohol, tobacco, stimulants, and narcotics; (2) get plenty of sleep and exercise; (3) eat a well-balanced diet; (4) receive the proper immunizations; and (5) avoid sharing toothbrushes, combs, hats, beverages, and food with others.

External Influences

The school is a community agency that cannot function appropriately in isolation. With that said, the range of problems associated with students does not only result from school, but also parents/family, neighborhoods, and larger community influences (e.g., consumerism, media, and environment). All those who advocate for students must realize that the complexity of today's health and social problems require all community stakeholders to take responsibility for the current situation and work together with the schools to improve the health of students. An important step to confronting these challenges is the need for local districts to establish a school health advisory council that includes members from all segments of the community (e.g., school personnel, medical professionals, non-profit organizations, and the business sector).

First Aid

First aid is the immediate, temporary care of an injured or ill person. Occasionally, during physical education classes or during school hours, injuries and illnesses occur. Therefore, a basic knowledge of first aid is important for physical education teachers and other instructors. However, a teacher should not attempt first aid if the procedures are unclear. A course in first aid is important for the classroom teacher, and they are readily available from the local American Red Cross.

The following are some common injuries and a brief description of their emergency treatments:

1. **Bone Fracture:** A fracture is a break in a bone. Fractures can be simple, multiple (many breaks in the bone), or compound (a break in the bone and the skin).

   Treatment: Immobilize, use ice to control swelling, and seek medical aid. In the case of a compound fracture, it is important to stop the bleeding.

2. **Traumatic Shock:** Traumatic shock is the severe compression of circulation caused by injury or illness. Symptoms include cool sweaty skin and a rapid weak pulse.

   Treatment: Minimize heat loss and elevate the legs without disturbing the rest of the body. Seek medical help.

3. **Sprain Injury:** A sprain is an injury to a joint caused by the joint being moved too far or away from its range of motion. Both ligaments and tendons can be injured in a sprain. Ligaments join bone to bone, and tendons join muscle to bone.

   Treatment: Guide the victim to rest, apply ice to the injury, and compression. The use of the acronym RICE—rest, ice, compression, and elevation—provides an easy way to remember the appropriate treatment for sprains.

4. **Strain Muscle:** A strain is a muscle injury caused by overwork.

   Treatment: Use ice to lessen the swelling and rest. Applying some heat after icing can be beneficial although opinion on the value of heat varies.

5. **Dislocation of a Joint:** In this type of injury, the bone becomes out of place at the joint. As a result, ligaments can be severely stretched and/or torn.

   Treatment: Immobilize and seek medical help. Some people advocate "popping" the dislocation back into place, but this can be risky for both the injured person and for the person giving the first aid (liability). Therefore, allow the medical professionals to put the joint back in place.

6. **Heat Exhaustion:** The symptoms of heat exhaustion include cold and sweaty skin, nausea, dizziness, and paleness. Heat exhaustion is not as severe as heat stroke.

   Treatment: Increase water intake, replace salt, and get out of the heat.

7. **Heat Stroke:** The symptoms of heat stroke include high fever, dry skin, and possible unconsciousness.

   Treatment: Attempt to cool off the body gradually, get into the shade, and seek medical attention immediately.

8. **Heart Attack:** The symptoms of heart attack include shortness of breath, pain in the left arm, pain in the chest, nausea, and sweating.

   Treatment: Elevate the head and chest, give cardiopulmonary resuscitation if indicated, and seek medical assistance. In the heart stops, apply resuscitation techniques. Resuscitation is a first-aid technique that provides artificial circulation and respiration. Remember the ABCs: A is for "airway," B is for "breathing," and C is for "circulation." Check the airway to make sure it is open, and check breathing and circulation.

9. **Seizures:** The cause of seizures is often epilepsy.

   Treatment: Clear the area around the victim to avoid injury during the seizure. Do not place anything in the victim's mouth; seek medical help after the seizure if necessary.

Competency 049: Physical Education

The teacher uses knowledge of the concepts, principles, skills, and practices of physical education to plan and implement effective and engaging physical education instruction.

Principles of Physical Education and Physical Activity

In 1986, the National Association for Sport and Physical Education (NASPE) appointed a committee to develop a working definition of the characteristics that physically educated people ought to exhibit (National Association for Sport and Physical Education 2009). As a result of this initiative, NASPE introduced the following definition. A physically educated person is someone who:

1. has learned skills necessary to perform a variety of physical activities
2. knows the implications of and the benefits from involvement in physical activity
3. participates regularly in physical activity, and values physical activity and its contribution to a healthy lifestyle

With this definition in mind, NASPE developed the National Standards for Physical Education:

Standard 1: Demonstrates competency in motor skills and movement patterns

Standard 2: Demonstrates understanding of movement concepts, principles, strategies, and tactics as they apply to the learning and performance of physical activities.

Standard 3: Participates regularly in physical activity.

Standard 4: Achieves and maintains a health-enhancing level of physical fitness.

Standard 5: Exhibits responsible personal and social behavior that respects self and others in physical activity settings.

Standard 6: Values physical activity for health, enjoyment, challenge, self-expression, and/or social interaction.

In order to help students achieve these standards, physical education teachers must have an understanding of the human body, and how physical activity can impact it. Knowledge of anatomy and physiology can guide teachers in the selection and implementation of games and physical activities appropriate for development. Anatomy describes the structure, position, and size of various body parts and organs. Because our bones adapt to fill a specific need, exercise is of great benefit to the skeletal system. Bones that anchor strong muscles thicken to withstand the stress put on it. Weight-bearing bones can develop heavy mineral deposits while supporting the body. Because joints help provide flexibility and ease of movement, it is important to know how each joint moves. Types of joints are ball and socket (e.g., shoulder and hip), hinge (e.g., elbow and knee), pivot (e.g., head of the spine), gliding (e.g., carpal (wrist) and tarsal (ankle) bones), angular (e.g., wrist and ankle joints), partially movable (e.g., vertebrae), and immovable (e.g., bones of the adult cranium).

Muscles are the active movers in the body. In order to properly teach any physical education activity, the functions and physiology of the muscles must be understood. Because muscles move by shortening or contracting, proper form should be taught so the student can get the most out of an activity. It is also important to know the location of each muscle. This knowledge will help in teaching proper form while participating in physical education activities. Understanding the concept of antagonistic muscles, along with the related information concerning flexors and extensors, is also vital to the physical educator. Imagine trying to teach the proper form of throwing a ball if you do not understand the mechanics involved. Knowledge of anatomy and physiology is also necessary to teach proper techniques used in calisthenics as well as all physical activities. Without this knowledge, exercise itself can cause harm to the body.

Exploration of movement activities through fun activities constitutes the main focus of the physical education curriculum in the early grades. However, the curriculum can provide for more organized activities like yoga or low impact aerobic exercise. Aerobic exercise involves both muscle contractions and movement of the body. Aerobic exercise requires large amounts of oxygen and when done regularly, will condition the cardiovascular system. Some aerobic exercises are especially suited to developing aerobic training benefits, with a minimum of skill and time involved. Examples of good aerobic activities are walking, running, swimming, and bicycling.

Benefits of an Active Lifestyle

The axiom "Use it or lose it" certainly holds true for the human body. Our bodies thrive on physical activity, which is any bodily movement produced by skeletal muscles and resulting in energy expenditure. Physical fitness enables a person to meet the physical demands of work and leisure comfortably. A person with a high level of physical fitness can enjoy a better quality of life and minimize the development of life-threatening diseases. Unfortunately, Americans tend to be relatively inactive.

Lack of activity can cause many problems, including weak muscles and heart, poor circulation, shortness of breath, obesity, coronary artery disease, hypertension, type II diabetes, osteoporosis, and certain types of cancer. Overall, mortality rates from all causes are lower in physically active people than in sedentary people. In addition, physical activity can help people manage mild-to-moderate depression, control anxiety, and prevent weakening of the skeletal system. By increasing physical activity, a person may improve heart function and circulation, respiratory function, and overall strength and endurance. All of these lead to improved vigor and vitality. Exercise also lowers the risk of heart disease by strengthening the heart muscle, lowering pulse and blood pressure, and lowering the concentration of fat in both the body and the blood. It can also improve appearance, increase range of motion, and lessen the risk of back problems associated with weak muscles, weak bones, and osteoporosis. On most days of the week, children should engage in at least 60 minutes of physical activity. Proper hydration is also important during physical activity. To help prevent dehydration during prolonged physical activity or when it is hot, people should consume water regularly during the activity and drink several glasses afterwards.

Evaluating and Monitoring Fitness Levels

One of the primary reasons for the teaching of physical education is to instill a willingness to exercise and encourage students to make good decisions about their health. Therefore, the evaluation of student performance and progress is becoming increasingly important and has, therefore, become an essential responsibility of the physical education teacher. In 2007, the Texas state legislature passed a law that all students from grades 3–12 will be measured once a year on the Fitnessgram (2009). The Fitnessgram is not a test of athletic ability, rather a health-related fitness assessment that uses criterion-referenced standards to measure physical health (i.e., muscular fitness, aerobic fitness, and flexibility). With regular physical activity all students should be able to achieve a score on the Fitnessgram that will place them within or above the Healthy Fitness Zone on all Fitnessgram test items. The idea is that all students should learn to assess their own level of fitness, interpret assessment results, plan personal programs, and motivate themselves to remain active throughout their lives.

The assessment plan for an elementary physical education program determines the degree to which students reach the identified goals. These critical objectives or "performance indicators" ensure that the teacher is focusing activities on skill development and improved performance during movement games and activities. To obtain good body management skills is to acquire, expand, and integrate elements of motor control. It is important that children not only manage their body with an ease of movement, but also realize that good posture and body mechanics are important parts of their movement process and patterns. In other words, a child with good motor control is a child who is confident and graceful.

Development of Motor Skills

Physical changes play a significant role in the development of children as they gradually gain control of the movements and functions of their bodies. As they develop physically, children refine their motor skills, enabling them to engage in increasingly complex movement lessons and/or activities. For teachers to be able to identify patterns of physical development, they must first assess the level at which students can control specific movement patterns and then create educational activities that are developmentally appropriate for their students' physical abilities.

Children between the ages of three and four have already mastered standing and walking. At this stage, children are developing gross motor skills, including the ability to hop on one foot and balance, climb stairs without support, kick a ball, throw overhand, catch a ball that has bounced, move forward and backward, and ride a tricycle. Children between the ages of three and four are also developing fine motor skills, such as using scissors, drawing single shapes, and copying shapes like capital letters. By age four or five, when most children enter school, they are developing the gross motor ability to do somersaults, use a swing, climb, and skip. These skills require a multitude of movement patterns with increasing coordination. In addition, children at this age can begin to dress themselves using zippers, buttons, and possibly tying their shoes. They can also eat independently using utensils. Children at this age are increasingly capable of copying shapes, including letters and numbers. They can cut and paste and draw a person with a head, body, arms, and legs. These fine motor skills develop quickly in children of this age. By age six, children can bounce a ball, skate, ride a bike, skip with both feet, and dress themselves independently. As the student develops year by year, the physical skills (both fine and gross motor) become increasingly complex and involve more muscles and more coordination. By age nine, children can complete a model kit, learn to sew, and cook simple recipes. By age ten, children can catch a fly ball and participate in all elements of a softball game.

Recognizing the basic milestones that most children will achieve by a certain age (i.e., Texas Essential Knowledge and Skills [TEKS]) will assist teachers in making decisions about academic lessons and tasks. In addition, teachers may be able to identify children who may not be reaching their developmental milestones with the rest of the class. In short, the physical ability of students to engage in simple to complex activities in school gradually increases as they develop.

During play activities, a child engages in meaningful movement patterns that utilize large muscle groups in the body. Movement education is the process by which a child is helped to develop competency in those general movement patterns. It has been defined as learning to move and moving to learn. Movement competency requires the student to manage his or her body through space, time, and direction with the ability to accomplish basic and specialized physical tasks and traverse various obstacles. Basic movement skills are necessary for a child's daily living, whereas specialized skills are required to perform sports and other complex activities that have very clear techniques.

Perceptual motor competency is another consideration in teaching body management. Perceptual motor concepts that are relevant to physical education include those that give attention to balance, coordination, lateral movement, directional movement, awareness of space, and knowledge of one's own body. Basic skills can be divided into three categories, locomotor, non-locomotor, and manipulative skills. A more complex movement pattern might include skills from each category. Locomotor skills describe the type of movement children have to master in order to travel or move within a given space. These include walking, running, leaping, jumping, hopping, galloping, sliding, and skipping. Non--locomotor skills are used to control the body in relation to the force of gravity. These are typically done while in a stationary position (i.e., kneeling or standing). Some of these activities include: pushing, pulling, bending, stretching, twisting, turning, swinging, shaking, bouncing, rising, and falling. Manipulative skills are used when a child handles, moves, or plays with an object. Most manipulative skills involve using the hands and feet, but other parts of the body may be used as well. Hand-eye and foot-eye coordination are improved when manipulating objects. Throwing, batting, kicking, and catching are important skills to be developed using balls and beanbags. Starting a child at a less challenging level and progressing to a more difficult activity is an effective method for teaching manipulative activities. Most activities begin with individual practice and evolve to partner activities. When teaching throwing and catching for example, the teacher should emphasize skill performance, principles of opposition, weight transfer, eye focus, and follow through. Some attention should be given to targets when throwing because students need to be able to catch and throw to different areas and levels. For detailed information on physical education activities for K–6 children, visit the PE Central website at *www.pecentral.org*.

Promoting Physical Fitness

Children in early childhood are not concerned with physical fitness; instead, they are interested in having fun. Based on this premise, a physical education program for this age group should reflect this interest. The child who is actively involved in fun physical activities will get the same benefits as children in a highly structured physical fitness program. To that end, it is important for K–6 physical educators to understand that programming activities that focus on the enjoyment of moving their bodies is much more important than being groomed for success at a specific event or sport.

Movement education enables the child to make choices of activity and the method they wish to employ. Teachers can structure learning situations so the child can be challenged to develop his or her own means of movement. The teacher is not the center of learning, but offers suggestions and stimulates the learning environment through guided discovery. If the teacher sets standards that are too high for the less talented students, they may become discouraged and lose motivation. On the other hand, if the teacher sets standards that are too low, the more talented students will become bored and also lose interest. Providing an array of options for learners is the best way to facilitate movement games and activities. This way, learners can identify which option or challenges are most appropriate and perform up to their developmental level with little assistance and/or cues from the teacher. Movement education attempts to develop the children's awareness not only of what they are doing but how they are doing it.

To teach a basic or specialized movement skill to a variety of learners, the instructor must present and use explanation, demonstration, and drill. Other students can do demonstrations, provided the teacher monitors the demonstration and gives cues for proper form. Drills are excellent to teach specific skills but can become tedious unless they are done in a creative manner. Using game simulations to practice skills is also an effective method to maintain interest during a practice session. Teachers must remember to use observation and feedback when teaching a skill or activity. Of course, positive feedback is much more conducive to skill acquisition than negative feedback.

Many physical education professionals have advocated for the Teaching Games for Understanding model as a sound philosophy regarding movement games education. It is a socio-constructivist teaching and learning approach to physical education that emphasizes the learners' engagement in the construction of knowledge, skills, and experience. This student-centered model is built upon critical thinking, problem-solving, observation, and debriefing the experience for specific learning outcomes (i.e., teamwork, sportsmanship, and skill performance). Strategies of this model can be implemented across a variety of physical education curriculum including adventure education, cooperative learning, fitness education, tactical games, and sports education.

Curriculum Requirements for Physical Education

The Texas Essential Knowledge and Skills (TEKS) comprises all the curriculum components in the area of Physical Education. Physical Education teachers are expected to implement the prescribed state curriculum (Texas Administrative Code, 2009b). In conjunction with the national initiative, The Texas Essential Knowledge and Skills (TEKS) requires children to demonstrate knowledge and skills for movement that provide the foundation for enjoyment, continued social development through physical activity, and access to a physically active lifestyle. All children are expected to develop muscular strength and endurance of the arms, shoulders, abdomen, back, and legs. They are also expected to become aware of how the muscles, bones, heart, and lungs function in relation to physical activity. The activities and skills for children in K–6 are designed to keep children active, to develop the fitness necessary for appropriate physical development, and to maintain a healthy body and mind. Some of the key skills and activities required in the state K–6 curriculum are listed below (Texas Administrative Code, 2009b).

Kindergarten

Children should be able to:

1. Play with other children within boundaries during games and activities
2. Develop muscular strength and endurance of the arms, shoulders, abdomen, back, and legs such as hanging, hopping, and jumping
3. Demonstrate knowledge of a variety of relationships such as under, over, behind, next to, through, right, left, up, down, forward, backward, and in front of
4. Roll sideways (right or left) without hesitating
5. Toss a ball and catch it before it bounces twice

First Grade

Children should be able to:

1. Demonstrate proper foot patterns in hopping, jumping, skipping, leaping, galloping, and sliding

2. Demonstrate the ability to work with a partner such as leading and following
3. Clap in time to a simple rhythmic beat; create and imitate movement in response to selected rhythms; jump a long rope; and demonstrate on cue key elements in overhand throw, underhand throw, and catch
4. Demonstrate proper foot patterns in hopping, jumping, skipping, leaping, galloping, and sliding
5. Demonstrate control in balancing and traveling activities

Second Grade

Children should be able to:

1. Demonstrate skills of chasing, fleeing, and dodging to avoid or catch others
2. Demonstrate mature forms of walking, hopping, and skipping
3. Demonstrate a variety of relationships in dynamic movement situations such as under, over, behind, next to, through, right, left, up, or down
4. Demonstrate simple stunts that exhibit personal agility such as jumping with one and two foot takeoffs and landing with good control
5. Demonstrate on cue key elements of hand dribble, foot dribble, kick and strike such as striking a balloon or ball with a hand

Third Grade

Children should be able to:

1. Demonstrate mature forms in jogging, running, and leaping
2. Demonstrate control and appropriate form such as curled position and protection of neck in rolling activities
3. Transfer their bodies on and off equipment with good body control such as boxes, benches, stacked mats, horizontal bar, and balance beam
4. Clap echoes in a variety of one measure rhythmical patterns
5. Demonstrate key elements in manipulative skills such as underhand throw, overhand throw, catch, and kick

Fourth Grade

Children should be able to:

1. Change speed during straight, curved, and zigzag pathways
2. Catch a football pass on the run
3. Jump and land for height and distance absorbing force such as bending knees and swinging arms;
4. Perform basic folk dance steps such as schottische (German folk dance), and step-together-step
5. Demonstrate key elements in manipulative skills such as volleying, hand dribble, foot dribble, and punt, also, striking with a body part, racquet, or bat

Fifth Grade

Children should be able to:

1. Demonstrate smooth combinations of fundamental locomotor skills such as running and dodging and hop-step-jump
2. Demonstrate the ability to contrast a partner's movement
3. Identify common phases such as preparation, movement, follow through, or recovery in a variety of movement skills such as a tennis serve, handstand, and free throw
4. Self-monitor the heart rate during exercise
5. Identify potentially dangerous exercises and their adverse effects on the body

Sixth Grade

Children should be able to:

1. Use relationships, levels, speed, direction, and pathways effectively in complex group and individual physical activities such as crouching low for volleyball digs, stretching

high during lay-ups, positioning for a soccer pass, or passing ahead of a receiver

2. Move in time to complex rhythmical patterns such as 3/4 time or 6/8 time
3. Hand and foot dribble while preventing an opponent from stealing the ball
4. Practice in ways that are appropriate for learning skills such as whole/part/whole; shorter practice distributed over time is better than one long session; or practicing is best in game-like conditions
5. Modify games/activities to improve the game/activity

Managing Instruction

Managing a large class of kids in a loud gymnasium or outdoor learning environment is no easy task. Therefore, a major goal of the physical education teacher is to have all students listen to directions prior to activity. The instructions should be short, to the point, and as clear as possible. A teacher who talks longer than 20 seconds during any single instructional period will soon find the class beginning to lose interest. This leads to an environment difficult to manage. For this reason, teachers should alternate short instructional episodes (including one or two points of focus) with longer periods of activity. Minimizing instructional content will reduce both student frustration and difficult situations to manage. Most students and teachers enjoy a learning environment that is organized, efficient, and allows a maximum amount of class time to be devoted to learning skills.

Management behavior routines must be enforced regularly by the instructor (especially early on); otherwise, the environment will always be chaotic and difficult to manage. Effective physical educators identify a consistent keyword to use with learners that commences a new activity (i.e., "Begin" or "Ready Go"). This implies encouraging youngsters to listen to the entire set of instructions before preparing for the next exercise. Since the keyword is not given until all directions have been issued, students cannot begin until they hear the selected keyword. Similarly, a consistent signal should be established for stopping an activity (i.e., "Freeze" or "Clap once… Clap twice… Clap three times…"). Whatever the signal, it must be practiced everyday so learners come to know the signal and it becomes second nature. Using an audio signal (i.e., whistle blast) and a visual signal (i.e., raising the hand overhead) may also be effective, since some youngsters may not hear the audio signal if they are engrossed in loud activity. Whereas a loud audio signal may be used to stop a class, a voice command should always be used to start the class. If children do not respond to these signals, the procedure must be practiced. Remember, if a teacher settles for less than full attention, students will fulfill those expectations of being chaotic and unmanageable.

Physical education teachers should also know how to divide students into teachable groups quickly. Simple games can be used to accomplish this such as "Back to Back" or "Foot to Foot" in which individuals get back to back (or foot to foot, etc.) with a partner as fast as possible. Students without a partner are instructed to go to the center of the teaching area (marked by a cone or spot) to immediately find someone else without a partner. If students are staying near a friend, teachers can tell the class to move throughout space using a locomotor skill and then find a different partner each time the body part is called. If arranging students in groups larger than two people, Whistle Mixer works effectively. When the whistle is blown a certain number of times, students form groups corresponding to the number of whistle blows and sit down to signify that they have the correct number of people in their group.

Physical education teachers need to use a consistent approach for dealing with undesirable behavior. "Time-Out" is generally used to deal with inappropriate behavior. The time-out approach moves youngsters out of the class setting and places them into a designated area when they misbehave. Being placed in the time-out area does not imply that the student is a "bad person," but rather that he/she has forgotten to follow the rules. When placing students in time-out, teachers should communicate to children that they are loved individuals, but their misbehavior is unacceptable, hence, the reason they are in time-out.

To minimize incidence of undesirable behavior, teachers are encouraged to develop a set of expectations and rules for the class. The plan's expectations should be no more than five items, posted in the teaching area for easy reference. The rules should be discussed regularly so children clearly understand what are the expected behaviors and consequences as follows:

First misbehavior—the student is warned quietly on a personal basis to avoid embarrassment.

Second misbehavior—the student is told to go to a designated time-out spot. The student must stay there until ready to reenter the activity and demonstrate the desired behavior.

Third misbehavior—the student goes to time-out for a longer period or the remainder of the period. The reward system is used to reward those students that follow the rules and comply with instructions, and as a way to motivate others to exhibit appropriate behavior.

Adaptive Physical Education

The Americans with Disabilities Act (2009) requires the placement of students in the least restrictive environment. For most "handicapped children," the least restrictive environment is the regular classroom, which includes participation in physical education activities. The challenge in teaching physical education to handicapped children is tailoring activities to fit each child. For example, blind or partially sighted students can participate in dance, and some gymnastic and tumbling activities. These students can also participate in some other activities with modifications. A beeper ball together with verbal cues can be used for T-ball or even for softball. If a beeper is not available, the teacher can put the student in position and assist in aiming and cueing when to hit the ball. For students using assistive devices like walkers or crutches, they can be allowed to hit the ball from a seated position and use the crutch to bat. If the child is unable to run, allow a substitute runner. Many games and activities can be modified for the handicapped child. Sometimes all it takes is a little ingenuity to change activities so handicapped students can enjoy participating.

References

Americans with Disability Act. 2009. Information and technical assistance on the Americans with Disabilities Act. www.usdoj.gov/crt/ada/adahom1.htm (accessed July 16, 2009).

Fitnessgram. 2009. Activity and fitness assessment and personal physical activity management. www.fitnessgram.net/home (accessed on June 29, 2009).

Healthy People 2010. Healthy People Website. www.healthypeople.gov/ (accessed July 16, 2009).

National Association for Sport and Physical Education. 2009. Physical activity guidelines published by the national association for sport and physical education. www.aahperd.org/NASPE/template.cfm?template=ns_index.html (accessed July 2, 2009).

National Institute of Mental Health. 2009. Eating disorders: Facts about eating disorders and the search for solutions. www.nimh.nih.gov/Publicat/eatingdisorders.cfm (accessed June 21, 2009).

PE Central. 2009. The premier website for health and physical education. www.pecentral.org (accessed May 27, 2009).

Shelov, S., and T. Remer. 2009. Caring for baby and young child: Birth to age 5. American Academy of Pediatrics. www.aap.org/publiced/BK0_ChildAbuse.htm (accessed July 8, 2009).

Texas Administrative Code. 2009a. Title 19, Part II Chapter 115. Texas Essential Knowledge and Skills for Health Education. www.tea.state.tx.us/rules/tac/chapter115/index.html (accessed May 22, 2009).

Texas Administrative Code. 2009b. Title 19, Part II Chapter 116. Texas Essential Knowledge and Skills for Physical Education. www.tea.state.tx.us/rules/tac/chapter116/index.html (accessed May 22, 2009).

U.S. Department of Agriculture. 2009. My food pyramid: Steps to a healthier you. www.mypyramid.gov (accessed June 7, 2009).

U.S. Department of Health and Human Services. 2006. Dietary Guidelines for Americans. www.health.gov/DietaryGuidelines/ (accessed June 29, 2009).

Competency 050: Theater

The teacher understands concepts, processes, and skills involved in the creation, appreciation, and evaluation of theater and uses that knowledge to plan and implement effective and engaging theater instruction.

When students are introduced to theater and its inherent creative and critical aspects, a gateway to a new world of perception and experience is opened to them. These perceptual experiences include the physical, emotional, intellectual, aesthetic, social, moral, and spiritual aspects of what it is to be human.

When they are involved in acting out plays students shift their perceptions from self to others through voice, physical action, and connection to others. Perceptions of reality expand as youngsters begin to interpret what they then see on television, at the movies, and on social media.

Fundamentals of Stage Directing

English Language Arts teachers may often serve as directors of school productions. They would find that developing the following skills would be very useful.

Conceptualization involves determining the class's approach to the play and what the play should say to the audience.

Blocking is planning and executing the patterns of onstage movement in a play. In theatrical parlance, the areas of the stage are as follows:

Upstage Right	**Upstage Center**	**Upstage Left**
Right Center	**Center Stage**	**Left Center**
Downstage Right	**Downstage Center**	**Downstage Left**

In this arrangement, "upstage" refers to the back of the stage, "downstage" refers to the section closest to the audience, and "left" and "right" refer to the actors' left and right as they face the audience.

Successful blocking grabs the audience's attention, unfolds the events with increasing urgency, and focuses the audience's attention on individual actors or small groups when necessary. For example, if a director of a realistic play wants to focus audience attention on a single actor without using special lighting, he or she might have the actor make a sudden movement, such as standing or sitting, or make a sound, such as a loud sigh or the thud of a chair on the stage.

Tempo is the pace of a play's movement and dialogue. A director should strive to maintain a brisk pace that moves the action along without confusing the audience. Every plot requires changes of tempo to create focus on dramatic high points.

Dramatic arc is the overall movement of the play from introduction and rising action to falling action and conclusion. A successful performance finds the appropriate rhythm of the play and follows it through the main stages of dramatic arc.

Exposition/Introduction–Introduces the main characters and sets the scene.

Inciting Incident–Presents the moment when a conflict arises, which will drive the rest of the story.

Rising Action–The intensity of events increases as the conflict grows.

Climax–The turning point occurs in which the situation changes for better or worse.

Falling Action–Suspense is prolonged as difficulties are confronted and questions are answered. The conflict often is overcome in this stage.

Resolution/Denouement–The remaining issues are settled. A sense of normalcy or peace is reinstated. Characters are reconciled and actions are validated. Sometimes future possibilities are presented.

Dramatic Performance

When initiating work on a dramatic production, teachers lead students to:

- understand and apply the creative process to the fundamental skills of acting and directing.
- understand and apply the creative process to skills of design and technical production.
- analyze and assess the characteristics and meanings of traditional and modern forms of drama.

Approaches to Acting

Actors try to portray a character in ways that fit the overall intentions of the play's author and the director. Actors must read the entire play carefully—several times, if possible—to understand the characters. Depending on the age of the actor, the teacher might need to highlight each actor's lines with different colors. Again, depending on the age of the students, the teacher may choose to use cue cards instead of having each actor memorize his or her lines. Each student actor should strive to become the character by thinking about that character's background, motivation, and emotional makeup. The actor should consider what gestures, movements, and speech inflections best express the character's personality. If the actor has done the background work and feels comfortable in the role, his or her performance will be more believable to the audience.

To help the actors develop their roles, the teacher can have them do improvisations in which they speak or interact with each other spontaneously in character. An actor can also practice speaking precisely, or correct elocution; projecting his or her voice so the audience can hear each line, speaking with an accent or different intonations, and performing various kinds of movements that suggest character traits. Storytelling, reciting poetry, and performing dramatic monologues also help improve diction and oral performance skills.

When rehearsing a scene with others, the actor needs to consider the following.

Relationship: How does the character feel about the other person or people in the scene? Does the character feel love or hatred? feel pity or remorse?

Conflict: The basis of every plot is conflict, so the actor must focus on the conflict in every scene. One character wants something, the other character wants the opposite—and only one can be successful.

Motivation: What background details account for the character's actions? Deciding on motivation will help the actor develop a performance that is consistent from start to finish.

Setting: Where is the character during each scene and how does the setting affect his or her reactions or emotions? What other people are around? Does the character feel safe or threatened?

Integrating Theater into Other Subjects

When creating long-term lesson plans, the teacher needs to be alert for instances where the planned dramatic production can be seamlessly echoed in another subject matter. This inclusion enlivens other subjects that might not be as appealing to the class. For instance, in set design, the use of mathematical formulas ensure that the individual pieces are in correct proportion to each other. Reading assignments might be about famous costume designers, similar plays, or actors who have played the youngster's part. Students could write about the specific roles either onstage or behind the scenes for which they are responsible. Social studies lesson plans can focus on the social and political issues presented during the time period of the play in production.

Stage Crew and Principles of Theatrical Design

The **stage crew** performs the various duties necessary for a successful performance. These duties involve the principles of theatrical design.

The *set designer* creates the background, scenery, and décor for the production.

The *costume designer* researches and designs the costumes for the characters.

The *lighting designer* controls the lighting. This involves manipulating the key light, or main light; the fill light, or the light that softens harsh shadows created by the key light; and the back light, which is used to visually separate the actors downstage from the background.

The *sound engineer* prepares and performs or directs sound effects, off stage voices, and incidental music.

The *props person* researches, locates, and distributes the various "props," or stage properties, necessary for the production.

The *stage manager* takes charge of stage instructions, oversees the stage crew, and handles the details of rehearsal.

Origins of Theater

As long as humans have been capable of communication, they have probably employed some form of drama and performance. Cave paintings supply evidence for the early use of costumes and masks to bolster mimetic performances, which, either as magic or prayer, functioned to encourage the productivity of nature.

Greek plays were probably ritualistic performances that might involve, for instance, a conflict between winter and summer, and that would include a combat, a death, and a resurrection. Later, Thespis, known as the founder of classical **tragedy** brought these early performances to the level of drama. He is credited with inventing a new breed of performer, the actor, who would engage the audience by impersonating one or more characters between the dances of a chorus.

China. The first performances in China were recorded about 1500 B.C.E., during the Shang Dynasty. Dance, music, and ritual were important elements in Chinese life. Temples were associated with performers and records of a raised stage have been found by archaeologists.

Medieval Theater in Europe originally began as a springtime religious observance. It was a communal and public event that drew large audiences to celebrate the teachings of the Old and New Testaments of the Bible. Religious theater was restricted by such elements as the liturgy, church calendar, and ecclesiastical dress. **Morality** plays were also performed during this time. They represented the conscience of the Middle Ages. After approximately 200 years, drama moved out of the church because the troupes were too restricted by the church's ruling. Historians document that women never performed in medieval plays for two reasons. First, male-dominated, rigidly hierarchical groups like clergy, craftsmen, and merchants predominated. Secondly, it was believed that boys with trained voices could produce more volume than women. During the Elizabethan era in England, theater was used for the first time as a commercial enterprise. The stage became lavish with detailed scenery and colorful costumes. There were two basic types of costumes, contemporary and symbolic. Symbolic costumes were worn to distinguish the important characters from the ordinary people. William Shakespeare created enduring characters and addressed timeless questions that still resonate for us today.

Italy's professional theater evolved from *commedia dell'arte* in the mid-1500s. This was a popular form of entertainment akin to street theater, designed to appeal to a mass audience.

France. Costumes, hairstyles, and makeup on the French stage mirrored popular fashions on the street or at court (1500–1700).

England's Charles II (1630–1685) marked the start of the modern proscenium playhouse, and repertory companies flourished.

Contemporary Theater. Many successful playwrights emerged from nineteenth-century Europe. These playwrights (influenced by Darwin and Comte) introduced stage realism and naturalism. In Russia, Konstantin Stanislavsky (1863–1938) developed an acting technique that came to be called "The Method" on account of its broad impact on the schooling of Western actors. Stanislavsky's approach to actor training was essentially psychological. In 1968, censorship of British theater was abolished. Modern American plays challenged theater audiences as well.

Getting Started

The use of drama can, and will, enrich learning at any grade level. Beginning experiences can include an activity you might call, "Follow Your Little Toe." Youngsters are directed to point their little toe and follow it around the room, using it as if it were an eye. A knee, nose, or ear could also be used to lead them to discover new ways of moving.

Simple improvisation, a loosely formatted activity in which students are given a location or a situation to create a scene, can be applied to a social studies or even a health class topic.

The "Story of Your Name" can be a homework assignment to be presented to the group, or an "improv" assignment in which the youngsters think of and deliver either a real story or an imaginary one. The rest of the group decides if it is real or not.

Other activities could include "Around the Fire," during which the class sits around an imaginary fire while the teacher tells the story of a myth (preferably without a book) and later gives openers for the youngsters to attempt, such as: "Where Clouds Come From," or "Giraffes Didn't Always Have Long Necks."

For social studies, teachers can create a large map of the United States (a string outline), preferably in a large space. Depending upon the class sizes, some activities can include: moving to the place where they were born; settling at the place from which their ancestors came; indicating places to which they have traveled.

With "Props in a Box" the teacher displays a collection of props from which a student selects three. That student then tells a story utilizing all three props. To help the students understand the use of perceived status throughout the world, the teacher can pin a playing card onto the back of each student and have them treat each other according to the status conferred on them by the level of the card. Or, each child may be handed a card, which is kept secret, and they themselves act in their own perceived status role. Starting with such simple activities would encourage growth to more sophisticated drama presentations.

Benefits

Good dramatic experience develops fluency in the reading of topics from all curriculum areas. Reading expression and performance gestures, stage presence and concentration, carry over during the rest of the students' lives. It is well documented that students' motivation dies as they progress through the grades. Drama brings the challenge to be creative and to have fun.

Using drama allows the students to take risks with language and helps them to connect their emotions with their cognitive abilities. Being involved in drama helps the youngsters to clear their perception of reality versus television, movies, and electronic communication. It also, very simply, allows them out of their seats.

ESL classes especially benefit from the use of drama because it gives students an opportunity to address, practice, and integrate reading, writing, speaking, and listening. Drama enriches youngsters' feelings and experience of the language.

The fun of drama beautifully influences the motivation of all students.

Rehearsal Strategies

Running a production means that teachers also deal with scheduling and organizing resources. It helps to list the resources available to the production. The teacher may need to check with school administrators and other teachers about the budget, equipment, and availability of school facilities. The teacher can then set priorities about choice of play, auditions, rehearsals, and performance.

Selecting a play. The play should be age appropriate for the students and approved by school administrators. Also, the stage should have the necessary technical capabilities for the production.

Holding auditions. Teachers encourage students to try out for the various roles in the play. Often, teachers will steer leading roles to older students who are capable of performing the parts, but this is optional.

Organizing a stage crew. The production will require crewmembers capable of handling sound, lighting, props, costumes, and other technical details. Students who act in one production may take stage crew positions in another.

Rehearsing. The teacher should oversee all the details of preparing the production, from holding rehearsals with the actors to arranging for stage crewmembers to practice their duties. The teacher must also monitor the students whose job is to acquire props, build sets, and create costumes. For a musical play, the teacher should insist that musicians join several rehearsals as well.

Answer Sheet

1. Ⓐ Ⓑ Ⓒ Ⓓ
2. Ⓐ Ⓑ Ⓒ Ⓓ
3. Ⓐ Ⓑ Ⓒ Ⓓ
4. Ⓐ Ⓑ Ⓒ Ⓓ
5. Ⓐ Ⓑ Ⓒ Ⓓ
6. Ⓐ Ⓑ Ⓒ Ⓓ
7. Ⓐ Ⓑ Ⓒ Ⓓ
8. Ⓐ Ⓑ Ⓒ Ⓓ
9. Ⓐ Ⓑ Ⓒ Ⓓ
10. Ⓐ Ⓑ Ⓒ Ⓓ
11. Ⓐ Ⓑ Ⓒ Ⓓ
12. Ⓐ Ⓑ Ⓒ Ⓓ
13. Ⓐ Ⓑ Ⓒ Ⓓ
14. Ⓐ Ⓑ Ⓒ Ⓓ
15. Ⓐ Ⓑ Ⓒ Ⓓ
16. Ⓐ Ⓑ Ⓒ Ⓓ
17. Ⓐ Ⓑ Ⓒ Ⓓ
18. Ⓐ Ⓑ Ⓒ Ⓓ
19. Ⓐ Ⓑ Ⓒ Ⓓ
20. Ⓐ Ⓑ Ⓒ Ⓓ
21. Ⓐ Ⓑ Ⓒ Ⓓ
22. Ⓐ Ⓑ Ⓒ Ⓓ
23. Ⓐ Ⓑ Ⓒ Ⓓ
24. Ⓐ Ⓑ Ⓒ Ⓓ
25. Ⓐ Ⓑ Ⓒ Ⓓ
26. Ⓐ Ⓑ Ⓒ Ⓓ
27. Ⓐ Ⓑ Ⓒ Ⓓ
28. Ⓐ Ⓑ Ⓒ Ⓓ
29. Ⓐ Ⓑ Ⓒ Ⓓ
30. Ⓐ Ⓑ Ⓒ Ⓓ
31. Ⓐ Ⓑ Ⓒ Ⓓ
32. Ⓐ Ⓑ Ⓒ Ⓓ
33. Ⓐ Ⓑ Ⓒ Ⓓ
34. Ⓐ Ⓑ Ⓒ Ⓓ
35. Ⓐ Ⓑ Ⓒ Ⓓ
36. Ⓐ Ⓑ Ⓒ Ⓓ
37. Ⓐ Ⓑ Ⓒ Ⓓ
38. Ⓐ Ⓑ Ⓒ Ⓓ
39. Ⓐ Ⓑ Ⓒ Ⓓ
40. Ⓐ Ⓑ Ⓒ Ⓓ
41. Ⓐ Ⓑ Ⓒ Ⓓ
42. Ⓐ Ⓑ Ⓒ Ⓓ
43. Ⓐ Ⓑ Ⓒ Ⓓ
44. Ⓐ Ⓑ Ⓒ Ⓓ
45. Ⓐ Ⓑ Ⓒ Ⓓ
46. Ⓐ Ⓑ Ⓒ Ⓓ
47. Ⓐ Ⓑ Ⓒ Ⓓ
48. Ⓐ Ⓑ Ⓒ Ⓓ
49. Ⓐ Ⓑ Ⓒ Ⓓ
50. Ⓐ Ⓑ Ⓒ Ⓓ
51. Ⓐ Ⓑ Ⓒ Ⓓ
52. Ⓐ Ⓑ Ⓒ Ⓓ
53. Ⓐ Ⓑ Ⓒ Ⓓ
54. Ⓐ Ⓑ Ⓒ Ⓓ
55. Ⓐ Ⓑ Ⓒ Ⓓ
56. Ⓐ Ⓑ Ⓒ Ⓓ
57. Ⓐ Ⓑ Ⓒ Ⓓ
58. Ⓐ Ⓑ Ⓒ Ⓓ
59. Ⓐ Ⓑ Ⓒ Ⓓ
60. Ⓐ Ⓑ Ⓒ Ⓓ
61. Ⓐ Ⓑ Ⓒ Ⓓ
62. Ⓐ Ⓑ Ⓒ Ⓓ
63. Ⓐ Ⓑ Ⓒ Ⓓ
64. Ⓐ Ⓑ Ⓒ Ⓓ
65. Ⓐ Ⓑ Ⓒ Ⓓ
66. Ⓐ Ⓑ Ⓒ Ⓓ
67. Ⓐ Ⓑ Ⓒ Ⓓ
68. Ⓐ Ⓑ Ⓒ Ⓓ
69. Ⓐ Ⓑ Ⓒ Ⓓ
70. Ⓐ Ⓑ Ⓒ Ⓓ
71. Ⓐ Ⓑ Ⓒ Ⓓ
72. Ⓐ Ⓑ Ⓒ Ⓓ
73. Ⓐ Ⓑ Ⓒ Ⓓ
74. Ⓐ Ⓑ Ⓒ Ⓓ
75. Ⓐ Ⓑ Ⓒ Ⓓ
76. Ⓐ Ⓑ Ⓒ Ⓓ
77. Ⓐ Ⓑ Ⓒ Ⓓ
78. Ⓐ Ⓑ Ⓒ Ⓓ
79. Ⓐ Ⓑ Ⓒ Ⓓ
80. Ⓐ Ⓑ Ⓒ Ⓓ
81. Ⓐ Ⓑ Ⓒ Ⓓ
82. Ⓐ Ⓑ Ⓒ Ⓓ
83. Ⓐ Ⓑ Ⓒ Ⓓ
84. Ⓐ Ⓑ Ⓒ Ⓓ
85. Ⓐ Ⓑ Ⓒ Ⓓ
86. Ⓐ Ⓑ Ⓒ Ⓓ
87. Ⓐ Ⓑ Ⓒ Ⓓ
88. Ⓐ Ⓑ Ⓒ Ⓓ
89. Ⓐ Ⓑ Ⓒ Ⓓ
90. Ⓐ Ⓑ Ⓒ Ⓓ
91. Ⓐ Ⓑ Ⓒ Ⓓ
92. Ⓐ Ⓑ Ⓒ Ⓓ
93. Ⓐ Ⓑ Ⓒ Ⓓ
94. Ⓐ Ⓑ Ⓒ Ⓓ
95. Ⓐ Ⓑ Ⓒ Ⓓ
96. Ⓐ Ⓑ Ⓒ Ⓓ
97. Ⓐ Ⓑ Ⓒ Ⓓ
98. Ⓐ Ⓑ Ⓒ Ⓓ
99. Ⓐ Ⓑ Ⓒ Ⓓ
100. Ⓐ Ⓑ Ⓒ Ⓓ
101. Ⓐ Ⓑ Ⓒ Ⓓ
102. Ⓐ Ⓑ Ⓒ Ⓓ
103. Ⓐ Ⓑ Ⓒ Ⓓ
104. Ⓐ Ⓑ Ⓒ Ⓓ
105. Ⓐ Ⓑ Ⓒ Ⓓ
106. Ⓐ Ⓑ Ⓒ Ⓓ
107. Ⓐ Ⓑ Ⓒ Ⓓ
108. Ⓐ Ⓑ Ⓒ Ⓓ
109. Ⓐ Ⓑ Ⓒ Ⓓ
110. Ⓐ Ⓑ Ⓒ Ⓓ
111. Ⓐ Ⓑ Ⓒ Ⓓ
112. Ⓐ Ⓑ Ⓒ Ⓓ
113. Ⓐ Ⓑ Ⓒ Ⓓ
114. Ⓐ Ⓑ Ⓒ Ⓓ
115. Ⓐ Ⓑ Ⓒ Ⓓ
116. Ⓐ Ⓑ Ⓒ Ⓓ
117. Ⓐ Ⓑ Ⓒ Ⓓ
118. Ⓐ Ⓑ Ⓒ Ⓓ
119. Ⓐ Ⓑ Ⓒ Ⓓ
120. Ⓐ Ⓑ Ⓒ Ⓓ
121. Ⓐ Ⓑ Ⓒ Ⓓ
122. Ⓐ Ⓑ Ⓒ Ⓓ
123. Ⓐ Ⓑ Ⓒ Ⓓ
124. Ⓐ Ⓑ Ⓒ Ⓓ
125. Ⓐ Ⓑ Ⓒ Ⓓ
126. Ⓐ Ⓑ Ⓒ Ⓓ
127. Ⓐ Ⓑ Ⓒ Ⓓ
128. Ⓐ Ⓑ Ⓒ Ⓓ
129. Ⓐ Ⓑ Ⓒ Ⓓ
130. Ⓐ Ⓑ Ⓒ Ⓓ
131. Ⓐ Ⓑ Ⓒ Ⓓ
132. Ⓐ Ⓑ Ⓒ Ⓓ
133. Ⓐ Ⓑ Ⓒ Ⓓ
134. Ⓐ Ⓑ Ⓒ Ⓓ
135. Ⓐ Ⓑ Ⓒ Ⓓ
136. Ⓐ Ⓑ Ⓒ Ⓓ
137. Ⓐ Ⓑ Ⓒ Ⓓ
138. Ⓐ Ⓑ Ⓒ Ⓓ
139. Ⓐ Ⓑ Ⓒ Ⓓ
140. Ⓐ Ⓑ Ⓒ Ⓓ
141. Ⓐ Ⓑ Ⓒ Ⓓ
142. Ⓐ Ⓑ Ⓒ Ⓓ
143. Ⓐ Ⓑ Ⓒ Ⓓ
144. Ⓐ Ⓑ Ⓒ Ⓓ
145. Ⓐ Ⓑ Ⓒ Ⓓ
146. Ⓐ Ⓑ Ⓒ Ⓓ
147. Ⓐ Ⓑ Ⓒ Ⓓ
148. Ⓐ Ⓑ Ⓒ Ⓓ
149. Ⓐ Ⓑ Ⓒ Ⓓ
150. Ⓐ Ⓑ Ⓒ Ⓓ
151. Ⓐ Ⓑ Ⓒ Ⓓ
152. Ⓐ Ⓑ Ⓒ Ⓓ
153. Ⓐ Ⓑ Ⓒ Ⓓ
154. Ⓐ Ⓑ Ⓒ Ⓓ
155. Ⓐ Ⓑ Ⓒ Ⓓ
156. Ⓐ Ⓑ Ⓒ Ⓓ
157. Ⓐ Ⓑ Ⓒ Ⓓ
158. Ⓐ Ⓑ Ⓒ Ⓓ
159. Ⓐ Ⓑ Ⓒ Ⓓ
160. Ⓐ Ⓑ Ⓒ Ⓓ
161. Ⓐ Ⓑ Ⓒ Ⓓ
162. Ⓐ Ⓑ Ⓒ Ⓓ
163. Ⓐ Ⓑ Ⓒ Ⓓ
164. Ⓐ Ⓑ Ⓒ Ⓓ
165. Ⓐ Ⓑ Ⓒ Ⓓ
166. Ⓐ Ⓑ Ⓒ Ⓓ
167. Ⓐ Ⓑ Ⓒ Ⓓ
168. Ⓐ Ⓑ Ⓒ Ⓓ
169. Ⓐ Ⓑ Ⓒ Ⓓ
170. Ⓐ Ⓑ Ⓒ Ⓓ
171. Ⓐ Ⓑ Ⓒ Ⓓ
172. Ⓐ Ⓑ Ⓒ Ⓓ
173. Ⓐ Ⓑ Ⓒ Ⓓ
174. Ⓐ Ⓑ Ⓒ Ⓓ
175. Ⓐ Ⓑ Ⓒ Ⓓ
176. Ⓐ Ⓑ Ⓒ Ⓓ
177. Ⓐ Ⓑ Ⓒ Ⓓ
178. Ⓐ Ⓑ Ⓒ Ⓓ
179. Ⓐ Ⓑ Ⓒ Ⓓ
180. Ⓐ Ⓑ Ⓒ Ⓓ
181. Ⓐ Ⓑ Ⓒ Ⓓ
182. Ⓐ Ⓑ Ⓒ Ⓓ
183. Ⓐ Ⓑ Ⓒ Ⓓ
184. Ⓐ Ⓑ Ⓒ Ⓓ
185. Ⓐ Ⓑ Ⓒ Ⓓ

Bilingual Generalist EC-6 (192) Practice Test

Questions 1–185

Instructions: Select the best answer.

5-hour time limit

1. Transitional bilingual education (TBE) is the program of choice for most school districts in the nation. This program is identified as a subtractive and early-exit program. Identify the rationale for the popularity of this program:

   (A) There is extensive research to support the effectiveness of the program.
   (B) The program allows for the mainstreaming of students in a relatively short period of time.
   (C) The program promotes the maintenance of both languages.
   (D) The program has been endorsed by legislators in Texas and in the United States.

2. The main difference between the dual language immersion programs in Canada and the structured immersion programs in the United States is that

   (A) contrary to the Canadian programs, the U.S. programs were designed for middle-class students.
   (B) the Canadian programs were designed to teach French and the American programs were designed to teach English.
   (C) the U.S. programs lead to bilingualism while the Canadian programs lead to monolingualism.
   (D) the Canadian programs lead to additive bilingualism while the U.S. programs lead to subtractive bilingualism.

3. School districts need to be sure that students have the communication skills at the social and academic levels to be successful before they are exited from the bilingual program. To ensure that students have the cognitive and linguistic skills to be successful, the Language Proficiency Assessment Committee (LPAC) evaluates the results of the following instruments:

   (A) a state-developed criterion-referenced test, a language proficiency test, and a norm-referenced achievement test
   (B) the Texas Observation Protocol (TOP), the STAAR, and the California Achievement Test (CAT)
   (C) a language proficiency test, the Reading Proficiency Test of English (RPTE), and the Texas Observation Protocol (TOP)
   (D) the Iowa Test of Basic Skills (ITBS), the Idea Proficiency Test (IPT), and the California Achievement Test (CAT)

4. Identify the similarities between the Language Proficiency Assessment Committee (LPAC) and the Admission Review and Dismissal (ARD) Committee.

   (A) Both are mandated by the federal Bilingual Education law.
   (B) The committees regulate admission and dismissal from the bilingual education and special education programs, respectively.
   (C) Both committees should have at least one parent, one legislator, and teachers.
   (D) The committees are regulated by the Individuals with Disability Education Act (IDEA).

5. One of the key provisions of the No Child Left Behind (NCLB) Act in regard to the education of English language learners is to

   (A) allow local autonomy in the implementation of services.
   (B) empower parents and children.
   (C) allow control of the federal government over the education process.
   (D) promote bilingualism in the United States.

6. In the transitional bilingual education (TBE) model, ESL is used as

   (A) a component of the program.
   (B) the program of choice to teach the content areas.
   (C) a pullout system to promote English development.
   (D) a way to avoid the use of L1 to teach the content areas.

7. Identify the statements that best describe TBE programs in the United States.

   (A) They are research-based and promote language maintenance.
   (B) They use native language instruction in conjunction with ESL instruction.
   (C) They promote bilingual and multicultural education.
   (D) They are considered late-exit and subtractive in nature.

8. The developmental bilingual education (DBE) program began in the 1970s as an alternative to the TBE model. These two programs might appear similar, but they have one key difference. What is the main difference between the two programs?

   (A) Contrary to the DBE program, TBE is considered a remedial program that promotes the maintenance of L1 and L2.
   (B) Contrary to the TBE program, the DBE is a late-exit program designed to maintain L1 and L2.
   (C) Contrary to the DBE program, TBE is an early-exit program designed to promote English and Spanish development among ELLs.
   (D) Contrary to the DBE program, TBE promotes literacy development in L1 and promotes the transfer of skills from L1 to L2.

9. In the last few years, two-way dual language programs are receiving support from mainstream groups. The main reason for this popularity is because the program

   (A) allows for the maintenance of L1 and L2.
   (B) allows the inclusion of children from mainstream groups.
   (C) is supported by the U.S. Department of Education.
   (D) is grounded in solid scientific research.

10. The key disadvantage of the pullout approach to teach English to ELLs is that children

    (A) might feel embarrassed about being placed in the ESL program.
    (B) might feel uncomfortable spending most of the time in mainstream classrooms.
    (C) can fall behind academically when they are pulled out for ESL instruction.
    (D) will not be able to learn English using this approach.

11. Convergent research shows that sheltered English instruction is more appropriate for students who are

    (A) field independent and have a strong foundation in L1.
    (B) at the intermediate or advanced proficiency level in English.

(C) native speakers of a language other than Spanish.
(D) already literate in their native language.

12. Traditionally, newcomer programs are designed to address the language and cultural needs of students

(A) from low socioeconomic backgrounds.
(B) from nontraditional backgrounds without prior schooling.
(C) who are from non-Spanish-speaking backgrounds.
(D) who are at the intermediate or advanced level of English proficiency.

13. The theory that best describes how the bilingual child organizes information in the brain is

(A) the common underlying proficiency.
(B) the separate underlying proficiency.
(C) the separate balloons theory.
(D) basic interpersonal communication skills.

14. Identify the main contribution of the landmark case of *Lau* v. *Nichols*:

(A) It mandated the creation of a bilingual education program in San Francisco.
(B) It empowered the Office of Civil Rights (OCR) to force school districts to provide better education to linguistic minority students.
(C) It guided other courts to find in favor of bilingual education.
(D) It resulted in the signing of a federal law mandating bilingual education in the United States.

15. As a result of the American Institute of Research (AIR) study of 1981,

(A) bilingual education was eliminated in California.
(B) the structured immersion program was introduced as a program option for ELLs.
(C) the Bilingual Education Act mandated dual language immersion for school districts in the nation.
(D) the Bilingual Education Act prohibited the use of federal funding to create transitional bilingual education programs.

16. The language acquisition process is affected by at least three main variables: sociocultural factors, language development, and academic development. Identify the most important sociocultural factors that can affect the acquisition of a second language in the United States.

(A) Self-esteem and the socioeconomic status of the native English-speaking groups
(B) The perceived social and psychological distance between the two groups
(C) Prejudice against the new group and the economic impact of social programs for ELLs
(D) Past injustices committed against the new group and the dropout rate in the district

17. To ensure cognitive growth and academic success in the second language, students should

(A) be exposed to a culture-free curriculum.
(B) be exposed to the importance of racial and linguistic harmony.
(C) be allowed to reach the threshold level in L1.
(D) become fully assimilated to the American way of life and the English language.

18. Identify one of the key characteristics of the first-language acquisition process.

(A) It is a lifelong process that usually ends around puberty.
(B) It is acquired subconsciously in contextualized and meaningful situations.
(C) The language is learned in meaningful situations with the use of direct corrective feedback from adults and caregivers.
(D) During the first two years, the language is taught deductively in a very supportive environment.

19. Identify the statement that best summarizes the research findings associated with the development of proficiency in L2 and the age of initial exposure to the language.

    (A) Children exposed to L2 before puberty develop near-native pronunciation.
    (B) Given the appropriate instruction, children who are exposed to L2 after puberty will develop similar language proficiency as those children who came into contact at earlier ages.
    (C) Children exposed to L2 after puberty master pronunciation, grammar, and reading better than younger children do.
    (D) Children may have advantages over adults in the mastery of pronunciation, but adults might have advantages in the acquisition of the abstract components of language.

20. According to Stephen Krashen, ELLs go through specific stages of second-language acquisition. These stages are preproduction, early production, speech emergence, and intermediate and advanced fluency. Identify the stage that students begin to understand written information accompanied by concrete objects and based on prior experiences.

    (A) Preproduction
    (B) Early production
    (C) Speech emergence
    (D) Intermediate and advanced fluency

21. Effective approaches for teaching English as a second language are

    (A) student-centered and communication driven.
    (B) sequenced based on the complexity of the grammatical structures and are teacher-controlled.
    (C) geared toward grammaticality with little emphasis on communication.
    (D) teacher-centered and multicultural in nature.

22. The language experience approach is a method developed to teach

    (A) English as a second and foreign language.
    (B) reading to language minority students.
    (C) writing skills for TAKS.
    (D) metacognitive strategies.

23. Identify the statement that best represents the rationale for the implementation of initial reading instruction in the student's native language.

    (A) Reading skills are transferable from L1 to L2.
    (B) Reading skills are identical in L1 and L2.
    (C) Reading skills are confusing for English language learners (ELLs).
    (D) Reading skills affect the cognitive process in bilingual students.

24. Healthy young children acquire their first language in natural settings with little direct language instruction. In the formal classroom environment, these conditions might be difficult to replicate. However, there are ESL methods that have attempted to replicate the L1 language acquisition process. These methods are

    (A) the language experience approach (LEA) and the community language method (CLM).
    (B) the total physical response (TPR) and the audio-lingual method (ALM).
    (C) the natural method (NM) and the total physical response (TPR).
    (D) the grammar translation method (GTM) and the direct method (DM).

Use the information in this scenario to answer the question that follows:

Scenario: Mike and Carla are fifth-grade bilingual students who were exited from the program a year ago. Both spent three years in the bilingual program, and performed well socially and academically while in the program. After a year in the regular program, Mike is performing well, as evidenced by his passing score on the most recent STAAR test. On the other hand, Carla is doing fine socially but not that well academically. She has difficulties handling the academic requirements in the regular English classroom. She feels depressed and wants to go back to the security of the bilingual education program.

25. Identify the statement that might explain the reasons for the difficulties that Carla is experiencing in the regular English classroom.

    (A) She mastered the basic interpersonal skills (BICS) but not the cognitive academic language proficiency (CALP) of the language.
    (B) She needs to go back to the bilingual classroom.
    (C) She does not have the verbal intelligence needed to do well in the regular program.
    (D) She mastered the CALP but still needs additional training to master BICS.

26. The development of second language proficiency is best achieved when

    (A) the language instruction leads to the development of functional communication skills in L2.
    (B) the language is taught deductively by involving students with activities in which they use language and derive language principles in a conscious manner.
    (C) instruction is contextualized and presented together with meaningful memorization drills.
    (D) students are exposed to idiomatic expressions in English and tongue twisters to facilitate communication.

Use the information in this scenario to answer the question that follows:

Scenario: Ms. Fuentes is a bilingual third-grade teacher in El Monte ISD. In her class, she has students of different English- and Spanish-speaking proficiencies. Every morning she reads from a Spanish reader that contains stories about the different ethnic and linguistic groups represented in the school community. Students are instructed to close their eyes and listen to the story. She uses dramatic reading and different tones of voice to highlight important parts of the story and to make the story more interesting. After this activity, she asks questions about the story. Later, she allows students opportunities to read the story silently on their own to identify the gist of the story.

27. What language skill(s) does Ms. Fuentes emphasize through dramatic reading?

    (A) listening and reading comprehension
    (B) reading comprehension
    (C) listening, speaking, reading, and writing
    (D) listening comprehension

28. Identify the theoretical framework that best describes how a native language is learned.

    (A) Language learning appears to be the result of some combination of innate ability and environmental influences.
    (B) Language is learned through imitation of older siblings, parents, and caregivers.
    (C) Humans learn languages in meaningful contexts and with reinforcement in the form of direct corrections.
    (D) Humans are innately endowed with fully developed language that is stored in the left hemisphere of the brain.

29. Marcos is a five-year-old student in the process of first language acquisition. He often produces statements like: This lollipop is the *bestest* Mom. Based on this speech sample, this child is

    (A) applying language rules.
    (B) experiencing language interference.
    (C) applying the concepts from L1 to L2.
    (D) imitating the speech sample of cartoons on television.

30. One of the most effective strategies or methods for students in the preproduction stage of language development is the total physical response (TPR). In addition to this command-based approach, teachers can promote language development by

    (A) the use of direct teaching instruction on the structure of the language.
    (B) modeling the language and contextualizing instruction through the use of concrete objects.
    (C) using questions that call for one short answer, like yes or no, and either-or questions.
    (D) using questions that call for open-ended answers.

31. Identify the most appropriate evaluation techniques that promote self-directed learning for ESL students.

(A) In the writing samples of beginner English language learners (ELLs), discuss the source of the problem and allow students time to figure out the type of correction(s) needed.
(B) In activities designed to polish the English pronunciation of advanced students, record their speech electronically and allow sufficient time for them to evaluate their own performance.
(C) In communication activities, provide immediate, specific, corrective feedback, emphasizing the areas in which improvement is needed.
(D) In communication activities, provide direct feedback and guide students to produce Standard English.

Use the information in this scenario to answer questions 32 and 33:

Scenario: Margarita is a limited English-proficient student at Cesar Chávez Elementary. She is fluent and literate in her native language, Spanish. She is experiencing academic problems in school and was referred for testing. A certified bilingual (Spanish-English) diagnostician administered the test. The diagnostician used a state-approved standardized achievement test to evaluate the child. Margarita scored 25 percent on the test. Based on this score, she was retested two weeks later and scored at 69 percent. The diagnostician was very puzzled by the results and retested her the following week. This time Margarita scored at 15 percent.

32. Based on Margarita's performance on the test, identify the key components of the testing process that must be evaluated before placement decisions are made.

(A) The reliability of the test
(B) The credentials of the diagnostician
(C) The accuracy of the testing instrument
(D) The content of the testing instrument

33. In addition to the results of the state-mandated instruments, what else should the LPAC consider before making placement decisions?

(A) results of the language proficiency tests in L1
(B) evaluation and input from peers
(C) formal evaluations conducted by parents
(D) the medical history of the child and input from parents

34. When analyzing and interpreting assessment data from culturally and linguistically diverse (CLD) students, assessors must take into account that

(A) the main objective of assessment is to make students feel valued and wanted in school.
(B) students go through different stages of development, and these stages should not affect the way that children are assessed.
(C) the students might express potential differently due to linguistic and cultural influences.
(D) students may have culture and language deficits that can preclude them from effective participation in the testing process.

35. One of the key problems associated with the use of standardized tests to measure the intelligence of culturally and linguistically diverse (CLD) students in grades 3 and up is that these tests

(A) are designed to measure achievement as opposed to intelligence and potential.
(B) are designed to measure content that has not been covered in class.
(C) overemphasize logic and mathematical skills at the expense of other indicators of intelligence.
(D) require a specific cultural framework and knowledge of academic language for students to be successful.

36. Modern assessment approaches for culturally and linguistically diverse (CLD) students use multiple assessment measures and contain the following key characteristic(s):

(A) The history of the physical development of the child and evidence of the legal status of the parent(s) in the country.

(B) Instruments are administered using Spanish.
(C) Instruments are validated for the population in question.
(D) A multidisciplinary team of professionals evaluates the data.

37. Identify the statement that best describes the value of portfolio assessment.

(A) It allows the collection of students' work throughout their schooling in the United States.
(B) It provides the opportunity to compete with other students.
(C) It provides teachers with an opportunity to collect confidential information about students.
(D) It provides students with a sense of ownership and participation in the assessment process.

38. Effective assessment practices generally share the following guiding principle:

(A) They are child-centered, ongoing, and collected as part of daily instruction.
(B) They are summative in nature and collected through instruments approved by the state.
(C) They are restricted to data gathered by competent bilingual diagnosticians.
(D) They emphasize student weaknesses and should promote self-monitoring.

39. Identify the statement that best describes the Texas Primary Reading Inventory (TPRI) and the Reading Proficiency Test of English (RPTE).

(A) Both instruments assess English reading development for different grade levels.
(B) Both instruments assess English and Spanish reading development.
(C) The TPRI assesses English reading development for ELLs, and the RPTE does the same for Spanish-speaking students.
(D) The TPRI assesses reading development for English dominant students in grades K–2, and the RPTE does the same for ELLs in grades 3 and up.

40. English language learners might have problems understanding the following statement: *All the gold in Fort Knox cannot make me change my opinion.* What type of knowledge should ELLs have to understand this statement?

(A) the concept of metaphor and allusion
(B) the concept of a simile
(C) the concept of an allusion
(D) the concept of a hyperbole

41. Identify the rationale for promoting literacy development in the students' native language.

(A) It facilitates and accelerates literacy development in the second language.
(B) It facilitates the acquisition of a second language in a fun and relaxed environment.
(C) It promotes the acquisition of academic language.
(D) It guarantees that English language learners (ELLs) will maintain their native language.

42. Mr. Lawrence reads a story to his kindergarten students in a very pleasant and natural tone of voice. Later, he uses a series of connected pictures representing events in the story. In addition to helping children understand the story, what other element is he teaching?

(A) The teacher is introducing the sound–symbol correspondence of the story.
(B) The teacher is filling the experiential gaps to be sure students can understand the story.
(C) The teacher is introducing sequencing and the story structure.
(D) The teacher is using developmentally appropriate practices because children at this stage cannot read on their own.

43. Identify the informal activities and/or instruments used to assess oral communication skills in pre-K students.

(A) teacher observation checklists, retelling stories, and anecdotal records
(B) multiple-choice tests, cloze tests, and an informal reading inventory
(C) audiotaped conversations, written cloze tests, and standardized achievement tests
(D) repetition drills, choral reading, and chants

44. One of the main functions of portfolio assessment for ELLs is to

(A) document social development and interaction with native English speakers.
(B) document progress toward language and content mastery.
(C) collect all assignments and daily activities completed during the day.
(D) collect all sample artwork and artistic manifestations of children.

45. Students who arrive at the threshold level of L1 have the following advantage:

(A) They have developed the positive self-esteem needed to acquire a second language.
(B) They have a deep understanding of culture and its implications for the acquisition of L2.
(C) They possess the foundation in L1 needed to transfer to L2.
(D) They can apply contrastive analysis theory to the acquisition of L2.

46. Identify the teaching guideline that best represents the principles of the student-centered approach for the teaching of language arts to ELLs.

(A) Support students' self-esteem by accepting their responses without questioning the value of the responses and their contribution to class discussion.
(B) In class discussion, guide students to monitor the linguistic behavior of their peers and provide corrective feedback.
(C) In communication activities, focus attention on meaning and/or the learning process instead of focusing attention on the correctness of grammar conventions.
(D) In communication activities, guide children to imitate the cultural and language patterns of native English speakers.

Use the information in this scenario to answer questions 47–49:

Scenario: Ms. Pedernales has a class that is composed of students from different cultural groups and linguistic levels. As part of her morning routine, she asks questions about the weather; the date; and the results of the basketball, football or baseball games, depending on the season. During the questions and answers, students are encouraged to respond verbally, nonverbally, or through a combination of both. To involve beginner ESL students, she uses yes/no cards to solicit responses from the group. Students really enjoy the daily morning activity, and they make an effort to watch the news or ask their parents for the information.

47. Ms. Pedernales follows student-centered practices and incorporates the following principles of learning covered on TExES examinations:

(A) assessment as part of instruction and lifetime learning
(B) developmentally appropriate practices and diversity
(C) teaching for meaningful outcomes and technology
(D) learner-centeredness and technology

48. Ms. Pedernales can address the linguistic diversity of the group by

(A) setting up cooperative learning groups organized homogeneously by linguistic levels, and including the ethnic groups represented in class.
(B) organizing peer support systems through heterogeneous grouping by linguistic levels.
(C) organizing intensive ESL classes for students and cross-cultural training for faculty members.
(D) making students aware of ethnic and linguistic differences among classmates.

49. After the initial activity, she uses the daily morning activities to teach the content areas. How can she use the content of the morning routine to teach mathematics?

(A) She can guide students to use role-play to imitate the way that television personalities present the weather and sports information.
(B) She can promote speaking ability by leading students to share important things that they have done during the weekend.
(C) She can ask students to write a summary of the weather data and predict the weather for the next day or for the week.
(D) She can use the results of the games and the performance of the teams to teach percentages.

50. Identify the statement that best describes the concept of sheltered English.

(A) It is a program designed to teach ESL and bilingual education to ELLs.
(B) It is the Canadian version of the bilingual education program.
(C) It is a program designed to teach ESL through instruction in the content areas.
(D) It is an example of a submersion program designed to promote bilingualism among students.

51. Identify the technique(s) that best represent the concept of sheltered English.

(A) speaking slowly in English and providing support in L1 as needed to promote comprehension
(B) using nonverbal communication to promote comprehension
(C) evaluating the mastery of the content taught at least once per week
(D) using visuals and hands-on activities and contextualizing instruction to ensure comprehension

52. In indirect instruction, the role of questioning is to guide students into discovery. Questions in this approach are used to

(A) refocus and probe for deeper analysis of the content.
(B) keep students engaged.
(C) promote equity and equality among linguistic minority students.
(D) promote deductive teaching.

53. Ms. Fuentes uses questioning techniques to motivate students to go beyond one-word answers and recall factual information. When students attempt to answer questions, she avoids the use of negative statements like "No, that's not what I have in mind" or "That's not what I was expecting"; rather, she leads students to the expected answer using cognitive coaching techniques. She expects students to reflect on their responses and show mastery of the content; but she is more interested in the mental process students use to arrive at the answer. Teachers who follow these teaching strategies model student-centered practices and the principles of

(A) behaviorist psychology.
(B) humanistic psychology.
(C) cognitive psychology.
(D) psychology of the oppressed.

54. The preview-review is one of the traditional strategies to ensure comprehension in the content areas. Identify the statement that best describes this strategy.

(A) English and L1 is used at the beginning of instruction.
(B) Translation is used as a teaching tool.
(C) L1 is used to introduce the content and to summarize instruction delivered in L2.
(D) L1 and L2 is strictly separated during instruction during the beginning, middle, and final part of instruction.

55. One of the key advantages of using learning logs in dual language instruction is to

(A) provide a comprehensive list of elements learned during a grading period.
(B) guide students to synthesize the content learned in class and identify areas in need of further support.
(C) develop an advanced organizer to communicate orally with teachers and peers.
(D) guide students to make oral presentations describing elements that they have learned in class.

56. When teachers explore the knowledge that children bring to the lesson and then provide additional details to prepare them for the content of the day, they are

(A) strengthening the language background of the child.
(B) expanding the schemata needed to comprehend new content.
(C) facilitating the process of second language acquisition.
(D) providing students with the vocabulary needed to understand the lesson.

57. The main purpose of semantic mapping is to

(A) teach geography concepts to ELLs.
(B) identify critical features of a given concept.
(C) establish connections between concepts in L1 and L2.
(D) present a graphic representation of a process.

58. Marisela develops a study guide to be sure that she synthesizes content and to check how much she knows about the content of a given class. What strategy is she using?

(A) cognitive
(B) social
(C) metacognitive
(D) memory

59. Joe is literate in his native language and he possesses a strong background in mathematics, social studies, and science. Once he came to the United States, he automatically began using the knowledge that he acquired in his native language as a foundation for learning new concepts in English. What strategy is he using?

(A) metacognitive
(B) cognitive
(C) social
(D) mnemonic

60. One of the most important strategies to help students gather information from textbooks is to

(A) teach the technical vocabulary needed to understand the content.
(B) teach the format used in textbooks and discuss how each part can increase comprehension.
(C) teach cognates in L1 and L2 and explain how this knowledge can facilitate the understanding of new concepts.
(D) provide a glossary of terms related to the content areas.

61. Identify the statement that best describes the relationship between the eight social studies strands and the TEKS in the implementation of the Texas curriculum.

(A) There is no connection between the TEKS and the social studies strands.
(B) The social studies TEKS have been used as a foundation for the development of the state curriculum.
(C) The strands apply to programs at the university level and the TEKS applies to K–12 curricula.
(D) The strands apply to programs at the high school level, while the TEKS applies to all grade levels.

62. The state curriculum officially introduces children to Texas history in

(A) prekindergarten.
(B) first grade.
(C) third grade.
(D) fourth grade.

63. Children in prekindergarten and kindergarten might have problems understanding how the Earth is represented in globes and flat representations because children at this age

(A) might not be developmentally ready to understand symbolic representations.
(B) might pay more attention to the colors and features of globes and maps than the concepts being taught.
(C) might not be interested in maps and globes.
(D) might have problems recognizing the Earth's features presented on the 12-inch globe representation.

64. To apply the concept of time zones, students need to have a clear understanding of

(A) the International Date Line.
(B) the Earth's yearly revolution.
(C) the concept of the meridians of longitude.
(D) the concept of the parallels of latitude.

65. The Sumerians, Akkadians, Babylonians, and Assyrians were some of the civilizations that flourished in Mesopotamia—the land between the rivers. What rivers are being alluded to in this statement?

(A) Nile and Amazon
(B) Tigris and Euphrates
(C) Nile and Indus
(D) Volga and Danube

66. Identify the modern-day country that encompasses most of the territory of ancient Mesopotamia.

(A) Iran
(B) Pakistan
(C) Kuwait
(D) Iraq

67. Identify two key historical concepts or characters of the Middle Ages.

(A) the Greek and the Roman Empires
(B) the feudal system and the Crusades
(C) Stonehenge and the rise of Islam
(D) the Renaissance and Alexander the Great

68. The most advanced pre-Columbian civilizations of Mesoamerica were the

(A) Aztecs and Incas.
(B) Maya and Aztecs.
(C) Toltecs and Pueblos.
(D) Olmecs and Iroquois.

69. Identify the statement that best describes the country of Iraq.

(A) It is a linguistically and ethnically homogeneous Muslim nation.
(B) It is a Muslim nation with multiple ethnic groups within its borders.
(C) It is located in Southeast Asia.
(D) It is a province of Pakistan.

70. If in the United States we are enjoying a warm winter, what season are the people of Brazil having?

(A) spring
(B) summer
(C) winter
(D) fall

71. The imperial forces of Japan attacked Pearl Harbor on Sunday, December 7, 1941. Once the attack began, the officer in charge called President Roosevelt and notified him of the attack. During the communication, the president was able to hear the noise of the bombs exploding and the struggle of the battle. Recently, a reporter from the *Dallas Morning News* was researching the details of the attack and found a transcription of the official diary of Emperor Hirohito, where he indicated the following: "The Imperial forces of Japan destroyed the American fleet in Hawaii Monday, December 8, 1941." If the attack occurred on December 7, why did the official document from the Japanese government indicate that the attack happened on December 8? Select the statement that best explains this discrepancy.

(A) The Americans knew that the attack was going to happen and assumed that it had happened the day before.
(B) The U.S. government had spies in Japan and they knew when the attack was going to take place.

(C) There is a one-day difference between the two regions.
(D) Emperor Hirohito learned about the attack the day after and he assumed that it happened on that day.

72. Indian tribes from the Central and Great Plains of Texas are better known than their counterparts from the Coastal Plains because

(A) they had a more advanced civilization.
(B) they were sedentary and built better ceremonial sites and permanent structures.
(C) they domesticated the horse, which made them better hunters and warriors.
(D) they had an abundance of food sources and were stronger.

73. Probably as a response to the war in the Middle East, OPEC cut the production of oil. As a result of this action, the cost of gasoline increased to almost $3.00 per gallon in 2005. What is the economic principle or statement that is best represented by this situation?

(A) During war, the prices of fossil fuels increase.
(B) The American economy is dependent on foreign oil.
(C) The law of supply and demand determines the prices of goods and services.
(D) OPEC was boycotting the United States.

74. The Fifteenth Amendment of the U.S. Constitution was ratified in 1870 to grant

(A) black women and men the right to vote.
(B) citizenship for blacks.
(C) freedom of slaves.
(D) black men the right to vote.

75. The U.S. Constitution was designed so that no single branch of the government—executive, judicial, or legislative—could exert full control over the other two. This unique feature of the Constitution is known as

(A) judicial review.
(B) the pocket veto.
(C) checks and balances.
(D) habeas corpus.

Use the information in this scenario to answer questions 76 and 77:

Scenario: Mr. Jamie Mackey has seven ELLs in his class who are having difficulties pronouncing English words containing the letters *sh* and *ch*. To support these students, he organizes small-group instruction to address their specific needs. He introduces pronunciation and vocabulary concepts through a chart. The chart is color-coded to guide students in the pronunciation of phonemes; i.e., he uses blue for the /sh/, green for /ch/, brown for /k/. Every week, he adds new words to the chart until he is satisfied that students have mastered the grapheme-phoneme correspondence. The chart for this week is shown on the next page.

76. Based on the information provided in the chart, what is the primary reason for the confusion that ELLs experience with these two phonemes?

(A) They cannot distinguish the difference between the two phonemes.
(B) They cannot pronounce either of the two phonemes.
(C) They might not be interested in learning these differences.
(D) The grapheme–phoneme correspondence is inconsistent.

77. What might be the advantages of using the chart on the next page to teach pronunciation?

(A) The chart provides examples of the graphophonemic consistency of English.
(B) The students become aware of the words that follow grapheme–phoneme correspondence and those that do not.
(C) The chart can be used to teach the intonation pattern of the language.
(D) Children get exposed to vocabulary words and develop graphophonemic awareness.

1. *sh*—/sh/	2. *ch*—/ch/	3. *ch*—/k/	4. *ch*—/sh/	5. *s*—/sh/	6. *t*—/sh/
shower	church	Christmas	chef	sure	caution
short	chart	chemistry	Chevron	sugar	contribution
shell	choice	chrome	Chevrolet	mission	communication

78. Identify the number of syllables and the number of phonemes present in the word *thought*.

(A) two syllables and three phonemes
(B) one syllable and three phonemes
(C) three syllables and six phonemes
(D) two syllables and three phonemes

79. Marcus can separate a word into its individual phonemes and put it back together to re-create the original word. However, he has problems separating words into syllables and identifying the syllable with the primary stress. Based on this scenario, Marcus needs additional support with

(A) phonological awareness.
(B) phonemic awareness.
(C) syllabication.
(D) word stress.

80. Mr. Rovira guides five-year-old children in the recitation of the following utterance—"**R**ound the **r**ugged **r**ock the **r**agged **r**ascal **r**an." Children have fun with the activity and try to say it without errors. What literary technique is he using?

(A) alliteration
(B) tongue twister
(C) nursery rhyme
(D) memorization drills

81. Ms. Thomas introduces new vocabulary words within the context of a sentence and through the use of visuals. Once children understand the concept linked to the word, she repeats individual words, pausing after each syllable. Once children can separate the word into syllables, she guides them to separate syllables into individual phonemes. What skills is Ms. Thomas introducing with the latter activity?

(A) the intonation pattern of the language
(B) phonological awareness
(C) vocabulary development
(D) pronunciation drills

82. When teaching the grapheme–phoneme correspondence of English, teachers must

(A) make the activity interesting to all students.
(B) monitor the children so they do not pronounce the letters with a foreign accent.
(C) create an atmosphere of cooperation among students from diverse ethnic and linguistic backgrounds.
(D) control the inconsistency of the grapheme-phoneme correspondence of English by presenting consistent sounds first.

83. Ms. Jefferson has guided first-grade students to read polysyllabic words until they can read them fluently. Later, students are asked to separate the words into syllables, and finally she guides students to identify the main stress in each word. What skill is Ms. Jefferson emphasizing?

(A) alphabetic awareness
(B) reading fluency
(C) phonological awareness
(D) syllabication

84. Ms. Jefferson also uses monosyllabic words to present the concept of onset and rhymes. Identify the pair of words that best represent this concept.

(A) *want-ed—walk-ed*
(B) *very—berry*
(C) *think-ing—eat-ing*
(D) *s-ank—b-ank*

85. The use of phonics instruction in conjunction with components from the whole language approach are typical for programs emphasizing a

(A) skills-based approach.
(B) balanced-reading approach.
(C) meaning-based approach.
(D) humanistic approach.

86. John Goodman used the term *miscues* in reading to describe the type of

(A) variation that occurs when children attempt to put words in writing.
(B) variation that occurs when children try to decode and guess the meaning of printed words.
(C) errors that occur when children try to communicate orally in their native language.
(D) discrepancy that occurs between the schemata of the child and the one intended by the author.

87. Identify the statement that best describes the advantages of using the language experience approach to teach reading to language-minority students.

(A) It provides the schema or experiential background to facilitate the comprehension of the story.
(B) It uses the vocabulary and the experience common to both language minority and mainstream students.
(C) It minimizes the possibility of errors due to idiomatic expressions from both L1 and L2.
(D) It facilitates reading by ensuring a positive match between L1 and L2.

88. Identify the main benefit of the shared book experience.

(A) Stories are shared in a warm, supportive environment.
(B) The whole class can read with the teacher.
(C) Children like big books.
(D) It contains attractive pictures and big letters.

89. Identify the statement that best describes sight words.

(A) Sight words are prevalent in environmental print.
(B) Sight words occur frequently in print.
(C) Children decode sight words using semantic and structural clues.
(D) Children have difficulty spelling sight words.

90. Knowledge of the two words used to create compound words can help students in the interpretation of the compound word. However, there are examples of compound words in which the meaning of the two components does not contribute to, and often interferes with, the interpretation of the new word. Identify the set of compound words that falls into this category.

(A) *doghouse*, *autograph*, and *boathouse*
(B) *greenhouse*, *White House*, and *mouthwash*
(C) *butterfly*, *nightmare*, and *brainstorm*
(D) *hotdog*, *birdhouse*, and *underground*

91. When teaching English to ELLs of Spanish background, Ms. Rico introduced a list of Greek and Latin prefixes common to Spanish and English. She explained the spelling patterns and the meaning of each of the prefixes. She presented examples of words that contain the prefixes, and led students to decode these based on the meaning of the prefixes. What decoding strategy is Ms. Rico using?

(A) contextual
(B) structural
(C) pictorial
(D) syntactic

92. Ms. Fuentes frequently leads students in choral reading to promote reading fluency. She also takes declarative statements from the story and asks students to change them to questions or exclamations. Students have fun generating these changes. What is the main purpose of the latter activity?

(A) To emphasize listening and speaking skills
(B) To teach the intonation pattern of the language
(C) To teach singing and music skills
(D) To make the class more enjoyable

93. By second grade, students are generally guided to discontinue the practice of pointing to the words being read. What is the rationale for this change of strategy?

(A) Students get tired of pointing to the words while reading.
(B) Students find this practice annoying and typical of younger children.
(C) This practice can interfere with the development of reading fluency.
(D) This practice is archaic and does not seem to help in the reading process.

94. Vocabulary development is a key predictor of success in reading. Identify a strategy that parents can use with preschool children to promote vocabulary development in a fun and relaxed environment.

(A) Use flash cards and concrete objects to introduce vocabulary words.
(B) Play a game where the parent and the child teach each other a new word every day.
(C) Play games where children have to name antonyms and synonyms.
(D) Ask children to memorize a list of vocabulary words every day.

95. The main purpose for teaching sight words is to promote instant recognition of characters and words. Instant recognition of words can improve students'

(A) reading fluency.
(B) decoding skills.
(C) reading comprehension.
(D) writing skills.

96. The main purpose of family literacy programs is

(A) to teach ESL to Spanish-speaking parents and to provide training in cross-cultural communication.
(B) to keep children busy while parents attend literacy classes.
(C) to empower parents to help and be involved in the education of their children.
(D) to empower child and adult English language learners by providing meaningful education.

97. Identify the factor(s) that most likely can affect the development of early literacy among preschool children.

(A) Parents read continuously to their children and have books available at home.
(B) Parents teach children to use the dictionary and guide them to select the best definition based on the context of the words.
(C) Parents have available reference materials and electronic translation programs to promote early bilingualism among children.
(D) Parents take their children to the library and bookstores to obtain books.

98. Mike is a four-year-old monolingual, Spanish-speaking child. His parents read Spanish books to him every day. As a result of their effort, Mike has mastered directionality in reading and basic decoding skills. He can also decode words by linking two syllables. Based on his literacy growth, what might be the next logical step for the parents to promote his growth?

(A) Stop reading to him to encourage self-sufficiency.
(B) Continue reading to him and introduce comprehension strategies.
(C) Continue challenging the child by introducing books for advanced first graders.
(D) Stop teaching Spanish reading and introduce English only.

99. The main purpose of an intergenerational literacy initiative is to

(A) improve the literacy development of adults and the community.
(B) use children as a reason to involve parents in school activities.
(C) promote literacy among children using the support of parents and other family members.
(D) improve reading skills beginning in preschool and continue improving throughout life.

100. Identify the steps that best describe the writing process.

(A) Develop an outline of the intended writing project, complete an initial draft, and edit for content.
(B) Complete an initial draft, revise for the accuracy of content, and publish.
(C) Brainstorm for ideas, develop an outline, complete an initial draft, edit, and publish.
(D) Write an initial draft, share it with peers, review for grammaticality, and publish.

101. In project-oriented activities, students are guided to produce knowledge instead of reproduce knowledge. Identify the strategy that best represents this difference.

(A) Students are presented with a problem, they are asked to discuss it, and they find possible solutions.
(B) Students recite the pledge of allegiance and later they discuss the meaning of the words.
(C) Students are presented with a problem and given three possible solutions to the problem.
(D) Students are given a list of solutions and a list of problems; they are supposed to match the two.

102. Identify the strategies to lead the child from the stage of learning to read to the stage of reading to learn.

(A) Expose children to different kinds of literature and vocabulary words specific to content areas.
(B) Introduce children to different kinds of text and how to scan to locate and retrieve information.
(C) Allow students to read without interruption for at least 20 minutes a day.
(D) Introduce the concepts of connotation and denotation in words and phrases.

103. Vocabulary development is a key predictor of success in reading in the content areas for all students, but especially for children new to the English language. Identify the best strategy to introduce vocabulary development for ELLs from diverse cultural and linguistic backgrounds.

(A) Teach content vocabulary through direct, concrete experience as opposed to definitions.
(B) Identify key vocabulary words in the content area and provide children with a translation of each word.
(C) Teach content vocabulary in a comparative fashion, contrasting the meaning of vocabulary words in the various languages represented in class.
(D) Deemphasize the importance of lexicon, introduce the words in context, and guide children to derive the meaning using context clues.

104. Mary, a well-educated teacher, visited one of her favorite English professors in college. After having lunch with him, she said good-bye to the professor and he replied with the following statement: "Good-bye and drive careful." Mary looked at him in shock and smiled. Why was Mary in shock?

(A) The professor looked old and unhappy.
(B) The professor exhibited faulty agreement in his speech.
(C) The speech of the professor was unintelligible.
(D) The professor used a colloquial expression.

105. The writing portion of the fourth-grade STAAR test has two components—a multiple-choice portion and a writing sample. The writing sample of the test is evaluated using a

(A) multiple-choice format.
(B) rubric with discrete language components.
(C) four-point rubric.
(D) six-point rubric.

106. A second-grade student began writing a composition about his friend in the following way: (1) George is my friend. (2) Mary is my best friend. (3) Rachel are my friends too. What type of support does this child need to write a more cohesive and standard writing sample?

(A) spelling and agreement instruction
(B) use of active and passive voice

(C) agreement and sentence connectors
(D) use of appropriate capitalization and punctuation

107. Identify the most appropriate strategy(ies) to meet the needs of children at the emerging stage of writing development.

(A) Identify errors in the writing sample and guide children to self-correct.
(B) Provide a prompt and guide children to write a composition based on it.
(C) Read stories and ask children to retell the story while you write it down.
(D) Allow the child to read for at least 30 minutes every day.

108. The main purpose of an interactive/dialogue journal is to allow

(A) children opportunities to practice speaking and writing skills.
(B) children opportunities to communicate freely in a written form.
(C) students opportunities to receive corrective feedback from peers.
(D) students opportunities to practice listening, speaking, reading, and writing.

109. Convergent research on linear versus curvilinear rhetorical patterns shows that Spanish-speaking English language learners and young children in general have a tendency to follow a curvilinear approach in writing. What strategies can teachers use to support these students?

(A) Teach pronunciation and application of grammar structures.
(B) Guide children to develop an outline for the story, and provide them with guiding questions to keep them focused on the topic and the audience.
(C) Provide a speaking checklist to help students stick to the topic.
(D) Provide examples of stories written in a linear fashion and ask students to modify them by adding their own information.

110. A rubric to rate English composition in kindergarten and first grade should not place heavy emphasis on the mastery of spelling because

(A) the use of phonemic and invented spelling is part of specific stages of writing development in children.
(B) the use of standard spelling is not important in the development of compositions.
(C) spelling addresses visual memory and should not be given great value.
(D) the development of standard spelling requires students to use structural and phonics rules effectively.

111. English writing samples from Spanish-dominant ELLs may contain which of the following key features?

(A) The stories are simple in content and written in a linear fashion.
(B) The stories might have complex sentence patterns and sophisticated words from Spanish.
(C) The stories might be perceived as disjointed and lacking logical sequencing.
(D) They might switch from Spanish to English within the same sentence.

112. In assessment, minimal pairs are used to teach and assess

(A) morphology.
(B) phonology.
(C) syntax.
(D) lexicon.

113. If a child is reading an average of 90 percent of the words correctly, he or she is reading at the

(A) independent level.
(B) frustration level.
(C) comprehension level.
(D) instructional level.

114. In compliance with the NCLB Act, Texas adopted an instrument to assess the English achievement of ELLs—the Texas Observation Protocol (TOP). The TOP assesses the listening, speaking, reading, and writing components of English. In addition to the writing samples required, this instrument uses _____ to assess the linguistic performance of children in English.

(A) a rating scale containing three options (agree, disagree, uncertain)
(B) a multiple-choice test with four choices (A, B, C, and D)
(C) a series of open-ended questions to guide the teacher in the collection of data
(D) a checklist identifying specific literacy components

115. Running records, teacher observations, and speaking checklists are examples of

(A) teacher-developed assessment instruments.
(B) informal literacy assessment.
(C) formal literacy assessment.
(D) objective literacy instruments.

116. In Ms. Waler's class, students were asked to interview family members to identify strategies they will use to solve a given mathematical problem. What might be the main benefit of this activity?

(A) It will provide a multicultural view for problem solving and will validate home cultures.
(B) It will validate the students' native language and achievements.
(C) It will free the teacher to address other administrative issues.
(D) It will establish the community as a guiding force in the development of the school curricula.

117. The main advantage of using hands-on activities in mathematics is to

(A) enhance students' ability to think abstractly.
(B) make the lesson more enjoyable.
(C) lead students to active learning and guide them to construct their own knowledge.
(D) promote equity, equality, and freedom for the diverse ethnic groups in the nation.

118. One of the reasons that might explain the low performance of English language learners in mathematics word problems is the lack of

(A) mathematical intelligence needed to do well in these kinds of tests.
(B) vocabulary development to understand technical terms and concepts in mathematics.
(C) a conceptual framework needed to do well in problems that require high-order thinking skills.
(D) interest and the ability to deal with abstractions and number concepts.

119. Children having problems deciding on the value of a dime versus ten pennies might be experiencing problems with

(A) centration.
(B) conservation.
(C) ordering or seriation.
(D) classification.

120. Perform the indicated operation: $(-36) - 11$.

(A) 47
(B) 25
(C) −47
(D) −25

121. Simplify: $6 \times 2 + 3/3$.

(A) 18
(B) 5
(C) 10
(D) 13

122. Simplify to a single term in scientific notation: $(2 \times 10^3) \times (6 \times 10^4)$.

(A) 12×10^7
(B) 1.2×10^{12}
(C) 1.2×10^8
(D) 12×10^{12}

123. Identify the mathematic properties involved in the following problem: $(6 + 2) + 5 = 6 + (2 + 5)$.

(A) Distributive property
(B) Associative property of addition
(C) Property of zero
(D) Associative property of multiplication

124. How many lines of symmetry do all nonsquare rectangles have?

(A) 0
(B) 2
(C) 4
(D) 8

Use the figure below to answer the question that follows. Assume that point *C* is the center of the circle. Angles *xyz* and *xcz* intercept minor arc *xz*. The measure of angle *xyz* is 40°.

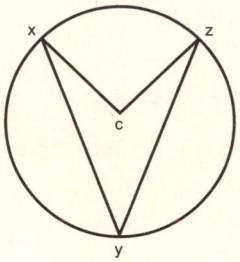

125. What is the measure of major arc *xyz*?

(A) 140°
(B) 280°
(C) 160°
(D) 320°

126. What is the approximate volume of the following cylinder?

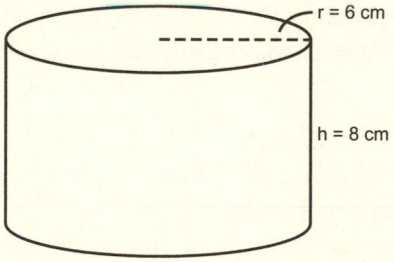

(A) 904 cm^3
(B) 301 cm^3
(C) 151 cm^3
(D) 452 cm^3

127. Mrs. Cameron plans to buy carpeting for her living room floor. The room is a rectangle measuring 14 feet by 20 feet. She wants no carpet seams on her floor, even if that means that some carpeting will go to waste. The carpeting she wants comes in 16-foot-wide rolls. What is the minimum amount of carpeting that will have to be wasted if Mrs. Cameron insists upon her no-seams requirement?

(A) 40 square feet
(B) 60 square feet
(C) 80 square feet
(D) 100 square feet

128. One of the key methodological considerations that teachers have to account for when developing thematic instruction for children in prekindergarten through grade 2 is

(A) the integration of all concepts.
(B) the development of age-appropriate instruction for children.
(C) the development of interesting and challenging activities for all learners.
(D) the integration of problem-solving strategies.

129. The earliest that teachers can introduce mathematics reasoning to children is

(A) first grade.
(B) kindergarten.
(C) third grade.
(D) second grade.

130. In the early grades, mathematic and spatial reasoning are introduced in learning centers through the use of manipulatives. What is the main advantage of using learning centers to introduce mathematic and spatial reasoning?

(A) Children explore and learn reasoning skills indirectly using concrete objects in informal settings.
(B) Children can play and enjoy the benefits of manipulatives.
(C) Children are taught mathematics concepts deductively using manipulatives and other concrete objects in an informal format.
(D) Children are exposed to the state curriculum in a highly structured learning environment.

131. The main value of using real-life situations to teach problem-solving skills involving mathematics is that the children in grades K–4 can see

(A) the connection between the school curriculum and mathematics.
(B) the value of mathematics in solving daily situations.
(C) that mathematics is an important part of the Texas curriculum.
(D) that the use of learning centers has a specific value in life.

132. The Texas TEKS requires a teacher to address the following four strands in art education:

(A) history, perception, performance, and creativity.
(B) creativity, emotion, Native American art, and European impressionists.
(C) perception, creative expressions, historical and cultural heritage, and critical evaluation.
(D) critical evaluation, visual arts and perception, color combinations, and body and finger painting.

133. Diego Rivera, José Clemente Orozco, and David Siqueiros are some of the best representatives of

(A) photorealism.
(B) muralists.
(C) surrealism.
(D) impressionism.

134. Identify the painter that best represents the cubism art movement.

(A) Salvador Dali
(B) Goya
(C) Michelangelo
(D) Pablo Picasso

135. The concept of value as an element of art describes the use of

(A) space to create perspective.
(B) line to highlight parts of a work.
(C) light to represent the mood of the artist.
(D) space to place objects on different planes.

136. Pitch is the relative _____ of a musical sound.

(A) duration or length
(B) loudness or softness
(C) high and low
(D) rhythm

137. Select the letter that contains the correct sequence of Kodaly rhythm syllables for this song line—"Happy Birthday to you!"

(A) Ta Ta Ta Ta Ta ta-a
(B) Ti Ti Ta Ta Ti Ti ta
(C) Ti ti ta ti ti ta ta
(D) Ti Ti Ta Ta Ta ta-a

138. The state song of Texas is

(A) "The Yellow Rose of Texas."
(B) "Texas, Our Texas."
(C) "God Bless America."
(D) "The Alamo."

139. Identify a modern popular music genre with a strong German, Mexican, and Czech influence.

(A) mariachi
(B) country
(C) tejano
(D) salsa

140. By ages four and five, children are generally able to perform somersaults, climb, and skip. They also begin dressing themselves using buttons and zippers. These kinds of activities represent an example of

(A) gross motor skills.
(B) required curriculum components in school.
(C) fine motor skills.
(D) a transition point from early childhood to adulthood.

141. The dance exercises more appropriate for children in grades 1–2 are

(A) walk and/or skip.
(B) run and/or skip.
(C) skip and slide.
(D) skip and step-hop.

142. The *E* in the acronym *RICE*, a treatment process for sprains, represents

(A) exercise.
(B) elevation.
(C) evaluation.
(D) expose.

143. Based on the Individuals with Disabilities Education Act (IDEA), children with crutches or any other types of assistive devices should

(A) not be allowed to participate in physical education activities.
(B) be allowed to participate like any other student.
(C) be provided with appropriate modification for participation in physical education activities.
(D) be provided with a special physical education class designed for them.

144. To complete an effective aerobic workout, exercise should be performed at an individual's target heart rate for a minimum of

(A) 15 minutes.
(B) 20 minutes.
(C) 30 minutes.
(D) 45 minutes.

145. Which of the following is a locomotor skill?

(A) bending
(B) catching
(C) throwing
(D) hopping

146. What percentage of a daily diet should be composed of carbohydrates?

(A) 20%
(B) 25%
(C) 40%
(D) 50%

147. The most appropriate and safe exercises for kindergarten and first-grade students are

(A) jogging and walking.
(B) games that require physical activity.
(C) games that require endurance.
(D) contact sports.

Use the information in this scenario to answer questions 148–150:

Scenario: Mr. Vargas organized a lesson to introduce sixth-grade students to the concept of marine habitats. As a focus, he presented two 25-gallon aquariums. Aquarium A has a variety of plants, 10 snails, and 25 unique varieties of small fishes. Aquarium B also contains a variety of plants, three snails, and five small fish of the same variety. He organized the students in groups of five. Once the groups were formed, students were asked to discuss the appropriateness of the combinations of plants and the number of animals. The ultimate goal is to predict the success of the habitats, including successful breeding, among the animals.

148. The main science objective of Mr. Vargas's lesson is to

(A) guide students to communicate with peers.
(B) promote scientific inquiry and problem-solving skills using scientific data.
(C) work in cooperative groups.
(D) keep students engaged and interested in the scientific concepts presented in class.

149. After a lengthy discussion, students agreed that Aquarium B had a better chance to establish and maintain a successful habitat. What information led students to make this decision?

(A) The size of the aquarium
(B) The ratio of plants and animals
(C) The number of plants
(D) The number of fish

150. Students also agreed that aquarium B had a better chance of successful breeding among the fish. What information did students use to arrive at this conclusion?

(A) The ratio of plants and fish
(B) The number of fish in each tank
(C) The size of the tanks
(D) The types of fishes in each tank

151. To make the science curriculum cognitively accessible to English language learners in grades K–2, teachers use thematic units and incorporate

(A) techniques from various foreign language methods.
(B) scientific exploration and hands-on activities.
(C) a variety of instructional strategies and sophisticated scientific tools.
(D) the use of chemicals and human specimens used by scientists.

152. George placed a metal spoon on an open flame and the spoon became so hot that it burned his hands. What scientific principle represents this type of energy transfer?

(A) Radiation
(B) Conduction
(C) Convection
(D) Kinetic energy

153. Vinegar is composed of two substances—acetic acid (a colorless liquid) and water. This combination of substances is an example of a

(A) compound.
(B) mixture.
(C) chemical.
(D) substance.

154. Traditionally, matter has been classified into three states:

(A) rock, soil, and minerals.
(B) ice, snow, and water.
(C) liquid, gas, and solid.
(D) nickel, lava, and magma.

155. The United States is probably the only industrialized country in the world that uses the English system of measurement in daily life, except for science and engineering. What is the rationale for using the metric system in scientific research and engineering?

(A) The metric system is widely used in the world.
(B) The English system is an archaic and outdated system used mostly in business.
(C) The metric system is more precise than the English system.
(D) The English system allows for the easy computation of measurements.

156. Living things are classified into five groups: monera, protista, fungi, plants, and animals. Some of these groups are unicellular, while the others are made up of multiple cells; however, there is only one group that has prokaryotic cells. What kingdom contains prokaryotic cells?

(A) Monera
(B) Protista
(C) Fungi
(D) Plants

Use the information in this scenario to answer questions 157 and 158:

Scenario: Corals are invertebrates that generally live in a symbiotic relationship with algae. Some of them build reefs, others do not. Most of them filter water to obtain nutrients for survival.

157. Based on this description, corals belong to which of the following kingdoms?

(A) Monera
(B) Animal
(C) Plant
(D) Fungi

158. The term *symbiotic* in this case means that corals

(A) are parasites attached to algae.
(B) share the same environment with algae.
(C) exchange services with other organisms.
(D) are living organisms.

159. The key function of the food chain in the ecosystem is to

(A) control the number of animals.
(B) preserve the types of plants in the habitat.
(C) maintain a balance among organisms.
(D) maintain a balance between fungi and dead matter.

160. Germaine, a fourth-grade student, notices that the shape of the east coast of South America can fit into the shape of the west coast of Africa. To demonstrate this, he cut off the South American map, placed it next to the map of Africa, and found an almost perfect match. He was amazed by his discovery and asked the teacher if Africa was once part of South America. What type of theory or scientific principle can the teacher introduce to make Germaine's discovery a teachable moment?

(A) theory of evolution of the species
(B) theory of intelligent design
(C) theory of transcontinental migration
(D) theory of plate tectonics

161. The main function of Earth's atmosphere is to

(A) protect and preserve life.
(B) prevent the contamination of Earth.
(C) create a vacuum between Earth's crust and its mantle.
(D) recycle water and gases.

162. Earthquakes are caused by

(A) thermal activity in the core.
(B) the movement of continental plates.
(C) the melting of rocks and minerals.
(D) the movement or rotation of Earth.

163. As a result of the *Plyer v. Doe* court case in 1982, the federal government guarantees

(A) bilingual education for all students in Texas.
(B) free public education for children of undocumented parents.
(C) free public assistance for bilingual education children.
(D) bilingual or ESL instruction in grades kindergarten to grade 12.

164. The federal government used which of the following to guide the implementation of bilingual education at the national level?

(A) federal laws
(B) the Equal Education Opportunities Act (EEOA)
(C) state laws
(D) the Lau Remedies

165. The Texas bilingual education law requires the Language Proficiency Assessment Committee (LPAC) to study results of assessment instruments used to determine causes for admission to or dismissal from the state's bilingual education program. Some of the tests used to set these standards are

(A) the State of Texas Assessment of Academic Readiness (STAAR) and a language proficiency test.
(B) the Reading Proficiency Test English (RPTE) and Texas Observation Protocol (TOP).
(C) the Tejas LEE and the Texas Proficiency Reading Inventory (TPRI).
(D) an oral proficiency test and the Texas Observation Protocol (TOP).

166. The terms *remedial* and *subtractive* bilingual education are used to describe the following type of program:

(A) late exit
(B) early exit
(C) dual language
(D) one-way dual language

167. In the 90/10 model of two-way dual language programs, identify the group that receives language services through an immersion approach.

(A) English language learners (ELLs)
(B) both ELLs and native English speakers
(C) native English speakers
(D) English as a second language students

168. One of the key elements that promoted the development of the *Structured Immersion Program* in the United States was

(A) the Baker and de Kanter study.
(B) the No Child Left Behind (NCLB) legislation.

(C) the Ramírez Study.
(D) Title VII of the Elementary and Secondary Education Act (ESEA).

169. The goal of the Structured Immersion Program in the United States is

(A) to make ELLs fully bilingual.
(B) to teach English to ELLs.
(C) to promote language maintenance among ELLs.
(D) to immerse students into their native language and culture.

170. One of the key limitations of using the *Concurrent Approach* in dual-language programs is:

(A) Teachers have to speak in both languages.
(B) Teachers have to learn to use the approach.
(C) The program violates the principles of language separation.
(D) The program does not provide for the teaching of all language skills.

171. English language learners experience problems understanding common idiomatic expressions in English because

(A) they might not have experience with idioms in their native language.
(B) they might not understand the meaning of idioms.
(C) idioms are not common in English and difficult to teach.
(D) idioms contain connotative language that makes them difficult to understand.

172. First-language acquisition is the result of

(A) environmental influences and innate abilities.
(B) innate abilities.
(C) repetition of language.
(D) imitation of the speech of parents and caregivers.

73. The holophrastic stage of first-language acquisition is similar to which stage of second-language acquisition?

(A) babbling
(B) preproduction
(C) telegraphic stage
(D) early speech production

174. Stephen Krashen's theory of second language acquisition has four hypotheses—the monitor, comprehensive input, natural order, and affective filter. Identify the school of psychology associated with the affective filter hypothesis.

(A) behaviorist
(B) cognitivist
(C) humanistic
(D) linguistic

175. Cognates are words with identical meanings in two or more languages. What is the main reason for the large number of cognates English shares with other Western languages?

(A) English and all other Western languages have a common origin.
(B) English and other Western languages have Greek and Latin influences.
(C) English and most Western languages have a common vocabulary.
(D) The strong influence of English in the world has resulted in English words being adapted into other Western languages.

176. Total Physical Response (TPR) is a method used to address the linguistic needs of students at the

(A) intermediate level of language development.
(B) advanced level of language development.
(C) advanced to high level of language development.
(D) beginning stage of language development.

177. The pidgin English spoken in Papua New Guinea is considered to be not a pidgin but a Creole because

(A) pidgin English has been used in the area for many years.
(B) pidgin English is the native language of a large number of people.
(C) pidgin English is the only language used in the region.
(D) pidgin English is used only for trading purposes.

178. Identify the concept that best explains the literacy development that some pre-school children experience prior to formal instruction.

(A) environmental print
(B) reading readiness
(C) developmental appropriate practices
(D) emergent literacy

179. **Scenario:** Ms. Lidia Morris, a first grade teacher, introduced her students to a list of common word segments and then had them add an initial letter or letters to create words. She illustrated the activity by providing the example of the word segment, *ank*, to which she added letters to create the words *bank*, *tank*, and *sank*. What literacy concept is Ms. Morris using?

(A) word puzzle
(B) onset and rimes
(C) minimal pairs
(D) fill-in-the-blanks

180. One of the theories that provides support for the implementation of late-exit bilingual education programs is the

(A) comprehensible input hypothesis.
(B) monitor hypothesis.
(C) threshold hypothesis.
(D) affective filter hypothesis.

181. What is the key advantage of using graphic organizers with ELLs to teach challenging content areas?

(A) Graphic organizers are interesting for ELLs.
(B) Graphic organizers provide linguistic clues to increase the vocabulary of ELLs.
(C) Graphic organizers can minimize the language demands required to master content areas.
(D) Graphic organizers provide reassurance to ELLs that English is not as difficult as it seems.

182. In education, the terms *bottom-up* and *top-down* are used to describe

(A) basic life skills concepts for children in pre-kindergarten.
(B) approaches used to study language concepts and reading.
(C) approaches used to teach listening comprehension to ELLs.
(D) strategies to divide the curriculum into smaller units to increase comprehension.

183. The main benefit for using *onset and rime* to teach reading is

(A) to compensate for the grapheme–phoneme inconsistency of English.
(B) to study the grapheme–phoneme correspondence of the English language.
(C) to find words that rime.
(D) to introduce idiomatic expressions.

184. One of the key differences between narrative and expository writings is

(A) the content of the idioms and cultural information used.
(B) the use of formal and informal language.
(C) the format used to present information.
(D) the use of connotative and denotative language.

185. In language arts, the terms *linear* and *curvilinear* are used to describe

(A) the teaching of geometric concepts.
(B) speaking and writing styles.
(C) the process used to read information presented in expository writing.
(D) the process used to read information presented in narrative writing.

Answer Key and Domain Competencies

Question Number	Answer	Domain Competency
1.	(B)	I-Competency 001
2.	(D)	I-Competency 001
3.	(A)	I-Competency 001
4.	(B)	I-Competency 001
5.	(A)	I-Competency 001
6.	(A)	I-Competency 001
7.	(B)	I-Competency 001
8.	(B)	I-Competency 001
9.	(B)	I-Competency 001
10.	(C)	I-Competency 001
11.	(B)	I-Competency 001
12.	(B)	I-Competency 001
13.	(A)	I-Competency 001
14.	(B)	I-Competency 001
15.	(B)	I-Competency 001
16.	(B)	I-Competency 002
17.	(C)	I-Competency 002
18.	(B)	I-Competency 002
19.	(D)	I-Competency 002
20.	(C)	I-Competency 002
21.	(A)	I-Competency 002
22.	(B)	I-Competency 002
23.	(A)	I-Competency 002
24.	(C)	I-Competency 002
25.	(A)	I-Competency 002
26.	(A)	I-Competency 002
27.	(D)	I-Competency 002
28.	(A)	I-Competency 002
29.	(A)	I-Competency 002
30.	(B)	I-Competency 002
31.	(B)	I-Competency 003
32.	(A)	I-Competency 003
33.	(D)	I-Competency 003
34.	(C)	I-Competency 003
35.	(D)	I-Competency 003

Question Number	Answer	Domain Competency
36.	(D)	I-Competency 003
37.	(D)	I-Competency 003
38.	(A)	I-Competency 003
39.	(D)	I-Competency 003
40.	(C)	I-Competency 003
41.	(A)	I-Competency 003
42.	(C)	I-Competency 003
43.	(A)	I-Competency 003
44.	(B)	I-Competency 003
45.	(C)	I-Competency 003
46.	(C)	II-Competency 004
47.	(B)	II-Competency 004
48.	(B)	II-Competency 004
49.	(D)	II-Competency 004
50.	(C)	II-Competency 004
51.	(D)	II-Competency 004
52.	(A)	II-Competency 004
53.	(B)	II-Competency 004
54.	(C)	II-Competency 004
55.	(B)	II-Competency 004
56.	(B)	II-Competency 004
57.	(B)	II-Competency 004
58.	(C)	II-Competency 004
59.	(B)	II-Competency 004
60.	(B)	II-Competency 004
61.	(B)	IV-Competency 023
62.	(D)	IV-Competency 023
63.	(A)	IV-Competency 025
64.	(C)	IV-Competency 025
65.	(B)	IV-Competency 024
66.	(D)	IV-Competency 025
67.	(B)	IV-Competency 024
68.	(B)	IV-Competency 024
69.	(B)	IV-Competency 024
70.	(B)	IV-Competency 025

(continued)

(continued)

Question Number	Answer	Domain Competency
71.	(C)	IV-Competency 025
72.	(C)	IV-Competency 024
73.	(C)	IV-Competency 026
74.	(D)	IV-Competency 027
75.	(C)	IV-Competency 027
76.	(D)	II-Competency 005
77.	(B)	II-Competency 005
78.	(B)	II-Competency 005
79.	(A)	II-Competency 006
80.	(A)	II-Competency 006
81.	(B)	II-Competency 006
82.	(D)	II-Competency 006
83.	(C)	II-Competency 007
84.	(D)	II-Competency 007
85.	(B)	II-Competency 008
86.	(B)	II-Competency 008
87.	(A)	II-Competency 008
88.	(A)	II-Competency 008
89.	(B)	II-Competency 009
90.	(C)	II-Competency 009
91.	(B)	II-Competency 009
92.	(B)	II-Competency 010
93.	(C)	II-Competency 010
94.	(A)	II-Competency 010
95.	(A)	II-Competency 010
96.	(C)	II-Competency 011
97.	(A)	II-Competency 011
98.	(B)	II-Competency 011
99.	(C)	II-Competency 011
100.	(C)	II-Competency 012
101.	(A)	II-Competency 012
102.	(B)	II-Competency 012
103.	(A)	II-Competency 012
104.	(D)	II-Competency 013
105.	(C)	II-Competency 013
106.	(C)	II-Competency 013
107.	(C)	II-Competency 013

Question Number	Answer	Domain Competency
108.	(B)	II-Competency 014
109.	(B)	II-Competency 014
110.	(A)	II-Competency 014
111.	(C)	II-Competency 014
112.	(B)	II-Competency 015
113.	(D)	II-Competency 015
114.	(D)	II-Competency 015
115.	(B)	II-Competency 015
116.	(A)	II-Competency 015
117.	(C)	II-Competency 015
118.	(B)	II-Competency 016
119.	(B)	III-Competency 017
120.	(C)	III-Competency 018
121.	(D)	III-Competency 018
122.	(C)	III-Competency 018
123.	(B)	III-Competency 018
124.	(B)	III-Competency 019
125.	(B)	III-Competency 020
126.	(A)	III-Competency 018
127.	(A)	III-Competency 022
128.	(B)	III-Competency 017
129.	(B)	III-Competency 017
130.	(A)	III-Competency 019
131.	(B)	III-Competency 019
132.	(C)	VI-Competency 046
133.	(B)	VI-Competency 046
134.	(D)	VI-Competency 048
135.	(C)	VI-Competency 046
136.	(C)	VI-Competency 047
137.	(D)	VI-Competency 047
138.	(B)	VI-Competency 047
139.	(C)	VI-Competency 047
140.	(C)	VI-Competency 049
141.	(A)	VI-Competency 047
142.	(B)	VI-Competency 049
143.	(C)	VI-Competency 049
144.	(B)	VI-Competency 049

(continued)

(continued)

Question Number	Answer	Domain Competency
145.	(D)	VI-Competency 049
146.	(D)	VI-Competency 048
147.	(B)	VI-Competency 049
148.	(B)	V-Competency 032
149.	(B)	V-Competency 038
150.	(D)	V-Competency 039
151.	(B)	V-Competency 031
152.	(B)	V-Competency 031
153.	(B)	V-Competency 028
154.	(C)	V-Competency 028
155.	(C)	V-Competency 028
156.	(A)	V-Competency 038
157.	(B)	V-Competency 038
158.	(C)	V-Competency 038
159.	(C)	V-Competency 038
160.	(D)	V-Competency 043
161.	(A)	V-Competency 043
162.	(B)	V-Competency 043
163.	(B)	I-Competency 001
164.	(D)	I-Competency 001
165.	(A)	I-Competency 002

Question Number	Answer	Domain Competency
166.	(B)	I-Competency 002
167.	(C)	I-Competency 002
168.	(A)	I-Competency 002
169.	(B)	I-Competency 002
170.	(C)	I-Competency 002
171.	(D)	I-Competency 002
172.	(A)	I-Competency 002
173.	(D)	I-Competency 003
174.	(C)	I-Competency 003
175.	(B)	I-Competency 003
176.	(D)	I-Competency 003
177.	(B)	I-Competency 003
178.	(D)	I-Competency 003
179.	(B)	I-Competency 003
180.	(C)	I-Competency 003
181.	(C)	I-Competency 004
182.	(B)	I-Competency 004
183.	(A)	I-Competency 004
184.	(C)	I-Competency 004
185.	(B)	I-Competency 004

Bilingual Generalist EC-6 (192) Practice Test

Answer Explanations

1. (B)

The transitional bilingual education (TBE) program uses native language instruction in conjunction with ESL instruction. Native language instruction is used to ensure that students are progressing academically at the same level as native English speakers. ESL is used to promote the English proficiency needed to be successful in the all-English classroom. Once this is accomplished, students are exited from the bilingual program. (A) is incorrect because there is no evidence to suggest that TBE is the best program. The Thomas and Collier study found that students in the one-way and two-way dual language programs outperformed students in other programs, including TBE. (C) is incorrect because native language instruction is used as a provisional component of this program. Once ELLs develop fluency in English, L2 instruction is discontinued; thus, the program does not promote language maintenance. TBE has been endorsed by legislators in Texas and elsewhere in the United States, but this is not the main reason for the popularity of the method. Legislators endorse the program because students can be exited after two to three years of treatment. **Competency 001**

2. (D)

The Canadian immersion programs are designed to promote bilingualism. In the early elementary grades, English-speaking Canadians are immersed in the second language (French). Later in the process, English is added as a subject; eventually the subject matters are taught in both languages. In the United States, students receive instruction in L1 while learning English; once students are fluent in English, L1 instruction is removed. (A) is incorrect because the Canadian programs were designed for middle-class students, while the American programs were designed for poor, disenfranchised language minority students. (C) is incorrect because the structured immersion programs in the United States are designed to teach English only, while in the Canadian model, the program promotes bilingualism. **Competency 001**

3. (A)

Option (A) provides a comprehensive classification encompassing all instruments approved by the state education agency (SEA) to assess social and academic language among ELLs. From this comprehensive list of tests, districts select the instruments that they want to use. Choices (B), (C), and (D) are too narrow in scope because they provide examples of the different options available in each of the categories. The STAAR is the new official state-developed criterion-referenced test to assess mastery of the Texas Essential Knowledge and Skills—the state curriculum. The RPTE is used in grades 3 and up to assess the development of English reading, and the TOP is used in kindergarten and up to assess skills of listening, speaking, reading, and writing in English. Both RPTE and TOP instruments were designed to comply with the accountability requirements of the No Child Left Behind legislation. The California Achievement Test (CAT) and Iowa Test of Basic Skills (ITBS) are examples of norm-referenced achievement tests. **Competency 001**

4. (B)

The ARD committee was created by the federal Individuals with Disabilities Education Act to regulate admission and dismissal from the special education program. The LPAC is an equivalent body created by the Texas Bilingual Education Act, which also regulates admission and reclassification, and provides follow-up services to students in the bilingual or special language programs. Choice (A) is incorrect because there is no federal law that mandates bilingual education; instead, we have Title III of the NCLB legislation, which provides funding to support ELLs. Choice (C) is incorrect because legislators are not part of either committee—ARD or LPAC. Both committees are composed of at least a parent, teachers, and administrators. In the ARD, the parents of the child become part of the committee; in the LPAC, a parent with a child in the program represents the other parents. (D) is incorrect because the federal special education program regulates only the ARD; the LPAC is regulated by the state bilingual education law. **Competency 001**

5. (A)

Under the NCLB Act, the implementation of services to ELLs becomes a state and district responsibility. The legislation requires states to ensure that ELLs do not fall behind academically and that they learn English to be successful in the all-English classroom. The states are required to design an accountability plan to document progress toward goal completion. Choice (B) is a strong distracter because the legislation attempts to empower students and to allow parents the option of accepting or rejecting participation of their children in the program. However, these two elements are not as important and all-encompassing as the program implementation presented in choice (A). Choice (C) is incorrect because the role of the federal government is to regulate the process to deliver services, not to assume full control of the process. Choice (D) is incorrect because the legislation does not endorse bilingualism as the goal. Actually, the words bilingual and bilingualism were purposely omitted from the legislation. **Competency 001**

6. (A)

In the TBE model, students receive content instruction in their native language to be sure that they do not fall behind academically. They receive English language development through ESL until they develop the proficiency needed to function in the all-English classroom. (B) is a strong distracter because content area English has become the program of choice in situations where dual language instruction is not feasible—in classrooms with students from multiple language backgrounds. Choice (C) is also a plausible answer because some programs might use ESL pullout to teach English, but this approach is an exception to the rule. (D) is another strong distracter because school districts have often used ESL techniques to avoid providing the dual language approach required in Texas. However, the true intent of TBE is not to replace dual language instruction with ESL. **Competency 001**

7. (B)

Choice (B) presents a traditional definition of TBE in which students receive native language instruction and ESL until they develop the proficiency needed to be successful in the all-English classroom. Research findings have been incorporated in the design of TBE programs; however, the second part of the statement is inaccurate because the model does not allow for language maintenance. Once students develop proficiency in L2, native language instruction is discontinued; thus, (A) is incorrect. (C) is incorrect because TBE is a compensatory education program and does not attempt to promote bilingualism or multiculturalism. (D) is not the best answer because TBE is not a late-exit program. Late-exit programs provide dual language support for a period of five to six years, while TBE provides only two to four years of L1 support. The program is subtractive in nature because it begins with two languages; at the end of the program, the second replaces L1. **Competency 001**

8. (B)

The developmental bilingual education program is an enriching, additive, late-exit program (five to six years) designed to promote bilingualism. TBE is a compensatory, subtractive, early-exit (two to four years) program designed to teach English and to get the child out of the program as quickly as possible. Based on these two program descriptions, (A) is incorrect because TBE does not promote language maintenance. (C) is also incorrect because TBE is not designed to promote two languages; plus, the use of Spanish makes the option too restrictive because TBE in the nation can apply to languages other than Spanish. Students must have a solid foundation in L1 to benefit and transfer elements to L2. Only the DBE program allows sufficient L1 support to develop this foundation; thus, (D) is inaccurate. **Competency 001**

9. (B)

The bilingual education program is often perceived as a compensatory program for undocumented immigrant students. Because the program does not provide service to mainstream students, community leaders may oppose the program. However, when a program like the two-way dual language program allows English-speaking children the option of becoming bilingual, suddenly it becomes a program for the gifted and the opposition to dual language instruction disappears. The two-way program allows for the maintenance of L1 and L2 (see choice (A)) but that is not the real reason why mainstream groups are supporting the program. (C) and (D) are not the best answers because some two-way programs are supported by federal funding and have a research foundation, but none of these features explain why the program is getting support from mainstream groups. **Competency 001**

10. (C)

In the pullout system, children are removed from the classroom to receive English language development for a determined period of the day. While the child is getting ESL instruction, he or she misses instruction in the content areas and can fall behind academically. Choices (A) and (B) describe elements that might be true but do not explain the key disadvantage of the pullout program. (D) is not a true statement because students in the pullout program are generally able to develop some levels of English proficiency, but at the expense of learning content. **Competency 001**

11. (B)

Sheltered English provides content and language instruction in contextualized situations to be sure students are able to understand the content. Because English is the only language of instruction, a minimum command of the language is necessary to obtain the full benefit of the program. Having a strong foundation in L1 (see choice (A)) and being literate in the language (see choice (D)) are good predictors of second language acquisition, but there is no direct connection with specific ESL methods like sheltered English. (C) is incorrect because the native language of the students plays a minimal role in the selection of ESL methods. **Competency 001**

12. (B)

Newcomer programs were designed to support students from nontraditional backgrounds who can benefit from a special language program designed to facilitate adjustment to life in the United States. Traditionally, newcomer programs provide linguistics and cultural activities to facilitate this adjustment. The socioeconomic status (see choice (A)) or the language background (see choice (C)) can be an important consideration for placement in the program, but the literacy status and the culture that the child brings to the process are more important considerations. (D) is incorrect because students at the intermediate or advanced level of English proficiency might not need the basic linguistic and cultural services of newcomer centers. **Competency 001**

13. (A)

The dominant theory of second language acquisition suggests that people store information in a language-free environment common to L1 and L2, the common underlying proficiency. Because language information is stored in a common environment, learning a second language does not diminish the mental capabilities of students. Proponents of the separate underlying proficiency (SUP) believe that L1 and L2 have to split the mental space, which can result in semilingualism or the inability to develop proficiency in either language. Research suggests that the SUP model (see choice (B)) does accurately describe what happens in the brain of a child learning a second language. (C) is incorrect because it makes reference to the SUP model mentioned in (B). (D) describes the social language, which does not have a connection with how the brain is organized. **Competency 001**

14. (B)

As a result of the *Lau* v. *Nichols* ruling, the OCR instituted the *Lau* remedies to force school districts to comply with the court ruling to offer meaningful education to ELLs. Choice (A) is incorrect because the court just mandated the district to offer meaningful education but did not specify the type of remedy. (C) is a true statement: at least two other cases (*ASPIRA* v. *NY* and *Serna* v. *Portales*) were decided based on the *Lau* ruling; however, these court cases affected only two states (New York and New Mexico) and the *Lau* remedies from the OCR affected the whole nation. (D) is a false statement because there has never been a bilingual education law mandating bilingual education. Title III of the NCLB legislation provides funding to support bilingual education programs. **Competency 001**

15. (B)

The AIR study compared the effectiveness of the bilingual and the English-only program and found no significant differences between the two. The research findings were questionable, but as a result of this finding, structured immersion was conceptualized as an option to address the language needs of ELLs. The term *structured immersion* refers to a program designed to teach English. The term was coined to avoid confusion with the bilingual immersion programs in Canada. (A) is incorrect because Proposition 227 mandated that bilingual education in California be eliminated. (C) is incorrect because the Bilingual Education Act has never identified dual language instruction as the program of choice. (D) is incorrect because the Bilingual Education Act of 1978 emphasized the transitional nature of bilingual education programs or TBE. The act also prohibited the use of federal funding to implement developmental or maintenance of bilingual education programs. **Competency 001**

16. (B)

The perceived social and psychological distance describes how ELLs see their relationship with members of mainstream groups. If they perceive themselves as socially equal, then second language acquisition becomes an easy task. However, if both groups perceive themselves as different, then it can lead to social isolation, which can hinder second language acquisition. Self-esteem, socioeconomic status (see choice (A)), prejudices (see choice (C)) and past injustices against the group (see choice (D)) can affect interaction with the group; but all these features are encompassed in the "perceived and social psychological distance" concept suggested in (B). **Competency 002**

17. (C)

The Canadian researcher Jim Cummins suggested that ELLs must arrive at a threshold level in their native language to transfer language and cognitive strategies from L1 to L2. The threshold level is reached when students develop a strong literacy foundation in their native language. A culture-free curriculum (see choice (A)), racial and linguistic harmony (see choice (B)), and assimilation (see choice (D)) might play a role in the language and cognitive growth of ELLs, but none of the choices individually can account for the cognitive and academic growth of ELLs. **Competency 002**

18. (B)

First language acquisition happens in a subconscious manner when children try to understand the world around them. Parents and caregivers teach language concepts indirectly through meaningful interactions in contextualized situations. Parents generally provide corrective feedback to children indirectly through modeling. (A) is incorrect because it presents a contradictory statement: language learning is indeed a lifelong process; therefore, it cannot finish at puberty. A first language is acquired subconsciously in meaningful situations, but direct corrective feedback is rarely used to support the process (see choice (C)). Choice (D) is incorrect because first language acquisition is not taught deductively, i.e., through direct instruction. **Competency 002**

19. (D)

Children who are exposed to the second language before puberty generally develop native-like pronunciation. On the other hand, adults generally rely on their native language as a foundation for the development of L2, which often leads to language interference at the phonological level. Adults are generally better at handling the grammar and abstract components of the language. Therefore, children have advantages over adults at the phonological level, but adults might have the advantage in all other areas. Choice (A) is a true statement but addresses only the phonological component of the language. Choice (B) is probably a true statement, but there is no empirical research to support it. Choice (C) negates research findings in the acquisition of a second language. Children exposed to the language after puberty might develop a better understanding of the abstract component of the language but they might lag behind in the development of pronunciation. **Competency 002**

20. (C)

Students at the speech-emergence stage communicate in phrases using words with high semantic value. They are also beginning to understand the print concept. They can understand speech and written communication presented in contextualized situations and accompanied with visuals. In the preproduction stage (see choice (A)), students lack basic language skills and might have to rely on nonverbal communication to get their point across. Thus, it is highly unlikely that they can understand written communication. In the early production stage (see choice (B)), students begin to communicate using language at the social level in everyday situations. Print awareness is taking place, but the main emphasis at this stage is the development of basic oral communication. The intermediate and advanced fluency stage (see choice (D)) represents a higher level of proficiency where students communicate using simple sentences; however, the language is not fully developed and their speech might experience language interference together with overgeneralizations. Their literacy development is beyond the basic recognition skills alluded to in the question. **Competency 002**

21. (A)

Effective methods to teach a second language should revolve around the child and his or her communication needs. The statement "student-centered and communication-driven" describes an effective approach to teaching a second language. (D) calls for the opposite, teacher-centered, and does not represent best teaching practices. (B) and (C) call for the teaching of a second language following a grammatical syllabus. Research does not support a grammar-based approach to teaching languages. **Competency 002**

22. (B)

The language experience approach (LEA) was designed to teach reading to children from non-mainstream groups as an alternative to the traditional basal readers. The basal reader contains stories written in a sequential format based on specific reading levels and representing middle-class values and experiences. The LEA can be used to teach foreign languages (see choice (A)), but it was not originally designed for that population. It emphasizes writing skills but not necessarily for TAKS (see choice (C)). Finally, there is no connection between LEA and the teaching of metacognitive strategies (see choice (D)). **Competency 002**

23. (A)

Research on second language acquisition suggests that a strong literacy development in L1 can facilitate the acquisition of similar levels of proficiency in L2. Language-specific variables, together with literacy and metacognitive strategies, can transfer from L1 to L2. Reading skills are not identical in L1 and

L2 (see choice (B)), but the strategies to develop the skills might be similar. Reading skills might be confusing for ELLs (see choice (C)) and can affect the cognitive process in bilingual students (see choice (D)), but they do not represent the rationale for the implementation of initial reading instruction in L1. **Competency 002**

24. (C)

The natural method (NM) and the total physical response (TPR) are modern adaptations of the direct method. The direct method imitates the way that babies acquire their first language. The TPR and NM use commands, nonverbal communication, and context to teach the language. The LEA is a method to teach reading, and the CLM is a method to teach foreign languages mostly to adults (see choice (A)). The audio lingual method is an ESL method that uses rote memorization and repetition drills to teach ESL (see choice (B)), none of which are effective strategies for children acquiring a first language. As the name suggests, the grammar translation method (see choice (D)) is used to translate from one language to another, a strategy rarely used to teach a second language. **Competency 002**

25. (A)

The BICS describes the social language that ELLs acquire after two to four years of exposure to the language. This type of proficiency is used in face-to-face communications and in highly contextualized situations. The CALP, on the other hand, describes the academic language required to do well in the content areas. It takes from five to seven years of meaningful exposure to the language to achieve this level of proficiency. Students who are exited from the bilingual program without developing CALP can experience academic problems in school. (B) and (C) contain opinions not directly supported in the scenario. (D) is incorrect because Carla is lacking academic language, not the social language component. **Competency 002**

26. (A)

Second language development is best achieved when instruction is geared toward meaningful and functional tasks in the language. This kind of approach can facilitate and increase the motivation for L2 learning. Deductive and inductive teaching can be used to teach a second language. However, inductive or indirect teaching seems to be more effective than direct instruction. (B) presents a convoluted and contradictory explanation involving inductive and deductive teaching. (C) looks correct until the term *meaningful memorization* is introduced. Memorization is not the best tool to promote proficiency in L2. Idiomatic expressions and tongue twisters are useful activities to promote basic communication skills but fail to go beyond that. **Competency 002**

27. (D)

Teachers use dramatic reading to make the story more interesting and to improve listening comprehension. Often teachers ask students to close their eyes to increase concentration and to listen for comprehension. Because students were instructed to close their eyes, reading comprehension is not the main purpose of the activity; thus, (A) and (B) are incorrect. Dramatic reading does not affect directly speaking or writing skills; thus, (C) is also incorrect. **Competency 002**

28. (A)

Nativists believe that humans are born with a mechanism that they call the language acquisition device (LAD), which gives humans the capability to acquire languages. However, for this mechanism to work, the child must be exposed to speakers of the language. Healthy children who are exposed to language in natural settings during the early years develop language. Yet children who are socially and linguistically isolated during the formative years can experience language delay or might not be able to develop adult-like language. Initially, children learn language through imitation with little direct corrections, but after age two, children generally develop language creativity and other techniques to improve language acquisition; thus, (B) and (C) are incorrect. Choice (D)

is incorrect because children are not born with language; rather, they have the mechanism to acquire it.
Competency 002

29. (A)

When children overgeneralize as in the example—*bestest*—they are in reality applying grammar rules, which indicates that they have passed the stage of mere repetition, and they are beginning to decode the grammar of the language. This overgeneralization is typical of native English speakers acquiring a language and does not show any kind of interference from a language. This statement eliminates choices (B) and (C). Choice (D) is incorrect, but it can be confusing for students taking the test because cartoons (*Rugrats*) often use this kind of overgeneralization to mimic the speech of children; however, the continuous overgeneralization typical of children cannot be attributed to cartoons on television.
Competency 002

30. (B)

Children in the preproduction stage of second language acquisition generally cannot communicate verbally. They are in the process of analyzing and "cracking" the language code. Thus, the use of commands, contextualizing instruction, and using concrete objects as teaching tools can promote language development. Choice (A) calls for the use of direct instruction on the structure of the language. This option might not be developmentally appropriate because students at the preproduction stage do not have the language skills necessary to benefit from direct instruction. Short answers like yes/no and either/or are usually used for students who are at the early production stage of second language acquisition (see choice (C)). Children in the preproduction stage (see choice (D)) do not have the language skills to understand and address open-ended questions.
Competency 002

31. (B)

The question calls for activities that promote self-directed learning. Advanced students generally have sufficient knowledge about the language to analyze the source of the errors and make their own corrections. Students at the beginning stage of second language acquisition might not have the knowledge to make their own corrections; thus, Choice (A) is incorrect. In communication activities (see choice (C)), ESL teachers do not provide direct corrective feedback; instead, they are encouraged to provide indirect feedback by modeling the structures in question. The same principle applies to (D); direct corrections are not the best tool during communication activities. However, teachers can take note of the grammatical problems and design a grammar lesson to teach the concepts.
Competency 003

32. (A)

Results of the test change are seen to in each administration; thus, the reliability of the instrument becomes the key issue in this question. Reliability is defined as the ability of the test to produce consistent results, which obviously does not happen in the scenario. The credentials of the diagnostician (see choice (D)) should not be part of the problem because he or she is bilingual and fully certified. The scenario does not provide negative information about the accuracy of the test, and it just indicated the instrument was approved by the state. Based on lack of information about the accuracy of the instrument, we can rule out choice (C). Choice (B) is incorrect because the scenario does not provide information about the content of the test.
Competency 003

33. (D)

Modern assessment practices call for the use of multiple assessment instruments to make instructional decisions. The medical history of the child and input from parents can yield vital information to develop a better picture of the child. Choice (A) is incorrect because the question calls for elements "beyond state-mandated tests," and the language proficiency tests are part of the state-mandated instrument. Evaluation and input from peers (see choice (B)) are not generally taken into account to make placement decisions. The input from parents is important, but generally they do not perform formal evaluations (see choice (C)) on their children. **Competency 003**

34. (C)

Culture shapes the way that children behave and perform in school. Linguistic limitations can also affect the ability of children to demonstrate capabilities and potential. The option of making students feel valued and wanted (see choice (A)) is a noble cause, but it should not be the main concern when assessing CLD learners. (B) presents a true statement when it indicates that students go through different stages of development, but that choice is invalidated when it says that these *should not* affect the way in which they are assessed. The term *cultural deficit* used in (D) invalidates the answer because CLD learners cannot be considered culturally deficient: They already bring with them their language and culture. **Competency 003**

35. (D)

Traditionally, standardized tests to measure intelligence and achievement contain middle-class values and experiences that might be foreign to CLD students. This mismatch can affect their performance in these tests. Choice (A) presents an opinion difficult to support and probably is inaccurate. Written tests of intelligence are generally norm-referenced tests designed to show general ability and potential. They are not designed to measure content covered in class (see choice (B)); thus, the fact that they do address class content should not be construed as a flaw. Intelligence tests often overemphasize logic and mathematics at the expense of other indicators of intelligence (see choice (C)), and this will create problems for all children. However, for CLD learners, the organization of the test and the values represented in the test constitute an additional and more important hurdle. **Competency 003**

36. (D)

Culture and language can affect the interpretation of assessment results for CLD student populations. For that reason, it is important to assess students using multiple instruments and to assemble a team with multiple areas of specialization (multidisciplinary) to be sure that results are interpreted accurately. The physical development of the child is important, but the legal status of the child is irrelevant (see choice (A)). Depending on the purpose of the assessment, some instruments should be administered in the students' native language but not necessarily in Spanish only (see choice (B)). The instrument should be validated for the intended population (see choice (C)); however, perhaps more important than that is how the results are finally interpreted. **Competency 003**

37. (D)

Portfolio assessment contains a sample collection of the students' work. Students are active participants in the gathering and organization of the portfolio, which provides a sense of ownership in the assessment process. (A) provides a generic definition of portfolio assessment, but it failed to present its real value. (B) presents a false statement because the main purpose of portfolio assessment is not to compete with other students. Portfolio assessment is used to document progress through a specific time frame and its content is commonly shared with parents; thus, its content is not confidential, as suggested in (C). **Competency 003**

38. (A)

Effective assessment practices are generally part of instruction, are ongoing, and are interpreted based on the developmental and cultural characteristics of the child (student-centered). It can be formative as well as summative (end product) (see choice (B)), but its data collection cannot be restricted to documentation collected using state-approved instruments. Data collection is not restricted to information gathered by diagnosticians (see choice (C)); parents and other personnel can provide valuable information for assessment. Assessment should promote self-monitoring (see choice (D)) but should not emphasize weaknesses only. Instead, assessment should capitalize on the strengths that children bring to the learning process. **Competency 003**

39. (D)

The TPRI was designed for English-dominant children to assess reading development in kindergarten through grade 2. In contrast, the RPTE was specifically designed for ELLs in grades 3 and up. (A) is a correct statement; both assess reading development, but the answer lacks specificity because it does not mention the groups or the grade levels addressed. (B) is an incorrect statement because the instruments do not address Spanish reading development. (C) is incorrect because TPRI was not designed for ELLs, and the RPTE was designed for all ELLs, not only for Spanish-speaking children. **Competency 003**

40. (C)

The idiomatic expression is alluding, or making reference, to Fort Knox, historically one of the main depositories of gold reserves in the United States. Listeners need to make a connection between the large amounts of gold Fort Knox had at one point and the implications of the statement. Choice (A) contains part of the answer, *allusion*, but includes the concept of a metaphor, which is not present in the statement. A metaphor is a figure of speech that makes a direct comparison of two ideas as in the statement, *You are my Venus*. In this case, the speaker is comparing someone to Venus, the goddess of love in Roman mythology. The concept of simile (see choice (B)) is not present in the statement. A simile is similar to a metaphor but makes an indirect comparison by using the words *like* or *as*—*You are like Venus*. A hyperbole (see choice (D)) is an exaggeration, like in the statement, "I am so hungry I can eat a horse." There is some degree of exaggeration in the statement, but it is not strong enough to be considered a hyperbole. **Competency 003**

41. (A)

A strong literacy background in L1 facilitates the transfer of skills to the second language, which will indeed expedite the development of literacy skills in L2. A strong L1 development facilitates the acquisition of a second language (see choice (B)), but it will not guarantee that it will be done in a fun and relaxed environment. The transfer of literacy skills from L1 to L2 (see choice (C)) goes beyond the transfer of academic language. Children also transfer metacognitive strategies and grammar concepts to the second language. A strong background in L1 can help in the preservation of the language (see choice (D)), but it cannot guarantee it. **Competency 003**

42. (C)

The use of pictures to represent events in the story can be used to represent the sequencing of events in the story. It can also be used to introduce visually the parts of the story, i.e., characters, setting, plot, climax, and resolution. Choice (A) is incorrect because the teacher is not connecting the pictures with the written text. Teachers can fill in the background knowledge of the students through visuals (see choice (B)); however, this activity is usually done as a prereading activity. Because the visuals were used as a postreading activity, we can believe that filling in the gaps was not the primary purpose of the activity. The teacher is definitely using developmentally appropriate practices (see choice (D)), but the ultimate intent of the activity goes beyond that. **Competency 003**

43. (A)

Checklists, retelling stories, and anecdotal records are examples of informal assessment measures commonly used to assess the development of communication skills among ELLs. The informal nature of these assessment strategies eliminates the stress associated with formal assessment procedures. Multiple-choice tests, cloze tests, and informal reading inventories (see choice (B)) are not generally used to assess oral communication skills. Audiotaping can be used to assess oral language development, but written cloze tests and standardized achievement tests (see choice (C)) are not. Repetition drills, choral reading, and chants (see choice (D)) are generally used to assess pronunciation, which is only one component of oral communication skills. **Competency 003**

44. (B)

One of the main functions of portfolio assessment is to document and analyze the growth of students. For ELLs, portfolios can be tailored to document the growth of language and content through a specific grading period. Teachers can show parents the kind of work done at the beginning of a grading period and at the end of it to provide evidence of children's performance. Portfolio assessment can be used to document social development and interaction with native English speakers (see choice (A)), but its main purpose goes beyond the social development of the child. Portfolio can be linked to the collection of assignments and daily activities (see choice (C)), but its real meaning goes beyond the mere collection of daily work and artistic manifestations (see choice (D)). **Competency 003**

45. (C)

The threshold level is defined as an advanced level of literacy development in a given language. Students who arrive at this level possess a solid foundation in language and can easily transfer those skills to the second language. Choice (A) is incorrect because there is no guarantee that students who have arrived at the threshold level will develop the positive self-esteem needed to acquire a second language (see choice (A)); nevertheless, there are indications that students who have been successful in L1 feel more comfortable dealing with L2. There is no indication to suggest that the mastery of L1 will lead to an understanding of culture and its implications for the acquisition of a second language (see choice (B)). The contrastive analysis theory alluded to in (D) requires students to have a deep understanding of L1 and L2, which ELLs obviously do not have. **Competency 003**

46. (C)

Teachers need to avoid direct corrections in communication activities. Direct corrections inhibit communication and can affect students' self-esteem. Instead, the emphasis should be placed on the content of the communication. Meeting the communication needs of children and tailoring instruction to address their needs are some of the most important principles of student-centered instruction. Supporting students' self-esteem and valuing students' contributions (see choice (A)) is positive, but we also need to be sure that students are getting accurate information and the same quality of content as students in mainstream groups. Teachers can guide ELLs to the expected answer, but accepting inaccurate responses is not an acceptable behavior for teachers. It is important to guide students to pay attention to the linguistic behavior of their peers and to learn from it, but it is not the role of children to provide corrective feedback (see choice (B)) to them. Students often imitate the cultural and language patterns of native English speakers (see choice (D)), but this does not emphasize the true meaning of the student-centered approach for teaching. **Competency 004**

47. (B)

When teachers develop activities to address the needs of students at different levels of language mastery and allow them to respond based on their language level, they are using developmentally appropriate practices by taking into account diversity and the stages of L2 development. Assessment and lifetime learning were indirectly addressed in the scenario, but details were too superficial to make (A) the best answer. Questions dealing with technology generally involve state-of-the-art devices and processes. Choices (C) and (D) mention television, but in this kind of test, television by itself does not capture the complete concept of technology as intended on TExES examinations. **Competency 004**

48. (B)

Organizing the support systems of students at various stages of language development creates a peer-support system where students can benefit from each other. Beginners and intermediate ELLs will get linguistic support from advanced students, and advanced speakers will reinforce what they know when they provide instructional support to them. Cooperative learning groups (see choice (A)) seem to be a good idea, but organizing them homogeneously prevents them from developing a linguistic support system. Organizing intensive ESL training for students and providing cross-cultural training for faculty members (see choice (C)) seems to be a long-range project that failed to address the immediacy nature of the question—how the teacher can address the linguistic diversity of the group. Making students aware of ethnic and cultural differences (see choice (D)) emphasizes differences among students and does not address positively the issue of linguistic diversity. **Competency 004**

49. (D)

The teacher can easily use the results of games to rank teams based on the percentage of games won and lost. She can also guide students to determine the average percentage of points scored by individuals or teams, and other mathematics comparisons. Choice (A) emphasizes language development, but it will be difficult to teach mathematics by just imitating weather and sports television personalities. (B) promotes language development without presenting a connection with mathematics. (C) emphasizes writing and forecasting weather based on patterns that indirectly address the mathematics (patterns) components, but the answer is not direct enough to constitute the best answer. **Competency 004**

50. (C)

Sheltered English focuses on the delivery of content in contextualized situations together with English language development. Students with different primary languages receive content instruction in English. However, teachers use a variety of strategies with the goal of facilitating comprehension and the acquisition of English and the content areas. The primary goal of the program is not to promote bilingual education (see choice (A)) but to teach English and content concurrently. There is no direct connection between sheltered instruction and the bilingual education programs in Canada (see choice (B)). (D) contains incorrect information because submersion does not lead to bilingualism. Contrary to sheltered instruction, in submersion, students are placed in the all-English classroom without any kind of linguistic support. **Competency 004**

51. (D)

One of the key features of sheltered English is the delivery of comprehensible input through hands-on, discovery learning, and contextualized instruction. Speaking slowly (see choice (A)), using nonverbal communication (see choice (B)) to promote comprehension, and checking for understanding (see choice (C)) are some of the features of sheltered English, but individually they do not represent the main concept of sheltered English. **Competency 004**

52. (A)

In indirect instruction, students are guided to discover and construct their own knowledge. However, teachers have to guide students to identify important concepts in the lesson. Questioning techniques are used to analyze and develop an in-depth knowledge of important components in the lesson. Questions can also be used to keep students engaged (see choice (B)), but their main purpose goes beyond keeping students engaged. Promoting equity and equality among linguistic minorities (see choice (C)) seems to be a commendable goal, but questioning in indirect teaching is designed for more specific purposes. Because indirect teaching by definition promotes inductive learning, (D) is obviously incorrect. **Competency 004**

53. (B)

Humanistic psychology takes into account all the physical, social, and emotional needs of the learners. Teachers who follow humanistic practices make students feel secure and supported. Choice (A) is incorrect because behaviorist psychology is based on reward and punishment and uses a teacher-centered approach. (A) is also incorrect because cognitive psychology is primarily concerned with the mental processes used in the teaching-learning process. It does not emphasize how the human or emotional component affects the learning process. (D) is completely incorrect because it refers to a book written by the Brazilian educator Paulo Freire. **Competency 004**

54. (C)

Preview-review is one of the traditional bilingual education strategies designed to teach content using two languages. In this strategy, the content is introduced in L1, the technical vocabulary and the lesson is presented in L2, and finally L1 is used again to review the content. The use of both languages at the beginning of instruction (see choice (A)) is incorrect because it does not specify the order and fails to indicate that L1 is used again at the end of the lesson. (B) is incorrect because translation is not used in this strategy. The concept of language separation (see choice (D)) is probably maintained in the preview-review strategy, but it is not the key characteristic of the strategy. **Competency 004**

55. (B)

Learning logs are used to guide students to summarize elements learned and to identify those who need additional support. By guiding students to summarize or synthesize the information, teachers help students strengthen their understanding of the concepts learned. Learning logs provide a list of elements learned (see choice (A)), but their value goes beyond a mere list of concepts. A learning log can be used as an advanced organizer to communicate with teachers and peers (see choice (C)) and as a guide for oral presentations (see choice (D)), but these are not the main objectives of learning logs. **Competency 004**

56. (B)

English language learners often have problems understanding content because they might not have the background information needed to internalize new concepts. By examining the knowledge that children bring to the lesson and providing the missing content, teachers expand the schema needed to acquire new content. The question deals with getting students to understand new content, not necessarily with language development (see choice (A)). Second language acquisition (see choice (C)) and vocabulary development (see choice (D)) will definitely help the child, but the question does not address language development by itself. **Competency 004**

57. (B)

Semantic mapping is a visual representation of interconnected characteristics or features of a given concept. This interrelatedness can be represented with words or visuals. For example, the concept of *landscape* can be linked to pictures of lakes, rivers, mountains, grass, trees, and other features that represent possible attributes of the concept. The word *mapping* can be linked to geography (see choice (A)); however, the intended meaning of the word goes beyond geography. People can use semantic mapping to contrast concepts in L1 and L2 (see choice (C)), but the process was not designed to accomplish that. (D) describes a possible type of mapping but does not represent the specific type of mapping required in the question—semantic. **Competency 004**

58. (C)

Metacognitive strategies describe ways to conceptualize how learning takes place. These types of strategies are divided into two classifications: organization and planning for learning, and self-monitoring and self-evaluating. Cognitive strategies (see choice (A)) describe techniques to improve understanding, increase retention of information, and apply new information. Social strategies (see choice (B)) describe techniques for learning from each other in social situations—peer or group format. (D) describes strategies for promoting rote memorization of facts. Some typical examples of this type of strategy are the use of songs, acronyms, and mnemonics to remember facts or rules. **Competency 004**

59. (B)

Cognitive strategies use techniques to improve retention of content and prior knowledge like information acquired in L1 as a foundation for acquiring new concepts. Metacognitive strategies (see choice (A)) describe the ability to conceptualize how learning takes place, not the actual transfer of information from L1 to L2. Social strategies (see choice (C)) describe ways to acquire new knowledge in social settings. The use of mnemonic devices is part of a rote memory strategy, which has no correlation with transferring content from L1 to L2. **Competency 004**

60. (B)

Information in a textbook is organized following a specific format that provides information different from the traditional narrative format used in children's literature. Students need to use resources like glossaries, indexes, text boxes, highlighted areas, graphics, and visuals to increase comprehension. Teaching technical vocabulary (see choice (A)), the use of cognates (see choice (C)), and the use of glossaries (see choice (D)) are good strategies for helping students gather information from textbooks, but individually they cannot account for the best answer. **Competency 004**

61. (B)

The social studies strands are systematically integrated throughout the social studies state curriculum in grades K–12. Choice (A) is incorrect based on the previous explanation. (C) and (D) are incorrect because the social studies strands are used in public education as well as in higher education. **Competency 023**

62. (D)

TEKS introduces social studies from the known to the unknown. Students begin studying themselves and from there go to the school, community, and finally to the state. The focus on TEKS for fourth grade is the history of Texas. Choice (A) is incorrect because TEKS is available only in K–12. For prekindergarten, teachers use instructional guidelines. (B) is incorrect because the focus of first grade is the school and the community. (C) is incorrect because in grade 3, the focus is the individual and how each affects the community. **Competency 023**

63. (A)

Choice (A) is correct because maps use symbolic representation, and children at that age rely mostly on concrete experiences for learning. The abstraction typical of maps' legends and other symbolic representations might not be developmentally appropriate for this age group. (B) is a plausible statement but not the best answer. Children initially will be inclined to use the globe as a toy and pay attention to colors, but eventually they will understand its function through classroom instruction. (C) is incorrect because it presents an opinion not supported in the scenario. (D) is probably a true statement. Children will have problems conceptualizing how the Earth can be represented in a small 12-inch globe, but this choice is not the best answer because it addresses only one component of the question—globe representation. **Competency 025**

64. (C)

The Earth is divided into 24 zones based on the meridians of longitude, which are determined using the rotation of the Earth and its exposure to sunlight. This rotation creates day and night, and consequently the concept of time. Choice (A) is incorrect because the International Date Line is only one of 24 meridians of the Earth. Choice (B) is incorrect because the term *revolution* describes the movement of the Earth around the sun, which affects the seasons but not necessarily the time zones. Choice (D) is incorrect because the parallels of latitude do not affect the time zones. **Competency 025**

65. (B)

The convergence of the Tigris and the Euphrates created a fertile region where some of the greatest civilizations of the world emerged. This part of the world has been called the Fertile Crescent and it is part of the area called the Cradle of Civilizations. Choice (A) is incorrect because the Nile gave birth to the Egyptian civilization, and the Amazon river is located in South America, far away from Mesopotamia. Choice (C) is incorrect because the Indus River is located in modern-day India. Choice (D) is incorrect because the Volga and Danube rivers are located in Europe. **Competency 024**

66. (D)

The country of Iraq is located in the region known as Mesopotamia. (A) is incorrect because the country of Iran is located east of the Tigris River. Choice (B) is incorrect because Pakistan is located further southeast of the rivers. Choice (C) is also incorrect because the Kingdom of Kuwait is located southwest of the area and south of Iraq. **Competency 025**

67. (B)

The feudal system characterized life in the Middle Ages. The attacks of the barbaric tribes forced people to live under the protection of a lord, usually within the walls of a castle. Muslim Turks took Jerusalem in 1095, and a year later, Christians began the Crusades to rescue the Holy Land. Choice (A) is incorrect because both the Greek and Roman empires are part of the Ancient World. Choice (C) is incorrect because one of the pair is part of the Ancient World—Stonehenge. Choice (D) is incorrect because Alexander the Great ruled the Ancient World. **Competency 024**

68. (B)

The Maya and the Aztecs occupied the area of Central America and Southern Mexico called Mesoamerica. Both groups were accomplished builders, astronomers, and mathematicians. Choice (A) is incorrect because the Inca civilization was not a Mesoamerican group. They developed an advanced civilization in South America, in present-day Peru and Ecuador. Choice (C) is incorrect because only the Toltecs were from Mesoamerica; the Pueblo Indians continue in present-day New Mexico in North America. Choice (D) is incorrect because only the Olmecs were a Mesoamerican group. The Iroquois civilizations developed in North America. **Competency 024**

69. (B)

Iraq is a Muslim nation with multiple ethnic groups within its borders. The largest groups are the Shi'a Muslims, Sunni Muslims, and the Kurds. (A) is incorrect. The multiple groups living in Iraq speak Arabic, Kurdish, Turkish, Assyrian, and other languages. Choice (C) is incorrect because Iraq is located in the Middle Eastern part of Asia. Choice (D) is incorrect because Pakistan is a Muslim country from the region but there is no political association between the two nations. **Competency 024**

70. (B)

Most of Brazil is located in the Southern Hemisphere, and the United States is located in the Northern Hemisphere; thus, if the United States is in winter, then in Brazil it is summer. Choices (A), (C), and (D) are incorrect based on the previous explanation. **Competency 025**

71. (C)

There is a difference of one day from Honolulu to Tokyo. Honolulu is located west of the International Date Line (IDL), while Japan is east of the line. That is, if we travel from Honolulu toward the west on December 7 and pass the IDL to get to Tokyo, we would get there on December 8. The attack was recorded on December 7, 1941, in Honolulu, but the equivalent date for Japan was December 8, 1941. (A), (B), and (D) are incorrect because they do not explain the real reason for the date confusion. Additionally, the scenario does not provide information to support the position that Emperor Hirohito was confused about the dates. **Competency 025**

72. (C)

The Apache and the Comanche domesticated the horse and became skillful hunters and warriors. These skills allowed them to fight the whites for many years for control of the Central and Great Plains of Texas. Choice (A) is incorrect because the tribes from the plains were nomads and did not develop an advanced civilization. (B) is incorrect because both the Comanche and the Apache were nomads and did not leave permanent constructions. (D) is incorrect because the tribes from the area had to hunt for survival and they had to move continuously to find adequate food supplies. **Competency 024**

73. (C)

Reducing the production of oil while keeping the same demand for the product creates an imbalance between supply and demand. This imbalance results in a price increase. (A) is incorrect. War generally increases the demand and prices in general, not only the price of fossil fuels. (B) is incorrect because the statement does not explain the economic principle required in the question. It just presents a true statement—the American economy depends on foreign oil. (D) presents an opinion that fails to address the true question. **Competency 026**

74. (D)

The Fifteenth Amendment granted black males the right to vote. (A) is incorrect because the voting right was given to black males only, not women of any race. (B) is incorrect because the Fourteenth Amendment granted citizenship to former slaves. (C) is incorrect because the Thirteenth Amendment granted freedom to slaves. **Competency 027**

75. (C)

The U.S. Constitution set up a system so that each branch has the power to control or regulate the power of the other two. Choice (A) is incorrect because judicial review addresses only the power of the judicial branch to review legislation enacted by Congress and signed by the president. If the legislation is unconstitutional, it can be invalidated. (B) is incorrect because it addresses the power of the president to veto or refuse to sign legislation approved by Congress. (D) is incorrect because habeas corpus is one of the civil rights that guarantees people the right to a quick trial by jury. **Competency 027**

76. (D)

A visual analysis of columns 4, 5, and 6 shows that the phoneme /sh/ can be represented by at least four different graphemes—*ch, s, ss,* and *t*—in words like ***ch**ef, **s**ure, mi**ss**ion,* and *caution.* The grapheme *ch* is also inconsistent. Column 3 shows that the grapheme *ch* represents the sound /k/. This inconsistency affects the ability of ELLs to separate the two phonemes. (A), (B), and (C) are incorrect because the scenario does not provide evidence to suggest that ELLs cannot establish a difference or pronounce the two phonemes, or that they might not be interested in learning the difference between the two. **Competency 005**

77. (B)

The chart provides examples of words that follow grapheme-phoneme correspondence. It also provides examples of words that use different graphemes to represent the sounds. This chart provides students with tangible information to help them deal with graphophonemic inconsistencies. (A) is incorrect because this particular chart places more emphasis on graphophonemic inconsistencies than on consistencies. (C) is incorrect because the chart presents words in isolation; thus, it cannot present information about the intonation pattern used in sentences or larger units. (D) is a plausible answer, but it does not capture the true intent of the activity. The chart is designed to deal with specific, inconsistent sounds only. **Competency 005**

78. (B)

The word *thought* is a very long word, but it is a monosyllabic word. It has three phonemes. The word contains two consonant diagraphs, *th* and *ght*, and a vowel digraph, *ou*, representing one sound each for a total of three sounds. (A), (C), and (D) are incorrect based on the previous explanation. **Competency 005**

79. (A)

The child is having problems with word stress and syllabication, and both terms are part of phonological awareness. (B) is incorrect because the child is not having problems with phonemic awareness. He has mastered the ability to separate phonemes and blend them back to re-create the word. (C) and (D) are incorrect because none of them individually explains the needs of the child. The reality is that the child needs support in both components; thus, (C) or (D) individually cannot be the correct answer. **Competency 006**

80. (A)

Alliteration is a technique to emphasize the connection between the consonant and the sound that it represents. In this particular case, the tongue twister is used to emphasize the sound of the /r/. (B) is incorrect because the technique goes beyond the use of a tongue twister. Tongue twisters are examples of alliteration and they emphasize pronunciation and fluency. (C) is incorrect because the utterance does not represent an example of traditional nursery rhymes. Nursery rhymes are short poems, stories, or songs written to entertain children. The most famous nursery rhymes are in the Mother Goose collection from England. **Competency 006**

81. (B)

The answer calls for syllabication and phoneme segmentation. Both concepts are part of phonological awareness. Choice (A) is incorrect because sentence analysis was not the primary concern in the scenario. The intonation pattern describes the rhythm and pitch used in phrases and sentences. (C) is incorrect because in the latter activity, the issue is the phonological analysis of words. Vocabulary development was emphasized in the first part of the scenario only. (D) is incorrect because the scenario does not address pronunciation at all. **Competency 006**

82. (D)

Teachers have to present the consistent sounds of English first to develop self-confidence among children. Once children master those initial grapheme-phoneme correspondences, they can attempt more challenging components. Choice (A) is incorrect because it deals with a generic well-accepted practice, but it does not address the question. (B) is incorrect because the alphabetic principle does not specifically deal with the issue of the development of foreign accents. (C) is incorrect because it failed to address the question. It is always important to create an atmosphere of collaboration among students, but this statement does not address the linguistic nature of the questions. **Competency 007**

83. (C)

Syllabication and word stress are part of the concept called phonological awareness. Choice (A) is incorrect because the activity goes beyond establishing the connection between letters and sounds typical of the alphabetic principle. (B) is incorrect because the development of fluency goes beyond the analysis of individual words. The development of phonological awareness is a prerequisite for the development of fluency. (D) is incorrect because the concept of syllabication is only one of two elements presented in the scenario—syllabication and word stress. **Competency 007**

84. (D)

Onsets represent the first phoneme of a syllable or a monosyllabic word like the words presented in choice (D). Rimes follow the onset, and are linked to the concept of word families. The rime *ank* can be used to create multiple words, like *blank, tank, rank,* and *flank*. Choices (A) and (C) are generally used to represent verb tenses and cannot be considered the typical rime or word family. Choice (B) is incorrect because the two words do not represent onset and rimes. Instead, the example of *very–berry* represents a minimal pair—two words that differ in only one phoneme. **Competency 007**

85. (B)

A balanced-reading approach uses best practices from both phonics and whole language. It also places emphasis on the use of authentic literature and the literature-based approach to construct meaning. Choice (A) is incorrect because the skills-based approach emphasizes mostly phonics instruction. (C) is incorrect because the meaning-based approach emphasizes mostly the whole language approach. (D) is incorrect because there is no connection between humanistic psychology and the question. **Competency 008**

86. (B)

Miscue analysis describes the variation that students produce in their attempts to read or decode words. Goodman suggested that only those miscues affecting meaning should be taken into account. (A) is incorrect because *miscues* is a term to describe reading not necessarily writing attempts. (C) is incorrect because Goodman does not identify miscues as errors, plus the concept does not apply to attempts to communicate orally, such as conversation. (D) is incorrect because there is no connection between miscues and the schema theory. **Competency 008**

87. (A)

The main reason for the creation of the language experience approach (LEA) was to eliminate the discrepancy between the background knowledge that the child brings to the reading process and the experiential background required to understand the story, i.e., the schema of the author. (B) is incorrect because it eliminates the need to discuss the schema of the story by exposing children to a common experience and guiding them to dictate a story using the experience. (C) is incorrect because students will use their own vocabulary in the story; if they use idioms, these are probably known to children in the group. (D) is incorrect because the main purpose of LEA is not to contrast L1 and L2. **Competency 008**

88. (A)

The overall purpose of the shared book experience is to guide children to be successful in reading and to develop an interest in learning to read. The story is read to the students in a very supportive environment using visuals to enhance comprehension. The main goal is to make reading an enjoyable activity and to motivate children to read on their own. (B) is incorrect because reading with the whole class is a by-product of the shared book experience, but it is not the main goal. (C) and (D) are true statements. Traditionally, books used in shared reading use big letters and attractive pictures, and children like big books, but these features are not the main reason for conducting shared reading. **Competency 008**

89. (B)

Sight words occur frequently in writing, and often the best way to teach them is by instant recognition. Choice (A) is not correct because environmental print does not necessarily contain sight words. Street signs and store names can have very unique names that cannot be taught as sight words. (C) is incorrect because sight words are taught to be recognized instantly, without analyzing their structural or semantic representation. (D) is incorrect because most sight words are short and easy to spell. Because they occur so frequently in reading, spelling is facilitated. **Competency 009**

90. (C)

The words *butterfly*, *nightmare*, and *brainstorm* may get students confused because they do not provide a reliable point of view to comprehend their meaning. (A), (B), and (D) are incorrect because they contain information to help children in the comprehension process. Words like *doghouse, underground,* and *mouthwash* provide clear definitional indications of the intended meaning. **Competency 009**

91. (B)

The analysis of the structure of the words for decoding and comprehension is definitely part of structural analysis. Choice (A) is incorrect because context goes beyond individual words. (C) is incorrect because pictorial clues describe any kind of visual information, like pictures and charts. (D) is incorrect because syntactic clues use whole sentences and determine meaning based on the position of words within sentences. **Competency 009**

92. (B)

When children change declarative sentences to questions or exclamations, they have to change the intonation pattern of the language. Choice (A) is incorrect because sentence transformations are not designed necessarily to teach listening skills. (C) is incorrect because there is no connection between the linguistic transformation requested and teaching singing and music. Conducting sentence transformation can be an enjoyable activity; however, making the class more enjoyable is just a derivative of the process. (D) is definitely incorrect. **Competency 010**

93. (C)

Pointing to the words as they are read is designed to establish the connection between speech and print. However, after the skill has been mastered, it is discontinued so students can engage in fluent reading. (A) and (B) are incorrect because they offer nonsubstantial reasons for the strategy change. (D) is incorrect because the practice of pointing to the words as they are being read is not archaic; it is indeed an effective practice for beginning readers. **Competency 010**

94. (A)

The use of flash cards with pictures representing concepts and concrete objects can definitely be effective in teaching vocabulary to preschool children. (B) is incorrect because parents can teach a word every day to the child, but the child might not be able to participate effectively because preschoolers generally do not have the vocabulary development to teach parents new words. (C) is also incorrect because preschoolers might not have the necessary vocabulary development to participate in a game dealing with antonyms and synonyms. (D) is incorrect because the practice of memorizing vocabulary is quite boring and ineffective for children of all ages. **Competency 010**

95. (A)

When children don't have to struggle to decode words, reading fluency is facilitated. (B) is incorrect because, by definition, no decoding is necessary when the reader recognizes the word instantly. (C) is incorrect because comprehension goes beyond the instant recognition of words. Readers have to analyze the schema of the writing and evaluate other elements to achieve reading comprehension. Instant recognition of words can improve spelling skills; however, it does not necessarily improve the writing process. **Competency 010**

96. (C)

A family literacy program involves family members, and its main goals are to emphasize the value of literacy and to support children's efforts in becoming literate. Choice (A) is incorrect because the goals of literacy go beyond teaching English to ELLs to provide cross-cultural communication. (B) is incorrect because the program is primarily aimed at promoting literacy among children. Teaching literacy to parents can also be part of the program, but it is a secondary goal. (D) presents a strong distracter because in a certain way, a family literacy program can empower children and adults; however, the option is too generic. **Competency 011**

97. (A)

Reading to children and having books available for them provide children with reading readiness skills and can promote interest in reading. (B) is incorrect because the use of dictionary skills might not be developmentally appropriate or interesting enough for preschool children. (C) is incorrect because the children might not be ready for electronic translation programs, and translation is not the best strategy for promoting literacy development. (D) is incorrect because getting books for children without additional support will not develop early literacy among children. **Competency 011**

98. (B)

Reading to children in any language can promote interest in reading and decoding skills. Promoting reading comprehension is the next logical step. Choice (A) is incorrect because reading to children should not be interrupted, especially during the preschool years. Actually, reading to children can be beneficial even for advanced readers. (C) is incorrect because the scenario does not provide evidence to suggest that the child is ready for more challenging first-grade books. (D) is incorrect because reading skills acquired in the first language can transfer to the second language. Additionally, students should be exposed to reading in the dominant language first. **Competency 011**

99. (C)

Intergenerational literacy programs are designed to involve parents and family members in the education of their children. Choice (A) is incorrect because the literacy development of adults and the community is neither the only nor the primary purpose of an intergenerational literacy program. Children are the most important component in this process. Involving parents is an important component of the program, but it is not the purpose of the program; thus, (B) is incorrect. Traditionally, intergenerational literacy initiatives are designed for the early grades, and successful programs can affect the child for life; however, the program traditionally does not go beyond the elementary grades; thus, (D) is incorrect. **Competency 011**

100. (C)

Brainstorming for ideas and developing an outline of the writing project are paramount for process writing. (A), (B), and (D) are incorrect because they do not contain brainstorming as the initial component of the process. **Competency 012**

101. (A)

When students are presented with a problem and they are asked to discuss it and provide solutions based on the information, they are creating or producing knowledge. (B) is incorrect because children are just reciting and analyzing the meaning of the words in the pledge of allegiance. (C) and (D) are incorrect because in both choices (and in choice B) students are selecting choices given to them, not creating new ones. **Competency 012**

102. (B)

The main purpose of reading to learn is to obtain content information efficiently and effectively. One way to accomplish this task is to make students aware of the format used in the content areas and to guide them to retrieve the information by reading for the main idea or scanning for information. Choice (A) is incorrect because it addresses only one component of the process—vocabulary development. (C) is incorrect because it does not address the issue of the complexity of expository writing. (D) is incorrect because it addresses only the issue of vocabulary development—connotation and denotation. **Competency 012**

103. (A)

The best way to teach vocabulary to ELLs is to present the word together with a visual or concrete representation—a word concept. The introduction of word concepts can avoid any possible cultural conflict with similar concepts in the students' cultures. (B) is incorrect because translation can teach the word but fail to teach the concept that the word represents. (C) is incorrect because it would be very difficult to teach every single word in a contrasting fashion. Plus, most ESL classes contain speakers of various languages, which makes this activity impractical. (D) is incorrect because with ELLs, we cannot deemphasize the role of vocabulary development. Using context alone to obtain meaning will not work for children new to the English language. **Competency 012**

104. (D)

The professor used a colloquial expression commonly used in Texas. In the expression *drive careful*, the adjective *careful* was used to modify the verb. In Standard English, adjectives cannot modify verbs; the expression requires an adverb to create the standard version—*drive carefully*. (A) and (C) are incorrect because the scenario does not provide evidence to substantiate the information. (B) is incorrect because the statement does not show faulty agreement in number. **Competency 013**

105. (C)

The writing sample of the STAAR test is evaluated holistically using a four-point rubric, where a score of 3 or 4 is required to show mastery. The actual score is a combination of the multiple-choice score and the score of the writing sample. (A) is incorrect because only one part of the test is evaluated with a multiple-choice format. (B) is incorrect because the writing sample is evaluated holistically as opposed to being evaluated with a rubric containing specific (discrete) language features. (D) is incorrect based on previous explanations. **Competency 013**

106. (C)

The three sentences can be combined with appropriate connectors to avoid repetitions. In this particular case, the conjunctions can be used to create compound sentences. Sentence 3 shows faulty agreement, which suggests that the child can also benefit from this kind of instructional support. (A) and (B) are incorrect because the writing sample does not show problems with spelling or the use of active and passive voice. (D) is incorrect because the writing sample does not show problems with capitalization and punctuation. **Competency 013**

107. (C)

Reading a story and asking a child to retell it promotes interest in writing. When the teacher writes down the dictated story, the child can see the connection of oral and written work. (A) and (B) are incorrect because the children at the emerging stage don't have sufficient command of written language to correct their own writing or write a composition based on prompts. (D) is incorrect because reading for 30 minutes a day without any kind of explicit or implicit writing support might not be effective for children at the emerging stage for writing. **Competency 013**

108. (B)

The use of interactive journals allows children opportunities to communicate in meaningful and real-life situations. (A) and (D) are incorrect because listening and speaking abilities are not emphasized in interactive journals. (C) is incorrect because corrective feedback is not encouraged in communication activities. Teachers can provide indirect corrective feedback through modeling. **Competency 014**

109. (B)

During the prewriting stage, students should be guided to develop an outline that reflects the order of the ideas in the composition. They also can benefit from guiding questions to keep them focused on the topic and the intended audience. Choice (A) is incorrect because learning about grammar structures and pronunciation will not necessarily affect the organization and coherence of the composition. (C) is incorrect because it addresses speaking ability as opposed to the writing process. (D) is a strong distracter but not the best answer. Modeling effective writing is always a good strategy, but examples only might not provide the necessary guidance to make permanent changes in the students' writing style. (B) is a better choice because it provides a strategy that, once learned, can be used in multiple future situations. **Competency 014**

110. (A)

Children go through predictable stages of spelling development. During the initial stages, children invent words and use phonics skills as a foundation for spelling, which often results in nonstandard spelling. (B) and (C) are incorrect because spelling might not be the most important element in writing, but it is definitely important for effective writing. (D) is incorrect because it does not address the question. It just indicates that spelling requires phonics and structural rules, but it does not say why a rubric should not place heavy emphasis on spelling. **Competency 014**

111. (C)

The English writing samples of ELLs from a Spanish background often follow a curvilinear progression and might include multiple stories embedded within the narrative. This deviation from the linear progression expected in English writing creates the impression that the story is disjointed and lacks coherence. Based on the previous explanation, Choice (A) is incorrect—children might not produce compositions following a linear progression. The composition of children might contain complex sentences and an occasional use of Anglicized words or even Spanish words, but these features do not represent the main characteristics of English compositions from Latino children. Based on this explanation, (B) and (D) are incorrect. **Competency 014**

112. (B)

In minimal pairs, students are required to identify whether two sets of words are different or the same based on the phoneme sequence contained in each word. For example, the words *vine* and *fine* are different because they differ in at least one phoneme, i.e., the /v/ and /f/. Choice (A) is incorrect because morphology is not taken into account when comparing the two words. (C) is incorrect because there is no connection between minimal pairs and syntax. (D) is incorrect because lexicon deals with vocabulary development, and minimal pairs attempt to test whether children can understand how phonemes change the meaning of the words. **Competency 015**

113. (D)

When children miss about 10 percent of the words in a passage, comprehension problems will occur. Children at the instructional level need continuous support and guidance from the teachers. Choice (A) is incorrect because students at the independent level of reading are able to understand 95 percent of the words. (C) is incorrect because the term *comprehension level* is not a technical descriptor for reading levels. (B) is incorrect because students at the frustration level can read less than 89 percent of the words correctly. With this low level of word recognition, they will have severe comprehension problems. **Competency 015**

114. (D)

The TOP contains a checklist of specific skills for teachers to document when these behaviors occur during observation. (A) and (B) are incorrect because the TOP does not contain rating scales or multiple-choice questions. (C) is incorrect because the TOP is a checklist identifying the specific linguistic features for observation. **Competency 015**

115. (B)

All three instruments, running records, teacher observations, and the checklist, are examples of informal assessment. Choice (A) is incorrect because at least one of the instruments, running records, is not a teacher-developed instrument. (C) is incorrect based on the information previously stated. (D) is incorrect because all three instruments require some level of subjectivity. **Competency 015**

116. (A)

People across the world solve mathematics problems using a variety of strategies and processes. When community members are allowed to share their problem-solving strategies, children get a broader view of mathematics concepts. (B) makes sense and the activity can validate students' native language and achievement, but these elements do not constitute the real purpose for inviting community members to share problem-solving skills. (C) is incorrect because freeing teachers from administrative tasks is not the real purpose of the activity. (D) is incorrect because an isolated activity with parents is not generally enough to make the community the guiding force in the development of school curriculum. **Competency 016**

117. (C)

Hands-on activities can make the curriculum more relevant and guide children to construct their own knowledge. Hands-on activities can probably lead children to think abstractly (see choice (A)), but the activity is not designed exclusively to accomplish this goal. Hands-on activities can make the class more interesting and enjoyable (see choice (B)), but they are not the reasons for the activities. (D) is incorrect because there is no evidence to suggest that hands-on activities can promote equity, equality, or freedom among students. **Competency 016**

118. (B)

Vocabulary development and the technical mathematics terms used in word problems can affect students' ability to comprehend and solve word problems. (A) and (C) are incorrect because there is no evidence to suggest that ELLs lack mathematics intelligence or the conceptual framework to do well in mathematics. (D) is incorrect because there is no evidence to suggest that ELLs might lack interest or the ability to do well in mathematics. **Competency 016**

119. (B)

Children in prekindergarten and kindergarten might have problems understanding the concept of conservation. They might pay attention to the quantity (10 cents) as opposed to the implied value of the currency. Choice (A) is incorrect because the issue of centration was not relevant in the question; centration refers to the tendency to focus on one characteristic while ignoring the others. (C) is incorrect because ordering and seriation did not play a role in the confusion of the child; seriation requires students to match two or more objects with two or more components in a sequence. (D) is incorrect because classification involves the simultaneous use of two or more variables to classify or categorize objects, and children were not required to classify objects in the scenario. **Competency 017**

120. (C)

When subtraction involves any negative numbers, a good rule to use is, "Don't subtract the second number. Instead, add its opposite." Using that rule, the original expression, (–36) – 11 becomes (–36) + (–11). To be "in debt" by 36, then to be further "in debt" by 11, puts one "in debt" by 47, shown as –47. **Competency 018**

121. (D)

When presented with a simplification problem involving several different operations, the universally accepted order of operations must be used. In this case, working from left to right, the multiplication (6×2) and the division ($3 \div 3$) must be completed first, giving $12 + 1$, or 13. **Competency 018**

122. (C)

The correct answer is 1.2×10^8. Because multiplication is commutative (factors can be multiplied in any order), multiply the 2 and the 6 (giving 12) and 10^3 and 10^4 (giving 10^7). Note: To multiply exponential expressions with like bases, add the exponents. This gives 12×10^7. That expression is not in scientific notation (the first number must be between 0 and 10), so change the 12 to 1.2, and 10^7 into 10^8 to "compensate." **Competency 018**

123. (B)

The associative property of addition states that the order of the addends do not affect the results. Choice (A) is incorrect because the distributive property addresses the combination of addition and multiplication and the question addresses only addition. (C) is incorrect because the property of the zero is not used in the question. (D) is incorrect because the question does not address multiplication. **Competency 018**

124. (B)

If you can fold a two-dimensional figure so that one side exactly matches or folds onto the other side, the fold line is a line of symmetry. The figure below is a nonsquare rectangle with its two lines of symmetry shown.

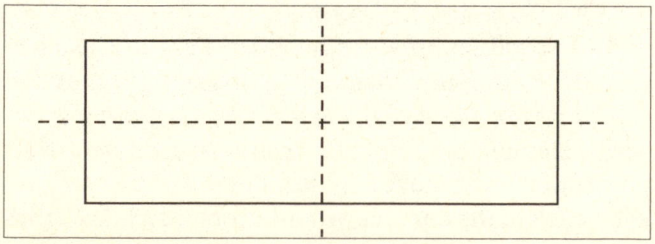

You might think that lines drawn from opposite corners are lines of symmetry, but they're not. The two halves would be the same size and shape, but wouldn't fold onto each other. Note that the question asked about nonsquare rectangles. Squares (which are rectangles) have four lines of symmetry. Based on the information provided, (A), (C), and (D) are incorrect. **Competency 019**

125. (B)

Angle *xyz* is an inscribed angle (its vertex is on the circle). Angle *xcz* is a central angle (its vertex is at the circle's center). When two such angles intercept (or "cut off") the same arc of the circle, a specific size relationship exists between the two angles. The measure of the central angle will always be double the measure of the inscribed angle. In this case, that means that the measure of angle *xcz* must be 80°. Thus, minor arc *xz* also measures 80°. Every circle (considered as an arc) measures 360°. That means that major arc *xyz* measures 280° (360 – 80). The explanation shows that (A), (C), and (D) are incorrect. **Competency 020**

126. (A)

The formula for finding the volume of a cylinder is: $V = \pi r^2 h$. This means that the volume is equal to pi (about 3.14) times the measure of the radius squared times the height of the cylinder. In this case, that's $3.14 \times 6^2 \times 8$, or $3.14 \times 36 \times 8$, or about 904. Note that the final answer is given in cubic centimeters. Based on this explanation, (B), (C), and (D) are incorrect. **Competency 018**

127. (A)

The only way carpet from a 16-foot-wide roll will cover Ms. Cameron's floor without seams is if she buys 20 feet of it. She can then trim the 16-foot width to 14 feet so that it fits her floor. Buying 20 feet of a 16-foot-wide roll means that she will have to buy 320 square feet. Her living room has an area of only 280 square feet (14 feet × 20 feet), so she'll be wasting 40 square feet (320 – 280), but no more.

Based on this analysis, choices (B), (C), and (D) are incorrect. **Competency 020**

128. (B)

Children in grades prekindergarten to grade 2 have unique developmental characteristics, like limited vocabularies and attention spans, that require appropriate planning to ensure that children benefit from instruction. (A), (C), and (D) are important considerations when planning instruction, but none of them is as important as planning instruction based on the developmental characteristics of children. **Competency 017**

129. (B)

TEKS requires children in kindergarten to explore and work with basic mathematic reasoning. In first grade and up, the level and sophistication of logical thinking increases in complexity. Based on prior statements, (A), (C), and (D) are incorrect. **Competency 017**

130. (A)

Learning centers allow children opportunities to explore mathematics reasoning in a play and low-anxiety format. (B) is incorrect because it addresses only one component of the benefit—the use of manipulatives. (C) is incorrect because, traditionally, learning centers are not used to teach deductively—direct teaching. Instead, students learn inductively through the use of manipulatives and the input from teachers. (D) is incorrect because learning centers do not use a highly structured format. On the contrary, learning centers are designed to be a low-anxiety environment where children can explore on their own. **Competency 019**

131. (B)

Children can see that knowledge of mathematics has a functional value in their lives. (A) and (C) are incorrect because most children cannot conceptualize that the activities that they do in mathematics are part of a school or state curriculum. (D) is incorrect because children in K–4 generally cannot make extrapolations between activities in the learning centers and their intrinsic value in life. **Competency 019**

132. (C)

Children are expected to be exposed to various forms of art, to study features of each, and to communicate using sensory-appropriate art terminology. They are also expected to produce artwork, and evaluate their own and the artworks from various groups. Based on the previous explanations, (A), (B), and (D) are incorrect. **Competency 046**

133. (B)

Diego Rivera, José Orozco, and David Siqueiros are the best representatives of the muralist movement in Mexico and perhaps in the world. Choice (A) is incorrect because photorealists do not use murals to present their work. Instead, canvases are generally used to create the artwork. (C) and (D) are incorrect because surrealism and impressionism do not use the social realism typical of the work of the Mexican muralists. **Competency 046**

134. (D)

Pablo Picasso is the best representative of cubism. Choice (A) is incorrect because Salvador Dali is linked to a different movement called surrealism. Both surrealism and cubism are art movements of the twentieth century. (C) is incorrect because Michelangelo is a painter of the Renaissance period and he used realism in his art. **Competency 046**

135. (C)

The values of light and darkness are used to create the three-dimensional quality of figures and to represent the mood of the artist. (A), (B), and (D) describe elements of art but the results of each are different from that produced by light and darkness. However, each of the choices provided correctly describes how these elements contribute to the creation of art. **Competency 046**

136. (C)

Pitch describes how high or low sounds are produced. Choice (A) is incorrect because it describes characteristics of rhythm. Based on this explanation, (D) (rhythm) is also incorrect. (B) is incorrect because it describes features of dynamics (volume)—loud and soft. **Competency 047**

137. (D)

The question addresses basic understanding of the standard Kodaly rhythm syllables. The three basic syllables included are *ta*, which would be notated as a quarter note on a staff; *Ti*, which would be notated as an eighth note on a staff; and *Ta-a*, which would be notated as a half note on the staff. If a person sings the common tune "Happy Birthday" to him- or herself, it should be apparent that the definite answer is (D). (B) is a good answer and would be the rhythm for the final statement if two notes were sung on the word *to*, which is often done. Choice (A) begins with the wrong note. (C) begins with the correct note but ends with the wrong note. **Competency 047**

138. (B)

In 1929, the Texas State Legislature adopted "Texas, Our Texas" as the state song. Choice (A) is incorrect. "The Yellow Rose of Texas" is a well-known song in the state. It is a patriotic song popularized by Texan soldiers during the American Civil War. (C) is incorrect because the song "God Bless America" is a patriotic song for the whole nation. (D) is incorrect because the Alamo is a patriotic symbol but not the title of a song. **Competency 047**

139. (C)

Tejano music has strong influences from the music and instruments of Mexican, German, and Czech immigrants. Choice (A) is incorrect because mariachi music is originally from Mexico with no specific influence from German or Czech groups. (B) is incorrect because there is no clear connection between the music from Mexico and country music. (D) is incorrect because salsa music does not have specific connections with Mexican, German, or Czech groups. Instead, salsa music has been influenced by Spanish, Indian, and African music. **Competency 047**

140. (C)

Performing somersaults, climbing, skipping, and dressing themselves require children to master fine motor skills. Based on this explanation, (A) is incorrect. (B) is a plausible answer but it is too generic in nature; thus it is not the best answer. (D) is incorrect because children will have to go through various years of development to arrive at the adult stage of development. **Competency 049**

141. (A)

The simplest steps used are "walk and/or skip" and are therefore appropriate for grades 1 and 2. The steps "run and/or skip" (see choice (B)) and "skip and slide" (see choice (C)) are more difficult and therefore are suggested for grades 2 and 3. Even more difficult is the "step-hop" (see choice (D)), and it is incorporated in dances appropriate for grades 3–6. **Competency 047**

142. (B)

Elevation is a key component to the RICE treatment process for sprains. The other components are rest, ice, and compression. Choice (A) is incorrect because one should not return to exercise until significant healing has been achieved, though bearing a tolerable amount of weight on the sprain has been shown to help quicken the healing process. (C) is incorrect because *evaluation* is not a technical term used in the treatment of sprains. (D) is incorrect because the sprain should be bandaged properly to prevent exposure and thus prevent re-injury. **Competency 049**

143. (C)

The ADA requires school districts to place special education children in the least restrictive educational environment; thus, an orthopedic handicapped student would be placed in mainstream classrooms. Students are required to receive physical education using appropriate accommodations to allow their successful participation. Choice (A) is incorrect because only in extreme cases are special education children excluded from participating in the school curriculum. (B) is partially correct, but it fails to mention the need to make accommodations for successful participation in physical education activities. (D) is incorrect because it adopts an extreme position not applicable to limited mobility. **Competency 049**

144. (B)

Cardiovascular exercise for a minimum of 20 minutes per session, as part of an exercise program, will lead to effective physical results with a proper nutritional diet. (A) and (C) are obviously incorrect based on the previous statement. Forty-five minutes (D) is an effective time period when performing lower-paced activities like a weight-lifting exercise session. **Competency 049**

145. (D)

Locomotor activities describe the types of movement that children use to move from one place to the other. In this case, hopping is the only choice that accomplishes this goal. Choice (A) is incorrect because bending is not a locomotor activity. (B) and (C) are also incorrect because they are manipulative skills. **Competency 049**

146. (D)

Complex carbohydrates should comprise at least half of the calories consumed for the healthy diet of an active person. Carbohydrates are the primary and most efficient source of energy for the body. Proteins should make up about 20 percent (see choice (A)) of the caloric intake of an active person. Based on the previous explanations, (B) and (C) are incorrect. **Competency 048**

147. (B)

Games involving physical activity are the best way to exercise children in kindergarten. Choice (A) is incorrect because, traditionally, jogging might be inappropriate for children at this early age. (C) and (D) are incorrect because contact sports and sports that require endurance are not developmentally appropriate for kindergarten students. **Competency 049**

148. (B)

Using high-interest activities like observing an aquarium can motivate scientific inquiry and problem-solving skills. Choices (A) and (C) are incorrect because both describe nonscientific objectives. Choice (D) presents a generic statement that fails to address the main scientific objective. **Competency 032**

149. (B)

A healthy aquatic system should have sufficient space and conditions to support life. Aquarium A has a large number of animals for a small 25-gallon aquarium. Overpopulation can pollute the environment and affect the balance of the ecosystem. The size of the aquarium (see choice (A)), the number of plants (see choice (C)), and the number of fish (see choice (D)) contribute to the success of the habitat, but individually, they cannot justify the students' decision. **Competency 038**

150. (D)

Fish of the same kind have a better chance of reproducing themselves. Aquarium B contains fish of the same kind, while aquarium A has different varieties. (A), (B), and (C) present elements that can affect the overall habitat, but they do not provide key information about the chances of successful breeding. **Competency 039**

151. (B)

The state curriculum requires students to engage in scientific exploration in grades K–12. Hands-on experimentation promotes active learning and is beneficial to all students, but it is especially important and developmentally appropriate for children in grades K–2. Choice (A) is incorrect because the incorporation of foreign language methods is a very broad statement, and it does not say specifically which method will be used or how it will be implemented. (C) is also incorrect because the statement is vague and does not describe the types of sophisticated tools. Traditionally, in K–2, the tools used are very simple and concrete. (D) is incorrect because the state curriculum does not require the use of chemicals and human specimens in the early grades. **Competency 031**

152. (B)

Conduction is a form of heat transfer. The metal of the spoon serves as a conductor of the heat emanating from the open flame. Choice (A) is too generic because radiation describes different kinds of energy produced naturally by the sun and artificially by microwaves and cellular phones. (C) is incorrect because it does not describe the type of transfer of energy presented in the scenario. However, convection is also a form of heat transfer carried through movement of matter. For example, the heating of water in a pan creates movement of the liquid from the bottom to the top, forcing cold water down to the bottom of the pan, where it is heated. **Competency 031**

153. (B)

A mixture is a physical combination of two or more substances that retain their own chemical properties; i.e., the mixture can be separated into the original substances—acetic acid and water. Choice (A) is incorrect because in a compound, the substances are chemically combined, and in the case of vinegar the substances are only mixed physically. (C) and (D) are incorrect because they lack the specificity required of the answer. **Competency 028**

154. (C)

Matter can change from liquid to solid to gas in a cyclical fashion. (A) is incorrect because all three represent examples of solid matter. (B) is incorrect because it presents only examples of the states and fails to address the stages represented. (D) is incorrect because it presents just examples of solid and liquid matter. **Competency 028**

155. (C)

The metric system is a very precise system that allows for the measurement of very small amounts of matter. For example, the metric system uses measurements divided into thousands (millimeters or milligrams), while the English system uses larger units of measurement, like inches and ounces. (A) and (D) contain perhaps true statements and opinions but they fail to address the question. (D) is incorrect; the English system does not have a simple way to compute measures. On the other hand, the metric system is based on 10 and the computations are a lot easier. **Competency 028**

156. (A)

The monera kingdom is composed of unicellular organisms and primitive cells called prokaryotic. (B), (C), and (D) are incorrect because all three have more sophisticated cellular systems called eukaryotic. **Competency 038**

157. (B)

Corals are invertebrates that fall under the animal kingdom. These small organisms can reproduce themselves sexually or asexually. Choice (A) is incorrect because unlike corals, the kingdom monera is made up of unicellular organisms with very rudimentary cellular organization. (C) and (D) are incorrect because corals are described in the question as invertebrates, a classification used exclusively for members of the animal kingdom. **Competency 038**

158. (C)

Corals live in a symbiotic relationship with algae because both exchange nutrients or other kinds of services in order for both to survive. Choice (A) is incorrect because corals are not parasites living off algae. Instead, parasites and corals provide support services to each other for their mutual survival. (B) and (D) might be true statements, but they do not define the term *symbiosis*. **Competency 038**

159. (C)

An ecosystem needs to have a balance among organisms to ensure the ability of the system to support life. (A), (B), and (D) are incorrect because they merely represent examples of how the system maintains a balance. **Competency 038**

160. (D)

The teacher can discuss the theory of continental drift, which gave rise to the current theory of plate tectonics. According to this theory, the crust of the Earth is broken down into several floating tectonic plates, which move and change locations. Choice (A) is incorrect because it describes how organisms evolve throughout history. It also alludes to the work of Charles Darwin. (B) is incorrect because it refers to the religious belief that the universe was created by a supreme being. (C) describes the process by which organisms living on one continent manage to migrate to other continents or to other regions within a continent. **Competency 043**

161. (A)

The main function of the atmosphere is to serve as a buffer between space and the Earth's crust. This buffer provides the ideal conditions to protect and preserve life on Earth. (B) and (D) present two functions that can be linked to the atmosphere, recycling water and gases; however, they fail to highlight the real function of the atmosphere. (C) is completely incorrect; the atmosphere is above the crust, not beneath it. **Competency 043**

162. (B)

The movement of the plates causes intense seismological activity near the faults, resulting in earthquakes. (A) and (C) have some merit because thermal activity can have some implications, but these choices do not provide specific answers to the question. (D) is totally incorrect; there is no known connection between the rotation of the Earth and earthquakes. **Competency 043**

163. (B)

Plyer v. Doe guarantees the right of undocumented children to free public education. Choices (A) and (D) are incorrect because the court case does not mandate bilingual education, specifically. Choice (C) is incorrect because the Plyer v. Doe decision covers only education services. **Competency 001**

164. (D)

The Lau Remedies contained information to regulate the implementation of bilingual education programs. The federal government established Lau Compliance Centers to ensure that the Lau Remedies were followed. Choices (A) and (C) are incorrect because the federal government does not control state legislation, and the United States government has not enacted legislation mandating bilingual education. Choice (B) is incorrect because the EEOA did not contain specific guidelines for program implementation. **Competency 001**

165. (A)

The LPAC examines the results from the reading and language arts portions of the STAAR test and the oral language proficiency test, as well as other indicators to make placement decisions. Choice (B) is incorrect because the RPTE and TOP are the instruments used to comply with the NCLB accountability system. The RPTE can be used as one of the instruments but at this point, it is not one of the required tests. Choice (C) is incorrect because the Tejas LEE and the TPRI are reading tests in Spanish and English, respectively, used only in grades prekindergarten to second grade. Choice (D) is incorrect because the TOP is not currently used to make placement decisions. **Competency 002**

166. (B)

The goal of the early-exit form of transitional bilingual education is to teach English (compensatory). Students begin with two languages and, at the end of the program, they make the transition to English only (subtractive). Choice (A) is incorrect because the late-exit model is considered an enrichment and additive program, since it allows for the maintenance of both languages. Choices (C) and (D) are incorrect because both are considered additive and enrichment programs. **Competency 002**

167. (C)

The 90/10 model represents the percentage for the minority and majority language, respectively. If 90 percent of instruction is delivered in the minority language, then native English speakers are immersed in the language and language-minority students are receiving the bulk of instruction in their native language. Based on this explanation, choices (A), (B), and (D) are incorrect. **Competency 002**

168. (A)

The Baker-de Kanter study (AIR study) analyzed the literature on the effectiveness of bilingual education programs. Results of the study were used as a foundation for identifying alternative programs to address the needs of ELLs. Choices (B) and (D) are incorrect because neither the NCLB nor the ESEA endorsed or mandated the implementation of the Structured Immersion program. Choice (C) is incorrect because the Ramirez report did not produce consistent data to support the need to implement the program. **Competency 002**

169. (B)

The main goal of *Structured Immersion* is to develop English proficiency as quickly as possible. Choices (A) and (C) are incorrect because traditionally the program does not provide instruction in the first language, nor does it try to address the students' native culture. Choice (D) is incorrect because the program does not immerse students in their native language or culture. **Competency 002**

170. (C)

In this approach, teachers switch from one language to the other within the same lesson. It violates one of the key principles in dual-language instruction, the separation of languages. Choices (A) and (B) are incorrect because it is academic that teachers have to learn and use both languages in instruction; however, the key issue here is when to use one language and not the other. Choice (D) is incorrect because this approach does not regulate or control teachers from delivering instruction in all language skills. **Competency 002**

171. (D)

Idioms are difficult because they contain implied or connotative language. Children have to grasp their implied meaning and the cultural allusions embedded in them to understand them. Choice (A) is incorrect because all languages have idiomatic expressions. Choice (B) is not the best choice because while it indicates that children have problems with idioms, it does not explain why. Choice (C) is incorrect because idioms are common in English and in other languages. **Competency 002**

172. (A)

First-language acquisition is the result of a person's innate abilities and support and stimulus received from interaction in the environment. Choices (B), (C), and (D) are incorrect because none of these components individually accurately explains the process of first-language acquisition. **Competency 002**

173. (D)

In the holophrastic stage, children use one word to communicate. The stage corresponds to the speech emergence of L2 where children communicate using single words to get their points across. Choices (A) and

(C) are incorrect because they describe stages of first language acquisition, not second language acquisition as the question calls for. Choice (B) is incorrect because the pre-production stage of L2 is equivalent to the babbling stage of first-language acquisition, where students do not produce meaningful words. **Competency 003**

174. (C)

The affective filter hypothesis falls under Humanistic Psychology. Humanistic Psychology views the needs of the learner as a prerequisite for learning. It hypothesizes that children must be relaxed to be able to benefit from instruction. Choices (A) and (B) are incorrect because neither Behaviorist Psychology nor Cognitive Psychology takes into account emotional components like the affective filter. Choice (D) is incorrect because the term "Linguistic" does not describe a school of psychology. **Competency 003**

175. (B)

The Greek and Roman empires had a great impact on Western civilizations and consequently on the language. A large number of cognates come from the languages of these two civilizations. Choice (A) is incorrect because Western languages do not have a common origin. Some, like English and German, are from Indo-European origin, while others like Spanish and French come from Latin. Choice (C) is incorrect because English and other Western languages do not necessarily have a common vocabulary. Choice (D) is incorrect because no language group can force other languages to adopt a common vocabulary. **Competency 003**

176. (D)

The commands and the modeling typical of the TPR are commonly used to address the needs of children new to a language. Choices (A), (B), and (C) are incorrect because the method might be too basic for students beyond the beginning stages of second language acquisition. Teachers might be able to use strategies from these methods with students at intermediate and advanced levels, but they must be very creative to meet the needs of these groups. **Competency 003**

177. (B)

Once a pidgin becomes the native language of a group, it ceases to be a pidgin, and it becomes a natural language identified as a Creole. Choice (A) is incorrect because the length of language usage is not the determining factor for a pidgin to become a Creole. However, a pidgin is a transitional language that eventually disappears or becomes a Creole. Choice (C) is incorrect because Pidgin English is not the only language spoken in New Guinea. Choice (D) is incorrect because the usage of the language does not play a role in a transition of a pidgin to a Creole. **Competency 003**

178. (D)

Emergent literacy describes how literacy can come about naturally when parents and caregivers expose children to literacy activities at home. Choices (A) and (C) are incorrect because the terms *environmental print* and *developmental appropriateness* do not explain how literacy develops prior to formal instruction. Choice (B) is incorrect because the term *reading readiness* suggests that reading emerges in stages that require the teaching and mastery of specific reading sub-skills. **Competency 003**

179. (B)

Onset describes the first letter of a syllable or a one-syllable word. The rime is the portion that follows the onset. Choices (A) and (D) are incorrect because word puzzles or fill-in-the-blanks are not literacy concepts nor are they used to describe the activity used in class. Choice (C) is incorrect because *minimal pair* is a sound discrimination or phonemic awareness activity to identify differences between two sets of words, like **pay** and **bay**. Teachers pronounce the two words and children determine if the words are the same or different. **Competency 003**

180. (C)

The threshold hypothesis suggests that children must arrive at a plateau in their native language in order to transfer skills from L1 to L2. The threshold level is usually obtained after four to five years of quality dual-language preparation. Choices (A), (B), and (D) are incorrect; the comprehensible input addresses the importance of delivering linguistically comprehensible information; the monitor hypothesis addresses the process that children follow to evaluate and monitor their linguistic performance; and the affective filter hypothesis deals with the role that emotions play in the language learning process. **Competency 003**

181. (C)

The visual clues provided in graphic organizers supplement information presented through language. Additionally, they provide a structure for instruction that can increase a student's ability to comprehend content. Choice (A) is incorrect because it provides generic and irrelevant information. Choice (B) is incorrect because increasing the vocabulary of ELLs is not the main reason for the use of graphic organizers. Choice (D) is incorrect because graphic organizers can provide comprehensible input for ELLs, but it cannot eliminate the complexity of the English language. **Competency 004**

182. (B)

The top-down approach for reading analyzes and teaches language by using whole units like passages and words, and then proceeds to address the smallest language components like syllables and sounds. The bottom-up approach does the same thing, but uses small language units like sound and letters to begin the process, and later expands to include larger units like sentences and whole passages. Choice (A) is incorrect because the terms are not related to teaching life skills to children. Choices C and D are incorrect based on the previous explanations. **Competency 004**

183. (A)

Through the introduction of word families like *ank* and *ang*, students learn to recognize and spell multiple one-syllable words. Based on the consistency of word families, teachers help students to cope with the letter–sound inconsistencies of English. Choice (B) is incorrect because onset and rimes are not designed to study, but rather to facilitate the grapheme–phoneme correspondence in English. Words created with the same rime can rhyme; however, finding rhyming words is the purpose for using onset and rime. Based on this explanation, Choice (C) is incorrect. Choice (D) is incorrect because there is no connection with the use of onset and rimes, and idiomatic expressions. **Competency 004**

184. (C)

Narrative writing communicates information in a more contextualized situation. It follows a predictable format with a beginning, mid-point and resolution. Expository writing, on the other hand, is more succinct, linear and hierarchical in orientation. Choices (A), (B), and (D) are incorrect because none of these issues can describe the difference between narrative and expository writings. **Competency 004**

185. (B)

Traditionally, the concept of linear versus curvilinear has been used to describe the way children organize and present information in writing; however, both concepts can also be used to describe the patterns used to communicate orally. In English, speakers traditionally favor a linear progression, while in other languages, periodic deviations from the main topic are permitted (curvilinear). Based on this explanation, Choices (A), (C), and (D) are incorrect. **Competency 004**

Index

Page numbers followed by *t* refer to tables

A

AAS (Angle-Angle-Side), 144
Absolute value, 127
Abstract paintings, 262
Academic Excellent Indicators System (AEIS), 45
Academic vocabulary
  science, 219
  social science, 171
Accelerated learning, 24
Accommodations and modifications, 33, 88, 89–90
Accountability measures, 10
Acquisition, vs. learning, 30
ACTFL (American Council for the Teaching of Foreign Languages), 32, 46–47
Activation energy, 230
Adaptation, of organisms, 242, 243, 289
Addition
  basic operation, 131
  decimals, 129
  fractions, 128, 129
  mixed numbers, 128
Adequate yearly progress (AYP), 45
Adventure Tales of America (Potts), 169
AEIS (Academic Excellent Indicators System), 45
Aerobic respiration, 238
Affective filter hypothesis, 30–31
Africa
  art, 263
  physical and cultural features, 198*t*
African Americans
  ebonics, 35–36, 60
  Ku Klux Klan threat, 183–184
  slavery, 182–183
Age, and second language acquisition, 31, 34
Air pressure, 249
The Alamo, 190
Alcohol use and abuse, 277–278
Algebra and patterns, 112–113, 134–141, 157
Algebraic expressions, 135–136
Algebraic inequalities, 141
Algebraic patterns, 135
Algebraic relationships, 137
Algebraic solutions, 137
Alliteration, 65
Alphabetic principle, 40, 67–70
Alphabetic writing system, 68
AMAOs (Annual Measurable Achievement Objectives), 10
Ambiguity, tolerance for, 33
American Council for the Teaching of Foreign Languages (ACTFL), 32, 46–47
American Indians, 177, 188, 189*t*, 263
American Institutes for Research (AIR) study, 23
Americanization, 8
American Revolution, 181–182
Americas, ancient civilizations of, 176–177
Analogies, 170
Anasazi, 177
Anatomy, 283
Ancient period of art history, 260
Ancient world, 172–173
Anecdotal records, 103
Angles, 145
Animals
  cells, 238
  life cycle, 237–238
  structure and functions, 236
Annual Measurable Achievement Objectives (AMAOs), 10
Anorexia nervosa, 280
Anxiety, and second language acquisition, 33
Apaches, 188
Aphasia, 63
Arabs, mathematical contributions, 157
Archimedes, 157
Area, 143–144, 146
Aristocracy, 207
Articles of Confederation, 182
Articulation problems, 63
The arts. *See* Fine arts (Domain VI)
ASA (Angle-Side-Angle), 144
Asia, physical and cultural features, 199*t*
A.S.P.I.R.A. v. New York, 13
Assessment
  alternatives for ELLs, 49, 107
  defined, 42
  language proficiency, 47–48
  literacy, 42–45, 102–106
  mathematics, 115–116, 125
  reading comprehension, 83, 84–85
  reading fluency, 80
  science, 225–226
  speaking ability, 60–62
  Texas state testing program, 44–45
  types, 42–44, 102–106
  visual arts, 258
  See also Texas Assessment of Knowledge and Skills (TAKS)
Assimilation, 8
Associative property of multiplication and addition, 134

Asteroids, 251
Atmosphere, 246
Atomic weapons, 187
Atoms, 227
Audience, 64, 97
Austin, Stephen, 190
Australasia, physical and cultural features, 199*t*
Authentic assessment, 42, 106
Authentic literature-based texts, 72
Autism, 279–280
Autocracy, 207
Automaticity, 79
Avenues, 169
Axioms, 151
Aztecs, 157–157, 177

B

Babbling, 59
Babylonians, number system, 156
Balance (art), 259
Balanced reading program approach, 20, 67, 72
Banking, 206
Barbizon School, 261
Bar graphs, 137
Baroque style, 261
Basal Metabolic Rate (BMR), 273
Basic interpersonal communication skills (BICS), 47–48
Basket weaving, 256
Beat, 264
Behaviorist theory of language acquisition, 29, 30
Bell-shaped curve, 105
Bernal, Joe, 15
Bias, in traditional children's stories, 82–83
BICS (basic interpersonal communication skills), 47–48
Big books, 39
Bilingual-bicultural education, 19
Bilingual education (Domain 1), 7–55
  accelerated learning, 24
  competencies, 7, 26, 36, 46
  critical pedagogy, 24
  cross-country comparison, 18
  federal laws, 8–11
  historical development, 7–14
  instruction, 46–52
  language and language acquisition, 26–36
  literacy, 36–46
  models, 18–21
  official endorsement of, 14
  state laws, 8, 14–17
  strategies, 24–25
  studies on effectiveness, 23
Bilingual Education and Training Act (Texas) (1981), 14
Bilingualism, statistics, 18
Bill of Rights, 184, 208–209
Bin Laden, Osama, 188
Binomials, 136–137
Biography, 74
Blood, 239, 272
Bloom's Taxonomy, 89
BMR (Basal Metabolic Rate), 273
Bolshevik Revolution, 186
Boston dialect, 60
Boston Massacre, 181
Boston Tea Party, 181
Bottom-up approach to reading, 39, 71
Briscoe, Dolph, 14
Brown v. Board of Education of Topeka, 12, 184
Bulimia nervosa, 280
Bunker Hill, battle of, 181
Burnet, David G., 190, 191
Burns, M., 148

C

Cabeza de Vaca, 188
Caddos, 188
CALLA (cognitive academic language learning approach), 22, 50–51
CALP (cognitive academic language proficiency), 47–48, 49
Canada
  bilingual education, 20, 21
  bilingualism, 18
Capacity, 150
Carbohydrates, 274
Castañeda v. Pickard, 13
Cells, 235, 238, 240, 272
Central America, physical and cultural features, 196*t*
Centration, 117
Ceramics, 256
CGI (cognitively guided instruction), 118
Chamot, A., 50
Chapter 89 Commissioner's Rules, 15–17
Charts, 165–168
Chávez, Cesar, 185
Checklists, 103
Checks and balances, 208
Chemical energy, 230
Chemical properties, of matter, 228
Chemical reactions, 229
Chemical sedimentary rocks, 247
Chicano Movement, 185
Child abuse, 278
Child development. *See* Development, human
China
  art, 262–263
  multilingualism, 18
Chloroplasts, 235
Chomsky, Norm, 57
Choral reading, 79
Chromosomes, 242
Circles
  area, 147
  circumference, 146
  diameter, 146
  radius, 146
Circuits, 231
Circulatory system, 239, 272
Circumference, 146
Citizenship, 209–210
Civil Rights Act (1964), 8–9, 13, 184–185
Civil rights movement, 184–185
Civil War, 183, 191–192
Classification (cognitive skill), 118
Classification of living things, 235–236
Classroom tests, 105–106
Clastic sedimentary rocks, 247
Clay, Mary, 80
Clef signs, 264–265
Climate, 249, 250
Cloze tests, 84–85

Cluttering, 62–63
Coahuiltecans, 188
Code switching, 20, 35
Cognates, 29, 169
Cognitive academic language learning approach (CALLA), 22, 50–51
Cognitive academic language proficiency (CALP), 47–48, 49
Cognitive development, 117–118
Cognitively guided instruction (CGI), 118
Cognitive strategies, 50–51
Cold War, 187–188
Collier, V. P., 23
Colonial period, 7, 178–181
Comanches, 188
Combination programs, 20
Comets, 251
Common multiples, 131
Communication, mathematical, 112
Communication disorders, 62–63
Communism, 207
Community environment, and second language acquisition, 34
Commutative property, 134
Compass rose, 195
Competition, 243
Composite numbers, 131
Compositions, scoring, 106
Compounds, 227
Compound words, 78
Comprehensible input, 30, 33
Computer-generated art, 256–257
Computer reading programs, 79–80
Concert etiquette, 269
Concord and Lexington, battle of (1775), 181
Concrete models, pattern identification using, 138
Concrete operational stage, 117, 118
Concurrent approach, 25
Conduction and conductivity, 227, 228, 230
Conferencing, 41, 42
Congress, 208
Congruence, 144
Connecticut Colony, 179, 180*t*
Connectors, 93
Connotation, 28
Conservation (cognitive skill), 117–118
Conservation of energy, 233
Consolidated alphabetic phase, 67
Constitution, U.S.
  amendments, 7, 12, 183, 184, 185–186, 206, 209
  Bill of Rights, 184, 208–209
  history, 182
  official language identification, 7
  power sharing between state and federal governments, 209
  role of, 208
Constitutional democracies, 207
Constitutional monarchies, 207
Consumers, 243
Content-based language programs, 50–51
Context clues, 76–77
Continental Congress, 181
Continental drift, 245
Contractions, 69
Contrast, 260
Convection, 230
Convergent questions, 84
Cooperative learning, 33, 51, 171
Copula deletion, 35
Copyright law, 269–270
Coral Way Elementary, 8
Core, earth's, 244–245
Coronado, Francisco Vázquez de, 188
Counting techniques, 132–133
Court cases, 11–13, 184, 208
Creolization, 34
Criterion-referenced tests (CRTs), 42, 44, 104
Critical pedagogy, 24
Critical-period hypothesis, 31
Critical thinking skills, 89
CRTs (criterion-referenced tests), 42, 44, 104
Crust, earth's, 244
Cuban missile crisis, 187
Cuban refugees, 8
Cubes, 144
Cubism, 262
Cultural differences, 61
Cultural diffusion, 204–205
Cummins, J., 31, 47, 48
Curvilinear approach, 61
Customary units of measurement, 150
Cylinders, 147

D

Data analysis, 112, 152–154
DBE (developmental bilingual education), 19, 23
D-Day, 187
Decentering, 118
Decimal numbers, 129–130, 134
Declaration of Independence, 181
Decoding clues, 76–77
Decomposers, 243
Decreolization, 35
Deductive reasoning, 151
Deflation, 206
Deforestation, 202, 247
Delaware Colony, 179, 180*t*
Democracy, 207
Denotation, 28
Density, 227
Dependent clauses, 94
Deposition, 202
Derivational morphemes, 28, 76–77
Descriptive writing, 97
Development, human
  cognitive development stages, 117–118
  language and language acquisition, 26, 27*t*, 29–33, 59–60
  literacy, 70–75
  mathematics, 116–118, 155–156
  motor skills, 284–285
  physical, 276–277
  reading, 37–38, 70–71
  visual arts, 255–256
Developmental bilingual education (DBE), 19, 23
Developmentally appropriate instruction, 116–118, 223–224
Dialects, 26, 35, 60
Dialogue journals, 99
Diameter, 146
Diana v. Board of Education, 12
Dictatorships, 207
Diet, 273–274
Differentiated instruction, 46–47
Digestive system, 239, 272

Disabilities, students with, 289. *See also* Special education
Discourse, 28
Discovery, age of (1400-1700), 174
Distributive property, 134
Divergent questions, 84
Diversity, 107
Division
basic operation, 132
decimals, 129–130
fractions, 129
DNA (deoxyribonucleic acid), 240, 241–242
Dolch words, 76
Double negatives, 35
Drafting, 41
Dramatic play, 63
DRTA (Directed Reading/Thinking Activity), 88
Drug use and abuse, 277–278
Dynamics (music), 265

E

Early childhood education, 37–40, 81, 116–118
Early-exit transitional bilingual education (TBE) programs, 9, 18–19, 23
Earth
atmosphere, 246
circumference and radius, 244
landform characteristics, 244
layers, 244–245
movement of, 250–251
tilt of, 250
Earthquakes, 245–246
Earth science, 244–250
Eating disorders, 280
Ebonics, 35–36, 60
Ecology, 243
Economic interdependence, 205–206
Economics, 205–206
Ecosystems, 243
Edges, 144
Editing, 41
Effectiveness of bilingual education, studies on, 23
Egocentrism, elimination of, 118
Egyptians, number system, 156
Eighteenth Amendment, 185–186
Eighth Amendment, 209
80/20 model, 20
Electricity, 231, 232–233
Electronic media, 100
Elementary and Secondary Education Act (ESEA) (1965), 9
Elements, 227
ELPS (English Language Proficiency Standards), 10–11
Emergent literacy perspective, 37
Emotional disorders, 279–280
Emphasis, 259
End-of-course (EOC) examinations, 44
Energy, 222, 229–233
England
American colonies, 7, 178–181
World War II, 186–187
English as a second language (ESL) programs and students
historical development, 8, 21–23
modifications, 33
program models, 18–21
strategies, 33
English for speakers of other languages (ESOL), 21. *See also* English as a second language (ESL) programs and students
English Language Acquisition, Language Enhancement, and Academic Achievement Act (Title III), 9–10
English language arts and reading (Domain II), 57–109
alphabetic principle, 67–70
assessment, 42–45, 102–106
competencies, 57, 65, 67, 70, 76, 79, 81, 86, 90, 95, 102
development stages, 37–38, 70–71
instruction methods, 20, 39–40, 67, 70–71
learning to read-reading to learn transition, 86
literacy development, 70–75
oral language, 57–64
phonological and phonemic awareness, 65–67
reading comprehension and application, 77–78, 79, 81–85
reading fluency, 79–80
reading speed and efficiency, 85, 86
research and inquiry skills, 86–89
viewing and representing, 100–102
word analysis and identification, 76–78
writing conventions, 90–95
written communication, 95–100
English Language Proficiency Standards (ELPS), 10–11
English-only movement, 14, 15
English-plus movement, 14
The Enlightenment, 180–181
Environmental print, 38
EOC (end-of-course) examinations, 44
Equal Educational Opportunities Act (EEOA) (1974)
Equal Protection Clause, 12
Equations, 140–141
Equilateral triangles, 146
Erosion, 245
"*Escuelitas*" program, 15
ESL programs and students. *See* English as a second language (ESL) programs and students
Estimation, 128, 133
Eukaryotic cells, 235
Eurasia, physical and cultural features, 197*t*
Europe, physical and cultural features, 197*t*
European Union (EU), 206
Evolution, 242
Excretory system, 239
Executive branch, 208
Exercise, 273, 283–284. *See also* Physical education
Exfoliation, 245
Expanded form, 127–128
Expanded notation, 128
Experiments
inquiry models, 215–216
interpretation of results, 217–219
safe and proper laboratory procedures, 213–215
tools and equipment, 219–220
Exponential notation, 127
Expository writing, 40, 97
Expression (music), 265

Expressive aphasia, 63
Extroversion, 33

F

Faces (solid figures), 144
Fairy tales, 82–83
False cognates, 29
Fats, 274
Federal government, 209
Federal laws, 8–11
Federal republics, 208
Federal Reserve, 206
Fifteenth Amendment, 183, 184
Fifth Amendment, 209
50/50 model, 20
Filmmaking, 256
Fine arts (Domain VI), 255–272
  competencies, 255, 264
  definitions, 255
  music, 264–271
  TEKS, 256
  visual arts, 255–263
First aid, 281–282
First Amendment, 209
Fitnessgram, 284
Fitness levels, 284
5-E model, 216–217, 218*t*
Flag, U.S., 210
Florida, first dual language program, 8
Flowcharts, 167–168, 170
Fluency, 79–80
Fluency disorders, 62–63
Food chain, 238
Food pyramid, 273–274
Force, 226–27
Foreign policy, 182, 187–188
Form (music), 265
Formal assessment, 42, 104–106, 125
Formal operational stage, 117
Formative evaluation, 43, 104
Fossilized language, 35
Fourteenth Amendment, 12, 183, 184
Fourth Amendment, 209
Fractions, 128–129
Free enterprise, 205–206
Freeze-thaw process, 245
Freire, Paulo, 24
French and Indian War, 181
French settlements, 189
Front-end estimation, 133
Frustration level, 103
Full alphabetic phase, 67
Functions, 135, 136, 139, 140
Fungi, 236

G

Galaxies, 250
Games, 119
Gases, 228
Genetics, 241–242
Genres, 72–75
Geography, 194–204
  definitions, 194
  deforestation, 202
  deposition, 202
  maps, 163, 194–195, 202–204
  mountains, 201–202
  regions, 195–200
  rivers, 200–201
  time zones, 195
Geologic faults, 245–246
Geology, 244–248
Geometry and measurement, 141–152
  angles, 145
  area, 143–144
  circles, 146, 147
  Greek contributions, 156–157
  grids, 148
  logical reasoning, 151–152
  measurement concepts, 148–149
  measurement systems and conversions, 150
  parallel lines, 145
  perimeter, 142–143
  perpendicular lines, 145–146
  points, 142, 144–145
  polygons, 146–147
  principles and properties of geometry, 142
  symmetry, 148
  TEKS, 112
  tessellations, 148
  translations, rotations, and reflections, 149
  triangles, 143, 144, 146, 147–148
  van Hiele theory, 142, 143*t*
  volume, 144, 147
Georgia Colony, 179, 180*t*
German language, 7
Germany, World War II, 186–187
Gettysburg, battle of, 183
Global aphasia, 63
Globalization, 205
Global warming, 247
Globes, 163, 194
Gogi apparatus, 235
Goliad, battle of, 190
Gonzales, battle of, 190
Gonzales, Rodolfo "Corky," 185
Goods and services, 205
Gothic architecture, 261
Goudvis, Anne, 83–84
Government and citizenship, 206–211
Grade equivalent score, 43–44
Graffiti, 262
Grapheme-phoneme correspondence, 26–28, 67–69
Graphic organizers, 49, 87, 170
Graphics, 88–89, 101–102, 164–168
Graphophonemic units, 40
Graphs, 137–139, 154, 164–165
Graves, Donald, 96
Gravity, 226, 246
Great Depression, 186
Greatest common divisor (GCD), 130–131
Greece, ancient
  art, 260–261
  mathematical contributions, 156–157
Greek roots, 169*t*
Grids (geometry), 148
Grid system (maps), 194
Groundwater, 246
Group investigation, 172
Guadalupe Hidalgo, Treaty of, 191
Guided oral repeated reading, 79

H

Habitual tense, use of, 35–36
Half-day alternating bilingual programs, 20–21
Hand-puppet shows, 64
Harmony (music), 265
Harmony (visual art), 260
Harvey, Stephanie, 83–84
Health (Domain VI), 272–282

body systems, 272–273
child abuse, 278
community participation, 281
competency, 272
diet and exercise, 273–274
eating disorders, 280
first aid, 281–282
health care, 280–281
human growth and development, 276–277
interpersonal relationships, 280
lifestyle changes, 272, 283–284
mental and emotional health, 279–280
safety and accident prevention, 278–279
school violence, 279
stress management, 274–275
substance use and abuse, 277–278
TEKS, 275–276
Health care, 280–281
Healthy lifestyle, 272, 283–284
Healthy People 2010, 280
Heart, 239, 272
Heat, 230
Heat transfer, 230–231
Hemoglobin, 239
Heredity, 241–242
Hernández v. Texas, 12
Hexagons, 146
Hindus, mathematical contributions, 157
Historical fiction, 73
History
Texas, 188–192
U.S., 178–188
world, 172–177
Hitler, Adolf, 186, 187
Hohokam people, 177
Holocaust, 187
Holophrasic one-word stage, 59
Home environment
early literacy importance, 38, 75
and second language acquisition, 34
Homographs, 78
Homonyms, 78
Homophones, 78
Houston, Sam, 190, 191
Human body
growth and development, 276–277
reproduction, 240
systems of, 239, 272–273
Human influences, on earth systems, 246–247
Humidity, 249
Hydrologic cycle, 248

I

Igneous rocks, 247, 248
Imitation, 57–58
Immersion programs, 19–21, 23
Immigrants, 7–8
Immune system, 239, 272–273
Immunizations, 281
Impressionism, 262
Improving America's School Act (1994), 9
Impulsiveness, and second language acquisition, 33
Incas, 177
Income tax, federal, 206
Indentured servants, 179
Independent clauses, 94
Independent reading level, 103
Individualized education program (IEP), 16
Inductive reasoning, 151
Industrial Revolution, 174, 175–176, 205
Inequalities, 141
Inferences, 84
Inflation, 206
Inflectional morphemes, 28, 76–77
Informal assessment, 42–43, 102–104, 125
Innatist theory of language acquisition, 29, 30–31
Inquiry and research skills, 86–89, 215–221
Instructional approaches
content-based language programs, 50–51
cooperative learning, 33, 51
differentiated instruction, 46–47
graphic organizers, 49, 87, 170
integrated curriculum, 49–50, 112, 122–125, 164, 263
literacy, 46–52
mathematics, 111–126
questioning techniques, 82, 84, 125, 126*t,* 223–224
reciprocal teaching, 24, 49, 88
scaffolding, 49, 115, 169
science, 223–224
sheltered English approach, 22, 51, 170–171
social science, 161–172
SQ4R strategy, 49, 87–88, 170
Instructional reading level, 103
Instrumental motivation, 34
Integers, 127
Integrated curriculum, 49–50, 112, 122–125, 164, 263
Integrative motivation, 34
Intelligibility, of speech, 60
Interactionist theory of language acquisition, 29, 31
Interlanguage, 34–35
Interpersonal relationships, 280
Intonation patterns, 65
Involuntary movement, 239
Iroquois, 177
Irrational numbers, 127, 157
Isosceles triangles, 46
Israel
bilingualism, 18
creation of, 187

J

Japan, World War II, 186–187
Jefferson, Thomas, 181
Jews, 187
Jigsaw groups, 170
Jim Crow laws, 184
Johnson, Lyndon B., 185
Journal writing, 41, 94, 99
Judicial branch, 208
Jumanos, 188

K

Karankawas, 188
Karplus, Robert, 215–216
Kennedy, John F., 185, 187
Kinetic energy, 229

King, Martin Luther, 184–185
Kingdoms, 235–236
Kodály method, 267–268
Ku Klux Klan, 183–184

L

Laboratory procedures, 213–215
LAD (language acquisition device), 57
"Lake effect," 250
Language acquisition, 26–36
  cognates/false cognates, 29
  development stages, 26, 27*t*, 29–33, 59–60
  factors influencing first language acquisition, 57
  factors influencing second language acquisition, 34
  imitation, 57–60
  interdependence of first and second languages, 48
  language components, 26–29
  social factors, 58
  variation and modification, 34–36
Language acquisition device (LAD), 57
Language across curriculum approach, 50
Language arts. *See* English language arts and reading (Domain II)
Language disorders, 62–63
Language experience approach (LEA), 38–39, 50, 92, 94
Language interference, 35, 61
Language logic, 41
Language play, 63–64
Language processing disorders, 63
Language proficiency
  assessment of, 47–48
  levels of, 46–47
  testing, 45
Language Proficiency Assessment Committee (LPAC), 17
Language transfer, 35, 48
Lapp, D., 37
Laredo School District, 15
La Salle, Robert de, 189
LAT (linguistically accommodated testing), 45, 89
Late-exit dual language programs, 19–21, 23
Latin roots, 169*t*
Latitude, 164, 194
Lau Remedies (1975), 14
Lau v. Nichols, 12
LEA (language experience approach), 38–39, 50, 92, 94
Learning, vs. acquisition, 30
Learning cycle model, 215–216, 218*t*
Learning environment, 120–121
Learning logs, 41, 99
Learning styles, 104
Legal issues, of bilingual education, 11–14
Legislative branch, 208
Levin, H., 24
Lexicon, 28, 58
Liberty Bell, 210–211
Life cycles, 236–238
Life science, 234–244
  adaptations, 242
  ecology, 243
  reproduction, 240–242
  structure and function of living things, 234–239
Light, 230, 232
Lightning, 231
Limited English proficient (LEP) students, identification of, 16–17
Lincoln, Abraham, 183
Linear functions, 135, 139, 140
Linear measurement, 150
Line graphs, 138
Lines, 142, 145
Lines of symmetry, 148
Lingua franca, 34
Linguistically accommodated testing (LAT), 45, 89
Liquids, 2258
Lisping, 63
Listening skills, 62
Literacy
  assessment, 42–45, 102–106
  development, 36–41, 70–75
  See also Reading; Writing
Literature, 72–75
Literature-based approach, 164
Local government, 209
Logical reasoning, 151–152, 155, 219
Longitude, 164, 194
LPAC (Language Proficiency Assessment Committee), 17
Lungs, 239, 272

M

Macroeconomics, 205
Magnetism, 226, 231
Maintenance bilingual education, 19
Manifest Destiny, 182
Manipulatives, 119, 121–122
Mantle, 244
Maps, 163, 194–195, 202–204
Marbury v. Madison, 208
Mariachi, 269
Marshall Plan, 187
Maryland Colony, 178, 180*t*
Marzano, R., 171
Mass, 150
Massachusetts
  bilingual education, 14
  Colony, 178, 180*t*
Mathematics (Domain III), 111–159
  analysis of teaching and learning, 122
  assessment, 115–116, 125
  competencies, 111, 127, 134, 141, 152, 154
  development stages, 116–118, 155–156
  and English language learners, 113–116
  geometry and measurement, 112, 141–152
  historical development, 156–158
  instruction, 111–126
  manipulatives, 119, 121–122
  number concepts and operations, 112, 123–124*t*, 127–134
  patterns and algebra, 134–141
  principles of, 111
  probability and statistics, 112, 113, 152–154
  processes, 154–158
  in real-life situations and connections, 118, 122
  standards for, 111–113

technology, 119–120
TEKS, 112–113, 122, 123–124*t*
terminology, 114
thematic units, 122–125
Matter, 227–229
Mayas, 157, 176
Mayflower Compact, 179
Mean, 153
Meaning, 59
Meaning-based reading approach, 67, 71–72
Measurement, 112, 113, 214–215
Media, 100–102
Median, 153
Medieval period of art, 261
Meiosis, 235, 240
Melody, 264–265
Mendez v. Westminster, 11–12
Mental health issues, 279
Metabolism, 273
Metacognitive strategy, 50
Metalworking, 256
Metamorphic rocks, 247, 248
Metric system, 150
Mexican Americans, civil rights movement, 185
Mexico
independence from Spain, 190
Texas War of Independence, 190–191
war with U.S. (1846-1848), 182, 191
Microeconomics, 205
Middle Ages (500-1400 CE), 173
Middle East, physical and cultural features, 198*t*
Midpoint, 105
Military, 207
Minerals, 248, 274
Minority/majority language program, 20
Miscue analysis, 71–72, 104
Mississippian people, 177
Mitochondria, 235, 238
Mitosis, 235, 240
Mixed numbers, 128–129
Mixtures, 228
Mnemonic devices, 87
Mode, 153
Modeling, 93
Modern fantasy, 73
Modifications and accommodations, 33, 88, 89–90
Molecules, 227
Monarchies, 207
Monera, 236
Money, 149, 206
Monitor hypothesis, 30
Monroe Doctrine, 182
Moon phases, 251
Morphemes, 28
Morphology, 28, 58
Motion, 226–227
Motivation, 34
Motor skills, 284–285
Mountains, 201–202, 244, 250
Movement, 260
Multicultural literature, 73
Multiplication
basic operation, 132
of binomials, 136–137
decimals, 129
fractions, 129
Muralists, 262
Musculoskeletal system, 239, 273
Music, 264–271
concert etiquette, 269
copyright law, 269–270
elements, 264–265
evaluation, 270
listening skills, 269
methods, 267–268
song repertoire, 268–269
TEKS, 265–266

N

Narrative writing, 40, 97
National Association for Sport and Physical Education (NASPE), 282–283
National Council for the Teaching of Social Studies (NCTSS), 161
National Council of Teachers of Mathematics (NCTM), 111, 122, 154
National curve equivalent (NCE) score, 43
National Organization for Women (NOW), 185
National Science Teachers Association (NSTA), 213
Native Americans, 177, 188, 189*t,* 263
Nativist theory of language acquisition, 29, 30–31
Natural numbers, 127
Natural order hypothesis, 31
NCE (national curve equivalent) score, 43
NCLB (No Child Left Behind) Act, 9–10, 45, 107
NCTM (National Council of Teachers of Mathematics), 111, 122, 154
NCTSS (National Council for the Teaching of Social Studies), 161
Negative numbers, performing operations with, 137
Nervous system, 239, 273
Newcomer centers, 22
New Hampshire Colony, 178, 180*t*
New Jersey
bilingual education, 8
Colony, 178, 180*t*
New Mexico, bilingual education in, 8, 14
New York Colony, 178, 180*t*
Nineteenth Amendment, 185
90/10 model, 20
Ninth Amendment, 209
Nitrogen cycle, 248–249
No Child Left Behind (NCLB) Act, 9–10, 45, 107
Nonfiction, 74
Non-linear functions, 135, 139
Norm-referenced testing (NRT), 42, 43, 105
North America, physical and cultural features, 196*t*
North American Free Trade Agreement (NAFTA), 206
North Carolina Colony, 179, 180*t*
Notes (musical), 264
Note taking, 87
NRT (norm-referenced testing), 42, 43, 105
NSTA (National Science Teachers Association), 213
Nucleus, 235
Number concepts and operations, 112, 123–124*t,* 127–134

Numbered heads together, 172
Number theory, 130–131
Nutrient cycles, 248

O

Obesity, 222, 273
Observation, 42, 103
Occasion, 99
Octagons, 146
Office for Civil Rights (OCR) Memorandum (1970), 13–14
Oil, 192, 206
Oligarchy, 207
Olmecs, 177
O'Malley, J., 50
Oñate, Juán de, 188
One-day alternating bilingual programs, 21
One-way bilingual education, 19
On-going assessment, 42, 107
Onset, 41
Open words, 59
Oral language, 57–64
Order of operations, 133
Orff Schulwerk method, 267
Organelles, 235, 238
Organic sedimentary rocks, 247
Organization of content, 87
Organs, 272
Ozone layer, 247

P

Pairing students, 79
Pair interviews, 64
Parallel lines, 145
Parallelograms, 147
Parks, Rosa, 184
Partial alphabetic phase, 67
Patriotic songs, 268
Patterns and algebra, 112–113, 134–141, 157
Peer review, 42
Pennsylvania Colony, 179, 180*t*
Pentagons, 146
Percentiles, 42, 43, 105
Percents, 130
Performance-based assessment, 42, 105
Perimeter, 142–143
Permutations, 154
Perpendicular lines, 145
Personality, and second language acquisition, 33
Personal journals, 99
Persuasive writing, 97
Phonation disorder, 62
Phonemic awareness, 40, 65–67
Phonemic stress, 65
Phonics, 39–40, 71, 90
Phonogram, 41
Phonological awareness, 65–67
Phonology, 26–28, 58
Photography, 256
Photorealism, 262
Photosynthesis, 230, 236–237, 238
Physical education, 282–289
  activities, 285–286
  adaptations for students with disabilities, 289
  class management techniques, 288–289
  competency, 282
  fitness levels, 284
  motor skills development, 284–285
  principles of, 282–283
  TEKS, 286–289
Physical science, 226–234
  electricity, 231, 232–233
  energy, 229–233
  force, 226–227
  gravity, 226
  magnetism, 226
  matter, 227–229
  mixtures, 228
  motion, 226–227
  solutions, 228
Piaget, Jean, 117–118, 223
Pickering, D., 171
Pictographic writing systems, 68
Pictorial graphs, 137
Picture books, 72
Pidginization, 34
Pie charts, 138
Pivot words, 59
Place value, 128
Planes, 142
Planets, 251
Plants
  cells, 238
  life cycle, 236–237
  photosynthesis, 230, 236–237, 238
  reproduction, 240–241
  structure and functions, 236
Plasmas, 228
Pledge of Allegiance, 210
Plessy v. Ferguson, 184
Plyler v. Doe, 13
Poetry, 74–75
Points, 142, 144–145
Polygons, 146–147
Portfolio assessment, 42, 103–104
Positive numbers, performing operations with, 137
Potential energy, 229
Potts, Jody, 169
Pragmatics, 28, 58
Pre-alphabetic phase, 67
Predation, 243
Predictions, 84
Prehistoric period of art, 260
Preoperational stage, 117
Pre-reading activities, 81
Presentations, oral, 64
Preteaching, 169
Preview-review approach, 25
Prewriting activities, 41
Prime factorization, 130
Printmaking, 256
Print media, 100
Prior knowledge, 81, 82, 84
Prisms, 147
Probability and statistics, 112, 113, 152–154
Problem solving, 112, 139, 155
Process writing, 41, 96
Producers, 243
Production, 205
Prohibition, 185–186
Projection systems, 99
Prokaryotic cells, 235
Proportional reasoning, 139–140
Proteins, 274
Protista, 236
Pseudo letters, 91
Public domain, 270
Publishing, 41
Pueblo people, 177
Pullout system for ESL instruction, 22
Punctuation, 93

Purpose, for writing, 99
Pythagorean theorem, 147–148, 156

Q

Quadrilaterals, 146
Questioning techniques, 82, 84, 125, 126*t*, 223–224

R

Radiation, 230
Radius, 146
Ramírez, D., 23
Range, 153
Rational numbers, 127
Raw scores, 105
Ray, 142
Raza Unida Party (RUP), 185
Readers' theatre, 80
Reading
  assessment, 42–45, 102–103
  comprehension and application, 77–78, 79, 81–85
  early reading approaches and activities, 37–40, 81
  fluency, 79–80
  instruction methods, 20, 39–40, 67, 70–71
  learning to read-reading to learn transition, 86
  phonological and phonemic awareness, 65–67
  speed and efficiency, 85, 86
  stages, 37–38, 70–71
Reading inventories, 103
Reading levels, 103
Reading Proficiency Test in English (RPTE), 45, 107
Reading readiness, 37
Realism, 261–262
Real numbers, 127
Reasoning, 112, 151–152, 155, 219
Receptive aphasia, 63
Reciprocal teaching, 24, 49, 88
Reconstruction Era (1865-1877), 183–184, 192
Rectangles
  area, 143, 146, 147
  perimeter, 142
  properties of, 147
Rectangular solids, 147
Reference maps, 194
Reflection (light), 232
Reflections (geometry), 149
Reflection strategy, 84
Reflective journals, 99
Refraction, 232
Registers, 26
Renaissance, 261
Repeating decimals, 134
Representations, in mathematics, 112
Reproduction, 235, 237–238, 240–242
Research and inquiry skills, 86–89
Resonance disorder, 62
Respiratory system, 239, 272
Reversibility, 118
Revising, 41
Revolution and Industry (1700-1900), 174
Rhode Island Colony, 178–179, 180*t*
Rhythm (music), 264
Rhythm (visual art), 260
Right triangles, 147–148
Riley, Bill, 14
Rime, 41
Rios v. Reed, 13
Rivers, 200–201, 244
Roanoke settlement, 178
Rock cycle, 248
Rock types, 247
Rococo, 261
Role plays, 169–170
Roman art, 261
Romanticism, 261
Roosevelt, Franklin D., 186, 187
Rotations, 149
Rounding, 133–134
Routine activities, 95
RPTE (Reading Proficiency Test in English), 45, 107
RubiStar, 270
Rubrics, 106, 270
Running records, 103, 104
RUP (Raza Unida Party), 185
Russia
  Bolshevik Revolution, 186
  Cold War, 187–188
  World War II, 186–187
Ryder, Martin, 24

S

Safety
  accident prevention, 278–279
  in laboratory, 213–215
San Antonio, 189–190
San Jacinto, battle of, 190–191
Santa Anna, Antonio López de, 190–191
SAS (Side-Angle-Side), 144
Scaffolding, 49, 115, 169
Scalene triangles, 146
Scanning, 86
Schizophrenia, 279
School nurses, 280
School records, 43
School Reform (1994), 9
School violence, 279
Science (Domain V), 213–253
  assessment, 225–226
  competencies, 213, 215, 221, 222, 223, 226, 227, 229, 232, 234, 240, 242, 243, 244, 247, 249, 250
  in daily life, 221–222
  earth and space, 244–252
  English language learner needs and supports, 213, 219
  instruction, 223–224
  life science, 234–244
  physical science, 226–234
  reproduction, 235, 237–238, 240–242
  safe and proper laboratory procedures, 213–215
  scientific inquiry, 215–221
  stereotypes about, 221
  unifying concepts and processes, 222–223
Scientific models, 223
Scientific notation, 127
Scribbling, 91
Sculpture, 256
SDAA (State-Developed Alternative Assessment), 44
Seal of the United States, 211
Second Amendment, 209
Sedimentary rocks, 247, 248
Segment, 142
Segregation, 184
SEI (structured English immersion), 22

Self-assessment, 42–43
Self-concept, 277
Self-efficacy, 277
Self-esteem, 33
Self-evaluation, 50
Self-monitoring, 50
Semantic clues, 76
Semantic mapping, 85
Semantics, 28, 58
Sentence builders, 93
September 11, 2001, 188
Seriation, 118
Serna v. Portales, 12
Seventh Amendment, 209
Sexual reproduction, 240–241
Sheltered English approach, 22, 51, 170–171
Show and tell, 64
Sight words, 39, 76
Silent sustained reading, 80
Singing, 268–269
Single teacher approach, 20
SIOP model, 22
6+1 Writing Traits, 96–97
Six Flags over Texas, 192
Sixteenth Amendment, 206
Sixth Amendment, 209
Skeletal system, 239, 273
Skill checklists, 42
Skills-based reading approach, 67, 71
Skimming, 86
Slavery, 182–183
Slope-intecept form, 140
Smith, Sperry, 117–118
Socialism, 207
Social realism, 262
Social science (Domain IV), 161–212
  competencies, 161, 172, 194, 205, 206
  economics, 205–206
  English language learner needs and supports, 169–172
  geography and culture, 194–205
  government and citizenship, 206–211
  history, 172–193
  instruction, 161–172
  TEKS, 161–163
Social settings, importance for language acquisition, 58
Social strategies, 51
Socioeconomic background, and second language acquisition, 34
Solar system, 251
Solids (geometry), 144, 147
Solids (state of matter), 228
Solutions, 228
Sound, 232
Sousa, David, 169, 213, 219
The South, 183–184
South America, physical and cultural features, 196*t*
South Asia, physical and cultural features, 199*t*
South Carolina Colony, 179, 180*t*
Soviet Union, 186, 187–188
Space science, 250–252
Spanish American War (1898), 186
Spanish language
  grapheme-phoneme correspondence, 26–28
  language interference, 61
Spanish settlements, 188–189
Special education
  IEPs, 16
  linguistic accommodation testing, 89
  State-Developed Alternative Assessment, 44
Speech, 57–64
Spelling, 40, 90–91
Spoken, vs. written English, 90
SQ4R (survey, question, read, reflect, recite, and review) strategy, 49, 87–88, 170
Squares
  area, 143, 146
  perimeter, 142
SSS (Side-Side-Side), 144
STAD (student teams achievement division), 171–172
Staff, musical, 264–265
Standard-based achievement tests, 44
Standardized testing, 42, 43–44
Standards. *See* Texas Essential Knowledge and Skills (TEKS)
STARR (State of Texas Assessments of Academic Readiness), 107
Stars, 250
"The Star-Spangled Banner," 210
State-Developed Alternative Assessment (SDAA), 44
State government, 209
State laws, bilingual education, 8, 14–17
State of Texas Assessments of Academic Readiness (STARR), 107
Statistics and probability, 112, 113, 152–154
Statue of Liberty, 210
Story grammar, 82
Story retelling, 83
Stress management, 274–275
Structural clues, 76–77
Structured English immersion (SEI), 22
Student teams achievement division (STAD), 171–172
Study skills, 86–87
Stuttering, 62
Submersion, 8
Substance use and abuse, 277–278
Subtraction
  basic operation, 131–132
  decimals, 129
  fractions, 128
  mixed numbers, 128
Suffixes, 169
Summarization, 87
Summative evaluation, 43, 104
Sun, 251
Supply and demand, 205
Supreme Court, 12, 184, 208
Surface water, 246
Surrealism, 262
Syllabication, 65
Syllabic writing system, 68
Symbols
  American, 210–211
  geographic, 195
  Texas, 192
Symmetry, 148
Syntactic clues, 76
Syntax, 28, 58
Synthesizing information, 84

T

TAKS. *See* Texas Assessment of Knowledge and Skills (TAKS)
Taxation, 206

TEA (Texas Education Agency), 97, 105
Teachers of English to Speakers of Other Languages (TESOL), 21
Teaching Games for Understanding model, 286
Team teaching, 20
Technology
  history of, 175–176
  mathematics, 119–120
  reading, 79–80
  social science, 164
  writing, 99, 102
Tectonic plates, 245
Tejano, 269
Tejas LEE (El Inventario de Lectura en Español de Tejas), 44
TEKS. *See* Texas Essential Knowledge and Skills (TEKS)
Telegraphic stage, 59
TELPAS (Texas English Language Proficiency Assessment System), 10, 11*t*, 45, 107
Temperance movement, 185–186
Temperature, 149, 228, 230, 249
Tenth Amendment, 7, 209
Terrorism, war on, 188
TESOL (Teachers of English to Speakers of Other Languages), 21
Tessellations, 148
Testing. *See* Assessment
Texas
  bilingual education history, 8, 14–15
  Chapter 89 Commissioner's Rules, 15–17
  economic activity, 201*t*, 206
  facts and symbols, 192
  geographic regions, 200, 201*t*
  history, 188–192
  Language Proficiency Assessment Committee (LPAC), 17
  music, 269
  Six Flags over Texas, 192
  testing program, 44–45
Texas, Our Texas, 269, 270
Texas Assessment of Knowledge and Skills (TAKS)
  accommodations, 89
  cognitive academic language proficiency, 48
  mathematics, 125
  purpose, 44, 104
  schedule, 44*t*
  Spanish version, 44
  writing portion, 98*t*, 106
Texas Education Agency (TEA), 97, 105
Texas English Language Proficiency Assessment System (TELPAS), 10, 11*t*, 45, 107
Texas Essential Knowledge and Skills (TEKS)
  health, 275–276
  mathematics, 112–113, 122, 123–124*t*, 154
  media, 100
  music, 265–266
  physical education, 286–289
  science, 220, 225–226
  social studies, 161–163
  visual arts, 256, 257*t*
Texas Learning Index (TLI), 44
Texas Observation Protocol (TOP), 44, 61, 107
Texas Proficiency Reading Inventory (TPRI), 44
TExES 192 Bilingual Generalist, EC-6 exam
  about, 1–2
  administration, 2
  format and content, 3–4
  registration fee, 2
  retakes, 6
  scoring, 4–5
  study tips, 2–4
  test-taking tips, 5–6
  when/where given, 2
Text, structure of, 86
Textbooks, for English language learners, 169
Textiles, 256
Thales, 156
Thematic maps, 194
Thematic units, 122–125, 164
Themes, in literature, 82–83
Theocracy, 207
Think-aloud strategy, 87
Think-pair-share, 172
Third Amendment, 209
Thirteenth Amendment, 183, 184
Thomas, W. P., 23
Threshold hypothesis, 31
Tides, 248
Tijerina, Reies, 185
Timbre, 265
Time, 149
Timelines, 166, 170
Time-outs, 288–289
Time zones, 195
Tissues, 272
Title I, Elementary and Secondary Education Act, 9
Title III, No Child Left Behind Act, 9–10
Title VI, Civil Rights Act, 8–9, 13
Title VII- The Bilingual Education Act, 9, 15, 23
TLI (Texas Learning Index), 44
Toltecs, 177
TOP (Texas Observation Protocol), 44, 61, 107
Top-down approach to reading, 39, 71–72
Traditional literature, 72–73
Transformations, 149
Transitional bilingual education (TBE) programs, 9, 18–19, 23
Translations, 149
Treaty of Paris (1783), 181–182
Triangles
  area, 146
  congruence, 144
  perimeter, 143
  properties of, 146
  Pythagorean theorem, 147–148
Truán, Carlos, 15
Truman Doctrine, 187
Turner, William, 261
Twenty-First Amendment, 186
Two-dimensional figures, 146–147
Two-way dual language immersion, 19–21, 23

U

United Farm Workers (UFW), 185
United Nations (UN), *The Use of the Vernacular Language in Education*, 8
United States

geographic regions, 200
government, 208–211
history, 178–188
rivers, 200–201
symbols, 210–211
University of Michigan, ESL field development, 21
U.S. v. State of Texas, 13

V

Vaca, Cabeza de, 188
Van Hiele theory, 142, 143*t*
Variables, 140
Venn diagrams, 170
Vertex, 144
Violence
at home, 278
at school, 279
Virginia Colony, 178, 179, 180*t*
Visual arts, 255–263
activities, 258
Africa, 263
assessment, 258
China, 262–263
classroom set-up, 258
definitions, 255
development stages, 255–256
elements and principles of, 258–260
evaluation, 263
integrated curriculum, 263
Native Americans, 263
styles and movements, 260–262
techniques and materials, 256–258
TEKS, 256, 257*t*
Visualization, 84
Visual media, 100, 101–102
Vitamins, 274
Voice disorders, 62
Volcanoes, 246
Volume, 144, 147, 150
Voluntary movement, 239

W

Wars
American War of Independence, 181–182
Civil War, 183, 191–192
French and Indian War, 181
Mexican-American war (1846-1848), 182, 191
Texas War of Independence, 190–191
World War I, 186, 192
World War II, 186–187, 192
Washington, George, 181
Water, 246
Water cycle, 248
Weather, 249–250
Weathering process, 245
Weight, 150
White House, 211
Whole language approach, 39, 50, 71–72
Wind, 249
Women's rights, 185
Word analysis and identification, 76–78
Word concepts, 59
Word families, 41
Word processing programs, 99, 102
Word stress, 61, 65
World history, 172–177
World War I, 186, 192
World War II, 186–187, 192
Writing, 40–41
audience, 97
conventions, 90–95
functions of, 97
occasion, 99
process of, 95–97
purpose, 99
systems, 68
technological tools, 99
types, 99

Y

Yalta Conference, 187
Ysleta del Sur, 189

Z

Zapotecs, 177
Zero, 137, 157

Notes

Notes

Notes

Notes

Notes